ORGANIZATIONAL DYNAMICS OF TECHNOLOGY-BASED INNOVATION: DIVERSIFYING THE RESEARCH AGENDA

IFIP – The International Federation for Information Processing

IFIP was founded in 1960 under the auspices of UNESCO, following the First World Computer Congress held in Paris the previous year. An umbrella organization for societies working in information processing, IFIP's aim is two-fold: to support information processing within its member countries and to encourage technology transfer to developing nations. As its mission statement clearly states,

> *IFIP's mission is to be the leading, truly international, apolitical organization which encourages and assists in the development, exploitation and application of information technology for the benefit of all people.*

IFIP is a non-profitmaking organization, run almost solely by 2500 volunteers. It operates through a number of technical committees, which organize events and publications. IFIP's events range from an international congress to local seminars, but the most important are:

• The IFIP World Computer Congress, held every second year;
• Open conferences;
• Working conferences.

The flagship event is the IFIP World Computer Congress, at which both invited and contributed papers are presented. Contributed papers are rigorously refereed and the rejection rate is high.

As with the Congress, participation in the open conferences is open to all and papers may be invited or submitted. Again, submitted papers are stringently refereed.

The working conferences are structured differently. They are usually run by a working group and attendance is small and by invitation only. Their purpose is to create an atmosphere conducive to innovation and development. Refereeing is less rigorous and papers are subjected to extensive group discussion.

Publications arising from IFIP events vary. The papers presented at the IFIP World Computer Congress and at open conferences are published as conference proceedings, while the results of the working conferences are often published as collections of selected and edited papers.

Any national society whose primary activity is in information may apply to become a full member of IFIP, although full membership is restricted to one society per country. Full members are entitled to vote at the annual General Assembly, National societies preferring a less committed involvement may apply for associate or corresponding membership. Associate members enjoy the same benefits as full members, but without voting rights. Corresponding members are not represented in IFIP bodies. Affiliated membership is open to non-national societies, and individual and honorary membership schemes are also offered.

ORGANIZATIONAL DYNAMICS OF TECHNOLOGY-BASED INNOVATION: DIVERSIFYING THE RESEARCH AGENDA

IFIP TC 8 WG 8.6 International Working Conference, June 14-16, Manchester, UK

Edited by

Tom McMaster
University of Salford
Salford, UK

David Wastell
University of Nottingham
Nottingham, UK

Elaine Ferneley
University of Salford
Salford, UK

Janice I. DeGross
University of Minnesota
Minneapolis, MN USA

 Springer

Organizational Dynamics of Technology-Based Innovation:
Diversifying the Research Agenda

Edited T. McMaster, D. Wastell, E. Ferneley, and J. DeGross

p. cm. (IFIP International Federation for Information Processing, a Springer Series in Computer Science)

ISSN: 1571-5736 / 1861-2288 (Internet)

ISBN 978-1-4419-4449-8   eISBN: 13: 978-0-387-72804-9
Printed on acid-free paper

9 8 7 6 5 4 3 2 1
springer.com

Contents

Part 3: Software Process Improvement

Part 4: Actor Network Theory

Part 5: Technological Interlude: The Case of RFID

Part 6: Firm Level Adoption Factors

Part 7: Position Papers

Part 8: Panels

Foreword

I am honored to be General Chair for the 2007 (10th) Working Conference of IFIP Working Group 8.6. I had some part in helping with the formation of this working group. Participating in this conference in Manchester reflects my interest in the working group and its research domain. The conference is also something of an anniversary, since the second conference of the working group was held nearby 10 years ago. I have some reflections on the formation and early conferences of the working group, the comparative advantage of being sponsored by IFIP and TC8, the reasons for WG 8.6, and the important contributions of the working group and this conference.

Reflections on the Formation of WG 8.6 and Early Conferences

I was Chair of the IFIP (International Federation for Information Processing) Technical Committee 8 (Information Systems) for two terms from 1990 through 1995. It was in 1993 when the proposal was made to form a new working group on Diffusion and Adoption of Information Technology. I supported the proposal and remember well how active and persuasive Priscilla Fowler and Linda Levine were in making the case for establishing a new working group.

I participated in the TC8 conference to ascertain the level of interest in the proposed working group and set in motion its organization. The conference was held in Pittsburgh, Pennsylvania, in October of 1993. The proceedings were published with Linda Levine as editor, *Diffusion, Transfer and Implementation of Information Technology* (North Holland, 1994). The working group was formally approved in 1994. Priscilla Fowler was appointed the first Chair of the working group with Karlheinz Kautz as Vice Chair and Chris Sauer as Secretary.

The first WG 8.6 Working Conference was held October 14-17, 1995, at Leang-kollen, Oslo, Norway. Unfortunately, I was not there. However, I attended the second WG 8.6 working conference at the Low Wood Hotel, Ambleside, Lake Windermere (near Manchester in the UK), June 25-27, 1997. The theme of the conference was "Facilitating Technology Transfer through Partnership: Learning from Practice and Research." The program chairs were Tom McMaster, University of Salford, and David Wastell, University of Nottingham.

Reflection: The Comparative Advantage of IFIP and WG 8.6

There are many organizations we can join and many conferences that we can attend. Why are we here at a conference sponsored by a working group of a technical committee of an international society? IFIP provides an excellent organizational framework for international cooperation. It is essentially a society of national computing societies with broad participation from countries with strong interest in information processing. Since the field of computing and information processing is large and diverse, IFIP has established technical committees for different areas of interest. IFIP TC8 is on the topic of information systems. Although the technical committee may sponsor conferences, most of its work is conducted by working groups on major topics within the field of information systems. WG 8.6 focuses on diffusion and adoption of information technology. It fits within an international organization free from national or region bias, and it is hosted within a technical committee on information systems that defines the general domain of interest. There is an infrastructure that provides an umbrella for working group activities and provides for the publication and sales of conference proceedings.

Reflection: The Reason for WG 8.6: Transfer and Diffusion of Information Technology

Any practitioner or academic researcher in the field of information technology systems comes face to face with the fact that technologies and systems with significant advantages are not adopted or face strong resistance. Before WG 8.6 was formed, there was already a body of research on adoption of innovations. Sometimes this research seemed to explain issues of information systems adoption but it did not appear to me and to others to be robust enough or comprehensive enough to deal with many of the problems we face with IT. In other words, we have some reasonably complex and somewhat unique situations, problems, and issues along with unique practitioner concerns. There is a need for academics in information systems to understand adoption and diffusion of information and communications technologies in organizations, the diffusion of system innovations, and the diffusion of software engineering innovations in building software and applications. There is also a need to foster dialogue between academics and practitioners and transfer research results to practice.

With over 10 years of research and conferences behind us, haven't the problems been solved? Unfortunately, technological innovations and diffusion continues to be difficult. The failure rate for new technologies and new systems remains high. In other words, there is still an important, viable mission for WG 8.6 in exploring issues of why some innovation efforts are successful and others fail. There is a need to continue to explore theoretical perspectives, methodologies, and organization issues.

Reflection: The Nature of WG 8.6 and the Value Added by this Conference

I started my academic career as a traditional positivist. It was in Manchester in 1984 at a conference on information systems research sponsored by WG 8.2 (Information Systems and Organizations) that I had an epiphany. My eye-opening experience did not convert me to a complete post-positivist and cause me to reject positivist research. Rather, it expanded my thinking to encompass a much broader range of research paradigms. I applied some of them in my own research.

WG 8.2 might have been organized with tight boundaries that excluded different research paradigms; it didn't happen that way. WG 8.6 was organized as a home for a diverse research agenda with openness for different research paradigms. This working conference continues the tradition. On behalf of us all, I thank David Wastell and Tom McMaster for the program that continues the spirit of open inquiry that has characterized WG 8.6. I second their thanks to those who have made the conference possible.

As I reviewed the papers in the proceedings, I was struck by the diversity. There were papers on topics I understand well and there were papers on topics that I had not thought of before or not understood very well. For example, for me, the six papers using actor network theory will clarify and expand my thinking relative to ANT. There are papers that advocate different approaches to research and open up a dialogue. An interesting innovation by the program chairs is the publication of 14 position papers that present interesting ideas but don't fit the traditional model of conference papers. In other words, the collection of papers in this volume can open minds and expand understanding.

Gordon B. Davis
Honeywell Professor of Management Information Systems, Emeritus
Carlson School of Management, University of Minnesota, USA

Preface

Welcome to the 10th Working Conference of IFIP WG 8.6 on the adoption and diffusion of information systems and technologies, and welcome to Manchester. In recent years, the frequency of these meetings has more or less stabilized into an annual event, but this has not always been so. The first four "official" 8.6 meetings[1] were held in Oslo, Norway (October 1995), Ambleside, UK (June 1997), Helsinki, Finland (December 1999), and Banff, Canada (April 2001). Gaps between gatherings of 20 to 30 months may seem a questionable start for an embryonic research group, but we have now stabilized inoto annual meetings with Sydney (2002), Copenhagen (2003), Leixlip (2004), Atlanta (2005), Galway (2006), and now Manchester (2007). The next meeting is planned for Madrid in 2008. The engine that originally sputtered into life is now purring and ticking over smoothly, thanks to all of those whose persistence, endeavors, and energies have made it so.

Events such as these cannot be staged without considerable help and advice from many others, and this is no less true of this particular meeting. We would, therefore, like to take this opportunity to acknowledge and thank those who have helped make this event possible.

Thanks to Yacine Rezgui, Director of the University of Salford's Informatics Research Institute (IRIS), for engaging IRIS as the principal sponsor and host of this event. Thanks are also due to Salford City Council in the guise of Mike Willetts (Head of ICT Services) for once again providing financial support (this is the third IFIP conference hosted in Manchester which the Council has sponsored), and to Bob Newbold of ISACA (Information Systems Auditing and Control Association) for generously sponsoring the conference reception. We would also like to express our gratitude to the various senior officers of the Working Group for helping bring this event to fruition, in particular Karlheinz Kautz, and also Linda Levine who has always been on hand with practical advice and invaluable feedback. Jan DeGross has again done a fine job in cutting and polishing the rough-hewn originals into a rather handsome published collection of papers.

We are also deeply indebted to members of the program committee. Our policy was to invite a set of people reflecting the international character of the Working Group as well as its aspiration to undertake relevant research, to bridge the much-bruited research-practice fissure. The committee is listed below. It reflects the constituency we sought,

---

[1]There had been a precursory IFIP Technical Committee 8 (TC8) meeting on the diffusion of information technologies held at Seven Springs, Pennsylvania, in October 1993. From this, WG 8.6 was formed and it was officially established as an IFIP group in 1994.

with both a broad international profile and a prominent representation of practitioners. We are particularly grateful to the individual members for their help in the reviewing and selection process, getting their comments back to us against rather tight deadlines.

The tireless work and endless patience of Elaine Ferneley is also acknowledged as the local organizing Chair. She kept our wandering minds focused on the task in hand and handled everything with aplomb: setting up the web site, arranging the all-important entertainment and victuals, as well as the technical facilities and the splendid venue. Her involvement in shaping the program was also much appreciated. Finally we would like to thank Mark Sanders and Kevin Blow at Salford University for their help in designing and running the conference web site, and to Nathalie Audren-Howarth of Salford University for fielding queries and performing other invaluable administrative tasks.

Tom McMaster and David Wastell
Program Co-Chairs, IFIP WG8.6, Manchester

CONFERENCE COMMITTEE

General Chair
Gordon B. Davis
University of Minnesota

Program Co-chairs
Tom McMaster
University of Salford

David Wastell
University of Nottingham

Organizing Chair
Elaine Ferneley
University of Salford

Program Committee

1 CONFERENCES AS EPISTEMOLOGICAL EXPERIMENTS: Purity, Plurality, and the Politics of Knowledge

David Wastell
Nottingham University Business School
Nottingham, UK

Tom McMaster
University of Salford
Salford, UK

1 INTRODUCTION

> *Ordnung ist heutzutage meistens dort, wo nichts ist.*
> *Es ist eine Mangelerscheinung*[1] – Brecht

So opens Feyerabend's (1993) seminal essay *Against Method.* The epigraph is apt for this commencement too, given the Conference theme which calls for diversification, in theory, method, and empirical contexts. The following amalgam of extracts gives the gist of Feyerabend's thesis:

---

[1] The translation is problematic, and we were certainly "lost" for a while. But with the help of two native German speakers, we hope that we have arrived at a satisfactory resolution. *Mangelerscheinung* was the trickiest element. Literally, it translates as "deficiency symptom," a medico-biological concept denoting the lack of some nutrient critical to physical well-being (e.g., a vitamin deficiency). Although the literal translation has a "clunky" feel, we decided to restrain poetic license and remain loyal to it, fearing the loss of relevant metaphorical content or the addition of spurious new meaning. We offer as our translation: "These days, order is mostly there where nothing is. It is a deficiency symptom." Presumably Brecht had a malaise of the soul in mind, not body!

Please use the following format when citing this chapter:

Wastell, D., and McMaster, T., 2007, in IFIP International Federation for Information Processing, Volume 235, Organizational Dynamics of Technology-Based Innovation: Diversifying the Research Agenda, eds. McMaster, T., Wastell, D., Ferneley, E., and DeGross, J. (Boston: Springer), pp. 1-12.

Science is an essentially anarchistic enterprise: theoretical anarchism is more humanitarian and more likely to encourage progress than its law-and-order alternative....This is shown both by an examination of historical episodes and by an abstract analysis of the relation between idea and action. There is only one principle that can be defended under *all* circumstances and in all stages of human development. It is the principle: *anything goes* (pp. 9, 18-19).

The attempt to increase liberty, to lead a full and rewarding life, and the corresponding attempt to discover the secrets of nature and of man, entails therefore the rejection of all universal standards and rigid traditions [imposed] upon research and upon any kind of knowledge-creating and knowledge-changing activity (p. 12).

Two points stand out here. First, that the argument for epistemological anarchy is empirical, as well as theoretical and ethical: it is carefully grounded on an extensive historical analysis of how science actually develops, using Galileo and the Copernican revolution as the primary exemplar. Recent sociological narratives of scientific practice would certainly bear out the same argument (e.g., Latour 1999); these accounts reveal working scientists as pragmatists and tricksters, far removed from the popular stereotype of the disinterested scholar uncovering *a priori* facts. Second, the indivisible linking of the causes of liberty and of science is also noteworthy: Feyerabend clearly connects dogma of method and theory not only with epistemological stasis but with human oppression too, hence the Brechtian grace-note. Let us end this salvo of quotes with yet another, this one from no less a figure in the scientific pantheon than Einstein. Feyerabend cites him as writing

The scientist [should] not be too much restricted in his construction of his conceptual world by the adherence to an epistemological system. He must therefore appear to the systematic epistemologist as a type of unscrupulous opportunist (p. 10).

If anarchism is such "excellent medicine for epistemology" (ibid p. 9), then it is surely worthwhile to check out the intellectual health of our community. Stoler (2002) introduces the idea of archives[2] as "epistemological experiments." She makes out the argument in the context of colonial archives; the general thesis readily extends, however, to other institutions and technologies of knowledge creation. This naturally includes conferences which, by design, leave an archival trace, in the durable form of books as well as more ephemeral documents (reviews, decision letters, minutes, e-mails, etc.). Stoler contends that scholars should view archives not as repositories to be passively mined for "facts" but as situated loci of knowledge production, "of taxonomies in the making, and of state authority." Archival scholarship thus moves from being an extractive enterprise to an ethnographic one: interest shifts to what constitutes the archive, what form it takes, the systems of classification it embodies, and so on. In other words,

---

[2]Such repositories are, of course, information systems in their own right, albeit exotic ones.

what does the archive as a cultural artefact reveal about the nature of the world which produced it, and of the ambient politics of knowledge.

Given its stated theme, it is particularly apposite to use this conference as an object of epistemological study! But first, we will take another anthropological detour.

2 PURITY, PLURALITY, AND THE POLITICS OF KNOWLEDGE

Through the concept of "dirt," understood generically as "matter out of place,"[3] Mary Douglas (2002) famously established a bridge between the sophisticated contemporary world and other cultures which we conventionally dub as primitive. What they taboo, we denounce as dirty! In both cases, a threat or danger to the existing social order is controlled, either through avoidance (e.g., taboo foods) or via the enactment of purification rituals (e.g., ritual bathing) whereby the pollution is cleansed. Characteristically, some form of extreme (and implausible) threat is invoked to shore up the threatened breach. Often this involves the precipitation of a natural catastrophe, thus co-opting Nature to defend what is merely human convention.

The association of danger with dirt is the key to this defensive structure. But what is classified as dirt or pollution is a matter of perspective and institutional interest: "there is no such thing as absolute dirt: it exists in the eye of the beholder" (Douglas 2002). Within limits, a messy or untidy house is not a threat to health, yet such disorder, and dirt in general, is viewed with a degree of revulsion that goes well beyond any possible material risk. As Douglas archly notes, "I doubt whether the perfunctory rituals of passing through water can really destroy bacteria, or that I can be infected by slightly damaged crockery." There is undoubtedly some instrumental basis for purification rituals, but this is often exaggerated. Pharmacologists may well seek to prove some medical basis for the prohibition against eating pork, but in another knowing aside, Douglas quips that, "Even if some of Moses' dietary rules were hygienically beneficial, it would be a pity to treat him as an enlightened public health administrator rather than a spiritual leader."

Turning back to epistemology and the sociology of science, there are intriguing implications. Is not the much-cherished peer-review process, for instance, a purification ritual? Certainly, in following a formalized and formulaic pattern, it has all the appearance of ritual. And dirt is absolutely integral to its operating rationale, which is based on the need to winnow good papers (technically sound, "make a contribution") from those which are deficient. The "pollution belief" that the latter are dirty and must be weeded out underpins the entire process. And lest readers consider this fanciful, we should reflect on the strength of the sense of alarm evoked by the idea of "letting in" defective papers. It is potent indeed. The quality of the journal (and indeed conferences in fields

---

[3]The phrase is often attributed to Douglas. In fact, it was first used by William James (1936) in *The Varieties of Religious Experience*: "Here we have the interesting notion of there being elements in the universe which may make no rational whole in conjunction with the other elements, and... can only be considered so much irrelevance and accident – so much 'dirt' as it were, and *matter out of place*" [emphasis added]. Douglas acknowledges this source (p. 203).

like our own,[4] which operate rigorous selection policies) must be protected at all cost from such defilement; disaster will ensue otherwise. But will it? Are "bad papers" really such a risk to our mental health and the purity of the corpus of scientific knowledge? Is not this abhorrence bought at a price that threatens intellectual vitality? Bad papers may fail to meet our epistemological standards, but they may yet contain ideas of value and interest, stimulating debate or otherwise destabilizing the *status quo*. Let us end this section with another pithy line from Feyerabend:

> There is no idea, however, ancient and absurd, that is not capable of improving our knowledge (p. 33)

3   AN OVERVIEW OF THE PAPERS

It may seem somewhat ironic, given these prefatory remarks, that we seem to have so meekly fallen in with the ordering conventions of science, and of those practiced in our field in particular. Despite our misgivings, we have adopted a "rigorous" review process based on full papers; we have fitted all into a common format like Chinese shoes, and the papers have also been clustered into subthemes. Perhaps on reflection we should have been more radical. But the politics of knowledge is no different from politics in general; it is the art of the possible. We have, therefore, chosen to innovate around the edges and to dabble in a little polemic, rather than attempting revolutionary change.

Overall, we received a total of 40 submissions, from which 21 full research papers were selected. Three forms of contribution were sought: full research papers, short position papers of a polemical nature, and panel proposals. All papers were blind-reviewed by two independent referees, and we as program co-chairs also read every submission. We saw much merit in many of the papers which failed to survive the formal review process, and the majority of authors were invited to revise and resubmit their submissions as position papers. We were delighted that almost all agreed. Together with the submissions originally submitted in this category, there are 14 position papers in all. Invited papers were solicited from several leading academics and from two practitioners, representing the public and the commercial sectors. Given the Group's commitment to relevant research, we were delighted that both Dave Carter and Gerry Pennell accepted these invitations, with a paper from Carter being published in the book. Bob Galliers' keynote address and two panel outlines complete the published collection.

Acknowledging the arbitrariness of any taxonomy, especially where there are multiple criteria, we have nonetheless attempted to classify the papers around what seemed to be a number of natural themes. Ordering is not always pernicious; indeed it is fundamental to the way our minds work. Douglas herself offers the following sanguine observa-

---

[4]Other disciplines do not. An inclusion agenda would seem to guide the selection of papers in other fields, with decisions based on abstracts and minimum criteria, rather than on full papers aping the "hard currency" of the journal article. Such rigorous sorting would seem inimical to scholarly debate and knowledge development. Why do we set such stall by having low acceptance rates; why is this good? To an outsider, it would seem perverse to mark prestige in this way. Surely a high rejection rate implies failure of the field, not its prosperity; such vice-like control hardly betokens open, vigorous discourse.

tion: "Dirt offends against order. Eliminating it is not a negative movement, but a positive effort to organize the environment" (p. 2). Five themes were descried and we shall briefly comment on the papers under each heading. Given the space limitations, we shall restrict our commentary to the full papers only. We will then stand back and take a critical view of the results of our *epistemological experiment.* To assess theoretical progress, we shall draw on Flynn and Gregory's (2004) survey of the prevalence of theory in IS research (based on IFIP WG8.2 conferences) supplemented by our own retrospections as WG 8.6 veterans. We were both involved in developing the program for the 1997 Conference, which provides a handy 10 year reference point (McMaster et al. 1997).

3.1 Keynotes and Invited Papers

Galliers provides an extended abstract of his keynote address in which he enthusiastically takes up the conference theme, arguing for greater diversity and innovation in method, as well as topic, in Information Systems research. Basing his arguments on recent critiques of injunctions to narrow our research focus (on the IT artifact and IS design), he highlights the expanding boundary of the field of Information Systems and what this means for the IS academy. He argues that it is only through a dynamic, exploratory, and transdisciplinary approach to our research (with concerns for societal, ethical, and global issues) that innovation and diversity will thrive.

Carter provides us with an intriguing account of how the City of Manchester is addressing in practical terms the "digital divide" and urban regeneration through the Manchester Digital Development Agency (MDDA). This draws together a number of interconnected "e-based" initiatives at local, regional, national, and European-wide levels. He describes in detail the Eastserve Project and how it addresses deprivation and social exclusion. The work of ONE-Manchester (Open Network E-Manchester) is also outlined. This partnership embraces various contiguous local government neighbors (Tameside, Salford, Oldham, etc.) as well as some private industry partners, and how these fit with national and European attempts to address similar problems of regeneration and social inclusion.

Truex and Holmström's stimulating essay is also right on the conference theme, addressing many of the issues which we have highlighted in our opening remarks. They too see the dangers of a totalizing tendency, which they dub the "*supremacist strategy*— a strategy aiming at establishing one theoretical approach as universally applicable." They call on IS scholars to drop their tools, hold their concepts lightly and update them frequently (the original exhortation comes from Karl Weick). Caution is not thrown entirely to the wind, however, and pollution anxieties still have a hold. Truex and Holmström warn that "we need to be particularly careful in the rush to find new or different theoretical lenses." Dilettantism or dogma; where lies the greater danger?

León discusses the merits of "open innovation" partnerships, with an emphasis on technology transfer (which he defines as the transfer of technical knowledge in its simplest form between a transmitter and a receiver). He describes three similar, but crucially different innovation models: the subcontracted model, the cooperative model, and the open community model. These are set in the context of European policy instruments for technology transfer. León advocates greater cooperation between governments, universities, and private sector organizations to exploit and benefit from such partnerships.

The distinction between factor and process perspectives is often made in delineating genres of IS research. Newman and Zhu are firmly committed to the latter paradigm. They hail the richer causal narratives yielded by longitudinal research that are able to map the shifts in project trajectories triggered by supervening events (critical incidents). The paper describes the application of their punctuated equilibrium model to the development of an information system in a major retail organization, highlighting the role of contextual forces in shaping dialectical change.

3.2 Novel Perspectives in Innovation Research

In response to the conference theme, we have tried to single out submitted papers in this first group which embody significant departures from the *vade mecum*, illustrating innovation in theory in the main but research methodology as well.

Bunker, Kautz, and Anhtuan focus on potential differences in organizational culture between the contexts of IS development and IS use, arguing that the vicissitudes of IS implementation could reflect incompatible assumptions, values, and skills. Differences in attitudes to managerial control were found to influence the contrasting fortunes of a time-sheet application in two neighboring settings, with the tool faring better where management control skills were more strongly developed compared to the more *laissez faire* regime. The treatment of skill as a dimension of culture is a distinctive feature.

An irony of the scientific method is that, although its epistemology is founded on the principle of replicability, replications are seldom carried out! Webb addresses this issue and presents a useful taxonomy of seven different forms of replication strategies involving different combinations of method, theory, and context. The methods-only extension, for instance, takes an existing theoretical question and tackles it using a different research approach. Webb illustrates this strategy by applying a grounded theory analysis to a model of multimedia systems development previously generated by a content analysis. In broad terms, similar results were found, strengthening the theory, although there were significant nuances.

Igira's paper is noteworthy for its use of activity theory, which has attracted desultory interest over the years within the IS discipline (see Flynn and Gregory 2004). The paper begins with a very thorough and readable account of CHAT (cultural historical activity theory), emphasizing its ability to address "the mutual shaping of context and work practice." There follows a fascinating description of the health-care system in Tanzania, which is used to illustrate the way that contextual influences from the management domain (e.g., the need to generate statistical information) create tensions at the operational level and how these have prompted the development of new local tools.

Whereas classic diffusionist accounts of innovation presuppose a hard-and-fast distinction between users and artefacts, SST (social shaping of technology), like its cousin ANT, emphasizes the dialectical relationship of the two. Burns and Light apply an SST approach to the design and use of software (in the form of "scripts") in call centers, showing how operational staff modified the scripts in order to adapt to local exigencies. In doing so, Burns and Light problematize the boundary between development and use, and underscore the nondeterministic nature of innovation processes.

In order to understand the barriers that all too often frustrate and obstruct organizational efforts to innovate, Bednar and Welch suggest complementing traditional methods with contextual analysis techniques. This entails a concentration on actors' individual assumptions, which when articulated can help those involved understand better the inherent complexities, and therefore the realization of such ambitions.

The novelty of Larsen and Levine is methodological rather than theoretical, and lies not so much in its individual elements, but in their combination. Their concern is the identity of the MIS field as a coherent discipline and on how this should be studied, in terms of its development over time and the diffusion of its core knowledge. Various methods are possible: classification and citation analysis, expert forums, etc. The authors conclude that all methods have a part to play and that a composite will give the most complete picture.

3.3 Software Process Improvement (SPI)

Since its inception, WG 8.6 has maintained a continuing interest in software engineering innovation. This theme unites the papers in this section. Börjesson, Holmberg, Holmström, and Nilsson are concerned that the conventional methods of SPI are founded on a problem-solving paradigm, which can stultify creative thought. They are interested in the potential of appreciative enquiry to stimulate a deeper level of critical reflection. Their case study, however, reveals that engineers find it difficult to let go of solution-oriented mental habits. The paper is also notable for its use of the punctuated equilibrium model that forms the basis of Newman and Zhu's invited paper.

Basili's goal–question–metric (GQM) approach is a well established SPI methodology. A novel feature of its deployment by Börjesson, Baaz, Pries-Heje, and Timmerås is its encasement in an action research framework. The rationale is to facilitate organizational learning and the evolution of the measurement mechanism over time. The results of a 6 year SPI initiative are presented and the paper ends with a reflection on the key lessons learned, including the need for well-defined goals and an iterative approach.

Conboy and Fitzgerald address agile methods, presenting a Delphi study on attitudes and beliefs. The results indicate that such techniques are, or appear to be, generally immutable and not, therefore, readily amenable to tailoring. Yet ironically, tailorability is the very essence of agility! Against a number of identified critical success factors for method tailoring, they highlight the deficiencies inherent in agile methods, concluding with recommendations for industry-based proponents and others who have an interest in such methodologies.

In an apparent contrast, the questionnaire study of the use of methods by Parsons, Ryu, and Lal confirms previous research showing that software technologies are characteristically deployed flexibly, adaptively, and contingently by developers. Their study also focuses on agile methods and techniques, and the findings show important gains in productivity and quality, which are accrued apparently without incurring extra cost.

3.4 Actor Network Theory (ANT)

A clutch of six papers in all feature ANT in different guises as the primary theoretical lens. We note in passing that ANT also sits atop Flynn and Gregory's "league table" of social theories in terms of its prevalence in WG 8.2's deliberations.

Elbanna takes the idea of "modalities" from Latour (1987). Like Newman and Zhu, she is concerned with shifting trajectories, or "drift," over the course of project life-cycles. Whereas positive modalities strengthen the formation of "black boxes," negative ones question the emergent *status quo*, and potentially move the project in different directions. This novel conceptualization is well-illustrated in a detailed account of an ERP implementation.

Linderoth discusses the interesting notion of whether technology should be made visible or invisible through built-in inscriptions that affect and change processes in the host organization. He presents three case studies, two of which provide contrasting accounts of visibility. The third case deals with another related ANT concept—in this case, whether or not the ICT system should become an obligatory passage point. He argues that organizations need to make special efforts in some cases to keep technology visible, thus maintaining a degree of control that might otherwise be lost.

Mohammed and Richardson attempt to combine contextualism with ANT in their study of the strategic processes entailed in constructing and implementing a customer services information system for a UK institute of higher education. They argue that the use of such a theoretical framework enables richer understanding and deeper insights into ICT implementation processes.

Rodon, Pastor, and Sesé provide a retrospective and interpretive account of the "black-boxing" of the network of actants which comprises the Port of Barcelona, along with a related interorganizational information system. The account covers an 11 year period. Their analysis uses the ANT concepts of problematization, interressement, enroll-ment, and mobilization to trace the translation processes through five phases between 1994 and 2005, during which time the system evolved and was eventually implemented.

Lin and Chiasson suggest that ANT concepts combined with innovation diffusion theory can provide a richer theoretical foundation for understanding the relationships among actors engaged in the diffusion of IT. Their study focuses on the technologies and contexts of a pilot study of mobile TV services being conducted in the UK.

In the final paper in this section, Vuokko and Kartsen present an ambitious attempt to integrate concepts from complexity theory with ANT. The theoretical exposition is particularly strong, lucidly articulating the inability of reductionist cause-effect models to account for complex, nonlinear processes. A case setting is described (hospital inten-sive care) where it is argued that their framework is required in order to address the complex work practices and interactions involved. The application of the framework is briefly outlined, although only at a very high level.

3.5 Technological Interlude: The Case of RFID

Radio frequency identification (RFID) technology has recently come to the fore as a potential breakthrough in the management of business supply chains. Huyskens and Loebbecke address the relatively slow progress of its adoption and elaborate an extended version of the technology acceptance model (TAM) as a generic factor model for studying adoption at the organizational level, rather than individual decision making. The model has three sets of factors: external influences, perceived benefits, and organi-zational characteristics. A case study in the fashion industry is presented. Some factors (coercive power, top management support) were found to play a more influential role than others.

RFID technologies are by their very nature immensely complex, and as such traditional research approaches are by and large inadequate for studying these new technologies. Brown and Bakru's thoughtful contribution provides a critique of traditional research methods, arguing that only the combination of process (or stage) models and IS diffusion research seems theoretically adequate for understanding such complex intra- and extra-organizational systems.

3.6 Firm Level Adoption Factors

The papers in this section share a concern with the adoption of technology at the level of the individual organization, and the factors which influence this. Vega, Chiasson, and Brown paper is of particular interest in two areas. Theoretically, it extends the core DOI (diffusion of innovation) model to address broader network-based influences, specifically those emanating from economic development policies. Addressing the role of government support is also timely given the increasing enthusiasm of the state for intervening in all public spheres. Such hubristic interventions often fail to deliver. The authors present a detailed case study illustrating a daunting range of structural factors which inhibit the effectiveness of such programs.

Zhang, Cui, Huang, and Zhang take up a similar theme, again assessing the effectiveness of governmental action. Their theoretical model is based on the technology–organization–environment (TOE) framework, extended with ideas from institutional theory. In a survey of firms in the Shanghai area, they find that the effectiveness of government action varies across sectors and by the type of ownership. Interestingly, local firms are more influenced by government action than enterprises with foreign investment.

Ramdani and Kawalek also draw on TOE in looking at the adoption of enterprise systems among a number of SMEs in the UK's Northwest region. They take a classic factor-based approach, derived from Rogers and others, in their study. Pointing out that there is not a single adoption model, they show that adoption factors in this sector differ from ICT studies in, for example, larger organizations. Their conclusions are presented as implications for software vendors which could assist them in improving their marketing efforts in this particular segment.

Finally, Abu-Samaha and Mansi provide us with insights into the challenges facing Jordan Telecom (JT) as it seeks to recapture ground lost to competitors and changing market demands. The strategy includes the adoption of new and emerging technologies such as microwave, VoIP, and wireless-based systems to compete with other commercial telecommunications providers. They provide a rich description of these technologies, as well as a brief historical perspective of JT and its marketing environment.

4   FINALE

Quoting from Larsen and Levine's final remarks, "In a rich field, many flowers bloom." A pretty enough trope, but we would do well to remember that the originator of the phrase was Mao Tze-tung shortly before wresting China back into the iron cage of central control! Certainly there are grounds for the anxieties expressed by Galliers, echoed by

Truex and Holmström, regarding what the latter dub as the supremacist tendency in our field. In scholarship in general, there are powerful institutional mechanisms exerting an ever tighter grip on what goes and what does not. Those of us in the UK currently engaged in RAE 2008[5] preparations know this only too well! In this audit-driven exercise, papers in top-ranking journals are prized above all else. But top-ranking journals are well-defended by powerful purification rituals, pride themselves on exclusivity, are run by elites, don't take risks with their reputations, and are typically main-stream and monoclonal. What place for the speculative, the idiotic, the unorthodox, the inter-disciplinary hybrid, the maverick? What place for dirt, in other words?

In her coda, Douglas offers the contrast between "dirt-affirming" and "dirt-rejecting" philosophies. She speaks approvingly of those who reject the hegemony of monistic systems of truth; pluralism and "healthy-mindedness"[6] are one and the same. She argues that we need dirt, indeed many religions sacralize the abhorred: "Purity is the enemy of change, of ambiguity and compromise" (Douglas 2002, p. 200). This is Feyerabend's credo too. Engineering also appreciates the epistemological importance of impurity; without mistakes and failures, there is no learning (Petroski 2006). Dirt is therefore to be celebrated, not to be spurned. How dirt-affirming and healthy-minded are we in our tiny niche of WG 8.6. Our epistemological experiment gives the opportunity to take stock. In our selection of papers, we have "worked around" the purity agenda in the interests of inclusion and plurality. Let us now assess the extent to which the Conference has achieved its overarching aim of diversification in theory, method, and empirical context. As noted above, we will use the 1997 conference as a rough baseline (McMaster et al. 1997).

Certainly we have a rich crop of papers, but overall how different is the landscape from a decade ago? Yes, there is some embellishment and the substantive content has moved on, but the main lineaments of our discourse have a remarkably familiar look. Mischief tempts one to say that the face is the same, just a little older! In terms of methodology, we have much the same mix of surveys, case studies, and action research. Domainwise, the majority of papers continue to address commercial rather than public organizations. This is despite the enormous increase in ICT expenditure in the public sector in recent years, and the critical role ICT is playing in driving forward the "modernization" agenda across the globe. Not a single paper explicitly addresses e-Government for instance, despite the burgeoning of this phenomenon, coming from nowhere in the last decade. Why this continuing infatuation with business, one is prompted to ask!

Perhaps theory provides the best indication of movement. In 1997, there were two main camps: DOI was the incumbent dogma and ANT was the new kid on the block. ANT may since have waxed but DOI seems still a powerful force, and they remain the chief protagonists. Indeed one does wonder, with more than a dash of irony, whether

---

[5]The Research Assessment Exercise is a periodic survey of research performance across the UK higher education sector, which regulates the allocation of much research funding. The last survey was conducted in 2001. This is not the place to rehearse the dysfunctions of the RAE; they are rich and varied, and much discussed elsewhere, for example, Elton (2000) and Pierce (2000). to name but a few!

[6]Again, a phrase from James (1936).

they have merely switched roles and that ANT has now become the new default position! It is surely salient that ANT is at the top of Flynn and Gregory's top ten. There is, of course, no explicit supremacist strategy at work here. Path dependency is enough to produce such conformity; it is easier to fit the mold than to break it, and we may need one of Newman and Zhu's "critical incidents" to punctuate this comfortable equilibrium. Perhaps our continuing failure to engage with practice, lamented by Truex and Holmström, will provide the needed crisis.

These authors go on to exhort us to drop our tools and hold our concepts lightly in order to straddle the gap with practice. This invites us to consider that redemption may lie not with more theory, but with less. Our enchantment with models and frameworks reflects our natural need to order the world. But while pastry cutters produce neat shapes, the form they create is the shape of the pastry cutter, not the pastry! Dirt is the source of change and renewal, the antidote to sterility and stagnation. Perhaps, then, we should loosen our attachment to frameworks and models with all their Euclidean orderliness, and dig in the dirt that their ceaseless ordering inevitably creates and sweeps from view. Ciborra (2002, p. 21) put it well: "How come researchers have come to privilege the geometry of a line connecting abstract concepts in a model while they remain blind to the *blurred reality that any, even slight, ethnographic study would have revealed*?" Ethnography and grounded theory may show the way to go. Latour (2004, p. 67) has uttered much the same *cri du coeur*, and it would seem fitting to leave the last word to the begetter of the new orthodoxy! Horrified by our fetishization of theory, he writes mordantly:

> My kingdom for a frame! Very moving; I think I understand your desperation. But no, ANT is pretty useless for that. Its main tenet is that actors themselves make everything, including their own frames, their own theories, their own contexts, their own metaphysics, even their own ontologies....So the direction to follow would be more descriptions, I am afraid.

References

Ciborra, C. *The Labyrinths of Information: Challenging the Wisdom of Systems,* Oxford: Oxford University Press, 2002.

Douglas, M. *Purity and Danger,* London: Routledge, 2002.

Elton, L. "The UK Research Assessment Exercise: Unintended Consequences," *Higher Education Quarterly* (54:3), 2000, pp. 74-83.

Feyerabend, P. *Against Method,* London: Verso, 1993.

Flynn, D., and Gregory, P. "The Use of Theories in 20 Years of WG 8.2 Empirical Research," in B. Kaplan, D. P. Truex, D. Wastell, A. T. Wood-Harper, and J. I. DeGross (eds.), *Information Systems Research: Relevant Theory and Informed Practice,* Boston: Kluwer, 2004, pp. 365-388.

James, W. *The Varieties of Religious Experience,* New York: Modern Library, 1936.

Latour, B. "On Using ANT for Studying Information Systems: A (Somewhat) Socratic Dialogue," in C. Avgerou, C. Ciborra, and F. Land (eds.), *The Social Study of Information and Communication Technology : Innovation, Actors and Contexts,* Oxford: Oxford University Press, 2004.

Latour, B. *Pandora's Hope: An Essay on the Reality of Science Studies,* Cambridge, MA: Harvard University Press, 1999.

Latour, B. *Science in Action*, Cambridge, MA: Harvard University Press, 2004.
McMaster, T. , Mumford, E., Swanson, E. B., Warboys, B., and Wastell, D. G. *Facilitating Technology Transfer Through Partnership: Learning from Practice and Research*, London: Chapman & Hall, 1997.
Petroski, H. *Success Through Failure: The Paradox of Design*, Princeton, NJ: Princeton University Press, 2006.
Pierce, N. "Why it Is Fundamentally Stupid for a Business School to Try to Improve its Research Assessment Exercise Score," *European Journal of Marketing* (34:1/2), 2000, pp. 27-35.
Stoler, A. L. "Colonial Archives and the Arts of Governance," *Archival Science* (2), 2002, pp. 87-109.

About the Authors

David Wastell is a professor of Information Systems at Nottingham University Business School. He began his research career as a psycho-physiologist before moving into information systems. His research interests are in public sector reform, innovation and design, management epistemology, and cognitive ergonomics. He has co-organized two previous IFIP conferences as well as the present meeting, and has extensive consultancy experience, especially in the public sector. David may be contacted at dave_wastell@hotmail.com.

Tom McMaster is a lecturer and researcher in the Informatics Research Centre at the University of Salford, Manchester, UK. Tom has a variety of research interests including technology transfer. He is a member of IFIP WG 8.2 and a founding member of IFIP WG 8.6, for which he co-organized the 1997 Ambleside event. He currently serves on the editorial boards of *Information Technology and People* and the *Journal of Information Systems Education*. Tom can be reached at t.mcmaster@salford.ac.uk.

Part 1:

Keynotes and Invited Papers

2 ORGANIZATIONAL DYNAMICS OF TECHNOLOGY-BASED INNOVATION: Diversifying the Information Systems Research Agenda[1]

Robert D. Galliers
Bentley College
Waltham, MA, U.S.A.

Tempora mutantur, et nos mutamur in illis[2]

This keynote address takes up the conference theme and argues for greater diversification and innovation—in method and topic—in Information Systems research and curricula design. Basing my arguments on my own—and others'—recent critiques of calls for a narrowing of our focus on the information technology artefact and IS design, I will highlight the expanding boundary of the field of Information Systems and what this means for the IS academy in terms of innovation and diversification in our research and teaching.

In some respects, and despite its relatively recent emergence as a field of study, Information Systems may go down in history as a field that has done more navel-gazing than any other. Following the publication of a paper in *MIS Quarterly*, which called for a return to the discipline's [*sic*] "core properties" (Benbasat and Zmud 2003), there was a crescendo of debate that argued pro and con (e.g., Alter 2003; King and Lyytinen 2006). But the debate did not start there. For example, back in 1970, Zani produced his "Blueprint for MIS," and in 1973, Langefors provided "a theoretical analysis" of Information Systems. Keen (1980) considered the field's reference disciplines and called

---

[1]This paper builds on and extends arguments published earlier (see Galliers 2003, 2006).
[2]"Times change, and we change with them" (quoted in Harrison, *Description of Britain*, Pt. III, Ch. iii, 1577).

Please use the following format when citing this chapter:

Galliers, R. D., 2007, in IFIP International Federation for Information Processing, Volume 235, Organizational Dynamics of Technology-Based Innovation: Diversifying the Research Agenda, eds. McMaster, T., Wastell, D., Ferneley, E., and DeGross, J. (Boston: Springer), pp. 15-18.

for a "cumulative tradition." In 1985, I myself went looking for "a paradigm" for Information Systems research (Galliers 1985). Soon afterward, my colleague at Bentley College, Mary Culnan, wrote on the "intellectual development" (1986) and "intellectual structure" (Culnan 1987) of MIS; Banville and Landry (1989) asked whether MIS could "be disciplined"; Backhouse, Liebenau, and Land (1991) considered the domain of the "discipline of Information Systems." More recently, Orlikowski and Iacono (2001) went ("desperately") to seek "the IT in IT research," and Weber (2003) was still desperate two years later. I could go on.

Why all this introspection? Another Bentley colleague of mine—Lynne Markus— poses the question: "What happens if the field of IS goes away?" (Markus 1999), a view echoed by Lucas (1999). For Markus, we are at a crossroads. Either we become one of the truly important fields in business, or—alternatively—different aspects of the field devolve into other subject areas of business. So concerned are some of our colleagues about the latter scenario that they argue for disciplinary purity—only by returning attention to the IT artefact, and focusing on IS design and development as the discipline's "core" (e.g., Benbasat and Zmud 2003, 2006) will we retain our place in the academic universe.

In this presentation, a contrary stance is taken. Developments in the field are viewed as a case of natural evolution. There is an implicit, early Kuhnian worldview underpinning Benbasat and Zmud's and Weber's arguments. A central feature of Kuhn's earlier consideration of scientific communities (Kuhn 1961) was the concept of paradigm—a monistic vision of science, which required revolution to take place in order for any movement from the core. Banville and Landry (1989, p. 49) develop the theme:

> [Adherents to this view] use the term paradigm as meaning [that] members of a scientific discipline...always know precisely the relevant research topics... the appropriate research methods and the proper interpretation of results.

The argument I put forth in my earlier work (Galliers 2003, p. 156) takes on a very different interpretation: "any field that is able critically to reflect on itself and range widely over related subject matter actually enhances its legitimacy." On reflection, Benbasat and Zmud are modernists, while I take a post-modernist stance.

> Postmodernism rejects boundaries and rigid genre distinctions. It emphasizes pastiche, parody, and bricolage. It favors reflexivity and self-consciousness, fragmentation and discontinuity, ambiguity. It places emphasis on the destructured, the decentered, and the absence of solutions. While much the same can be said of modernism, postmodernism differs in relation to its stance on these issues. Modernism—like postmodernism—presents this fragmented view of human subjectivity, history and the world we live in, but does so with a measure of angst. It presents this fragmentation as something tragic, something to be lamented and something to be concerned about. I see the arguments of Benbasat and Zmud, and Weber, among others, in this light. They, like many modernist thinkers, try to uphold the idea that we as a "discipline" should accentuate the unity, coherence, and meaning that they lament as being lost in much of recent IS literature that has somehow forgotten the "core"—which in

their terms is the IT artifact. Postmodernism, in contrast, doesn't lament the idea of fragmentation, provisionality, or incoherence, but rather celebrates all this. The world is meaningless? Let's not pretend that we can make meaning then, let's just play with nonsense; let's enjoy the incongruities, the range of stances we take, and the emergence—the new knowledge that arises from the confluence of ideas emanating from our different worldviews. Let's continue to explore terra incognita. Who knows what we might find. In other words: "Don't worry, be happy" (Galliers 2006, p. 326).[3]

This keynote presentation will develop the theme of emergence and innovation, emphasizing the need for a dynamic, explorative approach to the IS field—one that is transdisciplinary by its very nature, and one that ranges from user interaction with the technological artefact—yes—but one that has also expanded—most appropriately—to concern itself with, for example, societal, ethical and global issues (Galliers et al. 2007). This is how diversity and innovation in our field is to be found.

References

Alter, S. "The IS Core – XI: Sorting Out the Issues about the Core, Scope, and Identity of the IS Field," *Communications of the AIS* (12:41), November 2003, pp. 607-627.

Backhouse, J., Liebenau, J., and Land, F. "On the Discipline of Information Systems," *Journal of Information Systems* (now *Information Systems Journal*) (1:1), January 1991, pp. 19-27.

Banville, C., and Landry, M. "Can the Field of MIS be Disciplined?," *Communications of the ACM* (32:1), January 1989, pp. January, 48-60.

Benbasat, I., and Zmud, R. "Further Reflections on the Identity Crisis," in J. L. King and K. Lyytinen (eds.), *Information Systems: The State of the Field*, Chichester: Wiley, 2006, pp. 300-306.

Benbasat, I., and Zmud, R. "The Identity Crisis Within the IS Discipline: Defining and Communicating the Core's Properties," *MIS Quarterly* (27:2), June 2003, pp. 183-194.

Culnan, M. "The Intellectual Development of Management Information Systems, 1972-1982: A Co-citation Analysis," *Management Science* (32:2), February 1986, pp. 156-172.

Culnan, M. "Mapping the Intellectual Structure of MIS, 1980-1985: A Co-citation Analysis," *MIS Quarterly* (11:3), September 1987, pp. 341-353.

Galliers, R. D. "Change as Crisis or Growth? Towards a Transdisciplinary View of Information Systems as a Field of Study: A Response to Benbasat and Zmud's Call for Returning to the IT Artifact," *Journal of the Association for Information Systems* (4:6), 2003, pp. 360-376.

Galliers, R. D. "'Don't Worry, Be Happy...': A Post-Modernist Perspective on the Information Systems Domain," in J. L. King and K. Lyytinen (eds.), *Information Systems: The State of the Field*, Chichester: Wiley, 2006, pp. 324-331.

Galliers, R. D. "In Search of a Paradigm for Information System Research," in E. Mumford, R. Hirschheim, G. Fitzgerald, and A. T. Wood-Harper (eds.), *Research Methods in Information Systems*, Amsterdam: North-Holland, 1985, pp. 85-94.

Galliers, R. D., Markus, M. L., and Newell, S. (eds.). *Exploring Information Systems Research Approaches: Readings and Reflections*, Abingdon, Oxford: Palgrave, 2007.

---

[3]This quote draws heavily from Mary Klage's course syllabus on modern critical thought at the University of Colorado (http://www.colorado.edu/English/courses/ENGL2012Klages/pomo.html).

Keen, P. G. W. "MIS Research: Reference Disciplines and a Cumulative Tradition," in in E. R. McLean (ed.), *Proceedings of the First International Conference on Information Systems*, Philadelphia PA, 1980, pp. 9-18.

King, J. L., and Lyytinen, K. (eds.). *Information Systems: The State of the Field*, Chichester: Wiley, 2006.

Kuhn, T. S. *The Structure of Scientific Revolution*, Chicago: University of Chicago Press, 1961.

Langefors, B. *Theoretical Analysis of Information Systems*, Philadlphia, PA: Auerbach, 1973.

Lucas, H. "The State of the Information Systems Field," *Communications of the AIS* (1:5), 1999.

Markus, M. L. "Thinking the Unthinkable: What Happens If the Is Field as We Know it Goes Away?," in W. Currie and R. D. Galliers (eds.), *Rethinking MIS*, Oxford: Oxford University Press, 1999, pp. 175-203.

Orlikowski, W., and Iacono, S. "Desperately Seeking the 'IT' in IT Research," *Information Systems Research* (7:4), 2001, pp. 400-408.

Weber, R. "Still Desperately Seeking the IT Artifact," *MIS Quarterly* (27:2), 2003, pp. iii-xi.

Zani, R. "Blueprint for MIS," *Harvard Business Review*, November-December, 1970, pp. 95-100.

About the Author

Appointed as Provost of Bentley College in 2002, **Bob Galliers** was previously Professor of Information Systems and Research Director in the Department of Information Systems at the London School of Economics. Before joining LSE, he served as Lucas Professor of Business Management Systems and Dean of Warwick Business School in the UK, and earlier as Foundation Professor and Head of the School of Information Systems at Curtin University in Australia. Bob is editor-in-chief of *Journal of Strategic Information Systems*, and a fellow of the British Computer Society, the Royal Society of Arts, and the Association for Information Systems (AIS), of which he was president during 1999. He has held visiting professorships at INSEAD (France), University of St. Gallen (Switzerland), City University of Hong Kong, Institute for Advanced Management Studies (Belgium), National University of Singapore, Hong Kong Polytechnic University, and Bond University (Australia). He has published widely in many of the leading international journals on Information Systems and has also authored/edited a number of books, the most recent being *Exploring Information Systems Research Approaches* (Routledge, 2007), the third edition of the best seller, *Strategic Information Management* (Butterworth-Heinemann, 2003), *Rethinking Management Information Systems* (Oxford University Press, 1999), and *IT and Organizational Transformation* (Wiley, 1998). He holds an AB degree with honors in Economics from Harvard University, an MA with distinction in Management Systems from Lancaster University, and a Ph.D. in Information Systems from the London School of Economics. He was awarded an Honorary Doctor of Science degree by Turku University of Economics and Business Administration, Finland, in 1995. His research focuses in the main on information systems strategy and the management of change associated with the adoption and appropriation of ICT-based systems within and between organizations. Bob can be reached by e-mail at rgalliers@bentley.edu.

3 TURNING THE DIGITAL DIVIDE INTO A DIGITAL DIVIDEND: Some Experiences from Manchester, UK

Dave Carter
Manchester Digital Development Agency
Manchester, United Kingdom

Abstract   *This paper focuses on the ways that innovative applications of digital technologies are being developed in Manchester (in the North West of England) and in the UK's largest urban regeneration area, East Manchester, with the aim of tackling the "digital divide," reengaging citizens in civic life, and transforming the delivery of public services in the context of urban regeneration. The paper suggests that sustainable regeneration requires a much more holistic approach to urban development than has been the case in previous strategies and policies and can benefit from using digital technologies. In order to turn the digital divide into a "digital dividend," more emphasis needs to be placed on citizen engagement, empowerment and capacity building. This case study aims to provide examples of how a multi-agency partnership approach is working to tackle these challenges through the "ONE-Manchester" initiative (Open Network E-Manchester).*

Keywords   Digital divide, urban regeneration

1 URBAN REGENERATION IN MANCHESTER

Urban regeneration is an essential prerequisite for tackling social exclusion and economic restructuring. Cities across the world face similar challenges in terms of finding coherent and effective policies and strategies that will support and sustain economic growth and connect the opportunities created by economic growth with the needs of their citizens. The emergence of the information society has added new complexities to this process,

Please use the following format when citing this chapter:

Carter, D., 2007, in IFIP International Federation for Information Processing, Volume 235, Organizational Dynamics of Technology-Based Innovation: Diversifying the Research Agenda, eds. McMaster, T., Wastell, D., Ferneley, E., and DeGross, J. (Boston: Springer), pp. 19-29.

on the one hand adding to the speed and scale of change while on the other hand providing new tools and processes which can help to mitigate the impact of that change.

Manchester (in the North West of England) has experienced new economic growth developing side by side with persistently high levels of unemployment, poverty, and social exclusion. It has the third highest rate of multiple deprivation (apart from Liverpool and Knowlsley) and the highest rate of child poverty in the UK. This "tale of two cities" syndrome (as it has been referred to) threatens to undermine the longer term sustainability of economic development and growth. Manchester City Council has responded to this challenge by identifying information and communication technologies (ICTs) and digital media (referred to in this paper as digital technologies) as an important cross-cutting theme within its City-Region Economic Development Strategy and Plan. The aim is that digital technologies should be used to increase citizens' access to skills, jobs, and services and to support greater participation in civic life, including in the regeneration process itself.

A major influence on this approach is the experience gained in East Manchester where the City Council has formed an urban regeneration company (URC), New East Manchester (NEM) Ltd., a public-private-community partnership operating on a not-for-profit basis. An online community network, run in partnership with local citizens organizations and representatives, known as Eastserve was established here in 2001.

This is supported by a new city-wide initiative, the Manchester Digital Development Agency (MDDA), established in 2003 with the mission

> *To make Manchester a leading world class digital city, having one of the most competitive broadband infrastructures in Europe, attracting and sustaining investment in ICT and e-commerce across all sectors of the economy, generating new businesses, developing new learning cultures, promoting social inclusion and providing all residents with the skills and aspirations to play a full role in the information society.*[1]

The objective is that the Manchester city-region can become one of the most competitive yet inclusive e-enabled urban environments in the world, based on a world-class and comprehensive broadband infrastructure which is used to promote access, skills, jobs, and sustainable economic growth. Through the work of the MDDA the City Council and its local strategic partnership (LSP)[2] aim to ensure that local people can develop the skills required to participate fully in the emerging information society and to be able to take advantage of the new training and employment opportunities that are becoming available.

The Eastserve project[3] works with existing community based ICT access centers, known as UKOnline Centres, across the city and related projects which promote the take-up and use of digital technologies by small businesses and social enterprises. This work

---

[1]From the MDDA website, www.manchesterdda.com.
[2]See the Manchester Partnership website at www.manchesterpartnership.org.uk.
[3]See the Eastserve project website at www.eastserve.com.

builds upon national[4] and local[5] policy frameworks focusing on digital inclusion as well as good practice examples identified through national initiatives such as the UK Communities Online network.[6]

These initiatives are aiming to achieve real and lasting benefits for citizens around three key issues that need to be addressed within this approach:

- How new e-services can be developed which engage citizens, drive take-up of eGovernment services and support the regeneration of urban neighborhoods.
- What barriers to take-up are being identified and how these can be challenged through new working relationships being developed between city administrations, citizens, and businesses.
- Ways in which innovation, in terms of both technologies and business models, can support organizational transformation and be sustained.

2   CHALLENGING THE DIGITAL DIVIDE

Many residents in the East Manchester area use mobile phones rather than fixed telephone lines. The initial survey work undertaken by the area regeneration partnership (in 2001) revealed that more than 25 percent of homes no longer used land lines. This led to changes to the initial aims and objectives of the project which had been to provide PCs to households with dial-up Internet access. This meant that a system of wireless broadband connectivity was required, which then enabled households to access the Internet and on-line services.

More than 2,000 of the area's homes now have wireless broadband Internet connections, as well as 17 local schools, 8 "UKOnline" community access centers, and 10 public access points in libraries and other centers. They all connect to a 100Mbps licensed wireless backbone linking four tower blocks around the East Manchester area from where bandwidth is distributed over a wireless network.

Schools and public buildings receive an online community service, developed by Eastserve, and relay it to other residential locations. These locations are grouped in clusters and communicate with one another wirelessly via a radio dish antenna connected to a wireless bridge. This is one of the largest community based all-wireless broadband networks in Europe and the largest community regeneration initiative using digital technologies in the UK. In spite of being one of the poorest areas in the city, the take-up of broadband in the area is far higher than the city-wide rate and residents are using their new skills to improve their access to training and jobs. The project aims to be financially self-sufficient within 2 years.

---

[4]Department of Trade and Industry (UK), "Closing the Digital Divide: Information and Communication Technologies in Deprived Areas," Report by the Social Exclusion Unit Policy Action Team 15, DTI, London, March 2000.

[5]Manchester City Council, "Tackling The Digital Divide Project Report." MCC, Manchester, July 2002.

[6]Communities On-Line, "Local Connections: Making the Net Work for Neighbourhood Renewal," COL, London, 1999.

The initial evaluation of the impact of the project has shown that Eastserve users are

- more aware of job opportunities
- want access to more training
- more likely to seek work
- more likely to take part in other educational opportunities
- more likely to be looking for new challenges
- more interested in running their own businesses

Plans are now going ahead to expand the current user coverage from about 5,000 households to more than 10,000 households during 2007 and then to more than 50,000 households by 2010, expanding population coverage from around 20,000 people to more than 250,000. Over 40 percent of residents have now had basic ICT training because of Eastserve, more than double the rate of most areas in the city, and 20 percent of these are moving on to extended courses which provide opportunities for accreditation.

3   DIGITAL INCLUSION AND URBAN REGENERATION

Manchester is the UK's second largest metropolitan area outside of London, with a population of over 2.5 million in the Greater Manchester city-region. At its core is the City of Manchester, the first industrial urban area in the world and the "original, modern" city. Alongside the city's transformation from industrial to knowledge economy is the legacy of high levels of unemployment and poverty from the experience and impact of the economic restructuring of the 1970s and 1980s. Much of this legacy is concentrated in the traditional industrial manufacturing area of the city, in East Manchester. Once home to more than 100,000, its population has declined significantly, to less than 30,000 people.

East Manchester is a regeneration challenge of regional and national significance. An area of 1,100 hectares situated immediately east of Manchester's City Centre, East Manchester presents an opportunity for regeneration on a scale and diversity almost unprecedented in an English city. There are unique opportunities for the renaissance of the area as a focus for the knowledge-driven economy of the 21st century. These opportunities have been generated by

- A range of regeneration initiatives focusing upon East Manchester to address many of the physical, economic, and social problems in the area
- The stimulus provided by a buoyant economy within Manchester and the major investment attracted through the staging of the Commonwealth Games in 2002
- The strong commitment by government to the success of cities and to tackling the most acute areas of deprivation
- The strong partnership between the local community and national, regional, and local government

A key component of any regeneration challenge in the 21st century is the role of technology in its many forms. Digital technologies are having an ever-increasing effect on all of our lives and are essential to the development of a strong economic base and an improved quality of life for citizens within an area such as East Manchester.

In looking to expand this strategic approach across the whole of the city-region, Manchester City Council and its partners within the LSP have linked up with three neighboring municipalities, Tameside, Salford, and Oldham, and their strategic partnerships to create ONE-Manchester (Open Network E-Manchester). ONE-Manchester is a new partnership which brings together the public sector, private sector, and voluntary/community sector around the idea of "turning the digital divide into a digital dividend."[7] This is looking at the longer term sustainability of digital inclusion policies and practices by developing a new collaborative delivery mechanism for digitally enabled services and social networking. It also aims to provide a sustainable digital development model which can be used to create social capital and community cohesion by

- Building on the "sense of place" through the development of geographically focused digital action places
- Transforming community capability and developing innovative content through improved access to e-services and content with proposals for the NetStart program
- Ensuring sustainability through a new digital cooperative which would coordinate and support local, regional, and national initiatives and realize the benefits of the digital dividend

ONE-Manchester is about taking the experience gained on innovative digital inclusion projects in which the partners are involved, such as Eastserve in East Manchester and eTameside, and using this to create an exemplar to stimulate and support digital inclusion initiatives across the city-region, the region, and nationally. This is based on imagining a Manchester in which people have a real personal stake in digitally enabled living and a new sense of pride in their achievements as one of the most connected and cooperative communities in the world.

ONE-Manchester's aim is mainstreaming innovation by developing a dynamic collaborative platform which will enable people, both individually and collectively, to become stakeholders in a new way of social networking through the digital cooperative. People need to be able to share their skills and knowledge, develop new digital applications and services, and create added value in the form of a digital dividend. ONE-Manchester's proposal is based on the four core principles of social cohesion:

- Creating a common vision and a sense of belonging for all communities through imaginative uses of digital technologies to help to transform lives
- Ensuring that diversity is appreciated and positively rewarded through improved accessibility of digital technologies to support social networking
- Engaging people from different backgrounds through the use of digital technologies which enables them to have similar life chances

---

[7]This is the central theme of the ONE-Manchester Digital Challenge bid (www.manchesterdda.com/digitalchallenge/158/). The UK Digital Challenge site is located at www.digitalchallenge.gov.uk.

- Encouraging strong and positive relationships to be developed between people from different backgrounds in the workplace, in education, and within neighborhoods by using digital technologies to break down barriers and promote social cohesion

4   TRANSFORMING COMMUNITIES THROUGH NEIGHBORHOOD EMPOWERMENT

ONE-Manchester's idea of turning the digital divide into a digital dividend is about enabling everyone in the community, no matter how excluded and disadvantaged, to gain a stake in the knowledge economy and to use it to provide themselves with a better life, particularly in terms of work, skills, and health.

The first stage of ONE-Manchester's journey of transformation is to start where people are located. In some places people are starting to do things for themselves: making the most out of the great investment that has been made in specific areas to date, such as Eastserve and eTameside; taking the lessons of the digital pioneers who initiated digital development in Manchester over the past 20 years; getting users involved in generating their own content and using that to develop new e-services with a mutual aid ethos.

The next stage is to develop a new set of tools, building on these foundations to provide everyone with the capacity to use digital technologies to transform their lives. Whatever the technology—computers, mobile phones, digital TV, assistive technologies in the home—people want to be "ready," to be able to deal with the inevitable change that they will face in the future. Whoever is working with people—public, private, and voluntary sectors—there is an equal sense of needing to be better prepared, to be ready, to manage change and create a renewed sense of cooperation and partnership. There is a similar need to be able to use digital technologies as an effective tool in making this happen.

ONE-Manchester is, therefore, about building on this experience and using the partners' proven track record in delivering projects which transform people's lives, from Eastserve to the Commonwealth Games, to create a new, imaginative, and sustainable digital city-region.

We start off by taking people's real experiences of both the challenges and the benefits of using technologies in this way. We have illustrated these through a series of "user journeys" based on archetypes developed through community engagement and consultations.

This led to the three core elements of the ONE-Manchester strategy:

(1) the focus on the sense of place with geographically based digital action places where the effort is concentrated
(2) stimulating community engagement and social capital, including innovative content, with the NetStart program
(3) promoting mutual aid to reflect the cooperative nature of the best of what is possible in the digital age with the proposal for a digital cooperative which will be the centerpiece of the project's economic sustainability

These will be underpinned by focusing on technology and applications that enable delivery of national-local service agreements, known as local area agreements, in each local authority area.

The geographic focus based on digital action places will have the resources and processes to deliver personalized NetStart action plans to local residents and organizations. This process will be like setting up a franchise (e.g., a shop selling fair-trade goods): it has local flavor and focus but draws on central support/processes, the proposed ONE-Manchester services catalog, including training materials, equipment discount deals, guides to content, and technical support services.

NetStart provides people with the capability and connectivity to access content and services most relevant to them, with a particular reference to work/skills and health/ liveability. The precise size and shape of support will depend on need and funding available, but the aim is to ensure that delivery on the most flexible/adaptable basis possible.

All of this will fit together into what we see as a digital matrix, with the digital cooperative at the center and a commitment to make the city-region the UK's first "IP-City" with everyone, everything and everywhere connected using IP (Internet protocol). Backing this up the content/services access mechanism which we have called the "MyCommunity Gateway" will enable users to get to relevant content/services.

Each user journey starts with

- Engagement with the local digital action place with the method depending on locality and approach taken to engagement
- NetStart individual planning to determine needs and current digital capability to create personalized NetStart plans
- Access to content/services via the matrix digital cooperative, with membership options and the chance to build up and share in a digital dividend (a digital "divi")

The ONE-Manchester partnership will start to deliver this by implementing the first stage of establishing new digital action places (strengthening and building out from East Manchester) in the North Manchester, Central Manchester, and Tameside (Droylsden/ Ashton Corridor) Regeneration Areas in 2007 to be followed by a second stage in the Wythenshawe, the Salford Urban Regeneration Company (URC) area, and North Trafford and Oldham Regeneration Areas during 2008.

5   BENEFITS FROM TRANSFORMATIONAL PRACTICE

In an attempt to address the challenges presented by Manchester's industrial legacy and to ensure that economic growth can be sustained, ONE-Manchester is being developed on a multiagency basis to develop innovative eGovernment applications which will support

- service improvement through enhanced quality and delivery of services
- citizen engagement through the development of new models for service delivery and to engage citizens more effectively in strategic planning and consultation arrangements

- the development of new business models which will aid organizational transformation, including public-private partnerships and social economy enterprises

Social inclusion lies at the heart of this approach because large parts of the
Manchester city-region are still characterized by poor quality environment and poor
infrastructure, the economic hangover from industrial restructuring. People living here
cannot reach their full potential as a result of this. Educational attainment and skill levels
are low. Levels of poor health are among the highest in the UK and many residents live
in areas where crime and anti-social behavior levels are significantly above the regional
and national averages.

Worklessness rates are among the highest in the UK. Rates are more than 20 percent
in Manchester's, some 60,000 people, and in the core urban population of more than
900,000, about 150,000 people are affected. Of the 58 priority wards being targeted by
the new joint city strategy partnership initiative with the UK government's Department
for Work and Pensions (DWP), 43 of them are in the urban core.

This is why the ONE-Manchester bid is concentrating on mainstreaming digital
inclusion into the three priorities, or "spines", and linked into the local area agreement
blocks.

(1) *Reaching full potential in employment and education*: reconnecting people with
    opportunities to work, including for themselves, and to learn.
(2) *Creating neighborhoods of choice*: creating improved and sustainable environments
    where people are, and feel, safe, where they have access to jobs, good schools,
    health services and amenities.
(3) *Individual and collective self-esteem/mutual respect*: understanding what motivates
    people to behave in certain ways, what influences aspirations and attitudes, and how
    to best engage people in fulfilling their responsibilities toward achieving inclusion
    and cohesion.

Underpinning all of this is the belief that encouraging people back into work will
have the biggest impact on quality of life and self esteem, including increasing collective
self-esteem and mutual respect. Alongside this, we believe that health and environmental
factors also need to be given a high priority in our commitment to transforming lives and
communities. Sustainable communities require healthier, greener, cleaner, and safer life-
styles to be encouraged and nurtured.

To turn this around requires continued investment. As the recent review report of
developments in the New East Manchester NEM-URC area highlighted,

> *The NEM rock is halfway up the hill. There is much development planned. If*
> *support is not maintained it could just as easily roll back down the hill as reach*
> *the sunny uplands at the top. It is critical that all partners realise this and con-*
> *tinue to support NEM.* (ProfessorMichael Parkinson, Liverpool JM University).

Based on the regeneration experience to date, the consultation and engagement
undertaken with those who will be affected by the bid and the political commitment of
the civic leadership, to deliver. ONE-Manchester believes that this approach can and
will transform lives at three levels:

- First, mobilizing resources through the geographic focus of digital action places and dedicating these to deliver to the priority areas tailored to their specific needs.
- Second, by having content that is directly relevant to the needs of local people, and the service providers working to meet their needs, through the NetStart program.
- Third, by using the digital cooperative as a new model of mutual aid that will provide service users with the motivation to become more active participants in the process of transformation, supporting behavioural change with improved aspirations.

In addition, Manchester is in the first phase of the Building Schools for the Future (BSF) Program, while Tameside and Salford are starting programs in 2007, offering the opportunity with the Computers for Pupils scheme to create additional digital action places at each BSF school. The added value considerably enhances the potential for young people to fully achieve their potential and reduce the number of pupils not engaged in education, employment, or training. The additional presence of a PC in the homes of those young people eligible for equipment via Computers for Pupils creates more opportunity for entire families to access NetStart packs and engage in the digital cooperative. Enhanced opportunity via a combination of BSF and One Manchester is a significant element in the delivery of the "14-19 agenda" across the region.

Many people already know about lessons learned from innovative digital inclusion approaches in East Manchester. Initially ONE-Manchester will use that to roll out its proposal in the adjacent areas, with digital action places as the basis for digital inclusion in North and Central Manchester and West Tameside. The NetStart program will be used to generate greater awareness about ways of engaging people in these areas through digitally enabled social networking and about the benefits of joining the digital cooperative.

The next stage will be to develop operation of this digital inclusion model as a form of "franchise" arrangement within the Salford URC area and with pilot projects in North Trafford and Oldham. ONE-Manchester then intends to lead a roll-out program for digital action places across the city-region, the North West region, the three northern regions of England (known as the "Northern Way"), and nationally.

6   CONCLUSIONS

The experience gained through the Eastserve project has been used by the partners involved in the ONE-Manchester initiative to reevaluate and refocus their work around the eGovernment and citizen engagement agendas. For Manchester City Council, this has meant a greater understanding of the need to be more proactive in stimulating demand for eGovernment service delivery. Side by side with organizational trans-formation internally, the City Council is now working hard to promote take up of e-services through awareness campaigns, improved access to training, and the direct involvement of citizens in producing content for on-line services.

Eastserve is considering new ways to achieve sustainability including developing a major part of its activities as a social economy enterprise which would develop a new cooperative model for service delivery with citizen stakeholders. All of this experience suggests that key players in eGovernment, such as local and regional government bodies, need to take a more holistic approach to promoting and delivering greater access to, and take up of, information society technologies. Further work is now needed to identify and evaluate best practice, especially in terms of identifying what are the most effective ways of engaging citizen involvement and then sustaining it.

At the same time work is also needed on new delivery partnerships, looking not only at developing models of public-private partnerships but also at citizen partnerships and models of social economy enterprises. It is felt that there is significant scope to develop and test new organizational models which will play an important role in ensuring sustainability of these developments. One of the most important recommendations to come out of this work is the need for innovative approaches to tackling inequalities in the information society, the digital divide, for example by providing not only access to equipment, connectivity, and training, but also stimulating demand by developing good quality content and involving local citizens in generating that content.

City administrations also need to learn from these results and experiences, particularly in terms of involving citizens more effectively in the ongoing organizational transformation of public services. The Eastserve project has many implications for the way that public and community services are delivered, including eGovernment solutions, not only in local authorities but also in other areas (e.g., in East Manchester, the police and health services are also now implementing changes to the way they deliver services because of the experience of the Eastserve project).

This has led to policy recommendations being proposed by the Manchester Digital Development Agency (MDDA), which are being taken forward through the ONE-Manchester partnership at the local level, at the regional level through the North West eGovernment Group (NWeGG), at the national level as part of the UK government's Digital Challenge initiative, and through European networks such as Eurocities and Telecities.[8] In terms of defining new challenges for information society technologies and policies, the most important one is about how we engage with citizens to ensure that they can become active producers of online content and new e-services rather than passive consumers of what is there already (as outlined above).

It is felt that the transformation of urban living through the imaginative use of digital technologies can make a significant contribution to the EU's Lisbon objectives, especially as revised by the recent Report of the High Level Group,[9] in terms of jobs and growth. Cities act as motors of innovation and creativity for the economy and society as a whole and it is anticipated that this will increasingly be the source of future jobs and growth in the knowledge economy. At the same, time these technologies also provide opportunities to transform the lives of citizens, as highlighted in the EU's communication on the challenges to be addressed by a European Information Society Strategy up to 2010.[10] This is why the focus on tackling the digital divide and promoting digital inclusion is continuing to be seen as a priority, highlighting the need to ensure that citizens have the capacity, skills, and motivation to take advantage of these technologies.

---

[8]See the Eurocities web site at www.eurocities.org.

[9] W.   Kok (Chair), "Facing the Challenge—The Lisbon Strategy for Growth and Employment," Report from the High Level Group, Brussels, November 2004.

[10]European Commission, "Challenges for Europe's Information Society Beyond 2005," COM, 2004.

There are a number of specific lessons that be can learned from the Eastserve experience which it is hoped will be of use to similar projects being developed in other areas. First, the need to develop e-services that are based on the social, cultural, and economic needs of the neighborhoods. This requires a combination of detailed local research and real efforts to consult with and engage local people as an essential prerequisite for capturing user needs and involving users in the design and delivery of the new services. Second, the stakeholders in the project, especially the public sector, need to demonstrate a long term commitment to community engagement and capacity building and invest as much in the development of people's skills and confidence as in the technology being deployed. Third, the need to have an ongoing evaluation strategy that not only has the ability to identify weaknesses, and even failures, but also has the role of communicating these results directly into the strategic decision making process so that the project can adapt and evolve as quickly and effectively as possible, backed up by effective project management resources.

About the Author

Dave Carter is head of the Manchester Digital Development Agency (MDDA), and previously served as acting head of Economic Development from 2002-2004, at Manchester City Council. The MDDA coordinates information society initiatives across the city-region, including community-based broadband initiatives and the ONE-Manchester Digital Challenge proposal. The MDDA focuses on how digital technologies can support economic regeneration and social inclusion (for more information, see www.manchesterdda.com). He was the European Project Coordinator of the IntelCities (Intelligent Cites) Project, which was a £7 million project funded under the EU's FP6 IST program (2002-2006) in partnership with the University of Salford, Nokia, Cisco, Telecities, Eurocities, and 20 other European cities. Dave can be reached by e-mail at d.carter@manchesterdda.com.

4 DROPPING YOUR TOOLS: The Diversity of the Research Agenda in Organizational Dynamics of Technology-Based Innovation

Duane Truex
Georgia State University
Atlanta, GA, U.S.A.

Jonny Holmström
Umeå University
Umeå, Sweden

Abstract   *The debate between protagonists of different theoretical approaches continues in the Information Systems field, with little prospect of resolution. The debate is typically characterized by tendentious arguments as advocates from each approach offer a somewhat one-sided condemnation of other approaches. A recent debate in the* Scandinavian Journal of Information Systems (SJIS) *illustrates the manner in which IS researchers are polarized into opposing camps, each tending to view the other as inferior. Ironically further polarization is occurring in the manner various groups of IS scholars are simultaneously calling for order, discipline and clearer notions of the "core of the discipline" while other scholars call for greater research diversity. In order to overcome this polarization we advocate a strategy recommended by Weick (1996): Drop your tools, hold your concepts lightly and update them frequently. Three reasons for dropping our theoretical tools are suggested as a means for moving forward, both for individual researchers as well as for the research community as a whole.*

Keywords   Theory, research diversity, actor network theory, structuration theory

Please use the following format when citing this chapter:

Truex, D., and Holmström, J., 2007, in IFIP International Federation for Information Processing, Volume 235, Organizational Dynamics of Technology-Based Innovation: Diversifying the Research Agenda, eds. McMaster, T., Wastell, D., Ferneley, E., and DeGross, J. (Boston: Springer), pp. 31-42.

1   INTRODUCTION

In declaring that "technological innovation continues to be problematic for many organizations," the call to this IFIP Working Group 8.6 working conference on Organizational Dynamics of Technology-Based Innovation asks for researchers to offer up "alternative conceptual lenses and standpoints" to help understand "why the same technology that 'diffuses' in one context meets only resistance and rejection in others" and to better understand the "organizational dynamics of technology-based innovation" (McMaster and Wastell 2006). This request is made because the IFIP WG 8.6 community may be too closely associated with diffusion theory in its many forms. But the very nature of the request implies that theoretical diversity is a positive and helpful end for a research community. Interestingly this request to broaden the theoretical repertoire is articulated at a time when other voices are being raised for more narrowly defining "the core of the field," differentiating those theories and means of knowledge creation that are unique to our field and effectively bounding theoretical options rather than opting for diversification. The debate takes many forms with distinguished colleagues on either side, holding tenaciously to favored positions (Benbasat and Zmud 2003). We weigh in on this discourse by proposing a set of recommendations that are neither theoretical absolutes nor theoretical relatives, but suggest a reflexive view toward theory adoption, use, and diversification. To do this, we reference a recent debate in two IS research venues, the *Scandinavian Journal of Information Systems* (SJIS) and the *Journal of the AIS* (JAIS), in which we have had a voice.

Diversification and pluralism are important ideals to strive for, but we need to acknowledge that theoretical discourses tend to be centered on a limited set of theories that hampers the discourse. The influence of diffusion theory on the IFIP 8.6 community is one example, and there are others. There is too often a polarization between rival theories that does not push the discourse further. In order to overcome this polarization we advocate a strategy recommended by Weick (1996): Drop your tools, hold your concepts lightly and update them frequently.

This paper is structured as follows. First, in section two, we examine a recent debate in SJIS in which the topic of technological agency is used as a vehicle for illustrating the problem. The seven contributions to the debate are interesting in part because of the shadow of supremacist strategies that they cast. The debate illustrates the manner in which Information Systems researchers are polarized into opposing camps, both of which tend to view the other as inferior. In the third section, we advocate the strategy recommended by Weick (1996) in order to overcome the polarization into opposing camps: Drop your tools, hold your concepts lightly and update them frequently. We will put forward three reasons for dropping our tools: the focus on improving practice, the focus on building cumulative tradition in the mother discipline, and the focus on building cumulative tradition in the IS discipline. Finally, the paper concludes with an assessment of the relevance of dropping your tools of research as a means to move forward.

2   CONCEPTUALIZING THE RELATIONSHIP BETWEEN TECHNOLOGY AND ORGANIZATIONS: CONSEQUENCES OF SUPREMACIST STRATEGIES

The history of IS research has been characterized by the hegemony of the positivistic research tradition (Orlikowski and Baroudi 1991). There has been a clear tendency in the field to relegate "soft" research approaches to a secondary position compared to the "hard," positivist approach (e.g., Benbasat et al. 1987). However, Dutton (1988) has criticized Benbasat et al.'s interpretation of how qualitative case studies should be conducted because of the explicit bias toward quantitative methods. The preoccupation in the IS field with hard research approaches is manifest in the excessive reliance on positivist and quantitative strategies for IS research. Clearly, while paradigms should ideally serve as a lens to illuminate research issues, in practice they serve as blinkers to help achieve closure. A pluralist strategy would allow for different paradigms to be applied in a research situation. It would also allow for theoretical approaches to be a part of a contingent tool-box approach where their strengths could be used as appropriate (Landry and Banville 1992). In contrast, a supremacist strategy would seek to establish one theoretical approach as universally applicable and "best" in all situations (for a discussion see Fitzgerald and Howcroft 1998). In our view, the character of much of the current debate seeking to identify or establish agreement about the "center" or core of the IS discipline (Benbasat and Zmud 2003) has the character of the later strategy.

In a recent debate in SJIS, Rose, Jones, and Truex (2005) discuss the issue that has occupied center stage in IS research for decades: how do we conceptualize the relationship between technology and organizations? They raise a number of important concerns with existing approaches to this issue, and by highlighting these limitations; they challenge us to rethink our cherished assumptions to studying technology in context. With respect to the question of agency, Rose, Jones, and Truex argue that both the structuration theory (ST) and actor-network theory (ANT) perspectives are lacking in different ways. Structuration Theorists are seen to privilege human agency over techno-logical agency, while ANT theorists go too far in their assumptions of symmetry between humans and machines. Rose et al. (2005b) described this incompatibility between ANT and ST accounts of humans and machines as *the problem of agency* and suggested some guidelines for a more consistent, theoretical treatment of agency, and a metaphor for that theoretical development: "the double dance of agency." In doing this they are in a sense urging the IS community to drop their tools and to push the debate further.

The idea of the double dance of agency was critiqued by a number of researchers quite familiar with ANT, ST, or both. These critiques cover a range of concerns from challenging the attempt to rationalize the distinct positions in ANT and ST with regard to *agency*, to attacks on one of the theories, or attacks on the authors' mental state. Walsham (2005, p. 153) argues that, instead of building integrative agency theories, we should "encourage a thousand theoretical flowers to bloom." Orlikowski (2005, p. 183) suggests a distinction between human agency and material performativity as a way forward. Hanseth (2005, p. 159) denigrates the contribution of structuration theory, and privileges the contribution of actor network theory. He argues that ANT resolves central problems in the relationship of organizations and technology whereas structuration theory, typical of other social theories, is technology blind. Hanseth suggests that instead of focusing on symmetry, researchers should focus on the notion of *hybrid collectif* an idea McMaster and Wastell (2005, p. 174) echo, arguing that "only collectives can act." Hanseth sees the issue of symmetry to be a historical concern, one that is no longer in the forefront of theory development, insisting instead that researchers forget about symmetry and concentrate on hybrids and collectives. In response to the Rose, Jones, and Truex challenge to ANT theorists to be more specific about the way nonhumans act, McMaster and Wastell (p. 175) argue that this is really a nonissue in ANT. They counter that the challenge itself is expressed in a way that *separates and contrasts* humans and machines—precisely the dichotomy that Latour's project sets out to undermine. McMaster and Wastell pejoratively accuse Rose et al. of having a "symmetrophobic block" (p. 175) arguing that symmetry is not the same as equivalence.

There are many interesting elements in this debate, but a common thread we see are the contours of a *supremacist strategy*—a strategy aiming at establishing one theoretical approach as universally applicable. The unfortunate consequences of the supremacist strategy could be that we end up with a debate for or against a particular theory instead of what it can tell us in the ongoing discourse in our discipline. Two of the debate participants suggested alternate lines of reasoning.

Holmström (2005, p. 167) chooses instead to consider the historical context of theories and the likely trajectory for those theories in the domain of IS research; or, what came before and what comes next? He posits that researchers need to focus on more than a purist's notion of what came before (i.e., how Latour and Giddens formulated their ideas) but also on our own theoretical contribution (i.e., what comes next). Focusing solely on "what came first" may hamper any discussion on what comes next and the growth of the theory as a result.

Orlikowski (2005), in a terminological slight of hand, proposes to speak of "human agency" and "material performativity" in order to avoid falling into unfortunate polemical traps that hamper further understanding of technological changes. Unfortunately, however, changing our description of the nature of agency as invested in people or things does not change that nature. And as Langer and Turkle each independently illustrate in the domains of the visual arts, media, and language, our inclination as humans to personify technology does not make it human. (Langer 1953, 1957; Turkle 1984). Rather it *humanizes* technology so that we might more easily assimilate it into our value systems, routines, social structures, work, and, indeed, our collectifs.

Building a cumulative theory assumes common and agreed notions of the "problem" and potential alternative futures. To our thinking, the current tenor of the debate does not advance that goal. So in the next section, we focus on reasons for dropping the tools of theoretical certainty so we might find common ground and advance theoretical and methodological discourse.

3   THREE REASONS FOR DROPPING THE TOOLS

As the IS discipline has evolved with relatively permeable research boundaries over the years, the diversity in theoretical underpinnings has been essential to the evolution of our discipline. To this end, we find the challenges raised by Rose, Jones, and Truex to both researchers and practitioners to be relevant. The authors argue that when reference theories are taken into the domain of IS, different problems emerge. Among other things, they argue that there are correct and incorrect ways to use theories such that "what came first" or that being aware of what was really said in the original theories should guide use of the theory. But this is not enough. Rose, Jones, and Truex also point at the need for a continuous evolution of theories. In the following section, we build on this position by advocating for Weick's (1996) strategy, namely, to drop your tools, hold your concepts lightly and update them frequently. We will put forward three reasons for dropping our tools: *the focus on improving practice, the focus on building cumulative tradition in the mother discipline, and the focus on building cumulative tradition in the IS discipline.*

3.1 Focus on Improving Practice

In recent years, the IS community has come under severe criticism for conducting research that has little relevance for practice. The gist of the criticism is that IS academia operates in isolation from practice and the findings of academic research efforts do not influence practice. A dynamic perspective of the interaction between IS academia and practice will help us understand better how IS academia can influence practice. This process should be continuous and subtle (Koch et al. 2002), but as it stands today, this process needs to be strengthened. Moody (2000) defines relevant research as that which "addresses a practical need," and goes on to state that relevance and utility can only be evaluated by practitioners. However, since much research does not have direct or immediate relevance to practitioners, the question arises as to how those findings should be disseminated in a suitable form at such time as they do become relevant. While a journal like *MIS Quarterly* is found to be important to research, practitioner publications are often found to be more useful for teaching. This practice is slammed as being hypocritical by Robey and Markus (1998), who insist that academics be forced to "eat [their] own dog food."

While the lack of a cumulative tradition within IS research is often lamented (Benbasat and Zmud 1999; Keen 1991), there are voices arguing that a cumulative tradition may actually hinder relevance in an era of rapid change (Davenport and Markus 1999; Robey and Markus 1998). In fact, results that are highly relevant to pragmatic issues might be rejected as being irrelevant merely because they are presented in an inaccessible style (Robey and Markus 1998). Too often research is driven by researchers' own interests and the profiles of publication outlets rather than practical needs (Lyytinen 1999; Moody 2000). If academics work in isolation and then try to impose ideas on industry, they are bound to fail. IS researchers should, therefore, look to practice to identify research topics that are likely to be of future interest (Benbasat and Zmud 1999). Clearly, we need a change toward a greater appreciation for practical issues. To drop your tools, to update them and adjust them to face this challenge, is a part of this effort. In the SJIS debate, we could see no efforts in this direction. Rather, it reminds us of the analogy semiologist David Blair uses (after Ziff) when describing words as tools, whose meaning are determined *in use*. He illustrates with the notion of a screw driver, which is normally used as a tool for driving fasteners with an inclined plane, but which in a paint shop may be used to pry paint lids off cans or, in a street fight, may be used as a defensive weapon

(Blair 1990). If we allowed theories in IS to be more exposed to practice, we could also expect to see more creativity among IS scholars in adapting theories in relation to actual needs in practice. We would then indeed be "eating our own dog food."

The notion of theory and praxis also raises two related questions: (1) How does the theory "fit" the problem at hand? (2) Are there methodological issues arising form the choice of a theory? Gregor (2006) distinguishes between five interrelated types of theory: (1) theory for analyzing; (2) theory for explaining, (3) theory for predicting; (4) theory for explaining and predicting; and (5) theory for design and action. These types are all very different but share this in common: Research projects always begin with a problem or question of interest. We find this relevant to the call for papers of this WG 8.6 gathering wherein the conveners wish to consider alternative theoretical frameworks to those now closely identified with the work of this research community. It is relevant to the issue of IS *in practice* and IS research *as a practice*. In research fields, the focus of attention varies over time and theories come in and go out of fashion (Jones 2000). Given that a poor fit of theory-to-question or problem stands to result in misleading or uninteresting findings, we need to be particularly careful in the rush to find new or different theoretical lenses to apply to a domain of inquiry. This theme is more fully developed elsewhere (see Truex et al. 2006) and is raised only as a cautionary note in considering the call for theoretical diversity.

The second concern when considering the impact on practice is the effective match of theory and research method. Simply put, different theories are more or less amenable to different types of data, different means of acquiring data, and different means of in-quiring that data. Theory and methodology are fundamentally related issues such that we cannot consider the selection of theories without also considering what implications this may have on research methodology. This topic is also treated in a much fuller way else-where (see Truex et al. 2006). So again, we raise this as cautionary note because researchers need to be aware of the costs and implications of the choice of theory in con-sidering the impact on their own practice of research or the practice of IS design, development, and management.

We share the concern that IS academia operates in isolation from practice such that academic research efforts do not significantly influence practice in the same way as some of our other academic brethren such as computer science or system engineering. The way in which academics cling to pet theories and, too often, resist further adaptation of it, contributes to this unfortunate state of affairs. In our mind, a reconsideration of the value proposition our research offers and further consideration of the real needs or practitioners would help reduce our isolation and infuse the field with fresh insights.

3.2 Focus on Building on Cumulative Tradition in the Mother Discipline

Holmström (2005) finds the challenges raised by Rose et al. to both researchers and practitioners valuable. In particular, Holmström states that he

> find[s] the argument that there are correct and incorrect ways to use theories to be an interesting and important challenge to our field. When it comes to theories one cannot only take the good bits and leave the bad bits behind. If a

researcher does not understand enough of the theoretical tradition from its original setting, s/he is likely to open the work up to any of the same criticisms of that theory that have already been voiced in the original discipline.

However, the relation to the discipline wherein the theory of interest has emerged is rarely reflected upon. Even more rare is the effort to actually contribute to that discipline. An exception can be found in Truex et al. (2006) wherein the authors suggest that researchers, borrowing theories from other disciplines, have the responsibility to do so knowledgeably, with fidelity, and with current knowledge of the discourse surrounding those theories in the home discipline, but also that they have responsibility to actually attempt to further the discourse by use of the theory in a second discipline. They state

> When using a specific theory as a resource in the theorizing process, the researcher should be able to answer: What is the added value to the theorizing process when using theory x that is not added when using theory y? The answer to this question should be given considering the tradition of the field—what we know and what we don't know. To contribute to cumulative tradition, a piece of research has to step beyond that which we already know (p. 30).

For them, "there is a pressing need to pay attention to cumulative tradition when adapting theories to IS research." They illustrate via Keil's use of escalation theory how work in IS research settings may contribute to the cumulative tradition and feedback into the discourse in the home field. This is a way in which escalation theory can be dropped in order to pursue a better explanation of technological change. Such a willingness to adapt theoretical tools is rare but looks like a promising route to pursue.

Perhaps arguing that IS researchers need to make contributions back to the mother discipline is a tad arrogant and ambitious. But we are of the opinion that our field has made theoretical contributions that should be noted elsewhere. We see the development of extensions and refinements to escalation theory made by Keil and his colleagues or the refinement and extensions of Habermas' theory of communicative action by Klein, Lyytinen, Hirschheim, and others as examples.

3.3 Focus on Building on Cumulative Tradition in the IS Discipline

The key challenge for an IS researcher approaching a theory from another discipline for use within IS is to invest the time and effort to understand the theory in its native environment, to learn the vocabulary and underlying assumptions of the theory, to understand its weaknesses as well as its strengths, and to acknowledge its previous use. But while we need to be more reflexive about the ways in which we adapt theories to our field and to deepen our understanding about how and why any theory is adapted, the faithfulness toward original theories is only a part of such reflexivity. For this reason, we want to elaborate on the importance of considering not only a theory's historical context, but also the theorizing process' contribution to cumulative theory.

Weick (1995) points out that "theory is a continuum" and as theories move from visions to detailed constructs and propositions they lose some of their accuracy and become more of an approximation, but they also become increasingly useful to the discipline. Building on Weick's description of the theorizing process, Truex et al. explore how social theories should be adapted to IS research and argue that both the historical context of the theory and the contribution of the theorizing process to cumulative theory should be considered. This is in concert with Weick's idea of embedding your theoretical contribution in the context of what came before and what comes next (p. 389). This includes not only the life cycle of one's own research process but, more importantly, the ongoing discourse in the particular discipline in which one is immersed. Such development depends on the generalization that Yin (1994) labels as an "analytical generalization," where the researcher "is striving to generalize a particular set of results to some broader theory" (p. 36).

With this in mind, Rose et al. (2005a, 2005b) might be criticized for concentrating on what came before rather than what comes next. They ask us to remain faithful to the original ideas from Giddens and Latour. But, following Weick's idea of theorizing, we argue that there is an even higher standard. Namely, we must seek not only to remain faithful to the key elements in the original theory, *but also* to develop the theory further. This begs the question of how can one be faithful to an original theory and develop it further. We suggest that to be ready to drop your tools, then, is to be ready to develop them further in line with a theory-development ideal.

To illustrate, we use Orlikowski's efforts to adapt Giddens' notions to the realm of research on information technologies use. Orlikowski (1992), recalling "interpretive flexibility," emphasizes that "there is flexibility in how people design, interpret, and use technology, but that this flexibility is a function of the material components comprising the artifact, the institutional context in which a technology is developed and used, and the power, knowledge, and interests of human actors" as well as time (p. 421). To her credit, her adaptation is a development of Giddens' original ideas to the practicalities of IS. Even so, a problematic issue in Orlikowski's model is that she puts technology *between* human agency and structure, and thus reestablishes a dualism that Giddens' structuration theory overcomes (Jones 1998; Rose and Truex 2000). In a later work Orlikowski (2000) appears to recognize this and proposes a "practice lens" as a means of overcoming these inconsistencies, thus bringing her characterization closer in line to Giddens' intent.

However, an important point should not be missed: those who, like Orlikowski, adopt structuration theory for their research are adapting and, willingly or not, developing Giddens' original ideas as they fit them to the practicalities of IS. They are conducting a kind of action research project on the theory itself. Such work illustrates the challenges of adapting general theories of society to the particulars of organizational life and IT research.

Jones (1998), for example, describes problems involved with applying structuration theory when trying to be specific about how information systems are used in organizations. In an attempt to modify structuration theory, he tries "to move beyond the pure subjectivism of Giddens structuration and to incorporate a form of material agency" (Jones 1998, p. 299). This point is elaborated in the SJIS debate in which there are two basic positions. There are, on the one hand, arguments advocating the need to remain faithful to the main thrust of Giddens' original ideas. On the other hand, there are arguments advocating the necessity to adopt Giddens' original ideas to the particulars of IS research. A good researcher will be able to combine these two positions, but in order to do so will need to be open to the idea of dropping theoretical tools in order to contribute to cumulative tradition in IS.

4 CONCLUSIONS

This paper is influenced by the work of those scholars who have become sensitive to the need of further developing our explanations of technological change by adopting and trying on theories that have not been applied previously in the IS research arena. In so doing, they are effectively helping us all drop our tools and renew our ideas and the character of our discipline.

With this in mind, we ask: Why is it, then, that an approach such as ANT has failed to make a similar impact as have positivistic accounts of technological change? One reason can be found in the character of the intellectual debate surrounding ANT; the debate is concerned with arguments for or against ANT rather than what ANT can tell us. There are a number of such debates in our field. They are often characterized by tendentious arguments as advocates, protagonists of different theoretical approaches, offer a somewhat one-sided condemnation of other approaches. These debates have little prospect of resolution unless participants do not loosen their grip on their tools. The debate on technological agency illustrates the manner in which IS researchers can be polarized into opposing camps, each of which tend to view the other as inferior.

This casts a shadow of supremacist strategies over a discourse and the field loses as a result. For if we accept that theories shape what we notice and ignore and what we believe is and is not important and that, as Lyytinen and King (2004) assert, better theory is likely to contribute to stronger results, we are obliged to loosen our grip while exploring theoretical notions. It is our hope, accordingly, that as the IFIP WG 8.6 community seeks to cast a wider theoretical net over the issue of the organizational dynamics of technology-based innovation, by dropping a diffussionist-centric approach it may also focus on improving practice, focus on building cumulative tradition in the mother discipline, and focus on building cumulative tradition in the IS discipline.

In order for a community to have the capacity for ongoing renewal, it has to identify the elements holding it back. Today it seems as if the ways in which researchers hold on to theories and defend their usage is such an element, which pervates the field and is not limited to the IFIP 8.6 community. In order to make change happen, we believe that dropping the theoretical tools that hold us back is a key, but we need to do this in an informed fashion.

Acknowledgments

An earlier and less developed version of this paper was presented at and is represented in the on-line proceedings of the Action in Language, Organizations and Information Systems (AOLIS) Conference, Borås, Sweden, November 2-3, 2006.

References

Benbasat, I., Goldstein, D., and Mead, M. "The Case Research Strategy in Studies of Information Systems," *MIS Quarterly* (11:3), September 1987, pp. 369-386.

Benbasat, I., and Zmud, R. W. "Empirical Research in Information Systems: The Practice of Relevance," *MIS Quarterly* (23:1), March 1999, pp. 3-16.

Benbasat, I., and Zmud, R. W. "The Identity Crisis Within the IS Discipline: Defining and Communicating the Discipline's Core Properties," *MIS Quarterly* (27:2), June 2003, pp. 183-194.

Blair, D. *Language and Representation in Information Retrieval*, Amsterdam: Elsevier Science Publishers, 1990.

Davenport, T. H., and Markus, M. L. "Rigor vs Relevance Revisited: Response to Benbasat and Zmud," *MIS Quarterly* (23:1), March 1999, pp. 19-23.

Dutton, W. "Letter to the Editor, *MIS Quarterly* (12:4), December 1988, p. 521.

Fitzgerald, B., and Howcroft, D. "Towards Dissolution of the IS Research Debate: From Polarization to Polarity," *Journal of Information Technology* (13:4), 1998, pp. 313-326.

Gregor, S. "The Nature of Theory in Information Systems," *MIS Quarterly* (30:3), September 2006, pp. 611-642.

Hanseth, O. "Beyond Metaphysics and Theory Consumerism: A Comment to Rose, Jones, and Truex, 'Socio-Theoretic Accounts of IS: The Problem of Agency,'" *Scandinavian Journal of Information Systems* (17:1), 2005, pp. 159-166.

Holmström, J. "Theorizing in IS Research: What Comes First and What Comes After?," *Scandinavian Journal of Information Systems* (17:1), 2005, pp. 167-174.

Jones, M. "Information Systems and the Double Mangle: Steering a Course between the Scylla of Embedded Structure and the Charybdis of Strong Symmetry," in T. J. Larsen, L. Levine, and J. I. DeGross (eds.), *Information Systems: Current Issues and Future Changes*, Laxenburg, Austria; IFIP, 1999, pp. 287-302.

Jones, M. R. "The Moving Finger: The Use of Social Theory in WG8.2 Conference Papers, 1975-1999," in J. Baskerville, J. Stage, and J. I. DeGross (eds.), *Organizational and Social Perspectives on Information Technology,* Boston: Kluwer Academic Publishers, 2000, pp. 15-31.

Keen, P. G. W. "Relevance and Rigor in Information Systems Research: Improving Quality, Confidence, Cohesion and Impact," in H-E. Nissen, H. K. Klein, and R. Hirschheim *Information Systems Research: Contemporary Approaches and Emergent Traditions*, Amsterdam: North-Holland, 1991, pp. 27-49.

Koch, N., Gray, P., Hoving, R., Klein, H., Myers, M., and Rockart, J. "IS Research Relevance Revisited: Subtle Accomplishments, Unfulfilled Promise, or Serial Hypocrisy?," *Communications of the AIS* (8), 2002, pp. 330-346.

Landry, M., and Banville, C. "A Disciplined Methodological Pluralism for MIS Research," *Accounting, Management and Information Technologies* (2:2), 1992, pp. 77-98.

Langer, S. K. *Feeling and Form*, New York: Charles Scribner Sons, 1953.

Langer, S. K. *Problems of Art*, New York: Charles Scribner Sons, 1957.

Lyytinen, K. "Empirical Research in Information Systems: On the Relevance of Practice in Thinking of IS Research," *MIS Quarterly* (23:1), March 1999, pp. 25-27.

Lyytinen, K., and King, J. "Nothing at the Center? Information Systems as a Reference Discipline?," *Journal of the Association for Information Systems* (5:6), 2004, pp. 220-246.

McMaster, T., and Wastell, D. G. "The Agency of Hybrids: Overcoming the Symmetrophobic Block," *Scandinavian Journal of Information Systems* (17:1), 2005, pp. 175-182.

McMaster, T., and Wastell, D. "Organisational Dynamics of Technology-Based Innovation: Diversifying the Research Agenda," Call for Papers, IFIP WG 8.6 Working Conference, University of Salford, 2006 (http://www.ifip86-2007.salford.ac.uk/papers/).

Moody, D. L. "Building Links Between IS Research and Professional Practice: Improving the Relevance and Impact of IS Research," in W. J. Orlikowski, S. Ang, P. Weill, H. C. Kcmar, and J. I. DeGross (eds.), *Proceedings of the 21ˢᵗ International Conference on Information Systems*, Brisbane, Australia, December 10-13, 2000, pp. 351-360.

Orlikowski, W. J. "The Duality of Technology: Rethinking the Concept of Technology in Organizations," *Organization Science* (3), 1992, pp. 398-429.

Orlikowski, W. J. "Using Technology and Constituting Structures: A Practice Lens for Studying Technology in Organizations," *Organization Science* (11), 2000, pp. 404-428.

Orlikowski, W. J., and Baroudi, J. "Studying Information Technology in Organizations: Research Approaches and Assumptions," *Information Systems Research* (2:1), 1992, pp. 1-28.

Robey, D., and Markus, M. L. "Beyond Rigor and Relevance: Producing Consumable Research about Information Systems," *Information Resources Management Journal* (11:1), 1998, pp. 7-15.

Rose, J., Jones, M., and Truex, D. "The Problem of Agency Re-visited," *Scandinavian Journal of Information Systems* (17:1), 2005a, pp. 187-196.

Rose, J., Jones, M., and Truex, D. "Socio-Theoretic Accounts of IS: The Problem of Agency," *Scandinavian Journal of Information Systems* (17:1), 2005b, pp. 133-152.

Rose, J., and Truex, D. "Machine Agency as Perceived Autonomy: An Action Perspective," in R. Baskerville, J. Stage, and J. I. DeGross (eds.), *The Social and Organizational Perspective on Research and Practice in Information Technology*, Boston: Kluwer Academic Publishers:, 2000, pp. 371-390.

Truex, D. P., Holmström, J., and Keil, M. "Theorizing in Information Systems Research: A Reflexive Analysis of the Adaptation of Theory in Information Systems Research," *Journal of the AIS* (7:12), December 2006, pp. 797-821.

Turkle, S. *The Second Self: Computers and the Human Sprit*, New York: Touchstone Press, 1984.

Walsham, G. "Agency Theory: Integration or a Thousand Flowers?," *Scandinavian Journal of Information Systems* (17:1), 2005, pp. 153-158.

Weick, K. E. "Drop your Tools: An Allegory for Organizational Studies," *Administrative Science Quarterly* (41), 1996, pp. 301-313.

Weick, K. E. "What Theory Is Not, Theorizing Is," *Administrative Science Quarterly* (40), 1995, pp. 385-390.

Yin, R. K. *Case Study Research, Design and Methods* (2ⁿᵈ ed.), London: Sage Publications, 1994.

About the Authors

Duane Truex, an associate professor of Computer Information Systems (CIS) in the J. Mack Robinson College of Business at Georgia State University, researches the social impacts of information systems and emergent ISD. He is an associate editor for the *Information Systems Journal* and has co-edited two special issues of *The Database for Advances in Information Systems*. His work has been published in the *Communications of the ACM, Accounting Management and Information Technologies, Journal of the AIS, The Database for Advances in Information Systems, European Journal of Information Systems (EJIS), le journal de la Societé d'Information et Management (SIM), Information Systems Journal (ISJ), Scandinavian Journal of Information*

Systems, Journal of Arts Management and Law, IEEE Transactions on Engineering Management, and over 50 other assorted IFIP transactions and edited books and conference proceedings. Duane can be reached by e-mail at dtruex@gsu.edu.

Jonny Holmström is a professor of Informatics at the University of Umeå. His research interests include IT's organizational consequences and electronic commerce. Jonny's larger research program has examined how organizations innovate with IT, in particular how they adapt to using technological innovations such as decision support systems, client/server development, knowledge management tools, and groupware applications. Jonny is currently investigating how organizations in the process industry sector can develop sustainable competitive advantage through mindful use of IT, and how they develop effective partnership relations to cultivate such use. He has published his research in *Information and Organization, Information Resources Management Journal, Information Technology and People, Journal of the AIS, Journal of Global Information Technology Management, Scandinavian Journal of Information Systems,* and at major international conferences. He can be reached by e-mail at jonny.holmstrom@informatik.umu.se.

5 COOPERATIVE MODELS FOR INFORMATION TECHNOLOGY TRANSFER IN THE CONTEXT OF OPEN INNOVATION

Gonzalo León
Technical University of Madrid
Madrid, Spain

Abstract   *Universities and public research institutions (PROs) are increasingly required to address strategic needs defined by industrial sectors both from the education and research standpoint and contribute more intensively to the absorption of advanced technologies. Many countries rely on the reform of traditional structures of universities and PROs by creating specific centers of excellence to ensure long-term partnerships with industry. The need for stable university–industry partnerships focuses on the evolution from short-term instruments to long-term instruments for cooperation in the wider context of technology transfer (TT) embedded in technology development processes. Within this context, governments are looking for adequate policy instruments to offer more attractive funding conditions to increase institutional involvement in TT as a pre-requirement to increase the long-term stability of public–private partnerships.*

The specific situation in the European Union is addressed where steps toward fostering open innovation have been taken to overcome structural, institutional, and cultural rigidities. The analysis is focused on the short and long term instruments provided by the European Framework Program and other European initiatives. Specialized technology transfer structures, especially those targeting the creation of joint research centers, are among the most common approaches in the EU in order to facilitate the exchange of tacit and explicit knowledge and accelerate innovation.

The rationale behind the concept of open innovation applied to technology transfer and diffusion activities is addressed. Interest is focused on the identi-

Please use the following format when citing this chapter:

León, G., 2007, in IFIP International Federation for Information Processing, Volume 235, Organizational Dynamics of Technology-Based Innovation: Diversifying the Research Agenda, eds. McMaster, T., Wastell, D., Ferneley, E., and DeGross, J. (Boston: Springer), pp. 43-61.

fication of trends, drivers, and limits in the models used today for TT and their impact on the design of policy. From this analysis, new open models emerge for immature technologies where research and TT cannot be isolated.

Finally, although these elements can be found in any science and technology domain, information technologies offer a set of special features making it even more important to address TT activities in a cooperative way where universities facilitate the transference of immature technologies. Experiences on the deployment of grid services will be outlined in this context. This case illustrates the benefits of a close open cooperation amongst all stakeholders (industry, academia, and governments) to support TT and to speed up grid services deployment.

1   INTRODUCTION

The assumption that scientific and technical knowledge is increasingly generated, transferred, and diffused in socio-technical networks composed by different types of agents (both public and private institutions) is widely accepted by governments and institutions in all advanced countries (Albino et al. 2005; COM 2006b; Foray 2005b; Ormala et al. 2005). Individual entities no longer possess in-house all of the required knowledge to develop new, advanced, complex products and processes; it is necessary to create the right context to efficiently generate and share knowledge with potential allies (both public and private) in order to speed up technological innovation. As a consequence, governments are focusing their research and innovation policies and instruments on this new scenario. Institutional reforms in public systems are also pursuing the same strategy.

The transference of technical knowledge commonly known as *technology transfer*[1] (TT), has been usually described as a bilateral interaction between one entity acting as provider of the technical knowledge and another acting as receiver. Models for TT rely on the assumption that provider entities possesses all of the knowledge they need to support technology development and transference, while receivers select a single entity as provider for the required technology. Models have ben refined to cover specialized roles based on the inclusion of TT broker entities (Geroski 2000) and other complementary activities to facilitate the transference of tacit knowledge. A common but hidden assumption is that the technology to be transferred is mature enough to support a linear process where the technology does not need to be substantially modified during the transference process; TT is delayed until reaching a determined technology maturity level. Technology adaptation only comes from the adequacy of the use of the technology to the receiver's specificities and in its merging with other preexisting technologies.

Unfortunately, real scenarios are far from this ideal situation. It is more common to find a situation where technologies are developed by different partners and responsibility for integration into products, systems, or services. falls on the partners, with responsibilities spread over a complex network. In this context, TT and even final deployment

---

[1]Although the use of the term *knowledge transfer* seems more adequate to cope with other nontechnical aspects, *technology transfer* is used in this article to emphasize the transfer of technical knowledge.

processes start with immature technologies. TT is progressively embedded in complex innovation processes involving new technologies, new user communities, and new applications fields. To cope with this additional complexity, a more cooperative scenario, with additional contributing partners, learning processes, and feedback mechanisms, is required to reduce the associated risks.

Models to explain the complexity of the interactions in socio-technical networks are also becoming more complex. The work on clusters (Albino et al. 2005) and science parks has developed richer scenarios with different types of partner entities: leader firm, follower, subcontractor, manufacturing technology source, infrastructure supplier, client/user, university/research center, etc., each with different roles and responsibilities. Based on this, it is possible to analyze roles, information flows, and dynamic interactions where geographical proximity is only one factor among many.

Not all of the partners categories mentioned above play the same role in accelerating technical innovation. Universities, as basic agents of knowledge-based processes, could play a crucial role in the transference of immature technologies by emphasizing cooperation with industry and government. This was, in fact, the basis of the well-known triple helix model (Etzkowitz and Leysderdoff 2000), which has strongly influenced research, innovation policy design, and the role of the university in the last decade, and the subsequent need to extend it to TT activities. This is the basis for the policy trend to "open innovation" and the emphasis paid to knowledge sharing.

Within the context of open innovation, this paper will analyze the cooperation models used today paying attention to TT requirements. The recognition of the need to develop open cooperative technology transfer models is the basis for the approach addressed here. The analysis of the role of public research entities (PROs) and universities in immature TT activities will be addressed. This focus will allow describing the different types of policy instruments available today and institutional involvement in the European Union. Emphasis will be paid to long-term, stable partnerships, where TT can be addressed within a long time horizon. Although the analysis could be applied to all industrial sectors, the information technologies (IT) will be addressed specifically to tune the proposed models.

2 THE EVOLVING NATURE OF RESEARCH AND DEVELOPMENT AT THE PRIVATE SYSTEM

2.1 Challenges for the Innovation Process

Enterprises need to become competitive in a globalized world; this competitiveness goal relies on innovation to be sustainable. Today, private companies are challenged in their innovative processes due to three complementary factors.

1. *The need to cope with multidisciplinary approaches to deal with system complexity.* Speeded up by emerging technology convergence (i.e., in the emerging field of bio-nano-cogno), requirements for large system design, and new application fields, the probability of basing new products on technologies available in-house is very low. It seems better to join forces with other institutions if partnership for specific purposes can be created in a relatively short time.

2. *The need to create and to deliver solutions for real or potential customers in shorter periods of time.* Due to the faster pace of technological change, the need to anticipate future customers' needs with in-house personnel becomes a huge barrier that avoids relying in the use of internal teams for complex product development. As a consequence, immature technologies should be exposed to selected users in order to trigger feedback and to speed up maturation. Solutions also require closer interactions with users than in the past to cope with multicultural diversity challenges and trigger mutual learning processes.

3. *The need to increase organizational flexibility to reduce costs and to adapt the company to new markets and regulations.* The consequence is a rich emergence of more agile organizations where core businesses (with some previously identified key technologies) are retained while other non-crucial aspects are externalized. Under this approach, companies intend to identify what are or should be the key knowledge they must possess in-house and, simultaneously, to raise a network of external partners or experts to be used on demand for specific purposes. The ability to set up dynamic networks with select partners and in-house evaluation and absorption capabilities is a requirement for success.

Geographical proximity between firms related to specific sectors or technologies has been identified as one of the critical factors to speed up innovation. Researchers have proposed that the strengthening of links facilitates knowledge transfer and sharing (Karlsson et al. 2005). Keeping strong links over time calls for stability in relationships and mutual credibility.

As a consequence of the interaction of the three challenges mentioned above, innovation is addressed by combining knowledge from several entities: from basic knowledge providers, technology developers, pilot users or specialized entities for TT or marketing activities. This is the basis for the concept of open (technical) innovation. Nevertheless, the degree of "openness" found in the open innovation realm varies from industrial sectors, geographical contexts, or involved technologies. Cooperative frameworks, as an evolution of more traditional bilateral or soft networking schemes, should be stable enough to reach the mutual credibility to facilitate long-term partnerships in technology transfer.

Today, three types of open innovation models can be identified in business sectors: subcontracted, cooperative, and open community models. Notice that these approaches are compatible and that all of them could coexist in a given scenario. These approaches will be described from the TT perspective in next sections.

2.2 Subcontracted Innovation Model

Within the subcontracted innovation model, research and development needs for specific purposes of a company (acting as contractor) are totally or partially subcontracted to another company or to one public research center or university. This corresponds to the well-known model of contract research widely used by companies in past decades.

This case is characterized by a strong asymmetry between the client and the provider of the required knowledge. All property and exploitation rights of the subcontracted

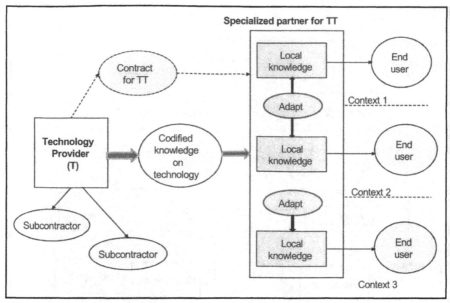

Figure 1. **Subcontracted Innovation Model**

activity lie with the contractor company with the exception of legal provisions in intellectual property legislation. If subcontractors are properly identified (in some cases or industrial sectors after a prequalification process), the three challenges defined above are addressed. Usually, multidisciplinarity requires signing several contracts with one or more entities.

The weakest point for this approach is the need to define in detail the components to be subcontracted in order to agree on time and money between parties. It precludes technological breakthroughs or, at least, very innovative solutions because subcontracted entities do not like to risk their contracts looking for solutions that are not clear. Furthermore, system integration and commercialization risks remains with the contractor. Again, this sharp distribution of roles and responsibilities is a constraint for innovative solutions.

It is theoretically possible to extend this model to cover technology transfer activities if developers rely on subcontracted, specialized entities to perform the transference activities in specific sectoral or geographical contexts. In practice, this model only works with very mature technologies when knowledge related to the target technology can be perfectly codified to be transferred to the specialized subcontracted unit. The extreme case is to agree on preexisting commercial structures for TT or diffusion. Figure 1 graphically depicts these interactions.

Notice that the technology provider does not have direct contact with end users. The specialized partner for TT (only one is represented in Figure 1) should have the necessary local knowledge to be able to have contact with end users in different contexts and to communicate feedback from the users to the provider. This structure is compatible with the use of other subcontractor entities during the technology development phases.

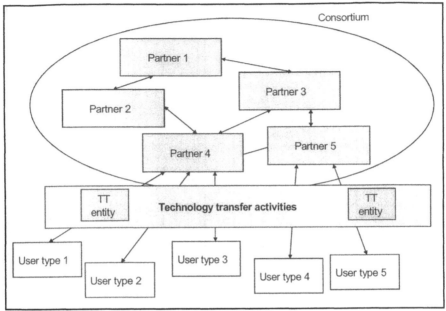

Figure 2. **Cooperative Innovation Model**

2.3   Cooperative Innovation Model

The cooperative innovation model is based on the need to share knowledge, risks, and benefits among a set of individual partners, both public and private. The set of partners agreeing to join forces to address a specific goal is called a *consortium* and this model is also known as consortia-based innovation. This model is widely supported by public administrations in Europe, well aware of the spillovers generated by national (or supranational) innovation systems.

Distribution of responsibilities within consortia is based on the specific scientific and technical capabilities of each partner. Usually, one partner assumes the coordinator's role while others perform specific tasks. Property and exploitation rights are also distributed on the basis of the work performed by each partner following rules approved by funding institutions. This model can also be combined with the subcontracted approach because one or more partners could have one or more subcontracted entities (up to a maximum percentage). This model has been mainly used for research and technology development activities. Figure 2 depicts the general elements and interactions associated to this model.

The application of this model to technology transfer activities is less straightforward. When TT is embedded into a larger process of technology development (as occurs in many R&D programs), activities like pilot experiences, demonstrators, structured feedback from users, etc. are addressed by the developers themselves. If an open cooperative model is used, those entities participating in the consortium assume some TT activities by distributing responsibilities according to their background and expertise.

In other cases, where TT is isolated from technology development due to specific complexities or lack of experience by developers, refinements of the open cooperative TT models are required. Notice that technology transfer activities are associated with some partners while others remain linked to pure technology development. As Figure 2 suggests, subcontracted specialized entities could support involved partners in carrying out TT activities; in other cases, these activities are supported by technology developers.

The weakest point for this approach is the need to ensure a good level of cooperation (even at the end of the activity) between partners to be able to exploit the results. The experience within the consortia-based approach used in the European Union advises creation of consortia structures where the role played by partners complements (but does not compete with) each other in the value chain. If cooperation among potential competitors is needed (e.g., to agree on an industry *de facto* standard in some technological domain), the time horizon for commercial exploitation is moved forward. Another difficulty stems from the fact that a single company cannot exploit all of the results by itself. As property rights are distributed for all involved partners, they should rely on others' interests. This constraint motivated use of this model only in cases where expected results were far from the market (historically, it was termed as precompetitive research) or when pre-agreements (even through the creation of specific legal entities) could cope with future exploitation aspects.

The full implementation of this approach of open innovation requires that governments play a more proactive role in stimulating cooperation through implementing specific policy instruments and favorable contexts. These instruments could support traditional collaborative research through individual projects, as similar instruments do in many other consortia-based R&D programs at the national and international level.

2.4 Open Community Innovation Model

An innovation model less often used in industry, but well known in the academic world, is based on open patents, publications, and stimulation to others' innovative solutions. This model can be found under the umbrella of *open communities*. These communities are understood in an international context where potential customers access immature versions and provide feedback to developers. In this context, different entities (in many cases, SMEs and public researchers) post their solutions, looking for wide acceptance and reuse. Sometimes, they compete with other open communities adhering to other types of solutions (i.e., another hardware platform or operating system in the case of the IT sector). Benefits come from rapid evolution of the field (as more entities participate, the faster is the evolution).

Large private companies were initially reluctant to sacrifice control of their R&D activities to gain more information, and they were not motivated to put their preexisting knowledge at general disposal. Nevertheless, given the time pressure to create markets for some types of specific products or solutions, large companies noticed that this model could dramatically increase the number of brilliant people involved in providing solutions, and the number of early customers and, ultimately, to speed up early product deployment.

Figure 3 schematically depicts the structure of this model driven by one (large) company generating a product incorporating elements contributed by several entities.

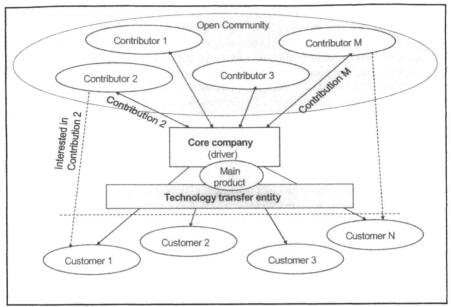

Figure 3. **Open Community Model**

These contributors could have a formal agreement with the core company to access the part of the technology they need if the information is open. Notice that technology transfer entities could be used or not. In this last case, the TT function is assumed by the core company or directly by some contributors (others delegate this responsibility to the core company).

2.5   Rationale for University–Industry Open Cooperation in Technology Transfer

Although all of the innovation models presented so far can be implemented by involving only private companies, it is becoming common to find universities and PROs involved in these kinds of partnerships. In some cases, governments have enforced this partici-pation through regulations in policy instruments as a mechanism to increase "vertebra-tion" in science and technology systems; in other cases, they participate because com-panies need to access the specialized knowledge required for specific projects.

The relationship between universities or PROs and enterprises in research activities has been deeply analyzed from several points of view in all advanced countries. Behind this interest lies recognition of its importance in building the so-called "knowledge society" by its positive impact in accelerating knowledge flows (Debackere and Veugelers 2005; Reichert 2006). The European Commission has devoted attention to this phenomenon in order to understand the strengths and weaknesses and to tune specific support policies (COM 2006a; EIRMA 2005).

The traditional approach, where universities create scientific knowledge to be used, incorporated in products or processes, and, finally, exploited by industry, refers to a linear model of innovation that has been demonstrated useless in a complex society. The new approach of open innovation relies on public–private partnerships, knowledge sharing and mutual learning (Ormala et al. 2005). In the new approach, universities find themselves as key stakeholders in an open innovation model where industry relies more and more on advanced knowledge to survive.

Policy instruments need to move further in promoting internal reforms in universities or PROs, or, by extension, in facilitating the creation of public–private partnerships (PPP) in a more general sense. PPPs in this contribution refer to stable agreements where universities, industries, and governments contribute to the creation of a sustainable agreement to support research and innovation in a predefined field. Sustainability is understood both from time and funding dimensions; in other words, partners should commit sufficient resources for actual science and technology progress during long periods of time. The analysis of this situation reveals the need to find a different basis for stable cooperation. In this context, the EU (EIRMA 2005) promoted the development of a guide to better practices for collaborative research between science and industry.

The PRO/university–industry research cooperation based on bilateral agreements can be theoretically extended to cover TT activities where universities are ready to provide extra knowledge on the technology developed (by themselves or by other entities) and they agree to support controlled experiences of technology deployment and early training. The relevant point from the university's view is to be convinced that TT fits their mission as a public research entity when it is framed in the wider context of knowledge creation and transfer.

Industry is also looking for academic partners to support TT-related activities. For private companies, universities are needed when the technology to be transferred to third parties implies at least one of the following features:

- The knowledge on the technology to be transferred is low in the target community (first phase of its life cycle). Universities could support dissemination by participating in educational activities where they can provide specific expertise and to motivate future clients.
- There is a need to tune the technology to specificities from the target community. In this assumption, universities participating in the initial phases of technology development could modify some aspects faster than others.
- The technology needs to be complemented with other technologies or elements not available at firms as technology developers. In this context, universities could support training for selected users, create educational material, participate as advanced users (acting as qualified early adopters) by providing systematic feedback to industry, etc.
- If the technology becomes a novelty in one application field, universities can provide useful cross-experience from other domains.

From the university perspective, the main problem is not identification of the potential benefits derived from their participation in TT activities, but rather their lack of motivation because the activity is not related to knowledge generation, the primary focus of university activity (unless they could exploit the acquired knowledge by themselves). To overcome this, TT activities could be embedded into conventional coopera-tive R&D projects or launched as complementary processes once the main R&D activities have been concluded.

The benefits of this cooperation for the involved academic entities increase when the collaborative framework is stable over time; then, is it possible to associate technology development to TT processes, to embed other knowledge-based activities, and to support future R&D triggered by the TT evaluation. Experience shows that it is not enough unless funding agencies modify their present policy instruments. This problem will be addressed in the next section in the context of the European Union.

3   EVOLUTION OF EU POLICY INSTRUMENTS FOR TT

3.1   Short-Term Instruments for University–Industry Research Cooperation

3.1.1 Assessment of Short-Term Instruments in the EU

Collaborative research has evolved in Europe to support industrial policies in a number of R&D programs like the EU Framework Program (FP) (COM 2006c), the EUREKA program, or the European Space Agency (ESA). In these cases, European countries have tried to promote intra-European cooperation among many types of European entities as a formula to speed up innovation. Due to its importance for universities, our attention will be directed at the FP instruments.

The recently completed FP6 had two different instruments for research cooperation: integrated project (IP), strategic targeted research project (STREP), and network of excellence (NoE). Universities actively participated in all of them. The single EU-FP instrument, where enterprises assume a secondary role, is the network of excellence. Within this instrument, the role of universities was even more relevant due to the type of long-term, fundamental research usually addressed in this FP instrument. In all cases, overlap between different FP instruments could occur.

All of the FP6 instruments mentioned above share a similar constraint: cooperation is limited to the duration of the R&D project (2, 3, or 4 years as a maximum). At the end of the project, the cooperation commitments (set up by formal contracts and consortium agreements) disappear and all partners are free to decide the next step according to their interests.

3.1.2 The Dissemination and Exploitation of Results in the FP6 Instruments

The concepts of *dissemination of results* and *exploitation of results* correspond to two different processes.

Dissemination of results refers to the explicit will to release part of the generated knowledge by using a wide range of mechanisms like workshops, papers in journals or congresses, training activities, books, media news, etc. It is assumed that the benefit of this process is not a predefined entity but generated knowledge that will benefit any researcher or institution.

Exploitation of results refers to the activities that partners involved in funded R&D activities can carry out to take advantage of the investment effort in new activities with economic relevance. Usually, exploitation is done after finishing the project framed by the provisions set in consortium agreements and Commission's contract for appropriability of the generated knowledge.

- *Networks of excellence* (NoE) were created to speed up knowledge generation by integrating the research agenda of multiple institutions (mainly PROs). It is obvious that setting up good mechanisms to ensure open dissemination of research results is a crucial factor in the assessment of the instrument; consortia agreements need to facilitate this dissemination in specific clauses.
- *Integrated projects* (IP) emphasize the closed exploitation of research results in the consortium partners by using the knowledge (both scientific and technological) generated during the project. It is also clear that the role and type of the different partners in a specific project limits the capabilities to exploit the generated knowledge. Industrial partners can access better the internal know-how to transform the results into a new set of products and processes.
- *Collective research projects* emphasize the development of common solutions for associations or groups of SMEs. Due to the low capacity of many of these participants, the research is carried out by other public or private entities, including universities.

The last monitoring report of EU FP6 (León et al. 2006) reveals that none of the FP policy instruments with the exception of collaborative research were designed by keeping TT activities in mind, and participants in R&D projects were not motivated to pay attention to TT and dissemination of results. However, these instruments could support some tasks related to the transference of the generated knowledge within the consortium to specific user entities in order to receive feedback and to tune the technology associated to pilot experiences. Other TT activities outside the consortium are not explicitly addressed.

Primary responsibility for the exploitation of results relies on the partners of every project, and the European Commission cannot interfere in internal agreements except when plans or commitments were explicitly included in the project tasks. FP instruments give enough capabilities to universities in using the results of their research because the participation is regulated and protected by the Commission's contract and consortium agreements where IPRs are defined by common participation rules. The case of academic partners in IPs is different than in NoEs because they assume that their concept of "exploitation" is different. The protection of the knowledge generated during the project by patents and, if possible, to licence them for industrial exploitation should be compatible with academic papers to justify their participation.

It is not common to find in IPs, STREPS, collective research, or even in NoEs too much effort (time and money) devoted to open dissemination of research results to non-experts. Furthermore, the evaluation of the project outputs in their institutions is never likened to TT activities but to the impact of academic papers. As a consequence, even when dissemination is addressed, it is understood as "peer dissemination" (to experts in the field) because personal promotion and recognition could depend on it. As a consequence, participants in FP6 do not devote time or effort to open dissemination of their work to nonexperts.

3.2 Long-Term Instruments for University– Industry Research Cooperation

Public administrations are convinced that the creation of stable university–industry relationships will facilitate the adaptation of the research agendas of public research groups to industry needs if this evolution is economically supported during long periods of time (COM 2006c). Simultaneously, enterprises will be more prone to demonstrate or incorporate advanced technology in their products or processes if the link to the science base is stable enough to allow feedback and adaptation. Behind it, public administrations have another objective in mind: to boost private investments in innovation by cofinancing a whole range of activities.

The consequence is the design of new policy instruments oriented to support long-term joint research ventures. The emphasis is not placed on the cooperation for one specific R&D project but the support for a wider research line during long periods of time with higher commitments of involved institutions. Over the years, many specific R&D projects and other activities (technology watch, post-graduate education, mobility, and technology transfer and diffusion) can be launched within the scope covered in the research line.

Looking for more stable PPPs, the EU promoted another mechanism: European technology platforms (ETPs). An ETP is a soft but long-term instrument led by European industries proposed during the execution of FP6 and in the preparation of FP7. The objective was to join a set of public and private institutions to agree on a long-term strategic research agenda (SRA) of up to 20 or 30 years and its associated roadmap in one specific domain. As a measure of the success, 36 ETPs were launched at the end of 2006. Notice that this instrument reinforces the role of industry in driving the research agenda.

The influence of ETPs heavily depends on their capability to attract all major stakeholders (basically, large industries) and other knowledge-intensive partners. Although resources are available to coordinate activities, the commitment of participants is not very hard. Nevertheless, there is a clear opportunity for participants to identify specific R&D projects and to receive funds by using other short-term instruments. Several European countries are creating national technology platforms as mirrors of the EPTs to address more local needs. Knowledge transfer is assured though public documents.

Universities assume a secondary role in ETPs because the leadership in SRA elaboration comes from large industries, but agreement on a common research agenda is a very important result to ensure that public and private entities will work in the same direction and facilitate TT in later stages.

Table 1 summarizes the main features of the instruments used in FP6 (including ETPs) affecting TT activities.

Figure 4 graphically represents the range of possibilities used today by universities to facilitate long-term agreements with industry: from the location of private research centers (usually in combination with some agreements to exploit technology created by the university) in their own premises, to well-known contract-research activities to research groups, to the exploration of other more innovative approaches like the temporal use of space in university research centers for specific activities or the creation of permanent joint legal entities (foundations, common enterprises, economic interest grouping, etc.).

Table 1. **Summary of Features of Short-Term Policy Instruments in the EU**

Feature/ Instrument	PRO-Industry Bilateral Research Subcontract	FP IP	FP STREP	FP NoE	Col Research for SMEs	ETP
Duration	1–3	3–4	2–3	3–4	1–3	undefined
Type of contract	Subcontract to one partner	Partner	Partner	Partner	Partner	associate
IP regime	Owned by contractor	Shared by Partners	Shared by Partners	Shared by Partners	Shared by partners	None
Responsibility of universities	Variable Limited to technical aspects	Reduced number of leaders	Variable Small percentage of leaders	High Leadership is common	Moderate	Variable
Independence of universities	Limited	Moderate	Moderate	High	Moderate	High
Type of TT activity	Low	Exploitation and dissemination	Exploitation	Dissemination	Education	Strategic agenda

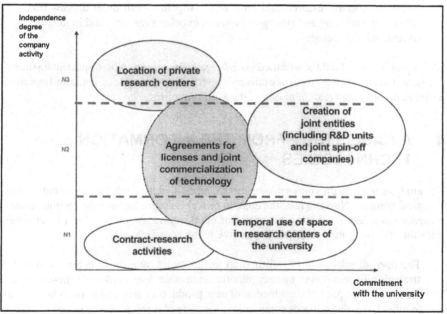

Figure 4. **Instruments for Long-Term Partnership**

In this context, joint research centers are the most useful mechanism to embed R&D and TT activities and are described as follows. A joint research center implies the creation of a common research infrastructure located within university premises to develop R&D activities closely linked to the interest of the enterprise (less common in other types of PROs). In some cases, more than one enterprise participates in the research center. The agreements imply long-term funding of a limited number of research lines which are decided with a strong influence of the enterprise. Indirectly, they try to boost more in-house research in the industrial sector. The creation of these entities is complemented through specific agreements on TT, dissemination, and exploitation of research results. European governments (both central and regional authorities) have defined support policies with specific funding for university-driven science parks where the location of some research institutions near potentially interested industries was also promoted to facilitate both explicit and tacit knowledge transfer.

Large multinational companies strongly supporting open innovation drive the creation of networks of joint (or supported by long-term agreements) research centers in several European countries. The effect is the need for a better complementarity in research topics and less dependence on funding from national or regional industries. These networks could have several levels of interdependence, but in a decade many excellent teams/centers could be involved in these ventures.

In this rich context, the EU has proposed the creation of the European Institute of Technology (EIT) (COM 2006c). The rationale behind it is based on the recognition by the European Council that

> a European Institute of Technology—based on top-class networks open to all Member States—will be an important step to fill the existing gap between higher education, research and innovation, together with other actions that enhance networking and synergies between excellent research and innovation communities in Europe.

EIT is proposing to fund the so called *knowledge communities*, where specific institutes or research groups belonging to one university with other external academic and business partners propose the creation of one of these communities.

4   A CASE STUDY FROM THE INFORMATION TECHNOLOGIES

The analysis made in previous sections can be applied, in principle, to any scientific and technical domain. Nevertheless, the domain of technologies for the information society presents some features that made the use of open innovation models for TT activities relevant. For the purposes of this paper, five features are relevant.

1. The open development of information technologies by a set of entities linked by strategic alliances is even more common than in other domains due to time-to-market pressures. The pace of introduction of new products or services is much faster than in other fields due to fierce competition, the pace of technical obsolescence, and the small window of time opportunity for a specific product.

2. Multidisciplinary approaches, especially in the deployment of telecom services, require early feedback from advanced users and the participation of different entities due to knowledge fragmentation, which increases the need to access, integrate, and consolidate external knowledge inside IT entities.

3. Entry barriers to innovation are lower than in other industrial sectors where capital investments are very high to obtain first results. This feature provokes a dynamic networking where ideas, people, and (immature) solutions are integrated looking for market anticipation. Cluster structures where private and public entities work closely together seem also adequate to facilitate rapid exchange of ideas.

4. The deployment of new IT services requires systematic feedback from end-users, who can accept high degrees of instability compensated by the access to very immature technologies. Academic entities play an important role in this area.

5. At the national and European level, IT is an exploratory field for testing new policy instruments to boost competitiveness: open public procurement models, national or supranational regulations concerning frequency allocation, property rights enforcement, or licenses linked to geographical deployment.

As a consequence of these features, the IT sector perceives the need of cooperation in a more acute way, promoting a close link betgween technology development, transfer, and diffusion. Although all open cooperative models are used, the IT sector offers several examples of success in using the open community models due to the possibility to rapid exchange of knowledge and solutions which contribute to the generation of software packages (i.e., in games, operating systems, specialized libraries, etc.) for a specific hardware or software platform or the deployment of advanced services. This approach is difficult to implement in physical (or hardware) product developments.

Universities and PROs can assume an innovative role due to the need to transfer and diffuse IT solutions to advanced users (mainly from academia) even in immature phases and also to give feedback to commercial equipment providers. Simultaneously, the emergence of a commercial market can be speeded-up based on the accumulated experience. In this context, open cooperative approaches with long-term public–private partnerships are common with the strong involvement of public authorities.

An example of advanced IT service deployment with a strong emphasis on TT is the deployment of massive grid-based services. Grid technology is a second step on top of the academic research networks deployed in the last two decades. Here, the need to access to huge supercomputers with massive data storage to conduct research in basic science (particle physics, climate change, structural biology, etc.) made cooperation with other entities for long periods of time necessary. From the service standpoint, maturation speed depends on the capability to transfer it in controlled scenarios. Notice that the required infrastructure for grid service deployment is based on high-speed networks and supercomputer pre-commercial equipment. Figure 5 summarizes the role played by the involved stakeholders.

Both national and European authorities have stimulated the deployment of high-speed academic research networks and grid services by financing investments and recurrent costs of the provision of grid services. Furthermore, the communications costs are

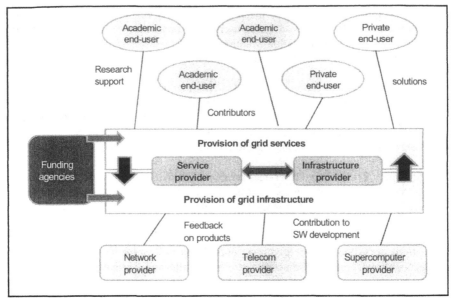

Figure 5. **Grid Services from the TT Perspective**

also partly supported for not-for-profit institutions. As an example of research-driven public procurement, it also triggered cooperation with the private sector by assuming that academic entities would accept a reasonable level of instability compensated by lower costs and experimentation capability. Universities, apart from their capability to offer advanced technical solutions (i.e., in network management, new generation of services, etc.), also participate as advanced users and help others (public and private) entities to adopt services.

Table 2 summarizes the characteristics of this case from the open cooperative models standpoint, where the evolution of embedded academic research networks is also presented as a hidden technology. Notice the coexistence of some of them.

The participation of large telecommunications and computer companies is also essential because public entities do not possess the capability to implement a large super-computer or to deploy an optical network. Participation of universities and public research centers was more focused on providing middleware solutions for specific purposes and the use of new services. This is a good example of TT embedded into technology development with the strong participation of advanced users.

The involvement of users from the private sector (at the first stage, participation was carried out through research departments but other engineering departments were progressively involved) offers another possibility to increase public–private cooperation. In this sense, the possible use of the academic network by private companies involved in FP consortia-based R&D projects is an example. The same situation is happening in the grid field.

Two levels of openness in cooperation can be identified. This case can be classified as a cooperative one with strong involvement of users (scientists) to provide the technological basis on top of high-speed networks. Simultaneously, the strong presence

Table 2. Open Cooperative Examples in the European TT Sector

Feature	Embedded Academic Research Network	Grid Technology
Open innovation models used	Subcontracted Cooperative	Extension of the open community models limited to public communities
Technology maturation	Moderate maturity level in networks, but both immature and mature services	Immature, both in basic components and in services
Involvement of universities and public research centers	Deep involvement at the beginning but responsibility was progressively transferred to specialized organizations	Yes, from the beginning until today; this role will be lower when technology matures
National governmental support	Communication costs Support to R&D projects access	Infrastructures costs like supercomputers or data management Support to R&D projects
European support	International communication costs FP development of advanced services	Use of academic research networks Support to FP projects
Instruments used	National R&D programs FP infrastructures, FP IP Public procurement	National R&D programs FP Public procurement
Embedded TT	Not in network technologies Yes in advanced services	Yes in grid technologies
Training and education approach	Not covered	Yes. User training covered in formal seminars
Public–private partnership	Yes, it derives from conditions in public procurement	With large multinationals
User's participation	Organized feedback to network operators User do not need to have a technical background	Organized distribution of responsibilities Technical users or scientists
Co-ordination structures	Yes, well structured at the national and European levels	Yes, based on a hierarchical structure for data management and access

of academic entities offers the co-existence with an open community model in the use of data once the technology has matured to emphasize services to scientific end users. It is still too early to extend it to other commercial users.

5   CONCLUSIONS

Governments and universities should work together to foster closer cooperation with private entities in the framework of open innovation models to increase knowledge generation, transfer, and use. Although all types of innovation models as presented in this paper are potentially useful, the right choice depends on the context, degree of maturity of the technology, and specific reward mechanisms from public administrations to stabilize long-term cooperation. A general trend characterized by an increasing involvement of universities in the participation of consortia-based policy instruments, where cooperation with industry is not restricted to specific research projects but applied in wider schemes, is noticed. A deeper institutional involvement of public universities has also permitted extending the range of TT cooperation between public and private sectors by assuming the role of advanced users. The growing management autonomy of public universities in the EU can facilitate the definition and implementation of new instruments adapted to their specific context without relying exclusively on instruments defined by public administrations.

Policy instruments provided by public administrations are also moving toward funding long-term partnerships because benefits cannot be obtained in the relatively short period of one R&D project, dissemination and exploitation is difficult to address in this context. The analysis of short-term and long-term instruments available in the EU for university–industry cooperation reveals a richer realm where many different approaches coexist and coevolve over time. The EU FP6 also promoted this change of trend with new participation instruments for a broader concept of innovation where education, research, and transference can be simultaneously addressed.

The sector of information technologies has been used as a pilot field due to the need to increase cooperation to speed up the deployment of advanced services. The case of grid technology and services demonstrates the usefulness of using cooperative open innovation models within the triple helix paradigm at the international level and the need to embed TT activities as a part of immature service deployment processes.

References

Albino, V., Carbonara, N., and Giannocaro, I. "Industrial Districts as Complex Adaptive Systems: Agent-Based Models of Emergent Phenomena," in C. Karlsson, B. Johansson, and R. R. Stough (eds.), *Industrial Clusters and Inter-firm Networks: New Horizons in Regional Science*, Cheltenham, UK: Edward Elgar, 2005.

COM. *Delivering on the Modernization Agenda for Universities: Education, Research and Innovation*, Brussels: Commission of the European Communities, 2006a (available online at http://ec.europa.eu/education/policies/2010/doc/comuniv2006_en.pdf).

COM. *Implementing the Renewed Partnership for Growth and Jobs: Developing a Knowledge Flagship: The European Institute of Technology*, Brussels: Commission of the European Communities, 2006b (available online at http://eur-lex.europa.eu/LexUriServ/site/en/com/2006/com2006_0077en01.pdf).

COM. *Proposal for a Regulation of the European Council and Parliament Establishing the European Institute of Technology*, Brussels: Commission of the European Community, 2006c.

Debackere, K., and Veugelers, R. "The Role of Academic Technology Transfer Organizations in Improving Industry Science Links," *Research Policy* (34:4), April 2005, pp. 321-342.

EIRMA. *Responsible Partnering: Joining Forces in a World of Open Innovation. A Guide to Better Practices for Collaborative Research between Science and Industry*, Paris: EIRMA, in cooperation with EUA, Pro Ton Europe, and EARTO, January 2005 (available online at http://www.eirma.asso.fr/f3/local_links.php?action=jump&id=796).

Etzkowitz, H., and Leysderdoff, L. "The Dynamics of Innovation: From National Systems and 'Mode 2' to a Triple Helix of University–Industry–Government Relations," *Research Policy* (29:2), 2000, pp. 109-123.

Foray, D. (rapporteur). "Globalization of R&D: Linking Better the European Economy to 'Foreign' Sources of Knowledge and Making EU a More Attractive Place for R&D Investment," Grupo de expertos de la Comisión Europea "Knowledge for Growth," April 2006.

Geroski P. A. "Models of Technology Diffusion," *Research Policy* (29:4-5), April 2000, pp. 603-625.

Karlsson, C., Johansson, B., and Stough, R. R. (eds.). *Industrial Clusters and Inter-Firm Networks: New Horizons in Regional Science*, Cheltenham, UK: Edward Elgar, 2005.

León, G. (Chairman), Calzarossa, M. (Rapporteur), Goericke, D., Olesky, E., Rogerson, S., Schmidt-Lainé, C., and Timperi, A. "Monitoring Report 2005: Implementation of Indirect Research Activities of the Sixth Framework Programmes of the European Community (EC) and the European Atomic Energy Community (EURATOM), October 2006 (available online at http://polaris.dit.upm.es/~gonzalo/Monitoring2005.pdf).

Ormala, E. (Chairman), Vonortas, N., Ayme, S., Cok, L., Donnelly, D., King, J., Mandl, C., Meyer-Krahmer, F., Llesky, E., Quintanilha, A., Stame, N., Tarrach, R., and Thys-Clement, F. "Five Years Assessment of the EU Framework Programme (1999-2003)," European Commission, 2005 (available online at http://ec.europa.eu/research/reports/2004/fya_en.html).

Reichert, S. "Research Strategy Development and Management at European Universities," European University Association, EUA Publications, Brussels, 2006 (available online at http://www.eua.be/fileadmin/user_upload/files/EUA1_documents/Research_Strategy.1150458087261.pdf).

About the Author

Gonzalo León is Professor in the Telematics Engineering Department at the Universidad Politénica de Madrid. His research activities focus on software engineering for telecommunications systems and on information technology transfer. Since 1986, Professor León has occupied several relevant positions in the Spanish Administration of Science and Technology: as Deputy General Director for International Relations on R&D, as Deputy General Director at the Office of Science and Technology attached to the Presidency of the Government. In 2002, he was appointed Secretary General for Science Policy at the Ministry of Science and Technology, responsible for the national R&D plan and industrial relations. He is chairman of the expert group on the follow-up of the Lisbon Strategy and vice president of the Space Advisory Group at the European Commission. Since 2004, he has served as vice president for Research at the Universidad Politénica de Madrid. He can be reached by e-mail at gonzalo.leon@upm.es.

6 PROCESS MODELING INFORMATION SYSTEMS DEVELOPMENT: The SellCo Case

Mike Newman
University of Manchester
Manchester England
Agder University College
Kristiansand, Norway

Shanshan Zhu
University of Manchester
Manchester, England

Abstract   We build on previous research to demonstrate how, with a combination of a socio-technical change model, a social process model, and punctuated equilibrium theory, we can describe and analyze a specific information system development project. In this paper, we focus on an information systems project that was being implemented in a UK retail organization where a new system was being implemented to replace the existing, failing one. Generally, the combination of these IS research models can provide us with a new, practical, and valuable way of understanding information systems development (ISD) as a social process. Despite the limitations associated with this type of research, this study attempts to contribute to the further understanding of process research into ISD.

Through our case study exemplar, several findings were generated. First of all, the project implementation context, including organizational context and external environmental context, was shown to play a significant role in the project implementation process. We show how social-technical equilibria can be perturbed by the critical incidents that occurred externally to the project. Furthermore, the ability of the project team in dealing with unexpected events was seen as a vital skill in ensuring the stability of a project. In contrast, drift is shown to lead to a degree of chaos. Third, the past project patterns or

Please use the following format when citing this chapter:

Newman, M., and Zhu, S., 2007, in IFIP International Federation for Information Processing, Volume 235, Organizational Dynamics of Technology-Based Innovation: Diversifying the Research Agenda, eds. McMaster, T., Wastell, D., Ferneley, E., and DeGross, J. (Boston: Springer), pp. 63-81.

similar patterns from other system processes, as suggested the literature, have significant impacts on current project patterns. Finally, when it comes to critical events that occur totally unexpectedly, we found that the knowledge generated from past project patterns or similar patterns from other systems may be of only limited use. Actors in our ISD drama were often reactive, not anticipatory.

Our approach illustrates the utility of the contextual process model in the study of ISD and, in particular, the distinction between project and work processes. The paper ends with suggestions which may be helpful to scholars in IS research as well as practitioners involved in IS projects.

Keywords   Socio-technical systems, social process, punctuated equilibrium, information systems, ISD, success and failure

1   INTRODUCTION

Despite the numerous methods and strategies designed to ensure information systems project success such as information systems development (ISD) methodologies, project management techniques, and software process improvement, it is still not possible to guarantee a successful project outcome for all interested parties. IS failures are legendary and have attracted the public attention in recent years due to a series of spectacular cases. For instance London Stock Exchange's Taurus paperless share settlement (see IT Cortex Statistics at http://www.it-cortex.com), London Ambulance Service's Computer-Aided Despatch System (LASCAD) (Beynon-Davies 1999), and French Railway Company SNCF's computerized reservation system, known as SOCRATE (Eglizeau et al. 1986; Mitev 1996) are all such examples. More recently, newspapers have reported on several notorious public sector cases in the UK such as the Passport Office, the Department of Social Security and the National Health Service.[1] The specter of IS failure continues to haunt both the academic and practitioner communities.

In particular, we investigate the parallel processes exhibited by the building events and the work (or legacy) events and focus on points of interaction. While it does not solve the success/failure conundrum, our analysis offers further insights and enables us to comment on theories such as escalation and de-escalation (Keil and Robey 1999) and the many factor, cross-sectional studies reported in the literature. This and other examples are the first steps in building our knowledge of ISD *from a process perspective.*

This study is guided by the following research questions:

* How can a combination of a socio-technical model, a social process model, and punctuated equilibrium theory be used to describe and explain the social dynamics of ISD in a retail organization?
* How can this application of the model contribute to our understanding of ISD research?

---

[1] "NHS IT Upgrade Set for Criticism," BBC News, June 16, 2006 (available online at http://news.bbc.co.uk/1/hi/health/5084596.stm).

This paper starts with a summary of the punctuated process model developed in a previous work (Newman and Robey 1992; Newman and Zhu 2005; Pan et al. 2006; Robey and Newman 1996). Next, we describe our research approach including a description of the case study used. This research focuses on an IS project that was being implemented in a UK retail organization, where the new system was implemented to replace an old, failing one. The next section describes the case study findings and these are analyzed using the *punctuated process model* and the implications for academics and project managers will be discussed. The paper ends with conclusions from the study and with a statement of its limitations.

2 SUMMARY OF THE PUNCTUATED PROCESS MODEL

Models of ISD and its environment can be applied to examine the IS implementation process, where the structure and content of the information system and its interaction with the environment can be described, analyzed, and communicated (De Abreu and Conrath 1993). In general, there are two identifiable streams in the literature: factor studies and process studies.

2.1 Factor Studies

A large number of IS implementation studies have tried to identify factors that are related to IS implementation success and failure (e.g., Burke et al. 2001; Kanter and Walsh 2004; Poon and Wagner 2001; Somers and Nelson 2001; Umble et al. 2003). This model and its later variants such as structural equation modeling remains as the largest research stream in the IS implementation literature; it uses independent and control variables and their associations with dependent variables (i.e., the project outcomes; Lyytinen 1987). The value of these studies is that they use cause–effect patterns to investigate IS implementation difficulties, and that they have provided valuable insight into the nature of IS problems (De Abreu and Conrath 1993).

Nonetheless, some researchers (e.g., Markus and Robey 1983; Newman and Robey 1992) noted that factor models have been of little practical utility in coping with IS problems, due to the lack of deep understanding of implementation process features (i.e., they only emphasize **what** factors are associated with outcomes, not **how** they shape those outcomes). Processes are largely ignored and are treated as a closed box.

2.2 Process Studies

ISD has long been seen as a socio-technical change process (Kwon and Zmud 1987), and can be "conceived as a sequence of episodes, punctuated by encounters, that follows patterns established in previous development work" (Newman and Robey 1992, p. 250). Studying the whole project implementation process can help researchers get a fuller, richer picture. Rather than focusing on technical features, process models focuses on social change activities by investigating sequences of critical incidents that link antecedent conditions with outcomes (Newman and Robey 1992). The punctuated equilibrium model is one of the theoretical frameworks that has been used by IS researchers to describe and explain organizational change patterns (Newman and Robey 1992; Newman and Zhu 2005; Robey and Newman 1996).

2.3 Conceptual Framework

Based on previous work (Newman and Robey 1992; Newman and Zhu 2005; Pan et al. 2006; Robey and Newman 1996), this study is constructed on three major frameworks: *Leavitt's socio-technical change model* (Figure 1), *a social process model* (Figures 2 and 3 showing a successful intervention), and a *punctuated equilibrium model* (Figure 4), and attempts to reach a sufficient understanding of a complex implementation process in its organizational and wider contexts. Leavitt's socio-technical change model is used to identity the relationships between structure, actors, technology, and task and their effects on IS implementation (Leavitt 1964). The social process model is applied to describe the project outcomes through the study of the entire implementation process (Newman and Robey 1992; Pan et al. 2006; Robey and Newman 1996) where the system change is seen as a construction of a sequence of incremental changes and critical incidents representing, respectively, equilibrium periods (stability) and disequilibrium periods (instability) within organizational and external contexts (Gersick 1991; Lyytinen and Newman 2005; Pettigrew 1990, 1992; Tushman and Anderson 1986). Finally, punctuated equilibrium theory is used to understand how change can occur. ISD is depicted as having relatively long, stable periods, punctuated with opportunities for change to the *deep structure* (e.g., a crisis such as a change in project leadership or major issues arising from software problems that lead to a radical change of approach).

Figure 2 depicts a critical incident (or event) that occurs during the project (i.e., building system) which produces a *gap* between the task and the technology. Not all events are critical but we designate those that are *critical* if they produce a gap in the

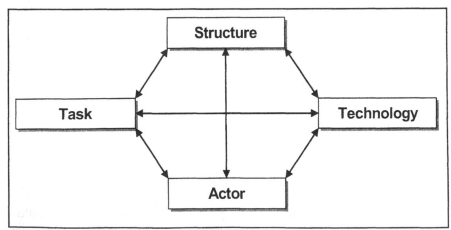

Figure 1. **Leavitt's Diamond (Adapted from Levitt 1964)**

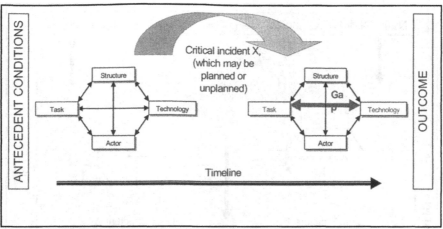

Figure 2. Social Process Model (Adapted from Leavitt 1964; Newman and Zhu 2005; Robey and Newman 1992)

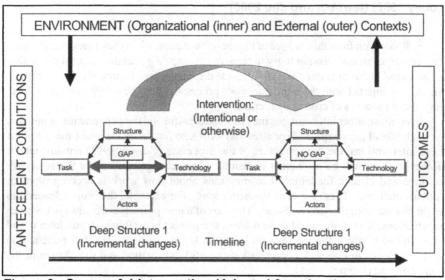

Figure 3. Successful Intervention (Adapted from Lyytinen and Newman 2005; Newman and Robey 1992; Newman and Zhu 2005)

socio-technical entity as above shows. For example, a pilot test of a new information system may cause major problems to the users of the test system (poor usability, slow response times etc.), resulting in a gap between the task and the technology. Critical incidents may be planned or unplanned. Gaps may persist for sometime.

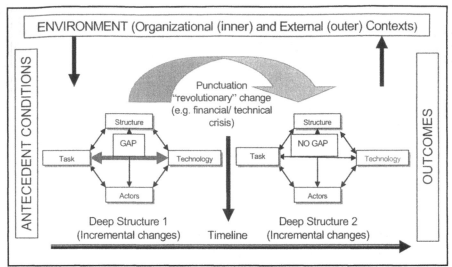

Figure 4. **The Contextual Punctuated Model (Showing a Successful Punctuation) (Adapted from Lyytinen and Newman 2005; Newman and Robey 1992; Newman and Zhu 2005)**

Following on from this, we see in Figure 4 that actors, when they recognize the gap, may construct an *intervention* to try to remove this gap (e.g., database redesign), which is *successful* in this example. We also include the elements of *context* (inner and outer), which may interact with the build and work processes (Pettigrew 1990 1992) as these may also be sources of critical incidences.

In contrast, other interventions may be unsuccessful and the gap remains or perhaps even additional gaps appear. Processes may drift into further chaos over time. In all of these interventions, the deep structure of the processes (Gersick 1991) remains intact. However, there will be infrequent occasions where changes will make the actors re-examine and change fundamental assumptions about how work is accomplished or systems are built. These are called *punctuations*. For example, the project leadership might change from user-led to IS-led. The start of a new project nearly always involves punctuations, first in the build system when the project is established, and later if and when the new information system replaces the legacy system. The full punctuation model is shown in Figure 4, depicting a successful punctuation and the change in the deep structure (Gersick 1991).

2.4 Parallel Process Model

Since social and organizational environments play such a significant role in IS implementation research, we add the final nuance to study work processes in parallel with IS building processes and the interactions between them. Newman and Zhu (2005), Pan et al. (2006) and Lyytinen and Newman (2005) introduced the **parallel process model** with the socio-technical entity concept (see Figure 5).

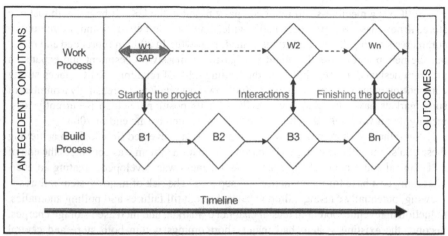

Figure 5. Parallel Process Model with Socio-Technical Entitites (Adapted from Lyytinen and Newman 2005; Newman and Zhu 2005)

In summary, shaped by an historical context (*antecedent conditions*), existing socio-technical arrangements continue until a *critical incident* (planned or, usually, unplanned) takes place which produces a *gap* between one or more of the S-T pairs. This is an unstable state and actors, when they recognize the problem, may attempt to design *interventions* which may remove the gap successfully or may fail and even result in multiple gaps (i.e., *unintended consequences*). In all of these cases there is no threat to the underlying *deep structure* although the model admits small *incremental, first order changes* to this deep structure. In contrast, some interventions (planned or unplanned) may produce *punctuations* (or *second order changes*) that produce a new, deep structure. Assembling the building team and delivering the final system to replace the existing work processes are both examples of common punctuations but there may be others as well that arise from sources that are internal or external. We now turn to illustrating the punctuated process model.

3   RESEARCH APPROACH

This study adopts a qualitative research approach with the support of an interpretive case study. The research site was a UK retail organization that will be referred to as the SellCo case throughout the report.[2] Data were collected to report how a database and data warehouse system (we label this the EPoS system) was developed through a set of stages over a 2 year period. The SellCo case was selected mainly opportunistically because of the high-level access the authors had in this organization, and, secondly, because the authors believe that this case could contribute to IS research through the application of the punctuated process model.

---

[2]Not its real name; Anonymity was a prerequisite of access to the company.

SellCo is a medium-sized retail company based in the UK. It began with just one store; it now has over 50 stores nationwide, a wholesale network, and a dynamic e-commerce system, all with ambitious plans for growth. In 2002, it rebranded and rolled out the new brand across the country as part of a massive investment and expansion program designed to keep SellCo at the leading edge of retailing. SellCo faces strong competition in the industry with many other low-cost retailers; increasingly a number of supermarkets have also challenged SellCo for its position. SellCo is currently loss-making, but it was looking to turn a profit of £1 million by the end of 2006.

Nevertheless, there were two key elements that prevented SellCo from achieving these goals. First, the existing DOS-based information system was coming to the end of its technical and functional life span as the business was developed, creating an ever-increasing cost base for maintenance and support. The risk of major system failures is growing, potentially causing a drop in sales through till failures and polling anomalies, reduction in revenue, potential loss of channel to market, and increased storage charges. Second, the existing system had major shortcomings within both store and central functions. Examples of these include insufficient visibility of holdings and locations of stock, insufficient ability to control prices and therefore margin, and insufficient control of markdown, resulting in high levels of reported stock loss.

This study focuses specifically on the new database and data warehouse system—the EPoS system (electronic point of sales)—that was being implemented in the organization to improve its efficiency and effectiveness.

The project implementation was still in progress by the time of the research but the system was being rolled out successfully to the stores. In order to comprehend different perspectives relevant to IS project, personnel at all levels within the organization were targeted, with five main stakeholder groups studied (system developers, end users, IT experts, management, and vendors). Over the period from March 2004 to August 2004, in total 11 semi-structured interviews were conducted *in situ* with actors from these user groups and some subjects were interviewed more than once for continuity purposes. We also did extensive documentary analysis as well as observing the subjects' interactions with technology. Where appropriate, we followed Klein and Myers' (1999) principles in collecting and interpreting data. For example, the principle of suspicion was employed using one subject's disclosure as a check against those from others. We also used mirroring techniques to tap into the subjects' life worlds (Myers and Newman 2007). Each interview transcript or set of notes taken from documentation analysis and observation was subjected to an intensive six-step process of data analysis. The research process started with the frameworks, explained earlier, describing socio-technical change, social process, and critical incidents associated with the IS project. Hence, the generation of concepts and frameworks forms an ongoing part of the data analysis as well as its conclusion.

4   CASE STUDY FINDINGS

The following is a brief narrative of the project, its antecedent conditions, context, and outcome. It was derived from the transcripts, documents, and observations.

4.1 Antecedent Conditions: Problems with the Legacy System

The legacy system in SellCo was a DOS-based system, which was used for stock control throughout the retail business. In general, the legacy system was successful with regard to meeting all of its original objectives. Over time, due to the outdated status of the hardware and software, the legacy system has been reported variously as very slow, unreliable, and inflexible, resulting in difficulties in carrying out management reporting, system support, and maintenance processes. As a result of the number of issues associated with the legacy system, a decision was made by the SellCo top management at the end of 2002 that an EPoS system would be implemented to replace the legacy system. In summary, the historical picture of ISD at SellCo was generally positive but the legacy systems were well past their sell-by dates (see Appendix A).

4.2 The New EPoS System

Generally, the main benefits identified were improved management information through better visibility of stock flow and sales through the business, improved merchandise management, in-store efficiency, affinity sales and promotions features, improved market stock control capability, higher quality of reporting and analysis through business objects for strategic planning, fully integrated system from warehouse to store, and improved security visibility and off-stock movement.

In contrast, there was some apprehension and resistance to change that surfaced as complaints from users who were familiar with the way the legacy system worked, and their jobs were normally organized around the legacy system's functionality. The user resistance was said to be attributed to the failure of users to initially take responsibility for their own training and also by the over-reliance on IT staff for problem solving. However, with the further training, store staff quickly adjusted to the easy-to-use graphical interface. The initial work appeared to be slower during the bedding-in period due to the change in work methods and increase in system functional complexity. This was soon overcome for the majority of users as the interface was similar to the Windows XP operating system.

4.3 The Project Implementation

4.3.1 The Selection of the System

The new EPoS system was bought from a UK software company as an off-the-shelf package with customized components built especially for SellCo. In selecting the system, the cost and the level of customization the vendor could undertake to the core product were the main considerations. Time was a tertiary factor, as the project had to be delivered in a slightly compressed time frame. However, management at SellCo expressed dissatisfaction with the vendor. This was due to a number of reasons. First, the vendor software had not been proven in a commercial situation. Second, the system delivered was not delivered in a test-friendly environment for SellCo as required. Third, instead of implementing the system with SellCo's perspective in mind, the vendor implemented it from their own perspective. Finally, before the system was delivered, the vendor failed to test the system adequately from a user or a store operator perspective. Generally these problems were solved by adding more specifications to the system required by SellCo and developing the software further.

4.3.2 The Project Team

The project team consisted of roughly 20 people, formed by using staff from different levels of the SellCo. The project manager represented SellCo's IT outsourcing company. The project leader from the IT department was in charge of project management. A business analyst from the management level was responsible for the alignment between the business and the new system. The IT manager was mainly responsible for system implementation, testing, and coordination of data transfer between the legacy system and the new system. The technical team dealt with extracting data from the current system, checking the accuracy of data, and providing interfaces to the new system. The IT Helpdesk team was to handle the new system testing and feedback. All of the store managers were responsible for the new system testing and feedback from their store staff.

4.3.3 The Project Schedule

This system implementation project started in 2002 and had one year in the planning stage and one year in the implementation stage. From mid-2003 to early 2004, the system was being implemented by the vendor. Training was provided afterward for the Head Office users, the store managers, the supervisors, and the IT experts. Testing was carried out in mid-2004, especially on the Head Office system, shop tills, and configuration. The pilot store system testing and roll-out was scheduled for late 2004, and the system was due to be rolled out to the rest of the stores in the following 2 months.

After testing, as planned, the system was to be rolled out to all the stores in two months on a one-by-one basis. However this was not on the original schedule: it was about 6 months behind although it was still within the financial budget. The system was a new product and unproven in a commercial situation. It had not been tested in a variety of retail situations.

4.4 General Case Interpretation

Figure 6 is a pictorial summary of the EPoS project trajectory (Langley 1999; Pentland 1999) using the punctuated process model. The project is seen as a punctuated equilibrium process, where critical incidents emerged at different levels at SellCo (i.e., in both organizational and external contexts), affecting the stability of the building process. The building process is presented as a sequence of socio-technical entities (represented by diamond shapes) and gaps (shown as thicker arrows) that may appear between the four components following the occurrence of critical events. The organizational work process is organized in a similar way. The mutual influences between these two parallel processes are also shown on the diagram, presented as thick black vertical arrows. These vertical arrows between the diamond shapes on the parallel processes demonstrate the significant points at which the two parallel processes intersected. Critical incidents generated gaps in the socio-technical components at the organizational work level process, which in turn resulted in gaps on the project level process. The equilibrium of the EPoS project was punctuated not only by the events in its organizational context such as new IT manager appointment, but also by the factors in its external environment, for example, the damage to the BT junction box, which was outside the control of SellCo.

The first row, "External context issues," the second row, "Organizational context issues," and the last row, "Build level issues," represent the critical incidents that occurred from its implementation context during the implementation process. The external context includes issues that are beyond the organizational boundary, such as industrial rivalry (e.g., competitive pressure), or even events outside the industrial boundary (e.g., government regulation). Organizational context takes account of planned or unplanned events that had significant impacts on the project implementation and also managerial decisions in relation to the implementation. Build management issues are issues that take place within or outside the project affecting the implementation process, such as a project team restructuring.

It is clear that the two parallel processes have significant influences over each other at some points (Figure 6). On the one hand, events on the organizational work process that need to be given priority can affect or delay the building process. On the other hand, incidents that occurred in the build process needed to be dealt with at the organizational work level. In the next two sections, the socio-technical entities on both the project level (Appendix A) and the organizational work level process (Appendix B) are selected and summarized with the associated critical events in order to give a clearer explanation.

We have identified two punctuations and one possible punctuation. The first punctuation is to the build system when the project team is established (B1) after it is recognized by senior management that the legacy systems are inadequate and must be replaced (outer and inner contexts). The second punctuation (also to the build system) comes later into the building process when a major IT person leaves SellCo (inner context) and the project team has to be restructured. A third possible punctuation involves both the work and build processes (W11 and B11) and arises from the ongoing testing crisis. At the time of writing it, was not possible to say if this crisis would be resolved successfully or lead finally to a system failure. Either way, it can be described as a punctuation.

Overall, the project appears to be still within budget, but it has been delayed by approximately 6 months. According to De Wit (1988), this could be considered as a project management failure, but it is not clear what would make the company cancel the EPoS project as it was crucial to their modernization efforts. However, the outcomes of this project cannot be predicted at this stage with total accuracy as they are dependent on the subsequent events. As the system appears to be rolling out successfully, we would expect that SellCo will be using the EPoS system in the near future. However, there are some clouds on the horizon: technical problems with the software could prove crucial to the success of the project.

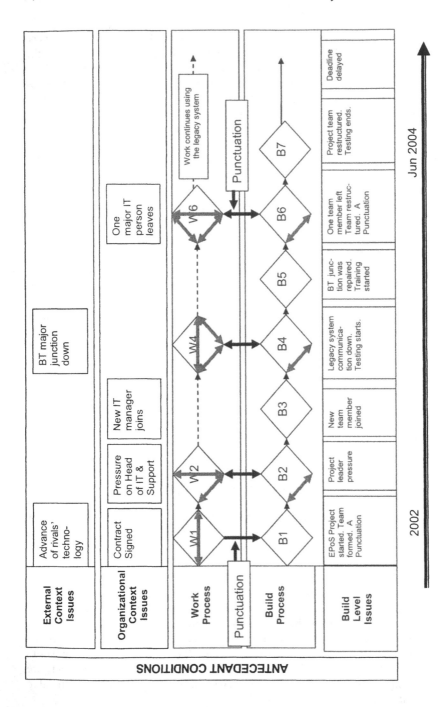

Figure 6. **General Structure of the EPoS Project Trajectory (see also Appendices)**

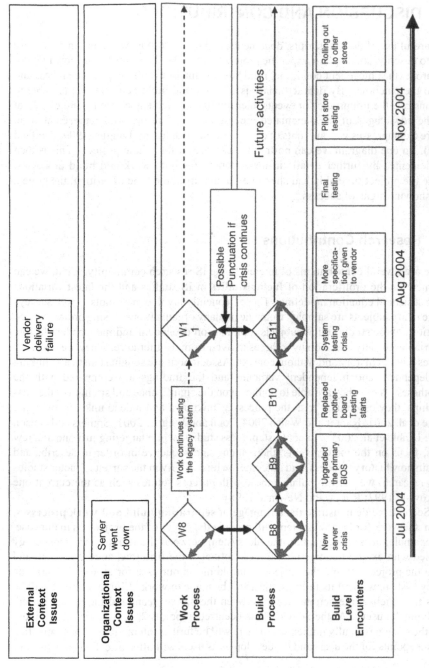

Figure 6. **General Structure of the EPoS Project Trajectory (Continued)**

5   DISCUSSION AND CONTRIBUTIONS

By careful use of our transcripts, documents, and observations, we found that we were able to describe and explain a specific project effectively. We could show how the project arose (the antecedent conditions) and how the major events shaped the process and led to the outcome. By detailed analysis of work and build activities we are able to demonstrate the importance of events, their timing and sequence (see Figure 6). What are the advantages of the punctuated process model? The pictorial representation in Figure 6 compresses vast amounts of data into a single diagram (Langley 1999; Pentland 1999). In one diagram we can portray the essence of the whole project. This is then supplemented by further details in the appendix for both work and build processes. While the project timetable had slipped by 6 months at the time of writing, the project was showing signs of success.[3]

5.1   Research Contributions

There are several contributions of interest to the IS research community. First, we can comment on the proliferation of **factor studies** in IS studies and the latest variations using structural equation modeling. These frequently involve mail shots or web surveys where many subjects are sampled from one or many organizations. Using ordinal-scaled questions, these studies elicit subjects' opinions on dependent and independent factors or variables loosely based on hypotheses derived from the literature. They are normally studies without history and without context. Associations are sought statistically linking the dependent and independent variables and the findings are compared with the hypotheses. While they are able to comment on the significance and strength of the relationships, they essentially treat the process as unknown and indeed unknowable (e.g., Burke et al. 2001; Kanter and Walsh 2004; Poon and Wagner 2001; Somers and Nelson 2001; Umble et al. 2003). In contrast, process studies, while targeting just one or a few cases, focus on the major events, their timing and sequence in order to describe and explain how history, process, and outcome are linked. Given the surfeit of factor studies in IS research, we need to balance these with process studies such as the current one (Olikowski 1992; Robey and Newman 1996).

Second, we demonstrate the advantage of **separating build and work processes**. Often, the work (or legacy) system will provide the origin of the project, as in our case. For example, at SellCo, gaps in the old system between the task and the technology coupled with external competitive forces motivated the firm to change its system and begin the project. While the project is unfolding, in our case for at least 2 years, the legacy system, with all its failings, must still be made to work. Moreover, there will be times that intense interactions occur between the project team and the legacy system involving the users. At the SellCo, these occurred at points 2, 4, 6, 8, and 11 in Figure 6. If the system is finally implemented there will be further interactions. These are often pressure points for the users and the developers as users will often be called upon to work

---

[3]Resources and access issues did not allow us to follow the project through to its conclusion.

on the existing system and help develop the new one. The punctuated process model enables us to detail these processes and their interactions, revealing the twists and turns of the project and showing how the outcome is linked to these.

Third, our process study is able to provide insights into the **patterning** effects of success and failure. By this we mean the historical patterns that develop and that are reinforced by repetition (see Robey and Newman 1996). That is why it is vital that the historical context of the project is revealed. SellCo was reported to have a relatively successful history of systems development and the legacy system, while it now had its limitations, was well-liked. In other words, there was a positive pattern of project work which would, other things being equal, render a successful outcome more likely. In other situations the opposite can occur and a company can enter a cycle of failure and rejection by the user community which without any decisive action to break the pattern would be repeated in any new project (e.g., Beynon-Davies 1999; Eglizeau et al. 1986; Mitev 1996; Robey and Newman 1996; see also IT Cortex Statistics at http://www.it-cortex.com).

Fourth, our study also provides insights in understanding the **complexity of success and failure in ISD** and concepts such as **escalation** and **de-escalation** (e.g., Keil and Robey 1999). By linking history, process, and context we can trace the trajectory of a project and show how the process is uniquely related to the outcome and how the various stakeholders can variously capture the rhetoric of success. For example, in a previous case (Newman and Robey 1992), the project was delivered five years late and four times over budget but was still believed by the managers to be a success. This and other examples indicate that escalation or the commitment of resources to a failing project and the demand to de-escalate such systems appear to be simplistic from a process perspective. In the case of SellCo, the EPoS system was essential to their future effectiveness and to abandon it prematurely would be to compound their problems. The time overruns might be escalating but they still needed the system. There was no escalation or de-escalation in the demand for the system: they could not abandon it.

Finally, for the research community, we acknowledge that case studies of this nature are highly labor intensive. However, other researchers should consider following a similar research paradigm as there is a clear dearth of such studies. Such studies will derive rich data sets and theoretical understandings. They offer plausible descriptions and explanations of ISD phenomena and greater transparency of the process (Klein and Myers 1999).

6   CONCLUSIONS AND LIMITATIONS

In the field of information systems development, many events, either expected or unexpected, may occur during the project process. Some critical issues related to ISD have been extensively discussed in the literature on organizational change, IS project implementation process, and IS success and failure. This research followed Lyytinen and Newman's, Newman and Zhu's, and Pan et al.'s approach, shown through the use of a contemporary case study (SellCo), that critical events occurring along the project process can affect the stability (i.e., equilibrium) of the project process. The equilibrium of the IS development process was influenced over time by critical events occurring around the build process, the organizational context, or the external context. The process itself in the case of SellCo was identified as a sequence of events where the connections between a preceding event and its consequences were depicted, where each of these events was analyzed by the interplay among its four components (i.e., actors, structure, technology, and task), and gaps were identified among the components in the case of critical incidents. The interactions between the organizational work process and build process were also analyzed. For example, we show that a misbalance on the organizational work level can generate a misbalance on the build level, and *vice versa*.

Through our case study, several findings were generated. First of all, in line with previous empirical studies, the project implementation context, including organizational context and external environmental context, was shown to play an essential role in the project implementation process. Process equilibrium can be seriously disturbed by the critical events that occurred in the implementation context. But this is hardly news. However, critical events do not necessarily have impacts over the project process equilibrium. Gaps between the components are generated by critical incidents, but the project process is still carried out on a daily basis (i.e., the project equilibrium is still maintained). Furthermore, we found that the ability of the project team in dealing with unexpected events is vital in ensuring the stability of a project process. In contrast, drift can lead to eventual chaos. Unquestionably, the past project patterns or similar patterns from other system processes, as have been suggested in much literature, have significant impacts on the present project patterns. We have shown how negative patterns can be reproduced. However, when it comes to the case that critical events occur totally unexpectedly, such as a natural disaster, the knowledge generated from past project patterns or similar patterns from other systems may be of little use. Process research, while long, complex, and resource-consuming, will surely provide further insights into the enigma of IS success and failure.

References

BBC News. "NHS IT Upgrade Set for Criticism," June 15, 2006 (available online at http://news.bbc.co.uk/1/hi/health/5084596.stm).

Beynon-Davies, P. "Human Error and Information Systems Failure: the Case of the London Ambulance Service Computer-Aided Despatch System Project," *Interacting with Computers* (11:6), 1999, pp. 699-720.

Burke, R., Kenney, B., Kott, K., and Pflueger, K. "Success or Failure: Human Factors in Implementing New Systems," unpublished paper, 1998 (available online at http://www.educause.edu/ir/library/pdf/EDU0152.pdf).

DeAbreu, A. F., and Conrath, D. W. "The Role of Stakeholders Expectations in Predicting Information Systems Implementation Outcomes," in M. R. Tanniru (ed.), *Proceedings of the 1993 Conference on Computer Personnel Research*, St. Louis, MO, April 1-3, 1993, pp. 408-415.

DeWit, A. "Measurement of Project Success," *International Journal of Project Management* (6:3), August 1998, pp. 164-170.

Eglizeau, C., Frey, O., and Newman, M. "SOCRATE: An Implementation Debacle," in J. Dias Coelho (ed.), *Proceedings of the 4th European Conference on Information Systems,* Lisbon, Portugal, July 2-4, 1986, pp. 1233-1244.

Gersick, C. J. G. "Revolutionary Change Theories: A Multilevel Exploration of the Punctuated Equilibrium Paradigm," *Academy of Management Review* (16:1), 1991, pp. 10-36.

Kanter, J., and Walsh, J. J. "Toward More Successful Project Management," *Information Systems Management* (21:2), 2004, pp. 16-21.

Keil, M., and Robey, D. "Turning Around Troubled Software Projects: An Exploratory Study of the De-escalation of Commitment to Failing Courses of Action," *Journal of Management Information Systems* (15:4), 1999, pp. 63-87.

Klein, H., and Myers, M. "A Set of Principles for Conducting and Evaluating Interpretive Field Studies in Information Systems," *MIS Quarterly* (23:1), 1999, pp. 67-94.

Kwon, T. H., and Zmud, R. W. "Unifying the Fragmented Models of Information System Implementation," in R. J. Boland Jr. and R. Hirschheim (eds), *Critical Issues in IS Research*, Chichester, England: John Wiley & Sons Ltd., 1987, pp. 227-251.

Langley, A. "Strategies for Theorizing from Process Data," *Academy of Management Review* (24:4), 1999, pp. 691-710.

Leavitt, H. J. *Managerial Psychology*, Chicago: University of Chicago Press, 1964.

Lyytinen, K. "Different Perspectives on Information Systems: Problems and Solutions," *ACM Computing Surveys* (19:1), 1987, pp. 5-44.

Lyytinen, K., and Newman, M. "Punctuated Equilibrium, Process Models and Information System Evolution: Towards a Socio-Technical Deep Structure of Information System Evolution," Unpublished Working Paper, Division of Accounting and Finance, University of Manchester, 2004.

Markus, L., and Robey, D. "The Organizational Validity of Management Information Systems," *Human Relations* (36:3), 1983, pp. 203-226.

Mitev, N. N. "More Than a Failure? The Computerized Reservation Systems at French Railways," *Information Technology & People* (9:4), 1996, pp. 8-19.

Myers, M., and Newman, M. "The Qualitative Interview in IS Research: Examining the Craft," *Information and Organization* (17), 2007, pp. 2-26.

Newman, M., and Robey, D. "A Social Process Model of User-Analyst Relationships," *MIS Quarterly* (16:2), June 1992, pp. 249-266.

Newman, M., and Zhu, S. "A Contextualised Socio-Technical Process Approach to ISD," in K. Soliman (ed.), *Information Management in Modern Enterprises: Issues and Solutions*, International Business Information Management Association, Lisbon, Portugal, July 5-7, 2005.

Pan, S. L., Pan, G., Newman, M., and Flynn, D. "Escalation and De-escalation of Commitment to Information Systems Projects: Insights from a Post-Implementation Evaluation Model," *European Journal of Operations Research* (173:3), September 2006, pp. 1139-1160.

Pentland, B. "Building Process Theory with Narrative: From Description to Explanation," *Academy of Management Review* (24:4), 1999, pp. 711-724.

Pettigrew, A. "The Character and Significance of Strategy Process Research," *Strategic Management Journal* (13), 1992, pp. 5-16.

Pettigrew, A. "Longitudinal Field Research on Change: Theory and Practice," *Organization Science* (1:3), 1990, pp. 267-292.

Poon, P., and Wagner, C. "Critical Success Factors Revisited: Success and Failure Cases of Information Systems for Senior Executives," *Decision Support Systems* (30:4), 2001, pp. 393-418.

Robey, D., and Newman, M. "Sequential Patterns in Information Systems Development: An Application of a Social Process Model, *ACM Transactions on Information Systems* (14:1), January 1996, pp. 30-63.

Somers, T. M., and Nelson, K. "The Impact of Critical Success Factors Across the Stages of Enterprise Resource Planning Implementation," in *Proceedings of the 34th Hawaii International Conference on System Sciences*, Los Aalmitos, CA: IEEE Computer Society Press, 2001.

Tushman, M. L., and Anderson, P. "Technological Discontinuities and Organizational Environments," *Administrative Science Quarterly* (31:3), 1996, pp. .439-465.

Umble, E. J., Haft, R. R., and Umble, M. M. "Enterprise Resource Planning: Implementation Procedures and Critical Success Factors," *European Journal of Operational Research* (146:2), 2003, pp. 241-257.

About the Authors

Michael Newman is Professor of Information Systems at the Manchester Accounting and Finance Group, Manchester Business School, University of Manchester, U.K., and is a visiting professor at Agder University College, Kristiansand, Norway, and NHH, Bergen, Norway. He has authored many academic articles in leading MIS and management journals including *MIS Quarterly*, *Information Systems Research*, *Journal of Information Technology*, *Journal of Management Studies*, *European Journal of Information Systems*, and and *Omega*. Mike's research focuses on the process of information systems development and he has conducted several empirical studies in a variety of organizations. He currently serves on the editorial board of *Journal of Information Technology* and *Information and Organization*, and has recently finished a term as associate editor for *MIS Quarterly*. He has held visiting positions at the University of Connecticut, Florida International University, Erasmus University, Rotterdam, and the Free University, Amsterdam. Mike can be reached by e-mail at MNewman@dom01.mbs.ac.uk.

Shanshan Zhu was an M.Sc. student at the University of Manchester and graduated in 2004. She began her doctoral studies in 2004 but left in 2005 to pursue a career as a consultant in the IT industry.

Appendix A.   Selected Summary of Project Trajectory (Build System)

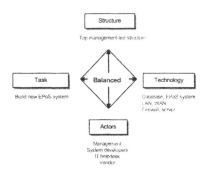

B1 – Antecedent conditions

SellCo is a medium-sized retail company based in the UK. It began with just one store; it now has over 50 stores nationwide, a wholesale network, and a dynamic e-commerce network, all with ambitious plans for growth. In 2002, it rebranded and is rolling out the new brand across the country as part of a massive investment and expansion program designed to keep SellCo at the leading edge of stock disposal retailing.

This study focuses on the new database and data warehouse system—EPoS system— being implemented at the organization. The new EPoS system is implemented to improve efficiency and effectiveness. It has six levels to track the stock at individual item level. It enables the company to have better market focus; the company can now pull data out of a database to see what items are selling well in which stores. Each till in the store will have a list of all stock item, therefore when ticket tags are missing, instead of contacting the head office to check the prices, they can just check from the till screen.

This project was led by top management. A **punctuation** to the build system.

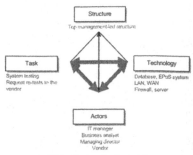

B11 – System testing crisis

As mentioned earlier, there are three types of testing: alpha stage (i.e., work or not), beta stage (further to more life cycle testing), and user acceptance stage (if the system works as it is supposed to). When delivering the system, instead of delivering the system in the user acceptance stage as specified, the vendor provided the system in the beta stage. Therefore in August 2004, when the project team started user acceptance testing on the Head Office system and the till system, many errors were identified. For example, a communication error occurred between the two systems, and till sales data could not be passed to the Head Office system.

A meeting held between the IT manager, business analyst, managing director, and vendor was held to discuss the problems. It was settled that more specifications would be given to the vendor and the system would be redelivered in two weeks.

In summary, gaps emerged between actors and task, and technology, and task and technology. This **may** produce a **punctuation** in the build system in the future.

Appendix B. Selected Summary of Organizational Trajectory (Work System)

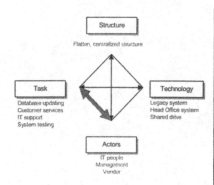

W11 – System testing crisis

As mentioned earlier, there are three types of testing: alpha stage (i.e., work or not), beta stage (further to more life cycle testing), and user acceptance stage (if the system works as it is supposed to). When delivering the system, the vendor provided the system at the beta stage.

Therefore in August 2004, when the project team started user acceptance testing on the Head Office system and the till system, many errors were identified. For example, a communication error occurred between the two systems, and till sales data could not be passed to the Head Office system.

A meeting between the IT manager, business analyst, managing director, and vendor was held to discuss the problems. It was settled that more specifications would be given to the vendor and the system would be returned in two weeks.

In summary, gaps emerged between actors and task components at the organizational work level.

Part 2:

Novel Perspectives in Innovation Research

7 AN EXPLORATION OF INFORMATION SYSTEMS ADOPTION: Tools and Skills as Cultural Artefacts— The Case of a Management Information System

Deborah Bunker
University of New South Wales
Sydney, Australia

Karlheinz Kautz
University of New South Wales
Sydney, Australia
Copenhagen Business School
Frederiksberg, Denmark

Anhtai Anhtuan
University of New South Wales
Sydney, Australia

Abstract   This paper explains the development of a skills-focused approach which can assist organizations to better anticipate hurdles to successful information systems adoption. This approach is utilized in an interpretive field study in an Australian information technology company. From a perspective that views information systems as tools, the approach is used to analyze the management control skills required to use a specific management information system. A skills match between the set of management control skills assumed by the tool maker and the skills possessed by the tool user shows why a group of users with a high degree of match adopted the tool, while another one with a low degree of match did not. The study demonstrates that the skills-focused approach is a valid and effective way of determining the appropriateness of an information system.

Please use the following format when citing this chapter:

Bunker, D., Kautz, K., and Anhtuan, A., 2007, in IFIP International Federation for Information Processing, Volume 235, Organizational Dynamics of Technology-Based Innovation: Diversifying the Research Agenda, eds. McMaster, T., Wastell, D., Ferneley, E., and DeGross, J. (Boston: Springer), pp. 85-99.

1   INTRODUCTION

Research indicates that many information systems and information technology implementations are not to the satisfaction of the adopting organizations. Larsen and McGuire
(1998) reported that half of all implementations are deemed unsuccessful or inappropriate. Unfortunately, the research into IS diffusion has not yet achieved very fruitful
outcomes for the IS community, in academia or industry. Research into this area suffers
from weaknesses, including bias and fragmentation (Kautz et al. 2005).

Taking a step back from current research directions, Bunker (2001) explored IS
adoption through an anthropological perspective. She argued that IS/IT are tools in
context and are created and used within a cultural framework. Tools inherit the cultural
values and assumptions of the creator's culture. As tools and the skills to use them are
closely related (Ayres 1978), the tool's cultural characteristics are manifested in skill sets.
Difficulties could thus emerge if the tool maker's assumptions about the context in which
the tool is to be used are not matched by the tool user's actual context. On this background, we outline a skills-focused approach to analyze tool maker and tool user contextual differences through the comparison of assumed and actual skills, which can assist
in anticipating hurdles to successful IS adoption.

This paper examines the validity of the approach by documenting an interpretive
field study of an IS adoption in an Australian IT company. In particular, the approach
is used to analyze the management control skills required to use a management information system. Three questions guide this research:

(1) What is the outcome of a skills match between the set of management control skills
     assumed by the tool maker and the skills possessed by the tool user?
(2) What factors in the user's process of tool indigenization appear to contribute to the
     resulting skills gap, if any?
(3) Is the skills-focused approach a valid and effective way of determining the appro-
     priateness of an information system?

The remainder of the paper is organized as follows: Section 2 provides the theoretical background and introduces the main concepts of the framework. Section 3 presents the research approach and method. Section 4 describes the setting of the case study
and section 5 includes and discusses our findings. We finish the paper with some conclusions in section 6.

2   THEORETICAL BACKGROUND AND FRAMEWORK

The current fragmented status and limited value of IS diffusion and adoption research
motivated us to explore alternative models for understanding IS adoption. Scandinavian
researchers (Ehn and Kyng 1984; Kammersgaard 1988) suggested a tool perspective on
the development and use of computer-based information systems. Bunker (1998, 2001)
specifically applied this perspective to IS adoption. Based on an anthropological approach to research in information systems, she developed an argument that views
information systems as tools that are created in a context, with a particular set of cultural
values and assumptions underpinning their creation. These cultural values and assumptions are manifested in skill sets.

2.1 Tools, Skills, and Organizational Culture as Their Context

Man is incomplete as a species and without tools—devices that aid in accomplishing a task or instruments used to perform an operation or necessary in the practice of a vocation or profession—**is unsustainable compared to any other species** (Stahl 2002). Technology is a sophisticated type of tool that is able to extend human capacity and even act as a substitution to achieve goals (Stahl 2002). Tools are created and used in context and are a reflection of human capacity and human culture (see Latour 1987; Winfield 1991; Winner 1986). They inherit the cultural values and assumptions of the tool maker's culture and consequently the intent and use of the tool is defined by that culture. It is a challenge for a tool user of a different culture to fully appreciate the original intent and representation of the tool.

For any tool, the mutual contingency of tools and skills is of importance for an understanding of technology as a function of human behavior (Ayres 1978). A tool requires skills not only to use it but also to understand the intent behind it. Ayres argues that technology not only involves the use of tools designed to complete an objective but also the set of skills that accompany tools. There is a natural affinity between tools and skills; human skills and the tools by which and on which they are exercised are inseparable. Skills always employ tools, and tools are such, always by virtue of being employed in acts of skill by human beings. A person's skills set is derived from the culture of which the person is a member (Bunker 2001). The same cultural derivation applies for tools. Thus, for a tool user to possess the skills to truly understand the intent and use of the tool, the user would have to subscribe to the cultural values and assumptions that are inherent in the tool (i.e, assumed by the tool maker). If tools are a visible manifestation of the assumptions and values that the IS discipline embodies, then information systems are those tools.

The term skill is commonly seen as the ability and knowledge used in order to achieve or do something. In the labour literature, skills are seen as the driver of job tasks, which then define job roles (Frizzell 1991). Jones and Whittaker (1975) comment that the mechanistic nature of the labor-industrial perspective on skills is constraining the proper examination of a person's skills set. Skills are a goal-directed, well-organized behavior that are acquired through practice with economy of effort (Proctor and Dutta 1995). The types of skill can be physical, motoric, and partially perceptual; or mental, cognitive, and perceptual; or a mixture of both (Jones and Whittaker 1975). Proctor and Dutta (1995) argue that the context partially determines skills acquisition. Skills go beyond the labor literature's mechanistic and physical portrayal and come as a dual-faceted entity featuring a mechanistic, technical dimension and an organic, cognitive component in which contextual, cultural factors play a role.

Sincoff and Sternberg (1989) report that contextual factors receive significant attention in psychology research. Here, Rosenbaum et al. (2001) argue that perceptual-motor skills are affected by context and the perceptual, cognitive, and motor domains work together to achieve skill acquisition and skilled performance (Carlson and Yaure 1990; Jones and Whittaker 1975). Given that skills are defined by mechanistic and organic components, it follows that a person's skills are embedded in the context in which they are learned. The context shapes the skill through its organic component. This again raises questions about the transferability of skills in other contexts.

In an IS environment, skills are critical. Zuboff (1988) talks of the IS environment as a "computer-mediated" environment where certain realizations about organizations' capabilities must be made. Information systems are not neutral tools and they embody essential characteristics that are bound to alter the nature of work within our factories and offices, and among workers, professionals, and managers. The profound effect of information systems on organizations and the strategy to deal with this relates to the type of skills present in the user organization: Mastery in a computer-mediated environment depends upon developing intellective skills.

Tools and their associated skills are developed and used in context. Cultural values and assumptions are inherent in tools and, consequently, their intent and use is defined by that culture. Organizational cultural theory helps to articulate precisely what is meant by culture and context, and how this impacts on IS adoption. Schein (1984) conceptualizes an organizational culture as having three distinct layers. The first layer holds the basic assumptions possessed by all members of that culture. These assumptions concern members' fundamental values of reality, human relationships, human nature, and the environment. They are taken for granted, subconscious, invisible, and most difficult to change.   The second layer holds the values to which members subscribe but are espoused, overt, and debatable, unlike basic assumptions. In the third and most visible cultural layer, labeled artefacts and creations, visual and tangible manifestations of culture are found, such as technology, art, and visible and audible behavior patterns. Schein's three layers of organizational culture form the contexts of both the tool maker and tool user in our model and complete the building blocks of our framework.

2.2 Management Control as a Significant Dimension of Organizational Culture

Culture is a multifaceted, complex phenomenon (Conner et al. 1987). Regrettably, prevailing IS research has taken a more for-granted view of the concept of culture (Avison and Myers 1995), which strips away the richness of this socially constructed phenomenon. While our research adopts an anthropological approach to studying information systems and organizational culture, it would consume more than one project to conduct complete cultural research. For that reason, the cultural focus undertaken here is further refined to a single yet important dimension of organizational culture, that of management control.

Inspired by Hofstede's (1991) work on dimensions of organizational culture, our analysis of the tool maker's and tool user's contexts has been confined to the culture of management control and the management control skills used with the tool under study—a dimension originally termed the loose versus tight control dimension. This is for two reasons. First, in the case study, the management control agenda of the tool user is most pertinent to its decision to adopt a practice management information system. Second, there is validity in concentrating on issues of management control because it complements the nature of the tool. The tool centers the time-based accounting of human resources, where standards of performance are monitored, analyzed, and set. To properly investigate the management control agenda in both the tool maker's assumed culture and the user's actual culture, we performed a further literature study to unearth common dimensions that could be used to provide specific focus for our investigation. Here, the work of researchers in organizational culture, organization theory, and organizational management was considered. As a result, five dimensions of management control were discovered,

Table 1. The Five Dimensions of Management Control

Dimension of Management Control	Literary Sources	Description
Standardization	Burns and Stalker 1966; Langfield-Smith 1997; Mintzberg 1979; Robbins 1983	The implementation of rules, standards, policies of engagement and operation
Policy compliance	Hofstede 1968; Mintzberg 1979; Tricker 1976	The measurement of performance and compliance, and the systems in place to motivate performance and compliance
Communication, interaction, behavior, and reporting	Burns and Stalker 1966; Hofstede 1968; Mintzberg 1979; Tricker 1976	The nature of the interaction and communication amongst members of all levels within the organization
Group divisions and its formalization (structure)	Burns and Stalker 1966; Mintzberg 1979; Robbins 1983; Tricker 1976	The formalization of organizational structure and job roles, the locus of decision making
Attitude toward control	Langfield-Smith 1997; Mintzberg 1979; Robbins 1983; Wieland and Ullrich 1976	Management and employee attitudes to meeting objectives and controlling resources, uncertainty, and variability

namely standardization; policy compliance; communication, interaction, behavior, and reporting; group divisions and its formalization; and attitude toward control. Table 1 provides details on each of these dimensions, including its literary sources and a brief description.

3   THE RESEARCH APPROACH AND METHOD

The research strategy reflects the researchers' relativist and constructionist assumptions. The research questions focus on the exploration and understanding of IS adoption using a skills-focused approach. Thus, the need for contextual respect is an influencing factor on our research strategy. Culture is not something that can exist as meaningful entries independently of consciousness and experience (Crotty 1998). Rather, culture is historically determined, related to anthropological concepts, and socially constructed (Hofstede et al. 1990). Hence, an abductive research strategy is used, its view of a socially constructed reality and use of thick descriptions (Blaikie 2000) enable the researchers to deal with all three research questions and properly respects the contextual and cultural aspects of this research.

As understanding human subjects and the world in which they live are only achievable through the interpretation of what subjects understand about themselves and their world (Lee 1994), we opt for an interpretive study. We gained an understanding of the IS adoption situation in the tool maker and user organizations by hermeneutically interpreting the text that was gathered in the data collection phase (Boland 1991) by attempting to make sense of the confused, incomplete, cloudy, and contradictory views (Myers 1997) of people through text-analogues in the form of transcriptions of all interviews and documentary texts. Data collected from in-depth interviews took the form of experiences, anecdotes, feelings, and statements of respondents. Eventually, following the hermeneutic circle of interpretation led us to a rich understanding of the tool maker and user contexts, the IS adoption that took place, and the skills required.

The strategy of inquiry was a case study featuring a tool user organization adopting a practice management information system developed by a tool maker organization. The research was conducted between the second-half of 2001 and the first-half of 2002. In-depth interviews were performed with four representatives of the tool maker (mainly consultants) and seven employees of the user organization (some managers using the information provided through the tool and other employees who, as timekeepers, were supposed to supply the tool with time information about their work). Documentary artefacts assisted with understanding the issues brought to the surface through the interviews. They were used as a way of triangulating the data, to verify the results. Artefacts included e-mails, memos, minutes of meetings, user manuals, presentations, training guides, and product marketing material.

A skills checklist was devised to facilitate the skills matching process. Using the checklist, the tool user's actual skills were checked against the tool maker's list of assumed skills. The checklist was categorized into the five cultural dimensions of management control.

4   THE CASE STUDY SETTING

4.1   The Tool User

Dataware[1] is a company spanning a number of sectors of the IT industry employing over 1,200 employees around Australia. The company had grown significantly from its inception in 1987 and had achieved a solid reputation. Its success in the 1990s attracted a multinational IT company, which bought it in 2001. Along with the purchase came a change in identity and management structure as well as a rationalization of existing divisions and the creation of new divisions. Every area of the company was affected by the downsizing.

Dataware was an esteemed employer. This was a reflection of the familial culture that existed before the purchase. The culture was reflective of a loosely controlled organization, where sticking to budget was not a priority. The company was very results-oriented, which contributed to its lack of concern for controlling costs while increasing revenue. Another characteristic of its culture was its enthusiasm for technological innovation. There was no hesitation in adopting new technologies that could assist it in its operations.

The major shake up in the company's size, structure, and identity after the purchase changed the organizational culture. The change was evident in the use of words. Rather

---

[1]On request to protect any identities, the names for the tool maker, the tool user, and the tool itself have been invented.

than describing the culture as *family* as before, terms such as *governance* and *company corporate* were used. There was a profound effect on employee morale after the purchase. With the downsizing continuing, the atmosphere was one of uncertainty. The company's **ITS (IT Services) Division** was not targeted intensely during the rationalization. It was responsible for the entire IT infrastructure and covered networking and communications, hardware, operating systems, and system applications for internal use. The staff were segregated into groups according to their function or service: a **Project and Development Group** managed all IT projects which dealt with the development of system applications for internal use; and a **Support Group** had the responsibility of supporting these applications and was in charge of maintaining and enhancing the networking infrastructure, operating systems, and hardware.

The division was mainly made up of system developers, system administrators, IT architecture specialists, project managers, and network engineers. The culture was similar to the rest of the company. The familial culture of optimism lingered for some time after the start of the rationalization process. However, with the introduction of a new practice management system, the culture transformed.

4.2 The Tool Maker

SixSoft is a publicly listed Australian company that has the practice management system called **STM** as its flagship product. Its services go beyond its systems to the technology, consulting, and training domains. The company boasts a global presence of over 1,600 employees and a client base of accounting and legal professions, the government sector, small and medium businesses, and large enterprises.

4.3 The Tool and its Adoption

STM was adopted by the commercial areas of Dataware in late 2000 to fulfil its requirements for supporting timekeeping. STM is designed for professional services firms to manage financial administration. It allows firms to record the time their employees spend on client work and subsequently bill the client based on those hours. Although SixSoft proclaimed that the system could be used in any professional services firm, it is interesting to note that it was originally authored as a solution for the legal profession.

During the initial adoption, the ITS Division was not part of the rollout because it did not charge for work performed for internal customers. In mid-2001, ITS management decided to implement a new version of STM for itself and installed the timekeeping module. It was seen as a way of formally monitoring staff with respect to their time at work. Instinctive and possibly unfounded management perceptions were meant to be replaced by official and factual evidence. The tool required all ITS staff to enter the time spent working.

As a tool for management, it would have been expected that ITS management would involve itself heavily with its introduction. Instead, hindsight made them realize how they failed to give the project the appropriate amount of managerial attention and significance. There was insufficient effort to define precisely what they wanted from the system, and how to go about achieving these objectives. The urgency of a timekeeping solution had put pressure on them to arrive at a resolution on time category definitions. Once STM was operational and staff entered their time into these categories, the definitions were found to cause confusion and subsequently underwent a series of revisions. Our analysis explains the phenomenon in more depth from the tool and skill perspectives.

5 FINDINGS AND DISCUSSION

We now present the tool maker's assumptions and the user's skills with regard to management control. We could not, however, identify any common assumptions and skills related to the group division and its formalization.

5.1 Skills Assumed by the Tool Maker SixSoft

Related to *Standardization*. The respondents stressed the importance of having organizational rules and policies that govern the way that business is conducted and employees work. They believed that the rules and policies must have clarity and be uniformly applied to the entire organization or organizational unit. They spoke about the need for a standard, accepted basis for recognizing business entities and events in order to record, control, and measure them properly. It was stressed that a common denominator has to be determined and used as the basis of performance measures in two critical aspects: budgeting and human productivity.

Clarity and uniformity are required for policies concerning where and how decisions are made and ratified. Without explicit conventions about executive powers, important decisions may be delayed, which could harm productivity. Based on these responses about standardization, the user must have the skills to develop clear and uniform measures of performance and decision-making policy.

Skills Related to *Policy Compliance*. SixSoft assumed that the tool user would have formal programs that motivate employees to enter their time sheets accurately and expediently. Any employee time that is either not calculated accurately or entered in a timely fashion represents an opportunity cost. The sales representative alluded to the use of key performance indicators (KPI) in order to motivate employees to time keep properly, accurately, and effectively. Any KPIs created to motivate timekeeping must be applied uniformly to all employees. In summary, the assumed policy compliance skill on a divisional level involved the setting up of motivational programs for timekeeping.

On the managerial level, managers are assumed to play a pivotal role in the division's financial and human performance. They are the visible manifestation of the division's policy compliance framework. They are there to enforce and encourage employees to time keep accurately. Managers should regularly review their staff's time sheets as the quality of their decisions is contingent on the data derived from their staff and they should be able to set and track a budget. Budgets are seen as a complex but critical goal. This is indicative of an ambitious culture where they "do it right and not just get it done." The budget will determine the scope with which employees can perform work. Budget performance is a key indicator of the organization's health. Managers need to understand how to spot trends, how to analyze data, and how to read the data analysis. This skill is about whether or not managers can act upon the information generated by and for them.

Managers have the need to know what their staff members are doing at all times. This requires managers to constantly monitor and review the projects and jobs that their staff members work on. Managers are assumed to be responsible for the completion of jobs and projects and, hence, should demand to know what staff are doing. STM provides managers with the visibility to examine employees' activities in an indirect and less inhibiting way. The constant monitoring and review of employees' work is also performed to detect obstacles that can be detrimental to the goal of productivity or chargeability. Information from STM and other sources should assist managers to foresee obstacles that lay ahead for their staff.

The four managerial skills related to policy compliance thus are review time sheets, set and track budget, monitor projects and jobs, and detect and clear obstacles to productivity.

Skills Related to *Communication, Interaction, Behavior, and Reporting.* Managers should be coaches and while being in a position of authority they should be in a mentoring role in order to support employees. Managers should be able to provide feedback to employees about their work performance. The managers' feedback provision follows from the view that they take interest in their employees and are keen to improve them. They should also communicate with the frankness of an open culture. Implementing a time accounting system can bring an atmosphere of mutual distrust, if the system and its introduction are not managed carefully. This can be avoided if STM is made open for all to access. Employees are then able to access and interpret issues using the same information as managers, who must be honest about financial and human performance. This enhances their relationship and facilitates mutual trust.

The three managerial skills here are being a coach and mentor, providing feedback to employees, and being frank about time accounting performance.

The respondents gave similar responses when asked about how staff members should do timekeeping. There are two steps to this process: to keep track of work each day and to enter this information into the system. For the first step timekeepers must recognize the work they performed "just a minute ago, an hour ago." They must be able to break down their day into pieces of work and understand the amount of time spent on each piece. The second step entails the processes that the timekeeper must think about in order to transfer a timed record of work into the system. The most difficult part of this process is to classify the time spent on each piece of work. The classification step involves identifying each piece of work, determining the client for which the piece was performed, and the type of work it was. Timekeepers are then asked to provide a description about each piece of work in the form of a narrative that allows others to be informed about the performed work.

While the skill of timekeeping appears mechanistic in nature, there is a context in which timekeepers record and enter their time. Timekeepers must understand that timekeeping is both in their own and their organization's interest. They are accountable to management, the organization, and to their clients.

Skills Related to *Attitude Toward Control.* Based on the assumption that STM is a tool with information open and visible to everyone, the user should not have any qualms over sharing information among employees. The idea behind such visibility is that an open culture encourages trust between management and employee and stimulates performance. Related to the user imperative to align revenues and costs closely to budget forecasts in an environment where professionals sell their expertise, the user must be aware of how much revenue is being generated through employees and how much cost is incurred. This information should then be compared with a budget to determine the user's performance.

In summary, the tool user must have two attitudinal skills: promoting information visibility and aligning revenues and costs to a budget.

5.2 Skills Possessed by the Tool User Dataware

Our analysis revealed that the ITS Division was split into two different subcultures: the Project and Development Group (PDG) and the Support Group (SG). Respondents who worked in the PDG, who performed project work lasting a longer period, saw significant benefit in STM. But respondents who worked in the SG had a consensus that STM's implementation was misguided and that it was not of much value. In terms of management control, differences were discovered between the subcultures in every sub-dimension.

Skills Related to *Standardization.* The implementation of STM was part of a broader objective for the division to become more regimented in the way it conducted its operations. ITS had an image problem for a few years as being disorganized and slow to act. The problem was exacerbated because ITS was a collection of teams, each with different responsibilities and goals. The solution was to find some common ground on which the teams could all interact successfully and appear as one to the organization.

In line with other projects to formalize the processes of the division, the STM implementation resulted in another formal standard. The focus was on how staff should identify pieces of work and classify them appropriately for timekeeping. The effect of introducing these rules was positive. Productivity increased and the organization started to appreciate the division's work. Accordingly, ITS appeared to possess skills of developing and disseminating policies, including those on decision making.

In terms of uniformity in performance measurements, however, ITS differed from SixSoft's assumptions. There was no suggestion of common measures using information from STM across the division. It appeared that the nature of each team's work shaped each manager's idea of performance. Only the PDG was concerned with the financial and human aspects of performance. This was indicative in the reports that project managers generated for their use and to show clients.

Overall, the division did not possess the skills of developing uniform standards for performance measurement. The varied nature of its work prevented it from reaching agreement on how performance should be defined. If we look at this situation from the perspective of the two ITS world views, only the PDG had its own uniform measures of performance that bear resemblance to SixSoft's assumed ones.

Skills Related to *Policy Compliance.* ITS used a KPI program for employees as its method of motivating employees to time keep. But the approach taken was fairly simplistic. Management enforced one KPI, which monitored whether each timekeeper submitted weekly time sheets by a certain deadline. The rationale behind this was not so much ensuring that timekeeping was observed; it was to diffuse the initial backlash from some staff about the new "Big Brother" tool and to demonstrate that management was serious about timekeeping. The tool maker's assumption that time capturing is a critical activity was generally not relevant to ITS. The PDG used time as a measure in managing their projects; for other work, timekeeping was secondary. The SG manager went as far as stopping the recording of his time. The division did not have the skills to effectively instil timekeeping in employee's KPIs.

Managers in the PDG were involved in ensuring that their employees complied with the timekeeping policy. They had an interest because the information they gained from employees through STM assisted them in managing their projects. One compliance approach was to review the time sheets to check that the allocation of hours was in line with the budget set for each project.

Budgets were crucial to the PDG. They defined the scope with which projects were performed in order to reach the organization's goals. The managers demonstrated skills of tracking budgets to check that project performance was to expectation and their skills in reviewing time sheets and tracking budgets reflected the discipline of project management. The managers recognized that they were accountable to the company and their clients, and they employed their skills as part of efforts to keep themselves and others informed. Hence, managers in the PDG possessed three of the four skills assumed: regularly reviewing staff time sheets, setting and tracking budgets, and monitoring and reviewing projects.

A different picture emerged from the SG. There was no management review of time sheets or monitoring of employees work on a daily basis. Trust and intuition of employees were the two major values that underpinned this management style. This went against the values of monitoring and reporting, which were manifested in STM. Furthermore, the SG did not charge for work or run explicitly to a budget. ITS' STM implementation had little bearing on SG work. This demonstrates that the SG did not possess the first three managerial skills that were assumed by SixSoft. Their work simply was not congruous with the type of structure and discipline expected.

With regard to the managerial skill of detecting and clearing obstacles, only the PDG managers seemed to possess it. Their concern for performance made it necessary to watch the welfare of their staff, using STM to detect possible anomalies in the staff's productivity patterns as an indication of possible delays to projects. The SG managers too were interested in the welfare of their staff; however, the rationale had less to do with maintaining performance and was more related to the camaraderie that existed in the teams.

On the whole, the PDG possessed all assumed skills in policy compliance on a managerial level. The SG did not possess any of the assumed skills.

Skills Related to *Communication, Interaction, Behavior, and Reporting.* ITS staff did not necessarily require a mentor or coach to guide them. Staff consisted mainly of senior professionals. The team managers promoted autonomy and self-guidance rather than dependence. This is not to say that no interest was taken in staff welfare. The managers believed that they and their staff were in teams where support was given to each other. This arrangement appeared to work well for most operations. From a timekeeping perspective, the lack of guidance had a negative impact. The hands-off approach to dealing with staff exacerbated problems with the classification of work in STM and the managers of both groups did not exhibit the assumed mentoring or coaching skills.

In terms of feedback to employees about performance, the nature of the PDG management meant that it was implicit in the policy compliance skills of monitoring, review, and budget tracking. Employees were kept up-to-date about their contributions with respect to the progress and performance of projects. On the SG side, STM was not used to prepare feedback for employees. Any feedback that was given appeared to only recognize workers of long hours. In conclusion, only the PDG possessed SixSoft's assumed skill of providing feedback on performance.

The assumed skill of talking openly about performance matters is related to the skill of providing feedback as it presumes that managers access and use STM. Hence, only the PDG managers possessed this skill.

The timekeepers from the PDG had a similar timekeeping style, which they performed according to the ITS standards. They recorded (on paper) the amount of time they spent on work in blocks of 15 minutes. Then, they identified the type of each piece of work, which was one of four standard types in ITS work. Next, they determined how to classify each piece according to the array of projects, clients, and codes set up in STM. The timekeepers also had a common view of the reasons for timekeeping. Timekeeping was focused on what their manager and client expected. This was what SixSoft assumed.

The SG timekeeping behavior followed a less stringent process. The first step normally saw a rough estimate on the amount of time to be spent on the work. The next step, the classification of work, was made simple. The bulk of work was allocated to only two categories—*support* and *administration*—with an aggregated time for each and no explanatory narrative. The way in which staff entered hours was more their decision than a process that management prescribed. The apparent flexibility in timekeeping in this group was indicative of the assumptions and values underpinning this skill. Essentially, it came down to the fact that the SG work was not financially focused. Another issue with STM in the SG was that it was viewed as a tool of scrutiny, which elevated an atmosphere of mutual distrust between management and some in the SG. The team was suspicious of management's motives behind STM. They felt that management had put a system in place to police them.

Ultimately, the analysis demonstrated that timekeepers in the SG were lacking timekeeping skills. Despite fulfilling the mechanistic system requirements, their incompatible organic view was at odds with the assumed skill sets for the use of STM.

Skills Related to *Attitude Toward Control.* There was a difference of opinion when the topic of visibility and open culture was raised with some respondents. One PDG manager was convinced that STM made more visible (for everyone) what all staff were actually doing, providing managers sanctioned access. However, it was only the ITS managers who were privy to most of the information. This went against the expectation of the company's CIO, who held the belief that all information related to time accounting should be made freely available to everyone in the company.

In ITS's STM implementation, the developer, who was responsible for determining the access list to information, decided on her own, not to make the reports freely available to all staff, in spite of a clear mandate from the CIO. The reasoning was that in an open culture, information could be abused. So far, no one has challenged this decision. To see visibility as a negative feature goes against SixSoft's assumption that openness to information creates an atmosphere of mutual trust between management and staff. Consequently, ITS failed to possess the skills of promoting visibility and an open culture.

With regard to the topic of budgeting and its importance in ITS, the split between the PDG and the SG was clear. Budgeting was a central part of the PDG's mission. For the SG, project and budget plans were irrelevant to their work and, therefore, their concerns for these issues were minor. While the PDG dealt with performance in terms of budgets using STM information, the SG did not. The divide between the two groups on the importance of budgeting highlights another split in skill sets. Only the PDG, motivated by issues that were assumed to drive budgeting, possessed the skill of promoting budget importance.

6   CONCLUSIONS

The contrast in the actual skills possessed by the two ITS groups highlights that the tool was only appropriate for one group (PDG) and explains some of the problems accompanying the adoption of this technical innovation. The organization faced a choice: change the tool to suit the SG or reconfigure the SG to suit the tool.

Beyond this result, the study demonstrates that the skills-focused approach is a valid and effective way of exploring IS adoption and it represents a step in a new direction for IS adoption research. The concept of skills, as a manifestation of organizational culture, could be used to articulate the differences in tool maker-tool user contexts.

The approach also has favorable consequences for industry. Tool users have an enhanced measure to determine the appropriateness of information systems. The assessment could assist them in devising proper indigenization plans with the intention of eliminating any skill gaps. For management of the potential tool users, the approach could become a tool to assess the organization's skill sets on varying levels of the organization and will allow management to be aware of the culture and capabilities that exist in the organization. This could be of benefit to their decision making. There are also positive implications for tool makers. They can become considerate of contextual factors that may inhibit customers' adoption of their products. The approach could arm them with a technique to assess the difference in their customer's skills and context compared to their own assumptions. This could influence how they design and implement the process of transferring their systems.

Our research on the tool maker side was not directly informed by the actual developers of the tool, but by the consultants responsible for its sale and implementation. Although this resulted in valuable insights about the skill-based assumptions made by the tool makers, the study might have benefitted from the involvement of the actual developers. Another limitation is that the research focused on a single dimension of organizational culture: management control. Expanding the cultural scope, especially with regard to other types of information systems, is a task for the future. There are opportunities to study IS adoption that employ different indicators for management control as used in this study. Future research could take on more dimensions of organizational culture. Learning about the impact that other cultural dimensions have on the skills-focused approach would be a constructive contribution to the overall development of the approach.

References

Avison, D. E., and Myers, M. D. "Information Systems and Anthropology: An Anthropological Perspective on IT and Organizational Culture," *Information Technology & People* (8), 1995, pp. 43-56.

Ayres, C. E. *The Theory of Economic Progress: A Study of the Fundamentals of Economic Development and Cultural Change*, Kalamazoo, MI: New Issues Press, Western Michigan University, 1978.

Blaikie, N. W. H. *Designing Social Research: The Logic of Anticipation*, Malden, MA: Polity Press, 2000.

Boland Jr., R. J. "Information Systems Use as a Hermeneutic Process," in R. Hirschheim (ed.), *Information Systems Research: Contemporary Approaches and Emergent Traditions*, New York: North-Holland, 1991, pp. 439-458.

Bunker, D. "Information Technology and Systems (IT&S) As Tools: Cultural Bias and the Implications for International Technology Transfer (ITT)?," in E. Hoadley and I. Benbasat (eds.), *Proceedings of the Fourth Americas Conference of the Association of Information Systems*, Baltimore, MD, 1998, pp. 818-820.

Bunker, D. "A Philosophy of Information Technology and Systems (IT and S) as Tools: Tool Development Context, Associated Skills and the Global Technical Transfer (GTT) Process," *Information Systems Frontiers* (3), 2001, pp. 185-197.

Burns, T., and Stalker, G. M. *The Management of Innovation*, London: Tavistock, 1966.

Carlson, R. A., and Yaure, R. G. "Practice Schedules and the Use of Component Skills in Problem Solving," *Journal of Experimental Psychology: Learning, Memory and Cognition* (16), 1990, pp. 484-496.

Conner, D. R., Fiman, B. G., and Clements, E. E. "Corporate Culture and its Impact on Strategic Change in Banking," *Journal of Retail Banking* (9), 1987, pp. 16-24.

Crotty, M. *The Foundations of Social Research: Meaning and Perspective in the Research Process*, St Leonards, Sydney: Allen and Unwin, 1998.

Ehn, P., and Kyng, M. "A Tool Perspective on Design of Interactive Computer Support for Skilled Workers," in M. Sääksjärvi (ed.), *Report of the Seventh Scandinavian Research Seminar on Systemeering*, Helsinki School of Economics, Studies B-74, 1984, pp. 211-242.

Frizzell, J. *Identifying Skills: In Seven Easy Steps*, Sydney: Australian Labour Research Centre, 1991.

Hofstede, G. H. *Cultures and Organizations: Software of the Mind*, London: McGraw-Hill, 1991.

Hofstede, G. H. *The Game of Budget Control*, London: Tavistock, 1968.

Hofstede, G. H., Neuijen, B., Ohayv, D. D., and Sanders, G. "Measuring Organizational Cultures: A Qualitative and Quantitative Study across Twenty Cases," *Administrative Science Quarterly* (35), 1990, pp. 286-316.

Jones, A., and Whittaker, P. *Testing Industrial Skills*, New York: Wiley, 1975.

Kammersgaard, J. "Four Different Perspectives on Human-Computer Interaction," *International Journal of Man-Machine Studies* (28:4), 1988, pp. 343-362.

Kautz, K., Zinner Henriksen H., Breer-Mortensen, T., and Poulsen, H. H. "IT Diffusion Research: An Interim Balance," in R. Baskerville, L. Mathiassen, J. Pries-Heje, and J. DeGross (eds.), *Business Agility and Information Technology Diffusion*, Boston: Springer, 2005, pp. 11-34.

Langfield-Smith, K. "Management Control Systems and Strategy: A Critical Review," *Accounting, Organizations and Society* (22), 1997, pp. 207-232.

Larsen, T. J., and McGuire, E. *information Systems Innovation and Diffusion: Issues and Directions*, Hershey, PA: Idea Group Publishing, 1998.

Latour, B. *Science in Action: How to Follow Scientists and Engineers Through Society*, Cambridge, MA: Harvard University Press, 1987.

Lee, A. S. "Electronic Mail as a Medium for Rich Communication: An Empirical Investigation Using Hermeneutic Interpretation," *MIS Quarterly* (18:2), 1994, pp. 143-157.

Mintzberg, H. *The Structuring of Organizations: a Synthesis of the Research*, Englewood Cliffs, NJ: Prentice-Hall, 1979.

Myers, M. D. "Qualitative Research in Information Systems," *MIS Quarterly* (21:2), 1997, pp. 241-242.

Proctor, R. W., and Dutta, A. *Skill Acquisition and Human Performance*, Thousand Oaks, CA: Sage Publications, 1995.

Robbins, S. P. *organization Theory: the Structure and Design of Organizations*, Englewood Cliffs, NJ: Prentice-Hall, 1983.

Rosenbaum, D. A., Carlson, R. A., and Gilmore, R. O. "Acquisition of Intellectual and Perceptual-Motor Skills," *Annual Review of Psychology* (52), 2001, pp. 453-500.

Schein, E. H. "Coming to a New Awareness of Organizational Culture," *Sloan Management Review* (25), 1984, pp. 3-16.

Sincoff, J. B., and Sternberg, R. J. "The Development of Cognitive Skills: An Examination of Recent Theories," in A. M. Colley and J. R. Beech (eds.), *Acquisition and Performance of Cognitive Skills*, Chichester, England: Wiley, 1989, pp. 19-60.

Stahl, B. C. "Information Technology, Responsibility, and Anthropology," in *Proceedings of the 35th Hawaii International Conference on System Sciences*, Los Alamitos, CA: IEEE Computer Society Press, 2002.

Tricker, R. I. *Management Information and Control Systems*, London: Wiley, 1976.

Wieland, G. F., and Ullrich, R. A. *Organizations: Behavior, Design, and Change*, Homewood, IL: Richard D. Irwin, 1991.

Winfield, I. *Organisations and Information Technology: Systems, Power and Job Design*, Oxford, England: Blackwell, 1991.

Winner, L. "Do Artifacts Have Politics?," in L. Winner (ed.), *The Whale and the Reactor: A Search for Limits in an Age of High Technology*, Chicago: University of Chicago Press, 1986, pp. 19-39.

Zuboff, S. *In the Age of the Smart Machine: The Future of Work and Power*, New York: Basic Books, 1988.

About the Authors

Deborah Bunker is a senior lecturer at the School of Information Systems, Technology and Management at the University of New South Wales. Her research interests are in IS philosophy, IS management, IS diffusion, and e-commerce/e-business. Deborah is a founding member and the current vice chair of IFIP TC 8 WG 8.6 on the adoption and diffusion of IT. Deborah can be reached at d.bunker@unsw.edu.au.

Karlheinz Kautz is professor in systems development at the Department for Informatics at the Copenhagen Business School. His research interests are in IT adoption, systems development, knowledge management, and software process improvement. Karl is a founding member and the former chairman of the IFIP TC 8 WG 8.6. Karlheinz can be reached at khk.inf@cbs.dk.

Anhtai Anhtuan has been a student for the degree of Business Information Technology (Honours) at the University of New South Wales and has been a research assistant for the project, building the basis for the research described here.

8   RE-SEARCHING COMMONALITY DIFFERENTLY: Subjectively Replicating a Theory of Multimedia Systems Development

Brian Webb
Queen's University of Belfast
Belfast, N. Ireland

Abstract   *Can subjective replication generate valid and worthwhile knowledge? A theory of multimedia systems development (MSD) generated using a content analysis method is tested using a grounded theory method. The theory—that two distinct communities of software engineers and graphic designers exist within MSD—is confirmed. In fact, the test finds more differences and less commonalities. This finding has implications for the development of MSD methodologies, and for the education and training of MSD practitioners. The conclusion is that subjective replication is worthwhile but must be done carefully because of problems with the application of methods in this relatively unexplored information systems research space.*

Keywords   Multimedia systems development, software engineering, graphic design, grounded theory, research methods, replication

1   INTRODUCTION

In their critique of information systems research Berthon et al. (2002) argue that "while much attention has been paid to methodological rigor and pluralism in MIS research, replication has received less attention. [This is because] in our rush for new knowledge, generation rather than replication, *search* rather than *re-search*, predominates" (p. 416).

Please use the following format when citing this chapter:

Webb, B., 2007, in IFIP International Federation for Information Processing, Volume 235, Organizational Dynamics of Technology-Based Innovation: Diversifying the Research Agenda, eds. McMaster, T., Wastell, D., Ferneley, E., and DeGross, J. (Boston: Springer), pp. 101-114.

In an effort to encourage more and better replication research, they present a framework "to conceptualize, structure and guide replication efforts" (p. 418). This framework seeks to "explicate the possible research combinations of problem, theory, method and context" and maps out various research strategies on a continuum from zero degrees of freedom (pure replication) to three degrees of freedom (pure generation). The various strategies are summarized as follows:

- *Pure replication.* This strategy constrains all three dimensions of the research to be as close as possible to the original study or studies. That is, the same theoretical framework, the same methodology and the same phenomenological context are employed. ("Pure replicative studies seem to be very rare in MIS, with literature reviews identifying no pure replicative studies in any of the major journals," Berthon et al. 2002, p. 423).

- *Context-only extension.* This strategy takes an existing theory and method and applies it in a different context (e.g., the use of SERVQUAL instrument within IS to measure user satisfaction; Parasuraman et al. 1988).

- *Methods-only extension.* This strategy takes an existing theory and context and links them through a different research method. (e.g., using a different method to measure service quality in IS; Van Dyke et al. 1997).

- *Theory-only extension.* This strategy takes an existing method and context but employs a new theory to explain the results (e.g., extending the technology acceptance model to explain information technology utilization behavior; Dishaw and Strong 1998).

- *Method/context extension.* This strategy takes a new method and context, but employs existing theory to explain the results (e.g., using an existing theory of IT enabled change to explain change in a different organizational setting, using a different research method; Manzoni and Angehrn 1998).

- *Theory/context extension.* This strategy takes an existing method but applies it to a new context and employs a new theory to explain the results (e.g., using alternative theories of software project management rather than simple escalation behavior to understand the dynamics of commitment to software projects; Keil et al. 2000).

- *Theory/method extension.* This strategy takes a new theory and method and applies them to an existing context (e.g., extending the TAM to investigate behavioral intention to use an information systems, while also using a different method of data analysis; Jackson et al. 1997).

Whereas "researchers working implicitly or explicitly within the objectivist tradition have stressed the need for replication and indeed its central role in science" (Berthon et al. 2002, p. 418) replication within the subjectivist tradition (Burrell and Morgan 1979; Lee 1991) is much rarer. In the subjectivist tradition, "replication is not concerned with accuracy (the building of an ever more accurate representation of some external reality) but depth of understanding (building richness of phenomenological experience" (Berthon et al. 2002, pp. 418-419). Although they discuss briefly the meaning of this statement, Berthon et al. readily acknowledge that their work "fits primarily into the objectivist tradition which accords replication a significant role in the research process" (p. 419) and they offer no further insights into how subjectivist replication may be done.

In this paper, the grounded theory method (Glaser and Strauss 1967) is used to test a published theory of multimedia systems development (Gallagher and Webb 2000). Since that theory was generated using a method of content analysis (Miles and Huberman 1994) and since all other research parameters remain constant, this is a methods-only extension. Thus the same problem is being investigated (differences and difficulties between software engineers and graphic designers in MSD), the same theory is being used to investigate that problem—Kuhn's (1970) theory of scientific communities or paradigms—and the same investigative context (the same data) and the same interpretive context (the same researchers) applies. Only the method is different.

Berthon et al. accept that "each dimension of research space can comprise sub-dimensions or levels." They therefore distinguish between data generation which is "methods of data production, including measurement issues, survey processes, interview techniques, observational protocols, etc." and data analysis which includes "textual analysis, statistical analysis, visual methods, etc." (p. 422). They give as an example of methods-only extension Pitt el al (1997), who responded to Van Dyke at al.'s (1997) extension of their earlier study of service quality (Pitt et al. 1995) by using the same data set and the same underlying theory, but changing the method of analyzing the data.

While "illustrations of the various strategies do exist in the literature but they are few and far between" (Berthon et al. 2002, p. 425), the goal is to make a contribution to knowledge by setting out an example of subjectivist replication in a way that is explicit and accessible to other researchers. This means identifying problems and limitations encountered. We also see value in testing a theory that has important implications for MSD methods development and project management, but that is yet to be tested, although 6 years old and cited in the literature (e.g., Lang 2003). The paper proceeds as follows. First, the test theory is outlined. Then we set out the test method, identifying points of departure with the method of data analysis used to generate the test theory. The test results are summarized and the limitations of the research acknowledged. Finally the implications of the research for IS researchers and MSD practitioners are discussed.

2   TEST THEORY

Multimedia systems development consists of a small number of generic steps—proposal, design, and production—analogous to the analysis and design phases of the software development life cycle; it involves iteration, prototyping, and top down and bottom up design. The field is characterized by complexity (of product and process), innovation (in products and processes), and methodological pluralism. Attempts to reconcile and manage multidisciplinary development teams have produced a plethora of domain-specific methods, some based on software engineering approaches (Constantine and Lockwood 2001), some based on a graphic design approaches (Mallon and Webb 2000), and some on hybrid approaches (De Troyer 2001).

Yet underlying tensions remain between the two disciplines (Lowe and Eklund 2002) and no single method is preeminent. A common feature of many of these methods is a desire to retain flexibility in response to the prevailing environment by means of contingency or cognitive fit (Fitzgerald et al. 2003), morphology (Baskerville and Stage 2001) design rationales (Firesmith and Henderson-Sellers 2002), and agile software development (Cockburn 2002). Nevertheless, there is evidence that many methodologies are not widely used in practice, or are not considered useful (Lang 2003).

Multimedia systems development is, by the very nature of the designed artefact, a multidisciplinary activity requiring the cooperation and collaboration of various professional communities, chief among which are software engineering and graphic design. Studies into multimedia systems development have identified underlying problems between software engineers and graphic designers (Barry and Lang 2001; Carstensen and Vogelsang 2001; Gallagher and Webb 1997, 2000; Lang 2003; Lowe and Eklund 2001).

Gallagher and Webb (2000) argued that two distinct communities (or paradigms) of software engineering (SE) and graphic design (GD) exist within multimedia development. They claim their theory can be used in method evaluation or feature analysis where "common elements can act as the basis of common criteria by which to judge methods, while non common elements can be used to derive features/method requirements that are specific to each community" (p. 65) and in methods integration when "method fragments [such as story-boarding] are combined to produce a single method for a particular context" (p. 67).

For Kuhn (1970), a paradigm represents a belief system that encompasses those concepts, models, assumptions, and metaphysical principles that are shared within each community (where a community is a distinct group of people composed of practitioners of a scientific speciality who have undergone a similar education and have drawn similar lessons as a result. Specifically, a paradigm (also referred to as a disciplinary matrix, or DM) may be defined as

- *Symbolic generalizations* (such as mathematical formula or scientific laws which are widely used by group members and readily justified by them)
- *Belief(s)* in heuristic and metaphysical models (preferred and permissible analogies and metaphors used to explain phenomena)
- *Values*, which are more widely shared among different communities than symbolic generalizations and models (for example a commitment to quantitative over qualitative methods)
- *Exemplars* or *paradigm as shared example* (examples of how theories are applied in practice; essential for group cohesiveness)

To generate their theory, Gallagher and Webb analyzed 12 textbooks and 20 semistructured interview transcripts using content analysis techniques drawn from Miles and Huberman (1994). Segments of "talk" within each text interview were coded using codes that indicated key themes. For example "DM-B" indicated the presence of a belief statement. Each source was analyzed systematically and a list of DM elements was compiled. Although 67 DM elements are common across both disciplines, suggesting nondistinct communities, 58 elements for software engineering and 54 elements for graphic design were identified as noncore elements (NCEs). The appendices to Gallagher and Webb's paper list each type of element for each discipline. This is helpful in this (test) context since it is possible for the interested reader to examine directly the correspondence of results produced in the development of the theory with the extensions to that theory reported below.

3   TEST METHOD

The theory—that two distinct paradigms exist—is unconfirmed if significant commonality is found between the two disciplines. Gallagher and Webb (2000) found some commonality but regarded it as weak. Because the main focus of Gallagher and Webb's study was on practitioners, only interview transcripts were analyzed as test data. At the practitioner level, differences between the two communities are most likely to be found, while commonalities that do exist are much more likely to be meaningful.

For the test analysis, two interview transcripts were unavailable (they simply could not be located) and, as both of these were from the same MSD community (software engineers), two graphic design transcripts were dropped. Parity of data sources was deemed important in our grounded theory analysis because of its reliance on the constant comparative analysis technique, where emerging concepts are scrutinized against similar and dissimilar concepts in order to tease out commonalities and differences in the data (Strauss and Corbin 1990). The semi-structured interview format, used in the original interviews, is given as Appendix A. Appendix B lists the 16 interviewees used to generate the test data.

A concept is a significant word, phrase, statement, or paragraph found in the transcript. At this stage the purpose of the analysis was simply to generate data that was descriptive of the phenomenon under study. No explicit attempt was made to search for and identify DM elements. An entry was created in the database by cutting and pasting the original text or by keying a summary of what was said. Each entry was given a label or name, its exact location in the transcript was identified, and three keywords recorded. In addition a memo was written further describing the concept (what Strauss and Corbin call an "operational memo"), or developing it analytically and conceptually (a "theoretical memo") and this was appended to the concept (database) record. Thus, while the concept records themselves were descriptive, each fostered analytical memos within which the original concept was further developed. Moreover the three keywords per concept provided a quick and easy way to compare concepts and an initial lead to categorization.

Although superficially similar to content analysis (a process of deconstruction and re-construction of data, using codes to represent units of text or talk), the open coding phase of grounded theory analysis differs significantly in the breadth and depth of its analysis. Content analysis is limited to a number of specific analytical techniques such as producing a contact summary sheet (Miles and Huberman 1994, p. 52), or developing codes using a mixture of an inductive approach and a "start list" approach (Miles and Huberman 1994, p. 58), but these techniques are neither informed by nor integrated with a particular methodological approach. Open coding, on the other hand, is intimately and inextricably bound up with the grounded theory method, and cannot be applied honestly except as part of that method. The application of open coding necessarily requires the application of associated and ancillary analyses. In addition to the constant comparison of data already referred to, these are theoretical sensitivity, theoretical sampling, and theoretical saturation.

Theoretical sensitivity "refers to the attribute of having insight, the ability to give meaning to data, the capacity to understand and the capability to separate the pertinent from that which isn't" (Strauss and Corbin 1990, p. 42). Sources of theoretical sensitivity are the literature, professional and personal experiences, and through continued interaction with the data itself. Theoretical sensitivity is a personal attribute of the researcher "it indicates an awareness of the subtleties of meaning of data" but it can be developed through techniques such as "stepping back from the data" and "maintaining an attitude of scepticism" (Strauss and Corbin 1990, p. 41) No such techniques accompany content analysis, although the stance may be assumed or even encouraged implicitly.

Theoretical sampling "is sampling on the basis of concepts that have proven theoretical relevance to the emerging theory [where] theoretical relevance indicates that certain concepts are deemed significant because they are repeatedly present or noticeably absent when comparing incident after incident" (Strauss and Corbin 1990, p. 176). Even where the purpose of a grounded theory study is not to produce a theory but, for example, to produce a rich or thick description of a phenomenon, theoretical sampling drives the analysis. Again no equivalent can be found in content analysis, even where codes are developed inductively. Identifying and developing codes using a start-list approach is incompatible with both theoretical sensitivity and theoretical sampling because of the imposition of *a priori* assumptions on the data.

Theoretical saturation is knowing when to stop. Theoretical saturation (Glaser 1978, pp. 124-126; Glaser and Strauss 1967, pp. 61-62) means that no new or relevant data seems to emerge during the analysis, indicating that the analysis is conceptually dense. The distinction between first and second level analysis (Miles and Huberman 1994), wherein data is developed into codes and then codes are developed into second level codes or patterns, suggests that patterns are the pinnacle of the analysis, but it is not clear how that pinnacle is achieved, or what it looks like when you get there. The grounded theory notion of saturation is more explicit, offering greater depth to the analysis.

Compared to content analysis, open coding conducted under the grounded theory method should produce more and better (more meaningful or conceptually dense) codes and the relationships between codes should be more easily developed. That is, the rudiments of a theory should already be in place at this stage of the analysis (Strauss and Corbin 1990). In the test study, 160 concepts were produced from 16 interview transcripts. This compares to 179 DM elements produced from 20 interview transcripts and 12 textbooks in the original Gallagher and Webb study. However, although interviews are regarded as a more relevant source of data, textbooks represent important repositories of accepted knowledge within the discipline (Kuhn 1970) and it is no surprise that the majority of DM elements identified in the original study came from this source.

This paper reports a methods extension by using open coding as an alternative to content analysis. It is not necessary for either of these approaches to be labeled a method in order to be able to justify this extension (although we argue that open coding can be considered a much better approximation to a method than content analysis). Rather, as was the case with Pitt et al. (1997) and Adams et al. (1992), the methods extension may be justified even where there is only a change to the techniques of data analysis. Berthon et al. cite both of these as examples of methods-only extensions where only the means of statistical analysis changed. For example, "Adams et al. used multiple-indicator structural equation modeling (LISREL), rather than multivariate regression of averaged scores, as the method of analysis" (Berthon et al. 2002, p. 424).

4   TEST RESULTS

The data analysis produced 160 concepts. These concepts were then compared directly to the list of DM elements produced by Gallagher and Webb. Since the ultimate purpose of the test was to test for the existence of two distinct communities of software engineering and graphic design in MSD, concepts were assigned to DM elements (by discipline) rather than vice versa. Assignment was on the basis of concept name, keywords description, and perceived fit with the DM element. Not all concepts could be assigned, and some concepts were assigned to more than one DM element. Table 1 shows the average number of concept occurrences per DM element per discipline.

The test data shows less commonality across all DM elements, for both software engineering and graphic design. This confirms the theory that there are distinct communities (major premise) and that the commonality that does exist is insignificant (minor premise). For example, whereas in the Gallagher and Webb study beliefs were found on average over five times in each software engineering transcript and over 3.5 times in each graphic design transcript, in the test study analysis this dropped to less than two times in each case. Some commonality clearly exists but this is as not strong. No symbolic generalizations or exemplars were found at all. Eleven belief statements and four value statements were found only in one or other of the disciplines, not both. Twelve value statements were not found in either discipline (see Appendix C for a full list of concepts by DM element).

Far fewer values were identified, reflecting in part the sequence of the analysis. As concepts were allocated to DM elements on the basis of best fit, they tended to be assigned as beliefs rather than values (where the distinction between beliefs and values was not always clear and beliefs were the first DM elements to be coded). Only the number of (distinct) sources (interview transcripts) within which a DM element was identified was recorded. In fact, a DM element may have multiple occurrences within the same source, which is an indication of depth of support for the target theory within discipline, rather than breadth of support across disciplines

Table 1. Average Number of DM Elements Found by Discipline

	SE/10	GD/10	SE/8	GD/8	SE Diff.	GD Diff.
Symbolic Generalizations	10	10	0	0	-10	-10
Beliefs	5.30	3.70	1.97	1.86	-3.33	-1.84
Values	2.95	3.75	0.95	0.66	-2.0	-3.09
Exemplars	10	0.10	0	0	-10	-0.10

GD = Graphic Design; SE = Software Engineering

5   LIMITATIONS AND IMPLICATIONS FOR IS RESEARCHERS

Berthon et al. (200, p. 4212) identify three primary IS stakeholder groups that may be interested in the application of their research framework: producers, consumers, and stewards. Each of these groups includes, but is not limited to, research practitioners. Yet Berthon et al. do not set out how their framework may be applied in each case. They claim that "the framework permits the planning of new research streams, the identification of opportunities, and the ensuing development of strategies and approaches to existing research streams" (p. 425), but there is little practical advise to researchers seeking to conduct subjectivist replication. This paper is an illustration and example of one approach to such research. It is intended to encourage more IS researchers to conduct this kind of research. Replication research is lower cost and lower risk than pure generation research, and the publication of more and better examples of such research can only increase the probability that such research will be undertaken in the future. However, there are practical difficulties and limitations that must be acknowledged.

Berthon et al. acknowledge that time inevitably changes both researcher and subject (p. 420). Although in a methods-only replication the data is held constant (the same data set is analyzed), subjective research is inevitably the product of the interaction of researcher and subject. So even, when the same researcher analyzes the same dataset, using the same method, some differences must be assumed because of time lapse. This highlights a weakness in the Berthon et al. framework, which is (necessarily) constructed on pure or ideal types. In practice, it is impossible to hold context parameters constant from study to study in social sciences research.

Berthon at al. cite two examples of methods-only extensions. In addition to Pitt et al. (1997), in which the same dataset was analyzed by the same researchers using a different method, they cite Adams et al. (1992), in which both the dataset and the researchers change. How can this be a methods-only extension to one degree of research freedom when two other parameters are also changed? More accurately, this is a methods/context extension (p. 424). Significantly, both examples of methods-only extension are in the objectivist tradition, with both using different methods of statistical analysis from the original studies. It is very much more difficult to replicate research settings in the subjectivist tradition.

One of the stated purposes of the Berthon et al. framework is to permit relevant stakeholder groups to classify and evaluate research. But if the framework itself is inconsistent—as with its treatment of method-only extensions—then it will be limited at best. At worst, an inconsistent or confusing framework, lacking clear definitions and examples, may only encourage the very misclassifications and inappropriate evaluations of research that it is designed to avoid.

6   IMPLICATIONS FOR MSD PRACTITIONERS

Whereas Gallagher and Webb (2000, pp. 65-66) postulate the possible contributions of the study to the development of MSD methods, specifically in the areas of methods evaluation and methods integration, we should now seek—on the basis of the results of this test—to moderate their assertions. With less commonality and greater differences than originally thought, it is even less likely that methods developed predominantly upon a common core of design will be successful. On the contrary, approaches that value and accommodate differences (while still also recognizing that some commonality does exist) are much more likely to be accepted by the two communities. Methods evaluation by way of a feature analysis of common and non-common elements remains perfectly feasible but requires some adjustments to the selection criteria to reflect stronger differences and weaker commonalities. Methods integration also remains possible but will be undermined where the basis of integration relies too heavily upon a common core of design, or upon a single design process or artefact (e.g., story-boarding).

Although Gallagher and Webb did not speculate upon the possible implications of their study for MSD practitioner education and training, the replication of their theory makes such speculation more justified. Given the very real differences between the two communities in terms of beliefs, values, and language, interventions to improve mutual understanding should precede any attempt to impose a particular methodology (new or existing). This is not to argue that the two communities should become more alike. On the contrary the challenges of MSD are most likely to be met where the distinctive capabilities and contributions of the two communities are fully recognized, but to call upon researchers, educationalists, method developers, and practitioners to study and act upon a better appreciation of what we now know to be the same and to be different about software engineering and graphic design approaches to MSD.

7   CONCLUSIONS

A theory of MSD is replicated along one degree of freedom of the Berthon et al. (2002) replication space: methods-only extension. Gallagher and Webb's (2000) theory, that two distinct communities of software engineering and graphic design exist within MSD, is confirmed but the test data indicates that the theory is understated. Less commonality and more differences were found between the two communities. This test has implications for methods development and for the education and training of practitioners, since the importance of the "common" element in any such initiative is questioned. A relatively neglected corner of the IS research space has been illustrated and further research outlined.

We conclude that subjective replication is worthwhile because it can be used to test theories that are important to IS practice. These theories may otherwise remain untested because of a lack of insight into how such testing may be done. However, the application of subjectivist replication must be done carefully. Test theories and test methods are often difficult to understand, to reconcile, and to demonstrate. Conceptual frameworks such as the one put forward by Berthon et al. can help the researcher but will be limited in their applicability until they themselves have been empirically tested.

References

Adams, D. A., Nelson, R. R., and Todd, P. "Perceived Usefulness, Ease of Use, and Usage of Information Technology: A Replication," *MIS Quarterly* (16:2), 1992, pp. 227-247.

Barry C., and Lang, M. "A Survey of Multimedia and Web Development Techniques and Methodology Usage," *IEEE Multimedia* (8:3), 2001, pp. 52-60.

Baskerville, R., and Stage, J. "Accommodating Emergent Work Practices: Ethnographic Choice of Method Fragments," in N. L. Russo, B. Fitzgerald, and J. I. DeGross (eds.), *Realigning Research and Practice in Information Systems Development: The Social and Organizational Perspective*, Boston: Kluwer Academic Publishers, 2001, pp. 11-28.

Berthon, P., Pitt, L., Ewing, M., and Carr, C. L. "Potential Research Space in MIS: A Framework for Envisioning and Evaluating Research Replication, Extension and Generation," *Information Systems Research* (13:4), 2002, pp. 416-427.

Burrell G., and Morgan, G. *Sociological Paradigms and Organizational Analysis*, London: Heinemann, 1979.

Carstensen, P. H., and Vogelsang, L. "Design of Web-Based Information Systems: New Challenges for Systems Development?," in *Proceedings of the 9th European Conference on Information Systems*, Bled, Slovenia, June 27-29, 2001, pp. 536-547.

Cockburn, A. *Agile Software Development*, Reading, MA: Addison Wesley, 2002.

Constantine, P. H., and Lockwood, L. A. "Usage-Centered Engineering for Web Applications," *IEEE Software* (19:2), 2001, pp. 42-50.

De Troyer, O. "Audience-Driven Web Design," in M. Rossi and K. Siau (eds.), *Information Modeling in the New Millennium*, Hershey, PA: Idea Group Publishing, 2001, pp. 442-461.

Dishaw, M. T., and Strong, D. M. "Supporting Software Maintenance with Software Engineering Tools: A Computed Task-Technology Fit Analysis," *Journal of Systems and Software* (44:2), 1998, pp. 107-120.

Firesmith, D. G., and Henderson-Sellers, B. *The OPEN Process Framework*, Reading, MA: Addison Wesley, 2002.

Fitzgerald, B., Russo, N. L., and O'Kane, T. "Software Development Method Tailoring at Motorola," *Communications of the ACM* (46:4), 2003, pp. pp. 64-70.

Gallagher, S., and Webb, B. "Competing Paradigms in Multimedia Systems Development: Who Shall Be the Aristocracy?," in *Proceedings of the 5th European Conference on Information Systems*, Cork, Ireland, June 19-21, 1997, pp. 1113-1120.

Gallagher, S., and Webb, B. "Paradigmatic Analysis as a Means of Eliciting Knowledge to Assist Multimedia Methodological Development," *European Journal of Information Systems* (9), 2000, pp. 60-67.

Glaser, B. *Theoretical Sensitivity*, Mill Valley, CA: Sociology Press, 1978.

Glaser, B., and Strauss, A. S. *The Discovery of Grounded Theory: Strategies for Qualitative Research*, London: Wedenfeld and Nicholson, 1967.

Jackson, C. M., Chow, S., and Leitch, R. A. "Towards an Understanding of the Behavioral Intention to Use Information Systems," *Decision Sciences* (28:2), 1997, pp. 357-254.

Keil, M., Mann, J., and Rai, A. "Why Software Projects Escalate: An Empirical Analysis and Test of Four Theoretical Models," *MIS Quarterly* (24:4), 2000, pp. 631-664.

Kuhn, T. S. *The Structure of Scientific Revolutions* (2nd ed.), Chicago: University of Chicago Press, 1970.

Lang, M. "Multimedia Systems Development: A Comparative Study of Software Engineers and Graphic Designers," *Communications of the AIS* (12), 2003, pp. 242-257.

Lowe, D. B., and Eklund, J. "Client Needs and the Design Process in Web Projects," *Journal of Web Engineering* (1:1), 2002, pp. 23-36.

Mallon, B., and Webb, B. "Structure, Causality, Visibility and Interaction: Propositions for Evaluating Engagement in Narrative Multimedia," *International Journal of Human-Computer Studies* (53), 2000, pp. 269-287.

Manzoni, J. F., and Angehrn, A. A. "Understanding Organizational Dynamics of IT Enabled Change: A Multimedia Simulation Approach," *Journal of Management Information Systems* (14:3), 1998, pp. 109-140.

Miles, M. B., and Huberman, A. M. *Qualitative Data Analysis: An Expanded Sourcebook*, London: Sage Publications, 1994.

Parasuraman, A., Zeithaml, V. A., and Berry, L. L. "SERVQUAL: A Multiple Item Scale for Measuring Customer Perceptions of Service Quality," *Journal of Retailing* (64), Spring 1988, pp. 12-40.

Pitt, L. F., Watson, R. T., and Kavan, C. B. "Measuring Information Systems Service Quality: Concerns for a Complete Canvas," *MIS Quarterly* (21:5), 1997, pp. 209-219.

Pitt, L. F., Watson, R. T., and Kavan, C. B. "Service Quality: A Measure of Information Systems Effectiveness," *MIS Quarterly* (19:2), 1995, pp. 173-187.

Strauss, A., and Corbin, J. *Basics of Qualitative Research: Grounded Theory Procedures and Techniques*, Newbury Park, CA: Sage Publications, 1990.

Van Dyke, T. P., Kappelman, L. A., and Prybutok, V. P. "Measuring Information Systems Service Quality: Concerns Othe Use of the SERVQUAL Questionnaire," *MIS Quarterly* (21:2), 1997, pp. 195-208.

About the Author

Brian Webb is a senior lecturer in Information Systems, School of Management and Economics, Queen's University of Belfast, N. Ireland. He is a former Distinguished Erskine Fellow, in the Department of Accounting, Finance, and Information Systems, Faculty of Commerce, University of Canterbury, New Zealand. He holds a Bachelor's degree from Queen's, an MBA from the University of Ulster, and a Ph.D. from University College London. Prior to becoming an academic, he worked as a systems analyst in both the United Kingdom and the United States. He may be contacted at b.webb@qub.ac.uk.

Appendix A: Interviews

Interviewee	Experience[†]	Education
GD1	12 years	BA Graphic Design
GD2	24 years	BA Graphic Design
GD3	20 years	BA Graphic Design
GD4	11 years	BA Graphic Design
GD5	08 years	BA Graphic Design
GD6	03 years	BA Visual Communications.
GD7	04 years	BSc Computing & Design
GD8	01 year	BA Visual Communications.
SE1	18 years	HND Computing
SE2	10 years	BSc Eng. MSc Computing.
SE3	14 years	BSc Eng. MSc Computing.
SE4	13 years	BSc Computer Science
SE5	06 years	BSc Computer Science
SE6	10 years	BSc Computer Science
SE7	01 year	BSc Computing & IS
SE8	03 years	BSc Computer Science

[†]Experience refers to total years experience in the referent field of graphic design or software engineering. As the number of years experience in the subfield of digital interactive multimedia was not always clear, this is not shown. In general, those with the least experience overall tend to be those with experience only in the multimedia field.

Appendix B: Interview Questions

[1] Attitudinal Information

Q1:   How would you define software engineering/graphic design?

Q2:   How would define multimedia?

Q3:   What is your attitude concerning the current state of these fields?

Q4:   What do you believe your field has to offer multimedia?

Q5:   What are the differences between your traditional field and that of Multimedia? What is the same?

[2] Development Activity

Q6:   Does multimedia development differ from traditional development within your field? (For example, the process?)

Q7:   Could you describe the multimedia development process (i.e., stages)?

Q8:   What are the most important aspects (stages) of this multimedia process? Why?

Q9:   Do you rely on a formal approach or methodology during a project?

Q10: Do you have any particular views on how multimedia development should be tackled?

Q11: What do you see as the key problems that are faced during multimedia development?

[3] Development Environment

Q12: How would you describe the nature of your development environment (for example, formal/informal; team/individual)?

Q13: If you undertake work as part of a team, do you have any particular attitudes or concerns regarding team development (for example, team leadership/team skills/team structure)?

Q14: What do you see as the essential characteristics of an ideal development environment?

[4] Project Management

Q15: How do you monitor/measure progress during a project? (Criteria for success? Formal reviews? Meetings?)

Q16: How would define the success/failure of a project?

[5] Design

Q17: How would you define the term/activity *design* within the context of your particular discipline?

Q18: How does this concept change within the context of interactive mMultimedia?

Q19: Do you have any particular views about how design should be carried out?

Q20: How would you distinguish good design from bad design?

Q21: What do you feel are the essential principles of design?

Q22: What factors influence design?

[6] Quality

Q23: How do you define *quality*?

Q24: How do you distinguish between high quality and poor quality?

Q25: If asked to evaluate the quality of a product, how would you approach this?

Q26: What particular aspects would you focus on?

Appendix C: Allocation of Concepts to Elements

	Theory Data (n = 10)	Test Data (n = 8)
Authoring packages/scripting languages [**Symbolic Gen.**]	10	10
A formalized design approach is worthwhile in some cases [**Beliefs..**]	9	22
Abstraction	3	321
Almost always the client doesn't know what they want	4	644
Analyze before design	4	232
Awareness of practical constraints	8	825
Choice of design method/strategy depends on nature of problem	10	523
Collaborative design	8	1024
Compromise	4	212
Decomposition	7	122
Design for change	4	112
Design for the lowest denominator	3	41
Design is a continuous process with no clear barriers to indicate where it begins and ends	2	25
Design is a creative problem solving activity	1	424
Design is a pivotal step in any development	7	135
Design is an iterative process—adding greater formality and detail	8	652
Design is open to interpretation	1	423
Design process is built up from theory, principles and/or heuristics	4	131
Design process is difficult to formalize and define	3	24
Design reviews are a good way to monitor progress	7	311
Design usually progresses from the higher levels to the lower levels	10	422
Designer's goal is to produce a representation or model of an entity that will later be built	6	353
Designers need direct contact with customers	7	233
Designers should avoid detail too early in the design process	6	211
Everything that is designed should be justified or have a reason for being	1	916
Fitness for purpose	1	212
Generate alternatives	4	71
It is generally good design practice to attempt some sort of design on paper first	5	61
It is vital to get agreement on the design specification as early as possible	2	221
Modularity	5	11
Planning—producing plans	2	411
Prescriptive design approaches are unhelpful	3	211
Prototyping	9	612
Separation of concerns	10	42
Some level of client/user involvement in the design process is required	7	632

	Theory Data (n = 10)	Test Data (n = 8)
Successful design requires the early involvement of all concerned.	7	42
Team effort in design can create problems	8	52
Testing is an integral aspect of designing	7	31
Accountability in design [Values..]	1	111
Accuracy	1	111
Appropriateness	5	8
Clarity	3	5
Coherence	2	81
Cohesion of design elements	1	3
Consistency	5	621
Elegance	4	12
Flexibility on part of the designer	4	7
Functionality	3	2
Independence of design components	3	2
Inventiveness/Innovation	3	622
Originality	1	9
Pragmatism	1	222
Precision	1	12
Professionalism	1	1
Readability	1	5
Relevance	1	2
Reuse	5	12
Robustness	7	1
Simplicity	6	432
Understandability	1	2
Usability	8	442
Visual aesthetics/appeal beauty	3	824
Analyze design cycle [Exemplars]	10	1

9 THE SITUATEDNESS OF WORK PRACTICES AND ORGANIZATIONAL CULTURE: Implications for Information Systems Innovation Uptake

Faraja Teddy Igira
University of Oslo
Oslo, Norway

Abstract   *This paper addresses the themes of work practices and organizational culture as situated actions and the implications for information systems innovation uptake. It reports on research being conducted in Tanzania that brings an ethnographic research approach to understanding relations between local health care practices and health information systems (HIS) development, by asking how health workers' practices and everyday actions are influenced by the context of their specific situation. The research is being conducted in the context of a globally distributed open source software project to introduce and enhance health information systems (HIS) in developing countries. Drawing on cultural historical activity theory, the study highlights the need for understanding each information system user's and each organization's specific and detailed work processes and how situational and organizational factors may come together with the HIS innovation processes in meeting the challenges discussed. In order to establish fully the potential of activity theory to HIS innovation processes, situatedness of work practices focusing on the organization context is emphasized.*

Keywords   Information systems, work practices, organizational culture, situated action, cultural historical activity theory, innovation uptake.

Please use the following format when citing this chapter:

Igira, F. T., 2007, in IFIP International Federation for Information Processing, Volume 235, Organizational Dynamics of Technology-Based Innovation: Diversifying the Research Agenda, eds. McMaster, T., Wastell, D., Ferneley, E., and DeGross, J. (Boston: Springer), pp. 115-132.

1   INTRODUCTION

Tanzania, like many other developing countries, has in recent years been attempting to develop and implement a health information systems (HIS) in the context of a globally distributed open source software project known as the Health Information Systems Programme (HISP) (see Braa et al. 2004; Lungo 2005). HISP aims at strengthening and further developing HIS in public health in an expanding network of developing countries including South Africa, Mozambique, Tanzania, Malawi, India, China, and Vietnam (for details, see Braa and Herdberg 2002; Braa et al. 2004). These HIS innovation initiatives are taking place in a context that is historically and culturally shaped (Bardram 1997); work practices (collection, storage, analysis, and transmission of routine health data throughout the health care administrative hierarchy) and health workers' everyday actions are influenced by the context of their specific situations. The work practices and existing health workers' actions are often in tension with situational, individual, and organizational factors of work. Organizational contexts in particular settings should be explored in depth to understand their effects on information systems innovation processes (Grudin 1996). Related to this, Avison and Myers (1995) highlight the importance of understanding organizational culture in IS development.

This paper presents useful perspectives on work practices and organizational culture as situated actions. The focus is on the local[1] situatedness of health workers' work practices as key sites for understanding the cultural-historical constitution of coexisting modes of practice and potentials for change. The relationship between work practices and organizational culture will be explored, as well as how organizational culture limits activities. The setting is the Tanzanian HIS (comprising the health facility level, district level, regional level, and the national level; see Figure 1). However, the focus in this paper is on the health facility level and district level because it is at these levels where health care work practices can be observed. The other levels (regional and national level) are more administrative in nature. The view is to understand how health workers' working practices and everyday actions are influenced by the context of their specific situations. Furthermore, the analysis explores the influence of climate on innovation uptake including the interaction between multiple organizational contexts. Cultural historical activity theory (CHAT) provides a potentially useful framework for understanding the mutual shaping of context and work practice. However, its ability to address the situated nature of work is limited.

The rest of the paper is organized as follows: Section 2 outlines a theoretical framework for the study of work practices and organizational culture, and the concepts from CHAT. Section 3 provides details on the context, setting and research methods. Based on the empirical work within the Coast region, section 4 describes the work practices and organizational culture that surround the HIS in Tanzania. Section 5 presents an analysis of the empirical data based on the key concepts drawn from CHAT. Finally, in section 6, concluding remarks arising from the study are presented.

---

[1]*Local* in this paper refers to the particular context, for example, the health care organization in Tanzania in this case.

2 CULTURAL HISTORICAL ACTIVITY THEORY (CHAT)

Originating in the former Soviet Union (Leontjev 1978; Vygotski 1978), cultural historical activity theory (CHAT) is a philosophical framework for studying different forms of human praxis as developmental processes with both the individual and social level interlinked (Engeström 1999c; Leontjev 1978). While individual actions can only be understood through the activity of which they are a part, activities are culturally and historically created and recreated. Human activities reflect real-life phenomena and not just theoretical constructs.

CHAT interprets work practices as activities and it explores the links between event and context. Therefore, using CHAT, the fundamental unit of analysis is the human work activity (Bardram 1997; Blackler et al. 2000). This human work activity reflects a number of people (subjects) working on a shared object (for example, health care data collection), not necessarily in the same time and place (for example, in different health facilities), to produce a joint outcome (for example, health care services improvement). In developmental processes using CHAT,

> [The] analysis is focused on the communication, coordination and collaboration required of members of teams and participants in networks to accomplish actions that are guided by *goals* of the actions at hand and to instantiate the *object of the activity* that motivates the activity system (Bratteteig and Gregory 1999, p. 168).

CHAT interprets social structures as both the production of human activities and the context for them (e.g., structuration theory; Giddens 1984). By acting in the world, human beings meet the objective world, which is experienced through the activity (Bardram 1997). Consequently, human work activity has the following characteristics: it is directed toward a material or ideal object that distinguishes one activity from another, it is mediated by artifacts (tools, language, rules, and procedures), and it is social within a culture (Bardram 1997).

On the other hand, Engeström (1987, 1999b) emphasizes that unexpected difficulties emerge in the execution of day-to-day tasks, causing people to change their activities and simultaneously change themselves. CHAT features the intimate relations between factors that mediate activity and the activities themselves (Blackler et al. 2000). Thus, activity theory avoids treating individuals as if they can be understood in isolation from their contexts, and the contexts as if they exist in isolation from individuals. Hence, in CHAT, "it is the *doing* of the activity in a rich social matrix of people and artifact that grounds analysis" (Kaptelinin and Nardi 2006, p. 9).

In summary, CHAT helps to analyze and describe the work people are doing, how they are doing the work and with whom, and how collective learning may occur, a description of which provides a picture of a particular organizational culture. Furthermore, CHAT offers a dialectical approach, open to change and recognition of the emergence of mundane innovation in everyday practice, with an emphasis on the social and holistic nature of individual and collective learning and human development. It is on this basis that CHAT is used for analyzing and discussing the local challenges in IS innovation uptake, focusing on work practices and organizational culture as situated actions.

2.1 Cultural Historical Activity Theory and Situated Actions

The term *situated actions* emphasizes the interrelationship between an action and its context of performance; it emphasizes the knowledgeability of actors and how they use common-sense practices/procedures to produce, analyze, and make sense of one another's actions and their local or situated circumstances (Doerry 1995). Every course of action is highly dependent upon its material and social circumstances focusing on interactions between actors and between actors and the environments of their action. By ignoring the influence of the environment on behavior, key features of the interaction between humans and the world are missed, such as the rich, nondeterministic nature of complex behavior. Situated action has been used as part of human–computer interaction studies (see, for examples, Bardram 1997; Suchman 1987). However, Nardi (1995) emphasizes that in addition to what situated action can help systems implementers understand, activity theory offers a set of perspectives on human activity and a set of concepts for describing that activity. These perspectives and concepts help to understand and describe the context, situation, and practice within a particular organization.

Studies have shown that information technology and information systems use is not a technical input–output relation between a person and the technology (Bardram 1997; Nardi 1995; Suchman 1987), that a much richer illustration of the user's situation is needed for IS innovation uptake. However, it is unclear how to formulate that illustration in a way that is not purely *ad hoc* (Nardi 1995). Here is where activity theory helps, by providing orienting concepts and perspectives. Activities within an organization are *post hoc* reconstructed and objectified so that they can be used in future. People work as collaborative actors in making sense out of the everyday world of actions. They (people) make use of embodied skills or past experiences to get them through a situation in the work practice. More importantly, participants in a situated action must define the work practice in the same way to maintain its success and stability (Kaptelinin 1992; Nardi 1992; Vygotsky 1978).

2.2 Organization Culture

An organization's culture refers to shared beliefs and values and has been described by Mullins (2002) as a reflection of how the organization is structured, how work is done, the aims of the organization, and how management and staff interact within the organization and with those outside. All of these aspects of organizational culture can be analyzed with CHAT. Furthermore, at the heart of organization development and improved performance is the need for effective information systems. IS innovation processes, however, do not take place in a vacuum but within the context of the organizational setting.

The organizational culture is not static. Over time, various groups such as employees, stakeholders, systems developers, and implementers help to influence it. The pervasive nature of organizational culture means that if change is to be brought about successfully, it is likely to involve change or shaping of the organizational culture. In a holistic system, any change will affect the organizational culture and the organizational culture will affect or constrain the change (Mullins 2002).

On the one hand, organizational culture has been found to play a significant role in IT management processes such as technology-driven change in organizations (Cabrera et al. 2001), groupware development and deployment (King 1996), and management of new systems development (Newman and Sabherwal 1996).

On the other hand, several researchers have encouraged the use of an organizational culture perspective for IS research (see, for example, Avison and Myers 1995; Dubé and Robey 1999; Iivari 2005; Nicholson and Sahay 2001; Robey and Azevedo 1994; Walsham 1993; Westrup et al. 2002). Some argue that IS researchers have to adapt insights from anthropology to study IS and organizational culture (Avison and Myers 1995; Westrup et al. 2002). Related work has explored a relativist position for the prospective IS research on organizational culture and change (Iivari 2005). Others have been influenced by the social theories, such as the theory of structuration (Giddens 1984; Orlikowski 1992). The conceptualization of organizational culture from a cultural perspective in IS research varies among researchers. Such concepts include organizational culture as lacking coherence as it is cross-cut by geographic, work-related, and other cultures (for example, Nicholson and Sahay 2001; Parker 2000). Others emphasize its homogeneity trend broadly enclosed within an organization's boundaries (for example, Robey and Azevedo 1994). This study acknowledges those who adopt the view of organization culture lacking coherence, while emphasizing that forces for harmony exist in any organization so that coordinated actions and collaboration in the organization's activities can take place. Although the organizational culture battle has been contested to a certain degree, particularly in IS research, there is still much to learn from studying organizational cultures. A situated action perspective, very broadly defined, constitutes a promising vehicle for such research.

3 CONTEXT, SETTING, AND METHODS

The study was directed by an ethnographic methodological approach (Aunger 1995; Hardon et al. 2001; Honigmann 1976) with the use of ethnographic interviews, participant observation, review of documents, informal talks, and discussion during the training and analysis of the information flows within the HIS in Tanzania. Ethnographic research methods provided details through the health workers' own words and descriptions of health facility situations, events, interactions, and observable behaviors for understanding how health workers' practices and everyday actions are influenced by the context of their specific situation. I was directly engagemented in the health facilities and thus played the role of participant observer. I am a member of the Tanzanian HISP team, and have thus played a central role in collaboration with health workers at all levels in the national health care system. The empirical material presented in this paper was collected during the periods from January to July 2005, and from February to April 2006.

In-depth semi-structured interviews were conducted with 32 members of the health sector in Kibaha and Bagamoyo districts. The interviewees were the people in charge of the health facility, the district information officers (DIOs), members of the council health management team (CHMT), the regional information officer and the HIS people at the Ministry of Health (MoH). Each interview was approximately one hour long and conducted in the local language, Kiswahili. Each interview started by introducing the purpose of the interview along with reassurances about confidentiality and the right of the interviewee to decline to answer any question to which s/he would prefer not to respond. After each interview, the interviewees were asked to provide a list of potential additional interviewees as well as to provide any documents of use to the study. Each interview was noted in a summary form and the summaries were extended immediately at the end of the day of each interview. The interviews took place within the health facility surroundings, mostly in health workers' offices as they needed to continue their daily health care activities.

Participant observation and informal talks were used to gather an impression of the health facilities surroundings and to understand health workers' working practices in depth and detail. Approximately 20 to 30 hours a week were spent doing the observations in different health facilities while documenting the observations in field notes. These observations involved a wide context of the health workers environments and thus allowed me to see and interpret the health care activities through intensive interaction, for example, by participating in day-to-day activities such as registering children for vaccination and weighing.

The documents reviewed include health performance reports at health facilities and the district level, the district plan reports and HIS implementation plan, the MTUHA guidelines manual and data documentation. I also analyzed the patients' records from various recording tools at the health facilities and district levels.

3.1   The Health Information System in Tanzania

Tanzania has achieved considerable expansion of health services since its independence in 1961. The health sector reforms initiated in 1993 have made some progress in improving health care services and resources throughout the country. However, there are problems with limited capacities for generating reliable data, analysis, storage, retrieval, dissemination, and use. As a consequence, decision-making in the health care system is not generally evidence-based.[2]

The current routine HIS in Tanzania is known by the acronym MTUHA (Mfumo wa Taarifa za Uendeshaji wa Huduma za Afya), covering both governmental, private, and nongovernmental organization (NGO) health facilities (MoH 1993). MTUHA's administration and reporting organization hierarchy has four levels: health facility level, district level, regional level, and national level (see Figure 1). The information within MTUHA is based on data collected at the health facility. The district level, being the main operation unit within the organization hierarchy, is responsible for planning, managing, and supervising all health facilities and health care programs within MTUHA.

---

[2]"WHO Country Cooperation Strategy: United Republic of Tanzania, 2002-2005" World Health Organizational Regional Office for Africa, Brazzaville (http://www.who.int/countries/en/cooperation_strategy_tza_en.pdf).

3.1.1 MTUHA Organizational Context and Working Practices

At the **health facility**, which is the origin of most routine health data for MTUHA, health workers collect data routinely on outpatients, inpatients, and maternal and child health (MCH). However, additional data in the health facility is obtained through working with the surrounding community through village health workers[3] (VHW), traditional birth attendants[4] (TBA), and community based distributors[5] (CBD) for contraceptives and school visits. The data collection and processing in health facilities consists of a set of MTUHA paper forms, register books (12 in number), tally sheets and different forms from donor funded programs such as tuberculosis, malaria, and immunization, mostly written in a mix of the Kiswahili and English languages. Reports are then prepared on weekly, quarterly, and yearly bases and sent to the district medical officer (DMO) (for details, see Lungo 2003; Mukama 2003; Rubona 2001). Data handling involves a group of health workers from different sections of the health facility who have been given responsibility for MTUHA. The group consists of the MCH coordinator, the OPD coordinator, etc., depending on the number of sections (services) available at the particular health facility.

At **the district level**, reports from the health facilities are aggregated into an overall district quarterly report and sent to the office of the regional medical officer (RMO) together with a copy of each health facility's annual report. One copy of the district quarterly report is also sent directly to the primary health care (PHC) secretariat, which is a section in the local government authority responsible for managing health centers, dispensaries, and village health posts. Since the beginning of MTUHA, the preparation of an overall district report was done manually through the use of the district processing file[6] (DPF) and involves a group of health workers who work together as a team. The team is composed of different coordinators for different health care service sections. In November 2004, the MoH implemented MTUHA data processing software[7] in all district health offices, which resembles the DPF in format.

At the **regional and national** levels, data processing is done with the help of a MTUHA computer software package. The regional level is responsible for sending quarterly reports to the national level on a floppy disk, based on further aggregation of the health data from the regional districts. Information on floppy disks from all regions is processed by the HIS unit staff at the MoH using a similar software package as the one installed at the regional level.

The overall information flows within the MTUHA system are summarized in Figure 1.

---

[3]People in the community responsible for reporting all activities going on in the community, such as, all newborn deaths.

[4]People in the community responsible for deliveries and reporting to the health facility on neonatal tetanus cases, registered children, children weighing and children behind their immunization schedule.

[5]People in the community responsible for distributing contraceptives to the community members and reporting to the health facility

[6]A manual database consisting of a collection of forms with specifications on what should be processed into a district quarterly report.

[7] Note: In this paper, the terms *software* and *database* are used interchangeably.

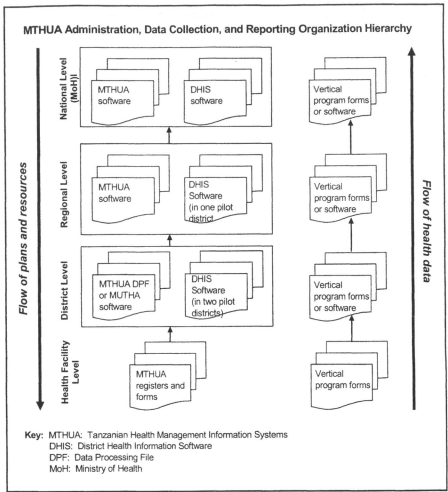

Figure 1. MTHUA Administration and Reporting Organization Hierarchy

3.1.2 HISP in Tanzania

In collaboration with the HIS unit at the MoH, HISP started piloting its activities in two health districts of Bagamoyo and Kibaha in the Coast region in July 2002. The activities included implementation of the DHIS software and training on computer and DHIS use, as well as conducting research on data collection, information flow, and use. (See Lungo 2005; Lungo and Nhampossa 2004; Kimaro and Nhampossa 2004;. For more details about HISP, see the proceedings of the IFIP WG 9.4 Working Conference on Enhancing Human Resource Development through ICT in Abuja, Nigeria, May 26-29, 2005.) At the time this paper was written, HISP was still conducting pilot studies of its activities in the Coast region.

4 SITUATEDNESS OF WORK PRACTICES AND ORGANIZATION CULTURE: CHALLENGES

This section presents the situatedness of work practices and organizational culture within the health care organization in Tanzania, focusing on the tensions around health workers' working practices due to situational, individual, and organizational factors of work including the interaction between multiple organizational contexts. While linking the work practices throughout the health care organization structure, the descriptions were categorized into three main groups: government health facilities, private health facilties, and district-level health facilities. Separation of the government and private health facilities is based on the difference in relations with other governmental organizations.

For the purpose of the present section, the elements of the health care system in Tanzania as an activity system are identified as follows:

- The health workers (doctors, nurses, and health managers) are the *subjects* who work together in transforming a shared object to an outcome.
- The primary and shared *object* of the health care workers is to attend patients coming to the health facility and the secondary object is the management of the health facility. At the same time, the functioning of the information system is a requirement due to demands from above and the need for information.
- The shared *outcomes* of these three objects are the improvement of health care services and the health situation of the population.
- In order to fulfil the health care organization's information needs, health workers attempt to control the functioning of an IS with the help of *tools* (register books, paper forms, pen, calculators, etc.).
- Activities are guided with certain *rules and division of labor* (each level is required to report at the end of each week (for weekly reports), after each three months (for quarterly reports), and yearly. One typical action of this activity is expressed at the health facility where health workers attend patients and collect routine data, which is often followed by another important action of preparing reports, which is often followed by sending them to the district level.
- Furthermore, there is a *community of practitioners* consisting of the coverage population, patients attending the health facility, and donor agencies.

4.1 Government Health Facility

4.1.1 Tensions between Primary, Secondary, and IS Work Practices and Resources

Health workers at the facility level are facing tensions between their primary work practices (patient care activities), secondary work practices (management of the health facility), and information systems work practices (data collection, report preparation and reporting). One health worker expressed this in the following way:

> *There are a lot of registers to fill in and many patients waiting...for example, a child crying, a pregnant mother waiting while tired—this makes the work difficult and complicated.* (Health Worker at Health Facility A)

This tension is partly due to lack of resources and skills for data collection, report preparation, reporting and storage, which was expressed by the health facility worker who said,

> *We need a calculator to help us in calculating the totals, especially on vacci-nation reports which are too many—you can't calculate them with your head.*
> (Health Worker at Health Facility B)

> *We had a calculator that we were given at the beginning of MTUHA, which is not working any more. We just use a mobile phone.* (Health Worker at Health Facility C)

> *We borrow a calculator from a teacher at the nearby school.* (Health Worker at Health Facility D)

> *We use our money for local transport when taking the reports to the district because if we wait they will say that we are lazy.* (Health Worker at Health Facility E)

The storage of data at the health facility depends on individual health workers' arrangement: some keep data on shelves, where it is being eaten by ants, and others keep data in boxes, where rats eat the papers. Consequently, the variation in storage makes access to data very difficult. In expressing the lack of proper arrangements for data storage, one health worker said,

> *We need somewhere to keep the register books and paper forms for easy access when we need the information.* (Health Worker at Health Facility F).

In addition to a lack of material resources, the lack of human resources and skills among health workers also causes tensions between the primary, secondary, and IS work processes. For example, in some of the health facilities visited there was only one health worker, so we had to stop the interview so that she could attend the patients to avoid long queues.

4.1.2 Demands from above and Health Facility's Needs: Creation of New Tools and Use of Old Tools

There are health facilities that provide more services than the data elements described in MTUHA forms and they are required to report on those services. In striving to fulfill the demands from above and the health facility's needs, health workers have to create new forms for data collection. For example, a table for registering medicines indicates only those which are being provided in drug kits (that is, for health centers and dispensaries), but the hospitals receive more medicines than those described in MTUHA forms.

Some use the old form, which was being used before MTUHA for collecting data on the MCH program. In expressing how this form (named MCH3) helps the health facility to collect the extra data required, one health facility worker said,

There was a form before MTUHA called MCH3 which they stopped distributing but found that the data in there are needed. We are asked to report on these data elements so we had to continue using MCH3 in order to be able to report to the district offices. (Health Worker at Health Facility B)

On the other hand, the DIO expressed this view of the MCH3 form:

Before MTUHA there was a form called MCH3. Health workers at the facility level find it easier to use than the current collection of registers books. (DIO).

4.2 Private Health Facilities: The Difference in Relations and Their Impact on Reporting Practices

All health facilities (government and private) in Tanzania are required to collect data using MTUHA data collection tools. Health workers in private health facilities collect the data they need for their daily management activities in a separate register book (designed by a particular private health facility) and do not necessarily follow the needs of MTUHA since they think data from MTUHA doesn't help them much as they don't get feedback from higher levels.

If I report to the DMO that my buildings are not well what will they do... they don't come to repair. So we also have to prepare our own registers [for management activities] especially on medicines consumption. (Private Health Facility in Charge)

On the other hand, private health facilities reported fewer numbers of patients than were actually attended. This is because they pay taxes to the Tanzanian Revenue Authority (TRA) according to the number of patients they are attending. The district health worker expressed this by describing her experience with private health facilities:

One day we were at one of the private health facilities and when we asked the in-charge how many patients he attends he said 3 per day, but while we were there we saw more than 10 patients coming. Then we asked him why have we seen more that 10 patients. He told us that he is doing that [reporting less] to avoid paying higher taxes to TRA because he is a retired person and the dispensary is his main source of income.

The above relational and operational differences between the private and government health facilities results in data interferring with business.

4.3 District Level

4.3.1 Demands from Above: Creation of New Local Tools for Data Collection

When it really comes down to the details of responding to their bosses' demands, the health workers effectively abandon the work processes and fall back on whatever embodied skills are available to them. When MTUHA started, it was declared that all the vertical programs would be using data colleted through MTUHA forms at the health facility level. After some time of operating different sections and departments such as the MCH department from the MoH started to demand data from the district level that are currently not collected through MTUHA forms (these are data that were previously collected before MTUHA, that is, before integrating the vertical programs). As a way of responding to the higher levels' needs, the district information officer (DIO) in collaboration with the district MCH in charge developed forms separate from MTUHA with the required data elements, which they distribute to all the health facilities in their specific district.

> *As the days went on, we are asked for other information that are not in MTUHA forms, which caused us to design our own forms and add more columns in MTUHA registers so that we could get the data the region coordinator is asking for.* (District MCH in Charge)

On the other hand, this adds more workload to health workers at the facility level who are busy attending patients with poor resources and infrastructure.

Health workers at the district level have to use data collection and processing tools from the MoH regardless of their limitations.

> *I have to use the MTUHA software regardless of its limitations because it is the order from the MoH.* (DIO)

However, the extra paper forms that the district level has designed for collecting information that is not in MTUHA paper forms and register books which the district receives from the health facilities has no place in the MTUHA database. In expressing the limitations of the MTUHA software, the DIO said,

> *In collaboration with the MCH coordinator we have designed paper forms, called* mapungufu ya MTUHA[8] *for collecting additional data on MCH activities that are missing in MTUHA register books used at the health facilities. These [additional data in the* mapungufu ya MTUHA *paper form] have no place in the MTUHA software and we can't modify the database.* (DIO)

4.3.2 Demands from above and District's Needs: Creation of New Local Tools for Data Analysis

There are some reports that are needed by the higher levels or for the district's activities, for example, a report on the top 10 diseases in the particular district. Currently it is very difficult to prepare such reports mainly due to deficiencies in the reporting. The quarterly reports, which the district level receives from the health facilities, have no diseases reports; the health facilities only report on diseases yearly, which means in the middle of the year you can't know the top 10 diseases for the district unless you go to the individual health facilities to collect data. In addition to the limitations on reporting the frequency

---

[8]*Mapungufu ya MTUHA* is a Swahili statement meaning "the lacks of MTUHA."

of diseases, there are no tool(s) to help the district health workers in sorting out the top 10 diseases from all the health facilities in a particular district. Each time the health workers at the district have to prepare a top 10 diseases report, they use a very big sheet of paper (joined papers which are pinned together), which they have given a Kiswahili name *mkeka* due to its size (big) resembling a local tool called *mkeka* used when sitting on the floor. On this sheet of paper, they list all of the health facilities in the district and the reported diseases. Then they count how many time the disease has appeared at each of the health facilities. When describing the process, the DIO said,

> *We have designed our own form called 'mkeka' to be able to find the top 10 diseases.* (DIO)

There are times when the district health workers have to use the previous year's diseases reports because of the difficulties in getting the current report.

> *Sometimes the community leaders call us to go to their community and report the diseases situation in our district but because the data is only being reported at the end of the year....sometimes we repeat the previous year's report because we don't have a tool to give us information on quarterly basis.* (District Health Worker)

5 DISCUSSION

Fundamental to the activity theory approach is that human capacities develop in collaboration with others, and people act upon their immediate surroundings (Engerström 1987). The idea of actors acting according to what is happening around them is the embodiment of situated action. The discussion on the situatedness of work practices and organization culture is based on two main arguments from activity theory: the relations between the organization and the overall object of its activities are mediated by its division of labor, and the relations between individuals and the organization of which they are a part are mediated by rules and procedures (Engerström 1999b). In this discussion, organization culture is perceived as expressed through the way the organization is structured, how work is done, the aims of the organization, and how management and staff interact within the organization and with those outside (for example, with the donor requirements through vertical programs and private health facilities with the TRA).

Health workers' work practices are physically situated within the environment and within the organization culture. The ethnographic data from this study indicates that situatedness is expressed through the *tensions* between primary health care work practices, secondary health care work practices, and IS demands, as well as the difference in relations between private and government health facilities. The local and situated construction of the HIS is archived by the interplay of the health care worker (at the health facility level, at the district level, at the regional level, and at the MoH), the tools (register books, paper forms, pen, calculator, etc.) and the infrastructure (the shelves for register books, the folders to keep paper forms, and transport for taking reports to the higher level).

5.1 The Division of Labor, Rules, and Procedures: Tensions in Work Practices

In providing health care and collecting health care data, several health care workers need to engage in the processes and take action within it (Korpela et al. 2004). Work in health care organizations can be described as distributed work among health workers as well as between the health care organizational hierarchies. HIS activities are mainly organized by managers at higher levels for the grassroots levels, for example, the CHMT organizing HIS activities for the health facilities. Distribution of work happens within a specific level, for example, the DMO distributing work between the district health workers. In practice, then, differently distributed tasks lead to different patterns of work practices, cause tensions for health workers, and limits other activities. In health facilities, for example, health workers have to perform mainly patient care, administrative, and secretarial tasks, which mainly involves paper work. At the district level, the DMO does mainly managerial activities while the DIO is supposed to deal with information issues (collecting reports from the health facilities and preparing the district reports). However, the distribution of work tasks includes problems such as some DMOs delegating emergence report preparation tasks and roles to DIOs, requiring the DIO to adjust his routine work practices, while some other DMOs do similar minor routine tasks themselves. This implies that the DIO assists the DMO in paper work or even attending patients in places where the district offices are located within the district hospital. Consequently, it is often the social connections and practical requirements that lead to a certain division of tasks and roles which might not be seen on any organizational charts or plans (Barley 1986), but has been noticed in the health care districts in this study.

On one hand, Tanzanian HIS is still relatively hierarchical with more emphasis on data collection and reporting at the health facility level. According to Markus (1983), organizational tensions and conflicts of authority are well known problems in hierarchical organizations. On the other hand, organizational hierarchy can create conflict trenches between DMOs and DIOs, higher levels and grassroots levels because of the politics related to distribution of work, resources, and power. Social factors can be the final battlefield where individuals use whatever skills and tools they have to fit situational factors. For example, health workers at the grassroots level designing their own data collection forms to fulfil the higher level's requirements, which in turn adds more workload, borrowing a calculator from a nearby school teacher so that they can prepare reports, using their money for transport to take the reports to avoid being seen as lazy.

When considering the contested, temporal, and evolving attributes of organizational culture (Avison and Myers 1995; Westrup et al. 2002), where there is room for development is in the area of how IS affects or mediates organizational culture and vise versa. To innovate IS in organizations requires a very careful exploration of the situatedness of the particular organizational culture in an organization. Equally, exploring organizational culture raises the issue of the environment in which organizations are found. The ethnographic data from this study show that as the days go on, there is a demand for extra data from the higher levels than what are being collected through a standardized IS tool (MTUHA in this particular case). Consequently, work practices and organization culture are subject to development and change over a period of time because of the learning going on within the organization. This change is normally incremental and evolutionary and is affected by both external and internal environmental factors. The importance is in understanding these factors and determining how they (factors) have had an impact on the development of the present work practices and organization culture.

5.2 When the Work Practice Is Disturbed

When the health care worker is asked for reports which s/he can't prepare with MTUHA tools, s/he creates other tools, for example, the use of *mkeka* at the district level to prepare the top 10 disease report, and the creation of new forms for collecting data requested by the higher levels. This is a disturbance, a deviation from the standard work practices of the IS. The situation continues to be a disturbance to the health worker, especially because similar events are repeated every day during routine data collection, each quarter during report preparation and reporting. The health workers do not stick to the routine MTUHA work practices and, therefore, they handle the disturbances. In handling the disturbance or the difficult as Engeström (1987 1999b) puts it, health workers change their activities and simultaneously change their skills. The health worker focuses on the disturbances and begins to search for tools to help in achieving the desired outcome (a required report, in this case the top 10 disease report, extra data on the MCH activities). In other cases, such as when the MoH or region level asks the district level about a certain report that is not collected and reported using MTUHA tools, the DIO does not conduct their reflective actions of how to report alone. They involve the district in-charges of particular health care programs (for example, involving the district MCH in-charge in this case) and health facility workers in the reflection actions, thus expanding the social scope and interactive basis of the actions. This usually results in the develop-ment of a new form for collecting and reporting the required information. The result in turn causes more tensions for the health workers.

The HIS innovation uptake in this case seems to be problematic as well because neither the organization nor the professional training within the health care system and within particular districts includes health workers training on HIS as a natural part of the normal work activity. Health care professionals rarely have detailed and profound knowledge about possibilities and restrictions of IS. Some health care workers may not be at all familiar with the importance of health data collection and use and this has already caused problems. "Knowledge and responsibilities are not always visible in the organizational structures but in the more or less hidden social networks" (Laine 2003, p. 5). It is also important to determine actual experiences from people within the organiza-tion in their adapting to the internal and external environments, for example, the private health facilities report fewer patients because they want to avoid paying higher taxes to the TRA.

6 CONCLUSIONS

In this article, we have examined the situatedness of work practices and organizational culture. Arguably this paper has addressed central themes in IS innovation uptake in both low income countries and developed countries. The situatedness of work practices and organization culture is expressed through the tensions between the shared objects (primary work practices, secondary work practices, and IS requirements) and the interaction between multiple organizational contexts within and outside the health care organization as an activity system. The identification and understanding of these tensions offers a step forward in current IS research in the HIS field. The division of labor, rules, and concrete procedures of the HIS are constructed historically and collectively, in collaboration between health care workers and their artifacts. The local and situated construction of the HIS also happens collectively. Coordination of activities requires commitment from individual health workers and health workers need to work across and around gaps in existing health care systems. The organization culture should not be seen as an obstacle to IS innovation uptake, but an aspect that is intimately linked to what we call the social, political, and economic aspects of people's lives and their relations with the organizations of which they are part. Unlike Egeström's approach to activity theory in developmental work research, which binds the individual, collective, and technological aspects of work together, this paper emphasizes the situatedness of work practices, focusing on the influence of the organizational context to actors' everyday work practices and actions. I consider this emphasis as the main theoretical contribution of the paper.

References

Aunger, R. "On Ethnography: Story Telling or Science?," *Current Anthropology* (36:1), 1995, pp. 97-130.

Avison, D. E., and Myers, M. D. "Information Systems and Anthropology: An Anthropological Perspective on IT in Organizational Culture," *Information Technology and People* (8:3), 1995, pp. 43-56.

Bardram, J. E. "Plans as Situated Action: An Activity Theory Approach to Workflow Systems," in *Proceedings of the ECSCW97 European Conference on Computer Supported Cooperative Work*, Boston: Kluwer Academic Publishers, 1997, pp. 17-32.

Barley, S. R. "Technology as an Occasion for Structuring Evidence from Observations of CT Scanners and the Social Order of Radiology Departments," *Administrative Science Quarterly* (31:1), 1986, pp. 79-108.

Blackler, F., Crump, N., and McDonald, S. "Organizing Processes in Complex Activity Networks," *Organization* (7:2), 2000, pp. 277-300.

Braa, J., and Herdberg, C. "The Struggle for District-Based Health Information Systems in South Africa," *The Information Society* (18:2), 2002, pp. 113-127.

Braa, J., Monteiro, E., and Sahay, S. "Networks of Action: Sustainable Health Information Systems across Developing Countries," *MIS Quarterly* (28:3), September 2004, pp. 337-362.

Bratteteig, T., and Gregory, J. "Human Action in Context: A Discussion of Theories for Understanding Use of IT," in T. Käkölä (ed.), *Proceedings of the 22nd Information Systems Research Seminar in Scandinavia (IRIS 22): "Enterprise Architectures for Virtual Organizations,"* Jyväskylä: University of Jyväskylä, Computer Science and Information Systems Reports, Technical Report TR-21, 1999, pp. 161-182.

Cabrera, A, Cabrera, E. F., and Barajas, S. "The Key Role of Organizational Culture in a Multi-System View of Technology-Driven Change," *International Journal of Information Management* (21:3), 2001, pp. 245-261.

Doerry, E. "Evaluating Distributed Environments Based on Communicative Efficacy," in *Conference Companion on Human Factors in Computing Systems, CHI'95*, Denver, CO, 1995, pp. 47-48(available online at http://www1.acm.org/sigchi/chi95/proceedings/doctoral/ed_bdy.htm).

Dubé, L., and Robey, D. "Software Stories: Three Cultural Perspectives on the Organizational Practices of Software Development," *Accounting, Management and Information Technologies* (9:4), 1999, pp. 223-259.

Engeström, Y. "Activity Theory and Individual and Social Transformation," in Y. Engeström, R. Miettinen, and R. Punamäki (eds.), *Perspectives on Activity Theory*, Cambridge, UK: Cambridge University Press, 1999a, pp. 19-38.

Engeström, Y. "Communication, Discourse and Activity," *Communication Review* (3:1-2), 1999b, pp. 165-185.

Engeström, Y. "Expansive Visibility of Work: An Activity-Theoretical Perspective," *Computer Supported Cooperative Work* (8), 1999c, pp. 63-93.

Engeström, Y. *Learning by Expanding: An Activity Theoretical Approach to Developmental Research*, Helsinki: Orienta Konsultit, 1987.

Engeström, Y., Miettinen, R., and Punamäki, R-L. (eds.). *Perspectives on Activity Theory.*, Cambridge, UK: Cambridge University Press, 1999.

Giddens, A. *The Constitution of Society*, Cambridge, UK: Polity Press, 1984.

Grudin, J. "The Organizational Contexts of Development and Use," *Computing Surveys* (28:1), 1996, pp. 169-171.

Hardon, A., Boonmongkon, P., Streefland, P., Tan, M., Hongvivatana, T., Geest, S. V. D., Staa. A. V., Varkevisser, C., Chowdhury, M., Bhuiya, A., Sringeryuang, L., Dongen, E. V., and Gerrits, T. *Applied Health Research Manual: Anthropology of Health and Care*, Amsterdam: Het Spinhuis Publishers, 2001.

Honigmann, J. J. "The Personal Approach in Cultural Anthropological Research," *Current Anthropology* (17:2), 1976, pp. 243-261.

Iivari, N. "The Role of Organizational Culture in Organizational Change: Idenfying a Realistic Position for Prospective IS Research," in D. Bartmann, F. Rajola, J. Kallinikos, D. Avison, R. Winter, P. Ein-Dor, J. Becker, J. Bodendorf, and C. Weihardt (eds.), *Proceedings of the 13th European Conference on Information Systems*, Regensburg, Germany, 2005.

Kapetlinin, V. "Human Computer Interaction in Context: The Activity Theory Perspective," in *Proceedings of the East-West Conference on Human Computer Interaction*, Moscow: ICSTI, 1992, pp. 7-13.

Kapetelinin, V., and Nardi, B. A. *Acting with Technology; Activity Theory and Interaction Design*, Cambridge, MA: MIT Press, 2006.

King, W. R. "Strategic Issues in Groupware," *Information Systems Management* (13:2), 1996, pp. 73-75.

Kimaro, H. C., and Nhampossa, J. L. "The Challenges of Sustainability of Health Information Systems in Developing Countries: Comparative Case Studies of Mozambique and Tanzania," in T. Leino, T. Saarinen, and S. Klein (eds.), *Proceedings of the 12th European Conference on Information Systems: The European IS Profession in the Global Networking Environment*, Turku, Finland, 2004.

Korpela, M., Mursu, A., Soriyan, A., Eorola, A., and Häkkinen, H. "Information Systems Research and Development by Activity Analysis and Development: Dead Horse or the Next Wave?," in B. Kaplan, D. P. Truex II, D. Wastell, A. T. Wood-Harper, and J. I. DeGross (eds.), *Information Systems Research: Relevant Theory and Informed Practice, Proceedings of the IFIP TC8WG8.2 International Conference*, Boston: Kluwer Academic Publishers, 2004, pp. 453-471.

Liane, S. "Social Networks and Organizational Structures During the Implementation Process of an Electronic Patient Record System," in *The 2003 European Computer Supported Cooperative Work Conference (ECSCW'03) Workshop on Social Networks*, Helsinki, Finland, 2003.

Leontjev, A. *Activity, Consciousness, and Personality*, Englewood Cliffs NJ: Prentice-Hall, 1978

Lungo, J. H. "Data Flows in Health Information Systems: An Action Research Study of Reporting Routine Health Delivery Services and Implementation of Computer Databases on Health Information Systems," M.Sc. Thesis, Department of Informatics, University of Oslo, Oslo, Norway, 2003.

Lungo, J. H. "The Potential of District Health Information Software in Tanzania," in A. Bada and O. Adelakun (eds.), *Social Implications of Computers in Developing Countries: Enhancing Human Resource Development through ICT*, Abuja, Nigeria. 2005, pp. 518-529

Lungo, J. H., and Nhampossa, J. L. "The Impacts of Legacy Information Systems in Reporting Routine Health Delivery Services: Case Studies from Mozambique and Tanzania," paper presented at the Eighth International Conference on Systems Science in Health Care, University of Geneva, Geneva, Switzerland, 2004.

Markus, M. L. "Power, Politics, and MIS Implementation," *Communications of the ACM* (26:6), 1983, pp. 430-444.

Mukama, F. K. "A Study of Health Information Systems at Local Levels in Tanzania and Mozambique," M.Sc.Thesis, Department of Informatics, University of Oslo, Oslo, Norway, 2003 (available online at www.ub.uib.no/elpub/NORAD/2003/uio/thesis02.pdf).

Mullins, J. L. *Management and Organizational Behavior* (6th ed.), Upper Saddle River, NJ: Prentice-Hall, 2002.

Nardi, B. A. *Context and Consciousness: Activity Theory and Human–Computer Interaction*, Cambridge, MA: MIT Press, 1995.

Nardi, B. A. "Studying Context: A Comparison of Activity Theory, Situated Action Models and Distributed Cognition," in *Proceedings of the East-West Conference on Human Computer Interaction*, Moscow: ICSTI, 1992, pp. 352-359.

Newman, M., and Sabherwal, R. "Determinants of Commitment to Information Systems Development: A Longitudinal Investigation," *MIS Quarterly* (20:1), March 1996, pp. 23-54.

Nicholson, B., and Sahay, S. "Some Political and Cultural Issues in the Globalization of Software Development: Case Experience from Britain and India," *Information and Organization* (11:1), 2001, pp. 25-44.

Orlikowski, W. J. "The Duality of Technology: Rethinking the Concept of Technology in Organizations," *Organization Science* (3:3), 1992, pp. 398-427.

Parker, M. *Organizational Culture and Identity*, London: Sage Publications, 2000.

Robey, D., and Azevedo, A. "Cultural Analysis of the Organizational Consequences of Information Technology," *Accounting, Management & Information Technology* (4:1), 1994, pp. 23-37.

Rubona, J. "Routine Health Information Systems that Operate in Tanzania," in *The RHINO Workshop on Issues and Innovation in Routine Health Information in Developing Countries*, The Bolger Center, Potomac, MD, March 14-16, 2001. Arlington, VA: Measure Evaluation, JSI Research and Training Institute, 2001, pp. 183-193.

Suchman, L. A. *Plans as Situated Actions: The Problem of Human–Machine Communication*, Cambridge, UK: Cambridge Press, 1987.

Vygotskij, L. S. *Mind and Society*, Cambridge, MA: Harvard University Press, 1978.

Walsham, G. *Interpreting Information Systems in Organizations*, Chichester, UK: Wiley, 1993.

Westrup, C., Liu, E., El-Sayed, H., and Al-Jaghoub, S. "Taking Culture Seriously: ICTs, Cultures and Development," in S. Krishna and S. Madon (eds.), *Information & Communication Techonologies and Development: New Opportunities, Perspectives and Challenges, Proceedings of the Seventh International Working Conference of IFIP WG 9.4*, Bangalore, India, May 28-31, 2002.

About the Author

Faraja Igira is currently a Ph.D. student at the University of Oslo, Norway, interested in studying information systems and cultural aspects. She holds a Master's in Informatics from the University of Oslo. Her current research is on organizational issues in the development and implementation of health information systems in low-income countries. Faraja can be reached by e-mail at farajam@ifi.uio.no.

10 USER-LED INNOVATION IN CALL CENTER KNOWLEDGE WORK: A Social Shaping Perspective

Beryl Burns
Ben Light
IS Organisations and Society Research Centre
University of Salford
Salford, United Kingdom

Abstract   So called "knowledge work" is seen as integral to post-industrial society and, for some, information and communications technologies (ICTs) are critical enablers of the associated practices. Many still propose the technologically deterministic route of rolling out ICTs and expecting that users will, and indeed can, "download" what they know into a system that can then be used in a number of ways. This approach is usually underpinned by the predominant assumption that the system will be developed by one group (developers) and used by another group (users). In this paper, we report on an exploratory case study of the enactment of ICT supported knowledge work in a human resources contact center which illustrates the negotiable boundary between the developer and user in local level innovation processes. Drawing upon ideas from the social shaping of technology, we examine how discussions regarding producer-user relations in innovation processes require a degree of greater sophistication as we show how users often develop (or produce) technologies and work practices in situ—in this case, to enable knowledge work practices and contribute to the project of constructing the knowledge component of professional identity. Much has been made of contextualizing the user; further work is required to contextualize the developer as a user and understand the social actors in ICT innovation environments who straddle both domains.

Keywords   Call centers, knowledge management, knowledge work, social shaping of technology, end user computing, innovation.

Please use the following format when citing this chapter:

Burns, B., and Light, B., 2007, in IFIP International Federation for Information Processing, Volume 235, Organizational Dynamics of Technology-Based Innovation: Diversifying the Research Agenda, eds. McMaster, T., Wastell, D., Ferneley, E., and DeGross, J. (Boston: Springer), pp. 133-147.

1   INTRODUCTION

So called *knowledge work* has been held up as integral to innovation efforts in the global knowledge economy, and call centers have become a key feature of this. Inbound call centers typically take the form of aircraft hanger style offices, populated with information and communications technologies (ICTs) and operatives that deal with a multitude of customer queries. The use of call centers has risen tremendously over the past 20 years, predominantly in response to the needs for globalization, the potential they offer for improving organizational efficiency, and the desire to become more customer facing in the light of the business hype surrounding customer relationship management (CRM) (Light 2003; Richardson and Richardson 2002). Call center workers often perform roles that, in more traditional organizational settings, would be performed by a number of people. Indeed, where outsourcing companies operate call centers, the workloads of employees can be distributed over a multi-organizational customer base so that they are most efficiently utilized. In order to further maximize the efficiencies to be had from the call center model, ICT-enabled surveillance is used extensively to monitor performance. For example, the automatic call distribution software used to allocate calls to agents is also used to measure performance in terms of length of time taken to answer calls, calls lost, revenue generated, and client data analysis (Taylor et al. 2002). Conventional call center agents have little or no officially sanctioned autonomy; scripts are built into ICTs to guide them through their interactions in an efficient and standardized fashion. Indeed, call centers could be seen as part of the trend toward "McDonaldization" (Ritzer 2004), the process by which the principles of the fast-food restaurant are coming to dominate aspects of work organizations and society because the dimensions of this phenomena resonate so highly with them: efficiency, calculability, predictability, and control. Call center workers are not supposed to be innovative.

In this study, we explore the ICT-related innovation processes in a call center environment, which we shall call CarePoint. At CarePoint, complex forms of knowledge and processes for the construction of knowledge are required to deliver the service in question. We look at the how a group of staff tailor and maintain an important knowledge artefact and how this facilitates its appropriation into the everyday practices in the call center. In doing this we are able to shed light on the links between the complimentary development and maintenance of an ICT innovation, different forms of knowledge, and the roles of users as developers in this environment. Our aim is to illustrate the negotiable boundary between development and use, and thus the arbitrary naming of developers and users in innovation efforts. In order to accomplish this, we lay out our theoretical basis in the next two sections. In the first section, we discuss perspectives on knowledge and knowledge making. In the second section, we introduce a social shaping lens, arguably an underused theory in studies of ICT innovation within information systems. We use this to highlight the negotiable boundary between development and use, and developers and users in innovation efforts. Following this, we introduce our approach to the field study and then we provide an interpretation of our findings. From this, we provide summary conclusions and some implications for research and practice as related to ICT facilitated knowledge work, user-developer relations, and the study of innovations from a social shaping of technology (SST) perspective.

2 KNOWLEDGE AND KNOWLEDGE WORK

Although there are those who privilege ICTs as *the* mechanism for capturing, storing, and disseminating knowledge, this approach has been challenged as lacking insight into different kinds of knowledge and its provisional situated nature (Blackler 1995; Fleck 1997; Marshall and Brady 2001; Sutton 2001). For example, knowledge may be

*   contingent, relevant to a particular context, widely distributed, shared, trivial, or accidentally acquired (Fleck 1997)
*   embodied, knowledge about how to do something, gained through doing
*   embedded, where routine arrangements are deployed
*   embrained, akin to the holding of conceptual skills and cognitive abilities
*   encultured, rooted in shared understandings
*   encoded, conveyed by signs and symbols (Blackler 1995)

Indeed, it has been further argued that greater insights can be gained by studying the processes of knowledge construction, rather than focusing upon describing and defining the different forms. Knowledge is mediated by various things, situated in a given time and place, provisional in that it is socially constructed, pragmatic in that it is purposive and object oriented, and contested as it has links with power and politics (Blackler 1995). Knowledge work also involves the distinct but interdependent process of knowledge creation, storage, retrieval, transfer, and application (Alavi and Leidner 2001). Blackler (1995), therefore, recommends that we focus upon the systems through which people achieve their knowing, on the changes that are occurring within such systems, and on the process through which new knowledge may be generated. The social shaping perspective we adopt here to study such knowledge seems particularly appropriate given its genealogy in the sociology of scientific knowledge (SSK). SSK proponents claim that the "natural world has a small or non-existent role in the construction of scientific knowledge" (Collins 1981, p. 3) and considers social influences on science and "while traditional sociology of knowledge asked how, and to what extent 'social factors' might influence the products of the mind, SSK sought to show that knowledge was constitutively social" (Shapin 1995, p. 289). The theories of SSK argue that *all knowledge* encased in science and technology studies is a social concept (Bijker et al. 1989).

The challenge is thus to show how particular practices and discourses sustain networks of power-knowledge relations (Knights et al. 1993). For example, historically, task-continuous status organizations were prevalent where functional and hierarchical differentiation coincided. In this environment, positions were defined by greater mastery of rules, ability, knowledge, and experience in production (Offe 1976). But modern organizations are said to exhibit more of a task-discontinuation structuring of status and the function of work performed (Hardy and Clegg 1996). The question, therefore, is how do these shifts occur and why? This all points to the need to go beyond simplistic notions of knowledge as a commodity to be extracted and transferred (Walsham 2001). Any sharing of knowledge has a political dimension. For example, it may be used in innovation appropriation processes to provide access to other relevant knowledge and artefacts and as a political tool in support of particular interests (Hislop et al. 2000). Knowledge informs and justifies how we act; when it is taken as "truth," especially when it is understood as neutral and authoritative, then it is powerful (Alvesson and Willmott 1996). As mentioned earlier, knowledge is situated and therefore it is necessary to understand that knowledge construction is somewhat predetermined by the fact of "growing up" in a society (Mannheim 2004), or indeed, in our case, an organization. Thus we have to be careful to avoid an excessively voluntaristic account of knowledge work in which actors are depicted as autonomous agents who possess sufficient resources to make their network a reality (Knights et al. 1993). Knowledge work is a complex, nonlinear, process involving a broad range of actors and intermediaries (Knights et al. 1993). The utilization and integration of "new" knowledge and artefacts with existing arrangements is an important aspect of the appropriation of innovations and thus this makes the control or possession of relevant knowledge important (Hislop et al. 2000).

Given this context, how might ICT-enabled knowledge working be performed in a call center environment that is often organized and managed according to a unitary organizational frame of reference? Moreover, given it has recently been argued that most ICT-based systems are still currently developed as static entities whose purpose is to model a dynamic world (Kanellis and Paul 2005) and that knowledge is provisional, then the implication is that innovation with ICTs in knowledge-intensive environments needs further investigation in terms of the role of users and developers in making such systems work in practice. In the next, section we introduce an SST lens to assist with this.

3   USER RELATIONS IN INNOVATION PROCESSES: A VIEW FROM SST

SST rejects technologically deterministic accounts of the construction and appropriation of technologies and recognizes the mutually constitutive nature, and negotiable boundary between, society and technology (for overviews, see Bijker and Law 1994; Mackenzie and Wajcman 1999; Pinch and Bijker 1987; Sørensen 2002 Williams and Edge 1996). From this perspective, technology applications do not have predictable, universal outcomes. Instead, technologies are conceptualized as being shaped as they are designed and used depending upon who is, and is not, involved along the way. Therefore, while they may change situations, the technologies themselves may be subject to change, resulting in intended and unintended consequences for that deemed the technology and that deemed the social arrangements with which it is meshed. However, as mentioned earlier, systems are often reported as being delivered as complete solutions, which are sufficiently specified *a priori*. The consequence of this is that many systems still fail and user involvement in the specification of systems is common practice even though, with this involvement, systems are still deemed to fail (Cavaye 1995). This has been termed the *design fallacy*, the presumption that the primary solution to meeting user needs is to build ever more extensive knowledge about the specific context and purposes of various users into technology design (Stewart and Williams 2005). Stewart and Williams argue that the problem with this thinking is that it privileges prior design, it is unrealistic and unduly simplistic, it may not be effective in enhancing design or use, and it overlooks opportunities for intervention. Indeed, it has been argued that the reality of the situation is that organizational features are products of constant social negotiation and consensus building and this means we need to rethink how ICTs are developed (Truex et al. 1999).

A further issue is that users are often not considered in their context and instead are often thought of, in systems development and use, as using a given ICT in isolation from other things (Lamb and Kling 2003). Developers, too, have often been seen as objective experts whose sole aim in life is to build the best system possible for an undifferentiated group of users. However, it is now increasingly recognized that such views are simplistic and that development and use is loaded with power and politics on both sides (Franz and Robey 1984; Markus 1983; Markus and Bjørn-Andersen 1987; Yourdon 1986). Yet, the two sides of users and developers in ICT efforts are still a key feature of IS research. We understand that power is exercised by developers over users (Markus and Bjørn-Andersen 1987), and that certain users may exercise power over developers (Howcroft and Light 2006), but users as developers exercising power has received minimal attention. Even the long tradition of end-user computing still predominantly refers to users, not as developers, but as users who happen to develop ICT-based systems. Users are rarely discussed in terms of any role they may have as a developer and developers are similarly usually not seen as users (Friedman and Cornford 1989), this despite case studies of users as developers and their valuable role in product development (Holmström 2001). Consequently, there are questions about whom users and developers are. We believe this is inextricably linked with the artificial distinction made between the social and the technical often seen in IS, when such distinctions are clearly socially constructed and negotiable (Bloomfield and Vurdubakis 1994).

Drawing upon SST, we would like to expand upon this in terms of the roles associated with work deemed social and technical. In sum, we think the boundary between the usage and production (or development) of that deemed social and technical, the socio-technical, is also negotiable (Rohracher 2005). Therefore, although discussions of producer-user relations have yielded many interesting and valuable insights, we think it might also be useful to emphasize the ongoing work that users put into socio-technical systems *in situ* (Fleck 1994; Rohracher 2005; Stewart and Williams 2005). Not only do they use such systems, they produce them in use too, as is the case here. This idea of innovation in use is well known within the social shaping of technology school. Such concepts include *innofusion* (innovation in the process of diffusion), *domestication* (the process by which artefacts are made to work *in situ*), and the *innovation journey*, or *innovation biographies* (the acknowledgment of nonlinearity and branching in such processes, potentially leading to radical deviations from original conceptualizations) (Fleck 1994; Rohracher 2005; Sørensen 2002; Stewart and Williams 2005). However, the distinction between users and developers usually remains. In this study, we focus upon how a group of users use and develop the scripts. In this case, we refer to the electronically codified content, processes, and procedures regarding human resource policies that are inscribed into a component of a call center information system. In the next section, we provide details of our approach to undertaking the fieldwork.

4 RESEARCH APPROACH

This study is part of a program of work that is exploring the deployment of ICTs in professionally populated environments. The findings are based on primary and secondary data drawn from one of the cases in the research program. The research approach is interpretive and qualitative through case study. The case study research method is largely acknowledged and is frequently used to conduct qualitative data informed research (Klein and Myers 1999; Orlikowski 1996; Walsham 1993, 1995). A range of techniques associated with the case study method were used given our concern for the social influence of ICTs within the company rather than solely those deemed *technical* (Myers 1997). CarePoint, the human resources contact center we have studied, employs 78 staff, only five of whom are male. The average age of the staff is 34 years. On arrival at the company, we were issued with identification badges and we were given authorized unaccompanied open access to CarePoint. A cross section of 14 members of staff, namely CarePoint's manager, policy makers, case workers, and a range of HR advisors, were interviewed and observed over a number of sessions during a 6-month period. At the start of each interview the study's purpose was explained and we made the participants aware that we intended to publish our findings and assured them that they and their comments would be annonymized. Our aim was to gain an overall picture of how the contact center operated focusing on several aspects concerning contact center work. This included various areas such as professional identity; the design, implementation and management of the IT system; surveillance issues related to the technology and general working practices and ergonomic arrangements. As a central feature of traditional call center work is the use of scripts, one aspect that we focus on in our study, our attention therefore turned to the use and development of scripts in an environment where workers were highly skilled and working in an area that could not always be dealt with in an expedient, straightforward fashion. Thus, questions related to the design, use, and housekeeping of the scripting artefact were asked accordingly. Questions from the initial interview protocol are shown in Table 1. From this point, we then branched off into other areas as the interview progressed, in the light of the interviewee's responses and our increasing familiarity with the area, empirically and theoretically. No one declined to be interviewed, and everyone was happy to have their thoughts shared with their colleagues.

The interviews were semi-structured with each interviewee encouraged to be candid and open. The time scale of individual interviews varied between 30 and 90 minutes; they were recorded and subsequently transcribed, providing 81 pages of transcription. Additionally, documentary evidence such as CarePoint policies were referred to as neces-

Table 1. **Initial Interview Protocol: Selected Questions**

- Please tell me about your role.
- How does your role sit with other roles in the contact center?
- Would you class yourself as working in a professional occupation?
- Please tell me about the IT systems you use.
- Can you give me some examples of how you use the IT systems?
- When might you not use the IT systems?
- How were the IT systems built?
- Who uses them?
- How do you maintain the IT systems?
- Given what we have talked about, is there anything else you think we should know about or anyone else we could talk to?

sary, which were collected from the company intranet and given to us by various employees during the process of our investigation. We also drew upon numerous sessions of nonparticipant overt observation and photographic evidence that was collected. Analysis and data collection were simultaneously carried out. This began with the aim of discovering the nature of the contact center agent's professional identity, their background, and their working environment. Data was then collected guided by Johnson's (2001) conceptual map of the characteristics of professions combined with a literature review of ICT use in organizations. The collected data was coded in relation to the literature and the features of the professions framework, and finally a subset of this related to knowledge was further unpacked, eventually leading to the identification of the analysis reported here.

5   CONSTRUCTING KNOWLEDGE AT CAREPOINT

CarePoint is an internal human resources contact center within an international health care product firm. The staff prefer CarePoint to be referred to as a contact center as opposed to a call center so as to get away from the traditional portrayal of a call center. This decision transpired because staff do more than deal with calls, the calls turn into transactions covering all human resource issues; therefore, contact center was chosen as a generic term to refer to phone calls that triggered transactions.

The contact center's function is to provide human resource support and advice to the 55,000 employees of the company. This work is undertaken by human resource professionals and involves advising on complex issues such as maternity leave, retirement policy, and staff recruitment. Employees will telephone the staff with a query, and it is their role to resolve it, escalating the caller to different levels of contact center workers as necessary. The center was set up in July 2003, with most of the staff recruited from within existing human resource roles throughout the company. However, two staff with experience of call routing and working in a call center environment were also recruited from elsewhere in the company. In both cases, the existing knowledge base of the staff was seen as crucial to the creation of this new organizational function. The majority of the staff within CarePoint are Chartered Institute of Personnel and Development qualified or are undergoing one of their programs of education. They regard themselves as professionals and consider human resources to be a profession.

The ICT-based system supporting the function was created from pieces of software from systems already in place throughout the wider organization. The system comprises a generic help desk application, a call logging system based on a customer relationship management package module, and a custom-developed staff scheduling system written in Microsoft Excel. In addition, call scripts are created in Microsoft Word using hyper linking and these are integrated with the customer relationship management module.

5.1   Users and Usage of the Development

CarePoint staff are the first obvious group of users within our case. They operate the ICT-based systems to provide advice to the employees who contact them for guidance. Such knowledge-based interactions mediate a number of things. A key artefact is the call flow model as shown in Figure 1 and it can be seen that Level 0 introduces another set of primary users, the employees and managers of CarePoint services. Level 0 is "self help," where line managers can solve minor problems and queries themselves by referring to the HR operating manual, Storenet, and other toolkits such as *Breakfast News* (a daily bulletin) via the intranet. CarePoint advisors then are organized across the remaining levels. Level 1, the advisory service, is split into two sections: Level 1a comprises a team of frontline advisors who should be able to answer a broad range of questions and initially take the calls. Level 1b comprises a team of senior advisors who have the ability to give more expert advice; a call that is referred to this level of staff should take no longer than 20 minutes to complete. The customer is put through a series of security checks, they are asked for their staff number and name, their details are then brought up and they are then asked to confirm their date of birth so as to ensure the advisor is speaking to the right person. If a call is more complex and exceeds 20 minutes, the customer is routed to the next level of agent, Level 2, comprising a team of case workers. Case workers deal with cases that exceed 20 minutes that need to be discussed in more detail, such as issues regarding discrimination or bullying. They make the choice on how to best support the line manager and if necessary they visit the customer on site. Case workers also go out on site and deal with any new or extra business as it arises, the formation of new sites of operations, for example. They also have particular respon-sibility for the development of the service; they look at how things can be done better. Level 3 hosts a team of policy owners; they deal with legal issues, set out various policies, are responsive to the needs of the business, and are accountable for the com-munication of changes in policy.

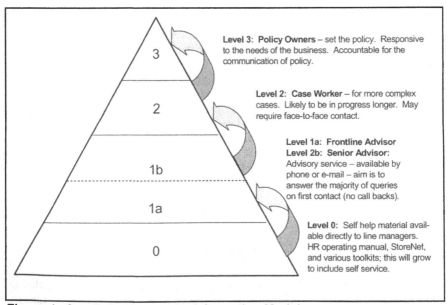

Figure 1. **CarePoint Conceptual Operating Model**

However, despite the internal structure of the contact center appearing to be task-continuous, in this case the staff's relationship to other members of departments is quite discontinuous. Level 1 staff may deal with high ranking managers throughout the organization based on their specialist encultured and embedded knowledge and by drawing upon the script as an encoded knowledge artefact. This means that when the call center was set up, working arrangements had to be altered bearing this in mind, as one employee explained.

> *We came from HR, which could be very complicated and we needed to give them the benefit of our experience, so 15 minutes for the average call, and Janet wanted it cut to 3 minutes and that's all you'll have and we had this ongoing debate, you know there's no way we can share our marvelous knowledge in 3 minutes and if you look at the call stats now we actually do it in 7 minutes.* (Adriana, Case Worker)

Indeed, the use of the knowledge component of the system, the scripts, is also optional. Cathy, a senior advisor, informed us that

> *It would generally be the advisors that would use the scripts, the stuff in scripts is fairly basic where a case is black or white, if it's a bit more grey and a bit more in depth then a bit more knowledge is needed.*

Even Level 1 advisors informed us that the scripts were used at their discretion.

> *I used the script regularly for the first 2 weeks while training, and sometimes I do still have to use them, but I have only been here 3 months, but because I come from an HR background I have prior knowledge of some issues, so that helps.* (Peter, Junior Advisor)

If the caller is a staff member, then advisors stick rigidly to company policy on what is discussed, referring the caller to the encoded knowledge in the scripts as necessary. However, if line managers call, advisors tend to draw upon encultured and embedded knowledge not recordable in the ICT-based scripts so they can give a more rounded discussion on the policy. The system is, therefore, used by more established members of staff in a supporting role if they are dealing with an unfamiliar case, with trainee staff using scripts in a supporting role, particularly in the first 2 weeks of training, and if they are new to the HR function. Case workers use the system to coach and develop advisors on legal issues and telephone manner and style, to learn from escalated and tribunal cases, and to probe the case issues and give guidance and advice. In addition, all advisors are encouraged to use the system in their spare time to further enhance their knowledge and skills on the various issues with which they have yet to deal.

5.2 Developers and Development in Use

So far, we have focused upon the users in our study. We now move on to consider the developers of a particular part of it, which the users think is the most important part.

Therefore, we focus upon the ICT-based scripts that underpin the contact center's operations. A central feature of traditional call center working is the use of scripts for the purposes of maximizing efficiency and reducing the need for skilled workers by imposing a standardized, prescriptive, innovation curtailing approach. Traditionally, third party companies or in-house developers throughout the requirements gathering process of the development cycle, or in response to user needs, produce call center scripts. At CarePoint, however, advisors take responsibility for constructing, modifying, and maintaining the scripts. From the outset, the scripts have been "built onto" as the need arises or as the need is identified by the users of the system, in order to reflect best practice and accommodate new pieces of legislation. This enables all users to "sing from the same hymn sheet," which is paramount as different advisors may interpret different situations and queries in different ways and, as CarePoint support the whole of the company with HR issues, some simple and some more complex and sensitive, it is important that the most accurate and best advice is given. Jane, a senior advisor, told us that

> *Senior ER advisors construct the scripting; we have to think about how the questions will be asked in various ways, and look at how these can be answered. The HR manual is also reconstructed as and when necessary. When the script is written it goes to the case workers to check their interpretation of the Q and A to make sure it is all done properly, then it is saved.*

In this case, users are also developers. As they are dealing with provisional knowledge, there is a need to constantly revise and sustain the scripts to build the base of encoded knowledge. It is a team effort to determine whether this happens or it just becomes encultured or embedded. As Helen, a team manager, commented,

> *It's a team effort though, we have meetings and if issues are raised regarding the scripts and they need to be altered, maybe a new query has been brought to light that we have no answer to, or maybe the answer to the question needed to be put into a different context, then it would be amended or written.*

However, the professional identity of the group is also seen as something to be maintained. All codifiable forms of knowledge do not end up being encoded into the scripts. Case workers have monthly meetings where they share their learning and decide with whom this will be further shared and how. The system may also not be developed further because of the temporally situated nature of the knowledge. For example, Heather, a junior HR advisor, informed us that

> *A useful tool we use is the Breakfast News that is communication between the teams about anything that needs to be shared...for instance we've got the Pope's funeral on Friday and we're starting to get calls about that, so everybody needs to give the same information. ....It doesn't go on the scripting because it's a one-off and it's not in the HR manual. People are querying the one-minute silence. It's a lot easier to update people this way than to update the scripting.*

Staff knowledge and expertise is a crucial element of working at CarePoint. Their professional identity is not only recognized by qualifications but in the main by an individual's knowledge and expertise. Jenny, the talent management administrator, told us that

> *There are a lot of people who have worked here for a long time and they've got a lot of knowledge about a lot of things and that's professional expertise, there are people here like that, their knowledge is so invaluable, so professional.*

Such knowledge constructed through dealing with various cases is shared by pulling out "key learning" from the cases, selectively sharing the findings in regular meetings, deciding if there is anything they need to share with other staff (formally and informally), and recording it, if necessary, in the scripts. One advisor described the system as a "time saving tool," another as a "learning tool." This process of selectively sharing and encoding knowledge is also a powerful political tool. Advisors unanimously agreed that the system enhances their professionalism, finding out information via the intranet is easier, it makes it possible for individuals to have a broader span of what information is available concerning the various issues they are dealing with as Melanie, a senior advisor, stated,

> *The system can pull up some wonderful information; it can tell you every minute of what's happening with a case...if you think about the responsibility we have got here, we support the whole of the company with HR issues, we are very powerful, the technology aids our power and knowledge...it enhances our professionalism, you know you could actually say that the technology in a way is your buddy because the system holds all the answers for you to enable you to do your job properly.*

Critically, though, the staff of the contact center control and enact the development of the scripts on their own terms, within the parameters of their role, of course. In doing this, they are able to present certain knowledge in an encoded format and label it as fairly basic, the black and white issues that lay people might be able to understand if they write it correctly and if support is there from them to interpret it as necessary. However, they also get to choose which knowledge remains embedded and enculured and in turn this mystifies their professional position. Ironically, the ICTs that the staff value so much are also distanced in some circumstances, even though they have developed them. They are badged as "not being capable of doing what they do," even though they have developed them, as part of the process of securing their professional identity.

6 CONCLUSIONS

SST affords a view of the differences of technological artefacts and offers a non-deterministic picture of the trajectory of a diffusion of innovations. Innovations do not have predictable, universal outcomes; as we show in our case, the adoption of the call center scripts is unpredictable. This is because products are appropriated in use through processes of domestication and innofusion. In our case, the sound, predefined arrangements of the contact center are domesticated by the employees and innofusion occurs. Moreover the trajectory is also ambiguous because of the differing relevant social groups involved in the appropriation of the artefact. The groups may flexibly interpret the artefact in question and provide differing levels of input into shaping the trajectory. For example, in our case, we see the relevant social groups of call center management; the HR professional groupings (as a group and as distinguished by the CarePoint operating model) and new employees have all taken differing perspectives of the technology and appropriated these in different ways.

In this paper we shed light on a group of users, who are also a group of developers, and how they get a knowledge artefact to work for them *in situ* through processes of innofusion and domestication. We also get insights into a different call center working "biography," which rejects ICT, process, and socio-geographic configurations based on typical arrangements. In our case, users develop a knowledge artefact for use by themselves, and others, in a variety of ways, and as with other innovation processes, this is political. Although, ICTs have been noted as heightening professional identities (Lamb and Kling 2003), and we see this in our case, it is also clear that considerable work goes into development *in situ* to fend off any encroachment such systems might enable. Lamb and Kling (2003) also state that, at the individual level, social actors exercise limited discretion in ICT choice and use, since, in organizational contexts, they articulate the preferences of a collection of actors. However, while we accept that this may be the case, we also show that individuals can have a high level of discretion as to whether they use particular features of an ICT: scripts are optional and often downplayed. Although it has been argued that larger systems might have more political support than smaller ones (Swanson and Dans 2000), our case affirms that smaller systems such as the one containing the script artefact can have a very high degree of political support, in this case, because of the desire to protect the professional identity of the group in question.

This study is more than a case of innovation in end-user computing and knowledge work though. Our findings have implications for user-developer relations more broadly. In Orlikowski and Gash's (1994) study, for example, it was found that *technologists* and *users* held different assessments of the value and function of a system. While we would certainly agree with this finding, our study suggests we need to think about user-developer relations a little more. In our study, the users were the developers too. The question is, when does one become the other, and vice versa? Our case is not isolated in this respect, work on innofusion, processes of innovation of the local level, implies users further developing a technology in use (Fleck 1994). In an ICT context, this is becoming ever more clear in the literatures on system workarounds (Rohracher 2005; Wagner and Newell 2006; Wagner et al. 2006; Wilson 2002) and packaged software customization where users have developed standalone applications to extract data from inflexible, enterprise-wide systems (Light 2001, 2005). The implication of this for research and practice is the need to consider the ongoing work, and actors who undertake this upon ICTs *in situ*. As Truex et al. (1999) state, systems need to be optimized for high maintenance effort. We would add this might be undertaken by users as developers rather than straight developers. Moreover, greater attention needs to be paid to the role of developers as users in the diffusion of innovations. Given the rise of social software, open source communities, and the packaged software industry, a broader consideration of ICT developers, as users is required. In each of these scenarios, developers may use the software as an application, but also as an artefact to fulfil a particular need—to sell to make a living, for example. Much has been made of contextualizing the user; further work is required to contextualize the developer as a user and understand the social actors in ICT innovation environments who straddle both domains.

References

Alavi, M., and Leidner, D. E. *"Review:* Knowledge Management and Knowledge Management Systems: Conceptual Foundations and Research Issues," *MIS Systems Quarterly* (25:1), 2001, pp. pp. 107-135.

Alvesson, M., and Willmott, H. *Making Sense of Management: A Critical Introduction,* London: Sage Publications, 1996.

Bijker, W. E., Hughes, T. P., and Pinch, T. *The Social Construction of Technological Systems: New Directions in the Sociology and History of Technology,* Cambridge, MA: The MIT Press, 1989.

Bijker, W. E., and Law, J. *Shaping Technology/Building Society: Studies in Socio-Technical Change,* Cambridge, MA: The MIT Press, 1994.

Blackler, F. "Knowledge, Knowledge Work and Organizations: An Overview and Interpretation," *Organization Studies* (16:6), 1995, pp. 1021-1046.

Bloomfield, B. P., and Vurdubakis, T. "Boundary Disputes: Negotiating the Boundary between the Technical and the Social in the Development of IT Systems," *Information Technology and People* (7:1), 1994, pp. 9-24.

Cavaye, A. L. M. "User Participation in System Development Revisited," *Information and Management* (28:5), 1995, pp. 311-323.

Collins, H. ""Stages in the Empirical Program of Relativism," *Social Studies of Science* (11), 1981, pp. 3-10.

Fleck, J. "Contingent Knowledge and Technology Development," *Technology Analysis and Strategic Management* (9:4), 1997, pp. 383-397.

Fleck, J. "Learning by Trying: The Implementation of Configurational Technology," *Research Policy* (23:6), 1994, pp. 637-652.

Franz, C. R., and Robey, D. "An Investigation of User-Led System Design: Rational and Political Perspectives," *Communications of the ACM* (27:12), 1984, pp. 1202-1209.

Friedman, A. L., and Cornford, D. S. *Computer Systems Development: History, Organization and Implementation,* Chichester, UK: John Wiley and Sons, 1989.

Hardy, C., and Clegg, S. R. "Some Dare Call It Power," in S. R. Clegg, C. Hardy, and W. R. Nord (eds.), *Handbook of Organization Studies*, London: Sage Publications, 1996, pp. 622-641.

Hislop, D., Newell, S., Scarbrough, H., and Swan, J. "Networks, Knowledge and Power: Decision Making, Politics and the Process of Innovation," *Technology Analysis and Strategic Management* (12:3), 2000, pp. 399-411.

Holmström, H. "Virtual Communities as Platforms for Product Development: An Interpretive Case Study of Customer Involvement in Online Game Development," in S. Sarkar, V. C. C., and J. I. DeGross (eds.), *Proceedings of the 22nd International Conference on Information Systems* New Orleans, LA, 2001, pp. 299-306.

Howcroft, D., and Light, B. "Reflections on Issues of Power in Packaged Software Selection," *Information Systems Journal* (16:3), 2006, pp. 215-235.

Johnson, D. G. *Computer Ethics* (3rd ed.), Upper Saddle River, NJ: Prentice Hall, 2001.

Kanellis, P., and Paul, R. J. "User Behaving Badly: Phenomena and Paradoxes from an Investigation into Information Systems Fit," *Journal of Organizational and End User Computing* (17:2), 2005, pp. 64-91.

Klein, H. K., and Myers, M. D. "A Set of Principles for Conducting and Evaluating Interpretive Field Studies in Information Systems," *MIS Quarterly* (23:1), 1999, pp. 67-94.

Knights, D., Murray, F., and Willmott, H. "Networking as Knowledge Work: A Study of Strategic Inter-Organizational Development in the Financial Services Industry," *Journal of Management Studies* (30:6), 1993, pp. 975-995.

Lamb, R., and Kling, R. "Reconceptualizing Users as Social Actors in Information Systems Research," *MIS Quarterly* (27:2), 2003, pp. 197-235.

Light, B. "Going Beyond 'Misfit' as a Reason for ERP Package Customisation," *Computers in Industry* (56:6), 2005, pp. 606-619.

Light, B. "The Maintenance Implications of the Customization of ERP Software," *The Journal of Software Maintenance: Research and Practice* (13:6), 2001, pp. 415-430.

Light, B. "A Study of Organizational Experiences of CRM Packaged Software," *Business Process Management Journal* (9:5), 2003, pp. 603-616.

Mackenzie, D., and Wajcman, J. (eds.). *The Social Shaping of Technology* (2nd ed.), Maidenhead, UK: Open University Press, 1999.

Mannheim, K. "The Sociology of Knowledge and Ideology," in C. Lemert (ed.), *Social Theory: The Multicultural and Classic Readings* (3rd ed.), Oxford, UK: Westview Press, 2004, pp. 213-216.

Markus, M. L. "Power, Politics, and MIS Implementation," *Communications of the ACM* (26:6), 1983, pp. 430-444.

Markus, M. L., and Bjørn-Andersen, N. "Power Over Users: Its Exercise By System Professionals," *Communications of the ACM* (30:6), 1987, pp. 498-504.

Marshall, N., and Brady, T. "Knowledge Management and the Politics of Knowledge: Illustrations from Complex Products and Systems," *European Journal of Information Systems* (10:2), 2001, pp. 99-112.

Myers, M. D. "Qualitative Research in Information Systems," *MISQ Discovery,* 1997 (available online at http://www.auckland.ac.nz/msis/isworld/).

Offe, C. *Industry and Inequality* (Translation of the German Edition of 1970), London: Edward Arnold Publishers Limited, 1976.

Orlikowski, W. J. "Improvising Organizational Transformation Over Time: A Situated Change Perspective," *Information Systems Research* (7:1), 1996, pp. 63-92.

Orlikowski, W. J., and Gash, D. C. "Technological Frames: Making Sense of Information Technology in Organizations," *ACM Transactions on Information Systems* (12:2), 1996, pp. 174-207.

Pinch, T., and Bijker, W. E. "The Social Construction of Facts and Artifacts: Or How the Sociology of Science and the Sociology of Technology Might Benefit Each Other," in W. E. Bijker, T. P. Hughes, and T. Pinch (eds), *The Social Construction of Technological Systems: New Directions in the Sociology and History of Technology*, Cambridge, MA: The MIT Press, 1987, pp. 17-50.

Richardson, H., and Richardson, K. "Customer Relationship Management Systems (CRM) and Information Ethics in Call Centers: 'You Are the Weakest Link. Goodbye!'," *Australian Journal of Information Systems* (9:2), 2002, pp. 166-171.

Ritzer, G. *The McDonaldization of Society* (4th ed.), London: Sage Publicatoins, 2004.

Rohracher, H. "From Passive Consumers to Active Participants: The Diverse Roles of Users in Innovation Processes," in H. Rohracher (ed.), *User Involvement in Innovation Processes: Strategies and Limitations form a Socio-Technical Perspective*, Wien, Austria: Profil, 2005, pp. 9-35.

Shapin, S. "Here and Everywhere: Sociology of Scientific Knowledge," *Annual Review of Sociology* (21), 1995, pp. 289-321.

Sørensen, K. H. "Social Shaping on the Move? On the Policy Relevance of the Social Shaping of Technology Perspective," in K. H. Sørensen and R. Williams (eds.), *Shaping Technology, Guiding Policy: Concepts, Spaces and Tools*, Cheltenham, UK: Edward Elgar, 2002, pp. 19-35.

Stewart, J., and Williams, R. "The Wrong Trousers? Beyond the Design Fallacy: Social Learning and the User," in H. Rohracher (ed.), *User Involvement in Innovation Processes: Strategies and Limitations from a Socio-Technical Perspective*, Wien, Austria: Profil, 2005, pp. 39-71.

Sutton, D. C. "What Is Knowledge and Can it be Managed?," *European Journal of Information Systems* (10:2), 2001, pp. 80-88.

Swanson, E. B., and Dans, E. "System Life Expectancy and the Maintenance Effort: Exploring their Equilibration," *MIS Quarterly* (24:2), 2000, pp. 277-297.

Taylor, P., Mulvey, G., Hymann, J., and Bain, P. "Work Organization, Control and the Experience of Work in Call Centers," *Work, Employment and Society* (16:1), 2002, pp. 133-150.

Truex III, D. P., Baskerville, R., and Klein, H. "Growing Systems in Emergent Organizations," *Communications of the ACM* (42:8), 1999, 117-123.

Wagner, E. L., and Newell, S. "Repairing ERP: Producing Social Order to Create a Working Information System," *Journal of Applied Behavioral Science* (42:1), 2006, pp. 40-57.

Wagner, E. L., Scott, S. V., and Galliers, R. "The Creation of 'Best Practice' Software: Myth, Reality and Ethics," *Information and Organization* (16:3), 2006, pp. 251-275

Walsham, G. *Interpreting Information Systems in Organizations*, Chichester, UK: John Wiley & Sons, 1993.

Walsham, G. "Interpretive Case Studies in IS Research: Nature and Method," *European Journal of Information Systems* (4:2), 1995, pp. 74-81.

Walsham, G. *Making a World of Difference: IT in a Global Context*, Chichester, UK: John Wiley and Sons, 2001.

Williams, R., and Edge, D. "The Social Shaping of Technology," in W. H. Dutton (ed.), *Information and Communication Technologies: Visions and Realities*, Oxford, UK: Oxford University Press, 1996, pp. 53-67.

Wilson, M. "Making Nursing Visible? Gender, Technology and the Care Plan as Script," *Information Technology and People* (15:2), 2002, pp. 139-158.

Yourdon, E. *Managing the Structured Techniques: Strategies for Software Development in the 1990s* (3rd ed.), Englewood Cliffs, NJ: Yourdon Press, 1986.

About the Authors

Beryl Burns is a research fellow at the Salford Business School, University of Salford, UK. Her research interests include the social and organizational aspects of information systems, surveillance technologies, and professional identity. Beryl can be reached by e-mail at B.J.Burns@ salford.ac.uk.

Ben Light is a senior lecturer at the Salford Business School, the University of Salford, UK. His research interests are concerned with the socio-technical nature of information and communications technologies in work organizations and society. Ben can be reached by e-mail at b.light@salford.ac.uk.

11 CONTEXTUAL ANALYSIS AS SUPPORT FOR SUCCESSFUL INNOVATION IN COMPLEX ENVIRONMENTS

Peter M. Bednar
University of Portsmouth
Portsmouth, UK

Christine Welch
University of Portsmouth
Portsmouth, UK

Abstract   *In order to survive and thrive, organizations need to adapt, reinvent them-selves, and innovate. However, many intentional efforts to bring about inno-vation do not succeed. In order to be successful, innovation requires the support of individuals throughout the environment in which it is emerging. In many cases, such support is not forthcoming for a variety of reasons. In this paper, the authors discuss a number of barriers that may inhibit the success of innovative practice. They then discuss a role for contextual analysis as the means to target individual engagement, and present an example of a method which could be used to conduct such analysis.*

1 INTRODUCTION

Innovation is associated with invention of novel artefacts; during the 1980s, mobile cell-phones were a significant *innovation*. However, the *Oxford Dictionary of English* defines innovation as "a new method, idea, product, etc." Technological innovations do not just relate to creation and exploitation of physical artefacts, but include behavioral, social, or thought processes—ways people in organizations think about things, or ways in which they carry out the organization's work. An example appears in Ciborra's (1993)

Please use the following format when citing this chapter:

Bednar, P., and Welch, C., 2007, in IFIP International Federation for Information Processing, Volume 235, Organizational Dynamics of Technology-Based Innovation: Diversifying the Research Agenda, eds. McMaster, T., Wastell, D., Ferneley, E., and DeGross, J. (Boston: Springer), pp. 149-161.

discussion of design in relation to strategic information systems. Drawing on a number of cases studied, he points to difficulties in exploiting the full innovative potential of new developments due to unexpected consequences: "events, behaviors and features of systems and the people who use them fall outside the scope of original plans and specifications" (p. 178). He suggests these systems are not so much designed as emergent—early adopters recognizing features that were initially overlooked or unplanned, but prove to be useful. In the second millennium, the "mobile" phone is surrounded by innovation, as much socio-cultural and fashion-oriented as technical, if not more so. Innovation-in-use is in focus here. Innovation involves creation of new information about resources, goals, processes, etc., and the existing stores of skill and competence residing in an organization represent at the same time potential for successful innovation and a constraint upon it (Pralahad and Hamel 1990).

Ciborra reminds us that there is always a knowledge gap to be addressed when tackling innovation, and that there are only two ways to bridge it: by incremental muddling-through (*bricolage*), or by radical learning processes which confront existing routines and core competences. The latter may be painful for individuals as well as organizations, as it involves moving out of a zone of familiarity to confront uncertainty (Ciborra 1993). Rogers (2003), in his well-known work on diffusion of innovation, highlights a number of attributes which appear to influence the rate of adoption. These include *complexity* (i.e., individual perceptions of how easy the novelty is to understand and use), *trialability* (i.e., the degree to which individuals have an opportunity to experiment on a risk-limited basis), and *observability* (i.e., the degree to which results of innovation can be viewed by others and described). We suggest that all of this may be resolved into one issue, which impacts upon the success of technological innovation, and this is the way in which individuals, and the organization in which they are located, deal with *uncertainty*. Michael (1985), cited in Schein (1992), refers to empirical evidence showing that managers' ability to tolerate uncertainty may be of great importance to organizational success during disturbance and change. People often react to conditions of uncertainty by seeking ways to simplify their problem-space. They may attempt to break down a complex problem into smaller ones, or make assumptions that ready solutions must exist if only they can be "found." Indeed, complexity is a phenomenon that arises through perceptions of actors involved in a scenario, who choose to regard it as complex. Checkland (1999) reflects that his early work with the soft systems methodology involved a movement away from perception of obvious problems to be solved, toward a perspective that there were situations regarded by some people as problematic.

Organizational problems, particularly where new initiatives are considered, are experienced as unstructured. Successful implementation of innovation is an inherently political process (Argyris 1990; Weick and Sutcliffe 2002). Weick (1995) discusses ways in which individuals transform a perceived problem-space that is unstructured (uncertain) into a *structured* uncertainty, through sense-making processes. In attempting to make sense of an unstructured problem, people try to move from a position of not knowing what to do, to a position of knowledge about a range of alternative possibilities from which a solution might be created (i.e., ambiguity). Unfortunately, organizational decision making is always subject to pressure of time. In many instances, this can lead to a desire to reach an early resolution of uncertainty, and thus to over-simplification of complex problem-spaces. A rush to early consensus on design or implementation of innovation may inhibit the process of emergence to which Ciborra (1993) refers.

In this paper, the term *contextual analysis* is used to mean inquiry into a number of contextual dependencies experienced by actors contemplating innovation/change. Examples of contextual dependencies include experiences of work roles, of political dimensions in the organization, or even of physical aspects of the work environment. The authors believe contextual inquiry to be useful in efforts to bring about beneficial change in human activity systems. Its benefit lies in the way in which it addresses the nature of transformation processes, and it may be conducted before, during, and after actions for change. Contextual inquiry may be useful in any environment actors choose to treat as complex. Traditionally, in scientific investigation, perception of complexity depends upon the qualities of the instrument used (e.g., a drop of water appears very simple until it is examined under a microscope, at which point the complex array of biological and chemical constituents contained within it emerges). We suggest contextual inquiry as an instrument enabling emergence of complexity in organizational situations. The authors agree with a widespread view (see Argyris 1990; Bateson 1972; Nissen 2007) that individuals need to become engaged with a process of innovation in order to support it successfully. We believe that collections of inquiries into multiple levels of specific contextual dependencies may lead to emergence of insights which provide support for engagement.

In the next section of this paper, the authors discuss barriers which many people have identified as inhibitors of successful innovation. Here, they are addressed together as a collective of contextual dependencies. We suggest how contextual analysis provides a key to overcoming them, and hence supports organizational members to bring about a necessary transformation of uncertainty into ambiguity. The following section outlines one method for contextual inquiry (the strategic systemic thinking framework), which supports individuals to explore these contextual dependencies and create new perspectives on innovation and change.

2 BARRIERS TO SUCCESSFUL INNOVATION

C. West Churchman (1971) has suggested that an inquiring system has the capability of asking itself what would be the characteristics of an inquiring system that did not function in accordance with the tenets of its own design. It is recognized in cybernetics that every distinct dimension of a complex system needs to be controlled in a way which is appropriate to its characteristics. This is Ashby's (1964) law of requisite variety. By analogy, every dimension of a complex problem space needs to be addressed with appropriate analytical approaches. We do not necessarily need a multiplicity of tools and techniques, catering for many different threads of problem spaces. What is required is exercise of human ingenuity to reflect and to adapt those methods available to us in appropriate ways (Ciborra 2002). We consider that individual engagement with innovative practice may be supported by methods that explore contextual dependencies. However, analysts wishing to adopt such methods first need to contemplate aspects of the problem space surrounding innovation. Since the problem space is unknown and uncertain in its boundaries, it is unlikely that a predefined archetype of method (which assumes a known problem) would suffice in itself without adaptation. Therefore, analysts need to develop an approach that specifically targets the needs of individuals from a particular inquiry, in a particular context. This approach needs to be designed to address those barriers to innovation which the analysts' preliminary investigations suggest to be present.

In business organizations, consultation can take place among stakeholders about initiatives that are planned. The question arises how far this is comprehensive, or represents a true attempt to establish dialogue, and how far the resultant opinions actually inform decisions about innovation. Some authorities (e.g., Argyris and Schön 1978, 1996) appear to suggest that individuals' views within an organizational setting are not always expressed effectively, nor are they necessarily acted upon. Change in behavior is much more difficult to achieve than mere descriptions of change. There is often a difference between our descriptions of what we think we do (what Argyris and Schön have called *espoused theories*) and what others can perceive that we do (our *theories-in-use*) (Argyris and Schön 1978). People do not always perceive or admit to this difference themselves. Efforts are required to surface these problematic issues in the form of inquiry into the informal and unconscious behavior of individuals (their intra-individual contexts) and the interactions between individuals (their interindividual contexts). The word *communication* could describe either a one-way process in which a message travels from sender to receiver, or a two-way process in which the receiver responds by providing feedback (see Grunig 1992). Communication processes might be symmetrical, reflecting equal degrees of engagement by the participants, or asymmetrical where one party is engaged or empowered to a greater degree than the other. Effective consultation on change requires a genuine engagement by both parties in a constructive and open dialogue. We believe that methods for inquiry are needed which provide specific support for creation of such a dialogue.

Two-way communication can provide for feedback between the parties. We frequently experience asymmetrical, two-way communication during political campaigns. Attempts may be made to persuade voters to a particular point of view through persuasive speeches. Sometimes "inconvenient" facts will be omitted or distorted in an attempt to engineer the goodwill of voters. In the course of the campaign, there may be opportunities for feedback, either directly (e.g., through hustings), or indirectly (through opinion polls). In contrast, two-way symmetrical communication would ideally involve dialogue between parties, who engage in an effort to interpret one another's contributions in order to promote a meeting of minds. Perfect symmetry in communication may be impossible to achieve. However, a participant in dialogue may perceive it to be more or less symmetrical. Each party could make an effort to put forward a truthful view, listen to the response of the other, and proceed to a discussion of areas of disagreement. Argyris (1990) has argued that the process of symmetrical two-way communication is a basic foundation which is a prerequisite for a learning organization to be built or sustained. We view symmetrical communication as a continuously changing process of inquiry, which is contextually dependent. Some aspects of contextual dependency are further developed later in this paper.

If managers are to promote support for a productive learning cycle in their organization, in relation to innovation, then individuals need to be motivated and empowered to think and express themselves, and to collaborate and share their ideas. Managers need to recognize a possibility that individuals could use their creative powers in ways that undermine such aspirations, or subvert them to other ends. Argyris (2004) draws attention to defensive strategies, which are sometimes adopted in organizations where conditions of great uncertainty are experienced. He points to an example from an empirical study by Van de Ven and Polley (1992), where colleagues pursued collusive action strategies of impression management. Here, members of a project team, together with resource managers, actively avoided recognizing errors and difficulties, so as to avoid embarrassment arising from the challenge of sense-making. One impact of these tactics was, of course, to inhibit opportunities for learning through trial and error, and reflection. Argyris highlights for us an ethical double bind, which he perceives to be involved. These individuals colluded in order to cover up disagreeable truths through feelings of loyalty to their colleagues and their organization, while attempting to show integrity by not exposing this process. We can turn to the work of Gregory Bateson (1972) for further illumination of situations where individuals are caught in a double bind. As conscious human beings, we have no choice but to reflect on our experience. The question for us all to address, however, is the form this reflection takes. Defensive strategies may tend to perpetuate the double bind in which individuals are caught. Bateson has suggested that an individual may need to adopt an observer perspective to enable herself to break out from such entrapment.

Organizational knowledge may not be distributed in a homogeneous way. Seely Brown and Duguid (2002), for instance, point out how communities of practice emerge within organizations. While organizations may develop a distinctive culture over time, it is also likely that there will be smaller groups within the organization who have more interests in common with each other than with colleagues generally. These clusters of individuals develop distinctive values and norms of their own. Sometimes, such a community within a particular organization finds more common ground with a similar community in the outside world than with their own colleagues. These authors point to examples where organizational knowledge has proved to be both "sticky" and "leaky" when it relates to innovation. If the prevailing paradigm by which members of a company make sense of their environment is nonconducive to inventions, those with creative ideas may be forced to set themselves apart. Their ideas do not then permeate the organization freely—their knowledge is sticky. However, through networks of practice they develop across organizational boundaries, ideas may leak from the organization to more receptive ground elsewhere (for discussion of Xerox PARC's failure to exploit GUI, which was subsequently taken up by Apple, see Seely Brown and Duguid 2002, p. 159).

What is clear from this is that managers' ability to develop and support an environment that promotes organizational learning, and helps to promote paradigm shift (Kuhn 1970), may be a key to success. It has been suggested that organizations can become "psychic prisons" in which individuals experience entrapment within their own constructed realities (Morgan 1997). Such entrapment prevents individuals and groups from espousing new knowledge if it conflicts with established and familiar patterns. Weick and Sutcliffe (2002) reinforce this when they suggest a need to promote a collective state of "mindfulness." More specifically, they suggest a need for on-going attention to existing expectations in the light of new experiences, and, simultaneously, engagement with creation of new expectations. A state of mindfulness would be characterized by a desire by individuals and groups to learn from their mistakes, a focus on disconfirming, rather than confirming behavior, and a respect for uncertainty. There would be a prevailing recognition that knowledge has limits, and that professional behavior and competence depend upon making explicit consideration of those boundaries.

An organization that successfully encourages a creative culture of mindfulness may be regarded as one that is able to support a constructive dialectic, between meaningful use of innovation and reflection upon that use. In a dialectical relationship between use and reflection on use, each element is subject to change. Reflection triggers change in use, and such change triggers further reflection. Lived human experience, and reflection upon that experience, seems to shape a double helix (further discussion of this double helix metaphor may be found in Nissen 2007). It is suggested that failures of innovative projects come about through lack of support for individuals and groups to engage in learning. We use the term *failure* here to mean a problematized difference between intended consequences and unintended (but recognized) consequences of design and action, *from a specific observer's point of view* (Markus and Robey 2004). This last point we consider to be most important because it highlights a further requirement for learning to take place. This is a *desire* to engage in learning activities (Bednar and Welch 2006). What incentive is required to induce individuals to espouse learning for change? What benefits would they derive and how might they become aware of these benefits? If intrinsic benefits to individuals are not apparent, can extrinsic inducements be appropriate? *Desire* for innovation may exist, but how is it to be articulated, assessed, and acted upon within the organizational context? If motivation is a necessary condition for adoption, then learning for meaningful use is an equally important aspect of socialization. In the words of Chris Argyris,

> It is not possible for human beings to engage *de novo* the full complexity of the environment in which they exist. Life would pass them by. Human beings deal with the challenge by constructing theories of action that they can use to act in concrete situations (2004, p. 8).

When an attempt is made to evaluate effectiveness in managing or designing organizational change, concepts of analysis become important. Good practice requires an understanding that addresses intrinsic and contextually dependent characteristics of organizational activities. An understanding can only come about through relevant evaluative and analytical strategies (Avgerou and Madon 2004). Evaluation can be described as a result of both inquiring and reflecting thought processes (i.e., mental activity intrinsically dependent upon a demonstrated, contextually dependent desire to explore a certain problem space). We see anaysis as an inquiry into the assumed-to-be unknown and/or a questioning of the assumed-to-be known. Evaluation, we suggest, is a consolidating process, where judgments are made, and assumed truths and knowledge are incorporated into some kind of hierarchy. Together, an analysis (i.e., creation of new knowledge) and evaluation (i.e., categorization of existing knowledge) represent closing of a learning circle. Any conscious reflection over the requirements for a higher quality learning circle could become a daunting exercise as it involves raising the quality of knowing. The concept of the learning organization, presented by Argyris and Schön (1978, 1996) is suggested as a means to reflect upon and reevaluate knowledge created by individuals within an organizational context. At this point, it is useful to consider the possibility of multiple orders of learning (see, for example, the discussion by Bateson 1972, p. 287). These are described by Argyris and Schön (1978) in terms of single or double loops. When an individual needs to solve an immediate problem (i.e., close a perceived gap between expected and actual experience), she may harness her sense-making processes within a context of existing goals, values, plans, and rules, without questioning their appropriateness. However, if she goes beyond this to challenge received wisdom and to critically appraise the assumptions previously applied, double-loop learning occurs. We view the resulting process as creating a productive learning spiral, and consider this to be essential to successful organizational innovation.

3   CONTEXTUAL ANALYSIS

We consider contextual analysis to offer a key to unlocking many of the barriers outlined above. Methods for analysis that specifically support exploration of contextual dependencies could lead to creation of alternative perspectives on innovation. The impact of innovation can be very significant for organizational development. Therefore, a high standard of analysis, uncovering needs and expectations that members of the organization have from the proposed innovation, is crucial. For example, evidence exists to suggest that an effective inquiry into the fit between information systems processes and business processes in a specific organization could make or break the business (Markus and Robey 2004). While any expenditure of resources faces an opportunity cost, we believe that time and money spent in promoting effective inquiry will be justified. The importance of organizational analysis, to make sense of possible business process enhancements through application of new ideas, routines, or technologies, cannot be overemphasized. Implementation practices have important consequences for the political and social systems within organizations.

One relevant example is Nestlé's attempt to introduce enterprise resource planning (ERP) systems in the late 1990s/early 2000s (see Worthen 2002). A clear business case could be made for systems to enable the company to act as one entity worldwide, and thus make cost efficiencies and manipulate its market power to greater effect. However, attempts to introduce SAP systems based on best practice in business processes were initially perceived by management as unsuccessful. Reflection by management highlighted lack of involvement of key stakeholders and concentration on technical matters as contributing factors. An independent analyst, whose assessment of the company potentially affected its share price, commented that the project "touched the corporate culture" and was thus a risk. Ultimately, the project was recommenced from scratch with a more inclusive approach. This case illustrates that, if inquiries conducted prior to, and during, introduction of an innovation are confined to a superficial examinations of goals, tasks, and decisions, the results may be very unsatisfactory. Successful implementation depends upon effective inquiry into a multitude of issues in the organizational arena forming the backdrop to any novel development (see Walsham 1993).

In order to overcome the problem of sticky knowledge relating to innovation, outlined by Seely Brown and Duguid (2002), everyone concerned in the organizational context requires enhanced understanding of the problem space. Who is supposed to create a better understanding, on behalf of whom, how, and of what? Experience suggests that expert-dominated (and/or management-imposed) solutions to organizational problems are not always bought into by the actors. This has led researchers to consider participative methods for engaging actors in creative processes. Examples can be seen in the field of information systems development, for example client-led Design (Stowell and West 1994) or the ETHICS methodology (Mumford 1994). In this type of approach, a focus is placed on a communication gap. It could be assumed that users simply do not have sufficient awareness of their own needs to be able to communicate them effectively to an analyst, and that if techniques can be found to bridge this gap, then all will be well. We argue that, while efforts to overcome the communication gap are worthwhile, this view still fails to address contextually dependent dimensions of complex organizational problem spaces. It is not simply that the users are unable to articulate their preexisting requirements, and therefore need a developed language and tools. First, they must be able to create an understanding of what those requirements might be, in relation to a problem space that represents their experience of working life. From our point of view, support for this creative process is vital to any vision of successful innovative practice. Furthermore, we believe that participation by actors is not sufficient; a genuinely collaborative approach is needed, in which actors own and control the inquiry for themselves. Analytical efforts must continue throughout the process of change. Those individuals in whose environments innovative artefacts, processes, or methods will reside must own and control the analysis, supported by professional facilitators, in order to be able to explore their understandings of their experiences.

The inherent complexities of organizational life, and the uncertainty associated with organizational contexts, lead us to highlight epistemological problems for a foundational view of knowledge. Opinions differ about the meaning of the term *knowledge*. As we focus attention on processes of knowledge creation and sharing, it is useful to consider this. A discussion is offered by Davenport and Prusak.

> Knowledge is a fluid mix of framed experience, values, contextual information, expert insight and grounded intuition that provides an environment and framework for evaluating and incorporating new experiences and information. It originates and is applied in the minds of knowers. In organizations, it often becomes embedded not only in documents or repositories but also in organizational routines, processes, practices and norms (Davenport and Prusak 2000, p. 5).

We view contextual analysis as an approach that addresses such problems and their implications for research into organizational systems. An analyst taking a relative view of knowledge needs to look critically at a series of exemplary approaches, which use different ontologies and epistemologies. For example, Information Systems research relating to contextual dependencies attempts, *inter alia*, to build on previous core research in information systems (e.g., by exploring ways in which contemporary open systems thinking can be applied to specific critical issues) (see Maturana and Varela 1980; Nissen 2007). Particular emphasis is placed on multiple sense-making processes, and ways in which these are played out within the frameworks of learning organizations. Some researchers have focused on individual or group managerial perspectives, such as where a business manager is a user (Carlsson 1993; Ciborra 1993). More recently, some efforts to deal with context have involved the use of actor-network theory (Latour 1999). Contextual dependency as a concept is relevant here because it supports a focus of inquiry on unique individuals, and their beliefs, thoughts, and actions, in specific situations and contexts. This kind of inquiry is intended to provide support to individuals in a contextually dependent creation of necessary knowledge. This in turn enables successful communication, analysis, evaluation, and, eventually, implementation of innovation.

We do not suggest that contextual analysis should necessarily replace other, traditional approaches to innovation. It is a complementary approach which may help those involved to avoid a conflict related to unproblematic assumptions of ontological beliefs and logical empiricism. For example, analysts sometimes hold unquestioned beliefs of unproblematic objectivity and truths. Like some of the traditional communicational theories, traditional approaches to organizational analysis may be based on assumptions around a sender-receiver model (see the earlier discussion). A contextual approach to analysis is intended to focus instead on individual perspectives. Thus an inquiry based on contextual analysis would not ask what an organization wants to achieve. Instead, it would support the actors to ask what they themselves want to achieve in the organizational context. For instance, they would question what roles and specific purposes their activities have; what makes their unique situations recognizable within the organizational problem space. The focus of inquiry is, therefore, individual assumptions and needs within the space of an open organizational system *from the actors' own points of view.* We describe this as a bottom up perspective on innovation. Contextual analysis, as an approach which tries to take contextual dependencies into consideration, may represent a response to escalation in complexity in organizational life.

In our view, approaches to analysis depend in practice on ways in which a problem space is framed, and by whom. This principle has been given thorough consideration by Ulrich (2001), in his extensive discussion of boundary critique. In soft systems methodology (Checkland 1999), for example, a consideration of individual *Weltanschauungen* (or world views) is required of those attempting to explore complex problem space. (For a contemporary discussion of the role of *Weltanschauungen* in analyses, see Bergvall-Kåreborn 2002.) With the help of analysis relating to narratives of mental constructs, relationships can be discussed within a more context-dependent framework of reasoning. One such approach is discussed next.

The strategic systemic thinking framework (Bednar 2000) aims to apply specially adapted methods to investigate how people construct understanding and meaning, and how need for knowledge, and new knowledge, are created by individuals within this process. The framework was originally developed through one of the author's experiences over a number of years in industry in dealing with complex problem spaces. Discussions later took place following a series of workshops for managers on systemic methods. These led to an initial view of a framework for contextual inquiry which has been developed over a number of years of further research. Basing inquiry in hermeneutic dialectics involves recognition of uncertainties and ambiguities inherent in socially constructed views of human activity. This type of inquiry seeks for transparency as well as clarity in investigations, in order to emphasize the self-awareness of individuals. Efforts to achieve precision, rather than transparency, involve a danger of separation between observations made and the unique perspectives of observer and observed (e.g., Maturana and Varela 1980; Nissen 2007). The intention behind SST is to promote inquiry into organizational knowledge creation and sharing, which avoids what Radnitzky (1970) describes as an artificial separation of theory and practice.

There are three aspects of inquiry using SST—intra-analysis, inter-analysis, and value analysis—which may be undertaken in any order and are iterative. Intra-analysis supports individuals in exploring their own perspectives on the perceived situation. A variety of methods such as rich pictures or brainstorming are used to support exploration of individual sense-making processes, and creation of individual narratives. Inter-analysis provides a vehicle for groups of people to communicate their individual narratives to one another, and attempt to create an understanding of each one. Members of the group then discuss one another's narratives in order to create a view of the range of different alternative opinions expressed in relation to the problem space. The purpose here is to create an enriched dialogue among actors without seeking a premature consensus. Value analysis, an examination of the known, inquires into what has been learned from intra/inter-analyses and attempts to relate it to a frame of reference. Actors conduct an examination of values influencing and constraining the analyses, consider prioritization from political and cultural perspectives, and assess risks. The overall purpose of SST is to support inquiry into multiple levels of contextual dependencies, in order to enable creation of new knowledge, communication of new perspectives, consolidation, and evaluation.

4 CONCLUSIONS

Contextual inquiry takes into account the messiness of everyday experience, and individuals' attempts to search for meaning through sense-making activity. Some approaches to organizational analysis are intended to simplify problem spaces, in a desire to steer a manageable path through rich and diverse sources. However, the authors of this paper propose instead a structured, systemic "complexification" through inquiry into contextual dependencies. Such an inquiry draws upon unique individual beliefs, actions, and perspectives in specific organizational situations, and the living history of an organizational group from each individual's point of view. However, it must be noted that we consider that methods seeking precision and clarity and those seeking transparency may be regarded as complementary to one another.

Processes through which people create and recreate their knowing are at once deeply personal, contextual and social. Knowing comes about through perception of change. This draws upon Bateson's (1972) idea of a "difference that makes a difference." Seely Brown and Duguid reflect on this point as follows:

> The background has to be in place for the information to register. The forces that shape the background are, rather, the tectonic social forces, always at work, within which and against which individuals configure their identity. These create not only grounds for reception, but grounds for interpretation, judgment, and understanding (2002, p. 139).

The contextually dependent nature of any problem description, including meaning and defined purpose, means that responsibility for understanding, sense-making, and creation of a problem redefinition cannot be delegated to an expert (or devolved upon any technique or technology). Every individual will perceive purpose and relevance from her/his own unique perspective, and must therefore take ownership of the problem space and be her/his own analyst. However, means are needed to support and facilitate people in their contextual inquiries, sponsored by management. This must then, by definition, involve some delegation. There is a paradox for us here, in that each individual's espoused theories and theories-in-use will be distinctive and cannot be resolved into a simple consensus (Argyris and Schön 1978). Therefore, in order to bring about a supportive environment for purposeful change, we need a recognition that this resolution cannot be achieved.

We have pointed to a number of factors which contribute to success or failure in making sense of, and responding to, uncertainty in complex problem spaces. We have demonstrated that a number of barriers exist within organizational environments which inhibit successful innovation and change. Our conclusion is that support for successful innovation in complex environments requires commitment from the main organizational protagonists. Promotion of commitment for change is in itself a political agenda, as recognized by both Argyris (1990) and Weick (Weick 1995; Weick and Sutcliffe 2002). An essential factor in the success of innovative projects may be a combination of individual and group sense-making processes which require support through constructive dialogue. We argue here that there is a need for managers to promote a culture of mindfulness so that a learning organization may be created. In an environment where uncertainty is embraced, rather than feared, and second order learning is fostered, successful implementation of innovation may be supported.

References

Argyris, C. *Overcoming Organizational Defenses: facilitating Organizational Learning*, Engle-wood Cliffs, NJ: Prentice Hall, 1990.

Argyris, C. *Reasons and Rationalizations: The Limits to Organizational Knowledge*, New York: Oxford University Press, 2004.

Argyris, C., and Schön D. A. *Organizational Learning*, Reading, MA: Addison Wesley, 1978.

Argyris, C., and Schön D. A. *Organizational Learning II: Theory, Method and Practice*, Reading, MA: Addison Wesley, 1996.

Ashby, W. R. *An Introduction to Cybernetics*, London: Methuen, 1964.

Avgerou, C, and Madon, S "Framing IS Studies: Understanding the Social Context of IS Innovation," in C. Avgerou, C Ciborra, and F. Land (eds.), *The Social Study of Information and Communication Technology: Innovation, Actors, and Contexts*, New York: Oxford University Press, 2004, pp 162-182.

Bateson, G. *Steps to an Ecology of Mind, Part III*, Chicago: University of Chicago Press, 1972.

Bednar, P. M. "A Contextual Integration of Individual and Organizational Learning Perspectives as Part of IS Analysis," *Informing Science* (3:3), 2000.

Bednar, P. M., and Welch, C. "Incentive and Desire: Covering a Missing Category," in *Proceedings of Mediterranean Conference on Information Systems: A Comparative Distinction of Mediterranean Information Systems*, San Servolo, Venice, Italy, October 5-9, 2006, pp. 53-61.

Bergvall-Kåreborn, B. "Enriching the Model-Building Phase of Soft Systems Methodology," *Systems Research and Behavioral Science* (19:1), 2002, pp. 27-48.

Carlsson, S. *A Longitudinal Study of User Developed Decision Support Systems*, Ph.D. Thesis, Department of Informatics, Lund University, Sweden, 1993.

Churchman C. W. *The Design of Inquiring Systems: Basic Concepts of Systems and Organizations*, New York: Basic Books, 1971.

Checkland, P. *Systems Thinking, Systems Practice: A 30-Year retrospective*. Chichester, England: Wiley, 1999.

Ciborra, C. U. *The Labyrinths of Information: Challenging the Wisdom of Systems*, Oxford, England: Oxford University Press, 2002.

Ciborra, C. U. *Teams, Markets and Systems: Business Innovation and Information Technology*, Cambridge, England: Cambridge University Press, 1993.

Davenport, T. H., and Prusak, L. *Working Knowledge: How Organizations Manage What They Know*, Boston: Harvard Business School Press, 2000.

Grunig, J E *Excellence in Public Relations and Communication Management*, Mahwah, NJ: Lawrence Erlbaum Associates, 1992.

Kuhn, T. S. *The Structure of Scientific Revolutions*, Chicago: University of Chicago Press, 1970.

Latour, B. *Pandora's Hope: Essays on the Reality of Science Studies*, Cambridge, MA: Harvard University Press, 1970.

Markus, M. L., and Robey, D. "Why Stuff Happens: Explaining the Unintended Consequences of Using IT," in K. V. Andersen and M. T. Vendelo (eds.), *The Past and Future of Information Systems*, New York: Elsevier, 2004, pp. 61-93.

Maturana, H., and Varela, F. *Autopoeisis and Cognition*, Dordrecht, Holland: D.Reidel Publishing, 1980.

Michael, D. N. *On Learning to Plan—and Planning to Learn*, San Francisco: Jossey-Bass, 1985.

Morgan, G. *Images of Organization*, Thousand Oaks, CA: Sage Publications, 1997.

Mumford, E. *Systems Design: Ethical Tools for Ethical Change*, Baskingstoke, England: Macmillan Press, 1996.

Nissen, H-E. "Beyond Double Helix Relationships to Understand and Change Informing Systems," *Informing Science Journal,* Special Issue: A Double Helix Relationship of Use and Redesign in IS?, 2007 (forthcoming).

Pearsall, J., and Hanks, P. (eds.). *The Oxford Dictionary of English* (2nd revised edition), Oxford: Oxford University Press, 2005

Pralahad, C. K., and Hamel, G. "The Core Competences of the Corporation," *Harvard Business Review* (68:3), May-June 1990, pp. 79-93

Radnitzky, G. *Contemporary Schools of Metascience*, Göteborg, Sweden: Akademiforlaget, 1970.

Rogers, E. M. *Diffusion of Innovation* (5th ed.), New York: Free Press, 2003.

Schein, E. H. *Organizational Culture and Leadership* (2nd ed.), San Francisco: Jossey-Bass, 1992.

Seely Brown, J., and Duguid, P. *The Social Life of Information*, Boston: Harvard Business School Press, 2002.

Stowell, F., and West, D. *Client-Led Design: A Systemic APproach to Information Systems Definition*, London: McGraw-Hill, 1994.

Ulrich, W. "Critically Systemic Discourse: A Discursive Approach to Reflective Practice in ISD, Parts 1 and 3," *The Journal of Information Technology Theory and Application* (3:3), 2001, pp. 55-106.

Van de Ven, A. H., and Polley, D. "Learning While Innovating," *Organization Science* (3:2), February 1992, pp. 92-116.

Walsham, G. *Interpreting Information Systems in Organizations*, Chichester, England: Wiley. 1993.

Weick, K. *Sense-Making in Organizations*, Thousand Oaks, CA: Sage Publicatoins, 1995.

Weick, K., and Sutcliffe, K. *Managing the Unexpected*, San Francisco: Jossey-Bass, 2002.

Worthen, B. "Nestlé's ERP Odyssey," *CIO Magazine*, May 15, 2002 (available online at http://www.cio.com/archive/051502/nestle.html).

About the Authors

Peter M. Bednar is originally from an engineering background and has several years of relevant industrial experience. Since 1997, he has been working as an academic. His research covers contextual analysis, organizational change, and information systems development, and he has published several book chapters and many articles in these fields. He is currently a senior lecturer in the School of Computing at the University of Portsmouth, UK, and is also affiliated with the Department of Informatics at Lund University, Sweden. He can be reached by e-mail at peter.bednar@ics.lu.se.

Christine Welch is a principal lecturer in the Department of Strategy and Business Systems, part of the Business School at the University of Portsmouth, UK. Her research interests include critical system thinking, contextual analysis, and knowledge management. She has published a number of articles in these fields. Christine is also a member of the board of the UK System Society. She can be reached by e-mail at christine.welch@port.ac.uk.

12

THE IDENTITY, DYNAMICS, AND DIFFUSION OF MIS[1]

Tor J. Larsen
Norwegian School of Management
Oslo, Norway

Linda Levine
Software Engineering Institute
Carnegie Mellon University
Pittsburgh, PA U.S.A.

Abstract   *This paper examines the key lines of inquiry that have been used in research focused on the identity, dynamics, and diffusion of MIS, as well as the strengths and weaknesses associated with each approach. We present five primary means: (1) citation analysis, (2) classification analysis, including meta-analysis, (3) editorials and opinion pieces, (4) historical surveys of previous work, and (5) forums. We use the term "line of inquiry" since this allows us some latitude in considering dissimilar approaches—methods as well as communication channels. Using examples from the published literature on the status of MIS, we define and illustrate the five approaches. Subsequently, we discuss the strengths and weaknesses of each. Where possible, we extend the discussion to consider the implications of these lines of inquiry for future research.*

Keywords   Management information systems, lines of inquiry, genre

---

[1]The authors are listed in alphabetical order but have contributed equally to the article.

Please use the following format when citing this chapter:

Larsen, T. J., and Levine, L., 2007, in IFIP International Federation for Information Processing, Volume 235, Organizational Dynamics of Technology-Based Innovation: Diversifying the Research Agenda, eds. McMaster, T., Wastell, D., Ferneley, E., and DeGross, J. (Boston: Springer), pp. 163-177.

1   INTRODUCTION

No end appears to be in sight for the longstanding discussions on the status of the field of Management Information Systems (MIS)[2]—its identity and its value, with respect to its role as a field, within the university, and in relation to industry practice (Alavi and Carlson 1992; Alter 2003; Avison 2003; Benbasat and Weber 1996; Benbasat and Zmud 2003; Briggs et al. 1999; Carr 2003; Ives et al. 2004; Lyytinen and King 2004; Robey 1996; Orlikowski and Baroudi 1991; Orlikowski and Iacono 2001; Paul 2002; Weber 1987, 2003; Westfall 1999). This self examination reveals two persistent themes. The first focuses on coherence in MIS and in framing questions such as: Does MIS have a core and overarching theory? A cumulative tradition? Are other disciplines referencing MIS? (See Baskerville and Myers 2002; Davis 2000; Pfeffers and Ya 2003; Vessey et al. 2002; Walstrom and Hardgrave 2001.) The second theme revolves around the matter of rigor versus relevance, which is also occasionally expressed as a debate between academic and practical concerns (Benbasat and Zmud 1999; Goles and Hirschheim 2001; Hirschheim and Klein 2003; Nurminen and Eriksson 1999; Robey and Markus 1998). If we are to come to grips with these issues we need to consider the approaches and assumptions that have grown up within our discourse.

Further refinement on the nature of MIS has examined its core and subareas. One approach distinguishes between the internalist view (Westin et al. 1994) and the externalist view (Whitley 1984). The internalist view builds on Kuhn's (1970) notion of a dominant paradigm in the tradition of normal science, which is interspersed with periods of revolution. This dominant paradigm takes the form of an overarching theory, which is subscribed to by a research community. The externalist view treats a discipline as a "complex network of interacting researchers whose ideas may stem from a number of disciplines who therefore form an intellectual community" (Vessey et al. 2002, p. 132).

Benbasat and Zmud (2003) argue that a definition of the IS artifact can serve as the platform for defining appropriate MIS research. Ives et al. (2004) present a strong counterargument. They advocate the field of MIS research is best seen as a "colonial system," where colonies have strong inner ties but loose outer connections. They assert that the glue in MIS is a common interest in information technology and information systems. Similarly, King (1993) describes the discipline of MIS as driven by "a shared interest in a phenomenal event—the rise and consequences of radical improvement in information technology....[and any] attempt to build a long-standing academic field on a phenomenon, especially a revolutionary phenomenon, will fail" (p. 293). As Fitzgerald (2003) aptly observes, "In IS, we stand with our backs to the technology, the computer, the machine or whatever, and look outward towards the world at large" (p. 227).

The purpose of this paper is to provide a preliminary examination of the key lines of inquiry that have been used in research focused on the identity, dynamics, and diffu-

---

[2]Different labels are used to refer to the field, for example: Information Technology (IT), Information Communication Technology (ICT), Information Systems (IS), Management Information Systems (MIS), and Information Management (IM). Knowledge Management Systems (KMS) is another term that is increasingly in use. Each term has its proponents; however, the terms are often used interchangeably. For the sake of clarity and consistency, we use the term Management Information Systems.

sion of MIS, as well as the strengths and weaknesses associated with each approach.[3] We have discerned five primary means: (1) citation analysis, (2) classification analysis, (3) editorials and opinion pieces, (4) historical surveys, and (5) forums. Loosely speaking, each of these represents a type of investigation—or in the case of forum, a place for discussion—into the identity and dynamics of MIS. We use the term *line of inquiry* since this allows us some latitude in considering dissimilar approaches—methods as well as communication channels. Using examples from the published literature on the status of MIS, we define and illustrate the five approaches; subsequently, we discuss the strengths and weaknesses of each. Where possible, we extend the discussion to consider the implications of these lines of inquiry.

2   LINES OF INQUIRY

The delineation of the five lines of inquiry has followed from earlier research we conducted on the identity and dynamics of the field of MIS using classification and citation analyses (Larsen and Levine 2005) and our reading of the related literature, as well as online discussion, on the identity crisis in MIS. Throughout our investigations, we have asked: What are the best avenues for examining the field of MIS? And which of these avenues and perspectives are reliant on formal methods (in data collection and analysis) in order to reach conclusions? The five lines of inquiry are addressed in the subsections that follow.

2.1   Classification Analysis

Classification studies constitute one of the major approaches to investigating patterns in research (Vessey et al. 2002). One specific instance employs meta-analysis techniques. Meta-analysis uses the common variables and relationships in empirical data to discern general and overarching patterns across different studies. Another classification approach takes a broader perspective and consists of analysis of topic or subject matter. This process involves selecting a topic and reviewing many journals and conference proceedings in order to find evidence of patterns, trends, similarities, and differences. The articles considered in a topical analysis may be either quantitative or qualitative and need not adhere to any common method.

   Vessey et al. (2002) perform a classification study pertaining to diversity in the IS field. They employ five dimensions of diversity: reference discipline, level of analysis,

---

[3] A point about the identity and dynamics of MIS and the role of a paradigm is in order. We considered the analytical approach that Pfeffer (1993) describes for verifying the existence of a disciplinary paradigm. Pfeffer forwards 14 variables that should be represented when a paradigm exists, including funding levels of departments, connection between productivity and pay, department-head turnover or average tenure, and cross-citation practices among fields. The general sentiment is that MIS does not have a paradigm. Hence, we concluded that the most rewarding approach would be to focus on key lines of inquiry—the means by which research issues, constructs, and variables have been investigated and communicated.

topic, research approach, and method. These dimensions are then individually refined into subcategories. They identify five top IS journals and code their articles, from 1995 through 1999, according to these dimensions and subcategories. This study approach is based on classification by inspection.

A more formal and rigorous instance of classification analysis is co-word analysis. Monarch (2000) surveys the history of research on co-word analysis. He describes the technique as revealing

> patterns and trends in technical discourse by measuring the association strengths of terms representative of relevant publications....A main tenet of co-word analysis is that the identified patterns of representative term associations are maps of the conceptual structure or knowledge network of a technical field and that a series of such maps produces a fairly detailed representation of the subject matter of a discipline....Co-word analysis enables the structuring of data at various levels of analysis: (1) as networks of links and nodes (nodes hold terms); links connect nodes, thereby forming networks; (2) as distributions of interacting networks; and (3) as transformation of networks over time periods (Monarch 2000, pp. 5-6).

A word about the distinction between co-word analysis and co-citation analysis is in order. Whereas co-citation analysis maps "the structure of a research field through pairs of *documents* that are jointly cited...co-word analysis deals directly with sets of *terms* shared by documents...and maps the pertinent literature directly from the inter-actions of key terms instead of from the interactions of citations" (Monarch 2000, pp.5-6, emphasis added; see also Small 1973). Co-word analysis shows links on the basis of content.

2.2   Citation Analysis

Citation analysis involves several types of study, including direct citation, co-citation analysis, and bibliographic coupling. Small (1973) observes that direct citation—the citing of an earlier document by a new document—and bibliographic coupling have received considerable attention. Bibliographic coupling links source documents. How-ever, in measuring co-citation strength, researchers measure the degree of relationship or association between papers as perceived by the population of citing authors. Further-more, because of this dependence on the citing authors, these patterns can change over time, just as vocabulary co-occurrences can change as subject fields evolve (Small 1973, p. 265). Small observes that many information scientists focus attention on the operation of document retrieval systems serving scientists in various fields. The scientists who are served by these systems comprise an *invisible college* (Crane 1972)—networks of scientists "in frequent communication with one another and involved with highly spe-cialized subject matters" (Small 1980, p. 183).

Culnan and Swanson (1986) use citation analysis to measure how MIS is evolving as a standalone discipline separate from its foundation disciplines of computer science, management science, and organization behavior. Their analysis studied 271 articles across seven outlets (six journals and one conference proceedings) over the period of

1980 through 1984. They concluded that (1) MIS remains less established than its foundation disciplines, (2) MIS is growing and maturing, in terms of output and cited references, and (3) there is no consensus as to a body of work integral to the field. Culnan (1986, 1987) examines trends in MIS research, and observes that MIS management issues have emerged as a subfield. Moreover, the traditional emphasis on technology and technical issues has been displaced by a strong organizational and managerial focus. Culnan considers the intellectual structure of MIS research, and based on co-citation analysis, she identifies five invisible colleges (or informal clusters of research activity): foundations, psychological approaches to MIS design and use, MIS management, organizational approaches to MIS design and use, and curriculum.

Citation analysis remains a popular means to investigation of the nature of the discipline. For example, Katerattanakul and Hong (2003) assess the quality of *MIS Quarterly* and compare this assessment to other journals of other disciplines. They conclude that *MIS Quarterly* ranks favorably in comparison with specialty journals and respectably among general journals (of specific disciplines).

2.3 Issues, Opinions, and Commentaries

The development of a field requires ongoing debate on its future direction and underlying assumptions. Sometimes this takes the form of thematic editorials. Issues, opinions, commentaries, and thematic editorials are usually based upon expertise and experience, rather than on empirical inquiry. Those who contribute to this discourse often play central roles in the field, as senior editors of leading journals, and as well-respected members of the research community. They are recognized for their valuable contributions made over the years. Some journals explicitly make room for ongoing discussion and occasionally or regularly accept papers falling under an issues and opinions category (e.g., *MIS Quarterly, Information Systems Research, Management Science,* and *European Journal of Information Systems*). Each journal takes a slightly different tact, so that a variety of labels are used for this purpose: issues and opinions, research commentaries, management insight, and editor's view.

An excellent example of an issues and opinions contribution on the development of the field of IS is Baskerville and Myers (2002). They propose that MIS has matured and now serves as a bona fide source of reference for researchers in other scientific fields. They declare (Table 1, p. 4) that research contributions in MIS include five bodies of knowledge, each with concepts, theories, processes, and applications; and typically, these research contributions are published in MIS journals. Baskerville and Myers posit a new reality where information technology and systems have become ubiquitous in the industrialized world and where many fields have developed a research interest in information and communications technology. By extension, they argue that rather "than conceptualizing the process of knowledge creation as unidirectional (being part of a food chain with IS at one end), we can conceptualize this process as multidirectional. IS scholars along with scholars in other fields can be seen as part of many knowledge creation networks throughout the world" (pp. 5-7). Baskerville and Myers' issue and opinion piece stimulated further dialogue, making it part of an ongoing conversation about the identity of MIS (Avison 2003; Katerattanakul et al. 2006; Kock and Davison 2003; Larsen and Levine 2006; Nambisan 2003; Vessey et al. 2005).

Another influential example of a research commentary is found in Orlikowski and Iacono's (2001) work on theorizing the IT artifact. They draw upon a review of articles published in *Information Systems Research*, from 1992 through 2002, and argue that the field has not deeply engaged its core subject matter—the information technology artifact. They maintain that IS researchers have largely been preoccupied with context, discrete processing capabilities, and dependent variables. As a result, researchers have neglected the IT artifact itself, or taken it to be unproblematic. Orlikowski and Iacono propose that IS researchers begin to theorize about the IT artifact. Their commentary succeeded in opening a dialogue on the nature of the IT artifact (Benbasat and Zmud 2003; Ives et al. 2004; Myers 2002).

A final note about issues and opinions is in order: these contributions càn vary substantially. For example, robust and extensive discussions of this type on the nature of a discipline can extend into theory development and be expressed in the form of a monograph or book (Checkland and Holwell 1998; Currie and Galliers 1999; Zmud 2000).

2.4   Historical Surveys

Historical surveys are conducted at various levels, including high-level explorations of MIS, as well as lower-level exploration of subareas within MIS. In addition, more extensive treatments of the history of technology are presented in monographs and books (Kurzweil 1999; Stork 1997). These histories of technology are beyond the scope of the present study.

An example of high-level exploration is found in Beniger (1986). According to Beniger, the degree of control a society can exert over life, production, people, money, and information has drastically changed. He describes how four levels of control have developed over time: life, culture, bureaucracy, and technology. In Beniger's view, the control revolution explains why modern economies have become distinctively more purposive systems. A major purpose of this revolution is to bring under control (of managers and politicians alike) society's ever faster material processing systems.

Davis (2000) examines the conceptual foundations of MIS, focusing on the set of high- level concepts and propositions that explain the rationale for structures, scheduling and accomplishment of tasks, and performance of activities. He identifies three approaches to the formulation of conceptual foundations, based on (1) *intersection*—where ideas are taken from any field, (2) *core*—where the focus is on distinct ideas within MIS, and (3) *evolution*—combining the notions of intersection and core.

Good examples of historical survey in a subarea—group support systems (GSS)—are found in descriptive evaluations by Fjermestad and Hiltz (1998, 2000). Their article published in 1998 addresses methodologies employed and results obtained in experimental GSS research. This systematization covers the period 1972 through 1998 and reports on approximately 200 controlled experiments published in 230 articles. The analysis is divided in two parts. Part I covers contextual and intervening factors. Part II presents an overview, synthesizing 1,582 hypotheses resulting from pairings of independent and dependent variables. In the article published in 2000, the authors perform a descriptive evaluation of 54 case and field studies from 79 published papers, spanning the years 1980 through 2000. These evaluations are purely descriptive and do not offer any conclusions.

One dimension of historical critique that is largely missing in the literature on the identity of MIS is reflection on the accuracy and veracity of predictions that have been made with respect to information systems. An exception is found on organizational structure and the role of middle managers. In 1958, Leavitt and Whisler anticipated that in the 1980s the use of mathematical programming, operations research, and simulation of higher-order thinking through computer programs would become part of the manager's daily routine. Use of the computer would alter managerial work and shrink the middle management layer. For decades these changes eluded us (Hunt and Newell 1971).

More recent developments confirm some of Leavitt and Whisler's predictions (Applegate et al. 1988). Today, the middle management population *is* reduced. Newly introduced management control systems, executive information systems, telecommunication networks, e-mail, topic-specific global databases, office automation, standard packages, data warehouses, and the multi-media web are just some of the IT services that have facilitated these changes. Leavitt and Whisler speculated that modern computer use would lead to centralization. Today, however, we see centralization, decentralization, and outsourcing occurring simultaneously. And, as the role of middle managers shifts from control (over the execution of planned activities) to feeding organizational innovation processes, the need for managers may climb again (Dutton and Ashford 1993).

2.5 Forums

Dialogue on the identity and dynamics of the discipline also occurs through forums where members of the community "talk" with one another. These forums include face to face conferences and virtual mediums such as listservs, discussion groups, and blogs. Virtual conferences are a hybrid. The degree of formality in forums varies. Conference presentations are the most formal; panels are somewhat formal; and listservs, discussion groups, and blogs are the most informal.

For example, at a recent conference, a panel discussion focused on the discipline of MIS (Larsen and Levine 2006). The panelists considered myths and taboos in the history of the field, interdisciplinary identities, intradisciplinary perspectives, and empirics on coherence and change.

Virtually, a 2006 dialogue on the ISWorld listserv focused on the search for a "bumper sticker" for MIS. The post spurred a flurry of roughly 140 responses. Subscribers who replied emphasized a wide range of issues, characteristics, and audiences for bumper stickers. Some focused on the need for a short and catchy message; others discussed the meaning of the field, and real differences between information systems and information technology.

Such debates on the identity of MIS are common, ongoing, and almost recursive—indeed, no end appears to be in sight for the now familiar, longstanding discussions on the status of the field.

2.6 Summary

In summary, Table 1 presents each line of inquiry and its major facets.

Table 1. **Lines of Inquiry and Their Major Facets**

Line of Inquiry	Definition/Purpose	Dataset	Method & Tools	Output
Classification	Classifies/codes categories of interest, typically topic variable, and research method. Includes co-word analysis and meta analysis.	Texts or keywords in articles, conference proceedings, etc.	Can be performed manually or via automated tools	Tables of codes, topic variables, and research methods Co-word analysis: clusters of terms Meta analysis: tables and graphs
Citation	Establishes relations among documents and includes (1) direct citation—citing of earlier document by new document, (2) bibliographic coupling: sharing of one or more references by two documents.	Publications (articles, conference proceedings)	As above	Relationships among documents (timeline, list, or tree diagram) Co-citation network: author or issue clusters
Historical Surveys	Allows reflection on the past and predictions for the future; presents patterns and trends. Recounts discrete elements (events and developments) in a larger context.	Events, records, documents, artifacts, interviews	Direct account or recording, statistical or interpretative analysis	Survey, account, or narrative as documented in mixed media
Issues, Opinions, and Commentaries	Wide ranging, subjective.	Author's experiences and reflections	Interpretive and analytical	Essay or editorial opinion
Forums	Includes face-to-face and virtual interactions: listservs, discussion groups, Wikis, blogs.	Authors' conducted research, experiences and reflections	Interpretive, analytical, conversational	Conference presentations and panels; informal communications

3　DISCUSSION OF STRENGTHS AND WEAKNESSES

In considering these lines of inquiry into the identity, dynamics, and diffusion of MIS—(1) classification analysis, (2) citation analysis, (3) issues, opinions and commentaries, (4) historical surveys, and (5) forums—we were obliged to ask a number of questions: What limitations are inherent in each line of inquiry? What are the strengths and weaknesses associated with each? How does each contribute to the dialogue on the identity and dynamics of the discipline?

3.1 Classification Analysis

Classification analysis has three key strengths. First, classification analysis (including meta-analysis) focuses on identifying phenomena that are shared across research results and synthesizes these findings in a coherent manner. Second, it contributes to a cumulative research tradition, which involves building upon other researchers' theories and replicating or extending those theories and analyses. Third, meta-analysis requires identification of specific, precise variables that are operationalized across studies. Thus, classification analysis allows for precision in discussions about the field of MIS.

However, some weaknesses apply to the pursuit of precision. The nature of classification analysis, as a method, is narrow; and its focus on similarities carries the risk that one may overlook differences in the richness of the real world. Similarly, a preoccupation with rigor may dominate and become a goal in its own right, so that the researcher loses sight of what is really meaningful. This poses a dilemma: the objective of a classification study is to classify, and so the results may be too narrow or they may be precise and crystal clear.

To date, classification analysis has been employed to a limited extent but use of this method may take off given increased availability of automated support (e.g., tools and databases).

3.2 Citation Analysis

Citation analysis builds upon the assumption that "the document is viewed as symbolic of the idea expressed in the text" (Small 1978, p. 327). The method of citation analysis provides insight into groupings or clusters of topics and authors in a manner that is not otherwise visible. Citation analysis is a good means to discern the role of reference disciplines with respect to MIS and its subfields.

Like classification methods, citation analysis is largely objective, factual, and based on data. However, interpretation is required in framing the research questions and facts, and in analyzing and communicating the results. This method offers a single, powerful lens on the dynamics of the discipline, but is also a limited, simplified, and partial view. By itself, it is insufficient to characterize the workings of the discipline—as it doesn't come to grips with the substantive content that makes up the datasets. The same may be said for classification analysis.

To date, citation analysis has been employed to a limited extent since this research is difficult and cumbersome to perform. The advent of tools and electronic databases offers dramatic opportunity for conducting this type of research.

3.3 Historical Surveys

Historical surveys allow for flexibility and can be performed in conjunction with other methods to yield quantitative results (e.g., Fjermestad and Hiltz 1998, 2000). Through reflection, historical surveys make us aware of our roots and sources, and can serve as a path to understanding the present course and directions for the future. A historical approach requires a long view. While events and phenomena invite reexamination, those who take a long view are less likely to reinvent the wheel.

Histories can be deceptive and give the appearance of objectivity by adopting a style that reports the "facts." However, we know that facts are always framed by an author's perspective and intent. Sometimes there is a slippery slope between an historical account and political discourse, which is closely tied to personal interests. History is written by the victor. In a related manner, histories can employ a theme or metaphor that is distorted or wrong-headed. For example, in Beniger's view, the control revolution explains why modern economies have become distinctively more purposive systems. But what if there is a better theory that explains power relations than this matter of control?

3.4 Issues, Opinions, and Commentaries

These treatments are wide ranging, impressionistic, subjective, innovative, and are not constrained by expectations of rigor or research methods. These contributions can open up a dialogue on future promising research activities or identify dead avenues. Issues, opinions, and commentaries may take the form of a colloquy—a conversation occurring within a print journal or across several journals (see discussion of the IS artifact in section 2.3). Since these contributions may lack data or direct evidence, they rarely build upon one another in an *empirical* manner, as part of a cumulative research tradition.

Conversations are an enigmatic phenomenon. Oftentimes, we debate the same issues over and over again, and it may feel as if we're thrashing. But, communities need to be nurtured in many strange ways—maturation is nonlinear. Progress and growth are a slow business. Discussion topics can be revisited for many reasons, including political refocusing, incomplete understanding, knowledge loss, and emergent information.

3.5 Forums

Forums allow for the push and pull of ideas. Face to face interactions, listservs, discussion groups, Wikis, blogs, and web-based forums are all push and pull, depending upon the intent of the speaker. Such forums support debate and information sharing and create interest and engagement. Virtual forums bring people together who would otherwise never be in contact.

The structure of discussion may repeat itself in conversational streams over time, so that the community doesn't appear to be learning even though its individual members are gaining an understanding of discrete topics. This is probably the result of people "coming and going." Virtual forums are also subject to "flaming" due to the unique nature of the medium, where it is easy to respond quickly and rashly.

Face-to-face conferences and panels offer a platform for focused exploration. However, these interactions can also fail to support community building and learning across events and over time.

4   IMPLICATIONS AND CONCLUSION

There is a long history of research on knowledge creation and diffusion, paradigms and scientific revolutions, as well as disciplines and field theory. For example, Crane (1972, p. 1) writes

> In the last two decades, dramatic increase in the scope and volume of scientific research have occurred, as may be illustrated by the fact that the amount of scientific literature is doubling approximately every ten years (De Solla Price 1963). For the scientist who needs to locate particular items of scientific information and for the documentation specialist who must make them readily available, the organization and management of this huge and expanding store of information is a serious problem. Increasingly radical solutions are being proposed. For example, some experts would like to scrap scientific journals and distribute their contents piecemeal. Information retrieval and delivery systems are being developed to enable scientists to locate information quickly and effectively.
>
> But in sharp contrast with the attention being paid to how knowledge is stored, distributed, and used, relatively little attention has been paid to why and how knowledge grows.

Thirty-five years later, we are still grappling with the problem of why and how knowledge grows. The focus of this article is more specific in that we are concerned with the body of knowledge of MIS and its identity, dynamics, and diffusion. Our charge, as professionals, is made even more challenging since in some universities the existence of MIS as a separate and distinct organizational unit is in question.

What have we learned from this preliminary investigation? We have confirmed that the identity and dynamics of MIS are of concern across these five lines of inquiry. Each line tackles this subject in its own manner, and in keeping with the essential properties and conventions (unspoken rules, values, and norms) of that approach. By necessity, greater reliance on structure and data are associated with the classification and citation studies—these studies could not be performed otherwise. On the more flexible side, issues, opinions, and commentaries are frequently a catalyst for debate about MIS and its purpose and core.

Each approach allows a lens on the field, where the plurality of perspectives constitutes a total view. Together, the lines of inquiry compose a Cubist painting. This *composite* is the closest we can get to a *complete* picture of the field. The present investigation has allowed us to think consciously about our repertoire—recognizing the various contributions derived from each approach, finally to realize that understanding comes through the amalgamation of the perspectives. At the start, intellectually, we knew this to be the case but we had not seen it expressed in specific and concrete terms.

Moreover, the contributions within the five lines of inquiry build a robust dialogue across the field of MIS, where diversity enhances the communications and interactions of the players. In a rich field, many flowers bloom. A single mode of operation and a unified view can lend focus, but can also become a straitjacket. Rather, we (the authors) are inclined to plurality and diversity even though this brings inevitable complications. While the field of MIS struggles with its identity and desire for a core, we see clear signs of an engaged and vibrant community.

There is a significant need for high quality classification and citation analysis studies. Today, there is simply too little of this. In the longer term, such studies would influence the formulation of future research activities. In addition, high-level analysis across deductive statistical approaches (as in meta-analyses) and inductive approaches (as in co-word analysis), will allow us to ferret out messages that otherwise cannot be detected. More historical surveys are needed to aid synthesis and direction for the future.

Greater emphasis on reflection is called for through commentaries and substantial editorials that do more than present mundane summaries of the articles included in a journal issue. We must target and encourage discussion, debate, and colloquy. More "wild goose chase" forum debates, such as the recent one on bumper stickers, spur lively discussion. This is not intended to replace the need for extended inquiry on key issues (What is information? What is an information system? What is the core of the field?). Where possible, it would be productive to introduce mechanisms that propel discussion into action. This might occur through sustained use of working groups, special interest groups, and societies. If we are to successfully wrestle with the challenges of our discipline, we must envision ourselves contributing to a network, which mirrors the vision and capabilities of the information systems that we study.

Future research into lines of inquiry, associated methods, and genre systems (Yates and Orlikowski 2002) will help to surface the conventions of each approach—so that biases and underlying assumptions may be clearly exposed. Such awareness will enable better critique and better evaluations of the claims and evidence employed in each approach.

If the "medium is the message," as McLuhan and Lapham (1994) state, future research might query the quality of the academic field of MIS in terms of the relative use of the five lines of inquiry. This would require data on how much each line of inquiry is used to convey MIS scholarship and a comparative rating of the lines of inquiry. By extension, one might pursue a contingency framework asserting that messages conveyed through the "right" medium have greater impact or influence than when those messages are conveyed through the "wrong" medium. Since all elements of this argument are subject to interpretation, this is particularly difficult terrain.

References

Alavi, M., and Carlson, P. "A Review of MIS Research and Disciplinary Development," *Journal of Management Information Systems* (8:4), Spring 1992, pp. 45-62.

Alter, S. "18 Reasons Why IT-Reliant Work Systems Should Replace 'The IT Artifact' as the Core Subject Matter of the IS Field," *Communications of the AIS* (12), 2003, pp. 365-394.

Applegate, L. M., Cash, Jr., J. I., and Mills, Q. "Information Technology and Tomorrow's Manager," *Harvard Business Review*, November-December 1988, pp. 128-136.

Avison, D. E. "Is IS an Intellectual Subject?," *European Journal of Information Systems* (12:3), September 2003, pp. 229-230.

Baskerville, R. L., and Meyers, M. D. "Information Systems as a Reference Discipline," *MIS Quarterly* (26:1), March 2002, pp. 1-14.

Benbasat, I., and Weber, R. "Research Commentary: Rethinking 'Diversity' in Information Systems Research," *Information Systems Research* (7:4), December 1996, pp. 389-399.

Benbasat, I., and Zmud, R. W. "Empirical Research in Information Systems: The Practice of Relevance," *MIS Quarterly*, 23(1), March 1999, pp. 3-16.

Benbasat, I., and Zmud, R. W. "The Identity Crisis Within the IS Discipline: Defining and Communicating the Discipline's Core Properties," *MIS Quarterly* (27:2), June 2003, pp. 183-194.

Beniger, J. R. *The Control Revolution: Technological and Economic Origins of the Information Society,* Cambridge, MA: Harvard University Press, 1986.

Briggs, R. O., Nunamaker Jr., J. F., and Sprague, R. "Exploring the Outlands of the MIS Discipline," *Journal of Management Information Systems* (16:3), Winter 1999-2000, pp. 5-9.

Carr, N. G. "IT Doesn't Matter," *Harvard Business Review* (81:5), May 2003, pp. 41-49.

Checkland, P., and Holwell, S. *Information, Systems and Information Systems: Making Sense of the Field*, Chichester, UK: John Wiley & Sons, 1998.

Crane, D. *Invisible Colleges: Diffusion of Knowledge in Scientific Communities*. Chicago, IL: University of Chicago Press, 1972.

Culnan, M. "The Intellectual Development of Management Information Systems, 1972-1982: A Co-Citation Analysis," *Management Science* (32:2), 1986, pp. 156-172.

Culnan, M. "Mapping the Intellectual Structure of MIS, 1980-1985: A Co-Citation Analysis," *MIS Quarterly* (11:3), September 1987, pp. 340-352.

Culnan, M. J., and Swanson, E. B. "Research in Management Information Systems, 1980-1984: Points of Work and Reference," *MIS Quarterly* (10:3), September 1986, pp. 289-302.

Currie, W., and Galliers, B. (eds.). *Rethinking Management Information Systems: An Interdisciplinary Perspective*, Oxford, UK: Oxford University Press, 1999.

Davis, G. B. "Information Systems Conceptual Foundations: Looking Backward and Forward," in R. Baskerville, J. Stage, and J. DeGross (eds.), *The Social and Organizational Perspective on Research and Practice in Information Technology*, Boston: Kluwer Academic Publishers, 2000, pp. 61-82.

De Solla Price, D. *Little Science, Big Science*, New York: Columbia University Press, 1963.

Dutton, J. E., and Ashford, S. J. "Selling Issues to Top Management," *Academy of Management Review* (18:3), 1993, pp. 231-244.

Fitzgerald, G. "Information Systems: A Subject with a Particular Perspective, No More, No Less (Response to Paul 2002)," *European Journal of Information Systems* (12), 2003, pp. 225-228.

Fjermestad, J., and Hiltz, S. R. "An Assessment of Group Support Systems Experimental Research: Methodology and Results," *Journal of Management Information Systems* (15:3), Winter 1998-1999, pp. 7-149.

Fjermestad, J., and Hiltz, S. R. "Group Support Systems: A Descriptive Evaluation of Case and Field Studies," *Journal of Management Information Systems*, (17:3), Winter 2000-2001, pp. 115-159.

Goles, T., and Hirschheim, R. "The Paradigm is Dead, the Paradigm is Dead...Long Live the Paradigm: The Legacy of Burell and Morgan," *Omega* 28(3), 2000, pp. 249-268.

Hirschheim, R., and Klein, H. K. "Crisis in the IS Field?," *Journal of the Association for Information Systems* (4:5), 2003, pp. 237-293.

Hunt, J. G. and Newell, P. F. "Management in the 1980's Revisited," *Personnel Journal* (50:1), January 1971, pp. 35-43, 71.

Ives, B., Parks, M. S., Porra, J., and Silva, L. "Phylogeny and Power in the IS Domain: A Response to Benbasat and Zmud's Call for Returning to the IT Artifact," *Journal of the Association for Information Systems* (5:3), March 2004, pp.108-124.

Katerattanakul, P., Han, B., and Rea, A. "Is Information Systems a Reference Discipline?," *Communications of the ACM* (49:5), May 2006, pp. 114-118.

Katerattanakul, P., and Hong, S. "Quality and Knowledge Contribution of MISQ: A Citation Analysis," *Communications of the Association for Information Systems* (11), 2003, pp. 271-288.

King, J. L. "Editorial Notes," *Information Systems Research* (4:4), December 1993, pp. 291-298.

Kock, N., and Davison, R. "Dealing with Plagiarism in the Information Systems Research Community: A Look at Factors That Drive Plagiarism and Ways to Address Them," *MIS Quarterly* (27:4), December 2003, pp. 511-532.

Kuhn, T. S. *The Structure of Scientific Revolution* (2nd ed.), Chicago, IL: The University of Chicago Press, 1970.

Kurtzweil, R. *The Age of Spiritual Machines: When Computers Exceed Human Intelligence*, New York: Penguin Books, 1999.

Larsen, T. J., and Levine, L. with Land, F., Myers, M. D., and Zmud, R. "The Identity and Dynamics of MIS," panel presentation in D. Avison, S. Elliot, J. Krogstie, and J. Pries-Heje (eds.),

The Past and Future of Information Systems: 1976-2006 and Beyond, IFIP 19th World Computer Congress, and TC8 Information System Stream, New York: Springer Science and Business Media, 2006, pp. 101-106.

Larsen, T. J., and Levine, L. "Searching for MIS: Coherence and Change in the Discipline," *Information Systems Journal* (15), 2005, pp. 357-381.

Leavitt, H. J. and Whisler, T. L. "Management in the 1980's," *Harvard Business Review* (36:6), November-December 1958, pp. 41-48.

Lyytinen, K., and King, J. L. "Nothing at the Center? Academic Legitimacy in the Information Systems Field," *Journal of the Association for Information Systems* (5:6), June 2004, pp. 220-246.

McLuhan, M., and Lapham, L. H. *Understanding Media: The Extensions of Man*, Boston, MA.: The MIT Press, 1994.

Monarch, I. "Information Science and Information Systems: Converging or Diverging?," in A. Kublik (ed.), *Proceedings of the 28th Annual Conference of the Canadian Association for Information: Dimensions of a Global Information Science*, 2000 (available online at http://www.slis.ualberta.ca/cais2000/monarch.htm).

Myers, M. D. "The IS Core—VIII. Defining the Core Properties of the IS Discipline: Not Yet, Not Now," *Communications of the Association for Information Systems* (12), 2002, pp. 582-587.

Nambisan, S. "Information Systems as a Reference Discipline for New Product Development," *MIS Quarterly* (27:1), March 2003, pp. 1-18.

Nurminen, M. I., and Eriksson, I. V. "Information Systems Research: The 'Infurgic' Perspective," *International Journal of Information Management* (19), 1999, pp. 87-94.

Orlikowski, W. J., and Baroudi, J. J. "Studying Information Technology in Organizations: Research Approaches and Assumptions," *Information Systems Research* (2:1), March 1991, pp. 1-28.

Orlikowski, W. J., and Iacono, C. S. "Research Commentary: Desperately Seeking the 'IT' in IT Research—A Call to Theorizing the IT Artifact," *Information Systems Research* (12:2), June 2001, pp. 121-134.

Paul, R. J. "Is Information Systems an Intellectual Subject?," *European Journal of Information Systems* (11), 2002, pp.174-177.

Pfeffer, J. "Barriers to the Advance of Organizational Science: Paradigm Development as a Dependent Variable," *Academy of Management Review* (18:4), 1993, pp. 599-620.

Pfeffers, K., and Ya, T. "Identifying and Evaluating the Universe of Outlets for Information Systems Research: Ranking the Journals," *Journal of Information Technology Theory and Application* (5:1), 2003, pp. 63-84.

Robey, D. "Research Commentary: Diversity in Information Systems Research: Threat, Promise, and Responsibility," *Information Systems Research* (7:4), December 1996, pp. 400-408.

Robey, D., and Markus, M. L. "Beyond Rigor and Relevance: Producing Consumable Research about Information Systems," *Information Resources Management Journal* (11:1), Winter 1998, pp. 7-15.

Small, H. "Cited Documents as Concept Symbols," *Social Studies of Science* (8:3), August 1978, pp. 327-340.

Small, H. "Co-citation Context Analysis and the Structure of Paradigms," *The Journal of Documentation* (36:3), 1980, pp. 183-196.

Small, H. "Co-citation in the Scientific Literature: A New Measure of the Relationship Between Two Documents," *Journal of the American Society for Information Science*, July-August 1973, pp. 265-269.

Stork, D. G. *HAL's Legacy: 2001's Computer as Dream and Reality*, Cambridge, MA: The MIT Press, 1997.

Vessey, I., Ramesh, V., and Glass, R. L. "Research in Information Systems: An Empirical Study of Diversity in the Discipline and ts Journals," *Journal of Management Information Systems* (19:2), Fall 2002, pp. 129-174.

Vessey, I., Ramesh, V., and Glass, R. L. "A Unified Classification System for Research in the Computing Disciplines," *Information & Software Technology* (47:4), March 2005, pp. 245-255.

Walstom, K. A., and Hardgrave, B. C. "Forums for Information Systems Scholars: III," *Information & Management* (39), 2001, pp. 117-124.

Weber, R. "Toward a Theory of Artifacts: A Paradigmatic Base for Information Systems Research," *Journal of Information Systems* (1:2), Spring 1987, pp. 3-19.

Weber, R. "Still Desperately Seeking the IT Artifact," *MIS Quarterly* (27:2), June 2003, pp. iii-xi.

Westfall, R. D. "An IS Research Relevance Manifesto," *Communications of the Association for Information Systems* (2:paper #14), September 1999 (available online at http://cais.aisnet.org/articles/2-14/article.htm).

Westin, S. M., Roy, M., and Kim, C. K. "Cross-Fertilization of Knowledge: The Case of MIS and its Reference Disciplines," *Information Resources Management Journal* (7:2), 1994, pp. 24-34.

Whitley, R. *The Intellectual and Social Organization of the Sciences*, Oxford, England: Clarendon Press, 1984.

Yates, J., and Orlikowski, W. "Genre Systems: Structuring Interaction Through Communicative Norms," *The Journal of Business Communication* (39:1), January 2002, pp. 13-35.

Zmud, R. W. (ed.). *Framing the Domains of IT Management: Projecting the Future Through the Past*, Cincinnati, OH: Pinnaflex Educational Resources, Inc., 2000.

Acknowledgement

The authors would like to thank Andrew Van de Ven for his helpful suggestions on an earlier version of this article.

About the Authors

Tor J. Larsen earned his Ph.D from the University of Minnesota in 1989. He has served as associate editor for *MIS Quarterly* and is currently a member of the editorial board for *Information & Management*. Tor's publications include articles in *Information & Management*, *Journal of MIS*, and *Information Systems Journal*. His research interests are in the areas of innovation, outcome, and research philosophy. Tor can be reached by e-mail at Tor.J.Larsen@bi.no.

Linda Levine is a senior member of the technical staff at Carnegie Mellon University's Software Engineering Institute. She is a member of the IEEE Computer Society, Association for Information Systems, National Communication Association, and cofounder and chair of IFIP Working Group 8.6 on Diffusion, Transfer and Implementation of Information Technology. Linda can be reached by e-mail at LL@sei.cmu.edu.

Part 3:

Software Process Improvement

13   USE OF APPRECIATIVE INQUIRY IN SUCCESSFUL PROCESS IMPROVEMENT: An Action Research Study[1]

Anna Börjesson
Ericsson AB and
IT University of Göteborg
Göteborg, Sweden

Lena Holmberg
Apprino
Göteborg, Sweden

Helena Holmström
IT University of Göteborg
Göteborg, Sweden

Agneta Nilsson
IT University of Göteborg
Göteborg, Sweden

Abstract   *Traditionally, software processes improvement (SPI) has been approached from a problem-oriented perspective, focusing on diagnosing and solving problems using methods such as the IDEAL model and DMAIC. In contrast, appreciative inquiry is an approach that focuses on what is best in an organization in order to further develop this to create a better future. It is, therefore, interesting to explore if and how software organizations familiar with problemsolving approaches can benefit from using appreciative inquiry. In this paper,*

---

[1]All authors have made an equal contribution to the paper and are listed in alphabetic order.

Please use the following format when citing this chapter:

Börjesson, A., Holmberg, L., Holmström, H., and Nilsson, A., 2007, in IFIP International Federation for Information Processing, Volume 235, Organizational Dynamics of Technology-Based Innovation: Diversifying the Research Agenda, eds. McMaster, T., Wastell, D., Ferneley, E., and DeGross, J. (Boston: Springer), pp.181-196.

we present an action research study conducted at the telecom company Ericsson in Sweden. Appreciative inquiry was used to facilitate an SPI initiative implementing a new process and tool for requirements and test case management. While the SPI initiative was considered successful, important lessons were learned regarding the application of appreciative inquiry. We conclude that the use of appreciative inquiry does not eliminate the dependence of other well-known key factors for SPI success. Also, the study indicates that the preference and satisfaction of problem-solving among individuals familiar with problem-oriented approaches may impede the use of appreciative inquiry.

Keywords   Appreciative inquiry, software process improvement, action research

1   INTRODUCTION

It is widely recognized that software process improvement (SPI) initiatives are complex (see Börjesson and Mathiassen 2004; Dybå 2000; Grady 1997; Humphrey 1989). Traditionally, SPI initiatives have been approached from a problem-oriented perspective, which typically focuses on what problems an organization is experiencing in its current situation and how to solve these problems. Typical examples of commonly adopted problem-oriented approaches are the IDEAL model (McFeeley 1996), capability maturity model (CMM) (Paulk et al. 1995), and DMAIC (Breyfogle 2003; Pande et al. 2000). The strength-based appreciative inquiry approach is in stark contrast to the problem-oriented focus underlying the SPI paradigm. Instead of focusing on problems, it emphasizes what works, the continuum, as the foundation. Appreciative inquiry started as an action research effort at Case Western Reserve University (Cooperrider 1986) and has since been successfully adopted as an organizational development approach by many organizations.

Whereas SPI initiatives and the use of problem-oriented approaches have been extensively studied, our knowledge about the ways SPI unfolds when using alternative approaches such as appreciative inquiry is limited. This paper reports from an action research study concerning the use of appreciative inquiry in an SPI initiative at the telecom company Ericsson in Sweden. In our study, the aim is to explore a particular SPI initiative and how it unfolds when appreciative inquiry is used instead of the commonly employed problem-oriented approaches. More specifically, our research questions are

- How does the use of appreciative inquiry influence known key factors for success in an SPI initiative?
- How does the use of appreciative inquiry impact individuals familiar with problem-oriented approaches?

The paper is structured as follows: Section 2 contrasts the appreciative inquiry approach with commonly known problem-oriented approaches, and considers key factors for SPI failure and success. Section 3 outlines our action research approach. Section 4 presents our empirical findings using encounters and episodes (Newman and Robey 1992) as the organizing principle. Section 5 discusses the empirical findings as a basis for understanding what happens when appreciative inquiry is introduced in a problem-oriented organization. Section 6 concludes the argument of appreciative inquiry for SPI initiatives.

2 THEORETICAL CONTEXT

SPI is today dominated by problem-oriented approaches like the IDEAL model (McFeeley 1996), the DMAIC model (Breyfogle 2003; Pande et al. 2000) and the CMM (Paulk et al. 1995). In this study, we let the IDEAL model represent a typical problem-oriented approach. The IDEAL model consists of five phases and provides software organizations with knowledge about how to organize SPI work. While highlighting both problems and possibilities, all phases (see Figure 1) aim at identifying and solving problems.

In contrast, appreciative inquiry is a strength-based approach (Cooperrider et al. 1995) consisting of five phases. Figure 1 shows the correspondence between the different phases in the IDEAL and appreciative inquiry models. While the two models look relatively similar, there are fundamental differences. For example, appreciative inquiry includes techniques to bring out the best of peoples' experiences and appreciate "what is" to create a collective awareness of the positive core. Grounded in experiences of success, future images of what might be are formed into a "dream." Opposite this, the IDEAL model includes techniques that focus on finding out what problems to solve and the desired future state. Another example is the difference in how learning is viewed: as an ongoing process (appreciative inquiry) or as an end-product (the IDEAL model). Figure 1 presents the IDEAL model, the appreciative inquiry model, and a possible mapping of their phases.

Recently, appreciative inquiry has been explored in relation to information systems. Although the objective of the approach is the same as in problem-oriented approaches (i.e., successful change), its emphasis on strengths is in stark contrast to traditional SPI paradigms.

Independently of the SPI model, there are well-known key factors that need to be considered when analyzing different SPI approaches and their applicability in different contexts. Wiegers (1998) claims lack of adequate management commitment is the first trap to avoid when starting to improve software processes. In a similar vein, Abrahamsson (2000, 2001) emphasizes management commitment as crucial for successful change. Other key factors are reactions to change (Weinberg 1997), the use of opinion leaders (Rogers 2003), user participation (Barki and Hartwick 1989), and the assimilation gap (Fichman and Kemerer 1999). The assimilation gap represents the difference between acquired and deployed improvements. Börjesson (2006) argues that a first and necessary step is a successful SPI deployment. Therefore, it is of great importance to address challenges related to the assimilation gap when introducing a change process in an organization.

3 RESEARCH METHOD

This paper reports from an 8-month (March – October 2006) action research (AR) study with the dual goal of improving implementation and use of new processes and tools in practice and contributing to the body of knowledge on the same theme. Collaborative practice research (Mathiassen 2002) supports the realization of this dual goal and supports the insider/outsider perspective (Bartunek and Louis 1996) which was a beneficial aspect of this research. The insider role (one of the authors works at the company) assured

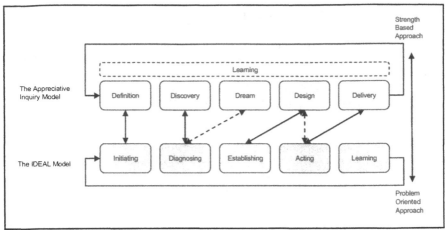

Figure 1. **The Appreciative Inquiry Versus the IDEAL Model**

primary access to data (Coghlan and Brannick 2001). The outsider role (represented by the other three authors) contributed with unbiased reflections.

AR has been introduced as a research method for solving practical problems while at the same time expanding scientific knowledge (Baskerville and Wood-Harper 1996; Susman and Evered 1978). We applied three characteristics of AR (Baskerville and Wood-Harper 1996): (1) the researchers were involved in solving practical problems, (2) the knowledge obtained was applicable in practice, and (3) the research was a cyclical process linking theory and practice. Action research is, however, also criticized and Baskerville and Wood-Harper (1996) summarize this critique as lack of impartiality of the researcher, lack of rigor, and consultancy masqueraded as research and results not being context free. In our study, we address this critique by using the insider/outsider role of researchers and by triangulation of data.

3.1   Research Site

This paper builds on an AR study conducted at the Swedish telecom company Ericsson. In particular, one product-developing unit was studied. The unit involves 65 skilled engineers, each with more than 15 years of experience working with the Japanese market. Traditionally, the engineers discuss SPI initiatives in terms of "problems" to solve. Over the years, problem-oriented approaches have shaped the mind-set among the engineers who appreciate the challenge of solving problems. The development unit comprise of a department with a department manager, a number of sections with section managers, and a development project with a development project manager (see Figure 2).

The aim of the SPI initiative was to enable all affected parts in the unit (shaded in Figure 2) to use the same tool (RequisitePro) and process for managing requirements and test cases. This was considered a challenge involving stakeholders with different interests. Moreover, instead of the commonly adopted problem-oriented approaches, this SPI initiative applied appreciate inquiry to facilitate the change process and to encourage a focus on strengths rather than problems in the units work practices.

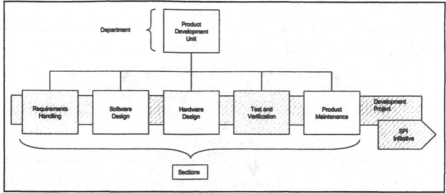

Figure 2. The Structure of the Development Unit Involved in this Study

3.2 Data Sources and Analysis

Several data sources were used (Patton 1987; Yin 1994) to increase rigor of the findings. Table 1 presents the data sources used in this study.

Table 1. Data Sources

Data Sources	Description
Direct involvement	The researchers were involved in workshops and meetings where the SPI initiative was initiated, planned, executed, analyzed, and evaluated.
Participatory observations	During workshops and meetings, three of the researchers took the outsider role (taking notes) while one of the researchers (the insider role) was directly involved in the activities.
Formal interviews	Six formal interviews were conducted. Each interview lasted for 30 minutes. During the interviews, two researchers asked questions while the two other researchers took notes.
Open-ended, semi-structured interviews	Due to the insider role, daily informal discussions concerning the SPI initiative were possible. These informal discussions allowed for insight in everyday practices at the company.
Project documentation	Due to the insider role, the research project had access to manager documentation, planning documents and progress reports.
Product documentation	Due to the insider role, the research project had access to the requirements and test product documentation.
Tool data	The research project had access to the RequisitePro tool, which was the tool implemented in the SPI initiative.

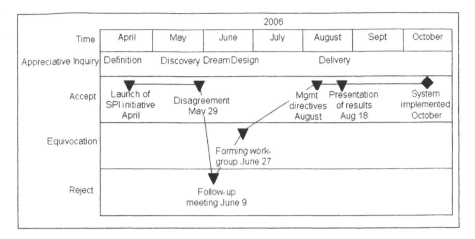

Figure 3. **Encounters and Episotes in the SPI Initiative (Episodes are illustrated as lines, which indicate the result of each encounter)**

We adopted Newman and Robey's (1992) social process model as a lens to organize and analyze our empirical findings. In this model, *antecedent conditions* are situations that existed before the change process. *Encounters* are events that mark the beginnings and ends of episodes. *Episodes* are longer periods wherein the pattern set within an earlier encounter plays out. Below, we present our findings using this model as the organizing principle.

4   THE SPI INITIATIVE

This section begins with describing the antecedent conditions (i.e., the situation and relationships between stakeholders before the initiation of the SPI initiative). Then we describe the encounters and episodes and how these led to the outcome of the SPI initiative (see Figure 3).

4.1   Antecedent Conditions

In March 2006, the management team of a product-developing unit at Ericsson made the decision to improve their requirements and test case management. To strengthen their operation excellence, the management team informally (with participation by one of the researchers in her role as the insider) analyzed possible improvement areas. The informal analysis revealed the following:

(1) Requirements were not managed by a known tool for requirements handling
(2) Test cases were managed by a high quality tool developed in-house, but only available for a limited number of engineers

(3) Requirements and test cases were not documented in a tool deployed by all engineers in the unit
(4) Managers and engineers working with requirements and test case had somewhat different views about how to accomplish the most efficient ways for handling requirements and test cases

4.2 Encounters and Episodes

Encounter 1: Launch of SPI Initiative. In early April 2006, the department manager started the SPI initiative through involving an experienced change agent who works with SPI at Ericsson and had been involved in several similar initiatives within different development units (previously referred to as the "insider"). The change agent was asked to commence the SPI initiative. The arrangement included an agreement to run the initiative using a new approach (i.e., appreciative inquiry), which had never previously been used in the company. Besides an interest in the SPI initiative and the success of this, the change agent and three associated researchers would also be able to explore how an organization familiar with problem-oriented approaches could benefit from this alternative approach. After an initial meeting, the understanding between the change agent and the department manager was that the definition phase (i.e., topic of choice) was decided in the development unit's management team. Consider this statement from the department manager:

We have now decided to improve our requirements and test case handling. It would be great if you could help us get started.

This statement led to the (unconscious) assumption of the change agent that the first step in appreciative inquiry (i.e., the *definition* phase) was completed. According to the department manager, a decision to improve had been taken. Based on this decision, the change agent took it for granted that the engineers within the unit were aware of the decision and agreed on this. In her view, and according to the department manager, they could now plan the SPI initiative in detail.

Episode 1: Acceptance. The first episode represented a period of acceptance during which the change agent enthusiastically planned different activities. Since the aim was to introduce appreciative inquiry and to explore how the SPI initiative unfolded as a result of this approach, the change agent formed a team of researchers including herself and three researchers with different backgrounds. A meeting was arranged with one of the section managers and the research team. At this meeting, the purpose of the project was discussed and a workshop, which would involve all unit stakeholders, was planned. A main goal of the project was declared: "Clear and simple product life cycle requirement and test case handling." The meeting had a positive atmosphere and as a result, stakeholders were summoned to a workshop. The main interest from the section manager was, of course, the SPI initiative itself, but he also showed an interest for the appreciative inquiry approach.

Well, if it this new approach can help make this improvement happen faster- and better- that would be just fine.

Encounter 2: Disagreement about "Determine What Should Be." Episode 1 led to the first workshop where all stakeholders attended, apart from the elsewhere-engaged department manager. Because the change agent took for granted that the first phase in appreciative inquiry (i.e., definition) was agreed upon, the workshop was arranged to proceed with the following phases. The goal of the workshop was to reach the result of a detailed plan of how the SPI initiative would continue towards implementation. At the workshop, during the second phase of appreciative inquiry (i.e., *discovery*), the participants enjoyed interviewing each other to discover positive experiences. In this phase, participants are expected to discuss and appreciate "what is." The participants seemed comfortable asking each other what they considered their strengths and their core competences. During the next phase (i.e., *dream*), the participants had a positive dialog about what they wanted to create. They all wanted to improve the requirements and test case management and they could all see the benefits of doing so. However, the participants sometimes found it difficult to express themselves in appreciative terms. For example, when asking the participants what they thought was the most positive aspect of an idea, many of them answered very briefly and one participant said

> *Why can't we tell what wasn't good? Why are we only allowed to tell what was positive?*

The discovery and dream phases were finished satisfactorily. The change agent (who was running the workshop) as well as the participants seemed to enjoy the opportunity of interaction between sections. However, when reaching the next step (i.e., *design*), it became apparent that people involved were in serious disagreement. In this phase, participants are expected to determine "what should be." In a discussion regarding generation and use of test case documents, some stakeholders expressed that they were not familiar with the referred material. Stakeholders from the section generating these documents did not agree on this and were quite irritated.

> *Yes, you are familiar with these documents—and you do read them!*

One of the section managers described the emotionally charged situation as follows:

> *Before the workshop it was assumed but not explicated that we should implement the RequisitePro tool to improve the requirements and test case management. In contrast, in previous project documents we were asked to provide suggestions of what to do about the requirements and test case management— as if we had actually a choice of what tool to use....Then we were summoned to the workshop, a rather large group of people from different units and with different interests....I felt irritated already before, and had decided that this was no good...and we had not had time do discuss or prepare beforehand how things should be done.*

At this point, it became clear to the change agent that the assumption that the definition was agreed upon was a mistake. Clearly, the participants did not fully share views. The definition had never been agreed upon and, therefore, participants could not agree on dreams and design. What also became clear was that there were tensions between stakeholders due to differences in previous investments and efforts.

Because of the disagreements and the insight that the definition phase was not yet established, it was not fully possible to complete the goal of the workshop. Instead, the workshop left key stakeholders with different issues to clarify before the SPI initiative could continue according to plans.

Episode 2: Rejection. The result of the workshop was a period of rejection on the part of the stakeholders. There were different views of whether an SPI initiative should take place at all, and if so, how it should be done. However, the department manager stood by the decision and supported the change agent in proceeding with the SPI initiative. With the aim of resolving the rejection, the change agent started planning for a meeting between some of the key stakeholders that had been in disagreement at the workshop.

Encounter 3: Follow-Up Meeting. Episode 2 led to the arrangement of a follow-up meeting. The meeting was suggested by the change agent and involved the two section managers responsible for requirements and test cases. This meeting was held in June with the aim of finding a way forward and resolving the tensions that had occurred during the workshop. The two section managers' ability to reflect in an unbiased way on what had actually happened at the workshop greatly facilitated the process of moving forward. At the follow-up meeting, one of the section managers said

> *We should, of course, have been more prepared—should have had a common agenda...it was stupid to even think that we could come to the workshop without having had discussions beforehand.*

At the follow-up meeting, the section managers agreed on the importance of proceeding with the SPI initiative, and agreed on the decision to arrange a second workshop. This workshop would emphasize the importance of the SPI initiative and the aim would be to get participants to proceed with the interrupted design phase and agree on "what should be."

Episode 3: Equivocation. After the follow-up meeting, the section managers conveyed the outcome of the discussions they had with each other and with the change agent to the rest of the group. There were no particular reactions in the group and most participants seemed to take a more neutral position waiting for the second workshop at which the design phase would continue.

Encounter 4: Forming the Work Group. Episode 3 led to the arrangement of the second workshop with all main stakeholders attending, except for the department manager. While most of the stakeholders had remained passive during the episode of equivocation, the department manager had reestablished the focus of the SPI initiative (i.e., he completed the definition phase). Stakeholders now agreed to implement RequisitePro and the SPI initiative could continue. Because of this basic agreement, workshop participants were able to discuss how to design and implement RequisitePro and its related processes. By focusing on the positive core and "what should be," workshop participants were able to agree on a concrete time plan based on the needs from the development project that was responsible for implementing the RequisitePro tool. At the workshop, it was clear that the attention from the project manager helped make a concrete time plan. Also, the workshop rendered in the creation of a work group that would manage the ongoing SPI initiative and deal with the details of design and delivery.

Episode 4: Acceptance. The stakeholders agreed on the work group and a period of acceptance came as a result. During this period, stakeholders were scheduled to leave for summer holidays, which put additional pressure on the work. At this time, the SPI initiative got assistance from another change agent specialized on the RequisitePro tool. The formal interviews, conducted after the SPI initiative was completed, show the importance of this additional change agent.

> *Without the help from our change agent we would never have been able to complete the transformation into RequisitePro in time...he helped us with all kinds of things from explaining to people how the tool works to help us with the actual work in RequisitePro.*

> *Our change agent made a great effort when one section experienced problems with transferring data and existing structures into RequisitePro.*

However, at this time, the SPI initiative was already running late and the change agent could not, on his own, bring it back on track before people returned from holidays. While tremendous progress had been made in some areas, there were still areas in which progress was slow.

Encounter 5: Management Directives. According to the time plan, the SPI initiative was supposed to be ready for demonstration in August. However, when returning from summer holidays, the project manager soon identified a lack of progress. Despite considerable help from the additional change agent, not all sections were performing according to the plan and the assigned working group had trouble managing this. During this period, the differences between the sections in terms of existing structures became apparent. Stakeholders realized that if this situation continued, they would fail to keep up with the time plan. Due to these difficulties, the project manager identified the risk of the project running late if resources were not reprioritized.

At this point, the project manager took an active role and, with support from the department manager, resources were reprioritized. In discussions with the section managers, it was emphasized how important the SPI initiative was and that high prioritization was necessary in the sections' everyday work.

> *We discussed what needed to be done and how we could solve the issue with requirements elicitation for the unit experiencing problems. This was very important for getting the process going again.*

Because of the project manager's early discovery of problems and management directives as a response to this, they could maintain the time plan and work could continue according to the plan.

Episode 5: Acceptance. Following the management directives, the SPI initiative continued smoothly. During this episode, the software developers and the delayed section worked together with the change agent to accomplish the transition to the RequisitePro tool. In addition, they made preparations for a first presentation of the system.

Encounter 6: Presentation of Results from the SPI Initiative. In August the first presentation of the result from the SPI initiative was held. This was the first time the full potential of the SPI initiative result was evaluated. The presentation was very successful and the overall feeling after the event was positive.

> *At this meeting I think we all got the feeling that "this will indeed work—we will manage and the system will improve our situation." This resulted in a very positive atmosphere within the whole project group.*

> *At this meeting all people were very positive! It felt like a springboard.*

Clearly, the presentation was appreciated and for the first time the different stakeholders got a shared view of the potential of RequisitePro. From an appreciative inquiry perspective, this was the time for delivery (i.e., the first time that stakeholders got a feeling for "what will be").

Episode 6: Acceptance. Following the presentation, RequisitePro was implemented and the sections had to use the same system for requirement and test case management. According to one of the software engineers, the idea of having one common system was important.

> *I think that having the sections using the same system is crucial. Now all people can see what is happening and more people can be involved in the process. Before it was only very few people that were aware of this process.... Also, the development of the system has made the sections to consider their test processes—the attributes involved—which is good for the common knowledge within and between the groups.*

Still, the RequisitePro tool has only been in use for a very short time and therefore it can be difficult to evaluate the full potential of the system, although most stakeholders seem to find the SPI initiative very successful.

> *I am very happy with the initiative. Of course, it has not been without struggle and disagreement—but why should it? Not only did we succeed in implementing a new tool, but we did it using a new approach, which nobody at the company had experienced before. Overall, the project has involved many people and we have learned a lot. After the demonstration of the system, I think we were all convinced that this is indeed an improvement and that the system will definitely serve its purpose. To me, this is what you can expect in an SPI initiative like this.*

It remains to be seen whether this project will be a success. We will know only when it is fully tested and when all people actually use it in their everyday work. But it looks very promising.

I think the project is a success. Even though we haven't had the chance to work with the system for very long I think it looks good. There is always a little resistance but after a while people start to realize the benefits with the system... also, we learned a lot from the process.

I think the result is very promising even though the process could have been better—but it was new to us all.

Overall, the SPI initiative was considered very successful. Despite limited use so far, benefits can already be seen and stakeholders are convinced that the implementation of RequisitePro will result in more efficient ways of working.

Outcome: Successful SPI Initiative. At the end of October 2006, a monthly steering committee meeting was held where one of the section managers involved in the SPI initiative was invited to report progress and outcome. In the presentation, it was made clear that the SPI initiative was considered very successful and that the new RequisitePro tool and its related processes would mean an increase in efficiency, quality, and visibility. According to the report, this increase in efficiency meant an estimated cost saving of approximately €80,000/year, which the steering committee considered a very good achievement.

5   DISCUSSION

In our study, the aim was to explore a particular SPI initiative and how it unfolded when a strength-based approach was used instead of the commonly employed problem-oriented approaches. More specifically we asked (1) how did the use of appreciative inquiry influence known key factors for success in an SPI initiative, and (2) how did the use of appreciative inquiry impact individuals familiar with problem-oriented approaches? The analysis provided us with a range of findings related to the use of appreciative inquiry in problem-oriented organizations. This section presents the findings, structured according to the two research questions. We conclude the section by suggesting further research in the area.

5.1   Appreciative Inquiry and Key Factors for Improvement Success

As can be seen in our study, the SPI initiative struggled with the same challenges as most SPI initiatives. When analyzing encounters and episodes, we see that traditional key factors such as management commitment, reactions to change, use of opinion leaders, and attention to deployment all had an impact on this SPI initiative. First, the commitment from management (Abrahamsson 2000, 2001) was an obvious key factor for the success of this SPI initiative. As Figure 2 shows, the established organizational structure clarifies who constitutes top management is (i.e., the department manager). The department manager was involved twice to sort out conflicts, make prioritizations, and give directives in favor of the SPI initiative. It is very likely that the SPI initiative would have failed without this effort from management. In addition, it is likely that attendance from the department manager at the two workshops would have facilitated progress of the SPI initiative. As recommended in appreciative inquiry, the whole system (i.e., all stake-holders) should ideally be present when engaging in activities such as workshops. This was indeed the ambition in this project, although due to unfortunate circumstances, the department manager was elsewhere engaged during both workshops.

Second, our study shows, in line with research on the topic, that negative reactions to change are natural (Weinberg 1997) and that these reactions can actually make an SPI initiative fail. In our study, negative reactions to change were apparent when stake-holders realized that they had very different perceptions of the current situation and that there had never been an agreement in relation to the definition of the project. In this, we discern unwillingness from stakeholders to fully comprehend the current situation, if this situation would lead to change. Despite a clear focus on strengths, in accord with appre-ciative inquiry, stakeholders struggled to negotiate and resolve unwillingness to promote change. This unwillingness can also be explained, if we choose to interpret going from problem-oriented to strength-based approaches as a major change, in terms of *radical change* (Weick and Quinn 1999).

Third, as in most SPI initiatives, opinion leaders proved crucial in this SPI initiative. Opinion leaders are individuals who provide information and advice to other individuals (Rogers 2003) and they are well known as key success factors for SPI implementation. In our study, the change agent introducing the SPI initiative as well as the appreciative inquiry approach was critical. In many encounters, the change agent had to moderate discussions to make progress when the stakeholders were in conflict. In addition, the change agent specialized in RequisitePro was highly appreciated among stakeholders. This change agent provided competence, advice, and a contribution to practical work. The final interviews revealed that this effort was of great assistance for progress in the SPI initiative. From this, we conclude that strong opinion leaders play an important role also when using appreciative inquiry as the approach for change.

Fourth, we see that acquired technology is not the same thing as deployed tech-nology (Fichman and Kemerer 1999). While the development unit had access to RequisitePro for a long period, nothing happened until people actually started using it. As in other SPI initiatives, conscious deployment proved critical in this project.

Based on experience from our study, the SPI initiative struggled with the same challenges as most SPI initiatives. When analyzing encounters and episodes, we learned that traditional key factors such as management commitment, reactions to change, use of opinion leaders, and attention to deployment all influenced this SPI initiative. These key factors need to be considered when analyzing different SPI approaches and their appli-cability in different contexts. This means that there was no indication that the importance of traditional key factors diminished when appreciative inquiry was used. Hence, we conclude that the use of appreciative inquiry does not eliminate the dependence on other well-known key factors for SPI success.

5.2   Appreciative Inquiry Versus Problem-Oriented Approaches

In the development unit being studied, all of the engineers were familiar with problem-oriented approaches and felt comfortable starting change processes based on problems to solve. As we see in many problem-oriented methods—for example, the IDEAL model (McFeeley 1996) or the DMAIC model (Breyfogle 2003)—phases are conducted to identify and find solutions to problems. The engineers in our study were accustomed to use these methods and enjoyed the challenges related to solving problems. It became apparent at the workshops that the majority of the engineers were less enthusiastic regarding the activity to "imagine what might be" or "determine what should be" while effortlessly engaged in identifying and solving problems.

While appreciative inquiry focuses on creating a collective awareness of the positive core, problem-oriented approaches do not seem to appreciate to collectively explore hopes and dreams. It was noticeable that there was a tension between the problem-oriented mind-set and the appreciative inquiry approach, which was an interesting feature of the study that became clear very early in the process.

Already in the beginning of the SPI initiative, there was unwillingness among stakeholders to emphasize positive experiences and talk in terms of opportunities rather than problems. Our attempt to shift the engineers' mind-set from solving problems to creating dreams proved a great challenge. Looking back at our attempt, it is plausible that we tried to implement a new approach without fully considering the basis of the problem-oriented mind-set. While appreciative inquiry has been successfully used in many organizations (Bushe 1995; Cooperrider et al. 2004), we conclude that the preference and satisfaction of problem-solving among individuals familiar with problem-oriented approaches may impede the use of appreciative inquiry.

Hence, there is the need of careful training and guidance to benefit fully from the approach and its strengths. It should be acknowledged that relatively little time was spent on introducing appreciative inquiry in this SPI initiative in order to adjust to the ordinary allocated resources of an SPI initiative at the company. It is therefore possible that the use of appreciative inquiry would have been more beneficial if the involved stakeholders had the opportunity to learn more about the approach in the early phases of the SPI initiative, or even before the process started.

5.3   Suggestions of Further Research

Accepting the potential of appreciative inquiry, one could imagine that comprehensive use of the approach could positively influence SPI initiatives, and perhaps influence key factors such as lack of management commitment and negative reactions of change.

To further develop our understanding whether *unified dreams* can overcome negative reactions to change, we suggest additional research. Our study indicates that appreciative inquiry needs to be introduced carefully to stakeholders. We recommend that future research attempts devote sufficient time and resources to communicate the identified need (i.e., the focus of the initiative), and to address the need firmly, focusing on positive possibilities. Our study indicates that it is important to avoid a problem-solving mode so that the SPI initiative is not led into the wrong mind-set from the start. It would also be interesting to investigate if and how training and guidance could help overcome the tension between appreciative inquiry and problem-oriented approaches.

6 CONCLUSION

This paper reports on an action research study at the Swedish telecom company Ericsson. The dual aim of the study was to improve implementation and use of new processes and tools in practice and to contribute to the body of knowledge about the use of appreciative inquiry. The focus of the study was to understand what happens when introducing appreciative inquiry in an organization familiar with problem-oriented approaches to conduct an SPI initiative. Whereas the SPI initiative was successfully implemented in the company, important lessons were learned regarding the use of appreciative inquiry.

*   The use of appreciative inquiry does not eliminate the dependence on other well-known key factors for SPI success.
*   The preference and satisfaction of problem solving among individuals familiar with problem-oriented approaches may impede the use of appreciative inquiry.

The study extends and complements current approaches to SPI by proposing appreciative inquiry with its strength-based characteristics. This approach translates insights from organizational development into specific knowledge about SPI initiatives by its stark contrast to the problem-oriented focus underlying the SPI paradigm.

References

Abrahamsson, P. "Is Management Commitment a Necessity After All in III: Software Process Improvement?," *Euromicro '00*, Maastricht, The Netherlands, IEEE Computer Society, 2000, pp. 246-253.

Abrahamsson, P. "Rethinking the Concept of Commitment in Software Process Improvement.," *Scandinavian Journal of Information Systems* (13), 2001, pp. 69-98.

Barki, H., and Hartwick, J. "Rethinking the Concept of User Involvement," *MIS Quarterly* (13:1), 1989, pp. 53-63.

Bartunek, J. M., and Louis, M. R. *Insider/Outsider Team Research (Qualitative Research Methods)*, Thousand Oaks, CA: Sage Publications, 1996.

Baskerville, R., and Wood-Harper, T. "A Critical Perspective on Action Research as a Method for Information Systems Research," *Journal of Information Technology* (11), 1996, pp. 235-246.

Breyfogle, F. W. *Implementing Six Sigma: Smarter Solutions Using Statistical Methods* (2nd ed.), Hoboken, NJ: John Wiley & Sons, Inc., 2003.

Bushe, G. R. "Advances in Appreciative Inquiry as an Organization Development Intervention," *Organization Development Journal* (13:3), 1995, pp. 14-22.

Börjesson, A. *Making Software Process Improvement Happen*, PhD Thesis, IT University of Gothenburg, Göteborg, Sweden, 2006.

Börjesson, A., and Mathiassen, L. "Successful Process Implementation," *IEEE Software* (21:4), 2004, pp. 36-44.

Coghlan, D. , and Brannick, T. *Doing Action Research in Your Own Organization*, Thousand Oaks, CA: Sage Publications, 2001.

Cooperrider, D. L. *Appreciative Inquiry: Toward a Methodology for Understanding and Enhancing Organizational Innovation*," unpublished Ph.D. Dissertation, Case Western Reserve University, Cleveland, OH, 1986.

Cooperrider, D. L., Barrett, F., and Srivastva, S. "Social Construction and Appreciative Inquiry: A Journey in Organizational Theory," in D. Hosking, P. Dachler, and K. Gergen (eds.), *Management and Organization: Relational Alternatives to Individualism*, Aldershot, UK: Avebury, 1995, pp. 157-200.

Cooperrider, D. L, Whitney, D., and Stavros, J. M. *The Appreciative Inquiry Handbook*, New York: McGraw-Hill, 2004.

Dybå, T. "An Instrument for Measuring the Key Factors of Success in Software Process Improvement," *Empirical Software Engineering* (5), 2000, pp. 357-390.

Fichman, R. G., and Kemerer, C. F. "The Illusory Diffusion of Innovation: An Examination of Assimilation Gaps," *Information Systems Research* (10:3), 1999, pp. 255-275.

Grady, R. B. *Successful Software Process Improvement*, Upper Saddle River, NJ: Prentice Hall, 1997.

Humphrey, W. S. *Managing the Software Process*, Reading, MA: Addison Wesley, 1989.

Mathiassen, L. "Collaborative Practice Research," *Information, Technology & People* (14:4), 2002, pp. 321-345.

McFeeley, B. *IDEAL: A User's Guide for Software Process Improvement*, The Software Engineering Institute, Carnegie Mellon University, Pittsburgh, Handbook CMU/SEI-96-HB-001, 1996.

Newman, M., and Robey, D. "A Social Process Model of User-Analyst Relationships," *MIS Quarterly* (16:2), 1992, pp. 249-266.

Pande, P., Nueman, R., and Cavanagh, R. *The Six Sigma Way: How GE, Motorola and Other Top Companies Are Honing Their Performance*, New York: McGraw-Hill, 2000.

Patton, M. Q. *How to Use Qualitative Methods in Evaluation*, Newbury Park, CA: Sage Publications, 1987.

Paulk, M. C., Weber, C. V., Curtis, B., and Chrissis, M. B. *The Capability Maturity Model: Guidelines for Improving the Software Process*, Reading, MA: Addison-Wesley, 1995.

Rogers, E. M. *Diffusion of Innovations* (5th ed.), New York: Free Press, 2003.

Susman, G., and Evered, R. "An Assessment of the Scientific Merits of Action Research," *Administrative Science Quarterly* (23), 1978, pp. 582-603.

Weick, K. E., and Quinn, R. E. "Organizational Change and Development," *Annual Review of Psychology* (50), 1999, pp. 361-386.

Weinberg, G. M. *Quality Software Management, Volume IV – Anticipating Change*, New York: Dorset House Publishing, 1997.

Wiegers, K. E. "Software Process Improvement: Eight Traps to Avoid, CrossTalk," *The Journal of Defense Software Engineering*, September 1998, pp. 9-12.

Yin, R. *Case Study Research*, Newbury Park, CA: Sage Publication, 1994.

About the Authors

Anna Börjesson has more than 10 years of practical experience working with software development and software process improvement. She has been working at Ericsson since 1998. Anna holds a Ph.D. in Software Process Improvement from the IT University of Göteborg. Anna is also a member of ACM and IEEE. She can be reached by e-mail at anna.borjesson@ ericsson.com.

Lena Holmberg holds a Ph.D. in Educational Research from Göteborg University. She has worked as a consultant for more than 10 years, recently specializing in strength-based development at Apprino. Lena also worked at the IT University during the start-up of the Software Engineering and Management program. She can be reached by e-mail at lena.holmberg@apprino.com.

Helena Holmström is Program Manager at the Software Engineering and Management Program at the IT University of Göteborg, Sweden. She is also affiliated with the University of Limerick, Ireland, where she is part of LERO, the Irish Software Engineering Research Centre. She holds a Ph.D. in Informatics from Gothenburg University. Helena can be reached by e-mail at helena.holmstrom@ituniv.se.

Agneta Nilsson is currently a lecturer at the faculty of Software Engineering and Management at the IT University of Göteborg. She holds a Ph.D. in Informatics from Göteborg University. Her research interests focus on IT implementation and change management in organizational contexts. Agneta can be reached by e-mail at agneta.nilsson@ituniv.se.

14 MEASURING PROCESS INNOVATIONS AND IMPROVEMENTS

Anna Börjesson
Ericsson AB and
IT University of Göteborg
Göteborg, Sweden

Anders Baaz
Ericsson AB
Göteborg, Sweden

Jan Pries-Heje
IT University of Göteborg
Göteborg, Sweden

Magnus Timmerås
Ericsson AB
Göteborg, Sweden

Abstract   *A major challenge in process improvement is to understand process innovation and improvement efficiency and use. How do we know that process innovations and improvements give organizational benefits? We need a mechanism for measuring. In this paper, we report from a longitudinal action research study at the telecom company Ericsson where a measurement mechanism was designed and successfully used in practice to understand, learn, and measure process efficiency. In the concrete, the measurement mechanism was built through empirical testing combined with using a goal–question–metrics (GQM) approach. The resulting measurement mechanism consists of four correlated metrics that indicate process use, process commitment, process learning, and process improvement. The same measurement mechanism can also be used to obtain feedback and evaluation, thereby allowing the organi-*

Please use the following format when citing this chapter:

Börjesson, A., Baaz, A., Pries-Heje, J., and Timmerås, M., 2007, in IFIP International Federation for Information Processing, Volume 235, Organizational Dynamics of Technology-Based Innovation: Diversifying the Research Agenda, eds. McMaster, T., Wastell, D., Ferneley, E., and DeGross, J. (Boston: Springer), pp. 197-216.

zation to determine process efficiency and use, and to determine the success of the process improvements.

Keywords   Software process improvement, process innovation, measurement, metric, GQM

1   INTRODUCTION

Since the early 1990s, several organizations have embraced the idea of software process improvement (SPI). SPI is, however, a very complex, resource-demanding, and long-term process where many have reported a very high failure rate (SEMA 2002). For example, Goldenson and Herbsleb (1995), in a study of 138 individuals from 56 organizations that had invested in SPI, found that 26 percent agreed that "nothing much has changed" and 49 percent declared themselves to be disillusioned. Another report by Herbsleb et al. (1994), however, reported between 500 and 700 percent return on investment from SPI. So SPI seems to be difficult, but definitely worthwhile. This leaves us with the immediate question: How do we know that process innovations and improvements give organizational benefits? We need a mechanism for measuring.

Metrics are required to understand, evaluate, take action, and follow up on progress. It is difficult to improve what we cannot measure. Dybå (2000) conducted an extensive literature review combined with a survey including 55 software companies, which revealed that one of six key factors for process improvement success is concern for measurements. This concern for measurements can also be found in Deming (1986), Grady (1997), Humphrey (1989), and Zharan (1998). Basili et al. (1994, p. 528) claim that metrics and measurement are "a mechanism for creating a corporate memory and an aid in answering a variety of questions associated with the enactment of any software process." Schaffer and Thomson (1992) argue there are six reasons why improvement programs fail and one of them is delusional metrics of success. Schaffer and Thomson promote the use of empirical testing that reveals what works in practice.

What is measurement then? The IEEE Standard 1061 (IEEE 1998, glossary) defines an attribute as "a measurable physical or abstract property of an entity." Fenton and Pfleeger (1997, p. 5) define measurement as a "process by which numbers or symbols are assigned to attributes of entities in the real world in such a way as to characterize them according to clearly defined rules." Kaner and Bond (2004, p. 4) elaborate on this definition and come up with the following definition: "Measurement is the empirical, objective assignment of numbers, according to a rule derived from a model or theory, to attributes of objects or events with the intent of describing them." Thus you measure up against a model or a theory. An example of a generally applicable model that can be used to measure against is CMMI (Chrissis et al. 2003), which defines a framework for software processes. Several examples of how to measure software processes exists. See, for example, Garmus and Herron (1995) or Florac and Carleton (1999) for discussions on the use of measurement as a means for evaluating software processes statistically. However, an alternative measurement strategy is to measure against a model tailored specifically to the needs of the organization such as GQM (Basili et al. 1994; Basili and Rombach 1988; Basili and Weiss 1984).

To define a mechanism for measuring process efficiency and use, from 2001 through 2006, we conducted a longitudinal action research project at the telecom company Ericsson. As the underlying theory we decided to use the GQM (goal–question– metric) approach defined by Basili and his colleagues (Basili et al. 1994; Basili and Rombach 1988; Basili and Weiss 1984) to define, empirically test, and iteratively improve a number of metrics for SPI. Using SPI approaches helps Ericsson improve their vital research and development (R&D) processes. The resulting measurement mechanism consists of four correlated metrics called *processment* (indicating process efficiency and use), process commitment, process learning, and process improvement. Together these four metrics give an answer to our research question: How do we know that process innovations and improvements give organizational benefits?

The study is presented as follows. Section 2 describes the theoretical context for our research. Section 3 explains the research method used. Section 4 gives an account of the study. Section 5 reports our analysis and discussions of the study performed and section 6 concludes the paper.

2   THEORETICAL CONTEXT

A metric can be defined as a quantitative characteristic of one or more attributes in relation to the software process, product, or project (Daskalantonakis 1992). A direct metric does not depend upon a measure of any other attribute (IEEE 1998, p. 2). Examples of direct metrics are: Number of lines of code in a program and number of defects found in a program. An example of a more complex metric is function points (Albrecht 1979; Albrecht and Gaffney 1993), which measure software complexity. Metrics can then be combined to answer more complex questions about quality and productivity increase, as for example: Number of defects/function point or number of hours/function point.

Basili et al. (1994) define a metric as a set of data, being either direct or complex. A measurement is the result of using one or several metrics to measure. In the literature, the distinction between metrics and measurements is often blurred. In this paper we have chosen to use metric and measurement as defined by Basili et al.

SPI and measurement has always been closely related. In the widely used SPI model CMM (capability maturity model), for example, "measurement and analysis" is a common feature for every key practice (Paulk et al. 1995). The newer CMMI model (Chrissis et al. 2003) has maintained this key role for measurement. In the European Bootstrap model (Kuvaja et al. 1994) for SPI, "process measurement" is one of the key features. That is also the case for the more recent ISO 15504 standard (2003, 2004, 2006). Thus measurements and model-based improvement are closely intertwined. However, an organization can also undertake SPI without a normative model. The Danish company Brüel and Kjær, for example, used existing defect reports to measure that they needed to improve requirements and testing and undertook a successful improvement program based on this measure (Vinter et al. 1998).

Measurements, however, are not only used for SPI. Measurements are a key part of software engineering. Nevertheless, the success rate is surprisingly low. Daskalantonakis (1992) found that only one out of ten industrial measurement programs were perceived to be positively successful, and Pfleeger (1993) found that only one out of three

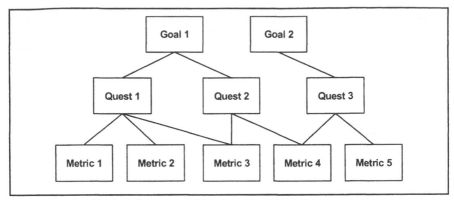

Figure 1. **Basili, Caldiera, and Rombach's GQM Approach**

measurement programs were continued after the second year. One of the approaches that seem to have had more success than the average is GQM.

GQM (goal–question–metrics) is a measurement approach developed by Basili and his colleagues (Basili et al. 1994; Basili and Rombach 1988; Basili and Weiss 1984) at the University of Maryland in cooperation with NASA. It is built on the assumption that for an organization to measure in a purposeful way it must first specify the goals for itself and its projects, then it must trace those goals to the data that are intended to define those goals operationally, and finally provide a framework for interpreting the data with respect to the stated goals (Basili et al. 1994, p. 2). The measurement model has three levels: the conceptual level (goal), the operational level (question), and the quantitative level (metric) (see Figure 1).

The process of using GQM consists of six activities.

(1) Elicit characteristics for the organization and projects including purpose, object, issue and viewpoint.
(2) Define goals from business plan and business goals.
(3) Break down goals to questions and then to metrics. The same metric can be used in order to answer different questions under the same goal or different questions for different goals. Metric data can be either objective (depends only on object and not viewpoint) or subjective (depends on both object and viewpoint).
(4) Measure and collect data.
(5) Conduct feedback sessions where measurement data are analyzed and synthesized.
(6) Package the measurement data so they become understandable and useful.

In Figure 2, we give example (derived from our own practice) on what the outcome of a GQM approach could be.

The GQM approach facilitates the process of defining valuable metrics to related questions and goals (Mashiko and Basili 1997). It is, however, also important to be familiar with related enablers and barriers having impact on the main goal. The literature on SPI and metrics reveal several promising reasons to understand success and failure of process innovations and improvements. Below we elicit four of the more dominant explanations.

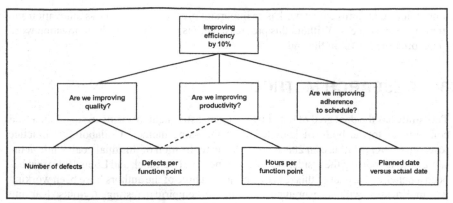

Figure 2. A GQM Example

Actual use of processes: Delone and McLean (1992) observe that information technology use is the most frequently reported measure of IT implementation success. Seddon and Kiew (1996) have modified IT use to IT usefulness. They argue a non-mandatory usage of an innovation is a good proxy of usefulness. Abrahamsson (2000) argues user satisfaction (i.e., level of satisfaction, fulfillment of the needs, solving experienced problems, and actual use) is valued as an important indicator of successful innovations and improvements. Rogers (2003) has shown that the rate of adoption is determined by the characteristics of an innovation perceived by the potential adopter, and not whether it has produced any advantages for competitors.

Commitment to process innovations and improvements: Commitment plays an important role for the outcome of innovations and improvements (Abrahamsson 2001; Grady 1997; Humphrey 1989; McFeeley 1996). Wiegers (1998) claims lack of adequate management commitment is the first trap to avoid. Successful process innovations and improvements depend on the commitment to the project from both managers and software developers (Humphrey 1989).

Ability to learn the process: Individuals in an organization that can learn from each other facilitate reflective practice and organizational learning. Argyris and Schön (1978) view knowledge as something acquired through experience and the way practitioners work, and claim that organizational learning contributes to organizational memory. In this sense, documented and accepted processes are one important part of an organizational memory. Merriam and Caffarella (1999) argue a more constructivist approach to learning emphasizing situated cognition, meaning that organizational culture plays a key role in learning and that learning cannot be separated from the situation in which learning takes place. Brown et al. (1989) share this view of learning as a product of the activity, context and culture. Another mechanism influencing the ability to learn is communities of practice (Leave and Wenger 1991; Wenger 1998), through which knowledge is designed and can be managerially instilled.

Progress in process improvement work: Grady (1997) states, based on lessons learned from industry failure analysis activities, that we seldom record adequate data to understand progress. This data is vital to understand environmental aspects that have effect on potential improvements. Börjesson (2006) has shown that progress of process innovation and improvement work is an important prerequisite to process innovation and improvement success. Without this progress, there is no chance for the innovation work to become successful in the end.

3   RESEARCH METHOD

This study has the dual goal of both improving measurement mechanisms in practice and contributing to the body of knowledge on the same theme. Collaborative practice research (CPR) (Mathiassen 2002) supports the realization of this dual goal, while at the same time supporting the insider/outsider perspective (Bartunek and Louis 1996) that has been a beneficial aspect of this research project. Three of the authors have been working within Ericsson with measurements definitions, empirical testing, try-outs, learning sessions, and data collection during the period 2001 through 2006 and have taken the insider role. The fourth author joined the research project in the final phases, taking the outsider role and contribring with analysis, discussion, and questioning in an unbiased way. The data collection design and research method used as presented below have helped us to answer the research question: How do we know that process innovations and improvements give organizational benefits?

The study is based on action research (Baskerville and Wood-Harper 1996, 1998; Galliers 1992; Davison et al. 2004) with a focus on understanding valuable mechanisms for measuring process efficiency and use. Baskerville and Pries-Heje (1999) argue that the fundamental contention of action research is that a complex social process can be studied best by introducing changes into that process and observing the effects of these changes. The authors collected data throughout the research project in iterative cycles as defined by Susman and Evered (1978). Figure 3 describes how we related the six GQM activities to Susman and Evered's cyclical approach in this study.

Table 1 summarizes the data sources used in the study. The many different data sources have facilitated triangulation (Patton 1987; Yin 1994) and analyses in an unbiased way.

Table 1. **Data Sources**

Data Sources	Explanation
Direct involvement	We were directly involved in and responsible for experimental testing, execution of the survey, and the result of the surveys
Open-ended, semi-structure interviews	We had informal interviews and discussions with practitioners who answered the surveys and with managers responsible for acting on the results
Process survey working group	We presented, analyzed, and discussed both survey and results with selected manager and senior practitioners
Process improvement steering groups	We presented, discussed, and suggested actions for managers on regularly held steering group meetings for process improvement issues
Questionnaires	We authored and sent out the questionnaires as defined in Figure 4

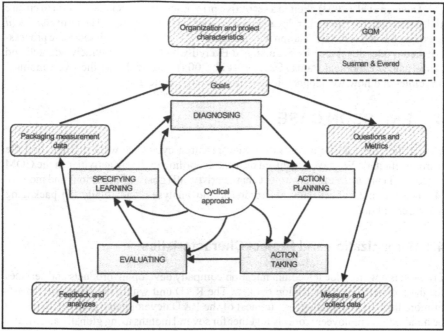

Figure 3. The Six GQM Activities and Susman and Evered's
Cyclical Approach

Table 2. Canonical Action Research Principles (Davison et al. 2004)
and Our Adaptation of Them

Principle	Adoption in this research project
Researcher-Client Agreement	Three authors work in industry and one in academia. There is commitment from the client (i.e., Ericsson) to support academic research and the researchers are committed to research results that are useful; thus one industry author is also working in academia.
Cyclical Process Model	Susman and Evered's (1978) cyclical action research method (Figure 3) was used.
Theory Principle	The GQM approach (Basili et al. 1994; Basili and Rombach 1988; Basili and Weiss 1984) was used as theory to build up and explain the measurement mechanism. Through all learning cycles, the theory in the form of the current GQM design was made explicit.
Change Through Action	One of the study's dual goals was to improve the measurement mechanism in practice at the client site.
Learning Through Reflection	The results from surveys were regularly analyzed and reflected upon in process survey working groups and steering groups for process improvement.

Davison et al. (2004) elicited a set of five principles and associated criteria to ensure and assess both the rigor and relevance of canonical action research. The term *canonical* is used to formalize the association with the iterative, rigorous, and collaborative process-oriented model developed by Susman and Evered which has been widely adopted and hence gained canonical status (Davison et al. 2004). Table 2 lists the five canonical principles and how we adopted them in this research project.

4   ERICSSON CASE

This section describes our case, the action research cycles we went through, and the learning elicited. We have organized the case according to the six activities in the GQM process: (1) organization and project characteristic, (2) goals, (3) questions and metrics, (4) measure and collect data, (5) feedback and analyses, and finally (6) packaging measurement data.

4.1   Organization and Project Characteristics

Ericsson is a worldwide telecommunication company developing products and services for the global telecommunication market. The R&D unit within the company consists of more than 16,500 employees. In most of the R&D development projects, there will be hundreds of employees working together for several months using globally and locally defined processes to facilitate efficiency in the product development. The R&D processes are vital for the company to stay competitive in a global market. SPI is a well-used approach to improve the R&D processes within Ericsson.

4.2   Goals

A measurement mechanism is necessary to stay focused on SPI and continuously improve the R&D processes. Measuring SPI and R&D efficiency is, however, a major challenge depending on several factors such as data collection difficulties (Humphrey 1989), system complexity (Albrecht and Gaffney 1993), and system size (Flaherty 1985; Humphrey 1989; Jones 1993, 1994). Figure 4 describes how Ericsson systematically has worked to overcome these measurement obstacles and define a measurement mechanism to understand and improve both SPI progress and R&D process efficiency and use. Each action research cycle (ARC) contributed to the goal of finding a measurement mechanism valuable for understanding Ericsson's SPI progress and R&D process efficiency and use. The main goal was discussed during the nine ARCs, but never changed. This indicated a strong will from the organization to understand and improve SPI progress and thereby the R&D process efficiency and use.

4.3   Questions and Metrics

Ericsson wanted to ensure that valuable SPI initiatives made progress and that the R&D processes were efficient and used. They also wanted to know how they could facilitate the actual use of their processes. To deal with these questions, Ericsson started to send

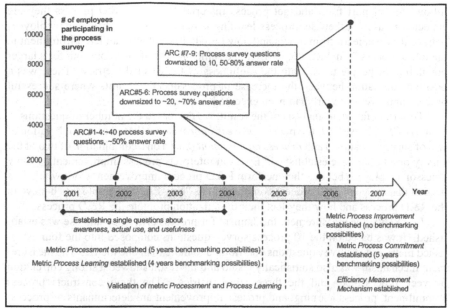

Figure 4. Action Research Cycles, Number of Process Questions, Answering Rate, and Established Metrics

out process survey questions to their employees. In the first ARC in 2001 (ARC#1), approximately 40 questions were defined based on three perspectives: awareness about the process, actual use (Delone and McLean 1992) and opinion about its usefulness (Seddon and Kiew 1996). The questions were also defined to understand change agent communication, process training satisfaction, and practice support. Initially there was no intention by the process survey project to combine questions into predefined metrics.

Six-point bipolar Likert scales were used for the majority of the process questions. A few process questions had nominal scales or only yes–no alternatives. Previous research indicates that reliability is highest when using five-point scales (Dybå 2000). The reason for using even-numbered scales was that our experience from other surveys in the same organization showed that a large number of the respondents only used the middle alternative. In order to get more information from these respondents, we choose the six-point scales, which require them to take a stand for either the negative or positive side.

During ARC#1 to ARC#4, we found it important to stabilize the questions to attain benchmarking effects over time, thereby obtaining commitment to the process survey. The number of process questions were, therefore, relatively stable (approximately 40) during this period. To further increase the answering rate and facilitate analysis of the result, we decreased the number of questions to approximately 20 in ARC#5. In ARC #5, the metrics *processment* (based on a combination of four of the survey questions) and *process learning* (based on a combination of two of the survey questions) were established. The definition of processment and process learning were inspired by Sigurd and Tedsjö (2005). Ericsson defines processment as "how Ericsson employees know, follow, get support from and get process material from the R&D process they are expected to use." Likewise, process learning is defined as "how Ericsson employees believe they can learn from others and how they believe others can learn from them in the R&D process." In ARC #6, we used the same number of questions, but for a larger population of people to validate the usefulness of the defined metrics. There was a positive correlation between the increase in processment and units where successful process improvement work had been executed.

To further facilitate analysis of the result, we decreased the number of questions to 10 in ARC#7. In ARC#7, the metrics *process improvement* (based on a combination of two of survey questions) and *process commitment* (based on a combination of two of the survey questions) were established. Ericsson interprets process improvement as "how Ericsson employees believe they perform R&D process improvement work where it is needed that are good" and process commitment as "how Ericsson employees believe in the R&D process and how they feel their organization promote the R&D process."

In ARC#8, the measurement mechanism for process efficiency and use was established. It was based on the 10 process survey questions composed into the four established metrics. No survey questions contributed to more than one metric. The measurement mechanism was also statistically tested and the result showed a strong correlation between processment and the three other metrics. The three constructs process commitment, process learning, and process improvement are determinants of processment. Based on a thesis work using the PLS-Graph tool for statistical analysis (Enskog 2006), we have calculated that the three constructs explain 76 percent of the variance of processment where numbers greater than 49 percent indicate strong correlation. Finally, in ARC#9, the same 10 survey questions was sent out to approximately 10,500 employees and the measurement mechanism (i.e., the four established metrics) was calculated and communicated to 168 different units.

Figure 5 presents the 10 process survey questions, the resulting metrics, the selection criteria, and how the measurement mechanism was described and deployed within Ericsson. A measurement mechanism had been established as a model to understand, improve, and follow-up R&D process efficiency and use.

4.4 Measure and Collect Data

For ARC#1 to ARC#4, we used a web-polling tool developed and maintained in-house by the process survey project. This home-made web-polling tool was used only for the process survey and no alignment or prioritizations were needed. For ARC#5 to ARC#8, another web-polling tool developed and maintained by Ericsson in general was used. Fortunately, web-polling solutions evolved during the early years of this decade, which meant that the work for the process survey project regarding using the new Ericsson web-polling tool was very limited.

In ARC#1 to ARC#5, the process survey was sent to approximately 500 employees. In ARC#6, the process survey was sent to approximately 1,000 employees. Two units, each consisting of 500 employees, participated in the survey to try out and unify the newly established metrics processment and process learning. In ARC#7, the process survey was again sent to 500 employees (one of the development units) to pilot the newly defined measurements process improvement and process commitment. In ARC#8, the

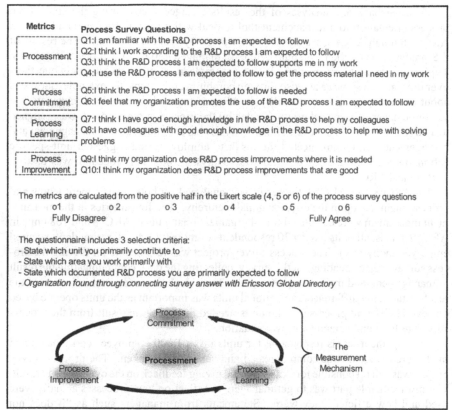

Figure 5. The Survey Questions, Metrics, Selection Criteria, and Resulting Measurement Mechanism

process survey was sent out to a broader Ericsson community, most of them working in Sweden, Ireland, Germany, and Spain (approximately 5,000 employees) to pilot the full measurement mechanism as shown in Figure 4. Finally, in ARC#9, the process survey was sent out to an even broader Ericsson community. It is planned that the process survey will be sent out biannually to establish benchmarking both for specific units and for Ericsson R&D as a whole.

4.5   Feedback and Analyzes

The result was analyzed through first identifying the positive (1–3) and negative (4–6) halves of each question (see Figure 5). Each metric was then analyzed through combining two or four questions. For example, the metric process commitment was calculated through the positive half of question five and the positive half of question six. This resulted in the metric explaining how many percentages were positive to both question five and question six (i.e., process commitment).

The feedback and analyses of the results changed focus during the study from process orientation to a management tool to deal with process efficiency and use. In ARC#1 through ARC#4, the analyses were made by process engineers. The results of the analyses were then communicated to management by the process engineers. Typically an analysis was made by looking at single questions, benchmarking questions over time, and, in some cases, also through combining questions; for example, questions about use and questions about skills. In ARC#5, the analysis involved managers and senior engineers. A special group, headed by the process survey project, was assigned to analyze the result. The result of this analysis was communicated to management and management then communicated the result to employees and suggested unit-specific actions to deal with the result. The same analysis group and procedure was used in ARC#6 and ARC#7.

In ARC#8 and ARC#9, the result was analyzed by both management teams and process engineers up in the organizational hierarchy. The four metrics in the measurement mechanism were calculated for 74 organizational units in ARC#8 and 168 units in ARC#9, that is, all units having 20 respondents or more (at least 20 respondents secured employee anonymity). The process survey project was responsible for driving the process survey project, sending out the survey, collecting the data, communicating the result to management, and maintaining the result. The calculation and communication of the result to the many different organizational units was important as the units operate based on several different processes. The units needed their specific result from the process survey to fully understand their own situation.

Management teams responsible for units up to 1,000 employees coordinated and made sure the result was communicated and actions were taken. The process survey project was still responsible for analyzing and giving feedback on the overall R&D result. The most valuable part was to get managers to reflect on how processes actually were used and how efficient they were. Statements from managers such as "It does not surprise me that my test engineers have such a low result" and "I'm happy to see that my initiatives to improve our way of working pay result" strengthened the belief in the result shown in the measurement mechanism. The measurement mechanism also revealed some less expected results. It was, for example, surprising to see how many employees felt a personal commitment to processes compared to how they believed their organization promoted the use of processes. Management has rather often argued the opposite (e.g., "our employees believe documented processes are not needed"). Furthermore, when making qualitative studies of specific units to understand the relation between ongoing SPI initiatives and metrics, we come to understand that there was an obvious correlation between the metric process improvement and ongoing SPI initiatives. We could find both increase and decrease in process improvement, which correlated to increase or decrease in SPI efforts.

4.6 Packaging Measurement Data

In ARC#1 through ARC#4, the process survey project packaged the metrics into a Power Point presentation available only for the process engineers. The presentation was approximately 100 slides. Selected parts of this package were made available for management through process improvement steering group presentations. These smaller presentations

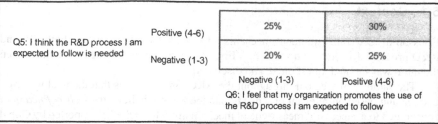

		Negative (1-3)	Positive (4-6)
Q5: I think the R&D process I am expected to follow is needed	Positive (4-6)	25%	30%
	Negative (1-3)	20%	25%

Negative (1-3)   Positive (4-6)
Q6: I feel that my organization promotes the use of the R&D process I am expected to follow

Figure 6. The Metric Process Commitment (Note that numbers are fabricated)

were available for all affected employees, but the result was not formally communicated to them.

In ARC#5 through ARC#7, the result was again packaged into PowerPoint presentations. The presentations were, however, downsized to approximately 30 slides focusing on the established metrics and benchmarking between units and over time. This downsizing and focus aimed to increase usability and understandability of the result in order to facilitate communication and action taking. It was also a natural result of fewer questions to analyze. In ARC#8 and ARC#9, the result was packaged into three different PowerPoint packages aiming to fulfill the communication needs for different target groups: one presentation of approximately 20 slides summarizing the overall R&D result, one presentation with approximately five slides plus one slide per unit having their own result as described in Figure 5, and one complete presentation of approximately 50 slides for the process engineers and upwards in the organizational hierarchy. This packaging of the results was defined and agreed upon before the process survey in ARC#8 was sent out. The communication packages were well received by the organization. Figure 6 shows how the process commitment metric was described in the communication packages.

One thing that we considered was whether there was any "self-selection" evident in the survey responses. Stated another way, were the people who took the time to respond to the survey exactly the ones who were the most "committed" and thereby unrepresentative of the population as a whole? As said earlier, we had a 50 to 80 percent response rate. We had many very positive but also quite a few very negative answers. Thus our closer-look analysis did not reveal any self-selection to be evident.

5   ANALYSIS AND DISCUSSION

Jeffery and Berry (1993) found four aspects to be of equal importance when evaluating the success of a measurement program: context, inputs, process, and product. *Context* refers to the organizational context in which the measurement program is situated. *Input* is about resources that go into the program. *Process* is the method used for designing and using the measurement program. *Product* is the outcome in the form of measurement data, reports, etc. In this section, we use these four aspects to analyze and discuss the success of the process survey project and to answer the research question: How do we know that process innovations and improvements give organizational benefits?

5.1 Context

Ericsson needed a measurement mechanism to understand and improve both SPI and R&D process efficiency and use. This Ericsson goal did not change over time, even though it was iterated, questioned, and discussed.

The stability of the goal throughout the ARCs implies to us that the goal was well defined and based on relevant organizational needs. We believe *the well-defined goal* contributed to a successful measurement mechanism. This belief is supported by Gopal et al. (2002), who used industry-wide survey data and regression testing to determine the influence of factors that may affect the success of a measurement program. They found the factor goal alignment to have great influence on success.

If the goal had been changed several times or contested by different stakeholders in the organization, then the suitability of our chosen GQM approach could have been questioned. But it worked very well for us in this case.

5.2 Inputs

The resources used in the process survey project did not change over time. Some were added, but there was a core of employees (two of the authors) that stayed current during the entire project. This made it possible to stabilize the questions and to attain benchmarking effects over time. Three of the four established metrics in the measurement mechanism were possible to analyze based on four or five years of benchmarking (see Figure 4). The combination of the same dedicated resources involved and the benchmarking possibilities facilitated receiving commitment to the process survey. It is well known that successful improvement initiatives are highly dependent on commitment (Abrahamsson 2001; Humphrey 1989). We believe *the use of the same resources throughout the process survey project* and *the longitudinal benchmarking possibilities* contributed to a successful measurement mechanism.

The process survey project did not spend any major efforts on what tools to use to collect the data. There was no discussion and prioritization about what features to include in the tool. We believe *the effort not spent on tools issues* contributed to a successful measurement mechanism.

The process survey project used an iterative approach to empirically test and try-out what worked in practice. Schaffer and Thomson (1992) argue empirical testing that reveals what works in practice is a useful approach to increase understanding of what works best. It was also possible to see a positive correlation between the increase in metrics and units with ongoing improvement initiatives. The measurement mechanism helped Ericsson measure whether process innovations and improvement gave organizational benefits or not. We believe *the iterative approach using empirical testing* contributed to a successful measurement mechanism.

5.3 Process

The GQM approach (Basili et al. 1994; Basili and Rombach 1988; Basili and Weiss 1984) helped us to structure and evolve the measurement mechanism. Figure 7 describes

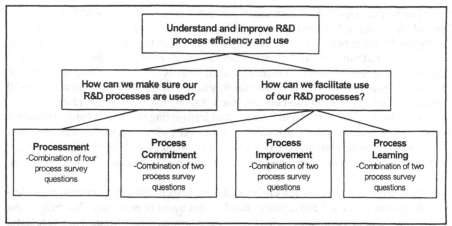

Figure 7. The Ericson GQM Adoption for Evaluating Process Efficiency and Use

how the GQM approach was adopted and used to identify valuable metrics for process efficiency and use.

The main goal for Ericsson was to understand and improve R&D process efficiency and use. SPI was the preferred approach to execute these improvements. The main goal represented the conceptual level in the GQM approach. The goal was then refined into two questions: How can we make sure our R&D processes are efficient and used? How can we facilitate use of our R&D processes? These questions represented the operational level in the GQM approach. Each question was then, based on empirical testing, refined into metrics. These metrics represent the quantitative level in the GQM-approach. We believe *the use of the GQM approach to structure and evolve a measurement mechanism* contributed to a successful measurement mechanism.

5.4 Product

The four metrics were empirically tested in practice and established as described in Figure 4. In parallel, as the metrics were established, the SPI and SPI-related literature focusing on improving software processes like Ericsson's R&D processes strengthened the belief in the importance of each metric. IT use and IT usefulness (Delone and McLean 1992; Seddon and Kiew 1996) strengthened the belief in processment. The importance of management commitment (Abrahamsson 2001; Grady 1997; Humphrey 1989) strengthened process commitment. Process learning was strengthened by organizational learning (Argyris and Schön 1978; Merriam and Caffarella 1999). Finally, process improvements was strengthened by the importance of progress reporting in SPI (Börjesson 2006; Grady 1997). The close relation between each metric and its relevance in the literature facilitated communication of the measurement mechanism. We believe *the strong correlation between the established metrics and established factors for successful process improvement* contributed to a successful measurement mechanism.

The four metrics in the measurement mechanism were calculated and deployed, as described in Figure 5, in as many as 168 organizational units in ARC#9. Managers analyzing the result believed in the result as shown through the measurement mechanism. They recognized similarities between the metrics and their own perception of the process efficiency and use situation. There was also, in ARC#6 and ARC#7, an identified positive correlation between the increase in processment and units where successful process improvement work had been executed. During the entire action research study, managers have been interested in viewing and interpreting the results from the process survey. The measurement mechanism, in both ARC#8 and ARC#9, was also well received by the organization when the result was communicated. We believe *the recognized similarities between the metrics results and reality* contributed to a successful measurement mechanism.

Furthermore, the measurement mechanism helped identify previous misunderstandings about personal and organizational commitment to processes. We believe *the recognized misunderstanding related to process commitment* contributed to a successful measurement mechanism.

Finally, the metrics process commitment, process learning, and process improvement explained 76 percent of the variance of processment. We believe *the strong correlation between the metrics in the measurement mechanism* contributed to a successful measurement mechanism.

6   CONCLUSIONS

This six-year action research project at the telecom company Ericsson aimed at answering the research question: How do we know that process innovations and improvements give organizational benefits? Ericsson wanted to improve both SPI progress and their R&D processes. The study answered the question by defining a successful measurement mechanism consisting of four correlated metrics. The use of this measurement mechanism made it possible for managers to understand the effects of process innovation and process improvement efficiency and use. Taking a step back we can summarize our lessons learned as follows:

We believe
- *the well-defined goal,*
- *the use of the same resources through-out the process survey project,*
- *the longitudinal benchmarking possibilities,*
- *the effort not spent on tools issues,*
- *the iterative approach using empirical testing,*
- *the use of the GQM approach to structure and evolve a measurement mechanism,*
- *the strong correlation between the established metrics and established factors for successful process improvement,*
- *the recognized similarities between the metrics result and reality,*
- *the recognized misunderstanding related to process commitment, and*
- *the strong correlation between the metrics in the measurement mechanism*

all contributed to a successful measurement mechanism, which then led to organizational benefits for Ericsson.

Finally, what can others learn from this study? First, a weakness in action research is the lack of specificity around how theory should be kept explicit through the action research cycles (Baskerville and Pries-Heje 1999). To overcome this weakness we found that the GQM approach worked well to make theory explicit and to update the theory when reflecting on the learning at the end of each action research cycle. Thus, in answering questions on benefit and improvement or similar questions, companies can use the GQM approach.

We believe the measurement mechanism with the four metrics (see Figure 5) is directly useful for other organizations pursuing improvement and asking the "does it pay off?" question. The usefulness of each of the four metrics will be as follows:

- Processment can be used as a measure of the quality of the process diffusion activity, in that it measures the degree to which employees have access to processes, know them, follow them, and are supported when doing so.
- Process commitment can show the extent to which employees have belief in the process and feel that the process is promoted by the organization.
- Process learning can show the extent to which employees believe they can learn from others and vice versa.
- Process improvement shows the employee perception of how they carry out relevant improvement work.

References

Abrahamsson, P. "Measuring the Success of Software Process Improvement: The Dimensions," in *Proceedings of the European Software Process Improvement (EuroSPI2000) Conference,* Copenhagen, Denmark, November 7-9, 2000.

Abrahamsson, P. "Rethinking the Concept of Commitment in Software Process Improvement," *Scandinavian Journal of Information Systems* (13), 2001, pp. 69-98.

Albrecht, A. J. "Measuring Application Development Productivity," in *Proceedings of the IBM Application Development Symposium,* Monterrey, California, October 1979, pp. 83-92.

Albrecht, A. J., and Gaffney, Jr., J. E. "Software Function, Source Lines of Code, and Development Effort Prediction: A Software Science Validation," *IEEE Transactions on Software Engineering* (SE-9:6), October 1979, pp. 639-648.

Argyris, C., and Schön, D. *Organizational Learning,* Reading, MA: Addison-Wesley, 1978.

Bartunek, J. M., and Louis M. R. *Insider/Outsider Team Research, Qualitative Research Methods* (Vol. 40), Thousand Oaks, CA: Sage Publications, 1996.

Basili, V. G., Caldiera, G., and Rombach H. D. "The Goal/Question Metric Approach," in J. Marciniak (ed.), *Encyclopedia of Software Engineering,* Volume 1, New York: John Wiley & Sons, 1994, pp. 528-532.

Basili, V. R., and Rombach, H. D. "The TAME Project: Towards Improvement Oriented Software Environments," *IEEE Transactions on Software Engineering* (14:6), 1988, pp. 758-773.

Basili, V. R., and Weiss, D. M. "A Methodology for Collecting Valid Software Engineering Data," *IEEE Transactions on Software Engineering* (10:4), 1984, pp. 728-738.

Baskerville, R., and Pries-Heje, J. "Grounded Action Research: A Method for Understanding IT in Practice," *Management and Information Technology* (9), 1999, pp. 1-23.

Baskerville, R., and Wood-Harper, A. T. "Diversity in Information Systems Action Research Methods," *European Journal of Information Systems* (7), 1998, pp. 90-107.

Baskerville, R., and Wood-Harper, A. T. "A Critical Perspective on Action Research as a Method for Information Systems Research," *Journal of Information Technology* (11), 1996, pp. 235-246.

Brown, J. S., Collins, A., and Duguid, P. "Situated Cognition and the Culture of Learning," *Educational Researcher* (18:1), 1989, pp. 32-42.

Börjesson, A. "Simple Indicators for Tracking Software Process Improvement Progress," in I. Richardson, P. Runeson, and R. Messnarz (eds.), *Software Process Improvement*, Berlin-Heidelberg: Springer-Verlag, 2006, pp. 74-87.

Chrissis, M. B., Konrad, M., and Shrum, S. *CMMI: Guidelines for Process Integration and Product Improvement*, Boston, MA: Addison-Wesley, 2003.

Daskalantonakis, M. "A Practical View of Software Measurement and Implementation Experiences Within Motorola.," *IEEE Transactions on Software Engineering* (18), 1992, pp. 998-1010.

Davison, R. M., Martinsons, M. G., and Kock, N. "Principles of Canonical Action Research," *Information Systems Journal* (14), 2004, pp. 65-86.

Delone, W., and McLean, E. "Information Systems Success: The Quest for the Dependent Variable," *Information Systems Research* (3:1), March 1992, pp. 60-95.

Deming, W. E. *Out of the Crisis*, Cambridge, MA: MIT Center for Advanced Engineering Study, 1986.

Dybå, T. "An Instrument for Measuring the Key Factors of Success in Software Process Improvement," *Empirical Software Engineering* (5), 2000, pp. 357-390.

Enskog, U. "Process Awareness and Use at Ericsson AB," B.Sc. Thesis, IT University of Göteborg, Sweden, 2006.

Fenton, N. E., and Pfleeger, S. L. *Software Metrics: A Rigorous and Practical Approach* (2nd ed.), Boston: PWS Publishing, 1997.

Flaherty, M. J. "Programming Process Productivity Measurement System for System 370," *IBM System Journal* (24:2), 1985, pp. 168-175.

Florac, W. A., and Carleton, A. D. *Measuring the Software Process*, Boston, MA: Addison-Wesley Professional, 1999.

Galliers, R. D. "Choosing an Information Systems Research Approach," in R. D. Galliers (ed.), *Information Systems Research: Issues, Methods, and Practical Guidelines*, Oxford, England: Blackwell Scientific Publications, 1992, pp. 144-162.

Garmus, D., and Herron, D. *Measuring The Software Process: A Practical Guide to Functional Measurements*, Englewood Cliffs, NJ: Prentice Hall, 1995.

Goldenson, D. R., and Herbsleb, J. "After the Appraisal: A Systematic Survey of Process Improvement, its Benefits, and Factors that Influence Success," Technical Report, CMU/SEI-95-TR-009, Carnegie Mellon University, Software Engineering Institute, Pittsburgh, PA, 1995.

Gopal, A., Krishnan, M. S., Mukhopadhyay, T., and Goldenson, D. R. "Measurement Programs in Software Development: Determinants of Success," *IEEE Transaction on Software Engineering* (28:9), September 2002, pp. 863-875.

Grady, R. B. *Successful Software Process Improvement*, Upper Saddle River, NJ: Prentice Hall, 1997.

Herbsleb, J., Carleton, A., Rozum, J., Siegel, J., and Zubrow, D. "Benefits of CMM-Based Software Orocess Improvement: Initial Results," Technical Report, CMU/SEI-94-TR-13, Carnegie Mellon University, Software Engineering Institute, Pittsburgh, PA, 1994.

Humphrey, W. S. *Managing the Software Process*, Reading, MA: Addison Wesley, 1989.

IEEE. *IEEE Standard 1061: Standard for a Software Quality Metrics Methodology*, Piscataway, NJ: IEEE Standards Department, 1998.

ISO/IEC TR 15504. *Information Technology—Process Assessment. Part 2-3*, International Organization for Standardization, Geneva, 2003.

ISO/IEC TR 15504. *Information Technology—Process Assessment. Part 1 and 4*, International Organization for Standardization, Geneva, 2004.

ISO/IEC TR 15504. *Information Technology—Process Assessment. Part 5*, International Organization for Standardization, Geneva, 2006.

Jeffery, R., and Berry, M. "A Framework for Evaluation and Prediction of Metrics Programs Success," in *Proceedings of the IEEE International Software Metrics Symposium*, Los Alamitos, CA: IEEE Computer Society Press, 1993, pp. 28-39.

Jones, C. *Assessment and Control of Software Risks*, Englewood Cliffs, NJ: Prentice Hall, 1994.

Jones, C. *Sources of Errors in Software Cost Estimating, Version 1.0*, Burlington, MA: Software Productivity Research, 1993.

Kaner, C., and Bond, W. P. "Software Engineering Metrics: What Do They Measure and How Do We Know?," in *Proceedings of the 10th International Software Metrics Symposium (METRICS 2004)*, Los Alamitos, CA: IEEE Computer Society Press, 2004.

Kuvaja, P., Similä, J., Krzanik, L., Bicego, A., Saukkonen, S., and Koch, G. *Software Process Assessment and Improvement. The BOOTSTRAP Approach*, Oxford, England: Blackwell Publishers, 1994.

Leave, J., and Wenger, E. *Situated Learning: Legitimate Peripheral Participation*, Cambridge, England: Cambridge University Press, 1991.

Mashiko, Y., and Basili, V. R. "Using the GQM Paradigm to Investigate Influential Factors for Software Process Improvement," *Journal of Systems and Software* (36), 1997, pp. 17-32.

Mathiassen, L. "Collaborative Practice Research. Information," *Technology & People* (14:4), 2002, pp. 321-345.

McFeeley, B. "IDEAL. A User's Guide for Software Process Improvement," Handbook CMU/SEI-96-HB-001, The Software Engineering Institute, Carnegie Mellon University, Pittsburgh, PA, 1996.

Merriam, S. B., and Caffarella, R. S. *Learning in Adulthood: A Comprehensive Guide* (2nd ed.), San Francisco: Jossey-Bass, 1999.

Patton, M. Q. *How to Use Qualitative Methods in Evaluation*, Newbury Park, CA: Sage Publications, 1987.

Paulk, M. C., Weber, C., Curtis, B., and Chrissis, M. B. *The Capability Maturity Model: Guidelines for Improving the Software Process*, Reading, MA: Addison-Wesley, 1995.

Pfleeger, S. L. "Lessons Learned in Building a Corporate Metrics Program," *IEEE Software*, May 1993, pp. 67-74.

Rogers, E. M. *Diffusion of Innovations* (5th ed.), New York: Free Press, 2003.

Schaffer, R. H., and Thomson, H. A. "Successful Change programs Begin with Results," *Harvard Business Review* (70), 1992, pp. 80-89.

Seddon, P. B., and Kiew, M-Y. "A Partial Test and Development of DeLone and McLean's Model of IS Success," *Australian Journal of Information Systems* (4:1), September 1996, pp. 90-109.

SEMA. "Software Engineering Management Analysis: Process Maturity Profile of the Software Community," Software Engineering Institute, Carnegie-Mellon University, Pittsburgh, PA, 2002 (updated maturity profiles can be found at http://www.sei.cmu.edu/appraisal-program/profile/profile.html).

Sigurd, G., and Tedsjö, J. "Making Use of Regular Process Surveys: A Case Study at Ericsson," B.Sc. Thesis, IT University of Göteborg, Sweden, 2005.

Susman, G., and Evered, R. "An Assessment of the Scientific Merits of Action Research," *Administrative Science Quarterly* (23), 1978, pp. 582-603.

Wenger, E. *Communities of Practice: Learning, Meaning, and Identity*, New York: Cambridge University Press, 1998.

Wiegers, K. E. "Software Process Improvement: Eight Traps to Avoid, CrossTalk," *The Journal of Defense Software Engineering*, September 1998, pp. 9-12.

Vinter, O., Lauesen, S., and Pries-Heje, J. "Preventing Requirements Issues from Becoming Defects," in C. Ghezzi and M. Fusani (eds.), *Proceedings of the Fourth International Con-*

ference on Achieving Quality in Software: Software Quality in the Communication Society, Venice: AQUIS, 1998, pp. 427-431.

Yin, R. *Case Study Research*, Newbury Park, CA: Sage Publications, 1994.

Zharan, S. *Software Process Improvement: Practical Guidelines for Business Success*, Harlow, England: Addison-Wesley, 1998.

About the Authors

Anna Börjesson has more than 10 years of practical experience working with software development and software process improvement. She has been working at Ericsson since 1998. Anna holds a Ph.D. in Software Process Improvement from the IT University of Göteborg. Anna is also a member of ACM and IEEE. She can be reached by e-mail at anna.borjesson@ericsson.com.

Anders Baaz joined Ericsson in 1993. He has been manager of a broad range of disciplines. In 2002, he was appointed general manager for the Mobitex business. At present he works with measuring operational excellence in development projects and processes. He holds an M.Sc. from Chalmers University of Technology in Gothenburg. Anders can be reached by e-mail at anders.baaz@ericcson.com.

Jan Pries-Heje is professor at Roskilde University, Denmark, and part-time at the IT University in Gothenburg, Sweden. Jan's main research interests are information systems development, software engineering, and software process improvement. He has carried out action research with industry on specific topics such as process improvement, high-speed software development, and metrics. He can be reached by e-mail at jan-pries-heje@ituniv.se.

Magnus Timmerås is an SPI change agent at Ericsson AB in Gothenburg, Sweden. Magnus has 10 years of experience working with SPI and SPI-related areas. He holds a B.Sc. in Psychology from Stockholm University and a University Degree in Electrical Engineering from Chalmers University of Technology (Gothenburg). He can be reached by e-mail at magnus.timmeras@ericsson.com.

15 THE VIEWS OF EXPERTS ON THE CURRENT STATE OF AGILE METHOD TAILORING

Kieran Conboy
Cairnes Graduate School
National University of Ireland
Galway, Ireland

Brian Fitzgerald
Lero Software Engineering Research Centre
University of Limerick
Limerick, Ireland

Abstract   *As stated in the conference theme, the failure of information systems and information technology projects remains stubbornly high. Agile methods have recently emerged as a new and seemingly popular alternative approach to systems development. Purveyors of these methods claim they solve many of the problems that have plagued the field for over 40 years, and there is now anecdotal evidence to suggest that these benefits are being realized and that diffusion of agile methods is rapidly increasing. However, a key factor in the diffusion of any technology or method is its ability to be customized. Innovative customization, tailoring, and fragmentation of systems development methods are viewed by many as a necessary step to avoid project failure like so many projects in the past. The ability to tailor any method is considered critically important given the complex and unique nature of each and every ISD environment, and in particular, one would logically expect that a method labeled as agile should be malleable. However, it is still unclear whether agile methods are amenable to tailoring. On one hand, purveyors of these methods advocate and often recommend tailoring. On the other hand, however, tailoring of agile methods has been described as a potential minefield due to the fact that their practices are interconnected, synergistic, and socially embedded in the development effort. This study develops a better understanding of agile method tailoring in practice through semi-structured delphi*

Please use the following format when citing this chapter:

Conboy, K., and Fitzgerald, B., 2007, in IFIP International Federation for Information Processing, Volume 235, Organizational Dynamics of Technology-Based Innovation: Diversifying the Research Agenda, eds. McMaster, T., Wastell, D., Ferneley, E., and DeGross, J. (Boston: Springer), pp. 217-234.

interviews with 40 ISD expert practitioners and academics. The study sought to ascertain their opinion on the tailoring of agile methods in general, and then honed in on specific critical success factors (CSFs) of tailoring, namely built-in contingency, clear rationale behind method practices, independence of method practices, and disciplined and educated tailoring of practices. The study found that these factors are largely ignored by the agile method movement except in rare instances, and concludes with a set of recommendations for agile method creators and users to ensure agile methods experience higher diffusion rates than at present.

Keywords   Agile method, tailoring, systems development, software development, delphi, expert opinion

1   INTRODUCTION

For the last 40 years, information system development (ISD) projects have been troubled by time and budget overruns, and inferior, ineffective systems, resulting in many dissatisfied customers, users, and developers. Many methods, method hybrids, and method variants have been developed and implemented in the hope of overcoming these problems, and yet at the start of this century the ISD community is still seeking what Brooks (1987) calls "the silver bullet." The late 1990s and early 2000s have seen the emergence of what are commonly referred to as agile methods. These seek to "restore credibility to the word *method*," and eradicate the problems that have plagued ISD for so long (Fowler and Highsmith 2001, p. 29). A number of methods are included in this family, the most popular being *eXtreme Programming* (XP) (Beck 1999), the *dynamic systems development method* (DSDM) (Stapleton 1997), *Scrum* (Schwaber and Beedle 2002), *Crystal* (Cockburn 2001), *agile modeling* (Ambler 2002), *feature driven design* (Coad et al. 1999), and *lean software development* (LSD) (Poppendieck 2001). These methods represent a popular initiative that complements the critique of formalized ISD methods over the past decade or so (Baskerville et al. 1992; Fitzgerald 1994, 1996), and have been well received by practitioners and academics alike. In fact, after 40 years of research showing that developers rarely adhere to formalized methods (Fitzgerald 1997, 1998; Hardy et al. 1995; Jenkins et al. 1984; Necco et al. 1987), there is now anecdotal evidence to suggest use of agile methods has been growing rapidly since their inception.

While there is general agreement across the ISD community regarding the increasing popularity of agile methods, there is a lot of uncertainty as to whether they should be fragmented or tailored. The ability to tailor a method is considered to be very important given that it is now accepted that no single method can provide an exact fit for the needs of every ISD project given the diversity and uniqueness of ISD environments (Brinkkemper 1996; Iivari 1989). One of the main reasons underpinning the lack of adoption of traditional methods is their lack of flexibility and malleability (Brinkkemper 1996; Iivari 1989). Apart from the fact that any method should be tailorable, the very name *agile* suggests that the method should be easily adjusted to suit its environment.

Some agile method texts and papers do highlight the ease with which agile methods can be tailored. Beck and Fowler's (2001, p. xi) text on planning XP projects authoritatively states that "no two XP projects will ever act exactly alike," and "once you get comfortable with the basic process, you will grow it to fit your situation more precisely."

Some studies have advocated an *à la carte* approach such as XP Lite, where an existing agile method is "defanged" and a subset method used (Stephens and Rosenberg 2003). Conversely, however, some state that the whole is better than the sum of its parts and that agile methods are only beneficial when used in their entirety and not tailored and fragmented (Beck 1999). Furthermore, Stephens and Rosenberg (2003) view the tailoring of agile methods as a potential minefield.

The objective of this paper is to review the current state of agile method tailoring. To achieve this, a set of method tailoring critical factors were drawn from the literature (section 2), and used as a lens to analyze what agile method literature exists in relation to each (section 3). The primary research approach is outlined in section 4, and describes how the researchers selected 40 ISD experts, ascertaining their opinions on the current state of agile method use regarding tailoring in general, as well as in relation to each exemplar. These findings are discussed in section 5.

2   CRITICAL SUCCESS FACTORS FOR METHOD TAILORING

The first factor of method tailoring cited in the literature is Iivari's (1989) notion of *built-in contingency*. Numerous studies advocate contingent use of methods, based on the belief that there is no single silver bullet method that is applicable in all circumstances (e.g., Avison and Wood-Harper 1991; Benyon and Skidmore 1987; Davis 1982; Gremillion and Pyburn 1983; Iivari 1989; McMaster et al. 1998; Naumann et al. 1980; Sullivan 1985; Vidgen and Madsen 2003). These studies have proposed many features or *situation dependencies* (Kumar and Welke 1992) of an ISD project environment which should be considered when selecting a method or part of a method. Such features include developer proficiency and experience, type of IS and customer, the development culture, and programming language. However, the concept of built-in contingency requires that the method itself contains an encompassing framework, allowing it to be adjusted to fit any context as well as providing guidance on the tailoring process, as opposed to being just one method to be selected from a pool of many.

Researchers have developed a variety of method engineering frameworks (e.g., Brinkkemper 1996; Cronholm and Goldkuhl 1994; Grundy and Venable 1996; Harmesen 1997; Harmesen et al. 1994; Smolander et al. 1990; Tolvanen and Lyytinen 1993;), all of which are designed to construct or "engineer" a development method according to stakeholders' needs, where methods are built from the ground up using "existing proven method fragments" (Fitzgerald et al. 2002, p. 150). This is an alternative approach to contingency-based use that suggests ISD projects may not always be fulfilled by a set of available methods due to the uniqueness of ISD situations (Brinkkemper 1996; Kumar and Welke 1992). Of the various method engineering frameworks in existence, almost all require that the *rationale behind these fragments be clear*, thus aiding the method creator. A further key attribute of a method amenable to engineering is that its *practices are highly independent*, allowing them to be separated and combined without fear of unknown knock-on effects (Kumar and Welke 1992; Stephens and Rosenberg 2003).

Finally, there is also evidence to suggest that while methods are tailored in practice, this is often done without adequate consideration being given to the practices being

Table 1. **CSFs of Method Tailoring**

Critical Factors	Literature
Contingency Built Into Method	Iivari 1989
Clearly Stated Rationale Behind Method and Practices	Brinkkemper 1996; Cronholm and Goldkuhl 1994; Grundy and Venable 1996; Harmesen 1997; Harmesen et al. 1994; Smolander et al. 1990; Tolvanen and Lyytinen 1993
Independent Practices	Brinkkemper 1996; Kumar and Welke 1992; Stephens and Rosenberg 2003
Disciplined and Educated Tailoring of Practices	Kumar and Welke 1992

dropped (Kumar and Welke 1992). Empirical research shows that method use in practice is rather limited (Fitzgerald 1996; Hidding 1996), and in fact, an empirical study by Fitzgerald (1998) found that only 6 percent of developers rigorously adhere to methods at all. This does not necessarily mean that all of these developers did not duly consider each practice or method before dropping them, but such a scenario is highly unlikely given that adherence is so low. The final exemplar, therefore, requires *disciplined and educated tailoring of practices*, whereby the ISD team test each practice or at leave give due consideration to the merits, demerits, and suitability of that practice before dropping it.

3   A CRITICAL CONSIDERATION OF METHOD TAILORING IN AGILE METHODS

3.1   Built-In Contingency

There is evidence to support the existence of contingency based approaches to agile method selection and tailoring across the literature, and some researchers have proposed situational characteristics upon which such selection efforts should be based (e.g., Boehm and Turner 2004; Koch 2005). These include team size, relationship with the customer, criticality of the system, dynamism of the environment, developer competency, team culture, and existing tools and processes. In some cases, the characteristics proposed are intended to be used to choose between agile methods (e.g., Koch 2005), while others aid the selection decision between agile methods and traditional plan-driven approaches (e.g., Boehm and Turner 2003).

However, a key exemplar proposed in Table 1 was that a method should guide the tailoring process through what Iivari (1989) calls "built-in contingency." From an analysis of the literature, it seems that agile methods have still not adequately dealt with this issue. The creators of each method still offer detailed, intricate, step-by-step instructions on how to follow their method, but although they acknowledge tailoring should be conducted, only Crystal offers recommendations as to how this should be accomplished (Cockburn 2001). This shortcoming of agile methods is similar to that of their traditional counterparts where the need for flexibility is acknowledged but not addressed. Therefore, an analysis of the literature would suggest that problems cited by Fitzgerald et al. (2002) in relation to traditional methods still hold true for the agile method movement: tailoring is still left to the intuition of developers, it is still carried out in an *ad hoc* fashion, and little is learned about tailoring across projects.

3.2 Clarity and Rationale Behind Practices

The method tailoring literature suggests that a method's practices should be clear and rational in order to aid tailoring decisions and processes. The existing agile method literature on this issue is scarce and what does exist is inconclusive. On one hand, there are a couple of dissenting texts which describe agile methods, and XP in particular, as irrational and vague (McBreen 2003; Stephens and Rosenberg 2003). In addition, quite a few also highlight the fact that some agile method practices are nonprescriptive, and represent a high level of abstraction, lending themselves to inconsistent interpretation and implementation (Abrahamsson et al. 2002; Boehm and Turner 2004; Koch 2005). On the other hand, however, there is at least one proprietary text to accompany every agile method, with an entire series of texts dedicated to XP. In many of these, a whole chapter is dedicated to each practice. Therefore, it is hard to argue that the creators of these methods are guilty of releasing them without adequate explanation of their constitution and rationale.

3.3 Independence of Practices

One of the most distinctive features of some agile methods is that their practices are not independent, but are instead very tightly coupled (Auer and Miller 2002), interdependant (Beck 1999), and synergistic (Martin 2003). As Beck (1999, p. 121) states, "any one practice doesn't stand well on its own….and they require the other practices to keep them in balance." Boehm and Turner (2004, p. 16) cite an unnamed "agilist" who dismisses partial use of agile practices and claims that "the pieces fit together like a fine Swiss watch." Stephens and Rosenberg (2003) liken this to a "self-referential safety net" (p. 81) where even if some practices add no value, it is impossible to remove them if they are necessary in order to hold the other ones in place. Stephens and Rosenberg state that "although XP is supposedly adaptable to a wide variety of projects, its authors have got it exactly the wrong way around" (p. 82). They consider this to be analogous to a house of cards or a circle of snakes:

> The tightly meshed nature of XP's practices and activities makes them like a ring of poisonous snakes, daisy-chained together. All it takes is for one of the snakes to wriggle loose, and you've got a very angry poisonous serpent heading your way (p. 82).

3.4 Disciplined and Educated Tailoring of Practices

Many efforts have been made to tailor agile methods to suit a variety of contexts such as large teams (Bowers et al. 2002; Cao et al. 2004; Crispin and House 2003; Kahkonen

2004; Lindvall et al. 2004), start-ups (Auer and Miller 2002), distributed development environments (Kircher et al. 2001; Stotts et al. 2003), greenfield sites (Rasmusson 2003), educational environments (Johnson and Caristi 2003; McDowell et al. 2003; Melnik and Mauer 2003; Wainer 2003), open source development (Kircher and Levine 2001), outsourcing arrangements (Kussmaul et al. 2004), and systems maintenance (Poole and Huisman 2001). However, there is little empirical evidence focusing specifically on the extent to which such tailoring is done in a disciplined and educated manner, and it is not known if teams evaluate all practices before deciding whether to adopt each or not.

4   RESEARCH APPROACH

This study involved a set of delphi interviews with experts in the field of ISD. The delphi method was originally devised "in order to obtain the most reliable opinion consensus of a group of experts" (Dalkey and Helmer 1963), and there are many reasons why the delphi method is desirable when conducting applied social research (see Dalkey and Helmer 1963; Linstone and Turoff 1975; Moore 1987). First, combining the judgment of a large number of people offers a better chance of getting closer to the truth. Second, it is easier to understand social phenomena by obtaining the views of the actors. Given the ambiguous interpretation and use of agile methods and the fact that they are socially oriented methods (Beck 1999; Koch 2005; Schwaber and Beedle 2002), this advantage is highly relevant in the context of this study. Finally, complex and ill-defined problems can often be addressed only by pooled intelligence, and such difficulties are prevalent not just in the field of agile methods, but also in the study of ISD and the study of agility across all disciplines.

There is no single prescribed format for conducting a Delphi study. It is "flexible in its design" (Okoli and Pawlowski 2004, p. 29) and, indeed, many hybrids and variants exist (Moore 1987). In this instance, the decision was made to invite 40 experts to take part in the study, all of whom accepted (see Table 2). Group size theory varies in its suggestions regarding the ideal number of delphi study participants. Some general rules-of-thumb indicate 5 to 10 people for a homogenous population, but 15 to 40 people for a heterogeneous population (i.e., people coming from different social and professional stratifications such as academics and practitioners, as is the case in this study) (Delbecq et al. 1975; Uhl 1983).

Verifying expertise is somewhat difficult as it can be judged by status, experience, or "a myriad of other things" (Brown 1968, p. 211). Amethodical selection of partici-pants or allowing every willing person to take part is considered highly unscientific (Clayton 1997; Sackman 1975), and so systematic classification and selection was conducted. The skills and background of experts required for this study are listed in Table 3, along with the basis for identification and selection. As well as selecting a mix of practitioners and academics, the selection process also ensured that at least half of the participants had experience using or researching traditional, pre-agile methods, so as to enable comparison and critical reflection. It is also worth noting that the minimum criteria were lower in relation to the selection of agile-oriented practitioners and academics, as more stringent criteria requiring 7 years industry experience or a large number of agile method publications is somewhat unrealistic given that these methods have such recent origins.

Table 2. List of Delphi Participants

Practitioner	Organization
Pekka Abrahamson	VTT Finland
Ben Aveling	Alcatel Australia
Sean Baker	Iona Technologies
Paul Bohan	American Power Conversion
Dave DesAutel	Accenture
Alistair Cockburn	Cockburn & Associates
Bill Curtis	TeraQuest
Niall Donnelly	Iona Technologies
Michael Freeley	Accenture
Tom Gilb	Gilb Consulting
Sean Griffin	Qumas
Brian Hanly	eXoftware
James Harte	PA Consulting
Ger Hartnett	Intel
Michael Hennessy	EDS
Liam Kidd	Dept. of Communications
Larry Lumsden	Curam Software
John McAvoy	Motorola
John O'Flaherty	MAC
Mary Poppendieck	Cutter Consortium

Academic	University
Ivan Aaen	Aalborg University
Richard Baskerville	Georgia State University
Michael Cusumano	Sloan MIT
Rob Fichman	Boston College
Guy Fitzgerald	Brunel University
Jim Herbsleb	Carnegie Mellon University
Mike Holocombe	University of Sheffield
Linda Levine	Software Engineering Institute
Kalle Lyytinen	Case Western Reserve
Angela Martin	University of Wellington
Lars Mathiassen	Georgia State University
Peter Middleton	Queens University Belfast
Mark Paulk	Carnegie Mellon University
Jan Pries-Heje	IT University of Copenhagen
Nancy Russo	Northern Illinois University
Helen Sharp	Open University
Ian Sommerville	Lancaster University
Duane Truex	Georgia State University
Laurie Williams	North Carolina State
Robert Zmud	University of Oklahoma

Table 3. Classification of Experts and Listing of Participants

Desired Background or Skill Set	Method of Expert Identification	Minimum Selection Criteria
Practitioners who have used agile methods	Membership of relevant societies (Agile Alliance, DSDM Consortium etc) Personal contacts	> 4 years agile method experience > 2 years agile project management experience
Practitioners who have worked in ISD, and are aware of agile methods	Membership of relevant societies (ITAA, Cutter Consortium etc) Personal contacts	> 7 years ISD experience > 3 years ISD management experience
Academics who have researched agile methods	Literature review of relevant academic and practitioner journals and conferences	≥ 3 agile method publications in refereed journal/conferences
Academics who have researched ISD and are aware of agile methods	Literature review of relevant academic and practitioner journals and conferences	≥ 5 ISD publications in refereed journal/ conferences

Data was collected through personal face-to-face interviews, which is considered the superior data gathering technique FOR interpretivist studies such as this (Yin 2003). Personal interviews are also well suited for exploratory research because they allow expansive discussions which illuminate additional factors of importance (Oppenheim 1992; Yin 2003). Also, the information gathered is likely to be more accurate than information collected by other methods since the interviewer can avoid inaccurate or incomplete answers by explaining the questions to the interviewee (Oppenheim 1992).

A guiding script was prepared for use throughout the interviews to establish a structure for the direction and scope of the research, to ensure the researcher covers all aspects of the study with each respondent, to manufacture some element of distance between the interviewer and interviewee, and to permit the researcher to compare and contrast responses (McCracken 1988). The researcher circulated the guiding questions in advance to allow participants to consider their responses prior to the interview. The questions were largely open-ended, allowing respondents freedom to convey their experiences and views, and expression of the socially complex contexts that underpin ISD and agile method use (Oppenheim 1992; Yin 2003).

The interviews lasted between 50 and 120 minutes, with the average length being approximately 85 minutes. The interviews were conducted in a responsive (Rubin and Rubin 2005; Wengraf 2001), or reflexive (Trauth and O'Connor 1991) manner, allowing the researcher to follow up on insights uncovered mid-interview, and adjust the content and schedule of the interview accordingly. Furthermore, the researcher kept a diary of questions asked during each interview, and analyzed their effectiveness, making refinements and additions to the set of questions prior to the next meeting. In order to aid analysis of the data after the interviews, all were recorded with each interviewee's consent, and were subsequently transcribed, proof-read, and annotated by the researcher. In any cases of ambiguity, clarification was sought from the corresponding interviewee, either via telephone or e-mail.

Coding is often used in qualitative research to provide structured and coherent analysis of qualitative data (Miles and Huberman 1999; Stake 1995; Wengraf 2001;

Rubin and Rubin 2005; Salkind 2006). This involves systematically labeling concepts, themes, and artefacts so as to be able to retrieve and examine all data units that refer to each subject across the interviews. The coding structure adopted in this research consisted of three distinct mechanisms. First, an ID code was attached to each piece of text extracted from a transcript (A1...A20 for academics and P1...P20 for practitioners) to ensure participant anonymity. Second, a classification schema was built to analyze the data from the delphi interviews as recommended by Rubin and Rubin (2005), Miles and Huberman (1999), Stake (1995), and Yin (2003). This mechanism acted as set of "intellectual bins" (Miles and Huberman 1999), which were then used to segment the data and remove any irrelevant data collected throughout the interviews. This process also considered the fact that some factors are repeated across various components of the framework, and these links were identified when coding and analyzing the data. Finally, pattern coding was used in order to "identify any emergent themes, configurations or explanations" (Miles and Huberman 1999, p. 41). This approach aims to aggregate and summarize the previous codes, identifying themes, and inferences across them all.

5   FINDINGS

5.1   General Perspectives on Agile Method Tailoring

Most respondents were of the opinion that agile methods are not designed with tailoring in mind. Some pointed to the religious undertones which often emanate from agile method creators and early adopters. A number recalled hearing methods such as XP and Scrum described as *bibles* (A1, A8, A9, P4, P7, P11, P12) and *doctrines* (A3, A10) and other religious connotations, indicating that these methods should never be tailored or even questioned. One practitioner recalled a conversation he had with what he called an *agile apostle*, where the practices of XP were continually referred to as *the 12 commandments* (P4). Three participants did note that such extremity was now rarer, and that even those driving the agile movement don't feel as *emotional* (P11, P17) about it anymore. However, some interviewees still believed that such compromising attitudes are often superficial, and that those behind the agile movement are as fanatical as ever:

> *We had one agile consultant on our project for a while, who said he wasn't an agile evangelist and believed in nothing more than a "try first" approach where XP practices are dropped if they are not working. After 6 months of working with him, I'd say his philosophy was "try first, and if it doesn't work then try harder."* (P7)

> *I keep hearing that that the agile method extremists are easing off a little these days. But I met one of them at a conference a month ago, and ever since he made reference to me and my team burning in the depths of hell if we didn't convert to agile, I'm not so sure.* (P12)

The dogmatic sentiments emanating from the creators of agile methods is typified by what some respondents identified as a fervent belief that the ISD environment should be tailored to the method rather than the method to the environment. While some respondents felt that *lubricating* (P3) the organization to the method is sometimes appropriate, others suggested that agile method *radicals* (A7) often take this to a ludicrous and unrealistic extreme:

> *I can see how organizational structures can be tinkered to get the best out of a method. But for God's sake, we worked on a consulting engagement for public sector bodies across the E.U. We were one project of about 30 that these bodies were dealing with, yet this guy came on board, and told us we should get them to change everything just for us. When we told him we were distributed across a continent, his only solution was "Get everybody in the same room." When we said a 40 hour week was not possible because the on-site customers we were given worked split shifts in their own organization, he said "Change it so they work 8 hours." When we said we couldn't do 2 week sprints because the government bodies worked on an 8 week testing schedule, he said "Get them to change it to 2 weeks!"* (P19)

Some research suggests that method purveyors should show the limitations of their method, and where it fits in with those already in existence (Benyon and Skidmore 1987; Iivari 1989; Naumann et al. 1980; Sullivan 1985). Most respondents indicated that purveyors of contemporary agile methods do not usually envisage their methods to be part of a larger ensemble, and pay little heed to alternatives. In fact, two respondents felt that on the rare occasions when a method's proprietary literature does mention alternative approaches, it is usually done to highlight their inadequacies and to accentuate the strengths of the new method being promoted.

Given that tailoring to context is essential to maximizing value and therefore agility, it is clear from the responses that the purveyors of agile methods need to encourage tailoring of their methods. It can be argued that some proprietary texts do concede that the method has limitations and is not suitable in all circumstances (e.g., Beck 1999; Cockburn 2001). If so, then the findings in this study suggest that this message needs to be conveyed to the ISD community in a clearer fashion than at present.

5.2   Built-In Contingency

Most contended that while some proprietary texts accompanying agile methods may state their limitations and where they are and are not appropriate, contingencies are rarely built in to guide the developers on how the method should be tailored to suit a particular project context. To illustrate this, one practitioner described his longing for a simple document accompanying an agile method, telling him "*if a circumstance exists do this step, if a different circumstance exists do this step, and so on*" (P5). All 20 practitioners described some form of tailoring they had conducted to adapt agile methods to a large organization or team, to a distributed environment, or to a critical system or public sector project. In 19 of those cases, the tailoring effort was done in an *ad hoc* manner or based on *intuition* (P6, P20), and was not in any way directed by any guideline inherent in the method being used. One practitioner described his experiences of tailoring without guidance:

We changed a lot of things about XP. It took a long time to perfect given we were flying in the dark, on a trial and error basis, but we got there. And I think we are more agile. I just wish the option to use these alternatives could have been part of the method. It would have saved a lot of time, effort, and uncertainty. (P1)

The absence of built-in contingency is not specific to agile methods, as this has been a problem associated with traditional methods as far back as the late 1980s (Iivari 1989). However, it is of more concern in an agile method context, given that agile theory demands that a method be as amenable to tailoring as possible.

5.3 Clarity and Rationale Behind Practices

Respondents noted two problems with current agile methods in relation to this exemplar which hinder the ability to tailor. First, two academics and one practitioner maintained that the level of abstraction across agile method practices is quite varied even within a single method, making it difficult to make a structured tailoring decision. One used XP as an example, describing the *pair programming* practice as *"prescriptive, operational, and detailed,"* while the *simple design* and *metaphor* practices are more abstract and open to wider interpretation (A3).

Second, quite a few felt that the rationale behind some agile method fragments is not always that clear, and as one practitioner stated, *"unless you understand the rationale, you can't make an informed decision about extending that step, tailoring it, [or] dropping it"* (P10). Of these respondents, six explicitly mentioned the *system metaphor* practice in XP as an example. However, it must be said that numerous practitioners and academics strongly disagreed, and felt that the rationale behind agile method fragments is usually explained clearly.

As stated earlier, the emergence of most contemporary agile methods has been accompanied by proprietary texts which clearly describe the purpose and rationale of the method's practices (e.g., Beck 1999; Cockburn 2001; Schwaber and Beedle 2002). Therefore, it is possible that the perceived lack of clarity regarding these practices is a function of something else, perhaps because on occasion these methods are being communicated second- and third-hand without the aid of proprietary documentation, a possibility raised by one respondent.

5.4 Independence of Practices

All of the respondents agreed that tailoring and fragmentation of today's agile methods is made increasingly difficult by the fact that many of their practices are highly inter-dependent and tightly coupled, confirming what some literature has already suggested (Auer and Miller 2002; Beck 1999; Martin 2003; Stephens and Rosenberg 2003). Various participants described these practices as being *interrelated* (A5, P7), *inter-connected* (P9), *fused* (P11), *meshed* (P8), *knitted* (A6), *tightly coupled* (P4), *tethered* (A13), *tied-in* (A19), and *synergistic* (A18), which together form a set of *checks and balances* (P6) or *cogs and pulleys* (P19). Even though one academic considered this to be an issue not specific to agile methods, but one that has *"plagued development since time immemorium"* (A7), he still conceded that it is certainly an issue exacerbated in contemporary agile methods.

It is also clear that such tight coupling is causing significant problems in practice. Many of the practitioners wanted to remove certain non-value-adding practices on past projects, but were reticent due to the embedded nature of these practices and uncertainty about knock-on effects. This reiterates Stephens and Rosenberg's (2003, p. 8) condemnation of what they called a "self-referential safety net," whereby no fragment can be removed, regardless of its limitations, due of the other fragments which are dependent on it. The fact that this hinders tailoring should be of some concern, and paves the way for the development of more modular and segmented agile methods. It also highlights an urgent need to learn more about what practices are interconnected and interdependent, as all 20 academics felt that, like so many other aspects of agile methods, very little is known as yet about such relationships and the knock-on effects the removal of practice will have.

5.5 Disciplined and Educated Tailoring of Practices

Despite the fact that agile methods are not conducive to tailoring, quite a few respondents ironically noted that current tailoring efforts in practice go far beyond *tweaking* (P5) and *fine tuning* (P1), and often see developers *"hacking off practices like body parts"* (P17). According to the respondents, this has resulted in a *sporadic* (P3) and *patchy* (P15) use of agile methods, where in many cases only a very small minority of practices are actually implemented. Academics spoke of their observations, with one concluding that *"its very rare to even see more than four or five [of the 12 XP practices] used"* (A9). Another spoke of 5 years of research looking at over 20 agile method projects, of which none employed "anything close" to the full range of any method's practices (A19).

This observation was supported by many of the practitioners' own experiences on their current or most recent project. Of 16 practitioners currently or recently working on an XP project, Figure 1 shows that in reality only 25 percent of those projects were adopting more than half of the practices.

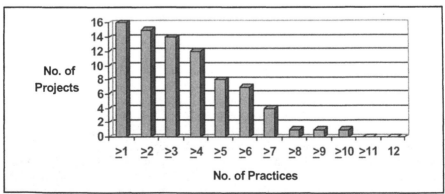

Figure 1. Sporadic Adoption of XP Practices

The fact that few practices are adopted is not that revelatory, as research has shown this to be true of method use in general (Fitzgerald 1997; Hardy et al. 1995; Jenkins et al. 1984; Necco et al. 1987; Powell et al. 1998). What is of greater concern is that many of the respondents believed that developers often do not have knowledge or experience of the practices they remove, and that there are many fragments "they know absolutely nothing about, but still love to drop" (A12). Of the 16 practitioners using XP, 15 conceded that many of the practices were dropped without due consideration, with only one stating that on his project, the pros and cons of each practice were debated before deciding whether to adopt or not (P20).

Although all participants agreed that method tailoring contributes to agility as a general rule, most did not believe this rule applied to the "*blind hacking of practices*" (A10), or when tailoring occurs just because the developers "*didn't feel like doing all of the practices*" (A17). As one of the interviewees contended,

> *Picasso has got to be the most agile guy there ever was- he mastered the traditional form and then he played with it.* (A5)

The need for diligent tailoring was considered to be even more imperative by one academic, given the uncharted nature of today's agile methods (A11). He argued that some of the flawed parts of older methods have been exposed through years of application, but that it was inexcusable for an ISD team to discard parts of agile methods when so little is still known about their use.

Linking this back to the discussion of agility theory, while customization and streamlining were considered important to maximize value and therefore agility, the general conclusion was that such efforts need to be done diligently, with due consideration given to each part of an entity before it is removed. It is clear from these responses that, in agile method practice at least, due diligence is often absent and ISD teams often take a minority of practices from a method without testing the other method fragments, or at least learning enough about them to justify their removal.

6 SUMMARY AND RECOMMENDATIONS

Rather than viewing method agility as being flexible and amenable to tailoring, there was a perception among respondents that agile methods are often incorrectly viewed as infallible and as possessing properties usually associated with a religion. The purveyors of these methods along with pro-agile consultants were seen by many as the primary drivers of these perceptions, although a few did concede such emotions were becoming less prevalent in the last couple of years.

The study also found that agile methods are not amenable to tailoring despite the fact that the ability to do so underpins the very meaning of what it is to be agile. The literature purported that contingencies should be built in to a method to guide the tailoring process, and these interviews found such contingencies to be distinctly absent. The findings also verified that the tightly coupled nature of agile method practices hinders the tailoring process, with numerous practitioners steering away from tailoring altogether for fear of knock-on effects. Many of the respondents also complained that despite the exis-

Table 4. Summary of Findings

CSF	Agile Method Deficiency
Built-in contingency	No built-in contingency apart from the Crystal family of methods.
Clearly stated rationale	Lack of clarity and rationale in some instances. Possibly caused by agile methods being passed on second and third hand.
Independence of practices	Low independence among agile method practice.
Disciplined and educated tailoring of practices	Indiscriminate culling of agile method practices in many cases.

tence of at least one proprietary text for each method, agile method practices sometimes lack clarity and the underpinning rationale is often unclear. It was felt that the vast majority of agile method tailoring efforts are haphazard and indiscriminate and, while it is now almost the norm to "hack off" huge parts of these methods, teams often fail to approach the tailoring process in a structured and rational manner, giving due consideration to practices before culling them.

The implication of this study is that those in practice need to develop agile methods which have built-in contingencies, independent practices, and a set of clearly stated rationale. While the research community can also play a vital role in the development, testing, and understanding of better agile methods, given that the agile method movement to date has been primarily industry-driven, it is logical to communicate these deficiencies primarily to this audience.

References

Abrahamsson, P., Salo, O., Ronkainen, J., and Warsta, J. *Agile Software Development Methods: Review and Analysis,* Espoo, Finland: Technical Research Centre of Finland, Vtt Publications, 2002.

Ambler, S. W. *Agile Modeling: Best Practices for the Unified Process and Extreme Programming,* New York: John Wiley & Sons, 2002.

Auer, K., and Miller, R. *Extreme Programming Applied: Playing to Win,* Reading, MA: Addison-Wesley, 2002.

Avison, D., and Wood-Harper, A. T. *Multiview: An Exploration in Information Systems Development,* Oxford, UK: Blackwell Scientific Publications, 1991.

Baskerville, R., Travis, J., and Truex, D. "Systems Without Method: The Impact of New Technologies on Information Systems Development Projects," in K. Kendall, K. Lyytinen, and J. I. DeGross (eds.), *The Impact of Computer Supported Technologies on Information Systems Development,* Amsterdam: Elsevier Science, 1992, pp. 241-269.

Beck, K. *Extreme Programming Explained,* Reading, MA: Addison-Wesley, 1999.

Beck, K., and Fowler, M. *Planning Extreme Programming,* Boston, MA: Addison-Wesley, 2001.

Benyon, D., and Skidmore, S. "Towards a Toolkit for the Systems Analyst," *The Computer Journal* (30:1), 1987, pp. 2-7.

Boehm, B., and Turner, R. *Balancing Agility and Discipline: A Guide for the Perplexed,* Boston: Addison-Wesley, 2004.

Boehm, B., and Turner, R. "Using Risk to Balance Agile and Plan-Driven Methods," *IEEE Software* (36:6), 2003, pp. 57-66.

Bowers, J., May, J., Melander, E., Baarman, M., and Ayoob, A. "Tailoring XP for Large Mission Critical Software Development," in D. Wells and L. Williams (eds.), *XP/Agile Universe*, Chicago, IL, August 4-7, 2002, pp. 100-111.

Brinkkemper, S. "Method Engineering: Engineering of Information Systems Development Methods and Tools," *Information and Software Technology* (38:4), 1996, pp. 275-280.

Brooks, F. "No Silver Bullet: Essence and Accidents of Software Engineering," *IEEE Computer* (20:4), 1987, pp. 10-19.

Brown, B. *Delphi Process: A Methodology Used for the Elicitation of Opinions of Experts*, Santa Monica, CA: Rand Corporation, 1968.

Cao, L., Mohan, K., Xu, P., and Ramesh, B. "How Extreme Does Extreme Programming Have to Be? Adapting XP Practices to Large-Scale Projects," in R. Sprague (ed.), *Proceedings of the 37th Hawaii International Conference on System Sciences*, Los Alamitos, CA: IEEE Computer Society Press, 2004.

Clayton, M. "Delphi: A Technique to Harness Expert Opinion for Critical Decision-Making Tasks in Education," *Educational Psychology* (17:4), 1997, pp. 373-387.

Coad, P., De Luca, J., and Lefebre, E. *Java Modeling in Color*, Englewood Cliffs, NJ: Prentice Hall, 1999.

Cockburn, A. *Crystal Clear: A Human-Powered Software Development Methodology for Small Teams*, Reading, MA: Addison-Wesley, 2001.

Crispin, L., and House, T. *Testing Extreme Programming*, Boston: Pearson, 2003.

Cronholm, S., and Goldkuhl, G. "Meanings and Motivates of Method Customization in Case Environments: Observations and Categorizations from an Empirical Study," in B. Theodoulidis (ed.), *Proceedings of the 5th Workshop on the next Generation of Case Tools*, University of Twente, Enschede, The Netherlands, 1994, pp. 67-79.

Dalkey, N., and Helmer, O. "An Experimental Application of the Delphi Method to the Use of Experts," *Journal of the Institute of Management Science* (9:3), 1963, pp. 458-467.

Davis, G. B. "Strategies for Information Requirements Determination," *IBM Systems Journal* (21:1), 1982, pp. 4-30.

Delbecq, A. L., Van De Ven, A. H., and Gustafson, H. *Group Techniques for Program Planning*, Glenview IL: Scott Foresman and Company, 1975.

Fitzgerald, B. "An Empirical Investigation into the Adoption of Systems Development Methodologies," *Information and Management* (34:6), 1998, pp. 317-328.

Fitzgerald, B. "Formalized Systems Development Methodologies: A Critical Perspective," *Information Systems Journal* (6:1), 1996, pp. 3-23.

Fitzgerald, B. "The Systems Development Dilemma: Whether to Adopt Formalized Systems Development Methodologies or Not?." in W. Baets (ed.), Proceedings of the Second European Conference on Information Systems, Nijenrode University, Utrecht, The Netherlands, 1994, pp. 691-706.

Fitzgerald, B. "The Use of Systems Development Methodologies in Practice: A Field Study," *Information Systems Journal* (7:3), 1997, pp. 201-212.

Fitzgerald, B., Russo, N., and Stolterman, E. *Information Systems Development: Methods in Action*, London: McGraw-Hill, 2002.

Fowler, M., and Highsmith, J. "The Agile Manifesto," *Software Development* (9:8), 2001, pp. 28-32.

Gremillion, L., and Pyburn, P. "Breaking the Systems Development Bottleneck," *Harvard Business Review* (61:2), 1983, pp. 130-137.

Grundy, J., and Venable, J. "Towards an Integrated Environment for Method Engineering," in S. Brinkkemper, K. Lyytinen, and R. Welke (eds.), *Proceedings of the IFIP TC8 Working Conference on Method Engineering: Principles of Method Construction and Tool Support*, London: Chapman & Hall, 1996, pp. 45-62.

Hardy, C., Thompson, J., and Edwards, H. "The Use, Limitations and Customization of Structured Systems Development Methods in the United Kingdom," *Information and Software Technology* (37:9), 1995, pp. 467-477.

Harmesen, F. *Situational Method Engineering*, Ph.D. Thesis, Twente University, Enschede, Netherlands, 1997.

Harmesen, F., Brinkkemper, S., and Oei, H. "Situational Method Engineering for I.S. Project Approaches," in A. A. Verrijn-Stuart and T. Olle (eds.), *Methods and Associated Tools for the Is Life Cycle*, Amsterdam: Elsevier Science, 1994, pp. 169-194.

Hidding, G. "Method Engineering: Experiences in Practice," in S. Brinkkemper, K. Lyytinen, and R. Welke (eds.), *Method Engineering: Principles of Method Construction and Tool Support*, London: Chapman & Hall, 1996, pp. 47-56.

Iivari, J. "A Methodology for I.S. Development as Organizational Change," in H. Klein and K. Kumar (eds.), *Systems Development for Human Progress*, Amsterdam: North Holland, 1989, pp. 197-217.

Jenkins, A., Naumann, J., and Wetherbe, J. "Empirical Investigation of Systems Development Practices and Results," *Information & Management* (7:1), 1984, pp. 73-82.

Johnson, D., and Caristi, J. "Extreme Programming and the Software Design Course," in M. Marchesi, G. Succi, D. Wells, and L. Williams (eds.), *Extreme Programming Perspectives*, Reading, MA: Addison-Wesley, 2003, pp. 47-59.

Kahkonen, T. "Agile Methods for Large Organizations- Building Communities of Practice," in T. Little (ed.), *Proceedings of the Agile Development Conference 2004*, Los Alamitos, CA: IEEE COmputer Society Press, 2004, pp. 2-11.

Kircher, M., Jain, P., Corsaro, A., and Levine, D. "Distributed Extreme Programming," in *Proceedings of XP 2001: Extreme Programming and Flexible Processes in Software Engineering*, Villasimius, Sardinia, Italy, May 2001, pp. 66-71.

Kircher, M., and Levine, D. "The XP of Tao: Extreme Programming of Large Open-Source Frameworks," *Extreme Programming Examined*, Reading, MA: Addison-Wesley, 2001, pp. 463-485.

Koch, A. *Agile Software Development: Evaluating the Methods for Your Organization*, Norwood, MA: Artech House, 2005.

Kumar, K., and Welke, R. J. "Methodology Engineering: A Proposal for Situation-Specific Methodology Construction," in W. Cotterman and J. Senn (eds.), *Challenges and Strategies for Research in Systems Development*, New York: John Wiley & Sons, 1992, pp. 257-269.

Kussmaul, C., Jack, R., and Sponsler, B. "Outsourcing and Offshoring with Agility: A Case Study," in C. Zannier, H. Erdogmus, and L. Lindstrom (eds.), *XP/Agile Universe*, Calgary, Canada, August 15-18, 2004, pp. 147-154.

Lindvall, M., Muthig, D., Dagnino, A., Wallin, C., Stupperich, M., Kiefer, D., May, J., and Kahkonen, T. "Agile Software Development in Large Organizations," *IEEE Computer* (37:12), 2004, pp. 27-34.

Linstone, H., and Turoff, M. "Introduction," in H. Linstone and M. Turoff (eds.), *The Delphi Method: Techniques and Applications*, Reading, MA: Addison-Wesley, 1975, pp. 3-12.

Martin, R. *Agile Software Development: Principles, Patterns and Practices*, Upper Saddle River, NJ: Prentice Hall, 2003.

McBreen, P. *Questioning Extreme Programming*, Boston: Addison-Wesley, 2003.

McCracken, G. *Qualitative Research: The Long Interview*, Beverly Hills, CA: SAGE Publications, 1998.

McDowell, C., Werener, L., and Bullock, H. "The Impact of Pair Programming on Student Performance, Perception and Persistence," in *Proceedings of the 25th International Conference on Software Engineering*, Portland, OR, May 3-10, 2003, pp. 602-607.

McMaster, T., Vidgen, R., and Wastell, D. "Networks of Association and Due Process in IS Development," in T. J. Larsen, L. Levine, and J. I. DeGross (eds.), *Information Systems: Current Issues and Future Changes*, Laxenburg, Austria: IFIP, 1998, pp. 25-34.

Melnik, G., and Mauer, F. "Agile Methods in Learning Environments: Lessons Learned," in F. Maurer and D. Wells (eds.), *XP/Agile Universe 2003*, New Orleans, LA, August 10-13, 2003, pp. 172-184.

Miles, M., and Huberman, A. *Qualitative Data Analysis*, London: SAGE Publications, 1999.

Moore, C. *Group Techniques for Idea Building*, London: SAGE Publications, 1987.

Naumann, J., Davis, G., and McKeen, J. "Determining Information Requirements: a Contingency Method for Selection of a Requirements Assurance Strategy," *The Journal of Systems and Software* (1:4), 1980, pp. 273-281.

Necco, C., Gordon, C., and Tsai, N. "Systems Analysis and Design: Current Practices," *MIS Quarterly* (11:3), 1987, pp. 461-476.

Okoli, C., and Pawlowski, S. "The Delphi Method as a Research Tool: An Example, Design Considerations and Applications," *Information & Management* (42:1), 2004, pp. 15-29.

Oppenheim, A. *Questionnaire Design, Interviewing and Attitude Measurement,* New York: Continuum, 1992.

Poole, C., and Huisman, J. "Using Extreme Programming in a Maintenance Environment," *IEEE Software* (18:6), 2001, pp. 42-50.

Poppendieck, M. "Lean Programming," *Software Development Magazine* (9:5), 2001, pp. 71-75.

Powell, T. A., Jones, D. L., and Cutts, D. C. *Web Site Engineering/Beyond Web Page Design*, Upper Saddle River, NJ: Prentice Hall, 1998.

Rasmusson, J. "Introducing XP into Greenfield Projects: Lessons Learned," *IEEE Computer* (20:3), 2003, pp. 21-28.

Rubin, H., and Rubin, I. *Qualitative Interviewing: The Art of Hearing Data*, Thousand Oaks, CA: SAGE Publications, 2005.

Sackman, H. *Delphi Critique*, Lexington, MA: D. C. Heath and Company, 1975.

Salkind, N. *Exploring Research*, Upper Saddle River, NJ: Pearson, 2006.

Schwaber, K., and Beedle, M. *Agile Software Development with Scrum*, Upper Saddle River, NJ: Prentice Hall, 2002.

Smolander, K., Tahvanainen, V., and Lyytinen, K. "How to Combine Tools and Methods in Practice: A Field Study," in B. Steinholtz, A. Sølvberg, and L. Bergman (eds.), *Lecture Notes in Computer Science, Second Nordic Conference Caise '90*, Stockholm, Sweden, 1990, pp. 195-214.

Stake, R. *The Art of Case Study Research*, Thousand Oaks, CA: SAGE Publications, 1995.

Stapleton, J. *DSDM: Dynamic Systems Development Method*, Harlow, England: Addison-Wesley, 1997.

Stephens, M., and Rosenberg, D. *Extreme Programming Refactored: The Case Against XP*, Berkeley, CA: Apress, 2003.

Stotts, D., Williams, L., Nagappan, N., Baheti, P., Jen, D., and Jackson, A. "Virtual Teaming: Experiments and Experiences with Distributed Pair Programming," in F. Maurer and D. Wells (eds.), *Extreme Programming/Agile Universe 2003*, New Orleans, August 11-14, 2003, pp. 129-141.

Sullivan, C. H. "Systems Planning in the Information Age," *Sloan Business Review* (26:2), 1985, pp. 3-11.

Tolvanen, J., and Lyytinen, K. "Flexible Method Adaptation in Case: The Metamodeling Approach," *Scandinavian Journal of Information Systems* (5:1), 1993, pp. 51-77.

Trauth, E., and O'Connor, B. "A Study of the Interaction Between Information, Technology and Society," in H-E. Nissen, H. K. Klein, and R. Hirschheim (eds.), *Information Systems Research: Contemporary Approaches and Emergent Traditions*, Amsterdam: North-Holland, 1991, pp. 131-144.

Uhl, N. *Using Research for Strategic Planning*, San Francisco: Jossey-Bass, 1983..

Vidgen, R., and Madsen, S. "Exploring the Socio-Technical Dimension of Information System Development: Use Cases and Job Satisfaction," paper presented at the 11th European Conference on Information Systems, Naples, Italy, June 19-21, 2003.

Wainer, M. "Adaptations for Teaching Software Development with Extreme Programming: An Experience Report," in F. Maurer and D. Wells (eds.), *XP/Agile Universe*, New Orleans, August 10-13, 2003, pp. 199-207.

Wengraf, T. *Qualitative Research Interviewing,* London: SAGE Publications, 2001.

Yin, R. *Case Study Research: Design and Methods*, Thousand Oaks, CA: SAGE Publications, 2003.

About the Authors

Kieran Conboy is a lecturer in Information Systems at National University of Ireland, Galway, Ireland. His current research focuses on agile methods for systems development as well as agility across other disciplines. Kieran's other research interests include systems analysis and management accounting in systems development projects. Kieran was a management consultant with Accenture, where he worked on a variety of projects across Europe and the United States. Kieran can be reached by e-mail at kieran.conboy@nuigalway.ie.

Brian Fitzgerald holds the Frederick A Krehbiel II Chair in Innovation in Global Business & Technology, at the University of Limerick, Ireland, where he is also Research Fellow and Science Foundation Ireland Principal Investigator. Brian's research interests lie primarily in the area of software development, a broad area which encompasses the use of development methods, globally distributed software development, agile methods, and open source software. Having worked in industry prior to taking up an academic position, Brian has more than 20 years experience in the software field. This experience was gained in a variety of companies (Citibank, Eircom, IDS Computing, Ridge Tool Company) in a number of countries (Ireland, Belgium, Germany). Brian can be reached by e-mail at bf@ul.ie.

16 THE IMPACT OF METHODS AND TECHNIQUES ON OUTCOMES FROM AGILE SOFTWARE DEVELOPMENT PROJECTS

David Parsons
Hokyoung Ryu
Ramesh Lal
Massey University, Albany
Auckland, New Zealand

Abstract   *Agile software development methods have become increasingly popular since the late 1990s, and may offer improved outcomes for software development projects when compared to more traditional approaches. However there has previously been little published empirical evidence to either prove or disprove this assertion. A survey carried out in March 2006 gathered responses from a large number of software development professionals who were using many different methods, both traditional and agile. A statistical analysis of this data reveals that agile methods do indeed improve outcomes from software development projects in terms of quality, satisfaction, and productivity, without a significant increase in cost. However, adoption of methods appears to involve a high degree of adaptivity, with many methods being used in combination and sets of techniques being adopted on an ad hoc basis. In this context, our analysis suggests that choosing specific combinations of methods can be particularly beneficial. However, we also find that successful adoption of an agile method is to some extent dependent on rigorous integration of certain core techniques.*

Keywords   Agile method, technique, software development

Please use the following format when citing this chapter:

Parsons, D., Ryu, H., and Lal, R., 2007, in IFIP International Federation for Information Processing, Volume 235, Organizational Dynamics of Technology-Based Innovation: Diversifying the Research Agenda, eds. McMaster, T., Wastell, D., Ferneley, E., and DeGross, J. (Boston: Springer), pp. 235-249.

1   INTRODUCTION

This paper provides some statistical analyses of a data set originally gathered using an online survey to determine the level of adoption of agile approaches by software development organizations. The survey, carried out in March 2006 by Scott Ambler, used mailing lists from both *Dr. Dobb's Journal* and *Software Development* magazine. A summary article was subsequently published on-line in September 2006 (Ambler, 2006c), and the raw data was made available for public access (Ambler 2006a). In this paper we view the original data from a number of new perspectives to explore some important questions about the effects of some key variables on the outcomes of software development projects. We begin by looking at previous studies that relate to the adoption and adaptation of agile methods and techniques. We then introduce the data set and methodology that we have used in this study. This is followed by an analysis of the data, from which we draw some conclusions and propose some further work.

2   AGILE METHODS AND TECHNIQUES

The mid-1990s saw the emergence of a set of informal analysis and design approaches known as *agile methods* (Highsmith 2002). While proponents of agile methods claim software development improvements, there is little empirical evidence to back this claim even though "agilists" emphasize that benefits would be experienced if these methods and practices were used (Anderson 2004).

2.1   Adopting and Adapting Agile Methods

Although agile methods tend to be quite prescriptive about the practices that they do or do not include, there is some information suggesting that methods and techniques are being adopted in a somewhat piecemeal manner (Aveling 2004; El Emam 2003; Hussman 2006). This is not inconsistent with the *intent* of these methods, since it is recognized that each software development project differs in its scale, scope, and technical challenges. Therefore agile methods encourage the chosen approach to be adapted to counter the various development conditions that apply to a particular development project (Keenan 2004; Mišic 2006). Integrating any new practice or software development process requires method tailoring to integrate it with existing processes and to match the organizational environment (Lindvall et al. 2004; Sfetsos et al. 2006). Sometimes it is necessary to stage the introduction of certain techniques because of dependencies between them (Beck and Andres 2005), while some authors propose extensions to certain methods to compensate for what they regard as their limitations. For example Stephens and Rosenberg (2003, p. 380) describe eXtreme Programming as an "anorexic process without effective contingency plans" and suggest a significant *refactoring* of the method. Others suggest that combining multiple agile methods may be more effective than using one method alone (Beedle 2006; Mar and Schwaber 2002). Choosing an appropriate method may also be problematical in practice. Datta (2006) proposes a framework known as the Agility Measurement Index (AMI) which can be used to determine the appropriateness of an agile method for a particular software development project, while Domingues et al. (2006) suggest a *suitability filter* for selecting specifically from agile methods. However, most software development teams do not have the depth of knowledge and skills to pick and choose different methods for different projects. The normal practice for software development is to adopt the most convenient or familiar method and then evaluate and improve it as it is being used to develop applications and systems. The implication of these issues is that methods may be adopted in ways that lead to extensive tailoring. This tailoring is likely to mean variations in the numbers and types of techniques adopted regardless of the label used to describe the umbrella agile method, or methods.

2.2 Choosing and Using Agile Techniques

Previous research has indicated that the selection of agile techniques within a method may be influenced not only by their perceived benefits but also by a range of problems and difficulties that certain techniques bring with them. A study by Sfetsos et al. (2006) identified pair programming and test-driven development to be the most significant success factors in outcomes from agile development, but noted that companies found problems adopting some other techniques such as common code ownership, on-site customer, 40-hour week, and metaphor. In contrast, Grossman et al. (2003) suggested that test-driven development was the most difficult and risky technique to adopt, as did a set of experiments at three different locations by George and Williams (2003). While many studies have highlighted the benefits of test-driven development, including defect reduction (Williams et al. 2003), a better testing process (Dustin et al. 1999) and higher quality (Bhat and Nagappan 2006), there are also some suggested drawbacks, such as a slower overall process (Bhat and Nagappan 2006; Canfora et al. 2006). Indeed some have suggested that this technique does not even, in fact, improve code quality (Muller and Hagner 2002). Further studies suggest that test driven development is not the only problematic technique. Others include simple design, pair programming, customer tests, and collective code ownership (George and Williams 2003; Mišic 2006). Paige et al. (2005) discuss some negative issues relating to increments, pair programming, and customer feedback in the context of building high-integrity systems (HIS). These studies show that there are many social, organizational, and technical factors that may influence why an agile technique may or may not be used by a particular software development team. This may explain why agile methods are not always adopted in full, but rather that certain techniques are adopted and methods are adapted.

Clearly, adopting an agile method in practice is not simply a case of taking a single method off the shelf and adopting its practices. Rather, it involves a process of selection and adaptivity. Given that practitioners are adopting various combinations of methods and techniques, the question that we try to address in this paper is which methods and techniques appear to provide the best outcomes. In the ongoing debate about the wisdom or otherwise of embracing agile methods (Boehm 2002; Nerur et al. 2005), empirical evidence such as the survey data used in this paper can make a valuable contribution to our understanding and assist software developers in building an appropriate methodology from the various agile methods and techniques on offer.

3   THE AGILE ADOPTION SURVEY DATA

The data set used in this paper was made available by Scott Ambler (2006a) and is based on an on-line survey. The Ambler survey repeated, with some changes, a similar survey carried out by Shine Technologies (2003). This original survey had only 131 respondents but Ambler's survey had 4,235 respondents.

Perhaps the most important aspect of both questionnaires is the four questions relating to the outcomes of software development projects, namely; productivity, system quality, cost, and stakeholder satisfaction. Ambler (2006c) endeavored to improve the original Shine survey in a number of ways. One important difference is that some Likert scale responses also included "I don't know" as a response for the four questions that related to outcomes, making it possible to discount these responses from our analyses. What is most interesting about the Ambler survey is that it introduced questions about the agile techniques that were being adopted, making it possible to do some analysis of which techniques were actually being used within the various methods. It also made it possible to see if the use of certain practices could be correlated with certain outcomes. In this paper, to explore the relationship between outcomes and agile methods and techniques, we focus on the outcomes as dependent variables, with the use of methods and techniques as independent variables.

In his original article, Ambler (2006c) drew some preliminary conclusions from the data. For instance, there was a correlation between knowledge of agile development and outcomes, so that the respondents who were more knowledgeable about agile approaches claimed to have better quality, productivity and satisfaction than those who were not. He also concluded that organization size was not a statistically significant factor in the levels of outcome attained from agile approaches. The most significant result claimed was that adoption of agile methods increases quality, productivity, and satisfaction, and that "adoption of agile processes has clearly been a resounding success" (Ambler 2006c, p. 3).

We do not intend to replicate all of these analyses in this paper, but prefer to explore additional features of the data. Ambler (2006c) did not attempt to provide a deeper analysis of any of the key variables that may have effects on the adoption of agile methods. This gave us an opportunity to mine the data set for some further insights into the effects of adopting agile methods and techniques, which is the main concern of this paper.

Looking at the data, we noted that many organizations are using more than one agile method. In fact nearly 16 percent of the respondents claimed to be using multiple methods, in some cases as many as seven (Table 1). This raised an obvious question about whether there is any benefit in adopting multiple methods for agile development.

We also noted that techniques and methods did not seem to be consistently used as one might expect with, in many cases, a lack of correlation between the stated use of a method and actual use of techniques that would normally be associated with that method. In other words, there were no consistent patterns between the stated methodology and the techniques actually being used. The 12 techniques included in the survey, and the number of respondents reporting their use, is shown in Table 2.

The lack of correlation between specific techniques and methods in practice led us to question: What is the underlying relationship between a methodology and a set of techniques?

Table 1. **The Numbers of Agile Methods Reported as Being Used by the Survey Respondents**

Number of Methods Used	Number of Respondents	Percentage of Respondents
No agile methods	2541	59.99%
One agile method	1019	24.06%
Two agile methods	500	11.80%
Three or more methods	175	4.15%
Total	4235	100%

Table 2. **The Numbers of Agile Techniques Reported as Being Used by the Survey Respondents**

Techniques	Number of Respondents	Percentage of Respondents
Active stakeholder participation	938	22.15%
Agile model driven development	260	6.14%
Code refactoring	1467	34.64%
Code regression testing	1383	32.66%
Colocation	447	10.55%
Common coding guidelines	1595	37.66%
Continuous integration	1113	26.28%
Database refactoring	416	9.82%
Database regression testing	407	9.61%
Pair programming	587	13.86%
Single sourcing	241	5.69%
Test driven design	959	22.64%

Given the data set provided, we were able to propose some initial, broad research questions that might be answered by this data. These research questions were

- Does the use of agile methods have a positive effect on outcomes (i.e., cost, productivity, quality, and satisfaction)?
- What are the most effective agile methods?
- What are the most effective agile techniques?

The following sections detail how these questions were addressed, using statistical analyses, in order to try to identify the most important success factors in agile development.

4   DATA ANALYSIS

We performed quantitative analyses of parts of the data set. To do this, the original data was re-coded and analyzed using SPSS (version 13.0). It was originally planned to use an analysis of variance, but Levene's test for heterogeneity of variance was found to be significant in most of the following analyses, suggesting that the data were not in fact suitable for analysis of variance. It would have been possible to transform the data but this would have made it difficult to interpret. For these reasons, the simple solution of using nonparametric analyses was adopted.

Several notes about the data set itself are needed here. First, the "don't know" responses from the original data have been regarded as "missing values" in the analysis. As a consequence, there are variations in the sample sizes in each analysis. Second, there were very small sample sizes for some responses, for example the dynamic systems development method (DSDM) was being used by only a handful of respondents. Finally, as mentioned above, quite a few respondents were using more than one agile method and various combinations of techniques (see Tables 1 and 2), so it is not straightforward to separate out the effects of a particular method or technique. For this reason, we chose to analyze both methods and techniques separately, and then if a particular agile method appeared to be the most effective, we planned to investigate the relationship between the method and the appropriate techniques in depth.

4.1   Question 1: Does the Use of Agile Methods Have a Positive Effect on Outcomes?

The first question we addressed in our analysis was whether the adoption of agile methods for software development might lead to better outcomes (i.e., in cost, productivity, quality, and satisfaction), as much of the literature on agile development has claimed. To do this we first explored the four outcomes, contrasting the non-agile method user group with the agile user group. The results of this analysis are shown in Table 3.

The results seem to indicate a positive response for the agile methods the respondents have employed. That is, all the three performance-related outcomes (i.e., productivity, quality, and satisfaction) indicate the benefits of agile methods, while there seems to be no great difference with regard to cost.

Table 3. **The Effect of Using an Agile Methodology**[†]

	Cost	Productivity	Quality	Satisfaction
No agile methods	3.01 (0.62)	3.40 (0.70)	3.55 (0.74)	3.40 (0.70)
Agile methods	3.05 (0.89)	3.88 (0.79)	4.02 (0.77)	3.95 (0.79)
Mann-Whitney U test	n.s.	$p < .01$	$p < .01$	$p < .01$

[†]Mean (s.d.) (min: 1 – much lower, max: 5 – much higher)

Table 4. **Outcomes Dependent on the Number of Agile Methods Used**[†]

	Cost	Productivity	Quality	Satisfaction
One agile method	3.03 (0.85)	3.83 (0.78)	3.98 (0.76)	3.89 (0.75)
Two agile methods	3.06 (0.92)	3.92 (0.77)	4.06 (0.76)	3.98 (0.82)
More than two agile methods	3.12 (1.03)	4.01 (0.86)	4.14 (0.80)	4.14 (0.84)

[†]Mean (s.d.)

This observation has been confirmed by the Mann-Whitney U test as shown in the bottom row of Table 3. Only the difference in the cost factor was not found to be statistically significant, supporting the interpretation given above.

Following on from this, a subsequent analysis was performed to identify what agile methods seem to be the most effective. To do this, we have to look at the data set with care. In many cases, the agile method user group reported that they used more than one agile method, so some developers are combining several agile development methods, either in different projects or within the same project. Therefore, to explore which agile methods are the most effective, we first investigated if any combinative use of agile methods (or, at least, employing more than one agile method) can have an effect on the four outcomes. The number of methods the respondents were using varied in the original data set, ranging from one to seven. However, to allow the sample size to be meaningful for statistical analysis, three classifications were considered: using one agile method, using two agile methods, and using more than two agile methods. Our results are summarized in Table 4.

In terms of the three performance-related outcomes (i.e., productivity, quality, and satisfaction), as shown in Table 4, it appears to be better to use more than two agile methods (mean 4.01 for productivity, 4.14 for quality, and 4.14 for satisfaction). However, further pair wise Mann-Whitney tests (at the level of $p \le .05$) revealed that while using two agile methods rated higher than using only one method, there appeared to be no significant further advantage in increasing the number of methods used beyond two.

4.2 Question 2: What Are the Most Effective Agile Methods?

Following on the result described above (i.e., that combining two agile methods might be beneficial in agile software development), we continued to analyze the results for adopting combinations of two agile methods. It was intended to see if any specific pair of methods could deliver better outcomes than the others. There were 24 different method pairs identified in the original data set, but many of these pairs were being adopted by a very small number of respondents, which took them beyond the scope of our data analysis. Figure 1 shows the 11 most commonly used pairs of agile methods, where more than 10 respondents reported using these pairs. However, only the most popular 6 pairs (with over 20 respondents) were considered in our analysis.

For this data, we applied the same nonparametric analysis (i.e., pairwise Mann-Whitney U tests) as we did with the previous set. The results of this analysis are shown in Table 5. In terms of both quality and productivity, there was a significant difference

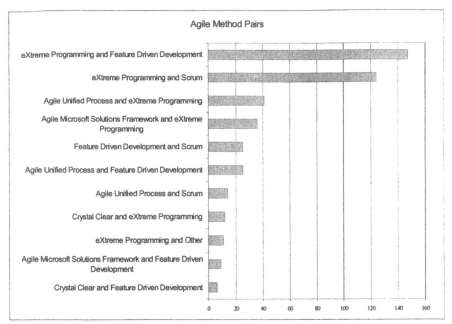

Figure 1. **The Most Commonly Used Pairs of Agile Methods**

Table 5. **Outcomes for the Six Most Commonly Used Pairs of Agile Methods**[†]

	Cost	Productivity	Quality	Satisfaction
XP/FDD	3.02 (0.89)	3.87 (0.70)	4.10 (0.75)	4.03 (0.77)
XP/SCRUM	2.91 (1.04)	4.10 (0.80)	4.30 (0.68)	4.05 (0.86)
XP/AGILE UP	3.26 (0.75)	3.87 (0.80)	3.82 (0.94)	3.97 (0.74)
XP/AGILE MSF	3.17 (0.95)	3.56 (0.82)	3.78 (0.87)	3.82 (0.73)
FDD/SCRUM	3.15 (0.88)	4.00 (0.69)	3.91 (0.53)	4.29 (0.78)
FDD/AGILE UP	3.00 (0.66)	4.04 (0.55)	4.00 (0.78)	3.79 (0.72)

[†]Mean (s.d.)

between the eXtreme Programming/Scrum combination and all the other pairs of methods. However there was no significant difference in either cost or satisfaction. This clearly tells us that the eXtreme Programming/Scrum combination is a good pairing of methods to adopt.

This result can be seen to make some sense in that eXtreme Programming (XP) is very much oriented towards technology based practices and programmer activity. In contrast, Scrum is more focused on agile project management aspects (Abrahamsson et al. 2002). In addition, Scrum is explicitly intended as a wrapper around other engineering approaches. Therefore XP and Scrum can be seen to be complementary from a practical point of view, supporting the claims made by Mar and Schwaber (2002).

Table 6. **Agile Techniques with Significant Benefits for Software Development Outcomes**[†]

	Productivity	Quality	Satisfaction
Active stakeholder participation	3.92 (0.76)	4.08 (0.73)	4.07 (0.76)
Agile model driven development	3.93 (0.82)	4.03 (0.82)	4.03 (0.79)
Code refactoring	3.91 (0.74)	4.09 (0.71)	3.92 (0.78)
Code regression testing	3.84 (0.75)	4.05 (0.71)	3.89 (0.77)
Colocation	3.99 (0.79)	4.08 (0.76)	4.00 (0.83)
Common coding guidelines	3.79 (0.76)	3.98 (0.73)	3.86 (0.77)
Continuous integration	3.97 (0.74)	4.11 (0.73)	3.99 (0.77)
Database refactoring	3.88 (0.78)	4.05 (0.74)	3.96 (0.83)
Database regression testing	3.78 (0.76)	3.98 (0.74)	3.86 (0.80)
Pair programming	3.97 (0.77)	4.15 (0.75)	3.99 (0.78)
Single sourcing information	3.93 (0.80)	4.00 (0.80)	4.00 (0.81)
Test driven design	3.95 (0.76)	4.18 (0.70)	4.01 (0.77)

[†]Mean (s.d.)

4.3 Question 3: What Are the Most Effective Agile Techniques?

Having undertaken some analysis of the effects of method choice on outcomes, we turned our attention to individual agile techniques. Since there are 12 different agile techniques covered in the original data, it was interesting to see if any of these provided greater benefits than others. The results of our analysis are shown in Table 6. The cost factor was eliminated in this analysis, because our main concern was to see what positive benefits a particular agile technique could bring.

To analyze this data, we first applied the same statistical approach that was used in the previous analysis. However, the ratings were uniformly high. Because of this overall ceiling effect, the small differences between means are not statistically evaluated. Nonetheless, several of the mean ratings given in Table 6 show a particularly interesting aspect. The techniques of colocation (3.99 in productivity, 4.08 in quality, and 4.00 in satisfaction, respectively) and pair programming (3.97 in productivity, 4.15 in quality, and 3.99 in satisfaction, respectively) appear to bring higher benefits for all three outcomes. Without further research, we cannot say for sure why these techniques appear to provide higher returns than some of the others. However, we can see support in the literature for the economic benefits of pair programming (Erdogmus and Williams 2003) and the importance of colocation (Bradner and Mark 2002).

5 THE RELATIONSHIP BETWEEN METHODOLOGY AND TECHNIQUE

Some queries executed against our data set seemed to suggest that the use of certain techniques among those respondents claiming to be using agile methods seemed to be very

Table 7. **Actual Use of Seven Core XP Techniques Among the Sample Claiming to Follow XP**

Agile Technique Used with XP	Number	Percentage of Sample
Active stakeholder participation	114	27.14%
Code refactoring	269	64.05%
Code regression testing	210	50.00%
Colocation	66	15.71%
Continuous integration	176	41.90%
Pair programming	183	43.57%
Test Driven Design (TDD)	180	42.86%

low. For example, test driven design, which from the agile methods literature one might expect to be a fundamental part of an agile approach, was only reported by between 40 and 50 percent of respondents, regardless of their chosen methods. This led us to explore in more detail the relationship between stated use of an agile method and actual use of agile techniques.

We decided to address this relationship by focusing on those respondents who claimed to be using eXtreme Programming as their agile method. There were two reasons for this. First, XP was the most popular agile method in the survey, with 23.4 percent claiming to be using XP. Second, our own analysis identified that XP appeared to be the most effective method, coupled with Scrum. Not all of the XP techniques specified by Beck and Andres (2005) were included in the original survey. Nevertheless, it would be reasonable to assume that those practitioners who claimed to be using XP would be using the core XP practices that were included in the survey. These practices would be active stakeholder participation, code refactoring, code regression testing, co-location, continuous integration, pair programming and test driven design, as shown in Table 7.

The sample size for this table was 420, which was the number of respondents who claimed to be using XP and no other method. Of these, only eight were using all of these techniques, and no single technique was being used by more than 65 percent of the sample. This result is somewhat surprising, suggesting that claiming to be doing a methodology did not necessarily mean that one was, in fact, following anything like the full set of techniques of that methodology. This seemed to go beyond the expected effects of adaptivity, and suggested an unreasonably low take up of some techniques. The obvious question that followed from this analysis was, what kind of effect might this limited use of core techniques have on the outcomes from using this method? We therefore chose to analyze which techniques might be the most important, given that many practitioners were using a subset of those recommended by the method. Our results are shown in Table 8. In order to gain a clearer result, in this analysis we combined the two techniques that focus on collaborative working, namely active stakeholder participation and colocation.

We applied a log-linear analysis to the data set for XP users to identify the associations between the techniques and their outcomes. The techniques that are ticked in Table 8 are those that have a significant association with the three performance-related

Table 8. **Techniques That Appear to Show the Most Benefit in the Context of XP**

Agile Technique Used with XP	Productivity	Quality	Satisfaction
Collaborative working	✓ (2)	✓ (2)	
Code refactoring	✓ (1)	✓ (1)	✓ (2)
Code regression testing		✓ (3)	
Continuous integration			
Pair programming	✓ (3)		
Test Driven Design (TDD)		✓ (4)	✓ (1)

outcomes. For each outcome, the number in parentheses shows the relative importance of that technique. For example, in the context of satisfaction, test driven design is the most important technique. Taking the three outcomes together, code refactoring appears to be the most important technique. In the context of XP, which is a code centric method, the importance of test driven design and refactoring can be understood as being crucial components of maintaining design integrity. The importance of collaborative working (in particular the XP practice of "real customer involvement") is also underlined by our analysis.

Our final analysis addressed a further question, namely, if XP users are not using all, or most, of the available techniques, does this have a negative effect on outcomes? For this analysis, we compared the outcomes from XP users based on the number of XP techniques (between zero and seven) that they had adopted. The results of this comparison are shown in Figure 2.

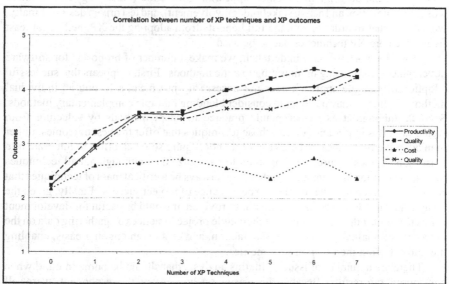

Figure 2. **Graph Showing the Correlation between the Number of XP Techniques Used and the Outcomes from Using the XP Method**

As we have already identified in earlier analyses, the effect on cost seems to be independent of the number of techniques adopted, but the other three performance-related outcomes show that the more techniques that are adopted, the better the resulting performance. Those respondents who claimed to be using XP but in fact were not using any of the seven techniques had particularly poor results, which is unsurprising.

This data was further analyzed using the same classification analysis employed previously, revealing that adopting more than five techniques results in the best performance in terms of all of the measures.

6   SUMMARY AND CONCLUSIONS

The adoption of agile methods appears from some of the literature to be an untidy process of partial adoptions and adaptivity. Against this background it is helpful to try to understand which agile methods and techniques may offer the best return on investment. In this paper, we have undertaken a statistical analysis of a data set based on an on-line survey about the adoption of agile methods. From our analyses, we have drawn a number of conclusions. We have shown that adoption of at least one agile method improves the outcomes of quality, satisfaction, and productivity over the use of non-agile methods, without a statistically significant increase in cost. We have also shown that the most effective way to apply agile methods is to combine more than one method together, and the most effective combination of methods appears to be eXtreme Programming and Scrum. We also looked at agile techniques and their outcomes and identified pair programming and colocation as the two most significant techniques when analyzed across all agile methods. However when we concentrated on an analysis of XP, the most important techniques for this method appeared to be code refactoring, collaborative working (colocation and active stakeholder involvement), and test driven design. Finally, we showed that in order to gain the full benefits from adopting the XP method, at least five of the core XP techniques had to be used.

From the work we have undertaken, we make a number of proposals for software development teams using or migrating to agile methods. First, it appears that successful adoption of an agile approach does not necessarily just mean selecting an individual method. Rather, it may be better to consider blending multiple complementary methods. Second, although it as an acceptable practice to adapt methods by selecting from techniques, it is important to select those techniques that offer the best outcomes, rather than adopting only those that are easy or do not require so much effort to integrate into existing processes. Third, it is important to recognize that, although not all techniques of an agile method are compulsory, there will always be a critical mass of techniques that should be adopted in order to offer the best chance of project success. Finally, given the insights that the data used in this paper has provided, it would be useful for development teams to monitor the effectiveness of their agile project practices by gathering data on the outcomes of quality, productivity, satisfaction, and cost on an ongoing basis, enabling them to carry out their own project metrics.

There are a number of issues with this analysis that should be borne in mind when considering our results. Because this was an on-line survey, the respondents were self selecting. We cannot, therefore, guarantee the validity of their responses. We are also unable to determine from the data whether respondents are reporting the use of multiple methods because different teams within their organization use different methods, or because individual teams are combining methods. We have also focused in this paper on agile methods and techniques. However the original survey includes questions about skill level and organization size, which Ambler has addressed separately (Ambler 2006c) but which we have not attempted to include in this analysis. In addition, further information about the respondents such as what type of organization they work for and what type of software systems they are developing is not available to us.

Ambler has himself summarized a number of issues with the survey (Ambler 2006b), including potential misunderstandings by respondents about feature driven development (FDD), which may make answers relating to this method unreliable, and the absence of the rational unified process (RUP) from the specified list of methods. This method appears a number of times in the "other" category within the survey but has not been discriminated in the analysis.

The results of our analysis appear to indicate a number of areas for future work. In particular, our quantitative analysis suggests a number of areas where field studies and qualitative analysis might be undertaken to further investigate issues such as how software development teams select, combine, and adapt agile methods in practice, and why particular subsets of techniques are selected from agile methods. There may also be scope for a further survey that might attempt to provide a finer grained discrimination of questions related to method and technique so that we might identify the ways that multiple agile methods are being used in practice. Finally, the original survey results are still available for public download (Ambler 2006a) and there are further aspects of the data, not considered in this paper, that could be analyzed from new perspectives.

References

Abrahamsson, P., Salo, O., Ronkainen, J., and Warsta, J. *Agile Software Development Methods: Review and Analysis*, Oulu, Finland: VTT Publications, 2002.

Ambler, S. "Agile Adoption Rate Survey," *Ambysoft*, March 2006a (available online at http://www.ambysoft.com/surveys/agileMarch2006.html).

Ambler, S. "Agile Adoption Rate Survey: Discussion of the Results," *Ambysoft*, March 2006b (available online at http://www.ambysoft.com/surveys/agileMarch2006.html#Discussion).

Ambler, S. "Survey Says: Agile Works in Practice," *Software Development Magazine*, August 3, 2006c (available online at http://www.ddj.com/dept/architect/191800169).

Anderson, J. D. *Agile Management for Software Engineering: Applying the Theory of Constraints for Business Results*, Upper Saddle River, NJ: Prentice Hall, 2004.

Aveling, B. "XP Lite Considered Harmful?," in J. Eckstein and H. Baumeister (eds.), *Extreme Programming and Agile Processes in Software Engineering: 5th International Conference*, Garmish-Partenkirchen, Germany, June 6-10, 2004, pp. 94-103.

Beck, K., and Andres, C. *Extreme Programming Explained: Embrace Change* (2nd ed.), Boston: Addison-Wesley, 2005.

Beedle, M. "Agile Enterprise," 2006 (available online at http://www.e-architects.com/AE/).

Bhat, T., and Nagappan, N. "Evaluating the Efficacy of Test-Driven Development: Industrial Case Studies," in *Proceedings of the 2006 ACM/IEEE International Symposium on Empirical Software Engineering*, Rio de Janeiro, Brazil, September 21-22, 2006, pp. 356-363.

Boehm, B. "Get Ready for Agile Methods, with Care," *IEEE Computer* (35:1), 2002, pp. 64-69.

Bradner, E., and Mark, G. "Why Distance Matters: Effects on Cooperation, Persuasion and Deception," in *Proceedings of the 2002 ACM Conference on Computer-Supported Cooperative Work*, New Orleans, LA, 2002, pp. 226-235.

Canfora, G., Cimitile, A., Garcia, F., Piattini, M., and Visaggio, C. "Evaluating Advantages of Test Driven Development: A Controlled Experiment with Professionals," in *Proceedings of the 2006 ACM/IEEE International Symposium on Empirical Software Engineering*, Rio de Janeiro, Brazil, September 21-22, 2006, pp. 364-371.

Datta, S. "Agility Measurement Index: A Metric for the Crossroads of Software Development Methodologies," in *Proceedings of the 44th Annual ACM Southeast Regional Conference*, Melbourne, FL, 2006, pp. 271-273.

Dominguez, J., Linecar, P., and Black, S. "Visualization of a Suitability Filter for Agile Methods," in R. Dawson, E. Georgiadou, P. Linecar, M. Ross, and S. Staples (eds.), *Software Quality Management XIV: Perspectives in Software Quality, Proceedings of the 14th International Software Quality Management Conference*, Southampton, UK, April 10-12, 2006, pp. 299-319.

Dustin, E., Raskha, J., and Paul, J. *Automated Software Testing*, Reading, MA: Addison Wesley, 1999.

El Emam, K. "Finding Success in Small Software Projects," *Agile Project Management Executive Report* (4:11), 2003.

Erdogmus, H., and Williams, L. "An Economic Analysis of Pair Programming," in L. Williams and R. Kessler (eds.), *Pair Programming Illuminated*, Boston: Addison-Wesley, 2003, pp. 221-236.

George, B., and Williams, L. "An Initial Investigation of Test-driven Development in Industry," in *Proceedings of the ACM Symposium on Applied Computing*, Melbourne, FL, March 9-12, 2003, pp. 1135-1139.

Grossman, F., Bergin, J., Leip, D., Merritt, S., and Gotel, O. "One XP Experience: Introducing Agile (XP) Software Development into a Culture That Is Willing but Not Ready," in H. Lutfiyya, J. Singer, and D. Stewart (eds.), *Proceedings of the 2004 Conference of the Centre for Advanced Studies on Collaborative Research*, Markham, Ontario, Canada, October 4-7, 2003, pp. 242-254.

Highsmith, J. *Agile Software Development Ecosystems*, Boston: Addison-Wesley, 2002.

Hussman, D. "A Fishbowl with Piranhas: Coalescence, Convergence or Divergence? The Future of Agile Software Development Practices: Some Assembly Required," in *Proceedings of the Conference on Object Oriented Programming Systems Languages and Applications*, Portland, Oregon, October 22-26, 2006, pp. 937-939.

Keenan, F. "Agile Process Tailoring and Problem Analysis," in *Proceedings of the 26th International Conference on Software Engineering*, Edinburgh, UK, May 23-28, 2004, pp. 45-47.

Lindvall, M., Muthig, D., Dagnino, A., Wallin, C., Stupperich, M., Kiefer, D., May, J., and Kahkonen, T. "Agile Software Development in Large Organizations," *IEEE Computer* (37:12), December 2004, pp. 26-34.

Mar, K., and Schwaber, K. "Scrum with XP," *Informit.com*, March 22, 2002 (available online at http://www.informit.com/articles/article.asp?p=26057&rl=1; article provided courtesy of Prentice-Hall).

Mišic, V. "Perceptions of Extreme Programming: An Exploratory Study," *ACM SIGSOFT Software Engineering Notes* (31:2), 2006, pp. 1-9.

Muller, M. M., and Hagner, O. "Experiment About Test-First Programming," *IEE Proceedings Software* (149:5), 2002, pp. 131-136.

Nerur, S., Mahapatra, R., and Mangalaraj, G. "Challenges of Migrating to Agile Methodologies," *Communications of the ACM* (48:5), 2005, pp. 73-78.

Paige, R., Chivers, H., McDernid, A., and Stephenson, Z. "High-Integrity Extreme Programming," in *Proceedings of the ACM Symposium on Applied Computing*, Santa Fe, New Mexico, March 13-17, 2005, pp. 1518-1523.

Sfetsos, P., Angelis, L., and Stamelos, I. "Investigating the Extreme Programming System: An Empirical Study," *Empirical Software Engineering* (11:2), 2006, pp. 269-301.

Shine Technologies. "Agile Methodologies Survey Results," Shine Technologies Pty. Ltd., 2003 (available online at http://agilealliancebeta.org/system/article/file/1121/file.pdf).

Stephens, M., and Rosenberg, D. *Extreme Programming Refactored: The Case Against XP*, New York: Apress, 2003.

Williams, L., Maximilien, M., and Vouk, M. "Test-Driven Development as Defect-Reduction Practice," in *Proceedings of the 14th International Symposium on Software Reliability Engineering*, Denver, CO, November 17-21, 2003, pp. 3-4.

About the Authors

David Parsons is a senior lecturer in Information Systems at Massey University, Auckland, New Zealand. Formerly an Enterprise Java consultant in the U.K., his research interests include agile methods, web application architectures and mobile learning. He can be reached by e-mail at d.p.parsons@massey.ac.nz.

Hokyoung Ryu is a lecturer in Information Systems at Massey University, Auckland, New Zealand. He is active in research on how new information and communication technologies such as interactive TV and mobile systems will change human social behavior. He can be reached by e-mail at h.ryu@massey.ac.nz.

Ramesh Lal is a researcher in Information Systems at Massey University, Auckland, New Zealand. He is currently working for his Ph.D., studying the adaptivity of agile methods using case studies across Australasia. He can be reached by e-mail at r.lal@massey.ac.nz.

Part 4:

Actor Network Theory

17 THE INERTIA OF ERP PROJECTS: Diffusion or Drift?

Amany R. Elbanna
Loughborough University
Leicestershire, UK

Abstract   *Models of the diffusion of innovation have received wide acceptance in IS research. Such diffusion models are typically based on the assumption that projects are either accepted or rejected by adopters, without recognizing or accounting for the negotiation, adaptation, and drift that take place during the implementation (Rogers 1995). This paper presents an alternative view, based on the actor network theory (ANT) concepts of translation, moving the token, and modality. This lens reveals that software implementation projects, such as enterprise resource planning (ERP), have no inertia in themselves. Instead, a project's fate depends on each move it takes and each party involved in handling that move. Every handling of the project by different parties could present either a positive modality (that strengthens it and pushes it forward on its track) or a negative modality (that weaken its initial form and drags it in a different direction). The findings provide an explanation of drift and an alternative view of the diffusion of innovation in the ERP case. This could be extended to other technological projects. The findings also invite practitioners to monitor the various movements of their projects and encourage academics to revise their endorsement of the previously dominant diffusion model. They also contribute to the drift argument by identifying and discussing one of the sources of drift.*

Keywords   Drift, ERP, diffusion of innovation, systems implementation, packaged software, case study, actor network theory (ANT)

Please use the following format when citing this chapter:

Elbanna, A. R., 2007, in IFIP International Federation for Information Processing, Volume 235, Organizational Dynamics of Technology-Based Innovation: Diversifying the Research Agenda, eds. McMaster, T., Wastell, D., Ferneley, E., and DeGross, J. (Boston: Springer), pp. 253-266.

1   INTRODUCTION

The implementation of enterprise resource planning (ERP) has a reputation for being notoriously problematic for organizations, as the large size and scale of the system and its organizational coverage make implementing it a challenging task. These implementation difficulties have been described as resembling "the prisoner escaping from an island prison" (Ross and Vitale 2000). The failure of many ERP system implementations has even led some organizations to bankruptcy and litigation proceedings (for example, in the Fox-Meyer case; see James 1997; Montoya 1998).

In addition to dramatic failures, research has also revealed that organizations end up with different results from their ERP systems as a result of changing the project scope and objectives (Lee and Myers 2004); customizing the system according to local needs (Alshawi et al. 2004; Markus et al. 2000); blocking some of the system functions (Elbanna 2006); or achieving a mix of legacy practices and new ERP-based practices (Wagner and Newell 2005). Research also shows that organizations implementing the same ERP package achieve different results, in ways that make their integration a very challenging task (Alshawi et al. 2004). The explanation of the occurrence of these variations in ERP adoption is beyond the capacity of the traditional diffusion of innovation model, typified by that proposed by Rogers (1995).

The traditional diffusion model, in its simplistic linear form, assumes a technology–push where users are invited to adopt the technology based on its technical merits (Rothwell 1992). From this perspective, the user's role is seen to be either to adopt or reject the project. Even when a need–pull is incorporated in the model, this adoption view has still been based on the same passive role of users as either accepting a project if it suits their needs or rejecting it if it does not (Rogers 1995). This assumes compliant and cooperative actors who are likely to adopt the project over time, which led to classification of adopters according to the time of adoption, such as eager minority, early majority, late majority, or awkward laggards (Baskerville and Pries-Heje 2001; Rogers 1995). In all cases, the underlying assumptions are based on a model of the project that assumes it has an in-built inertia which moves it forward and that the different parties involved can only accept or reject, without interfering in its direction.

The drift model, on the other hand, highlights the evolving nature of technology projects, which do not always follow a preplanned discourse. It gives more weight to organizational actors and allows them the possibility of moving the project from its initial discourse toward their own. In its extreme form, the drift model finds technology projects rather uncontrollable and liable to run away (Hanseth et al. 2001). In its modest form, it argues that technology projects are surrounded by surprises and emerging events that deviate it from the preplanned discourse and lead to unintended consequences (Ciborra 1999, 2000; Nandhakumar et al. 2003; Orlikowski 1992).

The underlying structure of technology drift continues to occupy many researchers who try to reveal how and why drift happens. This paper extends and complements research in this area. It focuses on examining the process of drift in ERP projects and revealing how and why drift tends to occur in such projects. To this end, it studies an ERP implementation in a sound international organization and applies actor network theory (ANT) to analyze the findings. ANT has been increasingly adopted in IS research to understand the emerging process of systems implementation. Researchers employing this approach have applied different concepts from the theory to reveal the complex character of IS implementation (Bloomfield et al. 1997; Klischewski 2000; Lilley 1998; Vidgen and McMaster 1996). These and other researchers also argue that applying ANT in diffusion studies provides an alternative, deeper insight on the technology adoption process that goes beyond the linear version of the diffusion model (Buscher and Mogensen 1997; Knights and Noble 1997; McMaster et al. 1997).

The paper consists of five sections after this "Introduction." The next section discusses the underlying assumptions of the translation model and contrasts it with the assumptions of the diffusion model in order to establish the theoretical background against which the data was analyzed. Section 3 presents the research methodology, followed by a section that describes and highlights some key findings of the case study using this methodology. Section 5 analyzes these findings applying ANT concepts. Section 6 provides a discussion and conclusion of the study.

2 THE TRANSLATION MODEL VERSUS THE DIFFUSION OF INNOVATION MODEL

Actor network theory has been developed to understand the construction of facts in science and technology. It has evolved incrementally over the years through the cooperative efforts of many scholars including Akrich, Callon, Latour, and Law among many others (Law and Hassard 1999).

The translation model at the heart of ANT is concerned with investigating the circulation of a *token*: a claim, order, project, idea, gadget, life style, product, or other artefact. The theory claims that network builders achieve their goals and those of their projects only through associations and alliances of faithful human and nonhuman actors. This model regards the spread in time and space of any token as being in the hands of people, each of whom may act in many different ways, for instance by dropping, modifying, deflecting, betraying, adding to, or appropriating the token (Latour 1991). It maintains that faithful transmission of a token is a rarity (Latour 1986). In this regard, ANT explicitly assumes that there is no intrinsic inertia in the token or the network builder project. Hence, everyone in the chain handling the project token gives it energy.

If the token is to move on, the project needs to find fresh sources of energy all the time as "you can never rest on what you did before" (Latour 1986, p. 267). For this reason, ANT denies the diffusion model's view of an actor as a medium that either resists or transmits the token. Instead, everyone is seen as doing something essential for the existence and maintenance of the token. As Latour (1986) elaborates, "the token changes as it moves from hand to hand and the faithful transmission of a statement becomes a single and unusual case among many, more likely, others." Thus, the translation model considers that "there are active members shaping and changing the token as it is moved," which means this model is not about the *transmission* of the same token but the *continuous transformation* of the token. It regards the stability of the token as an unusual circumstance.

According to ANT, translation is the mechanism by which the network builder recruits actors and ensures their faithful alliance. Callon (1986) suggested four inter-related *moments of translations* that actors may go through during the translation process: problematization, interessement, enrollment, and mobilization. He also noted that these moments do not represent stages and might not occur—or be detected—in this order, and that all or only some moments may be gone through. Problematization refers to the network builder's effort to divert the actors' attention from their initial goal toward the network builder's aims and to convince them that they cannot achieve their displaced goal without helping the network builder to pursue his or hers. It sets the network builder project as an indispensable or obligatory passage point to the actors if they want to achieve their displaced goal. Interessement is the action of interest building. Enrollment specifies the role the actors are required to play in the network and convinces them to accept it. Mobilization means moving the new actors to be part of the network.

Building on Greimas (1990), Latour (1987) illustrates that the network building project is like a sentence that could be made more of a fact or a fiction depending on how it is inserted into other sentences. By itself, a given sentence is neither a fact nor a fiction. It is made into one of these in later stages by others who intervene to add their own positive or negative modalities. Such modalities are "the sentences that modify (or qualify) another one" (Latour 1987, p. 22) and, depending on the kind of modalities, "people will *be made to go* along completely different paths" (Latour 1987, p. 25). Positive modalities are those sentences that lead a statement away from its condition of production down stream, making it solid enough to open up some other possible consequences (Latour 1987). In contrast, negative modalities are those sentences that lead a statement upstream in the opposite direction, toward its conditions of production. It does this to investigate and review the details of its production, instead of using it to render some other consequences necessary. The notion of modalities illustrates that the status of a statement depends on later statements.

Latour contrasted this version of the translation model to the diffusion model. He explained that the diffusion model views the displacement of a token through time and space as the usual expected action.[1] It assumes the transmission of the same token through others, and interferes only to explain the slowing down or acceleration of the token movement that results from other people's reactions. In this regard, the diffusion model views the token as having an initial force that is fully maintained and regards the network through which it passes as playing the role of the medium through which the token circulates. The slowing down or distortion of a token is then explained in terms of societal friction and resistance, such as poor communication, ill will, the opposition of interest groups, or indifference. The diffusion model, therefore, explains everything through either the initial force or the resisting medium.

3   RESEARCH METHODOLOGY

This study follows the interpretive tradition in IS research. It aims to answer questions about how and why ERP projects tend to drift and to provide explanations of the phenomena based on participants' experiences in real world situations. This is done by examining a case study of ERP implementation. Such case study research does not seek generalizations in a statistical sense, but aims to provide analytical insight and theoretical generalization.

---

[1]The contrast between the diffusion and translation models largely adopted in this paragraph is derived from Latour (1987).

In order to understand ERP implementation, data of an ERP project in a large reputable company in the food and beverages sector (which we will call Drinko) was collected between August 2000 and March 2001. Drinko owns many production, packaging, and sales sites in several countries, each of which represents a company or group of companies that operates in that local area. This study focuses on Drinko's business units (BUs) in only three countries, referred to here as EUK, EUB, and America, which include more than 25 BUs.

The data collection methods applied comprised interviews with various parties involved in the project; document reviews; and other communications with the project participants. Interviews lasted between 1 and 3 hours and followed general guidelines. Interviewees were encouraged to talk about the project, with questions asked only as triggers when needed (Bryman 1989). Interviewees were encouraged to drift during the interview and to talk more about whatever they felt was most interesting or important. Following the main interview, interviewees were contacted again via e-mail, telephone, or in-person for a short interview lasting between 30 and 60 minutes in order to clarify issues, explain positions, or comment on the progress of issues. Thirteen members of the ERP project teams were interviewed, in addition to two other members of the staff who were met several times before the formal collection of data. These included the project director, project manager, module managers, change managers, and project members from all of the implemented modules, as well as members from the external consultancy teams. Tape recording was not permitted, in line with the access agreement with the organization. To address this limitation, full notes were taken during each interview and extended directly afterward by the researcher, who added further observations and comments. Document reviews included project newsletters, corporate bulletins, internal reports, external consultants' documents and reports, and internal e-mails.

Data was analyzed following ANT's analytical conventions, for example grouped according to actors. A chart of actors was produced, followed by a few translation charts connecting the different actors and showing their diverse interests. The progress of each issue was followed and its settlement recorded. The negative modalities were traced backward to examine how the translation took place, and forward to understand how the project proceeded. Positive modalities were also identified but due to space limitations are reported only briefly here.

4   CASE STUDY

The ERP project studied for this case passed through many changes during the course of its implementation. The following subsections highlight some of these.

4.1 Changes to the Initial objectives

The ERP project started with three objectives. Quoting from the project plan and the company newsletter, they were: "To enable Drinko to meet increased worldwide demand profitably; to give people access to accurate information quickly so they can make good decisions fast; and finally to simplify core processes and systems across what have been traditionally regarded as separate regional operations." During the progress of the implementation, there was some confusion and a disparity of views regarding the purposes of the project. When each party started to work against its perceived objectives, the deliverables of the first stage of implementation varied significantly across ERP project teams as well as departments.

Senior management decided to hire an external consultancy to analyze the situation and provide an explanation for the varied nature of the deliverables. The consultants advised that different parties had made their own assumptions regarding the objectives of the project and hence worked to achieve certain deliverables that were not necessarily in harmony with those of other groups—or with the corporate overall vision of the system. In following up on this insight, and as a result of successive brainstorming sessions, the organization's senior management simplified the project objectives to a single one: to unify the business. This was complemented with a colored logo to reinforce the new objective.

4.2   Change of System's Scope and Reach

The initial scope of Drinko's ERP system encompassed all the organizational business units in many different locations. This included three main commercial arms within the organization, located in EUB, America, and EUK. However, America BU refused to join the project, arguing that this would complicate their ongoing plan to merge with a distribution company operating in the same market. ERP project management became engaged in intense negotiations with America BU to try to convince them to cooperate by joining the project. This would contribute to the realization of the project's plan and corporate executive management's aim of having a single system across the entire organization. The ERP project management failed to convince the American BU and had to exclude it from the project's scope, despite the major importance and large size of its market (Drinko's third largest). This meant the initially planned corporate-wide system ended up excluding nearly a third of the organization, leaving it to focus on only two of its companies: EUB and EUK. These had historically been isolated from each other, with EUB having an organizational reputation of lagging behind and being less competent than EUK (Elbanna 2007).

4.3   Change of System's Vision

The initial plan was to have a single ERP system encompassing all organizational operations, replacing 225 systems around Drinko. Yet, departments either refused to replace all of their current systems or insisted on buying different packaged software to complement ERP. This meant the project team had to work to interface its ERP system with several other software packages, such as Manugistics for production planning; a decision support system; and a number of business statistics and graphics packages. The initial plan also recommended that a single, shared service should be created to conduct routine accounting across the entire organization. The idea was that one group of staff would be responsible for most finance transactions, based in one location, which would lead to these tasks no longer being carried out independently in each company. EUK and EUB fought so fiercely over the location of the proposed service center that the continuation of the project was threatened by their dispute. Because of this, Drinko's senior management changed their position and allowed the project to have two shared services, one in each company.

4.4 Change of Orientation

The project started with many teams, including internal teams comprised of the organization's managers and employees together with two external teams from two consulting firms. One external team (here called Business Consulting) was responsible for the business side of the project and the other (Technical Consulting) for the technical side. The technical consultants kept a low profile within the organization as they focused on preparing the relevant technical capabilities of the system and the organization. In contrast, Business Consulting were more conspicuous as they pursued their business methodology on the implementation that aimed to bring a more business-oriented view to the ERP implementation.

Business Consulting competed with the internal change managers for the attention of corporate executives. For example, while maintaining frequent contact with Drinko's corporate executives, Business Consulting often conveyed the internal change managers' ideas as if they were their own and without giving credit to the change managers (according to change managers and the project manager). This initiated a war between the two parties that ended in the termination of Business Consulting's contract and a dependence solely on Technical Consulting for external implementation support. This change of the team structure led to a shift in the project's orientation from being a business project, as it was initially perceived, to becoming a primarily technical project.

4.5 Change of Configuration Assumptions

During the ERP implementation, an organization-wide transformation program was initiated to review the strategic structure of the organization. In its initial phase, the transformation program suggested to the ERP project that it was considering the separation of the supply and demand organizations, which would be something the ERP project would need to take into consideration in its system configuration processes. As the transformation program did not yet have any detailed view of how the supply and demand organization would be split, the ERP project had to configure the system according to its own working assumptions.

As the transformation program progressed and established a detailed view of how the separation between the supply and demand organizations would be done, the ERP project management discovered that their working assumptions were different from what had been finally decided by the transformation program. This meant the ERP system was configured for an imaginary organization that would never exist. Hence, it would need to be changed again to suit the final organizational design of the transformation program.

5   ANALYSIS

The following subsections present an account of drift in the investigated case study, given from an ANT perspective. In this analysis, it should be borne in mind that ANT considers *actor* to including a network comprised of more actors and networks.

5.1   System Objectives

The ERP project studied deviated from its originally planned objectives as it moved from the project office to involve the rest of the organization; its goals were translated differently in many of the networks through which it passed. For example, EUK sought to align the project to its interest in understanding EUB's operations, which shifted the project's objectives for this business unit to making transparent the hidden processes and data in EUB. On the other hand, EUB, with little experience of large business and systems projects, viewed the ERP project as a major challenge. EUB also viewed the project as a good opportunity to prove their efficiency and equal business capacity to the rest of the organization. In these ways, the ERP project's objectives drifted in EUB to become focused on installing an ERP and keeping up with the project's tough schedule.

For the operational planning department, this was seen to be a good opportunity to implement what they had always advocated but which had been resisted by business units: a sales plan for the entire organization. As a result, this team pulled the project's objective toward their prime aim of having one sales plan for the entire organization, seizing the ERP system's capability and the corporate executives backing of the project. The sales department problematized the project as an opportunity to solve their problems with warehouses and transportation as well as offering a way to bring together, stream-line, and "see through" end-to-end processes. This meant the sales team focused more on integration issues and emphasized the detailed design of warehouses.

In effect, each team translated the project objectives to suit their local interests. This led to considerable drift from the project's initial goals of meeting market demand profitably; improving the quality of information and speed of its flows; and simplifying processes and systems across the organization. Instead, the deliverables of each team varied according to its translation of the project, which put more weight and emphasis on their translated and displaced objectives.

As the teams' deliverables for the second phase varied considerably, Drinko's top management hired a third party to investigate the situation. This consultancy's report pointed to the dispersed understanding of the objectives between different teams and recommended the need to establish a solid objective for the project; in ANT terms, this could translate all the networks involved. This new objective problematized the project as an integration exercise aimed solely to unify the business. This focused objective made the project's goals immutable and put an end to the multiple translations and different modalities that occurred during the project's moves between networks.

5.2   Project Scope

As already indicated, the scope of the ERP project as initially planned and documented in the business case was to cover all BUs in the company. Yet when the time came to move the project token to the BUs, the American business unit opened the project's "black box" and returned it to the point of setting its objectives because they disputed and challenged these objectives. Through a series of translations, the American BU displaced the project team's interest in covering all business units and shifted the objectives toward reducing operational costs and increasing efficiency. They then presented their local interest of merging with another distribution company as an answer to the project's displaced objective. In doing so, America BU successfully translated the project management by convincing them that this business unit's proposed merger was more aligned to the corporate objectives than implementing the ERP system. This negative modality succeeded in shifting the project scope to exclude America BU from the corporate ERP implementation project. This effectively drifted the whole notion behind the implementation of ERP in the organization from being an organization-wide implementation to a system implementation covering only a few of Drinko's parts.

5.3 System Vision

A further area of change from the initial ERP plan was the use of other systems, which required interfacing them with ERP software. The project team's vision of implementing a single, integrated ERP had to be modified when the detailed design phase and consultation with end users in configuration sessions commenced. As the ERP implementation moved from the project office to the end users, the users returned to the point of initiation to discuss the technical reasons behind the decision to introduce the system.

Different users strongly advocated different reasons in favor of other systems that they were either using at that time or would like to acquire instead of the ERP. They disputed many ERP system functions, such as the operation planning processes, statistics and graphics, and the capacity for storing and analyzing information. Negotiations between the users' networks and the project team ended up favoring the use of other systems to carry out such functions. Thus, the users' negative modality meant the project team had to incorporate the implementation of other new systems, or the continuation of existing systems and building interfaces between them and the ERP system. This drifted the ERP project away from the initial plan.

Another deviation from the ERP implementation plan and what the system was expected to support was the configuration of the system to include two shared services. When the detailed design process reached the phase of approaching EUK and EUB, these business units shifted the project aim of implementing a single shared service for the organization to a discussion focused on the location of the proposed new ERP service center. Each unit insisted on the service center being located in its premises and indicated they would seriously question the intentions of senior management if they decided not to locate it in their country.

The implementation project ground to a halt while the project team waited for a resolution to the dispute about the location of the service center, with each party threatening to withdraw its commitment to the project if they did not win. Drinko's top management intervened to resolve the issue in a way that would satisfy both parties' explicit interests, in order to guarantee their commitment to push the project forward. This involved agreeing on a costly configuration based on having two service centers, one in each business unit. Although this decision was a deviation from what had been planned, it was a step forward in materializing the project. By guaranteeing the continuation of the BUs' commitment, this new plan sustained the project's inertia by maintaining its sources of energy.

5.4   Project Orientation

A major incident of drift was the shift in orientation from a business project to one focused on a technical software implementation. This occurred as a result of a battle between the external Business Consulting and internal change managers. The change managers were a traditionally influential network within the organization, accustomed to a close relationship with corporate executives. However, Business Consulting tried to highlight their role in the project to ensure future contracts within Drinko. It did this by approaching corporate executives directly, without consulting the change managers. Business Consulting also did not give credit to change managers when adopting ideas surfaced by change mangers during project meetings, and conveyed them to corporate executives as if they were the consultancy's own. This interference by Business Consulting in the corporate executive network threatened the power and prestige of change managers within the organization and was not tolerated.

The change managers problematized their interest in regaining their status by moving to get rid of Business Consulting. They did this by displacing the project management's strong interest in justifying the project's time and cost overruns, shifting it to helping the change managers in their dispute with Business Consulting. Change managers and project management aligned to open the consultants' black box and returned to the point of the consultancy's appointment in order to question their competencies, methodology, and implementation approach. They criticized Business Consulting of taking "an awful lot of time and producing little results." In doing so, they returned the project to the point of a choice of overall direction by advocating a new path based on the idea that "we have a system here to build." In this way, change managers eventually convinced corporate executives to chose what they thought was an organizationally less complicated and more straightforward technical implementation guided by Technical Consultants.

5.5   System Configuration

Organizational requirements for the ERP system configuration passed through several changes during the course of its implementation. While the ERP configuration process was underway based on assumptions representing the current organizational structure, the transformation program network was proceeding on its study of the strategic direction of the organization and the possible improvements to the organizational structure. This returned the ERP project to a discussion of basic organizational assumptions. The transformation program, despite its initial vague notion of separating the supply and demand organizations, translated the ERP project's interest in continuing top management support and displaced it to follow the transformation program's rough ideas on the future design of the organizational structure.

In following the negative modality of the transformation program's proposal for a new structure separating supply and demand organizations, the ERP project began to pursue a new, displaced goal. This led to a drift from its initial assumptions about organization structure. By the time the transformation program communicated its detailed final vision and plans for a new organizational structure, the ERP project found that the final version of the proposed separation between supply and demand was even different than their drifted assumptions. Being already translated to follow the transformation program's deliverables, in the hope of the continuation of management support, the ERP project drifted again to follow this different negative modality in order to accommodate the newly conveyed design for the organizational structure.

6   DISCUSSION AND CONCLUSION

The case study and its analysis described in this paper illustrate how this ERP project moved between many networks during its implementation. Actors that handled it contributed actively to its realization through their modalities. Each actor represented an important source of energy for the project. When actors disputed the project, the project came to a stand still to wait for fresh energy to push it into a direction, either the same as previously planned or a different route.

For instance, in the dispute regarding the location of the service center, business units succeeded in returning the project to the point of discussing the rationale behind the service center and what it represents organizationally. This negative modality led to a standstill that set the scene for a different direction for the project. Another example is the Business Consulting' challenge to change managers, which backfired by initiating fierce opposition to themselves and the discussion of their existence in the organization. The change managers succeeded in associating themselves with the project management, gaining more power and strengthening their modality. The negative modality of change managers and project management drifted the ERP project to termination of the consultancy's contract and shifted the project from a business orientation to what was perceived as a straightforward technical implementation.

Departments also contributed with negative modality that returned the ERP system back to the decision of acquiring it to dispute the value and functionality of the system itself. They argued for the introduction of their preferred alternative rather than the ERP system, including special software for graphics and statistics, Manugistics for production planning, and other existing and new systems. As a result, the project drifted from being viewed as a single system for the entire organization to an ERP system interfacing with many other software programs. Furthermore, the system objectives were frequently changed during its adoption by different teams and departments. Different networks tended to translate the objectives and pull it toward their organizational interest. Each team contributed with a different modality that shifted the project objectives into many directions.

In conclusion, the ERP's horizontal integration invited many parties to be involved in its implementation. As the project moved between different networks, it gained positive or negative energy from the different actors that contributed to it, either pushing the project forward along its initial plan or backward to the point of production to set a different direction. Negative modality that alters the initial plan represents the source of drift in ERP implementations.

The paper contributes to ERP implementation studies by providing a novel framework to conceptualize the drift in such integrated horizontal systems that are supposed to span the entire organization. It highlights the drifting course of ERP implementation and, more importantly, demonstrates that drift is inherent in such implementations. This helps to explain why researchers often find that merging companies that have implemented the same packaged ERP system is problematic, despite the initial perception that merging the same ERP system between organizations should follow a rather straightforward and predictable trajectory (Alshawi et al. 2004; Truex and Ngwenyama 2000).

The research emphasis on the importance of drift for the survival of technology projects illuminates some areas of significance for theory and practice. It demonstrates that a technology project needs a continuing stream of fresh sources of energy to keep it alive and to guarantee its circulation between networks. However, it is rare to achieve the submission of actors to the project's stated objectives during this circulation as in many cases they wish open its black box, dispute it, and return it to the decision-making process. This can translate the project differently and change its direction. As drift results from the occurrences of such negative modalities, it is necessary to accommodate them to guarantee actors' involvement and ongoing support, providing the required energy for the project's survival.

In this regard, but with a different analysis, this study also supports the proposition of Holmstrom and Stalder (2001) that technology projects succeed to disseminate when they are allowed to drift to suit different actors' needs. Such drift is required to give the project energy at points of disputes where actors successfully open its black box and discuss its production. Such disputes cannot be settled without a drift that allows the technology project to work for everybody. This stress on the continuous need for new sources of energy also provides an alternative view to the diffusion of innovation model. It shows the lack of inertia in IS implementation projects and that the possibility of drift always exists—unless a positive modality is guaranteed from the outset (which is an unusual occurrence).

On the practical side, project managers should be aware of the vast number of negotiations through which an IS implementation project goes, and the way actors' different modalities and positions can drag it in many different directions. With every move of a project, and with each new actor entering the network, there is the possibility of the IS implementation taking a different path. Keeping the project on its initial path requires maintaining the same translation from beginning to end. This is not realistic because different actors may join during the course of an implementation. In principle, actors could translate and bend the project in their way, indicating that drift should be considered as an embedded characteristic of IS implementations. It might also not be feasible to follow the initial path at critical points when new energy is needed to proceed. This is when drift can be in order, to guarantee actors' commitment and contributions. At every step of an implementation project, therefore, special care needs to be taken to monitor the moves being made in order to try to keep actors aligned in achieving desired mutual goals.

References

Alshawi, M., Themistocleous, M., and Almadani, R. "Integrating Diverse ERP Systems: A Case Study," *Journal of Enterprise Information Management* (17:6), 2004, pp. 454-460.

Baskerville, R., and Pries-Heje, J. "A Multiple-Theory Analysis of a Diffusion of Information Technology Case," *Information Systems Journal* (11), 2001, pp. 181-212.

Bloomfield, B. P., Coombs, R., Knights, D., and Littler, D. (eds.). *Information Technology and Organizations: Strategies, Networks, and Integration*, Oxford, UK: Oxford University Press, 1997.

Bryman, A. *Research Methods and Organization Studies*, London: Unwin Hyman, 1989.

Buscher, M., and Mogensen, P. "Mediating Change: Translation and Mediation in the Context of Bricolage," in T. McMaster, E. Mumford, E. B. Swanson, B. Warboys, and D. Wastell (eds.), *Facilitating Technology Transfer Through Partnership: Learning from Practice and Research*, London: Chapman & Hall, 1997, pp. 76-91.

Callon, M. "Some Elements of a Sociology of Translation: Domestication of the Scallops and the Fishermen of St. Brieuc Bay," in J. Law (ed.), *Power, Action and Belief: A New Sociology of Knowledge*, London: Routledge and Kegan Paul, 1986, pp. 196-233.

Ciborra, C. U. "Drifting: From Control to Drift," in K. Braa, C. Sorensen, and B. Dahlbom (eds.), *Planet Internet*, Lund, Sweden: Studentlitteratur, 2000, pp. 185-195.

Ciborra, C. U. "A Theory of Information Systems Based on Improvisation," in W. Currie and B. Galliers (eds.), *Rethinking Management Information Systems: An Interdisciplinary Perspective*, Oxford, UK: Oxford University Press, 1999, pp. 136-155.

Elbanna, A. R. "The Construction of the Relationship Between ERP and the Organization Through Negotiation," in *Proceedings of the 14th European Conference of Information Systems*, Goteborg, Sweden, 2006.

Elbanna, A. R. "Implementing an Integrated System in a Socially Dis-integrated Enterprise: A Critical View of ERP Enabled Integration," *Information Technology & People* (20:2), 2007 (forthcoming).

Greimas, A. J. *The Social Science: A Semiotic View*, Minneapolis, MN: University of Minnesota Press, 1990.

Hanseth, O., Ciborra, C. U., and Braa, K. "The Control Devolution: ERP and the Side Effects of Globalization," *The Data Base for Advances in Information Systems* (32:4), 2001, pp. 34-46.

Holmstrom, J., and Stalder, F. "Drifting Technologies and Multi-Purpose Networks: The Case of the Swedish Cashcard," *Information and Organization* (11), 2001, pp. 187-206.

James, G. "IT Fiascos and How to Avoid Them," *Datamation* (43:11), 1997, pp. 84-89.

Klischewski, R. "Systems Development as Networking," in *Proceedings of the Fourth Americas Conference on Information Systems*, Long Beach, CA, 1998, pp.1638-1644.

Knights,D., and Noble, F. "Networks and Partnerships in the Evolution of Home Banking," in T. McMaster, E. Mumford, E. B. Swanson, B. Warboys, and D. Wastell (eds.), *Facilitating Technology Transfer Through Partnership: Learning from Practice and Research*, London: Chapman & Hall, 1997, pp. 92-107.

Latour, B. "The Powers of Association," in J. Law (ed.), *Power, Action and Belief: A New Sociology of Knowledge*, London: Routledge & Kegan Paul, 1986, pp. 264-280.

Latour, B. *Science in Action: How to Follow Scientists and Engineers Through Society*, Cambridge, MA: Harvard University Press, 1987.

Latour, B. "Technology Is Society Made Durable," in J. Law (ed.), *Sociology of Monsters: Essays on Power, Technology and Domination* London: Routledge & Kegan Paul, 1991, pp. 103-131.

Law, J., and Hassard, J. (eds.). *Actor Network Theory and After*, Oxford, UK: Blackwell Publishers, 1999.

Lee, J. C., and Myers, M. D. "The Challenges of Enterprise Integration: Cycles of Integration and Disintegration Over Time," in R. Agarwal, L. Kirsch, J. I. DeGross (eds.), *Proceedings of the 25th International Conference on Information Systems*, Washington, DC, 2004, pp. 927-937.

Lilley, S. "Regarding Screens for Surveillance of the System," *Accounting, Management and Information Technology* (8), 1998, pp. 63-105.

Markus, M. L., Tanis, C., and Fenema, P. C. V. "Multisite ERP Implementations," *Communications of the* ACM, (43:4), 2000, pp. 42-46.

McMaster, T., Vidgen, T., and Wastell, D. "Technology Transfer: Diffusion or Translation," in T. McMaster, E. Mumford, E. B. Swanson, B. Warboys, and D. Wastell (eds.), *Facilitating Technology Transfer Through Partnership: Learning from Practice and Research*, London: Chapman & Hall, 1997, pp. 64-75.

Montoya, S. "Foxmeyer Files Suit Against SAP Software Company," *AP Wire*, August 27, 1998.

Nandhakumar, J., Rossi, M., and Talvinen, J. "Planning for 'Drift'?: Implementation Process of Enterprise Resource Planning Systems," in *Proceedings of the 36th Hawaii International Conference on System Sciences*, Los Alamitos, CA: IEEE Computer Society Press, 2003.

Orlikowski, W. J. "Learning from Notes: Organizational Issues in Groupware Implementation," MIT Sloan School Working Paper #3428-92, Center for Coordination Science Technical Report #134, Massachusetts Institute of Technology, Cambridge, MA, 1992.

Rogers, E. M. *Diffusion of Innovations* (4th ed.), New York: The Free Press, 1995.

Ross, J. W., and Vitale, M. R. "The ERP Revolution, Surviving vs. Thriving," *Information Systems Frontiers: Special Issue on the Future of Enterprise Resource Planning Systems* (2:2), 2000, pp. 233-241.

Rothwell, R. "Successful Industrial Innovation: Critical Factors for the 1990s," *R&D Management* (22), 1992, pp. 221-239.

Truex, D., and Ngwenyama, O. K. "ERP Systems: Facilitating or Confounding Factors in Corporate Telecommunications Mergers?," in *Proceedings of the 8th European Conference on n Information Systems*, Vienna, Austria. 2000, pp. 645-651.

Vidgen, R., and McMaster, T. "Black Boxes, Non-Human Stakeholders and the Translation of IT Through Mediation," in W. J. Orlikowski, G. Walsham, M. R. Jones, and J. I. DeGross (eds.), *Information Technology and Change in Organizational Work*, London: Chapman & Hall, 1996, pp. 250-271.

Wagner, E. L., and Newell, S. "Making Software Work: Producing Social Order via Problem Solving in a Troubled ERP Implementation," in D. Avison, D. Galletta, and J. I. DeGross (eds.), *Proceedings of the 26th International Conference on Information Systems*, Las Vegas, NV, 2005, pp. 447-458.

About the Author

Amany Elbanna is a lecturer of Information Systems at the Business School, Loughborough University, United Kingdom. She holds a Ph.D. in Information Systems from the London School of Economics. She also holds MBA and M.Sc. degrees in information systems. Her research interests include packaged software implementation, the project management of large IS projects, and the management of change associated with the adoption and appropriation of ICT. Amany can be reached by e-mail at a.elbanna@lboro.ac.uk.

18 MAKE TECHNOLOGY INVISIBLE, OR KEEP IT VISIBLE? The Role of Intra-organizational Transfer and Integration of Project Outcomes

Henrik C. J. Linderoth
Umeå School of Business
Umeå University
Umeå, Sweden

Abstract   *Today's organizational renewal and change is conducted primarily within projects (i.e., temporary organizations), and, in varying degrees, includes information and communication technology (ICT) systems that should mediate or trigger intended changes. However, the definite duration of a project process and the indefinite duration of ICT-mediated change processes cause challenges for the permanent organization when intra-organizational transfer of intended and emergent project outcomes would be managed. However, when studying the interaction between ICT and an organizational context, it is of crucial importance to also include the ICT in the analysis. Accordingly, the aim this paper is to uncover technology features and their consequences for the permanent organization when intra-organizational transfer of intended and emergent project outcomes is managed. In order to achieve the aim of the paper, three case studies of ICT projects are analyzed and discussed. The ICT features predefinition of processes to change and the ease of making the ICT into an obligatory passage point will have consequences for the permanent organization's management of intra-organizational transfer of intended and emergent project outcomes. The conclusion is that these features of ICT have an impact on arrangements to be made by the permanent organization in order to support the intra-organizational transfer and integration of intended and emergent project outcomes.*

Keywords   Organizational change, ICT, inscriptions, project management

Please use the following format when citing this chapter:

Linderoth, H. C. J., 2007, in IFIP International Federation for Information Processing, Volume 235, Organizational Dynamics of Technology-Based Innovation: Diversifying the Research Agenda, eds. McMaster, T., Wastell, D., Ferneley, E., and DeGross, J. (Boston: Springer), pp. 267-281.

1   INTRODUCTION

Today's organizational renewal and change is conducted primarily in temporary organizations (projects) (Ekstedt et al 1999; Lundin and Söderholm 1995; Söderlund 2005) and,
to a varying degree, includes information and communication technology (ICT) systems
that should mediate or trigger intended changes (Barrett et al. 2006; Boddy and Buchanan
1992; Henfridsson 1999). To organize an ICT-mediated change process in the organizational form of a project, however, is not without inherent conflicts between the task to be
solved (the IT-mediated change) and the organizational form used to solve the task (the
temporary organization). First, learning and knowledge development in the project process regarding emergent use of a system can challenge budgeted use of resources and
timelines (Linderoth and Lundqvist 2004). Second, the use of ICT systems in daily
practice regularly drifts away from original intensions and goals, no matter who defines
them (Ciborra 1996). This situation causes problems for determining goals at the
beginning of a project process when uncertainty is high (Kreiner 1995). Third, in contrast to the indefinite duration of ICT-mediated change processes (see Bresnen 2006;
Orlikowski 1996), temporary organizations have a definite duration. Thus, it can be
claimed that the fluidity of ICT-mediated change processes has implications not only for
the temporary organization, but also for the permanent organization that hosts the project.
Because ICT has the potential to transform a wide array of organizational processes and
structures, all of the change options are not known when a project is initiated. Rather,
change options emerge over time when actors enact and make sense of a technology (see
Orlikowski 1996; Orlikowski and Hofman 1997). Because of time and budget
constraints, therefore, all of the options for emergent changes and organizational development are not possible to realize within a single project. Thus the definite duration of the
temporary organization and the indefinite duration of ICT-mediated change processes
create a critical issue for the permanent organization: How can the intra-organizational
transfer of intended and emergent outcomes from an ICT-mediated change project be
managed?

When this inherent conflict arises between ICT-mediated change processes and the
temporary organization, no particular attention has been paid to the ICT itself. However,
when studying ICT in some organizational contexts, it is of crucial importance to include
the ICT in the analysis of outcomes of the interaction between the technology and the
organizational context (see Monteiro and Hanseth 1996; Orlikowski and Iacono 2001).
Thus, if deeper knowledge is to be gained about the challenges faced by the permanent
organization in hosting the ICT-mediated change project, the focus cannot be merely on
the inherent conflict between the change processes and the organizational form in which
the process is temporarily managed. It is well known in the ICT research literature that
ICT, in the shape of a blurred mixture of social and technical components, has an impact
on actors and their roles and relationships in the context in which a system is deployed
(Hanseth and Monteiro 1997; Monteiro and Hanseth 1996). But what impact do ICT
features have on challenges for the permanent organization when the intended and emergent outcomes from a project would be transferred to the permanent setting? This issue
has not received adequate treatment in the literature. Accordingly, the aim of this paper
is to uncover technological features and their consequences for the permanent organization when intra-organizational transfer of intended and emergent project outcomes is
managed. In order to achieve this aim, three ICT projects will be analyzed and discussed.

2 TRANSFER THE TEMPORARY TO THE PERMANENT

Bearing in mind the role of technology features and the inherent conflict between ICT-mediated change processes and the temporary organization, how can the problem be approached in a way that enhances the understanding of intra-organizational transfer of project outcomes? Concerning this overall problem, three questions can be raised. How can a successful transfer be viewed? Why does transfer occur? What is the impact of the technology features on the transfer?

The successful transfer of project outcomes can be viewed from a number of perspectives, such as ROI, achievement of goals, and perceived benefits. But a pragmatic stance is taken in this paper. A successful transfer of project outcomes is viewed as occurring when outcomes become an integrated and standard part of the operating system in the permanent organization (see Meredith and Mantel 2005). Accordingly, when ICT usage has triggered a change of organizational processes, integration is achieved, as an expression of a successful transfer of project outcomes. However, if integration is expressed in this manner for a successful transfer of project outcomes, why does integration of project outcomes occur? In the literature focusing on diffusion of innovations (see Rogers 1995), there is a basic assumption that there should be a fit between the characteristics of an innovation and an appreciation of these characteristics among potential adopters. This view has been criticized for neglecting the role of actors when innovations diffuse (Latour 1987). Latour (1986) claims that the 100th actor is as important as the first actor in a diffusion chain, and each actor can modify, adopt, neglect, or betray an innovation. Thus, Latour's idea that innovations are transferred along a chain of actors indicates that the organization hosting an ICT-mediated change project needs to add links in the chain after the termination of a project in order to facilitate intra-organizational transfer of project outcomes.

However, one basic claim in this paper is that features of the ICT will have an impact on the intra-organizational transfer of project outcomes. Accordingly, these features will have an impact on the *shape* of the links in the transfer chain. Thus, it will be of crucial importance to understand the various features of the ICT that have been implemented. In this paper, the concept of inscriptions, taken from actor network theory (ANT), is used as a tool to uncover technological features. Inscriptions refer to the technology designers' assumptions about the role of technology in a future context of use, about the context itself, and about potential users' capabilities and competencies (Akrish 1992). Designers' assumptions are inscribed into a technology in strong or weak modes, and, in the process of inscription, tasks are delegated to the technology and to the future user, respectively (Hanseth and Monteiro 1997; Latour 1991, 1992). However, the patterns of action inscribed in the new technology can cause conflicts with established norms and with actors' prevailing roles and relationships in a process (see Linde and Linderoth 2000; Orlikowski 1992, 2002). Patterns of action, for example delegation of tasks, can partly inform actors of future actions to be taken when ICT should be integrated into the permanent organization (Linderoth 2002b). Even if, for example, actors are knowledgeable about the task of identifying the process to change by means of the ICT and learn the actions to perform in order to integrate ICT usage into the permanent organization, a crucial question remains: To what extent have intended and emergent project outcomes been integrated when a project is terminated?

Intended and emergent changes may be realized to a greater or lesser extent before the project is terminated. Taking this into consideration, how can the integration of changes triggered by ICT be viewed? In the ideal ICT-mediated change project, it can be claimed that integration occurs when the technology has become an *invisible* part of the operating system, or is viewed as something that no longer needs to be considered a black box (Callon and Latour 1981). However, because optional changes—intended and emergent—may not be possible to implement during the project lifetime, viewing integration or a successful transfer of project outcomes as the creation of a black box is not without problems. To place issues related to ICT-mediated changes in the black box implies that these issues are no longer considered. However, Linderoth (2002a) argues that the concept of a black box can still be used if changes realized and integrated into the permanent organization are put in the black box, at the same time as issues of further optional changes are considered. Otherwise, the entire issue of ICT-mediated change is made invisible after the termination of the project. Accordingly, the challenge for the permanent organization is to consider issues not dealt with in the project, and to place accomplished issues in the project in the black box. But what organizational arrangements are needed in order to manage issues emerging from the project? And what role do inscriptions in the system play when designing the organizational arrangements? In the remainder of the paper, three ICT-mediated change projects are analyzed in order to uncover the impact of technological features on the formation of organizational arrangements that should facilitate an intra-organizational transfer and integration of intended and emergent outcomes of a project.

3   DATA COLLECTION AND CASE DESCRIPTION

One basic claim in the paper is that inscriptions, including the technology designer's delegation of tasks to technology respectively to the organization hosting the project, will have consequences for the intra-organizational transfer of outcomes from ICT-mediated change projects. Therefore, a crucial issue is the selection of cases that vary in the features of the ICT that is implemented. One such variation indicated is the delegation of tasks to technology respectively to the organization hosting the project. For one case, this means a system should be identified in which the processes affected are already inscribed in the system (i.e., delegated to the technology). In another case, a system should be identified where the processes affected are not identified (i.e., it is delegated to the host organization to identify processes to change by means of the technology). A third case is also included in the analysis. During its analysis, another dimension of technology features emerged as an explanation for actions that the permanent organization has to perform in order to achieve the intra-organizational transfer and integration of emergent and intended project outcomes. This dimension was the ease of making the ICT into an obligatory passage point (OPP), which, as described by Callon (1986, 1987), is something that actors must pass on the way to their goals. In the context of this paper, OPP refers to whether or not actors can avoid using ICT, and to how much effort is needed to avoid passing the OPP.

The first case is a longitudinal study of a project involving the implementation of electronic patient records (EPR) in a clinic at a university hospital. This clinic was the 11th of 21 clinics at this hospital to receive the new EPR system. The project process for our chosen case followed a traditional structure, the main tasks in the project process being adaptation and adjustment of the system and organizational routines, followed by a "big bang roll out." The project group was goal-oriented on the operational level. Some project group interviewees stated that the goal was to implement the system by 1 October 2002, but they also had more qualitative goals, as they stated that they should create a system as good as possible for the clinic. The overall goals of the hospital-wide implementation (e.g., to increase access to information, improve patient security, and improve efficiency) were, however, not often mentioned by interviewees. In our chosen clinic, the project ran for 1 year; we followed its progress during its last 6 months, interviewing a total of eight people: six from the project group, the chair of the steering committee (who was head of the actual clinic), and one from the hospital's central support unit responsible for the overall implementation of EPR in the hospital. Further data were collected by participant observation at project and steering group meetings, at demonstrations of the system for end users, and at two sessions of end-user education. Additionally, we had access to all protocols from meetings of the steering and project groups, as well as to the project description and other related material. Three additional follow-up interviews, with the former project manager, the head of the clinic, and the person in the central support function, were conducted 3 years after the termination of the project.

The second case is a longitudinal study of the implementation of telemedicine in a Swedish county, a process that was followed by the researcher from 1994 to the present. The overall goal of the telemedicine projects was to investigate potential consequences of the use of telemedicine along a number of dimensions such as competence development, patient service, and potential cost reductions. At the outset, two parallel projects, PAT (telepathology) and GT (general telemedicine), were running between 1996 and 1998. In the GT project, communication channels were established among two health centers and three clinics at a university hospital (dermatology; orthopedics; and diseases of the ear, nose and throat). In the PAT project, communication channels were established between two clinics at a university hospital (pathology and cytology) and two clinics at two county hospitals (surgery and gynecology). Since the terminations of the PAT and GT projects, there have been a number of small projects initiated as a consequence of the county's decision to support further investments in the technology. The main study was accomplished between 1994 and 1999. Data were collected through 62 semi-structured interviews and participant observation was employed in 18 project-group meetings. After the first study, informal contacts have been kept with informants in the actual settings, a few follow-up interviews have been conducted with representatives for the project settings studied between 1996 and 1998, two managers at a central support function have been interviewed and document studies have been conducted, and 1,800 telemedicine consultations that took place between June 2003 and January 2006 have been analyzed.

The third case is a retrospective study of a project implementing an e-learning system in a company in the telecom industry. The motive for the project was to control the process of distribution and use of training material in after-sales services (i.e., customer care centers and repair firms managing guarantee repair and other repair services). The company is operating in a highly competitive industry in which launches of new product models are essential for maintaining a competitive position. Thus, one critical activity is the early distribution of training material containing information about the functions and features of the new product model and how to detect errors. The purpose of the project was to implement a system in which information and repair advice regarding the company's new product models could be distributed to companies around the world that are responsible for warranties and after-sales services. Five interviews were accomplished with representatives for the project and the system vendor.

4   MAKE THE SYSTEM INVISIBLE, OR KEEP IT VISIBLE?

In section 2, a claim was made that the integration of project outcomes was completed when technology use was taken for granted—in other words, when technology was made invisible. This view was not without its complications, however, as the definite duration of a project implementing ICT-mediated change implied that opportunities of organizational change and development would probably remain after the termination of a project. Thus, a crucial issue for the permanent organization will be twofold: to make ICT invisible and to keep it visible. In this section, the work of the temporary organization and the permanent organization to make ICT invisible and keep it visible will be described and analyzed for the three selected cases.

4.1   Electronic Patient Records: More Visible than Wanted

In the electronic patient records (EPR) case, a large number of predefined, interconnected processes for change were inscribed into the system, meaning that system designers tried to get potential adopters to accept the designers' view on the organization of information flow. It should also be noted that laws and regulations prescribing the information to be documented and how it should be documented have a significant influence on the designers' inscriptions in an EPR system. In any case, the organization has the option of influencing the complexity of the project process, as the system consisted of five interconnected modules that could be implemented separately. At the time, however, it had been decided within the hospital that all modules should be implemented in the project. Hence, a main task for the project group became the identification of all processes affected, and then the adaptation and adjustment of these processes in accordance with routines inscribed in the system. In particular, project group members had to attempt to adapt the system without violating rules and regulations when inscribed routines would cause too many complications in the daily operations. Thus, the feasibility study (the identification of prevailing processes and their relationships) in the beginning of the project became rather comprehensive and was one important activity used to prepare the ground for a smooth integration by making the system invisible after the termination of the project, because misfits between the system and organizational processes would be very visible for end users. The project's feasibility study was one of the most thorough among projects that had been undertaken by the hospital at that time, and a manager in the central EPR support function stated that the feasibility study was one of the reasons for the project's success. Due to the comprehensive feasibility study, the project manager stated that they could already detect problems in their early stages that had been caused by mismatches between prevailing processes and system features, and for that reason, the project group could start working at solving some crucial problems in advance.

During the feasibility study and the remainder of the project process, a number of issues concerning further organizational development and change can be expected to be detected because of knowledge development and learning that occurs during the project process (see Orlikowski 2002; Robey et al. 2000). A crucial issue for the permanent organization is how the intra-organizational transfer of these project outcomes would be managed. An alternative is to exploit the knowledge developed in the project process by enhancing the scope of the project, which implies that more resources are needed and/or that timelines for the project are exceeded, as was the case in projects implemented in other clinics at this hospital. In the clinic studied, all issues that could cause an increase in the scope of the project were handed over to the clinic manager, who decided if a further project would be started. The manager in the central EPR function stated that matters had been handled differently. In another clinic that had implemented EPR (a clinic not included in the present study), the permanent organization dealt with emergent project outcomes by returning to the outcomes in clinic meetings (when coming activities were planned, for instance) whereas in other clinics, nothing happened.

It is not only important to mange the transfer and integration of emerging project outcomes, but, as previously noted, one of the project group's main tasks is to try to make the system as invisible as possible. Because the ICT becomes an obligatory passage point (Callon 1986, 1987) for everyone who must manage or retrieve patient-related information, all users of the system can make their own sense of the technology, which will guide their coming actions. Roughly expressed, in the extreme cases, users either use the system without further notice, or they actively try to bypass the system in order to make requested information available (e.g., by asking the secretary for printouts). Even if the work of the project is to make the system as invisible as possible for the end user, the large number of inscribed and interconnected processes in the system implies that the change from managing paper-based patient-related information to managing the information electronically will be highly visible. From an analytical point of view, transfer of intended project outcomes can be claimed to occur by *switching*. During a short period when the system is rolled out into the operations, the mode in which information is managed and retrieved would be switched from paper-based records to electronic records. If the transfer is successful, the system should become invisible and should not be considered further. However, because the system becomes an OPP, it will probably not become invisible, or will not be taken into consideration, for the sole reason that it has become an OPP! Even if the integration of the system could be regarded as successful immediately after the termination of the project, support is needed if the integration is to persist and if the system is to become invisible. This could, however, be a long process. In the case studied, immediately after the project was terminated, the project manager got a position as the one responsible for managing the system. In an interview three years after the roll out, she revealed that many of her activities concerned issues related to hardware and software problems, the training of new users, and further training of old users. Issues concerning further organizational development triggered by use of the system have been more or less absent, but those issues that appeared during the project process are still being dealt with. Issues concerning the EPR system at the university hospital are still highly visible, a matter that became clear during the autumn of 2006. It was reported in the regional broadcast news that surgery had been postponed at the hospital due to severe problems with the EPR system when it was upgraded.

As this EPR case has demonstrated, the intended outcomes—for example, that the system should become an OPP—and the emergent outcomes that evolve from learning and knowledge development can be considered for a long time after implementation of the system. Thus, the integration needs to be maintained in the permanent organization by establishing a function that has resources to cultivate the integration, thereby making the technology invisible, but also keeping it visible in order to exploit emergent project outcomes.

4.2   Telemedicine: Institutionalized Visibility

In the second case, the telemedicine system implemented is basically a videoconferencing system to which optical equipment can be connected. The work of identifying processes to change is delegated to the permanent organization, because the generic feature of the technology was just the possibility of transmitting live and frozen pictures in real time. When the permanent organization initiated the two projects in the clinics concerned, the search for processes to change was only undertaken in these clinics. It is the project group, however, to whom the responsibility falls for identifying potential processes to be changed. In PAT and GT, the two projects initiated in 1996, the project manager for the PAT project had a relatively clear idea about a few applications for the technology and actions to help realize the ideas. On the other hand, it was decided for the GT project that applications to be tested (processes to change) should be sought out during the project period. Depending on which optical equipment was connected to the telemedicine system, the number of possible processes in which to intervene was reduced. If an otoscope (ear camera) was connected to the system, for instance, interventions would be delimited to processes connected to ear-related problems. The search for processes in which to intervene, and the actual interventions were made throughout the project period and occurred even 2 or 3 years after the termination of the GT project, although none of the applications tested during this period was transferred and integrated into the per-manent organization. However, a spinoff from the first project was an initiation of a "one person project" in the Department of Dermatology, which had also been in the first project. A new application was identified, allowing the dermatologist to serve a hospital 140 km away via telemedicine, instead of sending her/him to this remote hospital by bus three or four times a week. The project was considered to be a great success, as the dermatologists' discomfort with catching the bus at 5:30 in the morning was removed, and today the department is one of the county's heavy users of telemedicine. In the PAT project, two applications identified at the outset—pathology conferences with two other hospitals—are integrated into the routine activities. Activities were established with a few more hospitals, even if the need for conferences occurs only two or three times per month at each hospital. A third application identified at the outset was tested, but it faded away due to lack of engagement by one party.

Although there was little intra-organizational transfer and integration of applications tested in the initial projects between 1996 and 1998, the county saw the potential useful-ness of the technology and supported a further investment in telemedicine infrastructure. During the 18 months following termination of the PAT and GT projects, actors interested in testing telemedicine could apply for money for equipment to initiate their projects, but overall coordination of the projects was lacking. In order to coordinate the further deployment of telemedicine and make it more visible, a support function, TeleMedLab, was established in 1999. Its assignment was to maintain the systems, test new technologies, support users, and promote use. The manager for TelMedLab states that many projects are completed in which participants are satisfied with the results, but when outcomes should be integrated into the daily praxis, nothing happens. He is also waiting for the breakthrough, as telemedicine has not yet become an important strategic issue for the county.

   In comparing the telemedicine case to the case of the EPR system, in addition to the dimension of need to identify process to change and decide how to organize changed processes, a further and rather obvious difference is how the system becomes an obligatory passage point. In the EPR case, the system becomes an OPP when it is rolled out and it is decided that all information related to patients should be managed via the system. But, as shown in the telemedicine case, the mere fact that the equipment is rolled out is no guarantee that the system will become an OPP. Because the technology functions as an intermediary for knowledge and information transfer, the telemedicine system is more fragile as an OPP. The actors have other alternatives; they can access information and knowledge, for instance, usually by sending the patient to a medical specialist. An essential part of the project group's work is thus to make the system into an OPP by convincing indispensable actors of the benefits of system usage, a goal that is aided by making appropriate organizational arrangements, like the creation of supporting routines (Linderoth 2002b). Based on developments in the telemedicine projects studied, it can be claimed that the OPP becomes rather stable if indispensable actors are convinced about the benefits of using the system, as occurs when actions are already tested in daily operations. For the same reason, the OPP can vanish immediately when the project is terminated, because appropriate organizational arrangements are not made and necessary decisions are not taken (e.g., to block or remove alternative paths of action). Thus, if the project group manages to establish the technology as an OPP, it can be claimed that the technology has become invisible or taken for granted. But, in order to facilitate further organizational change and development, the permanent organization needs to establish a function, like TeleMedLab, that will serve to keep the technology visible.

4.3 E-Leaning: Invisible for the Rest of the Organization

In the third case, the e-learning system implemented was originally developed for use in universities and similar contexts. The course provider can either develop the learning material on his/her own, or the vendor can assist in the development of a course. Furthermore, the course provider can choose how sophisticated the design of the course material should be, from a simple use of office tools, to flash animations for more advanced users. For the user, the interface reminds one very much of Windows Explorer. Further features of the basic version of the system are, for example, the possibility of seeing who is logged into a certain course, and opportunities for course participants to chat with each other. The content on the platform is managed by an administrator who, among other things, determines when materials should be released, views activities of registered users, and decides if a test should be passed before a user can proceed to the next level of the course.

The e-learning system is similar to the telemedicine system in that system designers have delegated to the host organization the task of identifying the processes to change. In this case, it means that the permanent organization's task is to identify processes where it has a need for learning and knowledge development, but course participants need not be physically present at one location. At the outset, the project group exhibited relatively clear problem recognition and had ideas about how to solve the problem of their lack control of how the information material for new product models was used and who used it. The clear problem recognition aspect was also confirmed by the vendor representative, who stated the project group had a very clear idea of what they wanted to achieve. In other organizations, the motives for implementing the system were very vague and the vendor had to help them identify the processes with which to start. The process of making the system invisible followed a traditional project management approach, based clear goals and subgoals and detailed work break down structures (see Packendorff 1995; PMI 1996). However, due to the project group members' problem recognition, the project was divided into four stages, which eased the integration. The first stage, the technical implementation of the system, was managed in accordance with traditional project management ideas. The integration of the change was, however, accomplished in the two following stages that were managed in the permanent organization, but still by the same people who accomplished the technical implementation project. The second stage was to create an organization for maintaining the system. A few people were assigned the responsibility for maintaining the system and they were located in the same building as the previous project group, a group nearly identical to the group responsible for the development of training material for use on a world-wide basis. However, integration could not be reached if the system not was promoted. Accordingly, the third stage was to identify and establish the role of the facilitators who would promote the system in their geographical regions and decide when the material should be released because a new product model could be launched at different times around the world. The fourth and final stage was an evaluation of the outcomes of the process.

The role of the facilitators in the present e-learning case could, in one sense, be considered similar to the role of the TelMedLab in the telemedicine case as the role of keeping the technology visible in order to facilitate integration and interorganizational transfer of project outcomes. But TeleMedLab should also facilitate the use of telemedicine in other processes than those originally intended. So, in another sense, the role of the facilitator in the e-learning case was similar to the role of the former project manager in the EPR project, to work for integrating intended project outcomes and to make the system invisible. Thus, in the e-learning case, it can be claimed that the function for integrating intended project outcomes was established, but the question remains: What about using the system in other processes than the intended ones? A representative for the steering group stated that the e-learning system could be used in other processes where there was a need for training and learning and participants were not physically present at the same location. However, someone has to work to achieve the intraorganizational transfer of emergent project outcomes and the further deployment of the system. By the time the third case was completed, no more initiatives had been taken.

Finally, in another sense, the e-learning system has the same features as the EPR system, because the transfer of intended project outcomes also occurred by switching the process to change, even if the switch was implemented after the temporary organization was terminated. In the EPR and e-learning projects, the systems became an OPP when they were rolled out, as indispensable information was inscribed into the systems and could only be accessed via the system (e.g., information about new products or patient related information). However, due to the fact that the e-learning system intervened in one process compared to the EPR system that intervened in a large number of inter-connected processes, the integration of intended project outcomes was managed by facilitators, and the work to maintain the system as an OPP was done by the group developing training material for new product models.

5 DISCUSSION

Two features of the ICTs studied here have consequences for the permanent organiza-tion's management of intra-organizational transfer of intended and emergent project outcomes: (1) predefinition of processes to change, and (2) ease of making the ICT into an OPP. Predefinition of processes to change means that the processes to change were inscribed in technology or that it was delegated to the host organization to identify processes to change. Predefinition of processes does not mean, however, that processes to change are specified in detail. Rather, the permanent organization is informed about where to start to search for processes to change by means of the ICT. In the EPR case, for example, all existing processes concerning the management of patient-related information were potentially affected. In the telemedicine and e-learning cases, pre-definition of processes to change had a much broader scope, and the actual knowledge about appropriate processes to change could be relatively low. When the predefinition of processes to change is discussed, two claims about implications for further action could be made: (1) When processes to change are inscribed into the technology, *there is an idea about what to do.* (2) When it is delegated to the organization to identify processes to change, *is there an idea about what to do*? If there is an idea about what to do, the temporary organization may be too focused on solving the task and the potential for generating emergent project outcomes may be reduced. A further question also could raised: Does a system that is determined *a priori* to intervene in a large number of organizational processes demand too much attention and too many resources from the temporary and permanent organization in resolving its integration issues, which, in turn, could imply that issues of further organizational development and change disappear from the agenda? When there is no clear idea about what to do, a number of outcomes may emerge, but with less focus on accomplishing something. Alternatively, the project may merely expand in scope, implying that budgets and timelines will be exceeded. In the former case, the permanent organization may need to stimulate emergent project out-comes (e.g., in the project's steering group); in the latter case, the permanent organization needs to ensure that there is a focus on at least one idea (e.g., through traditional project management methods), and that other emergent outcomes are managed. Thus, especially when the change processes not are predefined, it is crucial for the permanent organization to make arrangements for emergent outcomes from the temporary organization to be managed for further exploitation; otherwise, the technology becomes invisible when the project is terminated.

The second dimension—ease of making the ICT into an OPP—depends on two things: whether the information required could be inscribed into the new ICT, and whether alternative ways of accessing the information could be disconnected. If it is easy to make the ICT into an OPP, as in the EPR and e-learning cases, either the permanent or the temporary organization needs to investigate the actions needed to make technology invisible after it has become an OPP. If the ICT becomes an OPP in a single process, as in the in e-learning case, it is necessary to ensure that ICT contains updated and relevant information. But if the system becomes an OPP for a large number of interconnected processes, as in the EPR case, a general support function is probably required in order to support end users, due to the complexity of the ICT. If the ICT is an intermediary for information transfer, as in the telemedicine case, the system does not automatically become an OPP. A crucial task for both the permanent and the temporary organization is to make arrangements that support the use of the ICT (see Linderoth 2002b) and to decide if changes are needed in the permanent organization in order to reorganize activities to facilitate use of the new system, and to block alternative ways of action. Making the ICT into an OPP also implies that technology is made invisible, however. Therefore, the permanent organization needs to establish a function that should keep technology visible—a function that supports and initiates new projects, for instance.

The three projects studied here can be grouped in a matrix along the dimensions of technological features: predefinition of processes to change and ease of making ICT into an OPP (Figure 1). This classification of ICT can be used as a starting point when discussing generally what happens when an ICT-mediated change process is framed in a temporary organization. The initiation of a project can be seen as an attempt to domesticate the ICT-mediated change process, by reducing complexity and making the processes manageable. If processes to change not are predefined, it may be believed within the permanent organization that this will be done in the project (see Markus and Benjamin 1997), because the essence of a project is to manage clearly defined tasks in a goal-directed manner, an opinion which could be found in any basic text book on the subject. This also means that initiators of projects try to place the ICT in the upper part of the matrix, and most probably in the upper right square, regardless of the features of the ICT. When placing the ICT in the upper left square, it can be claimed that the aim is to make technology invisible after termination of the project, because

> ...something has to be transformed or changed as a consequence of the existence of the temporary organization, and therefore, these changes are to be achieved before the organization is terminated (Lundin and Söderholm 1995, p. 442).

Thus, managing the ICT-mediated change process in a temporary organization implies, *per se,* a risk of making technology invisible and losing further options for organizational change and the development of the permanent organization. This risk is highly evident for ICT when the predefinition of the processes to change is low. It can be claimed that the permanent organization should not follow the temporary organization in the predefinition of processes to change. Rather it is necessary for the permanent organization to obtain knowledge and information about emergent project outcomes in order to keep technology visible, a function that could be performed by the organizational arrangement suggested earlier in this section. However, if these knowledge and information links are not established, it is likely that the technology would become invisible.

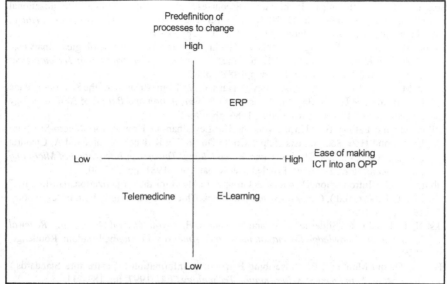

Figure 1. Dimensions of Technology Features

6 CONCLUSIONS

Organizing ICT-mediated change processes in a temporary organization creates challenges for the permanent organization regarding the intra-organizational transfer and integration of intended and emergent project outcomes, challenges that arise out of the inherent conflicts between the characteristics of change processes and project processes. The character of these challenges originates from features of the ICT that is implemented. By uncovering these features, the permanent organization can become informed about actions to take when the project is terminated, in order to facilitate the intra-organizational transfer of intended and emergent project outcomes. Furthermore, the framing of an ICT-mediated change project in a temporary organization implies that technology may be made invisible after the termination of a project, and that the opportunity for further organizational change and development may be lost. In order to keep technology visible, the permanent organization needs to make arrangements that support the visibility of technology. Any such arrangements will depend, of course, on the features of the ICT being implemented.

References

Akrish, M. "The De-scription of Technical Objects," in W. E. Bijker and J. Law (eds.), *Shaping Technology/Building Society*, Cambridge, MA: MIT Press, 1992, pp. 205-224.

Barrett, M., Grant, D., and Wailes, N. "ICT and Organizational Change: Introduction to Special Issue," *Journal of Applied Behavioral Science* (42:1), 2006, pp. 6-22.

Boddy, D., and Buchanan, D. *The Expertise of the Change Agent*, New York: Prentice Hall, 1992.

Bresnen, M. "Conflicting and Conflated Discourses? Project Management, Organizational Change and Learning," in D. Hodgson and S. Cicmil (eds.), *Making Projects Critical*, Houndmills, England: Palgrave Macmillan, 2006, pp. 68-89.

Callon, M. "Society in Making: The Study of Technology as a Tool for Sociological Analysis," in W. E. Bikjer, T. Hughes, and T. Pinch (eds.), *the Social Construction of Technological Systems*, Cambridge, MA: MIT Press, 1987, pp. 83-103.

Callon, M. "Some Elements of a Sociology of Translation: Domestication of the Scallops and the Fisherman of St Brieuc Bay," in J. Law (ed.), *Power, Action and Belief. A New Sociology of Knowledge?*, London: Routledge, 1986, pp. 196-233.

Callon, M., and Latour, B. "Unscrewing the Big Leviathan, or How Actors Macro-Structure Reality and How Sociologists Help Them to Do So," in K. Knorr-Cetina and A. Cicourel (eds.), *Advances in Social Theory and Methodology: Toward an Integration of Micro and Macro Sociologies*, London: Routledge & Kegan Paul, 1981, pp. 277-303.

Ciborra, C. U. "Introduction: What Does Groupware Mean for the Organizations Hosting It?," in C. U. Ciborra (ed.), *Groupware and Teamwork*, Chichester, England: John Wiley & Sons, 1996, pp. 1-19.

Ekstedt, E., Lundin, R., Söderholm, A., and Wirdenius, H. *Neo-industrial Organizing. Renewal by Action and Knowledge Formation in a Project-Intensive Economy*, London: Routledge, 1999.

Hanseth, O. and Monteiro, E. "Inscribing Behavior in Information Infrastructure Standards," *Accounting, Management & Information Technology* (7:4), 1997, pp. 183-211.

Henfridsson, O. "IT Adapting as Sense Making," Department of Informatics, Umeå University. 1999.

Kreiner, K. "In Search of Relevance: Project Management in Drifting Environments," *Scandinavian Journal of Management* (11:4), 1995, pp. 335-346.

Latour, B. "The Powers of Association," in J. Law (ed.), *Power, Action and Belief: A New Sociology of Knowledge*, London: Routledge, 1987, pp. 264-280.

Latour, B. *Science in Action*, Cambridge, MA: Harvard University Press, 1987.

Latour, B. "Technology is Society Made Durable," in J. Law (ed.), *a Sociology of Monsters: Essays on Power, Technology and Domination*, London: Routledge, 1991, pp. 103-130.

Latour, B. "Where Are the Missing Masses? The Sociology of a Few Mundane Artifacts," in W. E. Bijker and J. Law (eds), *Shaping Technology/Building Society*, Cambridge, MA: MIT Press, 1992, pp. 225-258.

Linde, A., and Linderoth, H. C. J. "Remove the Blinkers and Discover the Conflicting Programs of Action: A Dynamic Perspective on Management of 'Fuzzy' Projects," in D. P. Slevin, D. I. Cleland, and J. K. Pinto (eds.), *Project Management Research at the Turn of the Millenium: Proceedings of the PMI Research Conference 2000*, Drexel Hill, PA: Project Management Institute, 2000, pp. 357-368.

Linderoth, H. C. J. "Bridging the Gap between Temporality and Permanency," in K. Sahlin-Anderson and A. Söderholm (eds.), *Beyond Project Management: New Perspectives on the Temporary-Permanent Dilemma*, Malmö, Sweden: Liber, 2002a, pp. 224-240.

Linderoth, H. C. J. "Fiery Spirits and Supporting Programs of Action: The Keys to Exploration and Exploitation of Open Technologies," *International Journal of Health Care Technology and Management* (4:3/4), 2002b, pp. 319-332.

Linderoth, H.C. J., and Lundqvist, A. "Learn Not to Learn: Paradoxical Knowledge Creation and Learning in ERP Projects," in *Proceedings of Sixth International Research Network on Organizing by Projects (IRNOP VI) Conference*, Turku, Finland, August 25-27, 2004.

Lundin, R. A., and Söderholm, A. "A Theory of the Temporary Organization," *Scandinavian Journal of Management* (11:4), 1995, pp. 437-455.

Markus, M. L., and Benjamin, R. I. "The Magic Bullet Theory in IT-Enabled Transformation," *Sloan Management Review* (38:2), 1997, pp. 55-68.

Meredith, J. R., and Mantel, S. J. *Project Management: A Managerial Approach* (5ᵗʰ ed.), New York: John Wiley & Sons, 1995.

Monteiro, E., and Hanseth, O. "Social Shaping of Information Infrastructure: On Being Specific About Technology," in W. J. Orlikowski, G. Walsham, M. R. Jones, and J. I. DeGross (eds.), *Information Technology and Changes in Organizational Work*, London: Chapman & Hall, 1996, pp. 325-343.

Orlikowski, W. J. "The Duality of Technology: Rethinking the Concept of Technology in Organizations," *Organization Science* (3:3), 1992, pp. 398-427.

Orlikowski, W. J. "Improvising Organizational Transformation Over Time: A Situated Change Perspective," *Information Systems Research* (7:1), 1992, pp. 63-92.

Orlikowski, W. J. "Knowing in Practice: Enacting a Collective Capability in Distributed Organizing," *Organization Science* (13:3), 2002, pp. 249-273.

Orlikowski, W. J., and Hofman, J. D. "An Improvisational Model for Change Management: The Case of Groupware Technologies," *Sloan Management Review* (38:2), 1997, pp. 11-21.

Orlikowski, W. J., and Iacono, S. "Research Commentary: Desperately Seeking the 'IT' in IT Research—A Call to Theorizing the IT Artifact," *Information Systems Research* (12:2), 2001, pp. 121-134.

Packendorff, J. "Inquiring into the Temporary Organization: New Directions for Project Management," *Scandinavian Journal of Management* (11:4), 1995, pp. 319-333.

PMI. *A Guide to Project Management Body of Knowledge*, Drexel Hill, PA: Project Management Institute, 1996.

Robey, D., Boudreau, M-C., and Rose, G. M. "Information Technology and Organizational Learning: A Review and Assessment of Research," *Accounting, Management & Information Technology* (10:2), 2000, pp. 125-155.

Rogers, E. M. *Diffusion of Innovations* (4ᵗʰ ed.), New York: The Free Press, 1995.

Söderlund, J. *Projektledning och projektkompetens*, Malmö, Sweden: Liber, 2005.

About the Author

Henrik Linderoth currently holds a position as assistant professor at Umeå School of Business, Umeå University. His research interest is primarily focused on ICT-mediated change processes. Henrik has done studies of ICT use in the health care sector and is currently studying ICT use in the building and construction sector. He can be reached by e-mail at henrik.linderoth@ usbe.umu.se.

19 IMPLEMENTATION OF A CUSTOMER SERVICES INFORMATION SYSTEMS STRATEGY IN A HIGHER EDUCATION CONTEXT: An Integrative Perspective

Tayfour A. Mohammed
Helen J. Richardson
University of Salford
Salford, United Kingdom

Abstract   *Higher education institutions (HEIs) in the United Kingdom are undergoing strategic changes, not least being the introduction of a new fees scheme and the identification of information and communication technologies (ICTs) as central to their strategic vision. However, little is known about the contexts and processes of formulating and implementing information systems strategy to support university "customer" and "user" communities. This paper investigates the process of customer service strategy implementation as at GM University using an integrated perspective that conceptualizes the implementation process as a network formation, interconnected with both the strategy context and content. Our theoretical framework draws on both "contextualism" and actor network theory to understand the IS strategy implementation process. We demonstrate that IS strategy implementation is an emergent and dynamic process. Our conceptual framework provides us with an insight into the process of implementation that transcends the human strategic agency to the "collective" transformation process.*

Keywords   IS strategy, HEIs, contextualism, actor network theory

1   INTRODUCTION

In the past two decades or so, higher education in the United Kingdom has witnessed a considerable change resulting from a number of successive initiatives such as the edu-

Please use the following format when citing this chapter:

Mohammed, T. A., and Richardson, H. J., 2007, in IFIP International Federation for Information Processing, Volume 235, Organizational Dynamics of Technology-Based Innovation: Diversifying the Research Agenda, eds. McMaster, T., Wastell, D., Ferneley, E., and DeGross, J. (Boston: Springer), pp. 283-295.

cation reform act in the mid-1980s and the information systems and technology value for money study in the late 1990s (Clarke 2001). The result has been a greater expansion in the UK higher education sector in terms of both the number of students and institutions, shrinking budgets from government and funding councils, the emergence of nontraditional higher education institutions (HEIs) that are heavily reliant on information and communication technologies (ICTs) in addition to considerable changes in "patterns of demand and competition" for higher education (Allen et al. 2002; Gemmell and Pagano 2003; Richards et al. 2004).

In response to such changes, many universities embarked on strategic planning and "began to strategically re-focus their management efforts...and many have identified ICT as an essential function to survive in this environment" (Allen et al. 2002, p. 159). Huge investments have been made in computer-based information systems such as enterprise resource planning systems in the quest to achieve efficiency and effectiveness in back office integration (Allen et al. 2002; Pollock 2000), often with very little attention being paid to the front office service provision.

Although it is apparent that the UK HEIs need a sound strategic vision for information systems to meet the increasing challenges, it has been suggested that many HEIs are incapable of coping with such challenges because they are still using traditional strategic planning methods (Richards et al. 2004). A need, therefore, arises for a more integrative approach that addresses change in a more dynamic way (Dufour and Steane 2006).

This paper investigates the process of customer service IS strategy implementation at GM University (pseudonym) using an integrated perspective that conceptualizes the implementation process as an interconnected network formation, interacting with both the strategy context and content. We draw from both actor network theory (ANT) (see Callon 1987; Latour 1987; Vidgen and McMaster 1996) and contextualism theory (see Karyda et al. 2005; Pettigrew 1987; Walsham and Waema 1994) to examine the processes of enrolment and coalition building during IS strategy implementation and the mutual shaping process taking place between implementation processes and the content and context of the strategy. The basic thesis of this paper, therefore, is to show how the use of the theoretical framework, which combines ANT and contextualism, would enhance and further our understanding of the IS strategy implementation process.

The remainder of this paper is structured as follows: In the next section, we provide a review of literature on alternative perspectives in IS strategy implementation, followed by the theoretical framework; we then introduce our research methodology and the case background; this is followed by the analysis section and discussion of the major findings using the theoretical framework. Finally, we conclude by emphasizing the dynamic and emergent nature of strategy implementation and how ANT and contextualism can illuminate our understanding of the IS strategy implementation process.

2   LITERATURE REVIEW

The literature on strategic change or strategy implementation has been described as inconclusive and fragmented because it spans multiple disciplines (Dufour and Steane 2006).

The concept of *strategy* with respect to computer-based information systems has involved a variety of conceptualizations. Cavaye and Cragg (1993) distinguish between different forms of strategic use of IS such as IS as support for strategic decision making, IS as supporting or shaping an organization's competitive strategy, IS used as a tool to support and implement strategy, and IS as enabler for strategy formulation. Galliers and Leidner (2003) contend that information system planning is the "process by which IS strategies are formulated and/or emerge" (p. 27).

Dufour and Steane (2006) identify four paradigms in the strategy and strategic change implementation literature: the classical, the contingency, the behavioral, and the political. The basic premises of the classical or rational approach is that the whole strategic change process can be centrally *controlled* and that the "formulation and implementation" of change strategies "are two sequential and discrete stages" (Dufour and Steane 2006, p. 130). The basic emphasis here is on achieving *efficiency* through rational planning, rational decision making, use of rational tools and techniques, and the ability to recognize the gap between the planned and the implemented.

The classical approach has received a considerable level of criticism; for example, Dufour and Steane argue that it "fails to capture the interactive relationship between formulation and implementation as well as the political dimensions of change process... one of the main weaknesses...is its lack of descriptive validity" (p. 131). Clarke (2001) suggests that the classical approach is highly simplistic and its implementation questionable; it is based on the idea of a stable environment and any changes would thus destabilize strategic content. Another observation is that the classical model is grounded in a belief that change is a technical, nonpolitical activity, which proceeds in response to the directions of rational leaders (Dufour and Steane 2006).

The contingency approach to strategy implementation is based on a projected mismatch between the strategy and the contextual forces. Organizations, when implementing a strategy, have to choose between various structures and processes that achieve the best fit with both internal and external environments (Dufour and Steane 2006). Burnes (2004) argues that one problem with the contingency model is the inherent difficulty in identifying the critical situational variables. Dufour and Steane also maintain that the contingency approach neglects the behavioral and political issues in the strategy implementation process.

The behavioral approach considers the human actions and behaviors as well as the motivations for such actions and behaviors. The major emphasis in this approach has been on the organizational culture perspective. Clarke notes that organizational *culture* and *structure* are key factors to be considered in the process of IS strategy formulation and implementation. There is ubiquitous research that supports the culture–IS/IT strategy (for recent, comprehensive reviews of culture in IS research, see Kanungo et al. 2001; Leidner and Kayworth 2006). For Clarke, culture as a shared set of beliefs emerges from the social interaction of all organizational members, and change management is the underlying premise of IS strategy formulation and implementation.

The behavioral approach is criticized for its focus on internal organizational culture and the content of strategic change at the expense of seeking a broader, contextual explanation of strategic change (Dufour and Steane 2006).

The political perspective on strategic change implementation has gained popularity in IS/IT research. It focuses on the impact of power and influence on the implementation process by investigating the various sources of power such as technical skills and knowledge and the control over allocation of resources (Dufour and Steane 2006). The key element in the political approach is the proposition that technologies, and their "organizational consequences, are products of choice and negotiation by powerful individuals and groups within the organizations" (McLaughlin and Badham 2005, p. 836). Therefore, IS/IT strategy implementation in this case is understood as an emergent process that reflects the dynamics of the adopting context (see Dawson et al. 2000; McLoughlin et al. 2000).

Although the political perspective is seen as somewhat capable of bringing strategic change outcomes and processes to the organizational context, thereby attending to the cause and effect issues, it has been criticized for its neglect of the links between the two or of how networks are formed (Dufour and Steane 2006). We introduce an integrated perspective that attends to both the network formation and the links with both the context and content of strategic change.

3   THEORETICAL FRAMEWORK

Our theoretical framework draws on both contextualism and actor network theory to understand IS strategy implementation as a dynamic, contextual, and emergent process. In organizational politics and the IS/IT literature, change is commonly understood as both *negotiation* and *coalition building* processes which are dynamically intertwined (Koch 2001). It has been argued that, "when enrolling actors in a coalition, it is likely that the content of change program changes; change programs emerge from the intentions of the actors in the setting" (Koch 2001, p. 259).

Contextualism as a theoretical approach for understanding organizational politics and change historically developed from two main research streams. The first is the Warwick University research group (see Pettigrew 1987, 1990). The second is Aston University group (see Child and Smith 1987). Pettigrew (1987) believes that one major weakness in strategic change literature has been its narrow emphasis on issues such as the role of leadership as well as its "snapshot" nature. Consequently, he proposes that the contextualism perspective provide "holistic and dynamic analysis of changing" (Pettigrew 1987, p. 655). As applied to strategic change, contextualism is a multilevel theory that seeks to analyze and understand the *context*, *content*, and *process* of change as well as the interconnection between the three (Pettigrew 1987). According to Pettigrew, context comprises both the broader socioeconomic and the inner cultural, political, and structural contexts. Content, on the other hand, refers to the type or area of intended change (e.g., changes to the technology, business processes, structures, human resource, etc.). The process of change "refers to the actions, reactions, and interactions from the various interested parties as they seek to move the firm from its present to its future state" (Pettigrew 1987, p. 658).

We believe that research on strategy implementation could also benefit from concepts drawn from ANT to enhance our understanding of the dynamic and emergent nature of strategy implementation. Recent research in strategy by Steen et al. (2006) further support such arguments by contending that "strategy-as-action puts the human strategic actor center stage, actor-network theory propagates a further flexibility in the nature and characteristics of the actors involved" (p. 308). ANT is a social theory dedicated to understanding how change and order are negotiated (Scott and Wagner 2003). It focuses on understanding "socio-technical systems as negotiated order constructed, tested, and reproduced through action" (Kim and Kaplan 2006, p. 37). Conceptualizing the process of IS strategy implementation as a process of building a network of heterogeneous associations through the acts of enrolling various human and nonhuman actors, aligning and translating the divergent interests (Callon 1987; Steen et al. 2006) would enable us to highlight on the role of the hybrid or quasi-object strategic agency in the transformation process (Vidgen and McMaster 1996; Walsham 1997).

Over time, the strategic visions inscribed in computer-based information systems strategy would change as new actors join the network of aligned interests. Further, the formation and implementation of IS strategy involves an extensive persuasion for others to buy-in (Lee and Myers 2004).

Thus when combining ANT with contextualism, researchers are able to demonstrate the dynamic and emergent nature of IS strategy implementation as an ongoing process for the creation of heterogeneous associations that is believed to answer the question of how IS strategy emerges in practice and how it becomes stabilized (Steen et al. 2006).

The theoretical framework discussed in this section will be used to empirically study the process of implementing IS strategy in one of the UK HEIs (GM University). However, it is important to point out that what is reported here represents early outcomes of an ongoing implementation process; therefore, it may not be taken as conclusive.

4   THE CASE STUDY AND RESEARCH METHODOLOGY

This section provides a description of the case study and historical perspective of the implementation of an IS strategy in the case institution. In addition, it also describes the research design approach and methods used for collecting research data.

4.1 Research Design and Data Collection

The research design of this study is based on an interpretive ethnographic intervention (Corbitt 2000; Walsham 1993), in the Information Service and Technology Division (ISTD) at GM University. The case was mainly determined by the unique opportunity offered to the researcher to study the process of IS strategy implementation "in its context from initiation to implementation" (Nandhakumar et al. 2005, p. 226). Myers (1999) observes that the main difference between ethnographic research and case study research is the extent of the researcher's immersion in the context and the availability of participant observation field notes.

Ethnographic research is criticized for its lack of breadth and the difficulty of making generalizations from a single organization (Myers 1999). However, as Walsham and Wema (1994) point out, the problem of generalizing from a single case organization is related to interpretive epistemology, where the emphasis is not on statistical validity but rather on the plausibility of the findings. Lee and Baskerville (2003) proposed a framework for IS researchers to generalize their findings while enhancing the relevance of their research.

Our data sources include "in-action" field notes from participant observation, in-depth semi-structured interviews with project teams, informal social discussions with participants, and documentation such as minutes of meetings, project reports, training materials, and presentations. Access was granted on the basis of presenting a consultancy report from the findings of the intervention to the ISTD senior management.

The interviewees include project managers, the customer support center (CSC) manager, the first-line coordinator, the change management controller, business analysts, service delivery managers, and application developers. Interviews were designed to encourage interviewees to give their interpretations by directly narrating their stories about the ongoing processes in the IS strategy implementation. Therefore, interviews vary between participants based on their role in the implementation process. All interviews were tape-recorded and transcribed immediately after the interview. Interviews lasted between 60 and 90 minutes.

4.2 Case Study Background

GM is one of the largest universities in the United Kingdom, located in the northwest part of the country, with approximately 2,000 academic and support staff within the faculties and support services, as well as over 18,000 full-time students.

The Information Service and Technology Division (ISTD) of GM University provides library services, IT desktop services, PC hardware support, e-mail facilities, campus telephony network, and application development sustaining all University ICT and telecommunication services. The catalyst to change lay with the impression of ISTD senior management that these multiple services were proving inconsistent and did not provide the level of responsiveness that were increasingly demanded by customers. The main reason, according to the ISTD management, is because the services were based on a help-desk call management system (called SM) which was seen as increasingly outdated and unsupportable. The staffing model used in the enquiry desk was based on a part-time and rota basis, which was considered inefficient and lacking in continuity.

In October 2004, an external consultant (Mr. Davidson[1]) was appointed to review the overall enquiry service in order to deliver a holistic solution that would address the shortcomings of the current system and radically improve the quality of response provided to the customers and users. After a series of presentations and workshops, the consultant was able to convince ISTD senior management that if they were really looking for radical improvement in customer services, they should look beyond a simple replacement of the call management software. The result was the creation of a strategic change program called the *customer resolution information services project* (CRISP), which is strategically positioned as the implementation of a customer-focused strategy in the delivery of all services offered by ISTD. Therefore, apart from the replacement of the call management system, the scope of the strategic change program included service processes redesign and the adoption of best practices in service delivery and support such as British Standards (BS15000) and IT infrastructure library (ITIL). At the

---

[1]All names in this paper are pseudonyms in compliance with confidentiality and ethical agreements.

end of Mr. Davidson's contract in April 2006, a new staged-implementation plan was worked out with the newly appointed internal replacement project manager. This included the decision to implement new Internet protocol call center (IPCC) software for improved scripting and call monitoring and the relocation of first- and second-line support staff. In July 2006, Key Milestone 1 (KM1) became the official temporal vision of the strategy implementation process.

In the following section, we will analyze the data collected using our theoretical framework to show how networks of heterogeneous associations were formed, stabilized, and destabilized during the process of IS strategy implementation. We will also demonstrate how strategy emerges through the dynamic interrelationship with the content and context of the strategy.

5 ANALYSIS

In this section, we will apply our theoretical framework to analyze the case study outlined above. We focus primarily on the strategic vision of the CRISP under two periods: during external consultant Davidson's time and the post-consultant time when a new internal project manager took over. The emphasis is to show how the vision is transformed through processes of enrolment and translation used to form coalitions that align actor's interests as well as highlighting the interconnection between such process and the strategy content and context.

5.1 Actor Network Theory as a Process Theory

There is a general agreement among both strategic management and information systems scholars that process studies provide better understanding of how and why things evolve over time (Langley 1999). IS strategy implementation, for example, has been described as a process in which actors participated in a process of "persuasion, bargaining, and sometimes direct confrontation" for building coalitions that were constantly shifting (Lee and Myers 2004, p. 360).

Contextualism theory requires researchers to adopt a particular behavioral perspective or theory for analyzing the unfolding processes in their context (Karyda et al. 2005). In this paper, we argue that ANT is a qualified theory to illuminate the strategy implementation processes since recognizing that actions drive the processes requires not only the human agency but the collective agency of both human and nonhuman actors (Karyda et al. 2005).

Employing concepts such as *enrolment, translation, network stabilization*, and *black boxing*, ANT provides better ways of viewing strategy implementation or, alternatively, examining why such networks fail to establish themselves" (Walsham 1997, p. 469).

5.2 Process of Network Formation

The unfolding patterns of events in our case demonstrate how networks of aligned interest were formed around the strategic vision/strategy of both the consultant and the new project manager. The consultant used his knowledge and expertise in business process reengineering consultancy to develop a strategic vision for improving customer services and the internal project manager used contextual knowledge to forge a more conservative path to change.

Through a series of translations, the consultant specifies the divergent interests (Steen et al. 2006) to enrol a number of actants, such as the senior management team, the software vendor, service support application (SSA) and business support systems (BSS) packaged systems, ITIL standards, users group, ITIL training organizations, etc. For example, the senior management team expressed interest in efficient and effective customer support as well as their need for information on key performance indicators to move to activity-based costing, which is expected to enhance control over resource allocation. Such translation also enrols other allies, such as software vendors, process reengineering and project management software, ITIL training providers, etc. User groups and team leaders were enrolled as change champions through training activities that presented generic benefits from the suppliers' rhetoric.

Being described as "excellent in talking and selling his ideas," the consultant was able to form a coalition enrolling different actants into a stable network that sustained his strategic vision for almost two years. However, research indicates that, over time actors, their interests, and the strategic vision that drove the strategy implementation process would change (Lee and Myers 2004). Voices from all over ISTD were raised, showing concerns that, "*its two years since CRISP started and nothing tangible has been delivered yet*" (project team member). Another voice argued that, "*after six months I realized that he [the consultant] cannot deliver anything because as a project manager he fails to produce a project plan*" (associate director 1). The result was a decision to replace the consultant with a new project manager. Consequently, the network formed around his strategic vision was destabilized. The new project manager started creating his own network to assist in implementing KM1, which is expected to deliver something tangible.

5.3   Content of Strategic Change

ANT understands the strategy content as an outcome of negotiated interests between different actors (Lee and Myers 2004) rather than "as an outcome of a rational decision making process" (Markoczy 2001, p. 1015). As new actors enrol in the network, the contents of the strategy black box need to be renegotiated to translate the interests of new allies.

The new project manager believed that it was not possible for the ISTD to implement Mr. Davidson's radical transformation vision and instead he worked out his new strategic vision based on "quick fixes for quick wins"— in the short-run, there is a feeling that they must be seen to deliver and make incremental changes through learning and continuous improvements. The scale of change in KM1 as proposed by the new project manager includes IPCC implementation and limited aspects of a new application called business support systems (BSS): process and structural changes and the remaining modules of BSS, were to be considered in later phases of the implementation process.

Conceptualizing the implementation process as a network and coalition formation has illuminated the dynamic of interplay between the process of implementation and the content of strategy.

5.4 Context of Strategic Change

The study of strategic context has been an essential element in strategy and change research. Sahay and Robey (1996) describe context as "the social structure that both constrains and facilitates human agency directed toward the implementation and use of information systems" (p. 256), but with the capability to shape both the context and process of implementation. Actors in processes of stabilizing and destabilizing their networks of alliances draw on the context whether internal (cultural, structural) or external (competitive, technological) to inform their actions and interactions and by these very actions they created and maintained their networks. Therefore, "context shapes the outcome of the processes" (Karyda et al. 2005, p. 251).

In our case, as a result of the implementation, the senior management team saw an opportunity in the external technological development to enrol more allies into the implementation process to embrace the need for change.

We also get external change coming upon us, not least technology. Technology continues to change at a vast rate and it is difficult at times to integrate this properly into what we do, and I think we have to acknowledge that (Director 1).

Focusing on limited software implementation is a comfort zone for the current project manager compared to the sea-change in organizational culture demanded during Mr. Davidson's regime.

5.5 An Integrated Perspective

In the above analysis, we demonstrate that ANT as a process theory has the power to provide rich insights into the dynamics of strategy in action. However, the contextualism perspective on strategic change implementation requires taking into consideration the influence of strategy context on the implementation processes, and linking these processes to strategy content (Karyda et al. 2005; Pettigrew 1987).

Combining ANT with a contextualism perspective in investigating strategy implementation brings more emphasis on the interrelatedness between the process (network formation) and both the strategy content and context. Further contextualism may provide a window of opportunity to bring context into ANT analysis.

6   DISCUSSION

While the external consultant and the internal project manager both had a strategic vision for ISTD as a hub for customer services, their experiences with the project differ significantly. The theoretical framework combining ANT and contextualism allows better understanding of these differences. The analysis provided above suggests that these differences can be attributed to variations in communication strategy. The external consultant advocated a vision of radical transformation grounded in his expertise in business process reengineering consultancy. In the implementation process, he tried to communicate that message and sell his vision as the only possibility for customer service delivery, not subject to other interpretations. The consultant's inability to deliver weakened his voice since it meant failure to enrol other speakers. Project deliverables are very good speakers and representatives for themselves and the project sponsors, consequently the process of networking remains at the controversy stage. The consultant also attempted to lead the project team into believing that he had a very intimate relationship with the director and used that as a way of enforcing and communicating his vision, as evident from a statement by a member of the project team:

> *Knowing that you were working really hard on the project and hear some consultant...telling you that he had some intimate relationship with the director, that he said no one in the ISTD is good enough to do this job, you really got to believe in that and that didn't help.*

Relating the consultant implementation process to the content aspect of the strategy, we recognize that his emphasis on communicating his vision of implementing the whole change package at once explains why the strategy contents remained a black box. He refused to negotiate with others for an agreed set of deliverables over time and this would also explain why he failed to provide a project plan. As we indicated in the theoretical framework, having success in both the process and content of strategy implementation requires intelligent understanding of the implementation context. Looking at the way the consultant communicated his vision in the process of implementation and how he presented the content of his strategy, we see that he lacked an understanding of the context in which ISTD operates. Mr. Davidson, for example, demanded full resourcing, insisting on promises from the director that the project be the number one priority. He failed to appreciate the limited ISTD budget, the lack of overall strategic planning within ISTD, and the role of ISTD within the overall University strategic planning. Mr. Davidson seemingly shared his radical vision with some senior managers.

> *CRISP is not just about the implementation of a software solution; it is a radical transformation of how we handle customer services and the service desk* (Associate director 1).

However, in the context of the institution as a whole, change demanded that ISTD have some deliverables in place prior to the commencement of the new academic year, and his lack of contextual awareness resulted in improper connectedness and a flawed relationship between the implementation processes, the strategy content, and the contextual understanding.

The new project manager on the other hand, equipped with a thorough understanding of the implementation context, realized that, with the limited resource availability, the internal organizational cultural, and the political environment, it was not practical to implement the whole strategic content in one big-bang deliverable and took a more conservative route to change. Consequently, the content black box was opened for negotiation and the communication strategy focused on network building based on the fact that results speak louder than promises. The content is to be implemented using a phased approach with clear set of deliverables at each stage, then built on incrementally through a process of continuous improvement.

CRISP is the foundation for continuous improvement process and there is always a chance of making things better. Change is an ongoing process; we need to adapt continuously (New project manager).

Each deliverable indicates the enrolment of a new actant to the network, which can speak loudly of itself and the network it represents. Therefore, as the project continues delivering results, different actors, both humans and nonhumans, will engage in communicating the message. In this case, we moved from the situation in which the consultant as project leader is in the role of change agent to the position where we have "collectif" or hybrid change agency comprising of the project team (human) and deliverables (nonhuman). The experiences of the new project manager show us how actors draw on the context in the process of stabilizing their networks and context plays a major role in shaping the outcome (content) of that process (Karyda et al. 2005).

On a practical level, our discussion raised the question of how organizations make the best use of external consultants involved in change programs, requiring a decision on which responsibilities be given to consultants and which would be better kept in house.

7 CONCLUSION

Strategy implementation is a longitudinal and dynamic process that requires building and maintaining networks of allies over along period of time. However, keeping such allies over time often proves to be problematic because of the need to align with both the context and the content of the strategy. Applying a conceptual framework that combines ANT and contextualism theory provides us with better understanding and insight into the process of implementing strategy contents within a context.

Acknowledgments

The authors would like to thank Dr. Elaine Ferneley of Salford Business School for her helpful comments on an earlier draft of this paper. Thanks are also due to anonymous reviewers for their suggestions.

References

Allen, D., Kern, T., and Mattison, D. "Culture, Power and Politics in ICT Outsourcing in Higher Education Institutions," *European Journal of Information Systems* (11:2), 2002, pp. 159-173.
Burnes, B. "Kurt Lewin and the Planned Approach to Change: A Re-appraisal," *Journal of Management Studies* (41:6), 2004, pp. 977-1002.
Callon, M. "Society in the Making: The Study of Technology as a Tool for Sociological Analysis," in W. E. Bijker, T. P. Hughes, and T. J. Pinch (eds.), *The Social Construction of Technological Systems: New Directions in the Sociology and History of Technology*, London: The MIT Press, 1987, pp. 83-103.
Cavaye, A. L. M., and Cragg, P. B. "Strategic Information Systems Research: A Review and Research Framework," *Journal of Strategic Information Systems* (2:2), 1993, pp. 125-137.
Child, J., and Smith, C. "The Context and Process of Organizational Transformation-Cadbury Limited in its Sector," *Journal of Management Studies* (24:6), 1987, pp. 565-593.

Clarke, S. *Information Systems Strategic Management: An Integrated Approach*, London: Routledge, 2001.

Corbitt, B. J. "Developing Intraorganizational Electronic Commerce Strategy: An Ethnographic Study," *Journal of Information Technology* (15), 2000, pp. 119-130.

Dawson, P., Clausen, C., and Nielsen, K. T. "Political Processes in Management, Organization and the Social Shaping of Technology," *Technology Analysis & Strategic Management* (12:1), 2000, pp. 5-15.

Dufour, Y., and Steane, P. "Competitive Paradigms on Strategic Change: Mapping the Field and Further Research Development," *Strategic Change* (15), 2006, pp. 129-144.

Galliers, R. D., and Leidner, D. E. "Information Systems Strategy," R. D. Galliers and D. E. Leidner (eds.), *Strategic Information Management: Challenges and Strategies in Managing Information Systems* (3rd ed.), Oxford, England: Butterworth Heinemann, 2003, pp. 27-32.

Gemmell, M., and Panago, R. "A Post-Implementation Evaluation of a Student Information System in the UK Higher Education Sector," *Electronic Journal of Information Systems Evaluation* (6:2), 2003, pp. 95-106.

Kanungo, S., Sadavarti, S., and Srinivas, Y. "Relating IT Strategy and Organizational Culture: An Empirical Study of Public Sector Units in India," *Journal of Strategic Information System* (10), 2001, pp. pp. 29-57.

Karyda, M., Kiountouzis, E., and Kokolakis, S. "Information Systems Security Policies: A Contextual Perspective," *Computers and Security* (24), 2005, pp. 246-260.

Kim, R. M., and Kaplan, S. M. (2006), "Interpreting Socio-technical Co-evolution: Applying Complex Adaptive Systems to IS Engagement," *Information Technology & People* (19:1), 2006, pp. 35-54.

Koch, C. "BPR and ERP: Realizing a Vision of Process with IT," *Business Process Management Journal* (7:3), 2001, pp. 258-265.

Langley, A. "Strategies for Theorizing from Process Data," *Academy of Management Review* (24:4), 1999, pp. 691-710.

Latour, B. *Science in Action: How to Follow Scientists and Engineers through Society*, Cambridge, MA: Harvard University Press, 1987.

Lee, A. S., and Baskerville, R. L. "Generalizing Generalizability in Information Systems Research," *Information Systems Research* (14:3), 2003, pp. 221-243.

Lee, J. C., and Myers, M. D. "Dominant Actors, Political Agendas, and Strategic Shifts Over Time: A Critical Ethnography of an Enterprise Systems Implementation," *Journal of Strategic Information Systems* (13:4), 2004, pp. 355-374.

Leider, D. E., and Kayworth, T. "*Review:* A Review of Culture in Information Systems Research: Toward a Theory of Information Technology Culture Conflict," *MIS Quarterly* (30:2), June 2006, pp. 357-399.

Markoczy, L. "Consensus Formation During Strategic Change," *Strategic Management Journal* (22), 2001, pp. 1013-1031.

McLoughlin, I., and Badham, R. "Political Process Perspective on Organizational and Technological Change," *Human Relations* (58:7), 2005, pp. 827-843.

McLoughlin, I., Badham, R., and Couchman, P. "Rethinking Political Process in Technological Change: Socio-Technical Configuration and Frames," *Technology Analysis & Strategic Management* (12:1), 2000, pp. 17-37.

Myers, M. D. "Investigating Information Systems with Ethnographic Research," *Communications of AIS* (2:23), 1999.

Nandhakumar, J., Rossi, M., and Talvinen, J. "The Dynamics of Contextual Forces of ERP Implementation," *Journal of Strategic Information Systems* (14:2), 2005, pp. 221-242.

Pettigrew, A. M. "Context and Action in the Transformation of the Firm," *Journal of Management Studies* (24:6), 1987, pp. 649-670.

Pettigrew, A. M. "Longitudinal Field Research on Change: Theory and Practice," *Organization Science* (1:3), 1990, pp. 267-292.

Pollock, N. "The Virtual University as 'Timely and Accurate Information,'" *Information, Communication & Society* (3:3), 2000, pp. 349-365.

Richards, L., O'Shea, J., and Connolly, M. "Managing the Concept of Strategic Change Within a Higher Education Institution: The Role of Strategic and Scenario Planning Techniques," *Strategic Change* (13), 2004, pp. 345-359.

Sahay, S., and Robey, D. "Organizational Context, Social Interpretation, and the Implementation and Consequences of Geographic Information Systems," *Accounting, Management & Information Technology* (6:4), 1996, pp. 255-282.

Scott, S. V., and Wagner, E. L. "Networks, Negotiations, and New Times: The Implementation of Enterprise Resource Planning into an Academic Administration," *Information and Organization* (13), 2003, pp. 285-313.

Steen, J., Coopmans, C., and Whyte, J. "Structure and Agency? Actor Network Theory and Strategic Organization," *Strategic Organization* (4:3), 2006, pp. 303-312.

Vidgen, R., and McMaster, T. "Black Boxes, Non-Human Stakeholders and the Translation of IT through Mediation," in W. J. Orlikowski, G. Walsham, M. R. Jones, and J. I. DeGross (eds.), *Information technology and Changes in Organisational Work*, London: Chapman & Hall, 1996, pp. 250-271.

Walsham, G. "Actor-Network Theory and IS Research: Current Status and Future Prospects," A. S. (Lee, J. Liebenau, and J. I. DeGross (eds.), *Information Systems and Qualitative Research*, London: Chapman & Hall, 1997, pp. 466-480.

Walsham, G. *Interpreting Information Systems in Organisations*, Chichester, England: John Wiley & Sons, 1993.

Walsham, G., and Waema, T. "Information Systems Strategy and Implementation: A Case Study of a Building Society," *ACM Transactions on Information Systems* (2:2), 1994, pp. 150-173.

About the Authors

Tayfour A. Mohammed is currently a doctoral candidate and a graduate teaching assistant at the Informatics Research Institute, Salford Business School, Salford University. His research interests focus on call centers, CRM systems, and organizational aspects of IS implementation. He can be reached by e-mail at t.a.mohammed@pgt.salford.ac.uk.

Helen J. Richardson is a senior lecturer in Information Systems at Salford Business School. She can be reached by e-mail at h.richardson@salford.ac.uk.

20   THE DYNAMICS OF AN IOIS IN THE SEAPORT OF BARCELONA: An ANT Perspective

Juan Rodon
ESADE, Universitat Ramon Llull
Barcelona, Spain

Joan Antoni Pastor
Universitat Politècnica de Catalunya
Barcelona, Spain

Feliciano Sesé
ESADE, Universitat Ramon Llull
Barcelona, Spain

Abstract   *On the basis of a longitudinal interpretive case study, this paper explores the dynamics in the implementation of an industry interorganizational information system (IOIS). The paper covers 11 years (1994–2005) of the implementation process. We use the lens of actor network theory (ANT) to analyze the process of emergence, development, and progressive stabilization of a socio-technical network, that of the IOIS. We focus on the negotiations and translation of interests that occur during the implementation of the IOIS. By using ANT we develop a different reading of the implementation process, which we believe provides a holistic view of the implementation, and can be adapted and applied to similar implementation projects. ANT is suitable as it helps us trace the course of the implementation, and because of the nature of the IOIS and of the implementation process, which involves political negotiations.*

Keywords   Interorganizational information system, standard, implementation, actor network, case study

Please use the following format when citing this chapter:

Rodon, J., Pastor, J. A., and Sesé, F., 2007, in IFIP International Federation for Information Processing, Volume 235, Organizational Dynamics of Technology-Based Innovation: Diversifying the Research Agenda, eds. McMaster, T., Wastell, D., Ferneley, E., and DeGross, J. (Boston: Springer), pp. 297-314.

1   INTRODUCTION

The research presented in this paper is based on a longitudinal case study about the implementation of an industry interorganizational information system (IOIS) for the exchange of documents in the landside transport network of the seaport of Barcelona. Borrowing the concept of information infrastructure from Hanseth and Lyytinen (2006), this paper defines an industry IOIS as a shared, evolving, and heterogeneous installed base of IT capabilities built on standardized interfaces. An IOIS is shared in the sense that it is set up, organized, and used by firms in the same industry. It evolves as new companies integrate with it or as new types of exchanges become possible through the IOIS. An IOIS is not designed from scratch; the existing installed base has an inertia that influences the way the IOIS is designed. It is heterogeneous as it encompasses multiple technologies as well as non-technological elements (social, organizational, institutional, etc.) that are necessary to sustain and operate the IOIS. Finally, an IOIS usually embeds and supports data and process standards that are defined by the same industry actors (Markus et al. 2006).

Drawing upon actor network theory (ANT), we inquire into the interplay among diverse actors (public bodies, private organizations, artefacts, procedures, standards, etc.) during the emergence, development, and stabilization of the IOIS. ANT allows us to describe in detail how the large heterogeneous actor network that represents an IOIS is built. We contribute to the literature on IOIS: first, we examine both IOIS development and diffusion; second, we focus on an industry phenomenon, thus our outcome of explanation is at the industry level of analysis; and finally, we extend prior literature on IOIS at seaports by using the lens of ANT to analyze the process that leads to the progressive stabilization of an IOIS.

We first give an overview of the role of IOIS in seaports and the use of ANT in IOIS literature. This is followed by an introduction to the research approach. Next we present the analysis and interpretation of the case study. Finally, we discuss the results of the case and present concluding remarks.

2   LITERATURE REVIEW

2.1   Seaports and IOISs

A seaport is an interface between a sea transportation system on one side, and a land transport network on the other side. Whereas the shipping industry has developed standard procedures for the seashore interface, the development of land transport has been shaped by the local regulatory and organizational framework.

In the landside transport network, companies operate in different roles including port authority, shipping agents, terminal operators, stevedores, harbor master, freight forwarders, customs, rail/truck carriers, pilots, haulers, and clearing agents. There are two forms of interactions in the transport network: (1) operational interactions related with the physical transfer of cargo and (2) administrative interactions related with the supervisory and information based exchanges. Each member in the transport network operates as a supplier as well as a customer, and generates some kind of information that is to be transferred along the network (van Baalen et al. 2000). Traditionally, administrative interactions have been highly paper-intensive. Therefore, from a technical-economic perspective the standardization, rationalization, and automation of these interfirm data exchanges with IOISs may enhance the efficiency of the entire transport network (McMaster and Wastell 2005).

Prior research on IOIS in seaports has examined a diversity of topics: the transformation of the organizational efficiency and effectiveness that results from the development of the IOIS (Teo et al. 1997), the political and economical models of port communities (Wrigley et al. 1994), the implementation process and decision to adopt the IOIS (van Baalen et al. 2000), and the role of trade associations in the diffusion of the IOIS (Damsgaard and Lyytinen 2001). These studies have been informed by transaction costs theory, diffusion of innovations theory, and institutional theory, but they have scarcely focused on the socio-technical nature and longevity of the IOIS implementation, which is an aim of this paper. In order to fill this gap, we use ANT.

2.2 Implementation of IOISs through the Lens of ANT

Through the lens of ANT, the implementation dynamics of an IOIS may be regarded as the emergence, development and stabilization of an actor network. ANT assumes that the boundaries between the social and the technical can always be contested. Thus an IOIS may be viewed as a stabilized set of relations between humans and nonhuman artefacts (e.g., computers) and rules (e.g., laws, policies). ANT pays attention to the interplay between diverse human and nonhuman actors: how the diverse actors' interests are translated and inscribed into technical artefacts, and how actors form alliances in order to mobilize support (Walsham 1997). To create a stable system, the actors must be aligned. If such alignment does not occur, the system will not survive.

ANT is suitable to study the implementation of IOIS for the following reasons. First, ANT helps explore how actor networks are formed, hold together, or fall apart. Thus, it supports our emphasis on the process aspect of implementation. Secondly, since the nature of IOIS implementation is a political-negotiating process, ANT provides an analytical framework for studying power processes within a socio-technical context. Finally, given the evolving nature of IOIS, ANT is appropriate because it distances itself from the view that technologies are stable entities that are passed from community to community and then put into use (McMaster et al. 1997). Next we present the concepts from ANT that will be used in this paper.

2.2.1 Translation

ANT treats humans and artefacts as a single heterogeneous unit of analysis—an actor network—and translation refers to the way in which this network is formed. Translation means reconciling the different meanings that actors hold of a given phenomenon. During translation, actors negotiate or maneuver others' interests toward their own with the aim of enrolling actors into the network. Thus, the translation process has political implications: "The result [of translation] is a situation where certain entities control others. Understanding power relationships means describing the way in which actors are defined, associated and simultaneously obliged to remain faithful to their alliances"

(Callon 1986, pp. 224). For instance, within the context of IS development, during the process of translation actors interact with each other to work out a scenario of how the system will work and will be used. "To translate is to displace...[and] to express in one's own language what others say and want, why they act in the way they do and how they associate with each other: it is to establish oneself as a spokesman" (Callon 1986, p. 223). The process of translation goes through four moments: problematization (problem formulation), interessement, enrolment, and mobilization (Callon 1986).

- During problem formulation, an actor frames a problem or an opportunity and attempts to persuade other actors in the network that the problem/opportunity is worthy of having resources dedicated to it. It is crucial to find a solution that is of common interest for the participating actors, despite their diverse interests. Problematization culminates with the definition of a point—namely, an obligatory passage point—through which any actor with a stake in the network has to pass in order to attain its objectives.
- Interessement means that other actors become interested in the solution proposed. They change their affiliation to a certain group in favor of the new actor. "For all the groups involved, the interessement helps corner the activities to be enrolled. In addition, it attempts to interrupt all potential competing associations and to construct a system of alliances" (Callon 1986, p. 211). If interessement is successful, it confirms the validity of problematization.
- Enrolment concerns "the group of multilateral negotiations, trials of strength and tricks that accompany the interessements and enable them to succeed" (Callon 1986, p. 211). Latour (1987) suggests five strategies for enrolment: (1) cater to others' interests; (2) convince others that their usual ways are cut off; (3) to seduce them through a detour; (4) reshuffle interests and goals (displacing goals, inventing new groups or new goals, rendering the detour invisible, winning trials of attribution); and (5) become indispensable to others.
- Mobilization is about stabilizing the actor network by making durable and irreversible relations. The network results in a single actor, which can be treated as a black-box (Latour 1987, pp. 131).

2.2.2 Inscription

Inscription is the process whereby translations of one's interests are embodied into technical artefacts. That is, a translation presupposes a material into which it is inscribed: text, software, skill, etc. The inscription includes programs of action for the users, and it defines roles to be played by users and the system. When a program of action is inscribed into a piece of technology, the technology becomes an actor imposing its inscribed program of action on its users. Inscriptions vary in terms of (1) what is inscribed: which anticipations of use are envisioned; (2) how are these anticipations inscribed: what is the material for the inscriptions; (3) who inscribes them; and (4) the strength of the inscriptions: how much effort does it take to oppose an inscription (Monteiro 2000, pp. 79). "The strength of inscriptions, whether they must be followed or whether they can be avoided, depends on the irreversibility of the actor network into which they are inscribed" (Monteiro 2000, pp. 78).

Table 1. Set of Concepts of Actor Network Theory

Concept	Definition
Problematization	Process of alignment of the interests of a set of actors with those of a focal actor.
Interessement	Second moment of translation in which other actors become interested in the solution proposed. They change their affiliation to a certain group in favor of the new actor (Callon 1986).
Enrolment	Third moment of translation that concerns "the group of multilateral negotiations, trials of strength and tricks that accompany the interesse-ments and enable them to succeed" (Callon 1986, p. 211).
Mobilization	Last moment of translation that consists of stabilizing the actor network by making durable and irreversible relations.
Spokesperson	An actor that speaks on behalf of other actors.
Obligatory Passage Point	Moment that is fixed during problematization through which any actor with a stake in the network would have to pass in order to attain its objectives.
Inscription	Process whereby translations of one's interests are embodied into technical artefacts; that is, the way physical artefacts embody patterns of use.
Black-boxing	Process whereby an "assembly of disorderly and unreliable allies is... slowly turned into something that closely resembles and organized whole. When such a cohesion is obtained we at last have a black box" (Callon 1986, p. 131).
Irreversibility	Concept that captures the accumulated resistance of an actor network against change; irreversibility also reflects the strength of inscriptions.

Working on the basis of the concepts presented in Table 1, we explore the implementation of an IOIS in the context of a seaport by tracing how the creation and stabilization of the actor network unfolded.

3   RESEARCH METHODOLOGY

An exploration of the dynamics of IOIS implementation requires us to take a process approach, which typically involves longitudinal analysis. Since our emphasis is on understanding reality in a specific context, we opt to use an interpretive case study (Walsham 1995). This research approach is "aimed at an understanding of the context of the information system and the process over time of mutual influence between the system and its context" (Walsham 1993, pp. 14).

The empirical work was conducted by the first author over three different periods (see Table 2 for a description of periods, topics of inquiry, and informants). We collected data through semi-structured interviews (about 1 hour each), informal conversations, press documents, field site visits, meeting attendance, and meeting minutes. Within each period, data collection and analysis occurred recursively, thus guiding subsequent interviews.

Table 2. Data Collection Periods, Topics Being Inquired and Informants

Period	Interviews, Topics of Inquiry, and Periods	Informants
First (October–November 2001)	Number of interviews: 6 Topics: History of the standardization process and the decision to implement the IOIS, and the actors involved Period inquired: 1992–2001	PAB: CIO and IS workers IGC and TelFor: participants IOS CEO and CIO Two adopters of the IOIS: CEOs and CIOs
Second (January–March 2004)	Number of interviews: 10 Topics: Standard development; standardization organization, outcomes, and actors Period inquired: 1998–2004	TelFor: Six participants PAB: CIO and two IS workers Customs: Two managers
Third (March–November 2005)	Number of interviews: 27 Topics: Standard evolution and outcomes; IOIS implementation (design decisions and actions and adopters' actions); problems arising during the integration of preexisting systems with the IOIS Period inquired: 2000–2005	IOIS: CEO, marketing manager, IS consultants, and designers Nine port agents: CEOs, COOs, CIOs, developers, and users

The involved researcher role was adopted (Walsham 1995). Besides attending meetings and presentations, we provided participants with feedback in the form of presentations and reports after each of the three data gathering periods. We considered this feedback useful because: (1) it gave us an in-depth understanding of the phenomenon; (2) it was a way to contrast and validate our interpretation; and (3) it facilitated our subsequent access to the field.

We use ANT as a lens to retrospectively interpret, structure, and present the empirical data through a narrative that reveals how events occur over time. We focus on the implementation of the IOIS throughout its emergence, development, and stabilization. We split the case analysis into five chronological stages, which are chosen in accordance with the researchers' interpretation of the data gathered. We use italics to highlight the ANT terminology in the case.

4   CASE STUDY ANALYSIS

4.1   Stage 1: Emergence of the Standard (1994–1997)

During the early 1990s, within the framework of the elaboration of a quality plan in the port of Barcelona, some of the port agents[1] complained about the response time of

---

[1]The port agents are shipping agents, inland terminals, freight forwarders, depots, haulers, and clearing agents.

customs clearance and handling of goods at the port. These port agents had always considered that the inefficiencies in the document exchanges were Customs' fault. Customs, for its part, wanted to modernize its services. At that time, the most common mechanisms for document exchange were fax and courier services.

Framing this as a problem with the mechanisms of formal documentary exchange between port agents and public bodies, the Port Authority of Barcelona (PAB) created the Information Guarantee Commission (IGC) at the beginning of 1994 to standardize the document exchange procedures and to define EDIFACT messages for the documents that port agents had to submit to the PAB and Customs (private-to-public exchanges). The PAB thus successfully *translated* Customs' and the port agents' interests. By *enrolling* with the IGC, Customs would modernize its services and improve the response time of customs clearance. Their respective *interests would be realized* by going through the IGC's work in extending electronic data exchange to all the documentary formalities between the port agents and public bodies at the port.

Likewise, the PAB *rendered itself indispensable* for port agents by acting as a one-stop shop with Customs. Port agents (shipping agents) could send electronic messages (e.g., cargo manifests) to the PAB who would forward them to Customs. However, once the procedures and messages defined by the IGC were in place, they were not adopted. Because most of the port agents were small firms and did not have the IT capabilities, the new procedures and messages could not overcome the inertia of the already installed base of fax and courier services as document exchange mechanisms at the port.

4.2 Stage 2: Emergence of the IOIS (1998–1999)

The PAB, in order to overcome the lack of IT capabilities of port agents, then proposed the development of a common IOIS for the entire community in 1997. For the PAB, this IOIS was the *device that would interrupt* the port agents from existing fax and courier services, hence enhancing the adoption of private-to-public exchanges. On the other hand, port agents became *interested* as the IOIS would help them overcome their lack of IT capabilities. A new actor network had *emerged*, one that concerned the creation of the IOIS. The PAB performed a set of actions to keep port agents *interested* in the IOIS.

- In 1998, the PAB governing council dissolved the IGC to form the Telematic Forum (TelFor). TelFor was a standardization committee that would extend the work of the IGC to those processes between port agents—namely, private-to-private exchanges. TelFor's standard dealt with the syntax and semantics of the EDIFACT messages exchanged. TelFor's participants—port agents that were supposed to *speak on behalf* of their trade associations[2]—used a consensus-based approach. By enrolling in TelFor, the port agents had the opportunity to standardize their daily exchanges, which represented savings in their operations.
- The PAB developed a master plan that proposed building an IOIS, namely PortIC (Port Information and Communication System), which would coordinate the activity of firms in the landside transport network of the port and integrate all of the infor-

---

[2]Associations of shipping agents, clearing agents, port stevedores, and freight forwarders.

mation exchanged among port agents and public bodies. PortIC would implement the standard defined by TelFor, thus offering three types of services: (1) private-to-public exchanges; (2) private-to-private exchanges; and (3) real-time information services that allowed the documentary tracking of goods. The PAB presented PortIC as an opportunity to enhance the efficiency and competitiveness of the port community. As a shipping agent retrospectively observed: "It seemed [that PortIC] would bring a clear productivity increase in our operative model." The PAB invoked the vision of a "paperless port," and PortIC was supposed to *inscribe* this vision.

- The PAB showed port agents the threat of a new entrant if they were not competitive. That is, the PAB *displaced* the port agents' goals. The PAB's CEO stated to the press:

> The control of the information that the transport chain generates is vital to be in the market and we must maintain this advantage. If we lose the control of this information because a third party, whether a shipping company or a financial institution, manages it, our business will be finished.

- For the development of PortIC, a formula of open public tenders was used. The specifications of the call for proposals set a deadline of 6 months. This 6-month deadline was a *strategy* that, although seen as unrealistic, the designers of the system helped the focal actor (PAB) *keep port agents interested* in the IOIS. In September 1998, after the analysis and the evaluation of the tenders' proposals, the project was awarded to a joint venture by two IS consultancies.
- PortIC was conceived to give everyone access regardless of their in-house systems. As most of the firms in the community were users of the Internet, PortIC was Internet-enabled. That was supposed to *interest* port agents as it promised easy accessibility to PortIC. On the other hand, PortIC's designers *interested* the IS workers of those port agents by defining multiple data exchange formats and services (Figure 1). For those who did not wish to integrate the messages with their in-house applications, PortIC developed a standalone Java-based application (FrontEnd) that ran on a PC and could be used to generate and receive messages.
- In 1999, PortIC raised concerns among the potential adopters regarding data security and privacy because PortIC would centralize all information. These concerns were solved by *enrolling new technical actors* into the network and *inscribing certain programs of action*, namely a security policy, into the PortIC system: (1) the legal certainty was guaranteed by means of an electronic data exchange agreement between the parties, taking into account in a company's contract of adherence; (2) those using the FrontEnd application had a smartcard with a digital certificate issued by the Barcelona Chamber of Commerce; (3) messages generated from FrontEnd were encrypted using the SSL protocol; and (4) the PortIC computer system included an electronic certificate issued by the Chamber of Commerce, high availability firewalls, and control of access to the applications.
- Finally, actors *entered into a pact* on how to manage the IOIS once it was developed. In February 1999, the PAB, the trade associations, and the Chamber of Commerce, which represented importers and exporters, set up a company, named PortICCo, to manage the operation of PortIC when completed in May 1999. Actors'

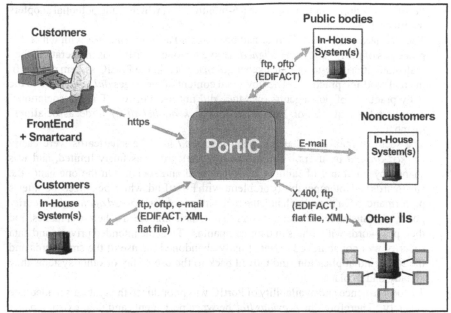

Figure 1. **Technical Actors Enrolled in the PortIC Actor Network**

interests would be realized with the implementation of PortIC. Through the trade associations becoming shareholders of PortICCo, all of the port agents in the port community *enrolled* the network. In that way they avoided any actor outside the community being able to control the *obligatory passage point*, PortIC. PortIC was *portrayed as an obligatory passage point* in the future: a node in the network through which all actors with a stake in the problem would have to pass.

4.3 Stage 3: Development toward Divergence (2000–2001)

By mid-2001, port agents were intensively using the information services and a significant percentage of the messages that the PAB received came through PortIC (private-to-public exchanges). Both networks—the information services and the private-to-public exchanges—became *black-boxes*. In the case of information services, which were used for documentary tracking of goods and statistical purposes, the port agents immediately *enrolled and mobilized* as any of the prior mechanisms required them to spend much more time gathering data. In the case of private-to-public exchanges, port agents *enrolled and mobilized* as they got faster responses from the public bodies when they used the IOIS. In addition, the PAB initially provided port agents with economic incentives to adopt these exchanges; thus, any alternative exchange mechanism would find it difficult to *resist* the new system.

On the other hand, since the PortIC system went live in 2000, the actor network that concerned private-to-private exchanges *developed toward divergence*. Some of the reasons were:

- PortIC's development finished with a 6-month delay, which made potential adopters mistrustful.
- The standard designed at TelFor had been treated as a *frozen actor* with which the processes of port agents were *aligned*. However, once PortIC was in operation, they realized that private-to-private exchanges *inscribed* in the PortIC system did not fit the real working practices. The flows and content of messages *did not adhere* to the daily practices of port agents; thus they did not use PortIC. Trade associations' representatives at TelFor had *failed to speak on behalf of* trade associations' members.
- The security measures that had been *inscribed* into the smartcards were easily *worked around* by users. The choice of smartcards was fairly limited, and was shaped by a number of failures, both technical and social. On the one hand, the smartcards had interoperability problems with FrontEnd, which penalized the latter's performance. On the other hand, the real patterns of use *worked against* the security policy. For instance, most of the users shared their smartcards, their user names, and their passwords with others in their companies. Thus the intended privacy and data security was not achieved. Users finally abandoned the use of the smartcards and the FrontEnd application, and moved back to the use of fax or other systems they already had in place.
- The performance and availability of PortIC was poor due to the system's inadequate capacity. Therefore, the *previous link* between port agents and their existing paper exchange mechanisms (fax), which PortIC *was supposed to weaken*, was actually strengthened as firms abandoned the use of PortIC to the detriment of prior exchange mechanisms.
- Moreover, at the beginning of 2000, one of the IS consultancies abandoned the project. The other consultancy took over responsibility for development of the entire system.

PortIC and the standard defined at TelFor had *failed as devices that cut the links* between port agents and prior exchange systems and procedures (installed base). The *inertia of the installed base worked against the stabilization of the PortIC actor network.*

In addition, a series of events occurred throughout 2000 and the beginning of 2001 that generated more *divergence*.

- PortICCo extended the scope of its services by linking inland transport network operations with those of the Barcelona airport. This idea of integration with other modes of transport was expected to enhance the service to existing customers (e.g., freight forwarders) by *weakening their links* with the systems they were using by that time (fax, Traxon, e-mail). However, once the integration was completed, it did not replace existing systems for airport operations. Freight forwarders were used to prior systems, which in addition had faster response times. On the other hand, some shipping agents felt upset as they considered PortICCo was giving value to freight forwarders beyond the boundaries of the port.
- PortICCo also implemented electronic payment services. However, these services proved unsatisfactory as PortIC did not support bank bills, the most widely used payment mechanism among port agents. None of these services were satisfactorily adopted and were thus discontinued.

- The CEO of PortICCo and the manager of international relations for the PAB commissioned a consultancy firm to design a strategic plan with the aim of transforming PortIC into a global IOIS, which would give service to complementary industries. This strategic plan was presented to new investors, two Spanish banks, who gave support to the initiative and became part of the shareholding of PortICCo. However, former shareholders (trade associations) considered banks' *interests* in doing business were *not aligned* with theirs, and perceived that banks could easily obtain control of the PortIC system—the *obligatory passage point*—in the future. Former shareholders also thought this initiative clashed with the initial idea of PortIC: to be a community project, not a project that went beyond the boundaries of the port community.

4.4 Stage 4: Sorting Out the Divergence (2001)

By mid-2001, the rate of PortIC usage for private-to-private exchanges was far from satisfactory. The PortIC system failed to live up to port agents' expectations. PortICCo's shareholders were dissatisfied with PortICCo management. They felt they had been deceived because PortICCo did not provide the promised service to the community. Various controversies sprang up concerning the development and use of PortIC. Consequently, the *translation process* backtracked to the *interessement stage*. The port agents did not visualize a port without an IOIS but disagreed with the way the IOIS should be implemented and the role of some of the actors (the managers of the IOIS). As the manager of an inland terminal noted, "If PortIC did not exist, we would have to invent it." Then PortICCo's shareholders and TelFor's participants made some changes.

4.2.2 Changes to PortIC

The board of directors of PortICCo replaced the CEO at the end of 2001. He had not been able to *tie up the various interests* in the new system and had failed to establish himself as a *spokesperson*.

The manager of international relations of the PAB was appointed as the new chief executive, and a new general manager and a marketing manager were hired. The new managers, who were under pressure to deliver rapid results, acted to sort out the situation.

- They decided to back-source the development of PortIC. From then on, PortICCo would be in charge not only of the operation of PortIC, but also of its development. The aim of this back-sourcing process (which was completed in 2003) was to provide *technical stabilization*.
- Although they did not abandon the project to transform PortIC into a global IOIS started by the former managers, they focused their attention on giving service to the firms in the community.
- They created the role of the consultant; someone who would be involved in understanding customers' demands and training needs and would also be fully involved in the TelFor activities. PortICCo and TelFor agreed that there was no need to use the smartcards to ensure security, thus this artefact was excluded. This measure

assured the *technical stabilization* of FrontEnd, and in turn the *social stabilization* as users accepted using FrontEnd.

4.4.2 Changes to TelFor

TelFor's participants considered that the standard had to *reflect the interests* of port agents if it was to be fully adopted. TelFor's governance and working procedures were changed. Until then, TelFor had been working with one main group with less than 20 people, who were involved in all of the standardization activities. The scope was too broad, which meant that members were not capable of deciding all of the issues that arose during standardization. Moreover, these people had jobs in their own companies, thus participating at TelFor represented extra hours. Therefore, they decided to change the organization of the standardization work: they set up a steering committee and 17 working groups, each of which would be responsible for a different part of the standardization process. Aiming to close the gap between the practices *inscribed* in the standard and the daily working practices, they put more emphasis on participation. They considered participation would enhance the further use of the IOIS. All the port agents, regardless of their size, were invited to participate in the process.

On the other hand, some private participants at TelFor promoted the creation of a Spanish committee with the goal of standardizing the private-to-public exchanges for most of the ports in Spain. This *new actor*, the Process Harmonization Group, was seen by big port agents as an opportunity to reduce their operating costs at the country level. On the other hand, the PAB and Customs perceived the *new actor as an opportunity* to provide better service to their customers (the port agents) and also to become leaders and promoters of a national standardization initiative. Finally, for TelFor, the Process Harmonization Group was an *opportunity* to extend the scope of its influence and to gain legitimacy.

4.5 Stage 5: Stabilization of the IOIS (2002–2005)

Between 2002 and 2005, the number of participants at TelFor rose from under 20 to over 130. We might attribute this to (1) the sustained leadership and enthusiasm of the chief of the regional Customs office, who was appointed president of TelFor in 2002, and (2) the organizing structure of TelFor, which offered opportunities for users to exert their influence. TelFor had become a dynamic committee in which port agents could make and develop proposals. The progressive involvement of new actors and the new structure helped *align the interests* of participants, and ultimately formed a *stable network* that reflected the working practices of the diverse port agents. *Inscriptions*, although they were paper-based, became *powerful*. All the (human) actors recognized and accepted TelFor's work; its focus was now directed to the outputs and no longer to its internal complexity. The standard transformed into a *black-box* and had a good deal of staying power.

On the other hand, to enhance the use of PortIC for private-to-private exchanges, both PortICCo and the PAB adopted new strategies to *stabilize* the actor network.

First, once the standard was *black-boxed*, the new PortICCo management selected small groups (constellations) of firms. More precisely, in September 2003, they launched the first partial import scenario with a constellation made of five port agents (a shipping agent, a freight forwarder, two haulers, and an inland terminal). They *aligned the interests* of the port agents in the constellation and those of the PortIC system. PortICCo introduced some changes to the system based on these firms' installed base (systems, uses of the system, message content, etc.). Once these constellations became *stable*, new actors—partners of these firms—*enrolled*. Therefore, the actions that PortICCo carried out aiming to *align* the different interests bootstrapped a self-reinforcing installed base of *actors*. As firms usually participate in more than one constellation, this *alignment process* has to occur more than once. However, successive alignments became easier as actors learned from experience.

Secondly, the PAB imposed a rule in May 2005 for some of the users of the port (holders of inland terminals, depots, shipping agents, and haulers). The reason for doing so was to increase the use of PortIC for private-to-private exchanges. This rule forced these companies to follow the standard defined at TelFor and use electronic means to submit the messages (PortIC was the only IOIS in the port) starting July 31, 2005. According to this rule, inland terminals had to refuse incoming or outgoing containers whose documentary process had not been submitted through PortIC. However, all of the *actors* complained. The inland terminals complained that this rule forced them to decide which hauler (customer) could enter and which could not. The freight forwarders argued this rule did not really penalize shipping agents, but haulers and in turn the shipper, their customer. The haulers claimed they were not ready to send and receive through PortIC. Thus this *inscription turned out to be weak as actors opposed the pattern of use*. The PAB postponed the implementation of the new rule for 2 months. Then the PAB *performed a sequence of trials* (e.g., made an agreement with an inland terminal to become a beta test site for the new rule, launched a training program for haulers) that allowed them to progressively *establish the desired behavior*. This shows that the *inscription* into the haulers' daily practices through training has proved to be *stronger* than through the rule.

As a result of PortICCo and the PAB strategies, the actor network seems to have gradually stabilized.

5   DISCUSSION AND CONCLUSION

Having described and analyzed the implementation of an industry IOIS in the port of Barcelona, we discuss several characteristics of the process.

As the case analysis shows, the implementation of the IOIS can be viewed as chains of translations that run sequentially or in parallel (Figure 2). Each translation process is triggered by a problem or an opportunity. For instance, in stage 1 we see two translation processes: the first one was triggered by the port agents' complaints about the service (e.g., response time) of Customs; the second was triggered by the low rate of adoption of the private-to-public exchanges standard due to the port agents' lack of IT capabilities. In response to an opportunity, the focal actor proposed a solution—create a standardization committee—to develop a common IOIS for the port.

On the other hand, we observe that a translation process may succeed or halt at any stage. When a translation succeeds—the case of the standard in stage 4—it becomes irreversible, that is, it is very difficult to go back to a point where that translation was only on among many and the translation may shape other translations—for example, the standard becomes a single aligned actor in the network concerning the implementation of private-to-private exchanges (Callon 1991, pp. 150). If the translation halts, then it may be necessary to backtrack. Prior alliances may weaken, translation may halt because of technical tensions as with the smartcards, or social tensions may create problems, as was the case with the project aimed at transforming PortIC into a global IOIS.

The problematization stage culminates in the definition of a situation, namely an obligatory passage point (OPP), that has to occur for all of the actors to satisfy their interests (Callon 1986). Considering the implementation of PortIC as the main OPP (Figure 3), we see that the different actors have to pass through it to avoid several obstacles or threats and to achieve their objectives. The OPP is directly in the path of the main focal actors, the PAB and PortICCo, who are powerful because of their control of the OPP.

	Problematization	Interessement	Enrollment	Mobilization
Stage 1 (1994-97)	P: Complaints about the service provided by Customs S: Standardization of private-to-public exchanges through IGC	* Private organizations wanted customs to improve. * Customs wanted to modernize their service and operations	* The PAB has power to impose the message flows and content to port agents at IGC * The PAB acting as one-stop ship with Customs	
	P: Low rate of adoption of private-to-public exchanges because there was a lack of IT capabilities S: * Idea: development of a common technical infrastructure for the whole community * Dissolution of IGC. Creation of TelFor to extend IGC's work to private-to-private exchanges.	* Port agents become interested as the common infrastructure avoid them from investing in new systems for their data exchanges * Port agents were interested in a solution that went beyond the private-to-public exchanges * New actors (importers/exporters, haulage contractors, etc) are identified to play a role at TelFor	* The PAB giving economical incentives to those using PortIC for private-to-public exchanges * The threat that represented that other organizations could enter the port and control the information * TelFor would use a consensus approach	
Stage 2 (1998-99)	P: A community vision: paperless port and improvement in the efficiency of organizations. S: Idea of PortIC (the OPP)	* The Master Plan is approved * Other port already had an IOIS	* The 6-month deadline was a tactic for enrollment into the actor-network * Use of Internet-based technologies to easy the access to PortIC (FrontEnd) * Inscribing a security policy in FrontEnd and in rules	
	P: There is need to manage the PortIC system S: Define a management model for PortIC	All the private stakeholders in the port community should be involved (trade associations, chamber of commerce).	* Create a company (PortICCo) * The trade associations are offered the opportunity to become shareholders. No external actors, except the Chamber of Commerce, becomes shareholder.	* Standard for private-to-public exchanges stabilizes
Stage 3 (2000-01)	P:* Port agents rejected the use of FrontEnd due to performance of smartcards (users worked around the security measures inscribed in FrontEnd) * Performance problem of PortIC S: Introduce small operative and strategic changes	* Remove smartcards from FrontEnd * Extension of PortIC to new actors (e.g. banks, airline services). This interessement failed	* The private-to-private exchanges inscribed in paper did not reflect real practices. The inscription became reversible (gap between standard for private-to-private exchanges and daily processes)	* Information services stabilize * Private-to-public exchange stabilize
Stage 4 (2001)	P: PortIC usage is less than satisfactory. Port agents start mistrusting the whole project, and are deceived with PortICCo management S: Introduce changes to PortICCo and TelFor	* General interests in the success of a community project such as PortIC * Port Agents interested in controling the project. Negotiations between focal actors and port agents	* Threat that new actors such as banks could control PortIC and consequently their business * The PAB coordinating the work of TelFor and financially supporting it * Creation of a new working structure at TelFor that fostered a wide participation, and that extend their work to a broader context	* Telfor organization and standard stabilize
Stage 5 (2002-05)	P: Lack of use of PortIC for private-to-private exchanges S: Strategies adopted by PortICCo and the PAB	* General interests in the success of a community project such as PortIC * Other seaports had similar initiatives running	* Aligning of constellations interests * The PAB defined a rule * Training programs for haulers * Beta-tester to show the good working of PortIC	* Private-to-private exchanges through portIC started stabilizing

P: problem/opportunity
S: solution to the problem/opportunity

Figure 2. **Translation Processes Throughout the Implementation Stages**

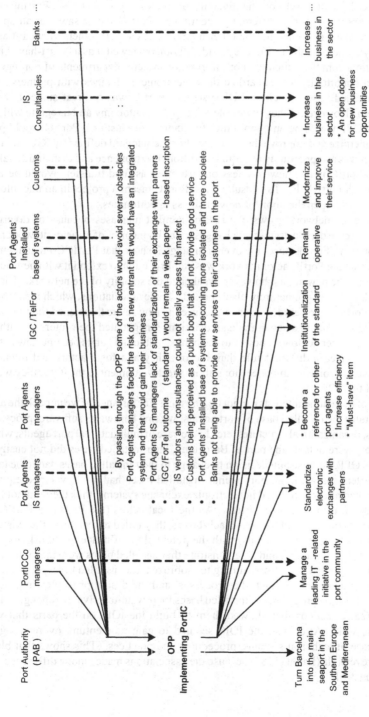

Figure 3. The OPP, Some of the Actors, Their Goals, and the Obstacles to avoid (based on Callon 1986)

On the other hand, the other actors may face more difficulties in passing through the OPP. These difficulties rely on the diversity of interests or objectives. For instance, managers of port agents had different perceptions of PortIC: some saw it as an opportunity to become a reference for the other members of the port, others viewed it as an opportunity to increase their efficiency, and still others viewed it as a "must-have" item (an imposition from their clients). For information systems departments of port agents, it meant an opportunity to standardize their electronic exchanges with partners. For existing installed bases—such as EDI systems—PortIC was a threat since it would replace them. However, if they were able to keep their autonomy and integrate with the PortIC, the OPP would be an opportunity for them. For Customs, PortIC would push them to modernize and improve their service. For the standard defined by IGC and later by TelFor, it was an opportunity to acquire additional permanence and to institutionalize. For banks, PortIC meant new business opportunities as fund transfers would be conducted through PortIC. For IS consultancies, PortIC meant a project in an unexploited sector that would open the door for new business opportunities.

As the actor network grows, the risk of conflict increases because of divergent interests. The case demonstrates that changes in the boundaries of an actor network have to be negotiated. For instance, the events in stage 3 show that PortICCo management considered that the PortIC actor network was stable enough to extend it with new actors (e.g., banks). The new actors, however, weakened the stability of the network. That is, the network had been prematurely black-boxed. Trade associations, which were shareholders of PortICCo, offered resistance because the new actors threatened their position in the network. Then in stage 4, trade associations renegotiated their interests with the focal actors in order not to lose power to the banks. Although banks became new actors, they finally played a different role than the one they and focal actors had intended. Banks would not control future decisions about the development of the IOIS, they would not control the OPP.

Some of the actors' interests cannot be foreseen. For instance, if we unpack the actor that constitutes the installed base of port agents, we find hardware, software, processes, developers, organizational structures, etc. In the case of multinational port agents, whose headquarters were outside the port of Barcelona, their installed bases did not easily go through the OPP, because any decision to change to their installed bases had to be taken in headquarters. In addition, port agents' installed bases had not developed equally: some firms had already invested in electronic exchange systems, thus they did not have any interests in using the new system. As the focal actors (the PAB and PortICCo) initially treated the installed bases as black-boxes, they failed to recognize the existence of some actors (e.g., multinationals) with the potential to influence the translation process. The events in stages 2 and 3 demonstrate that installed bases were unstable allies. In stages 4 and 5, the focal actors, aiming to mobilize these installed bases, decided that PortIC would adapt the artefact, the processes, and the design principles in order to accommodate the heterogeneity of installed bases for private-to-private exchanges. They adopted a set of actions that allowed them to build the IOIS on the parts that were functioning well. After that, the IOIS seemed to gain momentum, overcoming the installed base of technical systems, procedures and practices. This shows that black-boxing is reversible (Latour 1987) because the associations made among different actors are often unstable.

Finally, the case also shows that IT played a major role in the image-making strategy. That is, IT mediated the discourse of the promoters (Latour 1987). The focal actors, the trade associations, press articles, and consulting firms portrayed the PortIC systems as the inevitable direction to enhance the competitiveness of the port and create a paperless port, which meant more efficiency in terms of time, cost, and infrastructure optimization. This techno-economic view was attractive not only because of the consequences, but also because of the easy explanations for a successful story. The PortIC system was presented as being technically advanced. In addition, well-established IS consultancies would be in charge of the implementation. Thus, IT was a rhetorical instrument in the persuasion campaign carried by focal actors. However, this strategy finally failed in stage 3 when the project was close to collapse. Focal actors had not fully taken into account the role of other actors—the port agents' systems, interests, internal processes, skills, working habits, etc.—in shaping the implementation process. The focal actors' assumption had been that the implementation process would be mainly shaped and controlled by focal actors' designers, and port agents would adopt it.

This paper contributes both to IOIS research and management. First, this empirical paper adds to existing IOIS literature as it examines both development and diffusion, and studies an industry phenomenon. ANT's focus on how socio-technical actors are brought together in stable networks of aligned interests provides a holistic view of IOIS implementation. ANT has allowed us to trace the course of the implementation by focusing on the translation processes and to identify sources of disagreement between actors' interests, and between the actors and the medium in which the translation was inscribed. Second, this paper adds external empirical validity to the argument by Lyytinen and Damsgaard (2001) and McMaster et al. (1997) that IOIS implementation cannot only be explained by a fixed set of independent factors. Rather, complex dynamics and processes involving different actors (people, technologies, standards, and rules) may complement factor-based models in explaining the evolution and the outcome—success or failure—of IOIS. Third, we present a longitudinal case that provides additional empirical findings to the IOIS literature, and in particular to the small number of studies on IOIS in seaports. We explain how the different actors perform to keep the different interests aligned, and how they struggle to inscribe their interests into textual descriptions, training programs, rules, hardware, and software. Finally, although we cannot assure the generalizability of the case findings, we believe the implementation dynamics presented in the paper are not exclusively from this sector; thus the paper furnishes insights for researchers and managers involved in IOIS implementations.

References

Callon, M. "Some Elements of a Sociology of Translation: Domestication of the Scallops and Fishermen of St. Brieuc Bay," in J. Law (ed.), *Power, Action and Belief: A New Sociology of Knowledge?*, London: Routledge, 1986, pp. 196-233.

Callon, M. "Techno-Economic Networks and Irreversibility," in J. Law (ed.), *A Sociology of Monsters: Essays on Power, Technology and Domination*, London: Routledge, 1991, pp. 132-161.

Damsgaard, J., and Lyytinen, K. "The Role of Intermediating Institutions in the Diffusion of Electronic Data Interchange (EDI): How Industry Associations Intervened in Denmark, Finland, and Hong Kong," *Information Society* (17:3), 2001, pp. 195-210.

Hanseth, O., and Lyytinen, K. "Theorizing about the Design of Information Infrastructures: Design Kernel Theories and Principles," unpublished paper, 2006 (available online at http://heim.ifi.uio.no/~oleha/Publications/ISRinfrastructurefinal05-12-05.pdf).

Latour, B. *Science in Action: How to Follow Scientists and Engineers through Society*, Cambridge, MA: Harvard University Press, 1987.

Lyytinen, K., and Damsgaard, J. "What's Wrong with the Diffusion of Innovation Theory?," in Proceedings of the IFIP 8.6, Banff, Canada, April 8-10, 2001.

Markus, M. L., Steinfield, C., and Wigand, R. "Industry-Wide Information Systems Standardization as Collective Action: The Case of the U.S. Residential Mortgage Industry," *MIS Quarterly* (30:Special Issue on Standard Making), August 2006, pp. 439-465.

McMaster, T., Vidgen, R. T., and Wastell, D. G. "Technology Transfer—Diffusion or Translation?," in T. McMaster, E. Mumford, E. B. Swanson, B. Warboys, and D. Wastell (eds.), *Facilitating Technology Transfer Through Partnership: Learning from Practice and Research*, London: Chapman & Hall, 1997, pp. 64-75.

McMaster, T., and Wastell, D. G. "Diffusion—or Delusion? Challenging an IS Research Tradition," *Information Technology & People* (18:4), 2005, pp. 383-404.

Monteiro, E. "Actor Network Theory and Information Infrastructure," in C. Ciborra, K. Braa, A. Cordella, B. Dahlbom, A. Failla, O. Hanseth, V. Hepso, J. Ljungberg, and E. Monteiro (eds.), *From Control to Drift: The Dynamics of Corporate Information Infrastructures*, Oxford, UK: Oxford University Press, 2000, pp. 71-83.

Teo, H-H., Tan, B. C. Y., and Wei, K-K. "Organizational Transformation Using Electronic Data Interchange: The Case of TradeNet in Singapore," *Journal of Management Information Systems* (13:4), Spring 1997, pp. 139-166.

van Baalen, P., van Oosterhout, M., Tan, Y. H., and van Heck, E. *Dynamics in Setting Up an EDI Community*, Delft, The Netherlands: Eburon Publishers, 2000.

Walsham, G. "Actor Network Theory and IS Research: Current Status and future Prospects, in A. S. Lee, J. Liebenau, and J. I. DeGross (eds.), *Information Systems and Qualitative Research*, London: Chapman & Hall, 1997, pp. 466-480.

Walsham, G. "Interpretative Case Studies in IS Research: Nature and Method," *European Journal of Information Systems* (4:2), 1995, pp. 74-81.

Walsham, G. *Interpreting Information Systems in Organizations*, Chichester, UK: Wiley, 1993.

Wrigley, C. D., Wagenaar, R. W., and Clarke, R. A. "Electronic Data Interchange in International Trade: Frameworks for the Strategic Analysis of Ocean Port Communities," *Journal of Strategic Information Systems* (3:3), 1994, pp. 211-234.

About the Authors

Juan Rodon is an assistant professor in the Information Systems Department at ESADE, Universitat Ramon Llull. His research focuses on development of standards for interorganizational information systems (IOIS) and IOIS implementation. He can be reached by e-mail at joan.rodon@esade.edu.

Joan Antoni Pastor is an associate professor at the Universitat Politècnica de Catalunya. His research focuses on the ERP procurement and implementation and IS qualitative research. He can be reached by e-mail at pastor@lsi.upc.edu.

Feliciano Sesé is an associate professor in the Information Systems Department at ESADE, Universitat Ramon Llull. His main research interests are data modeling, studying the notion of information in the diverse information systems development approaches, and pondering over the circumstances which lead IS projects to success or failure. He can be reached by e-mail at feliciano.sese@esade.edu.

21   A DYNAMIC APPROACH TO CONTEXT IN DIFFUSION RESEARCH: An Actor Network Theory Study of Mobile-TV Service

Su-Yi Lin
Mike W. Chiasson
University of Lancaster
Lancaster, United Kingdom

Abstract   *Contextual studies of information technology diffusion offer an opportunity to understand both the production and diffusion of IT innovations. Using a case of mobile-TV in the United Kingdom, this paper uses actor network theory (ANT) to render context as the various cross-industry groups and technologies enrolled and translated into the construction and reinvention of the mobile-TV services. By focusing on the various cross-industry actors, context is recast as a dynamic environment composed of other actors' behaviors, and no longer as a set of static factors. Implications for diffusion research and practice are discussed.*

Keywords   Innovation diffusion theory, actor network theory, convergence service, mobile-TV

1   INTRODUCTION

Despite a call for more research on the context around information technology diffusion (Fichman 2004), including the technical and social production of IT innovations (Lyytinen and Yoo 2002), few have yet to heed this call. In addition, what context is, and how to address it in information systems research remains an open question (Avgerou 2001; Chiasson and Davidson 2005; King et al. 1994).

Please use the following format when citing this chapter:

Lin, S-Y., and Chiasson, M. W., 2007, in IFIP International Federation for Information Processing, Volume 235, Organizational Dynamics of Technology-Based Innovation: Diversifying the Research Agenda, eds. McMaster, T., Wastell, D., Ferneley, E., and DeGross, J. (Boston: Springer), pp. 315-330.

This paper provides a methodological and empirical glimpse into the use of actor network theory (ANT) to address the diffusion context, by recasting it as a dynamic interplay of various actors which affect and are affected by their enrolment into socio-technical relations. The case we examine is a pilot trial of a new IT-enabled service: mobile-TV. Mobile-TV is a convergence service that allows consumers to watch TV on-the-go. A more precise definition is TV viewing from a wireless pocket-sized terminal or phone in public and private environments, both as a personal TV set and as a tool to establish closer interaction with the content (Södergård 2003). Since the context of mobile-TV is composed of a network of actors—users, service providers, technology suppliers, and content providers—mobile-TV is a critical case to explore how various cross-industry actors, both human and nonhuman, enrol and translate interests in the construction and reinvention of an innovation.

The remainder of this paper is arranged as following. First, the literature on innovation diffusion theory (IDT) and on ANT is reviewed to identify both theoretical and empirical gaps. We then describe our methodology for examining a mobile-TV trial. Following this, we present our initial findings, tracing important events back to various human and nonhuman actors, including their partial enrolment into the emerging IT network, and issues that threaten to strengthen or weaken their future enrolment in the network. In the concluding section, we discuss the results and explore how our use of ANT addresses contextual studies of diffusion.

2   LITERATURE REVIEW

2.1   Innovation Diffusion Theory

The term *innovation* is generally understood to mean an idea, practice, or object that is perceived as new by adopters, and *diffusion* is defined as "the process by which an innovation is communicated through certain channels over time among the members of a social system" (Rogers 1995, p. 5). Few IDT studies, however, pay attention to the particular institutional context (a social system such as a firm, industry, or society) and how it influences the construction and diffusion of an innovation. Most IDT studies just focus on the process of diffusion and the penetration of innovation (Orlikowski and Iacono 2001).

Reviewing the literature, Rogers (1995) found that more than 70 percent of the diffusion research studied the characteristics of the innovators. Around 1 percent of the research concentrated on the attributes of innovations, but this topic has attracted considerable attention recently (Hackney et al. 2005; Hong and Tam 2006). Of note, three important attributes are considered to explain the rate of adoption: greater relative advantage (perceived need), technical compatibility, and reduced technical complexity (Bradford and Florin 2003). Less than 1 percent of the early literature was interested in the varying patterns of network links among two or more members of a system. Until now, only a few studies have examined the process of innovation diffusion within a changing institutional context (e.g., Geels 2005; Park and Yoon 2005).

Another limitation in IDT is that little research has been done from an organizational or industrial viewpoint. Brown (1981) commented that IDT studies emphasized the demand side for innovation marketing, and the economic studies of diffusion concentrated on price and profitability, although both supply and demand variables were analyzed. Therefore, growing studies have been carried out on the institutional and market structures that channel new technologies to users (e.g., Chiasson and Lovato 2001; Kodama 2005; Murase 2003). Nevertheless, these studies tend to be performed from the view of specific suppliers or adopters. An exploratory study of cross-industry innovation appears necessary given that the production of complex innovations occurs in alliances across organizations and industries.

2.2 Actor Network Theory

To address some of these limitations in the IDT research, we propose ANT as a systematic framework to analyze how the various actors alter relational ties with each other during the production and initial diffusion of an IT innovation. Unlike other network theories, ANT is known as the sociology of enrolment and translation, during which the interrelated roles of actors and their strategies are defined and negotiated (Callon 1986; Law 1992). Both human and nonhuman actors (e.g., IT artifacts) are treated equally. The temporary "maps of interests" and the "funnel of interests" and the compromises among actors interests, are helpful to understand how IT artifacts are produced and diffused. However, actor networks are unstable, subject to both production and deconstruction, as social orders collapse or reform (Law and Hassard 1999).

A few researchers have employed ANT in their IT innovation diffusion research. They highlight the diverse interests of actors as well as broader contexts on IT diffusion. Walsham and Sahay (1999) learned that the effects of geographical information systems (GIS) for decentralized administration in developing countries was strongly related to the interests of multiple agencies and local social values. Allen (2004) found that the actor networks of two early personal digital assistants (PDA) were not only affected by technologies but also redefined by management and practices external to the PC industry. Unlike the previous researchers, Oh and Lee (2005) examined how cross-industry actors forged alliances and how technology (re)shaped the interaction patterns between banks and mobile service providers. They also demonstrated how research could examine the effects of substitute technologies and customers as contexts on the diffusion of convergence services.

The actor network of convergence services leads to an issue in the linkage of IDT and ANT. While traditional IT innovation is usually developed by research and development designers with intended functions, the companies that produce IT products and services, including the convergence services in this case, often conduct market trials to assess and build the relative advantage of the innovation for adopters. The creation, distribution, and reinvention of innovation between suppliers and customers are, therefore, simultaneous. As recommended by Lyytinen and Yoo (2002, p. 387), "New alliances need to be forged and IS researchers should be actively involved in studies where technologies are being built and tried out—not after the fact when they enter the market."

This confirms a need to employ methodologies and theories to understand how actors in an industrial chain enrol and translate their diverse interests in the production, diffusion, and reinvention of an IT artifact.

3   METHODOLOGY

3.1 Study Design

To demonstrate the empirical possibilities of an ANT approach to study context in diffusion research, we examine how a new convergence service was shaped by the interaction of actors across time. The current case of a mobile-TV trial in Oxford is a pilot study of a larger research project, which is expected to capture changes in technologies and the market of mobile entertainment, in order to understand what and how the "triple diffusion" of an IT artefact—across producers, producer-to-user, and user-to-producer—occurs.

The case of the mobile-TV trial in Oxford, which is promised to offer 24 hour, live access to 16 TV channels, provides a setting in which to assess an ANT view of context for two reasons. First, the case appears to be the most comprehensive mobile-TV trial in the UK (Table 1). It continues for 6 months with a physical trial plan and provides a complementary result (Figure 1).

The second reason is that the actors in this case are spread across diverse industries. This industrial chain of mobile-TV covers a *network broadcaster* (Arqiva), a *mobile service provider* (O2), a *handset and technology supplier* (Nokia), several *content providers* (16 TV channels), hundreds of *adopters* (375 trial users), and the *digital video broadcasting-handheld* (DVB-H) *technology*. Arqiva and O2 rolled out the trial over the DVB-H technology. Sixteen TV channels were delivered digitally to 375 users who were equipped with Nokia 7710 smart phones for their feedback (Figure 2).

3.2 Data Collection

The data sources of our study include interviews with key participants from July to October 2006, and documentary analysis of news, articles, and company documents. First-hand data was collected from three in-depth interviews with the managers in charge of this trial for Arqiva, Nokia, and O2 as well as two interviews with the customers who

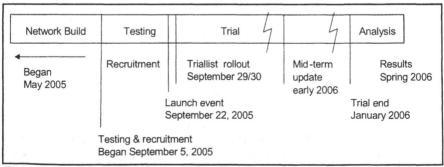

Figure 1. The Timeline of the Mobile-TV Trial in Oxford
(from D. Williams, "Oxford Mobile-TV Trial," 2005, http://www.o2.com/media_files/oxford_mobile_tv.pdf)

Table 1. The Milestone of Mobile-TV in the United Kingdom Up to 2006[†]

Time	Event	Milestone	Technology
January 2004	4Interactive, Endemol UK, and Vemotion offered end-to-end live programming of a new and round-the-clock show, accessed by some video-capable GPRS handsets.	The first TV-to-mobile service from terrestrial channels.	GPRS (2.5G)
May 2005	Orange launched its 3G mobile-TV service.	The first mobile-TV services using TV streaming via 3G.	3G
September 2005	O2 and Arqiva launched a mobile-TV trial over DVB-H in Oxford. Sixteen TV channels were delivered digitally to 375 users equipped with specially modified Nokia 7710 handsets.	The first trial of multi-channel TV broadcast directly to mobiles rather than one-to-one streaming via the mobile networks. The first trial to provide full-length TV shows.	DVB-H
November 2005	Vodafone UK and British Sky Broadcasting launched mobile-TV with 19 channels. All Vodafone's 3G users could use it free before the end of 2005. Afterward, some channels would be packaged and charged £5 monthly.	The first commercial mobile-TV service available on a wide range of 3G handsets.	3G
October 2006	Virgin Mobile, using BT's system, launches the first commercial broadcast mobile-TV service without charge to its pay-monthly customers whose bills are £25 or more. Pay-as-you-go users charge £5 monthly after the first 3-month free trial. However, only one handset provided by Windows mobile shop was workable.	The first commercial broadcast mobile-TV service.	DAB-IP[‡]

[†]Source: 3G News (2005), BBC News (2005), E-Consultancy (2004), and Meyer (2006)
[‡]Digital-audio-broadcast IP (DAB-IP) is an enhanced system using the same frequencies of digital audio broadcasting (DAB) to provide a limited number of TV channels.

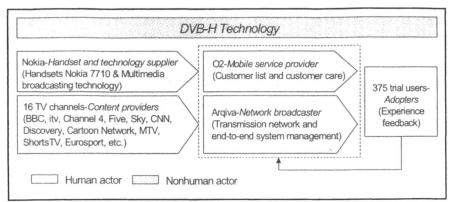

Figure 2. **The Industrial Value Chain of the Mobile-TV Trial in Oxford**

had experienced mobile-TV through their 3G phones in Birmingham and London. To protect their personal data, interviewees were anonymously analyzed except for those who agreed to disclosure. The managers were contacted via formal customized enquiry letters, while the customers were contacted via a web forum. Semi-structured questionnaires were designed and sent in advance (Table 2). These questions were developed based on concepts from ANT, such as enrolment and translation. The objectives of our research were explained in the letter or during the first visit. Documentary data were gathered from the websites of main companies and the search engine *Google* with the keywords "mobile-TV trial" and "Oxford."

3.3   Data Analysis

To analyze the data, we looked for statements and events that pointed to past, present, and future possibilities for enrolment and translation across participants. Our analysis disclosed that the interaction among the six actors could be divided into two phases. In the network-forming phase, the role and interests of each actor is identified. In the network-reshaping phase, the challenges and opportunities of actors in the future are analyzed (or predicted). We conclude by discussing further implications for research on the relations among innovation diffusion, actor networks, power, and contexts.

3.4   Method Limitations

Since the findings of this paper are based on a pilot case study, there are three limitations: the number of supplier interviewees, the sample requirements of customers, and the time spectrum of the mobile-TV trial. First, only one person in each supplier group is interviewed, so the interview opinions do not explore the full-range of positions and interests of those in charge of the mobile-TV business. To compensate, we have explore other documentary evidence to determine the interests and positions of the suppliers. Second, because of limited resources, our interviewees represent adopters of 3G mobile-TV users, not the actual DVB-H mobile-TV trial users in Oxford. Therefore, our findings are con-

Table 2. The Semi-Structured Questionnaire for Mobile-TV Suppliers and Customers

Interviewee	Question
Various Suppliers	• Does your company have any official definition about mobile-TV? • Does your company position mobile-TV as a mobile service or a member of TV family? • What motivated your company to launch or support mobile-TV? • What are the objectives of this trial in Oxford? • What roles did your company and your partners play in the alliance? Which one was the focal actor in this trial? Why? • Has your company had different or conflicting ideas with your partners? • What is the feedback from the trial users? • How does your company think about mobile-TV over DVB-H, 3G, or DMB? • Have you found any challenge after this trial? Do you have any plan to solve them? • Will you choose exclusive or multiple partners in each function when formal commercial mobile-TV is provided? Why?
Customers	• What is mobile-TV in your interpretation? • When and how did you learn about mobile-TV? • When did you first use mobile-TV? Why? • Which company services did you use? Why? Did you like it? Why? What handset did you use? Did you like it? Why? • When, where, how often, and how long did you use mobile-TV? Why? • Do you continue using it? Why? • Have you ever recommended your family or friends to use mobile-TV? Why? • Which score (1-5) do you rank the mobile-TV? Why? • Will you use mobile-TV in the future 12 months? Why? • Which pricing model do you prefer? How much money are you willing to pay? • When you watch TV at home/workplace/outdoors, what is your priority for TV sets, PCs, notebooks, mobile phones, others? • Any suggestion about services, content, and handsets? • What TV programmed genres do you prefer to watch through mobile-TV and TV? • IT usage behaviors and demographic data of interviewee

tradictory to the official results from O2 and Arqiva. Finally, although the mobile-TV trial is 6 months only, the production of mobile-TV and its diffusion among the supplier groups has been in development for years. To compensate, we expand our interviews and documentary evidence to gather additional historical data, consistent with ANT studies. Since we focus here only on these initial findings, we address some of the limitations in this study with continued study of the UK project, and a new project with Taiwanese mobile-TV projects.

4   FINDINGS

4.1   Phase 1: The Forming of Actor Networks

In this section, we use the mobile-TV trial in Oxford to illustrate how actor networks are forming through the enrolment and translation of diverse actor interests. Figure 2 illustrates the influence across suppliers and customers. It serves as a study of diverse participants' actions and reactions to the development and diffusion of an IT service. Table 1 provides a trace summary of the various actors, events, and influences supporting and competing with those involved in the TV trial in Oxford.

Despite the apparent solidarity of Figure 2, each actor group in the trial had unique interests that were enrolled and translated to produce temporary complements in joint action. We start with the DVB-H technology because it was the focal actor in the network of relationships.

4.1.1 DVB-H Technology: Nonhuman Actor

DVB-H is viewed as a broadcast (one-to-many downstream only) technology trans-mitting digital signals from towers to handsets, following the recognizable principles of digital terrestrial broadcast television. By investing in certain facilities through existing TV broadcast transmission, the actors involved in DVB-H mobile-TV believe that they can offer downstream channels at high data rates without a restriction on the number of concurrent viewers. Hence, the quality of video programs and the network efficiency are promoted as generally better than 3G, a two-way packet system that is considered to have limited capacity and significant transmission delays. As Mark Fowler, the business manager for Nokia UK mobile-TV, said,

> With DVB-H mobile-TV network, because it a true broadcasting, the same as
> the (terrestrial) broadcast TV at your home, everybody in the world can watch
> the same channels at the same time, but 3G mobile-TV wouldn't.

In this trial, the actors enrolled DVB-H technology to demonstrate its superiority with its potential competitors: 3G, digital audio broadcast over Internet protocol (DAB-IP), digital multimedia broadcasting (DMB), and MediaFLO.[1] However, customers who wished to watch DVB-H mobile-TV required new handsets with the DVB-H chips, so new relations (i.e., networks) were formed from the DVB-H handset suppliers to the trial users to test the new system. Therefore, the question—what "is" DVB-H technology—can be seen as a series of relations between actors. The trial could determine whether and how diverse interests of customers and suppliers are to be translated and enrolled into the DVB-H network. Figure 3 highlights these relations.

---

[1]DAB-IP, DMB, and MediaFLO are other competitive broadcast mobile TV technologies supported by different camps. Please refer to Shin (2005) and Qualcomm (2005) for further information.

4.1.2 Network Broadcaster: Arqiva

Arqiva, one of the two licensed mobile-TV network broadcasters in the UK, initiated the trial. Arqiva acted aggressively because it was hoping to imitate a successful business model in DAB (Figure 4). This business model began in 1998, when Arqiva and GCap Media invested in a joint venture, Digital One, to bid for the sole DAB spectrum license. Digital One then contracted with digital audio providers, wholesaled the digital audio service to interested retailers, and outsourced Arqiva to build and manage the network over the coming years.

Using its relations to exploit economies of scale and speed to market, Arqiva hoped to produce an obligatory passage point. It believed that mobile service providers would be unable to catch up to its existing advantage over the relations with TV channels and infrastructure in Oxford, to form an alliance with 16 TV channels and the mobile service provider O2. It hoped to earn nation-wide attention and recognition for its construction and management of the DVB-H broadcast system. This was a deliberate attempt to weaken competitive network relations, which had enrolled alternative technical standards. To do so, Arqiva needed to enrol other suppliers and customers. These include handset providers, mobile service providers, and content providers.

4.1.2 Handset and Technology Supplier: Nokia

Nokia, one of the largest handsets suppliers and a major promoter of the DVB-H technology, provided hundreds of free handsets and supported the multimedia broadcast technology in the trial. Nokia's aggressive role in this trial arose from their long-standing

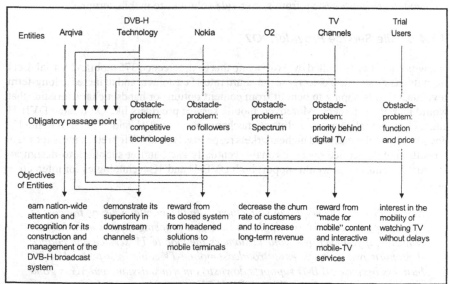

Figure 3.   The DVB-H Networks of the Mobile-TV Trial in Oxford in the Network-Forming Phase

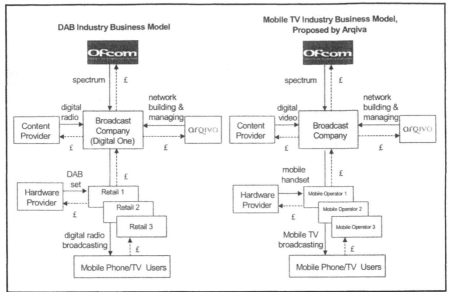

Figure 4. **The Business Model of DAB Industry and Mobile-TV Industry Proposed by Arqiva**

interest in mobile-TV over a 5-year period, and its all-out effort to back DVB-H against the other competitive technologies. As a the future reward, Nokia hoped that other suppliers and customers would use DVB-H for mobile video because Nokia was well prepared to provide a system from server-side solutions to mobile terminals.

4.1.4 Mobile Service Provider: O2

O2, which had been enrolled by Arqiva into this trial, screened 375 mobile-TV trial users from its customer list. To decrease the churn rate of customers and to increase long-term revenue, O2 was hoping to benefit from content options or handset characteristics that would lock-in customers. Moreover, mobile service providers like O2 treated DVB-H and 3G as complementary delivery mechanisms: DVB-H and 3G for mobile-TV downstream to the mass and niche markets respectively, and 3G for return messages. As a result, mobile service operators may eventually ask handset suppliers to design an affordable handset that would support both DVB-H and 3G technologies for interactive mobile-TV.

> *Mobile-TV could be helpful to stop churn....In the mobile industry, the cost of acquiring customers is very high, and the cost of losing them is even higher. However, if you ever give your customers the mobile-TV service, the chance they churn away is much less. Broadcast mobile-TV could [also] stimulate 3G business because DVB-H supports downstream transmission, and 3G is good at two-way transmission....When DVB-H TV users want to vote [their favorite participants on the game shows] or send messages [to their friends for real-*

time discussion], they have to use the 3G. ....Hence, mobile-TV might contribute only to mobile service providers, but it could raise in 3G revenue (Anonymous interviewee with Arqiva).

4.1.5 Content Providers: 16 TV Channels

In the trial, 16 TV channels provided free news, entertainment, sports, or documentary content to Arqiva. They were relatively passive participants in this trial because (1) programs are produced from an almost fixed cost, and were then easily digitized to match various platforms, and (2) mobile-TV needed time to get established, as compared with digital TV through terrestrial broadcasting. Thus, they responded to Arqiva's invitation from a lost cost and low benefit position. In the near future, however, content providers might be rewarded with two opportunities: "made for mobile" content and interactive mobile-TV services, which will redesign the process of producing and selling TV programs.

4.1.6 Adopters: Customers

From O2's customer list, 375 mobile phone users living predominantly in Oxford were selected. With free handsets to watch free mobile-TV, the trial users were obliged to participate in the trial and reply with their thoughts via monthly telephone questionnaires, focus groups, and users' daily diary. Without enough data to completely understand the variety of interests and experiences of customers, we conducted two interviews to find out how adopters perceived their experiences with mobile-TV. Our results show that, unlike the positive results released by O2 and Arqiva, our price-sensitive interviewees believed that mobile-TV was only "nice-to-have" on their 3G phones (Table 3).

Beyond sample size issues in explaining the differences, it is possible that the capture and presentation of data is a combined political-technical effect, used for the purposes of enrolling other actors. Further research into the production of evidence in this and other IT production studies is required.

4.2　Phase 2: The Reshaping of Actor Networks

After the trial, the actor networks were altered by three challenges. First, O2 was unsatisfied with the business model proposed by Arqiva (Figure 4), so a conflict of interests was emerging. Arqiva is being forced to change its strategy because mobile service providers are its present and future customers. Now the mobile-TV trial in Ireland is dominated by O2 with support from Arqiva.

The second challenge for mobile-TV at this time is that the government, a new actor, has not allocated the spectrum for DVB-H.

The key requirement is the availability of spectrum in order to operate this broadcast service. In the UK, at the moment, there is no allocated spectrum for DVB-H, and a decision is required from the UK government (Ofcom) about whether and when this will become available. ....There is a desire to have the spectrum available sooner given the progress being made in other parts of

Table 3. **Feedback from 3G and DVB-H Mobile-TV Users**

	3G Mobile-TV Users in Our Interviews	DVB-H Mobile-TV Users in Oxford
Whole reaction	Mobile-TV was "nice-to-have" on the 3G phones because the mobile-TV users were price-sensitive and uncertain about its value.	The majority of the users were in favor of mobile-TV, with 83% of them "satisfied" with the service, and 76% prepared to taking the service up within 12 months.
Motives for the first use	They used mobile-TV due to curiosity and free trial. Price was a key determinant on whether users would continue to use it. They were unsatisfied with the existing pricing model and agreed that a monthly fee with unlimited usage would be better.	N/A
Preferred location or time	They seldom watched mobile-TV at home but preferred to use it during the commute, waiting time, traveling overseas, and at lunch breaks.	They used mobile-TV mainly at home, at work and on the daily commute. Traffic demand was highest in the mornings, lunch times and early evenings.
Favorite genre of content	News was the most favorite genre for mobile-TV. The user behaviors of watching mobile-TV and TV were very different.	The most favorite genres were news, soaps, music, documentaries, and sports. During the lunch break, viewers preferred news, sports and their favorite daytime soaps. One third of the users were looking for "made for mobile" programming and even some long-form content (e.g., movies).
Rule of decision-making on continuing usage	The users could give up Vodafone free mobile-TV for O2 low-price promotion of mobile phone. The priority on content variety or system stability was depended.	A wide range of channels and well-known brand channels were wanted. Additional factors were ease of use and high-quality pictures/ sounds.

Source: O2 (2006), Slocombe (2006), and interviews for this paper.

Europe, as the UK could be left behind, although the regulators have been competing demands for the spectrum not only from mobile companies but also from TV channels to offer high-definition TV services (Anonymous interviewee with O2).

The third challenge for DVB-H mobile-TV is the difficulty of reconciling mobile service providers interests in a competing technology to the 2G-3G-4G route. The mobile service providers are the gatekeepers to user access, and most of them have invested significant money in upgrading their system from 2G to 3G, and even 4G. If the 4G technologies are perceived to provide better performance in both two-way data transmission and mobile-TV broadcasting, they may wish to defer investment and avoid being locked into the DVB-H network.

Finally, the feedback from the trial users is not only an outcome, but also a future influence on the reinvention of mobile-TV. At the same time, customer preferences are produced and formed through trials and initial customer adoption. The joint shaping of both producers and customers suggests that context is a constellation of actor influences and actions, changing as well as being changed by other actor behaviors. This raises new possibilities for the study of context in diffusion research, as discussed next.

5   DISCUSSION

The early IDT led us to infer that the speed and effect of diffusion was determined by relatively static and independent contexts, filled with factors. Our analysis of this case using ANT, however, suggests that the context is composed of various actors, defining their identities and changing their interests. The actor network composition and enrolments are dynamic, thus producing a fast-changing context for any particular actor, resulting in innovation with high uncertainty. A possible implication of this is that closer examinations of the forming and reshaping of actor networks could produce better understanding of how the current and future contexts affect the production and diffusion of innovations. Several substantive issues in our case highlight this possibility.

5.1   Linkages between Context and IT Production and Diffusion

The shape and form of IT production and diffusion depends upon the production and dissolution of actors and their engagement with each other. For example, despite the initial formation of the DVB-H network, its continuance depends on a number of future forces which could dissolve it. An instance is that the relative advantage perceived by suppliers in this trial was mostly the result of downstream speed and the unlimited connectivity of users to DVB-H technology. However, if O2 decides to focus on 4G mobile-TV because of its consistency with 2G and 3G networks, the DVB-H network might dissolve. Other forces like the spectrum lease delay or unenthusiastic user response may also alter the trajectory and continuance of DVB-H network.

5.2   Nature of IT Production and Diffusion Changes
as the Actor Network Grows

Even if an IT network doesn't dissolve, its shape and direction changes as new actors are attracted and enrolled into it, their interests both translating and affecting the network composition and direction. For example, if DVB-H becomes more widely accepted and used, DVB-H chip-design companies will become more involved in DVB-H mobile-TV if mobile service providers order customized handsets (e.g., big screen size, long battery life, and easy to use). This could prompt changes in content providers who come to see the medium as a new channel for their programming content. However, as the available content increases, the broadcast approach of DVB-H may become a limit on the available channels, which will then prompt other protocol suppliers and vendors to address this limitation, and so on.

5.3 Relations between Actors Positions and Relative Power

The positions and material circumstances of key actors determine the relative power of each in the network. An illustration is that content providers have a larger space to wait and see if DVB-H succeeds because (1) they can easily reformat their content for many mediums with low cost; (2) their lead time of producing content is relatively flexible, which allows them to alter ties with the other actors instantly if they change their mind; and (3) the well known content providers, supported by the user preferences for branded channels, acquires even more power to make conservative decisions. Specific events arising from this power relation includes Channel 4 refusal to broadcast live with Virgin Mobile-TV, and BBC's limiting involvement with mobile-TV producers to a year.

5.4 Surprises

ANT approaches to IT production and diffusion would also help in anticipating and explaining unanticipated changes in actor networks. For example, online users broke the separation between users and producers via blog, mobile video blog (MoVlog), or the other interactive and grassroots production systems. It is possible that mobile-TV could be used by amateurs and unknown producers to find audiences for their content through mobile service providers. The combination of voice, short messages, mobile-TV, or location-based services could bring in new approaches to interactive television. These new IT-based activities could churn and transform the contexts around entire industries, and may alter not only the production and diffusion of content but also the attention and interests among actors—customers, producers, and service providers. ANT thus opens up new possibilities for investigating how changes in actor positions and relations produce and render the contexts around IT production and diffusion.

6 CONCLUSION

This paper proposes that an ANT methodology could support two areas in diffusion research: the study of the dynamic diffusion process, and the role of many diverse players involved in the production and diffusion of IT innovations. In addition, the ANT methodology also contributes to our understanding of how adopters perceive their relative advantages in one or more networks, and how their involvement can reinvent the production and diffusion of innovations. To explore these possibilities through empirical data, a study of a mobile-TV trial in Oxford is provided. The findings show that combining IDT and ANT may provide a richer theoretical foundation in studying how the varying relations among actors affect the production and diffusion of IT innovation.

Future research is required to extend the coverage of contexts (e.g., 4G technologies) and actors (e.g., government) that influence the actor networks involved in the production and diffusion of mobile-TV. Furthermore, additional empirical studies could be conducted with other IT products or services, within different industries. Finally, it would be valuable to do a study of how adopters influence the reinvention of innovations by producers.

Reference

Allen, J. P. "Redefining the Network: Enrolment Strategies in the PDA Industry," *Information Technology & People* (17:2), 2004, pp. 171-185.

Avgerou, C. "The Significance of Context in Information Systems and Organizational Change," *Information Systems Journal* (11:1), 2001, pp. 43-63.

BBC News. "Major UK Mobile-TV Trial Starts," 2005 (available online at http://news.bbc.co.uk/1/hi/technology/4271474.stm).

Bradford, M., and Florin, J. "Examining the Role of Innovation Diffusion Factors on the Implementation Success of Enterprise Resource Planning Systems," *International Journal of Accounting Information Systems* (4:3), 2003, pp. 205-225.

Brown, L. *Innovation Diffusion*, London: Methuen, 1981.

Callon, M. "Some Elements of a Sociology of Translation: Domestication of the Scallops and the Fishermen of St Brieuc Bay," 1986 (available online at http://www.vub.ac.be/SOCO/tesa/RENCOM/Callon%20(1986)%20Some%20elements%20of%20a%20sociology%20of%20translation.pdf).

Chiasson, M., and Davidson, E. J. "Taking Industry Seriously in Information Systems Research," *MIS Quarterly* (29:4), December 2005, pp. 591-605.

Chiasson, M., and Lovato, C. "Factors Influencing the Formation of a User's Perceptions and Use of a DSS Software Innovation," *Advances in Information Systems* (32:3), 2001, pp. 16-35.

E-Consultancy. "UK TV-to-Mobile First for Endemol UK and Channel 4 as Live Broadcasts Are Sent to Mobile Phones," January 6, 2004 (available online at http://www.e-consultancy.com/news-blog/153837/uk-tv-to-mobile-first-for-endemol-uk-and-channel-4-as-live-broadcasts-are-sent-to-mobile-phones.html).

Fichman, R. G. "Going Beyond the Dominant Paradigm for IT Innovation Research: Emerging Concepts and Methods," *Journal of the Association for Information Systems* (5:8), 2004, pp. 314-355.

Geels, F. "Co-evolution of Technology and Society: The Transition in Water Supply and Personal Hygiene in the Netherlands (1850-1930)—A Case Study in Multi-Level Perspective," *Technology in Society* (27), 2005, pp. 363-397.

Hackney, R., Xu, H., and Ranchhod, A. "Evaluating Web Services: Towards a Framework for Emergent Contexts," *European Journal of Operational Research* (173), 2005, pp. 1161-1174.

Hong, S. J., and Tam, K. Y. "Understanding the Adoption of Multipurpose Information Appliances: The Case of Mobile Data Services," *Information Systems Research* (17:2), 2006, pp. 162-179.

King, J. L., Gurbaxani, V., Kraemer, K. L., McFarlan, F. W., Raman, K. S., and Yap, S. C. "Institutional Factors in Information Technology Innovation," *Information Systems Research* (5:2), 1994, pp. 139-169.

Kodama, M. "Technological Innovation through Networked Strategic Communities: A Case Study on a High-Tech Company in Japan," *Advanced Management Journal* (70:1), 2005, pp. 22-35.

Law, J. "Notes on the Theory of the Actor Network: Ordering, Strategy and Heterogeneity," 1992 (available online at http://www.lancs.ac.uk/fss/sociology/papers/law-notes-on-ant.pdf).

Law, J., and Hassard, J. *Actor Network Theory and After*, Boston, MA: Blackwell Publishers, 1999.

Lvytinen, K., and Yoo, Y. "Research Commentary: The Next Wave of Nomadic Computing," *Information Systems Research* (13:4), 2002, pp. 377-388.

Meyer, D. "Virgin Readies UK'ss First Mobile-TV Broadcasts," July 7, 2006 (available online at http://news.zdnet.co.uk/communications/0,1000000085,39278338,00.htm).

Murase, E. M. *Keitai Boomu: The Case of NTT DoCoMo and Innovation in the Wireless Internet in Japan*, unpublished Ph.D. dissertation, Stanford University, 2003.

O2. "Oxford Mobile-TV Trial Reveals Strong Consumer Demand for Multi-Channel Broadcast TV onto Their Mobile," Press Release, January 17, 2006 (available online at http://www.o2.com/media/press_releases/press_release_1298.asp).

Oh, S., and Lee, H. "How Technology Shapes the Actor–Network of Convergence Services: A Case of Mobile Banking," in D. Avison, D. Galletta, and J. I. DeGross (eds.), *Proceedings of the 26th International Conference on Information Systems*, Las Vegas, NV, 2005, pp. 483-493.

Orlikowski, W. J., and Iacono, C. S. "Research Commentary: Desperately Seeking the 'IT' in IT Research—A Call to Theorizing the IT Artifact," *Information Systems Research* (12:2), 2001, pp. 121-134.

Qualcomm. "MediaFLO FLO Technology Brief," May 6, 2005 (available online at http://www.qualcomm.com/mediaflo/news/pdf/flo_whitepaper.pdf).

Rogers, E. *Diffusion of Innovations* (4th ed.), New York: The Free Press, 1995.

Park, S., and Yoon, S. "Separating Early-Adopters from the Majority: The Case of Broadband Internet Access in Korea," *Technological Forecasting and Social Change* (72), 2005, pp. 301-325.

Shin, D. H. "Prospectus of Mobile-TV: Another Bubble or Killer Application," *Telematics and Informatics*, 2005, pp. 1-18.

Slocombe, M. "UK Mobile TV Trials Get Mixed Response," January 18, 2006 (available online at http://digital-lifestyles.info/display_page.asp?section=distribution&id=2927).

Södergård, C. (ed.). "Mobile Television—Technology and User Experience: Report on Mobile-TV Projects," VTT Publications, 2003 (available online at http://virtual.vtt.fi/inf/pdf/publications/2003/P506.pdf).

3G News. "Vodafone UK and SKY Team Up To Launch SKY Mobile-TV," 2005 (available online at http://www.3g.co.uk/PR/Nov2005/2133.htm).

Walsham, G., and Sahay, S. "GIS for District-Level Administration in India: Problems and Opportunities," *MIS Quarterly* (23:1), March 1999, pp. 39-66.

Williams, D. "Oxford Mobile-TV Trial," 2005 (available online at http://www.o2.com/media_files/oxford_mobile_tv.pdf).

About the Authors

Su-Yi Lin is a Ph.D. student in the Department of Management Science at Lancaster University. Su-Yi's research examines the interactions among societies, technologies, and management issues. Her interests include IT diffusion, convergence services, e-commerce, digital content, change management, and the social effects of the Digital Age. Su-Yi can be reached by e-mail at s.lin5@lancaster.ac.uk.

Mike Chiasson is a senior lecturer in the Department of Management Science at Lancaster University. Mike's research examines the relationships between institutional contexts and the development and implementation of information systems. His work includes action research, user involvement, IT diffusion, privacy, outsourcing, and social foundations of IS development and use. Mike can be reached by e-mail at m.chiasson@lancaster.ac.uk.

22 WORKING WITH TECHNOLOGY IN COMPLEX NETWORKS OF INTERACTION

Riikka Vuokko
Helena Karsten
University of Turku
Turku, Finland

Abstract   *Contemporary issues such as increases in operational scope, connectivity, and dynamism in organizations have meant also a corresponding increase of complexity in producing everyday interaction. A simple task on the individual level can be approached as a part of complicated whole or even as adding to complexity on the organizational level. In this paper, we compare two strong metaphors for studying complex nonlinear interaction in heterogeneous networks: complexity theory and actor-network theory. Both examine socio-technical phenomena as evolving in ongoing negotiations of participants within complex networks. Understanding complex networks can add to our understanding of relationships between social actors and technical artefacts, that is, of information systems in use. As an example, we introduce a study of work practices in intensive care. We argue that this work is carried out as multiple and interdependent interactions further generating complexity in a network of humans, technical artefacts, and other materials. In such socio-technical networks, work practices, new technology, and work processes are negotiated or made irreversible through the actions of participants.*

Keywords   Actor network theory, complexity theory, work practices, intensive care

1   INTRODUCTION

Research often strives for rationalization or simplification by ordering, dividing, and excluding in order to abstract or to reduce real world phenomena (Mol and Law 2002). But what if simplicity and complexity, or order and complexity, are not opposites? What if

Please use the following format when citing this chapter:

Vuokko, R., and Karsten, H., 2007, in IFIP International Federation for Information Processing, Volume 235, Organizational Dynamics of Technology-Based Innovation: Diversifying the Research Agenda, eds. McMaster, T., Wastell, D., Ferneley, E., and DeGross, J. (Boston: Springer), pp. 331-342.

production of organizational working life is a more complex matter, for the lack of a better word? At work, a phenomenon that is simple for one actor on a local level can be viewed by others as complicated or even as adding to complexity. Carrying out a specific task in an organizational process can be approached as a simple thing. But what if many actors carry out these same tasks, or if the single tasks add up to a more complicated whole? Then work can be approached as complicated and consisting of various clearly defined components, such as work processes, roles, and tasks, that add to the "system" as a whole. The perspective changes even more when we try to understand the organizational dynamics of a system that consists of a large number of interacting and overlapping parts whose actions cannot be predicted but who can share and retain information of their past and whose development can be seen as a continuum. Our object of study can be then described as complex.

Cilliers (1998) emphasizes that the notions *complex* and *complicated* have different meanings. A computer, for example, can be a complicated system that constitutes of a multitude of parts, but its functioning can be described and understood through its parts. A brain, for example, is a complex system that cannot be fully analyzed through understanding its components. The interactions within the system, with other systems, and with its environment are too complex to be understood simply by cutting up the system. Cilliers (p. 2) states that "complexity entails that, in a system, there are more possibilities than can be actualized." In the opinion of Mol and Law (2002, p. 1), "there is complexity if things relate but don't add up, if events occur but not within the process of linear time, and if phenomena share a space but cannot be mapped in terms of a single set of three-dimensional coordinates."

Contemporary trends and issues, such as changes occurring in the operational scope of organizations; increases in computing power and connectivity between people, applications and devices; and increased dynamism, uncertainty and discontinuity in organizational life have all contributed to the growth of complexity in working environments (Cohen 1999; Desai 2005; Jacucci et al. 2006; Merali 2004). As organizations change, the study of organizational dynamics needs new approaches. Traditional frameworks of technological innovations, such as diffusion of innovations (Gallivan 2001), approach socio-technical change from the perspective of individual autonomy and individual adoption or rejection, although that is hardly the case in organizations with a multitude of interconnected actors. Complexity is an increasingly common research theme in economics, organization science, and social theory (Anderson 1999; Jacucci et al. 2006), and although it is not entirely new in information systems either, the lack of a practically defined methodology has hindered its use (Merali 2004).

Information systems have been described as webs of socio-technical elements composed of both social and technical items (Kling and Scacchi 1982) or, for example, as work systems (Alter 1999) but applying complexity theory would mean a paradigm shift away from the classic definition of information systems as consisting of discrete components or subsystems to an approach of dynamically engaged and interconnected systems or networks of systems (Jacucci et al. 2006; Merali 2004). Anderson (1999, p. 217) states that modeling nonlinear outcomes of many interacting components and interdependent variables has proved to be difficult as "simple boxes-and-arrows causal models are inadequate." We propose that combining complexity with a network metaphor would increase understanding about the relationship between actors, technological artefacts, and information systems in use, or technology-in-practice (Orlikowski 2000).

Orlikowski argues that structuration theory (Giddens 1984) does not sufficiently describe technology as structure similar to social structures and as enabling or constraining action. Such an interpretation contradicts Giddens' original definition of structures as modalities of action, as memory traces. We argue that actor-network theory and complexity theory could provide a deeper understanding of socio-technical relations, or of information systems in use as complex and parts of working context.

Introducing new technologies to a working context can have manifold consequences. Star (1992) calls technological implementation a "Trojan door" with unexpected consequences, while she describes how the action and actors are dependent on their motivation, location, and causality of events as well as on their situated and distributed cognition. It is part of human nature to attempt to control system complexity and uncertainty (Tan et al. 2005) as an unknown creates discomfort and, especially in organizations, feelings of insecurity and powerlessness. Tan et al. (2005) note that although it is not always possible to control complex behavior, it may be possible to develop an understanding of its characteristics. Even in routine computing, individual tailoring and fitting occurs, and negotiations of shared work practices are needed. Karsten (2003) states that inter-dependencies between organizational actors and interdependencies between work tasks are being constantly formed and dismantled in working environments—especially when change "has become a way of life in organizations" (p. 437). According to Desai (2005), most naturally occurring processes are complex and an actor manages by being adaptable. In an organizational context, when dealing with complex situations, flexibility and adaptability are needed in a sense "that systems or processes are not frozen because they are too tightly constrained nor are they dysfunctional such that they disintegrate due to too little order" (Desai 2005, p. 34).

A recent topic in science and technology studies, and especially in studies framed with actor-network theory (Latour 2005; Moser and Law 2006) is complexity. In heterogeneous and socio-technical networks, all kinds of elements can interact in producing the social and the technical (Latour 2005; Law 1992). Knox et al. (2006) base the fascination of networks or network metaphor on the ubiquity of networks in the contemporary world, and state that one of the founding questions in network approaches is rearticulation of social relations as action and performance. The network metaphor has made it possible to address the mobility and complexity in social systems, and to describe socio-technical artefacts and relations.

Our research interest is to examine the dynamics and totality of interaction in a socio-technical network, which in our case is an intensive care unit in a university hospital. Orlikowski (1996) feels that complex work situations, environmental, technological, and organizational premises can facilitate patterns of working which cannot be "explained or prescribed by appealing to *a priori* plans and intentions" (p. 65). Instead, she continues, emergent change of working practices is approached as ongoing and grounded activities of organizational actors. This view demands reconceptualizing the use and development of information systems in the light of rising complexity (Jacucci et al. 2006). Heterogeneous socio-technical elements, such as system specifications and requirements, high costs and risks, several stakeholder groups with divergent interests, a large group of potential users, and different organizational resources like skills, may increase the level of complexity when implementing large-scale systems (Star and Ruhleder 1996) in established institutions (Chae and Lanzara 2006, Tan et al. 2005). Here, we examine the theories of complexity and actor networks to compare what kind of conceptual tools they could provide for studying socio-technical change in an institution with a long history. We then briefly introduce our research proposal for studying interactions in an intensive care unit where human and nonhuman actors engage every day in multiple ways.

2   APPROACHING COMPLEXITY

2.1   Complicated or Complex?

Jacucci et al. (2006) propose that the complexity of any technology utilization in contemporary organizations should be addressed from socio-technical and organizational viewpoints in environments where there are systems consisting of large numbers of self-organizing agents that interact in a dynamic, nonlinear fashion and share a path-dependent history (Cilliers 1998). To explore how intensive care nurses might experience working in an environment that consists of complex connectivity between various types of actors, the classic systems paradigm view is no longer sufficient (Merali 2004). According to Merali (2004), in the systems paradigm, information systems are conceptualized as holistic, well-defined systems that have clear boundaries that they strive for stability. Such systems can be complicated in that they consist of many components. In contrast to this, complex systems cannot be sufficiently understood by dividing them to components or subsystems. Merali describes the new information technology in organizations as a facilitator of complex, adaptive systems that have different features and that connect a diversity of entities through various and multiple channels. Behavior of a complex system is hard to predict because it is nonlinear and emergent (Anderson 1999; Kim and Kaplan 2006).

According to Cilliers (1998), complex systems are often systems that are grappling with their environment. There is a need to adapt to a changing environment simply to survive and to develop further. In order to adapt and to respond to changes, complex systems have to be able to gather and store information for future use, and to self-organize when necessary. Merali identifies five characteristics of complex adaptive systems grounded in a connectionist definition of networks. First, complex systems consist of interconnected "nodes" or actors that can communicate with each other and process information. Second, from the connectivity between a network's actors emerges a topology of the network. Third, as each actor within a network both constitutes and uses it, information circulating within a network gives rise to potential complexity, that is, to emergent diversity of information. The same message can be transmitted through various connections within the network, and the message is prone to change into multiple versions because the the interpretations given at different nodes by different actors. Fourth, the local action and the information diversity in a network can give rise to emergent global behavior, especially if we consider the actors of a network to have bounded rationality or limited knowledge and free will to take action. Fifth, boundaries are not useful in defining complex systems as holistic units. The relationship between a network system and its environment is reflexive and ambiguous. This relationship is also prone to change in time as a network's connectivity is dynamic.

Merali's (2004, p. 419) definitions of complex adaptive systems are grounded in complexity theory: "The 'science of complexity' is concerned with studying how collective behaviors of the focal system as a whole arise from the nonlinear interactions of its constituents with each other and with the environment." According to Merali, ontological constructs based on complexity theory would suggest a focus on complex network systems and on the dynamic and emergent properties within them. Epistemologically, this would mean studying such systems in their own environments, and focusing on emergent phenomena. This would also suggest describing network "dynamics in continuous time, as histories rather than snapshots" (Merali 2004, p. 439).

Complexity theory has not been used much in information system research but some examples can be found. Tan et al. (2005) combine complexity theory with chaos theory to outline the complexities of service delivery systems in health care organizations. Chae and Lanzara (2006) combine complexity theory with institutional theory to study large-scale technological change. Kim and Kaplan (2006) and Merali (2002) inspect the use of technology as or within a large complex system that includes the organization and its actors. Moser and Law (2006) combine complexity theory with actor-network theory to explore meaning and relevance of information in health care decision making. Kaghan and Bowker (2001) study the nature of socio-technical systems by comparing different research traditions of complexity and network metaphor. Kaghan and Bowker, Kim and Kaplan, and Moser and Law also suggest that complexity theory and actor-network theory are studying the same phenomena.

2.2 Studying Networks with Actor Network Theory

Actor network theory (Callon 1991; Latour 1991, 1992, 2005; Law and Callon 1995) has been used to study and describe large and complex networks of technological innovation and change. Especially in so-called "after ANT"—that is, the last 10 years' update in actor-network theory—there has been considerable attention given to complexity issues (Moser and Law 2006). In general, networks constitute a relevant social group (Bijker 1995) of actors that negotiate and interact with each other to solve a shared "problem." For example, in our study, the main social actors are the nurses and doctors. There are also other relevant actors in intensive care units such as technical artefacts, organizational rules, and scripts (Law and Callon 1995).

Howcroft et al. (2004) contend that a new technology is conceived when a relatively stable heterogeneous network of aligned interests is created and maintained. Development and implementation of technologies involves the building of alliances between various actors and this includes individuals and groups, as well as "natural" entities such as machines. Thus, both the social and the technical are involved as the actors are enrolled into a network. As the network evolves, the nature of the project and the identities and interests of the actors are themselves transformed (Law and Callon 1995). The results of the transformation process, translation, are subsequently inscribed into technologies (Walsham and Sahay 1999). Translation refers both to the process and the result of action (Latour 1991).

Black-boxing (Callon 1991; Howcroft et al. 2004; Kaghan and Bowker 2001) is another key process in actor-network theory that describes the effects of closure. When a phenomenon or a subnetwork becomes irreversible or has frozen elements, it is black-boxed or "closed" by drawing boundaries around it. This makes it possible for other actors within the network to treat the black box as a simple input/output device whose internal organization or operational rationality is indifferent to them. Black boxes are outcomes of socio-technical negotiations and as such, they can later be opened or renegotiated if new challenges appear within the network.

According to Scott and Wagner (2003), during the negotiation processes, many actors become involved and present varied interpretations of future. Translations are often accompanied by compromises and only some interests survive obligatory passage points. The temporalities that survive these trials develop strong characteristics of irreversibility. This indicates that if a translation of, for example, new working practices succeeds, it will be hard to cancel the development later on. Howcroft et al. argue that the emerging inscriptions (Akrich 1992) show the rationalizing effect of technology in a sense that social actors receive them as standardization or constraints of behavior. Scott and Wagner also note that durable time (Latour 1991) comes with a cost: the negotiations and compromises can become a hindrance to future development.

3   COMPARING COMPLEXITY THEORY AND ACTOR-NETWORK THEORY

Both complexity theory and actor-network theory deal with connected assemblages, that is, networks of interconnected nodes (Cilliers 1998; Latour 2005). From the interactions between the heterogeneous members of a network appear emergent properties shaping the future development. According to Kim and Kaplan (2006) and to Kaghan and Bowker (2001), both theories describe the unexpectedness of a change influenced by the local or situational features. Actor-network theory approaches the world as socio-technical, and in complexity theory the world is fundamentally organic.

These networks (Cilliers 1998; Latour 2005) are relatively stable but not in any way frozen in time or space. Instead, developing further is a continuum. Complexity theory does not describe an end-point that could be reached and in actor-network theory the process of translation is never-ending, the multiple and complex "ordering" is never finished (Moser and Law 2006). Both theories acknowledge, however, that the networks or the actions of networks' members can be constrained by previous choices and that, in a sense, networks are defined by path-dependency.

In complexity theory, it is not relevant to define the boundaries of a system or a network (Cilliers 1998; Merali 2004). More relevant is to explore the permeability of boundaries. In an organizational setting, this could mean studying how working over department or unit barriers is arranged and carried on. In actor-network theory, weight is put on defining a network or the group of "us" by setting clear boundaries. Non-members or "anti-group" (Latour 2005) have a role in underlining the differences between those included in and those excluded from a network.

Complexity theory provides a usable metaphor. Complex adaptive systems were first an area of interest in studies of organic systems, linguistics, and artificial intelligence (Anderson 1999; Cilliers 1998; Merali 2004). The idea of complex adaptive systems was used in laboratory experiments as simplification devices (Merali 2004; Mol and Law 2002), and the metaphor is "stretched" when studying individual agents and action in social settings (Anderson 1999; Kim and Kaplan 2006).

Network has been a prevailing metaphor for studies emphasizing connectedness in, for example, information science, organization science, and sociology (Castells 2000;

Cilliers 1998; Kling and Scacchi 1982; Merali 2004; Latour 2005). A network is dynamic, and has flexibility and adaptability to survive. In a network metaphor, interconnectivity has been described as negotiable, as voluntary or open-ended, or even as unpredictable. As such, the metaphor has fitted well to describe contemporary organizations and the changes in working life. In research, it means recognition of fragmentation and complexity (Knox et al. 2006).

The network metaphor has been criticized for a lack of clear definitions, or for having multiple meanings (Cohen 1999; Doolin and Lowe 2002; Kaghan and Bowker 2001; Latour 2005). There is no agreement about what kind of nodes and relations comprise a network. As such, power relations can be left undefined or even neglected when using the network metaphor. Kaghan and Bowker (2001) criticize that rationalist or functionalist approaches in network theories have tendencies of determinism, for example, when professionals or managers are portrayed as the "brains" that lead and regulate a change process. The network metaphor has also been criticized because it lacks the power to describe how change actually happens. Knox et al. (2006, p. 134) state this as follows: "As soon as the network itself becomes a blueprint for spatial relations, that is, as soon as it stops challenging and starts prescribing, then the productive capacity of the network is diminished."

Actor-network theory has been criticized from various viewpoints (Howcroft et al. 2004). First of all, there is the notion of symmetry. In actor-network theory, social and technical, or human and nonhuman, actors are seen as inseparable and thus they should be studied using same concepts. This has been seen as a radical explanation but at the same time intellectually and morally problematic as it allows human actors to be reduced to mere objects (Howcroft et al. 2004; Walsham and Sahay 1999). Latour (2005) explains that relevant actors within a network or in a given situation are all those present and participating without which it would be problematic to perform the task at hand. Thus, for example, to hit a nail, the hammer is as essential as the human actor with the knowledge to use the hammer.

Claims have been made that actor-network theory concentrates on micro-level or local studies, leaving out macro-level or global considerations (Howcroft et al. 2004; Knights and Murray 1994). This implies that social structures are not taken into consideration and that only a limited number of possibilities are accepted for the process of translation. Of the possibilities or technological trajectories available, only some are chosen, but actor-network theory does not clearly tell who or what is responsible of this choosing, or how the choices are later evaluated (Kim and Kaplan 2006). This is connected to the criticism that actor-network theory has an amoral stance as there is no regard to social consequences of technological choice, or about the inclusion or exclusion of members in a network. Star (1991) has described such irreversible networks of technological change as "networks of the powerful." Claims have been made that actor-network theory has a flat ontology because it takes institutions into consideration while studying how networks are constituted (Doolin and Lowe 2002; Knights and Murray 1994; Rose and Jones 2005). Similarly, it leaves out gender issues in technological change narratives (Howcroft et al. 2004).

Another characteristic common to in complexity theory and actor-network theory is that neither is a clearly defined theory, ready-to-use (Callon 2005; Cilliers 1998; Walsham and Sahay 1999). Instead both have been revised and further developed (Kaghan and Bowker 2001; Kim and Kaplan 2006).

4   STUDYING COMPLEXITY IN INTENSIVE CARE

Nursing work practices are being reformed as nurses are utilizing information technology in their working environment, for example, using electronic patient information systems. The work practices consist of a complex set of both standardized and situational arrangements—partly grounded in laws—that nurses carry out in their everyday work. An intensive care unit is a small component in the overall structure of health care, but at the same time, it is a complex system that involves surgeons and assisting physicians, anesthesiologists, nurses, supporting staff, and multiple mechanical or electronic devices. These actors are influenced by their roles, skills, and personality as well as hospital guidelines and situational arrangements. Berg (2004, pp. 36-37) describes the interwoven nature of information technology and care practices to be "such that it actually makes no sense to speak of the "consequences" or "impact" of information technology" as the development is "too complex for identifying such simple, causal lines." In the intensive care wards in Turku University Hospital, the co-construction of organizational practices and the use of information technology have not been previously studied from the perspective of complex interaction. Nursing documentation practices have been studied from the perspective of ethical issues in relation to intelligent systems and that of the possibilities of data mining of electronic patient records (e.g., Suominen et al. 2005, 2006). In intensive care, there are situations that require rapid action and care. It is essential to study how the nursing work practices are carried out *in situ*, how the nurses take action based on the information both from the situation and from electronic sources, and, in general, how information technology can be used to support nursing work.

In this study, we explore nurses working in three information environments (Lamb et al. 2003) as in intensive care there are different ways to arrange working, and various developmental stages of receiving and utilizing work information. First, in the intensive care unit for children, we can inspect a situation where work practices are being carried out "in the old way" and the use of electronic systems is still a matter under consideration. Second, the intensive care unit for adult patients already has experience using information technology as the various information systems have been a part of the everyday routine for some time now. It is possible in this environment to observe how information technology and other technological artefacts are being used together in care work.

From these initial cases, interesting questions arise. Using information technology affects working arrangements and organization of work. One aspect of technology use is that it can make work processes more transparent while at the same time hiding other aspects of work. Nurses have admitted feelings of losing their grip on the work when the care information has been transformed into electronic data. Based on a description of work practices, we can reflect on the differences of work practices in an environment where information technology is already in routine use and is considered an inseparable part of daily work with an environment only beginning to consider its use. In this context, we can study how information technology supports nurses' action-taking and decision-making.

While our aim is to understand how technology is used, it is not sufficient to only state that electronic records are used to support nursing work. More important is to find how textual and symbolic information is used, and what other type of information might be available to support fluid working. Both complexity theory and actor-network theory would suggest mapping out what other technologies are used and how these add to the picture of everyday working in the intensive care unit: what constitutes the integrated environment of interaction between heterogeneous actors? Furthermore, to assess further changes in work, it is important to inspect what information technology hides and reveals in the work, and how nurses react to these changes—for example, do they work around the problem situations, or does large-scale deconstruction of working practices take place? Or do they simply render technology to more simplified units through black-boxing it?

Third, in intensive care, the next step in health and medical informatics is the utilization of intelligent systems to receive technical support for daily care work. Intelligent systems are contemporary phenomena adding to rising complexity at work. Intelligent systems have largely stayed as a topic for more mathematically oriented research (e.g., Fenton et al. 2001), and in information systems they have attracted only moderate interest. No single reference sufficiently covers the research of intelligent systems from the viewpoint of supporting work practices and workers' action taking. Complexity theory suggests studying how interaction occurs in nonlinear fashion, how the actors adapt to changing environment, and how the actors are able to transform their practices, that is, the kind of new practices that emerge from action. Further, complexity theory suggests studying how emergent features are then transferred within the network and either what kind of diversity emerges, or what kind of path-dependence may constrain the development.

The plan is to carry out data gathering and analysis with qualitative ethnographic methods (e.g., Strauss and Corbin 1998) that aim for understanding a phenomenon in its everyday working context by observations and interviews. Using ethnographic methods fits well to theories of complexity and actor networks (Kaghan and Bowker 2001; Knox et al. 2006; Latour 2005) as in the former, emphasis is on emergent action in its environment, and in the latter, ethnographic analysis has longer traditions. The network metaphor provides a challenge to rigidity and as such it is a significant tool for analysis. The complexity metaphor allows us to analyze on-going interaction in open networks. Together, they make it possible to construct a picture of how large socio-technical networks are produced, and reproduced when innovations are introduced in them.

To summarize the conceptualization of our study plan, the main concepts derived from complexity theory and actor-network theory that will be used to guide the data gathering and the data analysis are listed in Table 1.

Table 1. **Conceptual Tools for the Study**

	Concepts for Studying Intensive Care Working
Actor-network theory	• Actor, actant (social and technical) • Network of shared interests • Transformation processes (translation, black-boxing)
Complexity theory	• Complex, nonlinear interaction • Self-organizing nature (reflexivity) • Adaptation to changing environment or situation • Bounded rationality of local action (path dependency) • Emergent interaction, emergent knowledge

5   CONCLUSIONS

In this paper, we have described work as carried out in multiple and interdependent inter-actions that further generate complexity in a network of humans, technical artefacts, and other materials. In such socio-technical networks, work practices as well as new tech-nology or work processes are negotiated, constructed, and made irreversible through the actions of participants. The actors can respond to their environments in many unpredict-able ways, so emergent behavior may result at various levels of the system. We argued that, for example, structuration theory has not been able to sufficiently describe the nature of information systems in use, and that combination of complexity theory and actor-net-work theory could provide an important new approach for studying changing work prac-tices and innovations in contemporary organizations. We have also shown how this could be carried out by introducing our study in an intensive care context where new innovations are part of continuous change and negotiation of how work is best carried out.

References

Akrich, M. "The De-Scription of Technical Objects," in W. E. Bijker and J. Law (eds.), *Shaping Technology/Building Society. Studies in Socio-technical Change*, Cambridge, MA: The MIT Press, 1992, pp. 205-224.

Alter, S. "A General, Yet Useful Theory of Information Systems," *Communications of AIS* (1:13), 1999.

Anderson, P. "Complexity Theory and Organization Science," *Organization Science* (10:3), 1999, pp. 216-232.

Berg, M. *Health Information Management: Integrating Information Technology in Health Care Work*, London: Routledge, 2004.

Bijker, W. E. *Of Bicycles, Bakelites, and Bulbs. Toward a Theory of Sociotechnical Change*, Cambridge, MA: The MIT Press, 1995.

Callon, M. "Techno-Economic Networks and Irreversibility," in J. Law (ed.), *A Sociology of Monsters: Essays on Power, Technology and Domination*, London: Routledge, 1991, pp. 132-161.

Castells, M. "Toward a Sociology of the Network Society," *Contemporary Sociology* (29:5), 2000, pp. 693-699.

Chae, B., and Lanzara, G. F. "Self-Destructive Dynamics in Large-Scale Technochange and Some Ways of Counteracting It," *Information, Technology & People* (19:1), 2006, pp. 74-97.

Cilliers, P. *Complexity and Postmodernism: Understanding Complex Systems*, London: Routledge, 1998.

Cohen, M. "Commentary on the Organization Science," *Organization Science* (10:3), Special Issue on Complexity, 1999, pp. 373-376.

Desai, A. "Adaptive Complex Enterprises," *Communications of the ACM* (48:5), 2000, pp. 33-35.

Doolin, B., and Lowe, A. "To Reveal Is to Critique: Actor-Network Theory and Critical Information Systems Research," *Journal of Information Technology* (17), 2002, pp. 69-78.

Fenton, W. G., McGinnity, T. M., and Maguire, L. P. "Fault Diagnosis of Electronic Systems Using Intelligent Techniques: A Review," *IEEE Transactions on Systems, Man, and Cybernetics* (31:3), 2001, pp. 269-281.

Gallivan, M. J. "Organizational Adoption and Assimilation of Complex Technological Inno-vations: Development and Application of a New Framework," *Data Base for Advances in Information Systems* (32:3), 2001, pp. 51-85.

Giddens, A. *The Constitution of Society*, Cambridge, UK: Polity Press, 1984.

Howcroft, D., Mitev, N., and Wilson, M. "What We May Learn from the Social Shaping of Technology Approach," in J. Mingers L.Willcocks (eds.), *Social Theory and Philosophy for Information Systems*, Chichester, UK: Wiley, 2004, pp. 329-371.

Jacucci, E., Hanseth, O., and Lyytinen, K. "Introduction. Taking Complexity Seriously in IS Research. Information," *Technology and People* (19:1), 2006, pp. 5-11.

Kaghan, W. N., and Bowker, G. C. "Out of Machine Age? Complexity, Socio-Technical Systems and Actor-Network Theory," *Journal of Engineering and Technology Management* (18:3-4), 2001, pp. 253-269.

Karsten, H. "Constructing Interdependencies with Collaborative Information Technology," *Computer Supported Cooperative Work* (12:4), 2003, pp. 437-464.

Kim, R. M., and Kaplan, S. M. "Interpreting Socio-Technical Co-Evolution: Applying Complex Adaptive Systems to IS Engagement," *Information, Technology & People* (19:1), 2006, pp. 35-54.

Kling, R., and Scacchi, W. "The Web of Computing: Computer Technology as Social Organization," *Advances in Computers* (21), 1982, pp. 1-90.

Knights, D., and Murray, F. *Managers Divided: Organization Politics and Information Technology Management*, Chichester, UK: Wiley, 1994.

Knox, H., Savage, M., and Harvey, P. "Social Networks and the Study of Relations: Networks as Method, Metaphor and Form," *Economy and Society* (35:1), 2006, pp. 113-140.

Lamb, R., King, J. L., and Kling, R. "Informational Environments: Organizational Contexts of Online Information Use," *Journal of the American Society for Information Science and Technology* (54:2), 2003, pp. 97-114.

Latour, B. *Reassembling the Social. An Introduction to Actor-Network Theory*, Oxford, UK: Oxford University Press, 2005.

Latour, B. "Technology is Society Made Durable," in J. Law (ed.), *A Sociology of Monsters: Essays on Power, Technology and Domination*, London: Routledge, 1991, pp. 103-131.

Latour, B. "Where Are the Missing Masses? The Sociology of a Few Mundane Artifacts," in W. E. Bijker and J. Law (eds.), *Shaping Technology/Building Society. Studies in Socio-Technical Change*, Cambridge, MA: The MIT Press, 1992, pp. 225- 258.

Law, J. "Notes on the Theory of the Actor Network: Ordering, Strategy, and Heterogeneity," *Systems Practice* (5:4), 1992.

Law, J., and Callon, M. "Engineering and Sociology in a Military Aircraft Project: A Network Analysis of Technological Change," in S. L. Star (ed.), *Ecologies of Knowledge: Work and Politics in Science and Technology*, Albany, NY: State University of New York Press, 1995, pp. 281-301.

Merali, Y. "Complexity and Information Systems," in J. Mingers and L.Willcocks (eds.), *Social Theory and Philosophy for Information Systems*, Chichester, UK: John Wiley and Sons, Ltd., 2004, pp. 407-446.

Merali, Y. "The Role of Boundaries in Knowledge Processes," *European Journal of Information Systems* (11:1), 2002, pp. 47-60.

Mol, A., and Law, J. "Complexities: An Introduction," in J. Law and A. Mol (eds.), *Complexities. Social Studies of Knowledge Practices*, Durham, NC: Duke University Press, 2002.

Moser, I., and Law, J. "Fluids or Flows? Information and Qualculation in Medical Practice," *Information, Technology & People* (19:1), 2006, pp. 55-73.

Orlikowski, W. J. "Improvising Organizational Transformation Over Time: A Situated Change Perspective," *Information Systems Research* (7:1), 1996, pp. 63-92.

Orlikowski, W. J. "Using Technology and Constituting Structures: A Practice Lens for Studying Technology in Organizations," *Organization Science* (3:3), 2000, pp. 398-427.

Rose, J., and Jones, M. "The Double Dance of Agency: A Socio-Theoretic Account of How Machines and Humans Interact," *Systems, Signs & Actions*, (1:1), 2005, pp. 19-37.

Scott, S. V., and Wagner, E. L. "Networks, Negotiations, and New Times: The Implementation of Enterprise Resource Planning into an Academic Administration," *Information and Organization* (13), 2003, pp. 285-313.

Star, S .L. "Power, Technology and the Phenomenology of Conventions: On Being Allergic to Onions," in J. Law (ed.), *A Sociology of Monsters: Essays on Power, Technology and Domination*, London: Routledge, 1991, pp. 26-56.

Star, S. L. "The Trojan Door: Organizations, Work, and the 'Open Black Box,'" *Systems Practice* (5:4), 1992, pp. 395-410.

Star, S. L., and Ruhleder, K. "Steps Towards an Ecology of Infrastructure: Design and Access for Large Scale Information Spaces," *Information Systems Research* (7:1), 1996, pp. 111-134.

Strauss, A., and Corbin, J. *Basics of Qualitative Research: Techniques and Procedures for Developing Grounded Theory*, Thousand Oaks, CA: SAGE Publications, 1998.

Suominen, H. J., Lehtikunnas, T., Hiissa, M., Back, B., Karsten, H., Salakoski, T., and Salanterä, S. "Natural Language Processing for Nursing Documentation," paper presented at the Second International Conference on Computational Intelligence in Medicine and Health Care (CIMED), Lissabon, Portugal, June 29-July 1, 2005.

Suominen, H. J., Lehtikunnas, T., Hiissa, M., Back, B., Karsten, H., Salakoski, T., and Salanterä, S. "Theoretical Considerations of Ethics in Text Mining of Nursing Documents," paper presented at Nursing Informatics 2006, Seoul, South-Korea, June 11-14, 2006.

Tan, J., Wen, J., and Awad, N. "Health Care and Services Delivery Systems as Complex Adaptive Systems," *Communications of the ACM* (48:5), 2005, pp. 36-44.

Walsham, G., and Sahay, S. "GIS for District-Level Administration in India: Problems and Opportunities," *MIS Quarterly* (23:1), 1999, pp. 39-65.

About the Authors

Riikka Vuokko is a Ph.D. candidate in Turku University and TUCS. Her thesis topic is "Mobile Computing in Home Care: Longitudinal Study of Organizational Implementation." That work focuses on describing the emergent work processes after an implementation, and social issues such as interpretations of control, efficiency, and professional ethics. She participates in the Louhi project on text mining nursing documentation in intensive care (for additional information on the project, see http://www.med.utu.fi/hoitotiede/tutkimus/tutkimusprojektit/louhi/). Riikka can be reached by e-mail at riikka.vuokko@utu.fi.

Helena Karsten is a professor in Information Systems, with a focus on information technology and work, in the Department of Information Technology at the University of Turku, Finland. She is the leader of Zeta Emerging Technologies Adoption Laboratory in TUCS (see http://www.tucs.fi/research/labs/zeta.php). Her research interests include the interweaving of work and computers, the use of IT to support collaboration, and social theories informing theorizing in information systems. She is an associate editor for *The Information Society* and an editorial board member of *Information Technology & People*. Helena can be reached by e-mail at eija.karsten@cs.utu.fi.

Part 5:

Technological Interlude: The Case of RFID

23   RFID ADOPTION: Theoretical Concepts and Their Practical Application in Fashion

Claudio Huyskens
Claudia Loebbecke
University of Cologne
Cologne, Germany

Abstract   *Technology vendors increasingly praised RFID technology to improve tracking and replenishment in supply chain management (Vervest et al. 2004). Many companies, especially retailers, announced plans for quick RFID adoption. Despite obvious technology advantages, RFID adoption made only little progress in today's supply chains. This paper explores the discrepancy between RFID announcements and reality. From a literature review, the paper derives three theoretical concepts and ten associated factors of organizational technology adoption and diffusion. It then describes the RFID adoption by a fashion retailer that started with an RFID pilot and stretched the RFID roll-out process over several stages. In the description, the paper also briefly touches upon RFID diffusion in the fashion supply chain. Finally, the paper discusses to what extent each of the ten factors derived from the literature apply to RFID adoption and diffusion in the fashion industry. It discovers some factors, crucial for adoption and diffusion and others which play only a minor role. The paper closes with some conclusions and suggestions for further research.*

Keywords   Organizational technology adoption and diffusion, RFID, fashion industry, case study

1   INTRODUCTION

Since World War II, radio frequency identification (RFID) technology has been used for varying purposes ranging from detection of hostile warplanes to highway toll collection (Landt 2005).

Please use the following format when citing this chapter:

Huyskens, C., and Loebbecke, C., 2007, in IFIP International Federation for Information Processing, Volume 235, Organizational Dynamics of Technology-Based Innovation: Diversifying the Research Agenda, eds. McMaster, T., Wastell, D., Ferneley, E., and DeGross, J. (Boston: Springer), pp. 345-361.

The U.S. Department of Defense announced in the early 1990s that RFID technology held the potential to revolutionize "In-Transit-Visibility" and the "Total Asset Visibility" in supply chains (Kolleda 2005). The DoD's subsequent support for the technology encouraged many technology vendors to also push forward RFID development for commercial purposes (Liard 2003).

However, the value of RFID technology for managing business supply chains has only been recognized in recent years. The business press has since proclaimed that RFID marks a commercial innovation with the potential to soon replace barcode technology in the supply chains of numerous industries (*The Economist* 2003).

Incited by those developments and promises, companies from varying industries planned RFID adoption aiming to exploit cost saving potentials and new business opportunities (McGinity 2004). Early press releases by companies, such as METRO Group, Wal-Mart, and Tesco, outlined ambitious timelines for the implementation of RFID along their entire supply chains (Collins 2006).

However, several years after the first releases, very few projects have been completed, indicating that the process of RFID adoption and diffusion along supply chains is more complex than generally anticipated.

This paper attempts to clarify how the process of RFID adoption by companies and industry diffusion occurs and which factors are relevant in the process. It proceeds with a methodological argument for the case study approach for analyzing organizational adoption and industry diffusion issues. A review of the theoretical underpinnings of organizational adoption and diffusion of technology fuels the selection of theoretical concepts and associated factors for analyzing RFID adoption and diffusion. The paper describes the RFID adoption at Kaufhof Department Stores AG (Kaufhof), a German fashion retailer and subsidiary of METRO Group, and the RFID diffusion along the fashion supply chain. The discussion investigates to what extent existing theory on technology adoption and diffusion corresponds with the observed actions taken by Kaufhof and in the fashion industry. The paper closes with some conclusions and an outlook to future research.

2   RESEARCH METHODOLOGY

This paper utilizes a three stage research strategy to investigate the process of organizational RFID adoption by Kaufhof and RFID diffusion in the fashion industry.

In the quest for theoretical guidelines to set up a research design, we drew on the technology adoption and diffusion literature (see section 3). A longitudinal single fieldwork case study served as research method in order to adequately reflect the complexity of reality in an approach to explain the "how" in the technology adoption and diffusion process (Galliers 1992; Yin 2003). According to Yin's (1981) case study typology, this paper stresses the exploratory character.

In a second stage, we collected mainly qualitative data in the field. We gathered data from Kaufhof and its supply chain partners during the entire project between 2003 and 2006. In particular, we conducted semi-structured interviews with senior executives and project managers. The interviewees included a Kaufhof manager in charge of logistics, a Kaufhof manager heading all RFID related projects, and the managing director of METRO Group Information Technology. The interviews covered the overall adoption process. The questions emphasized participating organizations and their objectives, the measurement of fulfillment, and the respective implementation stage and schedule. During an industry event on RFID, we also acquired insights from IT managers and CIOs of fashion manufacturers regarding their RFID projects.

Additional data collection efforts involved publicly available company and market data (Benbasat et al. 1987). Minutes of meetings provided information concerning inter-organizational events not allowing direct observation. Financial reports added to the information base as they provided information on the project context, objectified measures, and official objectives tied to the adoption of RFID technology.

Ongoing data collection during the entire duration of the project assured the inclusion of management perspectives prior to project launch, during the pilot, and during the roll-out. The informal interview settings gave respondents the opportunity to be frank about their perceptions and impressions of the project. Reviewing results for inconsistencies and ambiguities and, if necessary, rechecking with interviewees reduced the risk of misconceptions. Finally, we presented the final case to METRO Group and Kaufhof executives to be corrected in terms of factual content.

In a third stage, we analyzed to what extent the theoretical arguments selected from the organizational technology adoption and diffusion literature corresponded with the RFID adoption and diffusion experiences gathered by Kaufhof and the fashion industry.

Admittedly, the single case study method lacks some generalizability compared to multiple cases or quantitative cross-sectional methods. However, the more appropriate representation of the adoption and diffusion processes weighs against that weakness.

3 THEORETICAL FOUNDATIONS: ORGANIZATIONAL TECHNOLOGY ADOPTION AND DIFFUSION

Rogers and Shoemaker (1971, p. 154) define adoption of innovations in general as "the relative speed with which an innovation is adopted by members of a social system." More specifically, Agarwal et al. (1997, p. 347) define organizational adoption of IS as the "first successful system using a new information processing technology." The information system may be used for either a product or an internal process.

Rooted in the field of social psychology, Fishbein and Ajzen (1975) with their theory of reasoned action (TRA) offer a marketing-oriented theoretical starting point for explaining customer adoption. Following TRA, individuals exhibit attitudes and conform to subjective norms. A combination of those elements determines the behavioral intention of individuals, which in turn causes behavior.

Davis, Bagozzi, and Warshaw (1989) employ the underlying argument of TRA and adapt the model to technology by proposing a technology acceptance model (TAM). Their main contribution lies in proposing perceived usefulness and perceived ease of use as concrete individual perceptions that replace the abstract beliefs forming attitudes in TRA. However, Bagozzi, Davis, and Warshaw (1992, p. 664) limit the causal structure of their model, indicating that "actual usage may not be a direct or immediate consequence," especially in case of problematic objects of behavior (e.g., adoption of specific software applications). Owing to this, Venkatesh and Davis (2000) later refine the model integrating social influence by third parties and cognitive processes by the individual into

TAM2. Applications of TAM2 include mandatory adoption contexts abstracting from free will, an assumption of TRA and TAM. However, TAM and TAM2 build on behavioral assumptions intended for individual adoption rather than contexts of organizational adoption.

According to Brown et al. (2002), in organizational contexts behavioral arguments exert less influence on actual adoption than in individual settings. Karahanna, Straub, and Chervany (1999) show that different drivers determine the adoption intentions of technology users and organizational adopters. For example, attitudes determine users' intentions with regard to adopting Windows in organizations, while normative pressure determines the intentions of actual organizational decision makers.

Institutional theories offer another research stream to explain organizational adoption and diffusion of technology. Zmud (1984) and Cooper and Zmud (1990) argue that rational organizational adoption decisions aim primarily at organizational goal achievement, which implies the subordinate objective of technological efficiency as technology adoption driver. This argument is in line with the finding of Brown et al. that organizational perception of usefulness differs from that of individuals (i.e., it relates to efficiency as opposed to individual goal achievement and satisfaction).

Resource dependency theories (Pfeffer and Salancik 1978) offer arguments concerning the power over resources. They are especially applicable, as supply chain contexts require technology adoption by all involved companies. Iacovou, Benbasat, and Dexter (1995) consider the existence of resources (e.g., IT sophistication) to determine organizational readiness for technology adoption. Small organizations often have fewer IT resources. In their resource dependency argument, Hart and Saunders (1997) indicate that interorganizational relationships comprise stronger and weaker partners with regard to resource allocation. They conclude that stronger organizations may drive the adoption of interorganizational technologies, while weaker organizations can only comply with adoption.

Westphal, Shortell, and Gulati (1997) and Konsynski and Tiwana (2004) identify either problem solving or the creation of business opportunity as a trigger for the adoption of total quality management, especially in interorganizational networks.

Overall, the different theoretical streams offer three groups of factors affecting organizational adoption: *external influences, perceived organizational benefits*, and *organizational characteristics* (Matta and Moberg 2006). Table 1 illustrates the three categories involving a total of ten factors influencing organizational technology adoption and diffusion.

3.1   External Influences

In the supply chain context, organizations adopt a technology or even a specific information system either due to coercive power imposed by a dominant organization (Iacovou et al. 1995; Jeyaraj et al. 2006) or based on free will (Moore and Benbasat 1991). The coercive power exerted by dominant companies has played a role in the adoption of electronic data interchange (EDI) in the supply chain (Hart and Saunders 1997; Premkumar 2000; Webster 1995) and in the adoption by electronic trading communities (Allen et al. 2000; Gerst and Bunduchi 2005). Depending on the supply chain, the question of which player has a dominant position varies from manufacturers in the automotive in-

Table 1. **Factors Influencing Organizational Technology Adoption and Diffusion**

Concept	Factor
External Influences	Coercive Pressure
	Isomorphic Pressure
	Information Availability
Perceived Organizational Benefits	Integration Efforts
	Standards Availability
	Quality of Service
	Financial Benefits
Organizational Characteristics	IT Commitment
	Top Management Support
	Organizational Size

dustry (Gerst and Bunduchi 2005), to wholesalers in pharmaceuticals (Naert and Swinnen 1977), and to retailers in fast moving consumer goods (Loebbecke 2004).

Adoption of innovative technologies exerts pressure on industry peers to follow the adoption. Such isomorphic pressure is exercised by capital markets (DiMaggio and Powell 1983; Haunschild and Miner 1997) and has been found in the context of adopting enterprise resource planning systems (Benders et al. 2006). Isomorphic pressure naturally threatens competitive advantages acquired by early movers (Clemons and Wang 2000).

Further, information availability on potentially relevant technology matters to potential adopters (Jeyaraj et al. 2006; Matta and Moberg 2006). Not only information on the existence of technology, but also information on potential solutions and the availability of adaptation and implementation know-how drive adoption. Concerning interorganizational relationships, information availability plays a role in EDI adoption (Walton and Gupta 1999; Shah et al. 2002) and in adoption of electronic markets by organizations (Dai 2002).

3.2 Perceived Organizational Benefits

Adoption of innovative IS along the supply chain and across interorganizational interfaces requires stronger integration efforts than IS adoption in intra-organizational environments (Iskandar et al. 2001; Briggs et al. 2003). McKeen and Smith (2002) investigate such adoption-related integration efforts in the context of enterprise application integration, Lee and Sohn (2003) concerning electronic marketplaces, and McLaren, Head, and Yuan (2002) with regard to EDI.

The availability of standards influences adoption because standards reduce the integration risk of multiple technological solutions implemented in a supply chain (Church and Gandal 1993; Kauffman and Techatassanasoontorn 2005). With regard to interorganizational information systems, EDI standards (Chwelos et al. 2001; Markus et al. 2006), standards for electronic marketplaces (Christiaanse and Markus 2003), and web services standards (Chen 2003) are relevant in adoption decisions.

Process innovations often build on preexisting systems. Therefore, they need to deliver comparable quality of service, avoiding interruptions or delays in the flow of information (Pitt et al. 1995; Watson et al. 1998). Insufficient service quality has a negative influence on adoption (Pitt et al. 1995). For instance, quality of service influences EDI adoption and diffusion due to its effect on performance (Ramamurthy et al. 1999).

Financial benefits, determined by the return on initial investments and the required operating costs, add to perceived organizational benefits (Eastin 2002; Matta and Moberg 2006).

3.3 Organizational Characteristics

Organizational IT commitment and top management support influence organizational adoption of innovative information systems (Cooper and Zmud 1990; Karahanna et al. 1999) as studied in the contexts of EDI (Premkumar et al. 1997), e-procurement technologies (Kauffman and Mohtadi 2004), electronic market platforms (Thatcher and Foster 2002), and open systems (Chau and Tam 1997).

Organizational size influences the adoption based on larger technology budgets and technological know-how (Kimberly and Evanisko 1981; Lai and Guynes 1997). Organizational size was found to be an adoption determinant for EDI (Iskandar et al. 2001; Premkumar et al. 1997), open systems (Chau and Tam 1997), and electronic markets (Palmer 2004).

4   RFID ADOPTION AT KAUFHOF AND DIFFUSION IN THE FASHION INDUSTRY

For more than a decade, increasing competition in the fashion industry put pressure on wholesale and retail prices and consequently on margins (*WIPO Magazine* 2005). The number of fashion cycles grew from 4 to 14 per year. Fashion manufacturers and retailers reacted to the challenges by increasingly considering innovative supply chain technologies such as RFID, without yet adopting them. They aimed at process and customer service improvements (Kurt Salmon Associates 2005). The multi-tier fashion supply chain comprised manufacturers, distributors, and retailers. It involved merchandise of varying price, packaging, and trends. Vendor managed inventory and seasonless retailing were barely feasible as supply chain members did not share sufficient data.

The following case covers RFID adoption at the department store chain Kaufhof (see also Loebbecke and Huyskens 2006) and describes the diffusion of RFID in the fashion industry (see Table 2 for the organizations involved and Figure 1 for the timeline of the Kaufhof RFID project).

In 2005, Kaufhof, a subsidiary of the world's third largest retailer, METRO Group, earned €69.2 million (1.92 percent operating margin). With 19,500 employees, it served more than two million customers who visited its more than 140 stores every day (METRO Group 2005). Kaufhof generated about half of its €3.6 billion turnover in the fashion sector.

Table 2. **Organizations and Their Functions in the Kaufhof RFID Project**

Organization	Function
METRO Group	Retailer
Kaufhof	Retailer
Gerry Weber	Manufacturer
Esprit	Manufacturer
Triumph	Manufacturer
METRO Group Information Technology	Shared services
EPCglobal	Industry association
GS1	Industry association
Impinj Inc.	Technology vendor

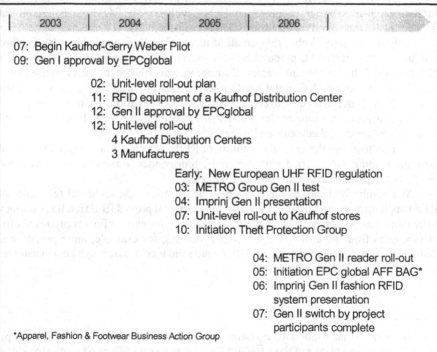

| 2003 | 2004 | 2005 | 2006 |

07: Begin Kaufhof-Gerry Weber Pilot
09: Gen I approval by EPCglobal

      02: Unit-level roll-out plan
      11: RFID equipment of a Kaufhof Distribution Center
      12: Gen II approval by EPCglobal
      12: Unit-level roll-out
          4 Kaufhof Distibution Centers
          3 Manufacturers

            Early: New European UHF RFID regulation
            03: METRO Group Gen II test
            04: Imprinj Gen II presentation
            07: Unit-level roll-out to Kaufhof stores
            10: Initiation Theft Protection Group

                  04: METRO Gen II reader roll-out
                  05: Initiation EPC global AFF BAG*
                  06: Imprinj Gen II fashion RFID
                        system presentation
                  07: Gen II switch by project
                        participants complete

*Apparel, Fashion & Footwear Business Action Group

Figure 1. **Timeline of Kaufhof's RFID Project**

4.1 The Kaufhof–Gerry Weber RFID Pilot

As Kaufhof considered a potential RFID adoption, it initiated an interorganizational RFID pilot with Gerry Weber[1] in July 2003 (Loebbecke and Palmer 2006). According to Wilfried Kanzok (2004), Head of Logistics Central Functions at Kaufhof, the main goal of the project running between July 1 and November 30, 2003 (see also METRO Group 2005), was to test the practical viability of RFID in everyday business. In detail, the project aimed at (1) investigating the efficiency improvement potential through RFID by accelerating and simplifying supply chain workflows, (2) analyzing the RFID potential for reducing supply chain shrinkage and increasing productivity through asset tracking, and (3) assessing the overall profitability of RFID investments.

Before approaching those objectives, Kaufhof and Gerry Weber had to make a decision with regard to the RFID *frequency*. Parallel utilization of the two available frequencies—high frequency (HF)[2] and ultra high frequency (UHF)[3]—would have implied redundant sets of equipment. In 2003, the International Standardization Organization (ISO) standardized only HF for unit level and for item level. Therefore, Kaufhof and Gerry Weber selected HF for both levels, even though the decision brought some limitations, such as shorter reading range. Hence, with the METRO Group RFID roll-out in November 2004, Kaufhof also used UHF for logistic units.

In the pilot, Gerry Weber shipped all of its merchandise contained in the Kaufhof product assortment from its production facilities via logistics service provider Meyer & Meyer to a Kaufhof distribution center. Kaufhof then distributed the merchandise to two selected stores. Gerry Weber and Kaufhof tested the full range of processes along the supply chain, from production, to tagging items and units,[4] various controls of incoming and outgoing goods, tracking and localization, inventory management, shelf management, theft prevention, and checkout (see Figure 2).

In order to assess the general suitability of RFID, Kaufhof and Gerry Weber tested how the reading rates varied with materials, transponder proximity, and speed and number of products traveling through RFID gates.

As a result, the Kaufhof–Gerry Weber pilot indicated the technical feasibility of RFID implementations along the fashion supply chain. It proved RFID reading accuracy to be more than 99 percent even under real-life circumstances. It further promised efficiency gains from enhancing supply chain processes, for example, more precise and faster inventory management (Kanzok 2006) and sales increases through better customer service (Loebbecke and Palmer 2006).

---

[1]Gerry Weber International AG is a German fashion and lifestyle company. In its 800 shops, Gerry Weber generated sales of about €400 million and 8 percent EBIT margin with a workforce of almost 1,700 in 2005.

[2]HF in this context refers to 13.56 MHz frequency, as used by Kaufhof, not to the entire HF band.

[3]UHF here refers to the 868 MHz frequency used by METRO Group and Kaufhof, and not to the entire UHF band.

[4]As key RFID code identifier on the tag Kaufhof and Gerry Weber used standardized European Article Number (EAN) along with proprietary product codes

Figure 2. **RFID Supply Chain Stages and Processes in the Kaufhof–Gerry Weber Pilot**

However, the pilot also raised concerns regarding transponder costs, readability, and standardization. Kaufhof opted to participate in initiatives to solve those issues and to continue to adopt RFID on a small and manageable scale in order to pursue RFID roll-out in phases rather than opting for an immediate full-scale implementation.

4.2 Kaufhof's RFID Adoption on Unit Level

In February 2004, METRO Group Information Technology, a METRO Group shared services department, crafted a plan to adopt RFID on logistic units destined for Kaufhof and Metro Cash & Carry.[5] Experiences from the METRO Group Future Store supermarket and the Kaufhof-Gerry Weber pilot along the fashion supply chain informed and justified the decision by METRO Group's board.

As a consequence of the executive decision, Kaufhof continued its RFID implementation in the regional distribution center in Neuss in November 2004.[6] Over a period of eight months, Kaufhof equipped four additional distribution centers. It reconfigured

---

[5]METRO Cash & Carry, a sales division of METRO Group, operates wholesale markets.

[6]The Kaufhof distribution center, entirely equipped with RFID technology, had already been the lynchpin in delivery to the METRO Group's Future Store supermarket (Loebbecke 2004) and in the Kaufhof–Gerry Weber pilot.

associated business processes, which no longer required manual counts of outgoing or incoming goods.

While Kaufhof had utilized HF RFID in its pilot, METRO Group and Wal-Mart focused on UHF for their unit-level RFID operations. Varying frequencies among RFID systems were challenging not only within METRO Group, but also along a multi-tier fashion supply chain. Looking for a resolution, METRO Group and Kaufhof, together with Wal-Mart, other user companies, and university labs engaged EPCglobal, an international nonprofit organization. In December 2004, EPCglobal approved the generation II (Gen II) standard. Gen II specified a UHF frequency range and thereby settled the open issue.

Following an internal debate over the switch to Gen II, in March 2005, METRO Group's Information Technology unit conducted lab trials in its Innovation Center in Neuss, Germany. Based on its own experiences, the downward compatibility of the standard, and presentations by RFID innovator Impinj Inc, METRO Group decided to adopt Gen II for its distribution centers (Wolfram 2006b).

Kaufhof followed METRO Group in the adoption of Gen II for RFID on unit level, even though the standard did not operate with the HF transponders used in the pilot.

4.3   Toward Kaufhof's RFID Adoption on Item Level

Driven by positive experience and increasing standardization, Kaufhof began to approach RFID at the item level. Transponder cost and readability again were crucial as Kaufhof proposed to tag and process about 70 million textile items per year.

The affordability threshold of transponder cost at €0.10 had not yet been achieved (Kanzok 2004). But the cost had decreased substantially since 2003, to about €0.15 in October 2006. Concluded Wilfried Kanzok (2006), "it took us about three years to improve the tag quality and to bring the tag cost down; it seems that we are not that far away from actual item level roll-out being economically feasible for fashion goods."

Transponder readability had also improved tremendously for two main reasons since the Kaufhof–Gerry Weber pilot: (1) European regulators allowed stronger energized UHF equipment in early 2005, thereby facilitating wider reading ranges; and (2) in June 2006, Impinj Inc. presented fashion-specific RFID systems capable of reliable near- and long-field reading independent of previous inhibitors. This development assured further utilization of existing equipment in distribution centers and stores.

While METRO Group engaged in overall RFID standardization across industries, Kaufhof focused on establishing fashion industry RFID standardization of data transfer and processes. Kaufhof considered such standards necessary for item-level RFID adoption. Such standards would allow monitoring not only the number of blouses in inventory, but also their respective colors and sizes.

In May 2006, Kaufhof co-initiated the EPCglobal Apparel, Fashion & Footwear Business Action Group (AFF BAG). In its standardization efforts, the group also incorporated approaches by the Virtual Interindustry Commerce Solutions Association and American Apparel & Footwear Association.

At the end of 2006, the transponder costs were continuously decreasing, readability issues were almost settled, and industry RFID standardization was on the way (Speer 2006). Kaufhof decided to approach the adoption of item-level RFID using UHF (Wolfram 2006a).

4.4 Supply Chain RFID Diffusion

Approaching an RFID-enabled end-to-end supply chain, Kaufhof increasingly approached *diffusion to fashion manufacturers*. Between December 2004 and June 2005, it invited Gerry Weber and the fashion manufacturers Esprit and Triumph to participate in unit-level RFID adoption. Kaufhof and the manufacturers applied RFID to perform (1) the check-out of units from the manufacturer, (2) the check-in at Kaufhof's distribution centers, and (3) the so-called "cross-docking," where suppliers' shipments to distribution centers were directly—without any further storing—repackaged to orders and further distributed to recipients. To guarantee working interorganizational processes, Kaufhof kept barcodes in use as a backup.

Kaufhof originally anticipated that manufacturers would only reluctantly adopt RFID due to the associated costs and possible lack of know-how. To its surprise, several manufacturers rushed forward to adopt RFID, even before infrastructure standardization was approved. For a while, they even successfully continued with Gen II incompatible HF equipment. In contrast Kaufhof's initial RFID partners, Gerry Weber, Esprit, and Triumph, followed the EPCglobal path and switched to Gen II upon availability.

In order to foster RFID *diffusion to small fashion retailers*, Kaufhof wanted to be able to suggest a business case taking into account their often limited financial resources. It gratefully acknowledged technology conglomerates, telecommunication providers, and large software vendors, who developed out-of-the-box plug-and-play RFID systems with reduced complexity, especially geared toward the needs of smaller retailers (Wearden 2004).

By September 2006, Kaufhof and competing retailers as well as manufacturers of all sizes had adopted RFID in logistics. The established end-to-end RFID logistics infrastructure facilitated new applications along the supply chain.

5 DISCUSSION

The discussion follows the theoretical concepts and their associated factors of organizational technology adoption and diffusion as outlined in section 3. It investigates the role of external influences, perceived organizational benefits, and organizational characteristics for Kaufhof's RFID adoption and for the RFID diffusion in the fashion industry.

5.1 External Influences

Kaufhof conducted a rational decision-making process toward RFID adoption. As an RFID pioneer in fashion, it experienced no coercive pressure from other supply chain participants. However, as a METRO Group sales division, Kaufhof participated in the METRO Group RFID strategy. Therefore, Kaufhof's RFID adoption was not entirely independent.

Once Kaufhof had adopted RFID, it convinced additional supply chain partners to join. In contrast to Kaufhof, smaller or more hesitant companies experienced coercive power exercised by the large, powerful fashion retailers.

METRO Group and Kaufhof were innovators concerning the trial and adoption of RFID. Therefore, the adoption could not be specifically attributed to isomorphism in retailing or in the fashion industry. However, the early ambitious implementation schedules issued by the world's largest retailers such as METRO Group and Wal-Mart combined with positive feedback from the capital markets suggested some isomorphic adoption tendencies for late movers in RFID.

Kaufhof's adoption was justified with information and expertise gathered from several differently organized external sources. Through its parent METRO Group, Kaufhof benefitted from the expertise of a number of technology vendors and technology consultants, who participated in the METRO Group Future Store Initiative (Loebbecke 2004). Kaufhof received the necessary information from technology vendors who envisioned a large market potential for RFID in the fashion industry and therefore were willing to cooperate. Finally, Kaufhof exploited its membership in industry organizations and associations and took advantage from their know-how concerning infrastructure and business processes.

5.2 Perceived Organizational Benefits

To adopt RFID, Kaufhof had to integrate hardware with software and to adapt inter-organizational business processes along the supply chain. It reduced necessary integration efforts by adopting RFID in stages. Learning from its own pilot, Kaufhof stretched adoption over time. It first adopted RFID on the unit level and then on item level, thus mitigating integration risks.

Kaufhof decided on the adoption of RFID at a time when the RFID-related standardization of infrastructure, frequency, numbering, and business processes were still rudimentary. Nevertheless, being aware of the necessity and importance of standards, Kaufhof opted for active participation in the standardization processes. Well known for its RFID pilot, it earned the role of an RFID opinion leader, which gave it a strong voice in the standardization process. Only after the approval of standards did Kaufhof pursue a full-fledge RFID implementation, thus reducing the risks of island solutions along the fashion supply chain.

RFID only added an innovative component to Kaufhof's existing supply chain management system. Therefore, the quality of service played only a subordinate role even though reading rates of 100 percent at fast speed and bulk reading were conditional to adoption. Backup solutions guaranteed the overall quality of service. For instance, in the transition phase, Kaufhof maintained barcodes as backup for RFID to assure high quality of service.

Due to the extended implementation period, Kaufhof could not assess the financial benefits prior to project finalization. However, based on the pilot and its business case, Kaufhof had positive expectations regarding the long-term financial benefits of its RFID endeavor.

5.3 Organizational Characteristics

Beyond bundling its IT competences in the METRO Group Information Technology unit, METRO Group also signaled IT commitment both internally to Kaufhof and its other sales divisions, and externally to technology partners and supply chain participants.

Internally, METRO Group signaled commitment by allocating resources. Reaching beyond company boundaries, METRO Group and Kaufhof participated in technology events and issued press releases and executive statements concerning RFID. METRO Group's and Kaufhof's commitment to IT raised the willingness by Kaufhof's partners to join them on the long and challenging RFID adoption path.

Similar to the institutional commitment, the executive managers of both METRO Group and Kaufhof exhibited personal commitment and support for the RFID project. They gave high priority to activities supporting RFID adoption and developing RFID diffusion strategies. For instance, METRO Group's Board Member Zygmund Mierdorf joined the board of GS1, an association that standardizes RFID business processes.

Kaufhof's size and buying power in fashion retailing supported its role as opinion leader and its coercive power along the fashion supply chain. Potential partners became eager to participate in the RFID initiatives of METRO Group and Kaufhof. Even hesitant manufacturers jumped on the RFID bandwagon in order to not lose their position as supplier to Kaufhof. Other manufacturers adopted RFID to increase their chance to newly enter Kaufhof's supply chain.

6   CONCLUSIONS AND FURTHER RESEARCH

This paper described the case of organizational RFID adoption by Kaufhof and of RFID diffusion in the fashion industry. It analyzed and discussed theoretical concepts and associated factors from the literature as they could play a role in the organizational adoption process.

The case of Kaufhof and the fashion industry only partly supported the literature on organizational technology adoption and diffusion.

With regard to external influences, the most powerful entity in the supply chain was not exposed to coercive pressure from other supply chain members, but, as a subsidiary, it experienced coercive pressure to adopt the strategy of the parent company. Due to the specific context of industry innovators, isomorphism appeared not to exist. However, the availability of technology and business process information seemed to drive adoption, especially in the case of early adoption where best practices did not yet exist.

Concerning perceived organizational benefits, a successive adoption process allowed circumventing prohibitively high integration efforts. Infrastructure and business process standards for fashion accelerated RFID adoption, while leaving enough differentiation potential to RFID applications. With barcode technology serving as backup, the quality of service provided with the RFID technology was sufficient throughout the adoption and diffusion phases. Early RFID adoption and the resulting opportunity to shape the industry's technology development path led to perceived financial benefits.

Referring to organizational characteristics, size implied bargaining power, which exerted pressure on upstream supply chain members to also adopt RFID. Internal and external commitment and top management support for the RFID project depicted convincing, trust-building signals to potential partners.

Overall, this paper illustrated and investigated RFID adoption and diffusion from the perspective of a powerful industry leader. Extending our qualitative work and accepting obvious limitations of factor models for analyzing complex stories, future research may want to tackle the perspectives of small manufacturers or technology vendors. Also, it could analyze organizational RFID adoption issues in the context of closed systems where RFID adoption and operation are independent of other organizations. Finally, when sufficient data from the field is available, quantitative research could attempt to confirm that the identified factors influence RFID adoption across industry boundaries.

References

Agarwal, R., Tanniru, M., and Wilemon, D. "Assimilating Information Technology Innovations: Strategies and Moderating Influences," *IEEE Transactions on Engineering Management* (44:4), 1997, pp. 347-358.

Allen, D., Colligan, D., Finnie, A., and Kern, T. "Trust, Power and Interorganizational Information Systems: The Case of the Electronic Trading Community TransLease," *Information Systems Journal* (10:1), 2000, pp. 21-40.

Bagozzi, R., Davis, F., and Warshaw, P. "Development and Test of a Theory of Technological Learning and Usage," *Human Relations* (45:7), 1992, pp. 660-686.

Benbasat, I., Goldstein, D., and Mead, M. "The Case Research Strategy in Studies of Information Systems," *MIS Quarterly* (11:3), 1987, pp. 369-386.

Benders, J., Batenburg, R., and van der Blonk, H. "Sticking to Standards: Technical and Other Isomorphic Pressures in Deploying ERP-Systems," *Information and Management* (43:2), 2006, pp. 194-203.

Briggs, R., De Vreede, G., and Nunamaker Jr., J. "Collaboration Engineering with ThinkLets to Pursue Sustained Success with Group Support Systems," *Journal of Management Information Systems* (19:4), 2003, pp. 31-64.

Brown, S., Massey, A., Montoya-Weiss, M., and Burkman, J. "Do I Really Have To? User Acceptance of Mandated Technology," *European Journal of Information Systems* (11:4), 2002, pp. 283-295.

Chau, P., and Tam, K. "Factors Affecting the Adoption of Open Systems: An Exploratory Study," *MIS Quarterly* (21:1), 1997, pp. 1-24.

Chen, M. "Factors Affecting the Adoption and Diffusion of XML and Web Services Standards for E-Business Systems," *International Journal of Human-Computer Studies* (58:3), 2003, pp. 259-279.

Christiaanse, E., and Markus, L. "Participation in Collaboration Electronic Marketplaces," in *Proceedings of the 36th Annual Hawaii International Conference on System Sciences*, Los Alamitos, CA: IEEE Computer Society Press, 2003.

Church, J., and Gandal, N. "Complementary Network Externalities and Technological Adoption," *International Journal of Industrial Organization* (11:2), 1993, pp. 239-260.

Chwelos, P., Benbasat, I., and Dexter, A. "Research Report: Empirical Test of an EDI Adoption Model," *Information Systems Research* (12:3), 2001, pp. 304-321.

Clemons, E., and Wang, Y. "Special Issue: Technology Strategy for Electronic Marketplaces," *Journal of Management Information Systems* (17:2), 2000, pp. 5-7.

Collins, J. "METRO is Back on Track," *RFID Journal* 2006 (available online at http://www.rfidjournal.com/article/articleprint/2762/-1/385/).

Cooper, R., and Zmud, R. "Information Technology Implementation Research: A Technological Diffusion Approach," *Management Science* (36:2), 1990, pp. 123-139.

Dai, Q. "Business Models for Internet-Based B2B Electronic Markets," *International Journal of Electronic Commerce* (6:4), 2002, pp. 41-72.

Davis, F., Bagozzi, R., and Warshaw, P. "User Acceptance of Computer Technology: A Comparison of Two Theoretical Models," *Management Science* (35:8), 1989, pp. 982-1003.

DiMaggio, P., and Powell, W. "The Iron Cage Revisited: Institutional Isomorphism and Collective Rationality in Organizational Fields," *American Sociological Review* (48:2), 1983, pp. 147-160.

Eastin, M. "Diffusion of e-Commerce: An Analysis of the Adoption of Four e-Commerce Activities," *Telematics and Informatics* (19:3), 2002, pp. 251-267.

Fishbein, M., and Ajzen, I. *Belief, Attitude, Intention and Behavior: An introduction to Theory and Research*, Reading, MA: Addison-Wesley, 1975.

Galliers, R. "Choosing Information Systems Research Approaches,," in R. Galliers (ed.), *Information Systems Research: Issues, Methods and Practical Guidelines*, Oxford, England: Blackwell Scientific, 1992, pp. 44-162.

Gerst, M., and Bunduchi, R. "Shaping IT Standardization in the Automotive Industry: The Role of Power in Driving Portal Standardization," *Electronic Markets* (15:4), 2005, pp. 335-343.

Hart, P., and Saunders, C. "Power and Trust: Critical Factors in the Adoption and Use of Electronic Data Interchange," *Organizational Science* (8:1), 1997, pp. 83-103.

Haunschild, P., and Miner, A. "Models of Interorganizational Imitation: The effects of Outcome Salience and Uncertainty," *Administrative Science Quarterly* (42:3), 1997, pp. 472-500.

Iacovou, C., Benbasat, I., and Dexter, A. "Electronic Data Interchange and Small Organizations: Adoption and Impact of Technology," *MIS Quarterly* (19:4), 1995, pp. 465-485.

Iskandar, B., Kurokawa, S., and LeBlanc, L. "Business-to-Business Electronic Commerce from First- and Second-Tier Automotive Suppliers Perspectives: A Preliminary Analysis for Hypotheses Generation," *Technovation* (21:11), 2001, pp. 719-731.

Jeyaraj, A., Rottmann, J., and Lacity, W. "A Review of the Predictors, Linkages, and Biases in IT Innovation Adoption Research," *Journal of Information Technology* (21:1), 2006, pp. 1-23.

Karahanna, E., Straub, D., and Chervany, N. "Information Technology Adoption across Time: A Cross-Sectional Comparison of Pre-Adoption and Post-Adoption Beliefs," *MIS Quarterly* (23:2), 1999, pp. 183-213.

Kauffman, R., and Mohtadi, H. "Proprietary and Open Systems Adoption in E-Procurement: A Risk-Augmented Transactions Cost Perspective," *Journal of Management Information Systems* (21:1), 2004, pp. 137-166.

Kauffman, R., and Techatassanasoontorn, A. "Is There a Global Digital Divide for Digital Wireless Phone Technologies?," *Journal of the Association for Information Systems* (6:12), 2005, pp. 1-46.

Kanzok, W. Interview conducted on March 11, 2004, Kaufhof AG, Cologne, Germany.

Kanzok, W. Interviews conducted on July 3 and August 16, 2006, Kaufhof AG, Cologne, Germany.

Kimberly, J., and Evanisko, M. "Organizational Innovation: The Influence of Individual, Organizational, and Contextual Factors on Hospital Adoption of Technological and Administrative Innovations," *The Academy of Management Journal* (24:4), 1981, pp. 689-713.

Kolleda, D. "Achieving In-Transit Visibility (ITV): A Study of Technology on ITV in the Department of Defense," U.S. Army War College, Carlisle, PA, 2005 (available online at http://www.strategicstudiesinstitute.army.mil/Pubs/display-papers.cfm?q=11).

Konsynski, B., and Tiwana, A. "The Improvisation-Efficiency Paradox in Inter-Firm Electronic Networks: Governance and Architecture Considerations," *Journal of Information Technology* (19:4), 2004, pp. 234-243.

Kurt Salmon Associates. "Moving Forward with Item-Level Radio Frequency Identification in Apparel/Footwear," Kurt Salmon Associates, New York, 2005 (available online at http://www.apparelandfootwear.org/UserFiles/File/RFID/White_Paper-VICS_AAFA_RFID_v11.pdf).

Lai, V., and Guynes, J. "Organizational Innovation: The Influence of Individual, Organizational, and Contextual Factors on Hospital Adoption of Technological and Administrative Innovations," *IEEE Transactions on Engineering Management* (44:2), 1997, pp. 146-157.

Landt, J. "The History of RFID," *IEEE Potentials* (24:4), 2005, pp. 8-11.

Lee, J., and Sohn, M. "The Extensible Rule Markup Language," *Communications of the ACM* (46:5), 2003, pp. 59-64.

Liard, M. *The Global Markets and Applications for Radio Frequency Identification and Contactless Smartcard Systems* (4th ed.), Venture Development Corporation, Natick, MA., 2003.

Loebbecke, C. "Modernizing Retailing Worldwide at the Point of Sale." *MIS Quarterly Executive* (3:4), 2004, pp. 177-187.

Loebbecke, C., and Huyskens, C. "Weaving the RFID Yarn in the Fashion Industry: The Kaufhof Case," *MIS Quarterly Executive* (5:4), 2006, pp. 109-119.

Loebbecke, C., and Palmer, J. "RFID in the Fashion Industry: Kaufhof Department Stores AG and Gerry Weber International AG, Fashion Manufacturer," *MIS Quarterly Executive* (5:2), 2006, pp. 15-25.

Markus, L., Steinfield, C., Wigand, R., and Minton, G. "Industry-Wide Information Systems Standardization as Collective Action: The Case of the U.S. Residential Mortgage Industry," *MIS Quarterly* (30:5), 2006, pp. 439-466.

Matta, V., and Moberg, C. "The Development of a Research Agenda for RFID Adoption and Effectiveness in Supply Chains," *Issues in Information Systems* (7:2), 2006, pp. 246-251.

McGinity, M. "RFID: Is this Game of Tag a Fair Game?," *Communications of the ACM* (47:1), 2004, pp. 15-18.

McKeen, J., and Smith, H. "New Developments in Practice II: Enterprise Application Integration," *Communications of the Association for Information Systems* (8), 2002, pp. 451-466.

McLaren, T., Head, M., and Yuan, Y. "Supply Chain Collaboration Alternatives: Understanding the Expected Costs and Benefits," *Internet Research: Electronic Networking Applications and Policy* (12:4), 2002, pp. 348-364.

METRO Group . *Annual Report*, 2005 (available online at www.metrogroup.de).

Moore, G., and Benbasat, I. "Development of an Instrument to Measure the Perceptions of Adopting an Information Technology Innovation," *Information Systems Research* (2:3), 1991, pp. 192-222.

Naert, P., and Swinnen, R. "Regulation and Efficiency in Drug Wholesaling," *The Journal of Industrial Economics* (26:2), 1997, pp. 137-149.

Palmer, J. "Electronic Markets and Supply Chains: Emerging Models, Execution and Performance Measurement," *Electronic Markets* (14:4), 2004, pp. 268-269.

Pfeffer, J., and Salancik, G. *External Control of Organizations: A Resource Dependence Perspective*, New York: Harper and Row, 1978.

Pitt, L., Watson, R., and Kavan, C. "Service Quality: A Measure of Information Systems Effectiveness," *MIS Quarterly* (19:2), 1995, pp. 173-187.

Premkumar, G. "Inter-Organizational Systems and Supply Chain Management: An Information Processing Perspective," *Information Systems Management* (17:3), 2000, pp. 56-69.

Premkumar, G., Ramamurthy, K., and Crum, M. "Determinants of EDI Adoption in the Transportation Industry," *European Journal of Information Systems* (6:2), 1997, pp. 107-121.

Ramamurthy, K., Premkumar, G., and Crum, M. "Organizational and Interorganizational Determinants of EDI Diffusion and Organizational Performance: A Causal Model," *Journal of Organizational Computing and Electronic Commerce* (9:4), 1999, pp. 253-285.

Rogers, E., and Shoemaker, F. *Communication of Innovations* (2nd ed.), New York: Free Press, 1971.

Shah, R., Goldstein, S., and Ward, P. "Aligning Supply Chain Management Characteristics and Interorganizational Information System Types: An Exploratory Study," *IEEE Transactions on Engineering Management* (49:3), 2002, pp. 282-292.

Speer, J. "Supply Chain Case Study," *Apparel Magazine*, February 1, 2006, (available online at www.apparelmag.com/articles/feb/feb06_8.shtml).

Thatcher, S., and Foster, W. "B2B E-Commerce Adoption Decisions in Taiwan: The Interaction of Organizational, Industrial, Governmental and Cultural Factors," in *Proceedings of the 36th*

Annual Hawaii International Conference on System Sciences, Los Alamitos, CA: IEEE Computer Society Press, 2003.

The Economist. "The IT Revolution: The Best Thing Since the Barcode," *The Economist*, February 6, 2003.

Venkatesh, V., and Davis, F. "A Theoretical Extension of the Technology Acceptance Model: Four Longitudinal Field Studies," *Management Science*, (46:2), 2000, pp. 186-204.

Vervest, P., van Heck, E., Preiss, K., and Pau, L. "Introduction to Smart Business Networks," *Journal of Information Technology* (19:4), 2004, pp. 225-227.

Walton, S., and Gupta, J. "Electronic Data Interchange for Process Change in an Integrated Supply Chain," *International Journal of Operations and Production Management* (19:4), 1999, pp. 372-388.

Watson, R., Pitt, L., and Kavan, C. "Measuring Information Systems Service Quality: Lessons from Two Longitudinal Case Studies," *MIS Quarterly* (22:1), 1998, pp. 61-79.

Wearden, G. "Microsoft Readying RFID Products," *ZDNet UK*, June 24, 2004 (available online at http://news.zdnet.co.uk/emergingtech/0,1000000183,39158619,00.htm).

Webster, J. "Networks of Collaboration or Conflicts? Electronic Data Interchange and Power in the Supply Chain," *Journal of Strategic Information Systems* (4:1), 1995, pp. 31-42.

Westphal, J., Gulati, R., and Shortell, S. "Customization or Conformity? An Institutional and Network Perspective on the Content and Consequences of TQM Adoption," *Administrative Science Quarterly* (42:2), 1997, pp. 366-394.

WIPO Magazine. "Intellectual Property in the Fashion Industry," *WIPO Magazine*, May-June 2005 (available online at http://www.wipo.int/sme/en/documents/wipo_magazine/5_2005.pdf).

Wolfram, G. Interview conducted on September 15, 2006, METRO Group, Duesseldorf, Germany, 2006a.

Wolfram, G. Presentation at National Retail Federation Conference, New York, January 27, 2006b.

Yin, R. "The Case Study Crisis: Some Answers," *Administrative Science Quarterly* (26:1), 1981, pp. 58-65.

Yin, R. *Case Study Research: Design and Methods* (5th ed.), Thousand Oaks, CA: Sage Publications, 2003.

Zmud, R. "An Examination of Push-Pull Theory Applied to Process Innovation in Knowledge Work," *Management Science* (30:6), 1984, pp. 727-738.

About the Authors

Claudio Huyskens is a Ph.D. candidate at the Department of Business Administration and Media Management at the University of Cologne. He works primarily on RFID utilization in supply chains and the phenomenon of IT outsourcing via the Internet. His biography and publications are available at www.mm.uni-koeln.de; he can be reached by e-mail at claudio.huyskens@uni-koeln.de.

Claudia Loebbecke holds the Chair of Business Administration and Media Management at the University of Cologne, Germany. In 2005-2006, she was President of the Association for Information Systems (AIS). She serves as Senior Editor of the *Journal of Strategic Information Systems*. Her curriculum vita and publications are available at www.mm.uni-koeln.de. Claudia can be reached by e-mail at claudia.loebbecke@uni-koeln.de.

24 INFORMATION SYSTEMS INNOVATION RESEARCH AND THE CASE OF RFID

Ann Brown
Cass Business School, City University
London, United Kingdom

Anjali Bakhru
Open University Business School
Milton Keynes, United Kingdom

Abstract   *Radio frequency identification (RFID) is a complex ICT application. Adoption by organizations has been relatively slow. This paper assesses the contribution that research into information systems adoption and diffusion can make to understanding and predicting the diffusion of RFID. The paper concludes that traditional research methods are inappropriate for such applications. Information systems stage research and diffusion research offer more promising models.*

Keywords   Radio frequency identification, RFID, technology adoption, technology diffusion, process research

1   INTRODUCTION

Radio frequency identification (RFID) is not a new technology. Example applications date as far back as the 1950s (Twist 2005). Interest in this technology began to accelerate during the late 1990s mainly as a consequence of the high rate of development in the various constituent technologies that combine to create one type of RFID application. An RFID system is a combination of several technologies: wireless communications, computer hardware, electronic storage, and software programs. These elements operate

Please use the following format when citing this chapter:

Brown, A., and Bakhru, A., 2007, in IFIP International Federation for Information Processing, Volume 235, Organizational Dynamics of Technology-Based Innovation: Diversifying the Research Agenda, eds. McMaster, T., Wastell, D., Ferneley, E., and DeGross, J. (Boston: Springer), pp. 363-376.

together to capture and process data on individual items and their movements by an electronic tagging system. The system collects real-time information on mobile items (people or products or assets) for storage and subsequent analysis by computer. It is already clear that its potential application is to a variety of uses across different sectors. RFID has been called a revolutionizing technology with multiple uses and potential applications. Nonetheless it has been characterized by a relatively slow rate of adoption (Angeles 2005; Reiner and Sullivan 2005; Saunders 2005).

There is a considerable body of work into information systems innovation research. This has led to a number of theories on information technology adoption and diffusion. What do these theories suggest about RFID? What help does this work provide in explaining and forecasting the progress of RFID adoption? This paper aims to assess the contribution of IS innovation research in understanding the progress of RFID adoption and diffusion.

This paper starts with a description of the characteristics of the RFID technology. The following three sections apply the work carried out by IS researchers into IT innovation to RFID technology within the three approaches: traditional IT adoption research, process modeling, and diffusion studies.

2   CURRENT STATE OF RADIO FREQUENCY IDENTIFICATION (RFID) TECHNOLOGY

The business potential of RFID is not seriously questioned. The collection and analysis of real-time information on mobile items (people, products, or assets) has many obvious applications that seem certain to yield significant business value in terms of cost savings and enhanced service levels.

The most widely discussed applications are those dealing with the supply chain and retail business (Angeles 2005; Kopalchick and Monk 2005; Twist 2005; Wilding and Delgado 2004b). The application developed by Scottish Courage, a brewer in the United Kingdom, demonstrates the value of this type of application (Wilding and Delgado 2004a). RFID keeps track of mobile items. The company has used RFID technology for managing the movement of the barrels in which it delivers the beer to its customers. The technology offers a way to attach a label (tag) to any physical item containing unique information about that item (in this case, the barrel). This can then be read by or in some cases updated by a receiver (reader) placed at some distance from the tag. Wireless technology is used to achieve communication between tag and reader, when the tag is not in view. The data on every tagged item in the system can be fed in real time from this network of readers into a computer management system to be processed. The tags provide a unique identification for individual items, providing their location and the option of considerable additional information about the item if required and cost effective. The brewery now knows the location and progress of each of its 1.9 million containers. Information is collected by readers at several stages—at the brewery, upon delivery to the customer, during audits, and following return as an empty. This is a typical example of asset tracking. The benefits flow from the increased visibility of the containers and are predominantly cost saving and service level enhancements. For example, theft, loss, and container cycle time have all been significantly reduced, quality issues solved as a consequence of traceability, and there are fewer errors of distribution.

2.1 Rate of Adoption

It is generally agreed, however, that widespread adoption has been slow (Angeles 2005; Reiner and Sullivan 2005; Saunders 2005). Retailers in the United Kingdom have been investigating the technology for some years. Sainsbury's (the UK supermarket chain), for example, started a pilot study in 2000. *Computer Weekly's* quarterly online survey of UK IT directors on technology adoption by UK businesses in June 2006 found that only 8 percent of businesses were using it in any guise (including pilot schemes) with a further 11 percent investigating its potential. These figures were virtually unchanged in the September 2006 survey. A similar pattern is reported in the United States. A survey sponsored by NCR Corporation in May 2006 found that adoption rates in the United States were modest and unlikely to change significantly (Kilcourse 2006). The results showed that only 9 percent of retailers had an implementation time line in place and most of these were at the pilot stage. The much higher figure of 44 percent for manufacturers was attributed to the effect of mandates by retail trading partners, of which U.S. retailers Wal-Mart and Target were the most frequently cited partners.

Numerous reports in the press over the last 2 years show the caution with which business is treating this technology. Many retailers, for example, seem aware of the technology (Kilcourse 2006) and have investigated RFID technology (through pilot schemes) but have decided to defer adoption until the technology achieves a higher level of performance and/or becomes cheaper. Neither Sainsbury's (Cray 2005) nor Exel (a logistics company) consider that there is or will be a business case for any application for some years to come (*Computer Weekly*, February 2005). Estimates for the widespread adoption by companies of RFID applications include 2010 and beyond.[1]

2.2 RFID Technology Elements

An RFID system is composed of four main elements, drawing on four types of technologies: the tags, the wireless enabled receiver/transmitter, standards for product codes and tag/reader equipment, and the computer information system that processes the data delivered by the RFID system. These technologies are undergoing continuous development (Angeles 2005; Smith and Konsynski 2003; Twist 2005). Hence, performance in terms of capacity, reliability, accessibility, and costs are constantly changing with consequent effects on total system performance. There are as yet no globally agreed standards. Most readers are compatible with only a single manufacturers tag (Twist 2005). Organizations like GS1 UK (headquartered in Brussels, Belgium, and Princeton, New Jersey) are attempting to get corporate support to drive the adoption of global supply chain standards, but have not yet achieved this.

An individual application of RFID can be viewed as one proprietary network based around the system of readers and tags. Tags interact with the network at any point where there is a reader. Information flows from the tag via the reader into the computer system supporting the network. No tags from other networks will be recognized. A network can

---

[1]These estimates are from personal communications with Mr. Cray, the IT business partner at Sainsbury's, and from presentations at the GS1 UK EPCGlobal Conference in London, June 2005.

be for many individual users (for example, the Oyster card system for payment by passengers on the London Underground train system), for one specific application within an organization (for example, Scottish Courage's barrel tracking system), or for an application common to a group of organizations (for example, suppliers to Wal-Mart). These networks require that the class of tagged items all be in the system in order to deliver value. Tracking all but a minority of containers at Scottish Courage, for example, would be of value but the real payoff comes from tracking every container. Hence, the system components can be considered largely infrastructure in that the major investment has to be made for all components of the system up front.

RFID technology has a wide range of potential uses. By 2004, Sainsbury's had identified over 18 separate applications within their operations (Cray 2005). The most promising ones were asset tracking (of trolleys) and employee tracking into and out of company sites (Symmons 2005). Vince Cerf, chairman of Icann (an Internet corporation for assigned names and numbers) and cocreator of the transmission control protocol (TCP), has suggested that the adoption of RFID by groups such as EPCGlobal could "create an internet of things" (*Computer Weekly*, November 2006a). The parallel with the Internet underlines not only the variety of possible uses for which the technology is already being considered, but raises the possibility of more innovative applications that will only become clear when the technology has reached a higher level of diffusion.

The community interest in and optimism about the future of RFID is large, diverse, and active. The public activity of the relevant community members has been prolonged and intense through conferences (such as the GSI UK EPCGlobal Conference in London in June, 2005), trade press (*Computer Weekly* and *RFID Journal*), and academic journal articles (Angeles 2005; Reiner and Sullivan 2005; Saunders 2005; Wilding and Delgado 2004a, 2004b).

Potential or actual applications of RFID include (Smith and Konsynski 2003):

- Item tracking (e.g., inventory, containers, mail parcels, books, people)
- Asset tracking (e.g., railway coaches, supermarket trolleys)
- Identification for Security (e.g., smart cards)
- Item labeling (e.g., information on "sell by" dates or to identify products as genuine)
- Contactless payments (e.g., public transport systems, motor way tolls)

The benefits cited vary according to application and context, and include reduction in accidents or losses, error reduction resulting in increased safety, cost reduction, efficiency gains, fraud prevention, customer service enhancement, and the targeting of recalls.

2.3 Characterizing RFID Adoption

From this description it becomes possible to identify those factors in relation to RFID technology that are critical to the business case and adoption decision.

- Cost: installation involves both high up-front and operating costs
- Technical performance: current performance is adequate only for some of the potential applications

- Interdependence of the operators
- Knowledge base: new knowledge and expertise required for installation and ongoing operational management
- Complexity: wide variety of applications involving differing levels of technical and operational complexity
- User base: large and active community of specialist experts and groups supportive of the application of the technology

For an individual RFID application, there is a very significant infrastructure cost required in installing the whole network of readers, software, and tags. The organizational costs of operational changes may also be substantial. In addition, even moderate applications, such as the Scottish Courage barrel tracking system, generate an enormous amount of extra data that has to be stored electronically, processed quickly, and integrated into other organizational information systems if it is to create value. The Scottish Courage application, for example, required readers at 26 depots and on 600 vehicles generating over 30m per keg or barrel of movements annually (Wilding and Delgado 2004a). Storage and computing power and new software have to be installed to meet these additional demands. Operational costs are not insignificant. An unusual facet of an RFID system is the issue of the price of RFID tags relative to the cost of the underlying product to which it is to be attached and to the potential savings. The tags incorporate a chip that stores the data and an antenna that transmits/receives information. Chips can be relatively simple, containing as little as an ID (passive), or highly sophisticated, containing a large amount of information that can be updated at every reader point. Tag costs reflect the degree of sophistication. Chip capacity is rising and costs reducing in line with Moore's law (Moore 2003), but tag costs are still considered far in excess of that required for many applications to be cost effective.

At present, the level of technical performance presents a number of problems. At an interview in August 2005, Sainsbury's IT managers concerned with this technology commented that the wireless communications link can be a weak part of the system (Symmons 2005). In their experience, it failed to reach far and could produce false reads due to local interference from, for example, metallic objects. For Sainsbury's, the reliability of the read/write function was critical to the business case. In their view, error rates were still too high. The survey sponsored by NCR Corporation in May 2006 (Kilcourse 2006) found that companies considered the technical challenges to be significant. These included problems with attaching RFID tags to products, poor read rates, and interference from other wireless devices that are in use in the RFID-enabled facility.

RFID applications deliver value from the performance of the system as a whole. All facets of the system are highly interdependent. Hence the work of all operational staff is also highly interdependent. If one operator makes a mistake, the performance of the whole suffers.

To develop a new application of RFID, an organization requires specialist expertise for both the installation of the new technology and its effective operation. The lack of agreed technical standards exacerbates the complexities inherent in installation and implementation of new systems. The concern with the complexities of implementation is manifest in the many long running pilot projects of RFID supply chain applications that have been reported in the trade press. Marks & Spencer (a UK clothes retailer), for example, have been running pilots since 2003 (Collins 2004, 2005; Marks & Spencer 2003, 2005) and announced their move to a full system in late 2006 (*Computer Weekly*, November 2006b). Sainsbury's considered RFID as early as 2000. Rolls-Royce (a UK defense equipment manufacturer) started planning for the use of RFID in 2004 mainly to meet the demands of the U.S. Department of Defense for RFID compliant supply chain by 2007 (*Computer Weekly*, October 2006). The company was still in the trial stage at November 2006.

Complexity of installation varies between applications. For example, supply chain applications, such as those announced by Wal-mart and Marks & Spencer, involve many organizations, which increases the problems of implementation. However, this use of RFID for this type of application is simple in concept, being in effect a replacement for bar code technology, and at present appears to create little organizational change. For other types of RFID applications, such as asset management and contactless payments the implementation stages could be less complex.

3   TRADITIONAL IS ADOPTION RESEARCH AND RFID

Traditional approaches to IS adoption research are concerned with understanding the drivers of adoption of information and communication technology applications within target populations of individual users or organizations (Fichman 2004; Gallivan 2001; Jeyjaraj et al. 2006). The research question is, "What factors facilitate or hinder adoption and diffusion of IT-based innovation within a population of potential adopters?" (Fichman 2004). The goal of IT innovation research has, therefore, been to provide advice to managers on how to gain acceptance of new information technology investment at either the personal level of the user or at the organizational level of new project investment. The primary aim of this research is the development of models that represent as closely as possible the adoption process itself rather than models that focus on the deployment of specific ICT applications.

The research approach has been to model the adopter process of individuals and organizations based on a core set of theories and frameworks that seek to explain their behavior (Gallivan 2001). Jeyjaraj et al. (2006) carried out a review of empirical work in this tradition published in the main IS journals between 1992 and 2003. Their results confirmed Gallivan's (2001) view that the work tended to draw on a core set of theoretical frameworks. Of these Rogers' (2003) innovation diffusion theory (IDT) was one of the few to be applied at both the individual and the organizational level (Jeyjaraj et al. 2006). The technology adoption model (TAM) developed by Davis (1989) and based on the theory of reasoned action (Fishbein and Ajzen 1975) and its variants, is probably the most widely applied model at the individual user level.

The dominant paradigm is positivist and works on the assumption that the more organizations and individuals possess of the right characteristics, the more likely is it that the IT innovation will be adopted. Fichman (2004, p. 315) expresses this as follows:

> This paradigm is typified by the desire to explain innovation using economic-rationalistic models, whereby organizations that have a greater *quantity* of what might be called the "the Right Stuff" (i.e., greater innovation-related needs and

abilities) are expected to exhibit a greater *quantity* of innovation (i.e., greater frequency, earliness or extent of adoption).

Models are usually quantitative and seek to predict the value of such quantities as perceived system use, intention to use, rate of adoption, and actual system use (Jeyaraj et al. 2006). These become the dependent variables used as surrogates for quantity of innovation.

Theory has proposed a wide range of factors that could influence adoption (the independent variables). Jeyaraj et al. (2006) categorize these into four groups: environmental descriptors, organizational characteristics, individual (variables describing individual user characteristics), and innovation, which deals with the technology characteristics. Hence these models tend to focus on the characteristics of the adopters, whether these are individuals or organizations. The (innovation) variables describing the technology application are generic and focus on the general benefits that the ICT application might bring, rather than a specific description of what the ICT application will do. For example, TAM includes the subjective measures of perceived usefulness, while IDT incorporates that of perceived competitive advantage. This is not an approach that could incorporate the unique characteristics of an application like RFID.

Empirical work establishes numerical measures of these quantities and tests the model for predictive power, with data collected for individual ICT applications at a specific time and context (Chau and Tam 1997; Cho 2006; Fang et al. 2005; Mun et al. 2006; Venkatesh and Davis 2000). The research based on the technology adoption model is typical of this type of research. It was originally developed with the aim of creating a model to predict and explain user adoption of individual applications in the workplace. The standard methodology for the empirical work in TAM studies is to set up a study that seeks to explain "a specific behavior (usage) toward a specific target [IS application] within a specific context [organizational situation]" (Davis et al. 1989). Typically users are introduced or trained to use a new IS application and then a questionnaire is administered to find out their intentions for adoption (Cho 2006; Fang et al. 2005; Mun et al. 2006; Venkatesh and Davis 2000). Many of the variables, both independent and dependent, tested in this way are constructs largely based on self assessment. The model is measured by how much variance in intentions it explains. Most organizational studies take the same approach with different choices of independent variables (Chau and Tam 1997). Others use case material but have similar goals, namely the identification of the factors that lead individual organizations to adopt specific applications. Each study produces results for one type of IS application for one situation (organization, business unit, work group). More recent research has attempted to improve the performance of these types of models through adding variables or creating composites of previous work (Gallivan 2001; Venkatesh and Davis 2000; Venkatesh et al. 2003). Venkatesh et al. (2003), for example, created the unified theory of acceptance and use of technology (UTAUT) to predict individual user response to new technology drawing on eight existing models (including TAM) in common use. Their empirical work tested this model and found that it gave a higher explanatory power than each of the eight individual models.

Like all modeling activity, this is a simplification of what actually happens. There are a number of concerns with this approach. Theoretical problems include the pro-innovation bias (Fichman 2004; Jeyjaraj et al. 2006) resulting from the fundamental assumption that technology adoption is beneficial. The reliance on self assessment introduces recall bias, in which respondents misrepresent or have forgotten their behavior (Jeyjaraj et al, 2006; Szajina 1996). The reliance on rational decision making does not fit the experience of many researchers (Nutt 2002). Use of survey data is a poor way to capture behavior changes over time. The assumption of voluntary adoption decisions does not match many situations where adoption is mandated. Nonetheless there is substantial agreement that this approach has achieved some success (Fichman 2004; Gallivan 2001; Jeyjaraj et al. 2006). The models developed within the dominant paradigm have proved stable with good predictive ability for some circumstances. This poses the question: for what conditions and questions do these models work adequately?

Gallivan's (2001) review of the performance of traditional adoption research frameworks established that studies that showed strong explanatory power were those in which individual users voluntarily decide whether to use personal tools such as word processing, which also do not require extensive specialized knowledge (Cell 1 in Table 1). In his classification matrix, based on Fichman (1992), traditional adoption models have achieved less success in situations where adoption is mandated by the organization (Table 1, Cell 2) and situations where either there is a high level of user interdependence or the application requires considerable effort to learn to use it (Table 1, Cell 3). But traditional models fit least well for situations in which the ICT application is complex, requires a high level of coordination across users and departments, and is mandated by the organization (Table 1, Cell 4).

As the previous section established, RFID has both characteristics of high user interdependency and a high knowledge burden and hence falls into Cell 4. Traditional adoption models are likely to prove a poor guide to organizational adoption decisions with respect to RFID. Moreover the pro-technology bias of traditional methods is inappropriate for RFID for which, currently, the cost and performance factors present significant barriers to adoption.

Table 1. Classification Matrix for Traditional Innovation Adoption Research (adapted from Fichman 1992)

		Locus of Innovation Adoption	
		Individual User	**Organization**
Class of IS Technology to Be Adopted	Type 1: Low user interdependencies and low knowledge burden	Cell 1: Traditional adoption	Cell 2: Organizational mandate
	Type 2: High user interdependencies or high knowledge burden	Cell 3: Knowledge burden	Cell 4: Organizational mandate and knowledge burden

4 PROCESS MODELING AND RFID

Traditional IT adoption research takes a mechanistic view of organizations. This world-view hypothesizes a series of factors that directly drive the adoption decision. It makes the assumption that each factor is an independent variable and does not take account of any interactions between them. It conceptualizes adoption as determined at one point in time, ignoring the dynamic nature of an information systems project and the effect of changing conditions. The measures of adoption tell us little about the final business value achieved. For Cell 4 type ICT applications, the decision to purchase is but the start of a potentially lengthy process of installation and implementation. Implementation of new, complex technology is not a routine operation. Examples abound of IS applications that have been bought by organizations but never deployed (Attewell 1992). It is this process of implementation that determines whether the application is ever fully adopted and the level of business value achieved through its deployment.

Process models offer a way to understand organizational implementation (Gallivan 2001; Soh and Markus 1995). They focus on the sequence of events over time, which appear to lead to an outcome and seek to explain how and why an individual information systems outcome has occurred (Newman and Robey 1992). For process models, factors or categories may or may not help to produce the outcome. Outcomes are not dependent variables but "the 'final cause' of preceding events" (Newman and Robey 1992, p. 251). Stage research models seek to represent this time-related behavior and their relevance to innovation research has been noted by many (Rogers 2003; Tornatzky and Fleischer 1990).

According to Tornatzky and Fleischer (1990), adoption proceeds through a number of stages with successful implementation signaled when it has achieved widespread deployment and complete exploitation for business value. The process of technological innovation is "neither a single event nor even a small number of discrete events" (Tornatzky and Fleischer 1990, p. 27). Individuals and organizations may revisit some stages many times before the new technology reaches total acceptance.

Rogers' (2003) five stage model of adoption and implementation was an early attempt at representing the innovation process in organizations. Although the decision to purchase (Rogers' Stage 3) is an important turning point, adoption cannot be said to have taken place until implementation has been achieved, at least to the extent that some employees make use of the applications on some level. Cooper and Zmud (1990) adapted this to a six-stage model for IS applications. For this line of research, user adoption is of less interest than the extent to which the application is used. This is a combination of breadth of impact and the extent to which the application is assimilated by the organization. Breadth of impact is measured by the number of workgroups, departments, and/or individuals that adopt it (Gallivan 2001). Depth of impact is a more intangible concept. It encompasses the degree to which the application reaches into and changes existing processes and organizational routines (Gallivan 2001; Swanson and Ramiller 1997). Complete assimilation has occurred when routinization (Tornatsky and Fleischer 1990), or confirmation (Rogers' Stage 5) or infusion (Cooper and Zmud's Stage 6) is reached. The potential value of the new application can be thought to lie on a continuum (stretching from negative, if unsuccessful, to positive, when fully assimilated). Both success and business value will be affected by the scale of change required in organizational routines and retraining requirements for members of staff. For this approach, adoption is not an automatic benefit (as it is for traditional methods).

This approach gives a description of RFID technology that fits the current situation more closely than the traditional theory. The characteristics of knowledge burden and range of applications with differing levels of complexity noted in section 2 underline the significance of the implementation stage for this technology. Moreover, individual RFID applications require substantial investment for the infrastructure (i.e., at Stage 3— purchase) and may take years to install. Rogers' stage model captures these character-istics. However, process theory offers little practical direction for research design or research method. It is a relatively high-level theory that can be applied in many ways.

For example, Gallivan uses this theory when he creates a three-stage model representing innovation, adoption, and implementation and applies this framework to two case examples. The aim of the empirical research is to capture insights into the imple-mentation process. A case-based approach is used to investigate the views of the key stakeholders. The model is complex and the empirical work time consuming. The results support other work into implementation but are not linked to the special characteristics of the ICT application being studied. The aim is similar to traditional IT adoption research in that it seeks to identify those generic factors that affect adoption and assimilation, so as to be in a position to offer advice on how to support and ensure adoption. It could be considered an extension of traditional studies in that it widens the analysis to include the important stage of implementation.

There is less empirical research in the process or stage modeling tradition and the reason for this is simple. Models can span a wide range of factors, are complex, difficult to apply, and tend to produce results that are difficult to interpret.

5   IS DIFFUSION RESEARCH AND RFID

Traditional diffusion theories model how innovations spread both within and between organizations (Rogers 2003; Tornatzky and Fleischer 1990). Diffusion represents a series of individual adoption decisions. Traditional theories assume an equal opportunity to adopt provided there is a demand, that the rate of diffusion depends on the effectiveness of communication between suppliers and potential adopters. It emphasizes the role of signaling, that is, spreading the word about the existence and potential benefits of a new innovation (Attewell 1992). It assumes that institutional factors of either supplier or adopter are not significant in the adoption decision and that the adoption decision is made by an individual using rational decision criteria. There is an implicit assumption that if there is a good case for adoption for one user, then this applies to the rest of the target population of adopters.

Less attention has been paid to diffusion in the IS literature. IS researchers, such as Swanson and Ramiller (1997) and Attewell (1992), who have worked on the subject of the diffusion of IS applications have all argued that many IS applications diverge from the characteristics assumed of innovations for traditional theories like Rogers'. For Cell 4 ICT applications and RFID in particular, these assumptions do not hold. For most RFID applications, many individuals will be involved in the decision. Implementation will involve gaining new technical knowledge. This requires more than knowledge transfer. According to Attewell (1992, p. 6), "implementing a complex new technology requires both individual and organizational learning." Complex technologies interact with existing systems in multifaceted ways and organizations master them through using them, not via knowledge transfer. Attewell suggests that the rate of diffusion will accelerate when mechanisms exist to support this learning process. He proposes a knowledge barrier theory of diffusion for complex ICT, in which it is the progressive lowering of know-how barriers that determines the rate of diffusion, not the development of communication channels. Case examples on the spread of computing through the two decades illustrated how the decision varies between organizations depending on their circumstances.

Swanson and Ramiller agree with Attewell as to the significance of the learning requirements for complex ICT applications. However, for them, it is the uncertainty surrounding new ICT that differentiates it most sharply from the traditional description of innovations. "New technology often arrives on the market in an immature state, puzzling as to its benefits, future prospects and long term form" (Swanson and Ramiller 1997, p. 459). They propose an alternative model of the diffusion process for applications like RFID. They suggest that the key factor is the ongoing perceptions and beliefs of the community with material interests in the new IS application which determines the rate of diffusion. This community is made up of those IS practitioners that become knowledgeable about the new technology, the business managers for which the new technology may be of value, consulting firms, academic researchers, user groups, industry pundits, technology vendors, and conference organizers (both academic and trade). These groups create the current dominant view (organizing vision) of how and where the technology can be used, its potential business value, and, most significantly, support the learning process that potential adopter organizations must go through. The vitality and level of public activity of this heterogeneous group offers a guide to the current state of the innovation. The community's discourse is carried out via such outlets as conferences, trade publications, journal papers, consultant's offerings, the business press, and exemplar cases of adoption. A high level of very visible activity creates the conditions for diffusion.

This theory of diffusion focuses on the individual technology and its characteristics. According to this view, an effective description of technology diffusion would require a model specific to the technology. Such a model would incorporate such factors as the business case, implementation issues, risks, and community beliefs and attitudes.

As noted in section 2, RFID technology conforms to this description. The business case is still uncertain for many applications and it carries a high knowledge burden. Nonetheless, the organizing vision currently being generated by the interested parties is dense and optimistic. Further work using this theory would require the development of a framework that would describe the factors specific to RFID technology that might affect the organizational adoption decision.

6 CONCLUSION

Adoption and diffusion of complex ICTs such as RFID are far from simple processes. This paper has emphasized that traditional research methods are unlikely to build useful models of this behavior given their inability to capture the complexity involved. Alternative research approaches are, however, likely to be more promising. Both IS process research (stage models) and IS diffusion research have identified significant factors that are likely to affect the rate of adoption and diffusion of these complex types of ICT. The research issue shifts toward choosing applications that will yield business value and, at the same time, achieve successful implementation. Central to understanding this potential, however, is an appreciation that increasing rates of adoption and diffusion of RFID technology are likely to depend on factors external to the firm. While adoption decisions traditionally take place in relative isolation within an organization's boundaries, adoption decisions regarding RFID will be affected by the decisions of others. The rate of diffusion will ultimately depend not only on the characteristics of the technology but also on the larger community of actors interested in or knowledgeable about the application.

References

Angeles, R. "RFID Technologies: Supply-Chain Applications and Implementation Issues," *Information Systems Management* (22:1), Winter 2005, pp. 51-65.

Attewell, P. "Technology Diffusion and Organizational Learning: The Case of Business Computing," *Organizational Science* (3:1), 1992, pp. 1-19.

Chau, P., and Tam, K. Y. "Factors Affecting the Adoption of Open Systems: An Exploratory Study," *MIS Quarterly* (21:1), March 1997, pp. 1-26.

Cho, V. "A Study of the Roles of Trusts and Risks in Information-Oriented Online Legal Services Using an Integrated Model," *Information and Management* (43:4), January 2006, pp. 502-520.

Collins, J. "Marks & Spencer Expands RFID Trial," *RFID Journal* , February 20, 2004 (available online at http://www.rfidjournal.com/article/articleview/791/1/1/).

Collins, J. "Marks & Spencer to Extend Trial to 53 Stores," *RFID Journal*, February 18, 2005 (available online at http://www.rfidjournal.com/article/articleview/1412/1/1/).

Computer Weekly. "Computer Weekly CIO Index: Technology Adoption," June 2006, p. 12.

Computer Weekly. "Computer Weekly CIO Index: Technology Adoption," September 2006, p. p. 14.

Computer Weekly. "Logistics Firms Hold Back but Are Key to Wide Scale RFID Roll-Out," February 2005, p. 10.

Computer Weekly. "Rolls-Royce Fires Up RFID Trail to Meet US Army Supply Chain Orders," October 2006, p. 14.

Computer Weekly. "The End of the Web as We Know It," November 2006a, p. 24.

Computer Weekly. "M&S Ready to Start National Roll-Out of Item-Level RFID," November 2006b, p. 5.

Cooper, R. B., and Zmud, R. W. "Information Technology Implementation Research: A Technological Diffusion Approach," *Management Science* (36), a1990, pp. 123-139.

Cray, T. IT Business Partner, Sainsbury's. Personal communication, 2005.

Davis, F. "Perceived Usefulness, Perceived Ease of Use Interface, and User Acceptance of Information Technology," *MIS Quarterly* (13:3), September 1989, pp. 319-340.

Davis, F., Bagozzi, R., and Warshaw, P. "User Acceptance of Computer Technology: A Comparison of Two Theoretical Models," *Management Science* (35:8), 1989, pp. 982-1003.

Fang, X., Chan, S., Brezezinski, J., and Xu, S. "Moderating Effects of Task Type on Wireless Technology Acceptance," *Journal of Management Information systems* (22:3), 2005, pp. 123-157.

Fichman, R. "Going Beyond the Dominant Paradigm for Information Technology Innovation Research: Emerging Concepts and Methods," *Journal of the Association for Information Systems* (5:8), 2004, pp. 314-355.

Fichman, R. "Information Technology Diffusion: A Review of Empirical Research," in J. I. DeGross, J. D. Becker, and J. J. Elam (eds.), *Proceedings of the 13th International Conference on Information Systems*, Dallas, TX, 1992, pp. 195-206.

Fishbein, M., and Ajzen, J. *Belief, Attitude, Intention and Behavior: An Introduction to Theory and Research*, Reading, MA: Addison-Wesley, 1975.

Gallivan, M. "Organizational Adoption and Assimilation of Complex Technological Innovations: Development and Application of New Framework," *The DATABASE for Advances in Information Systems* (32:3), 2001, pp. 51-85.

Jeyaraj, A., Rottman, R., and Lacity, M. "A Review of the Predictors, Linkages and Biases in IT Innovation Adoption Research," *Journal of Information Technology* (21:1), 2006, pp. 1-23.

Kilcourse, B. "The 3rd Annual *RFID: How Far, How Fast — 2006 Benchmark Study*," report by Retail Systems Alert Group, sponsored by NCR Corporation, May 2006 (downloaded from NCR's website in November 2006).

Kopalchick III, J., and Monk, C. "RFID Risk Management," *Internal Auditor* (62:2), 2005, pp. 66-72.

Marks & Spencer. "Marks & Spencer Develops Intelligent Clothing," Press Release, April 7, 2003 (available online at http://www2.marksandspencer.com/thecompany/mediacentre/pressreleases/2003/com2003-04-07-00.shtml).

Marks & Spencer. "Background to Marks & Spencer's Business Trial of RFID in its Clothing Supply Chain," Press Release, February 18, 2003 (available online at http://www2.marksandspencer.com/thecompany/mediacentre/pressreleases/2005/com2005-02-18-00.shtml).

Moore, G. "No Exponential Is Forever...But We Can Delay Forever," presentation to 2003 IEEE International Solid-State Circuits Conference, February 2003 (available online at at http://www.intel.com/research/silicon/mooreslaw.htm).

Mun, Y. Y., Jackson, J., Park, J., and Probst, J. "Understanding Information Technology Acceptance by Individual Professionals: Towards an Integrative View," *Information and Management* (43:3), 2006, pp. 350-363.

Newman, M., and Robey, D. "A Social Process Model of User-Analyst Relationships," *MIS Quarterly* (19:2), June 1992, pp. 249-266.

Nutt, P. *Why Decisions Fail*, San Francisco: Berrett-Koehler Publishers Inc., 2002.

Reiner, J., and Sullivan, M. "RFID in Healthcare: A Panacea for the Regulations and Issues Affecting the Industry?," HealthCare Purchasing News Online, June 2005 (available online through http://www.hpnonline.com/).

Rogers, E. *Diffusion of Innovations* (5th ed.), New York: The Free Press, 2003.

Saunders, A. "Can Smart Tags Deliver?," *Management Today*, February 9, 2005, pp. 50-53 (available online at http://www.clickmt.com/public/news/index.cfm?fuseaction=fulldetails&newsUID=467e3a73-9051-41e6-a38d-015f67cffb08).

Smith, H., and Konsynski, B. "Developments in Practice X: Radio Frequency Identification (RFID)—An Internet for Physical Objects," *Communications of the Association for Information Systems* (12), 2003, pp. 301-311.

Soh, C., and Markus, L. "How IT Creates Business Value: A Process Theory Synthesis," in J. I. DeGrosss G. Ariav, C. M. Beath, R. Hoyer, and C. Kemerer (eds.), *Proceedings of the 16th International Conference of Information Systems*, Amsterdam, 1995, pp. 29-41.

Swanson, B., and Ramiller, N. "The Organizing Vision in Information systems Innovation," *Organization Science* (8:5), 1997, pp. 458-474.

Symmons, N. IT Partner, Supply Chain Management, Sainsbury's. Personal communication, 2005.

Szajina, B. "Empirical Evaluation of the Revised Technology Acceptance Model," *Management Science* (42:1), 1996, pp. 85-92.

Tornatzky, L. G., and Fleischer, M. *The Processes of Technological Innovation*, Lexington, MA: Lexington Books, 1990.

Twist, D. "The Impact of Radio Frequency Identification on Supply Chain Facilities," *Journal of Facilities Management* (3:3), 2005, pp. 226-239.

Venkatesh, V., and Davis, F. "A Theoretical Extension of the Technology Acceptance Model: Four Longitudinal Field Studies," *Management Science* (46:2), 2000, pp. 186-204.

Venkatesh, V., Morris, M., Davis, G., and Davis, F. "User Acceptance of Information Technology: Towards a Unified View," *MIS Quarterly* (27:3), September 2003, pp. 425-478.

Wilding, R., and Delgado, T. "RFID Demystified: Supply-Chain Applications," *Logistics & Transport Focus* (6:4), May 2004a, pp. 42-48.

Wilding, R., and Delgado, T. "The Story So Far: RFID Demystified," *Logistics & Transport Focus* (6:3), April 2004b, pp. 26-31.

About the Authors

Ann Brown is a senior lecturer in Information Management at Cass Business School, City University. Her research is on information systems in organizations, with a special focus on the problem of obtaining business value from information and communications technology. Ann can be reached by e-mail at a.p.brown@city.ac.uk.

Anjali Bakhru is a lecturer in Strategic Management at the Open University Business School in the United Kingdom. Her research encompasses resource-based evolutionary approaches to competitive advantage, and she has undertaken research on the challenges of new market entry with respect to on-line markets. Anjali can be reached by e-mail at a.bakhru@open.ac.uk.

Part 6:

Firm Level Adoption Factors

25 EXTENDING THE RESEARCH AGENDA ON DIFFUSION OF INNOVATIONS: The Role of Public Programs in the Diffusion of E-Business Innovations

Arturo Vega
Mike Chiasson
David Brown
Lancaster University Management School
Lancaster, United Kingdom

Abstract   *Given the important but largely unstudied role of contextual influences on the diffusion of innovations, theories and methodologies which take context into account are increasingly relevant. One such approach, the system of innovation approach (SIA), considers context as a network of organizations and groups involved in the production and diffusion of innovations. In addition to the focal innovation, these organizations and groups are influenced by other contexts, and so the further study of their diffusion settings extends the diffusion research agenda. To this end, we focus on a subset of the public programs involved in the diffusion of e-business innovations to small- and medium-sized enterprises (SMEs). E-business applications are complex innovations, and the need for outside assistance is especially significant for SMEs because they often lack the knowledge and resources to strategically adopt, modify, and use e-business applications. To understand how these programs influence e-business adoption, we used theories that examine the contexts around public program interventions in order to explain its form and outcome. The empirical findings suggest that many public programs fail to effectively deliver interventions because program personnel work in contexts that restrict their focus and ability to completely assess SME business needs.*

Please use the following format when citing this chapter:

Vega, A., Chiasson, M., and Brown, D., 2007, in IFIP International Federation for Information Processing, Volume 235, Organizational Dynamics of Technology-Based Innovation: Diversifying the Research Agenda, eds. McMaster, T., Wastell, D., Ferneley, E., and DeGross, J. (Boston: Springer), pp. 379-392.

Keywords   Research agenda, context, e-business, systems of innovation approach, SMEs,
                    diffusion of innovations, public programs

1   INTRODUCTION

A review of the diffusion literature illustrates an increasing need to study contextual
influences around adoption and diffusion. Few attempts have been made to broaden the
research agenda to include institutional contexts such as suppliers, knowledge, supply-
push, and government (e.g., Attewell 1992; King et al. 1994).

One approach to context is the systems of innovation approach (SIA) (e.g., Edquist
2005). The SIA recasts innovation as a network of participants and innovations jointly
and sometimes remotely involved in the production and diffusion of intermediary innovations, leading to a focal innovation. The SIA suggests an extended research agenda
examining the intermediary systems that affect the production and diffusion of
innovations. These can include university–industry links, consultancy accreditation,
assessments of public assistance, immigration laws, perception of organizational
decision-takers on systemic issues, professional and trade association roles, support
centers, assistance brokerage, and online collaborative strategies, to name a few.

Following this extended research agenda, we decided to study one systemic issue:
public programs and their influence on e-business adoption by SMEs. Given the broad
scope and resources consumed by such programs, which includes e-business awareness,
project management, SME training, and consultancy support, there is an increasing
interest in the impact of these initiatives on the adoption and use of e-business
applications (European Union 2001; OECD 2004). The topic is relevant for both
developed and emerging economies which are involved in e-business diffusion (CEPAL
2007).

Academics have, so far, given little attention to the study of public programs for e-
business innovation in SMEs. We identified two research studies that have examined
policy choices to engage SMEs in e-business technology (Gengatharen et al. 2005; Hira
2002), and research that generally examines information technology government programs (Yap and Thong 1997). Both types of research (i.e., choice and evaluation) are
valuable first steps in this area of research. To complement this, we study public program
delivery, its influence on e-business adoption by SMEs, as well as program personnel
behavior and the context around them. We focus specifically on consultancy support
programs. We conclude that public program delivery is affected by a number of
contextual influences that inhibit the adequate assessment and delivery of tailored
programs to an SME. We also conclude that additional theories and methodologies are
needed to study context systemically, including the systems of innovation approach.

Our paper is organized as follows. Section 2 explores theory relevant to the study
of e-business adoption by SMEs, including the SIA. Section 3 provides a general
theoretical model to study e-business adoption in SMEs. The model includes program
and SME contexts, diffusion of innovations, and the stages of program intervention. The
research methodology is explained in section 4. In section 5, there is a description of the
findings of a case study, which is analyzed and described in section 6. Finally, we
conclude by examining the applicability of the theoretical model to study and evaluate
program interventions.

2 RESEARCH AGENDA FOR E-BUSINESS INNOVATION IN SMES

The *diffusion of innovations theory* (DOI) (Rogers 2003) defines diffusion as the process in which an innovation is communicated through certain channels over time among the members of a social system. For simple innovations, the DOI can be conceptualized as the transmission of information from change agents to adopters, and the use of incentives to increase the creation of critical mass. However, most innovations are **complex** (Attewell 1992; Eveland and Tornatzky 1990), including e-business applications. In these cases, the diffusion of complex innovations requires a study of the various contextual influences from participants around the adopter, in the creation, implementation, reinvention, maintenance, and coordination of innovations.

For example, a booking system for the lodging sector could require other participants to support its adoption and use, such as an application service provider who hosts the application. To be successful, the on-line booking application will require the careful design of its functionality, through studies of multichannel sales. Any problems in the available bandwidth or the lack of marketing resources would fail to produce and diffuse a usable and useful innovation. Finally, the application's value will depend on the trained and skilled use of the application by motels, restaurants, and museums to create joint tourist packages.

The *system of innovation approach* (SIA) considers that innovation success and failure could be located in any part of a complex system of participants, producing many intermediate innovations for a focal innovation to diffuse. A failure could be the result of missing or inappropriate activities, organizations, institutions, or linkages (Edquist 2002). The SIA takes into account not only the proximal causes described in the last paragraph, but also the **causes of these causes**, in any part of the system. Policy intervention is required to complement or correct these **systemic failures** which inhibit the effective production and diffusion of innovations (Lundvall and Borras 2005; Nyholm et al. 2002).

As an example with the diffusion of e-business applications and SMEs, there could be a lack of marketing expertise in a region which could affect the shaping and delivery of an e-business system. In response, a publicly funded program could be introduced to address this knowledge gap. This could include the use of university students with marketing expertise. This initiative would link marketing expertise in academic organizations to e-business adoption activities in an SME. However, the SIA approach does not often stop at the public program intervention—the first contextual layer. It can further investigate the context around the context by, for example, exploring the evaluative and compensatory mechanisms of the public program, and how it influences the behavior of the students in their consultancy interventions.

In terms of practical implications, the SIA suggests that the context around the SME affects the diffusion of e-business innovations, and that this context also has its own context. As a result, there could be numerous causes that contribute to an inadequate set of resources to assist in the effective production and diffusion of innovations. For instance, the lack of marketing knowledge available for SMEs could have multiple causes. To mention only some, there may be few marketing consultants in the region, SMEs may not have the economic capacity to employ or contract these resources, SMEs may be unable to find them or they may not know how to select proper consultants.

The implications for public policy are the consideration of the contextual systems around the SME, and where the policies need to be targeted in concert with other initiatives, to produce a working innovation system. For instance, the supply and access to marketing knowledge could be increased in several ways, depending on the contextual influences around the SME: creating marketing programs in universities, increasing the quality of these programs through the selection of skilled workers, subsidizing student placements, establishing consultancy accreditation schemes, softening immigration laws to attract skilled marketing people, improving the working and living conditions of these professionals, subsidizing training for consultants, and sponsoring quality awards for marketing consultants. It may also be the case that there are so many contextual gaps preventing the production and delivery of innovations that any policy initiative will do little if anything for e-business adoption.

In terms of the specific literature on e-business adoption by SMEs, there is a potential to inform the research on e-business innovation in SMEs using the SIA. The literature so far has studied only a few systemic issues related to the adoption of e-business by SMEs. For example, consultancy accreditation (Morgan et al. 2006), the role of governments and industry actors to stimulate the adoption of sector applications (Dierckx and Stroeken 1999), the availability of technical facilities and support services related to information technology (Jansen 1998), and industry cooperation for the development of standards (McGowan and Madey 1998).

In general, the systemic approach to innovation extends the research agenda not only on e-business and SMEs, but also for the adoption and diffusion of other complex technologies. We turn next to a theoretical model that guides our various studies of public program interventions in the adoption of e-business innovations by SMEs.

3   THEORETICAL MODEL

Various theories can be drawn upon to examine the contextual influences on the diffusion of innovations. Traditional diffusion of innovations research defines an **adoption process** (agenda-setting, matching, redefining, restructuring, clarifying, and routinizing) as a sequence of stages through which decision-making units pass in evaluating and adopting innovations. Despite its great value, it is a general theory, which was not specifically developed either for e-business or SMEs. In most cases, the DOI has to be complemented by the **factors of adoption** of specific innovations and specific types of adopters.

For instance, SMEs tend to be centralized in the chief executive officer or owner to makes decisions. This will bias the perceived attributes of an application toward this one person (Grandon and Pearson 2004). In cases where a chief executive officer decides not to adopt an application during the matching stage of adoption, a **barrier** is created. On the other hand, if the decision-maker decides to adopt the innovation, the redefining and restructuring stage would be quick, which would be a **motivator**.

In addition to the implications of the DOI and the e-business innovation in the SME literature, public programs represent an important influence on SME adoption. "Policy intervention is an ongoing, socially constructed and negotiated process, not simply the execution of an already-specified plan of action of expected outcomes" (Long 1999, p. 4). In terms of the process of implementing public programs, program officers select recipients, design interventions, deliver policies, connect their work with other programs, follow-up client processes, and evaluate outcomes. These various stages can be considered **program processes**.

The effect of program processes and adoption processes are interrelated. On the one hand, the decisions and outcomes of the program officer are influenced by the adoption process. For example, the *design* of the assistance must take into account the *stages* of the SME's adoption process that need support. On the other hand, the decisions and outcomes across the adoption process are influenced by program processes. For instance, the *clarifying stage* could be deficient because of poor *delivery* of the program assistance. So, the program process is influenced by the program context and adoption processes, and the adoption process is influenced by the factors of adoption and by the program processes.

In addition to adoption processes, the program context affects the working conditions and capabilities of the public worker. For example, **bureaucratic routines** can create both barriers and motivators in the delivery of public programs, and their ability to assess and monitor program outcomes. Lipsky (1980) explains various program contexts of public service workers and the effects that they have on the execution of their work. Public service workers grant access to government initiatives and provide services within them (e.g., program consultants and public assistance brokers). These workers often have significant discretionary judgement given the fact that their work tends to be complicated and subjective (Argyris 1964). Additionally, they have relative autonomy given the taken-for-granted assumption that they agree on the goals of the program organization. In this reality, policies tend to be made at the **street-level**, and not from the heads of policy agencies (e.g., Juma and Clarke 1985; Lipsky 1980).

In general, the **contexts** around program consultants are complex and tend to negatively affect the quality of their work. There are often inadequate resources to meet client demand, in terms of time, knowledge, information, and budget. Public workers operate in an environment in which there is a constant displacement of ambiguous and competing goals (e.g., client-centered, social engineering, and program-centered goals). This issue is more problematic because of ill-defined performance targets. Given this climate, however, program consultants also have a position of relative power over the client because they control the benefits of their service, and have the capacity to deny or to make access more costly. In some cases, the benefits of the programs cannot be found elsewhere. Adding to the difficulties of program evaluation, clients may manipulate or evaluate positively poor programs in order to have access to the agency's services in the future.

In this environment, workers can also become alienated because their services are only a part of a wider need. This can reduce their motivation, resulting in an alienation from their work and clients. For example, a program worker could develop a software application based on a deficient functional specification given by the client. Another consequence is the disconnection between the work of the bureaucracy and the next stages of the process of the clients. For example, an information technology strategy could have been successfully defined in a program workshop, but the decision-taker of the SME did not have the knowledge to manage the rest of the adoption process. Finally, the pace of the work is another dimension of the program workers that tends to be alienated from clients. This is represented when the response time of public services becomes too long because of the excessive and confusing work that the same customers generate.

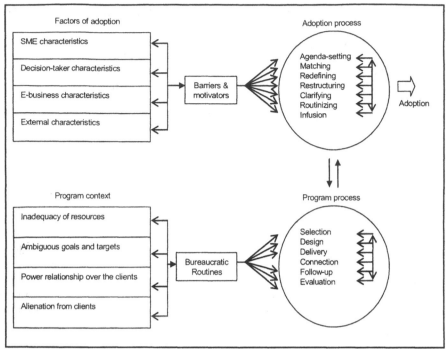

***Figure 1.* Theoretical Model to Explain Public Program Intervention in SMEs**

Figure 1 shows the entire theoretical model. In this paper, however, we focus primarily on the public programs and their effect on SME adoption of e-business applications, with only moderate references to other contextual influences on program and SMEs. After reviewing the literature of e-business adoption by SMEs, we decided to classify the factors of adoption in four groups: SME characteristics, decision-taker characteristics, e-business characteristics, and external characteristics. In one way or another, most of the research is located in this classification (see Thong 1999). Note that we are considering one more stage in the adoption process, *infusion*. Infusion measures the extent of use of an application in organizations by measuring the types of transactions and the quantity of transactions per type. Interestingly, this addition is supported by research on the adoption of e-business systems in SMEs (Cooper and Zmud 1990).

4   RESEARCH DESIGN

To investigate the public program influence on the adoption of e-business innovations in SMEs, we chose a case study methodology (Yin 2002). We focus on the experiences of SME adopters and program officers in the delivery of public programs. In doing so, we studied the phenomenon within its real context. To understand the events and experiences of participants, we interviewed decision-takers in SMEs to determine the outcomes of the adoption processes. We also interviewed program consultants to figure out how they designed and delivered the services to the SMEs. Finally, we interviewed program directors and reviewed program files to understand and determine the program processes and outcomes in several SME cases. The theoretical model was used from the beginning, but as a way to organize our questions and participants' answers.

The unit of analysis was the individual policy interventions. In addition, the embedded unit of analyses were the stages of the adoption process and the stages of the program process. So, the gathering of information focused on how these complex and interdependent stages developed over time.

The case studies were based on two programs supporting SMEs, both delivered by one university but from different departments. The projects are co-funded by public organizations and the university. Whereas one of the programs is focused exclusively on information technology support, the other gave business assistance to some e-business adoption processes. The information technology support is normally given by student placements, and the business assistance is delivered by a pool of consultants that work for the university. The seven SMEs that participated in the study were direct beneficiaries of these programs. In addition to these two programs, we contacted the director of another program from a different university and the program manager of an entire regional plan, both oriented to e-business innovation in SMEs. These contrasting cases and programs represent excellent sources of data for the research.

The research is based on the study of adoption and program processes. Process research (Mohr 1982) implies an understanding of what events occurred throughout time, with the purpose of analyzing a causal order to these events. For these reasons, the research entailed the use of qualitative methods, in our case, semi-structured interviews and documentary evidence.

All of the participants are located in England. As part of the field work, we completed 16 interviews, of which 13 were tape recorded. The three interviews that were not tape recorded were summarized in text and sent to the interviewees for their corrections and conformity. Given space limitations, we focus on the detailed explanation of one case in our findings, drawing initial conclusions to consider in our other cases.

5 EMPIRICAL FINDINGS

This section describes the program and SME case, through the relevant opinions of some of its participants. For confidentiality reasons we use letters to name the SMEs and the program (e.g., SME B), and we give only the job positions of the participants (e.g., managing director, etc.). These findings will be analyzed in detail in next section using a part of the theoretical model described in section 3.

5.1 The SME Assisted and the E-Business Initiative

The company assisted was SME A. However, it was a joint venture formed by SME B and SME C. The start-up was a third-party e-marketplace for the building supplies sector. SME B is an expert on Internet information systems and SME C is a distributor of architectural hardware, a subsector of the building supplies segment. The managing director of SME B was the managing director of the venture, SME A.

The e-business model was based on resale agreements with brick-and-mortar shops. The gross profit of the venture was the difference between the selling price of SME A to its customers and the buying price from the shops. The shopping basket of each client of the e-marketplace could include products from different shops. However, the delivery to the customers of SME A was made directly from the warehouses of the shops. As a result, the delivery charges to the clients varied depending on the shop.

5.2   The Development of the Initiative

The partnership started in the middle of 2002. Once the application was developed and the company recruited eight or nine shops, SME A made an initial market research. At that point, the results of the research were considered promising by the partners. In the middle of 2003, SME A received public consultancy support from program A and received loans from two financial institutions. At the beginning of 2004, the company used the loans to develop a marketing strategy. Despite of the recruitment of more shops, the sales results were not as expected. One year later, SME A employed a student on an MBA summer project to try to improve the competitive position of the company. However, the venture remained unprofitable. The company closed down in the middle of 2006. For the managing director of SME B, the collapse of the venture was caused by the lack of knowledge of the whole building supplies sector of SME C. The managing director expressed that the personnel of SME C only knew about the architectural hardware subsector and that this affected all of the marketing initiatives of the company.

5.3   The Program and the Assistance

The purpose of program A was to provide coaching and mentoring to SMEs on several business subjects, using e-learning techniques and traditional face-to-face teaching methods. The program was run by a university and employed an e-learning platform and several full-time employees to deliver the services. Program A was partly funded by a public organization and the university. The program had major problems finding clients for its funds.

The requirement of SME A was quite open: to increase the web traffic and the conversion and retention rates of the clients based on modifications of the web presence. The company expected recommendations around the core e-business model, unless other expensive and important issues were needed for it to survive. The consultant for the program built his recommendations based on the analysis of the operation of other e-marketplaces (e.g., Amazon.com) and on his personal experience. Apart from his work in the university, the program consultant was the sole trader of a company that provides web design and development as well as basic marketing services. The total time employed for the entire program process was around 1 week.

The first advice of the program was related to the delivery charges. The recommendation was to use one group of conversion factors based on the total weight of the products of the shopping baskets. This advice was rejected by the managing director because he considered it impossible for SME A to absorb the economic differences of the charges. Secondly, the program advised the company to display the e-marketplace by shops on the web site. In spite of the fact that SME A accepted this recommendation, it was later rejected and replaced with a presentation of product categories, from the MBA project's recommendations. The managing director trusted the advice of the MBA student because it involved 8 weeks of comprehensive work, was based on empirical data, and was clearly expressed in a detailed report. Additional advice of the MBA project was also used to change the commercial name of the venture. The final recommendation of the program was related to the look and feel of the application. This advice was implemented by the partners.

The assistance was evaluated via a form from the public organization that co-funded the program, about 6 months after delivering the service. This is a simple form that asks for basic information such as the increase in sales, the jobs created and safeguarded, etc. In theory, these numerical indicators are to be attributed exclusively to the assistance. For example, the form indicates an increase in sales of £ 67000. Finally, at the moment of the interview, the consultant of the program was unsure about what advice was implemented by SME A.

6 ANALYSIS AND DISCUSSION

This section uses the theoretical model presented in section 3 to analyze and discuss the information described in the previous section. We start identifying the barriers and motivators that affected the adoption process of the SME. Then, we review the outcome of the assistance and give recommendations about the possible actions that could have improved program assistance. Finally, we examine the context that surrounded the program in order to determine the factors that influenced the program processes.

6.1 Barriers, Motivators, and the Adoption Process in the SME

Three organizational and venture-related **barriers** were identified in the case. There was a lack of business know-how of SME C about the entire building supplies sector. There were restricted financial resources to continue with the venture. There was also missing business knowledge which prevented the effective design of certain aspects of the web presence (e.g., presentation of the e-marketplace and definition of the commercial name). On the other hand, the technical knowledge of SME B was an important **motivator** for the adoption of the application. These three barriers and the motivator are **SME characteristics** affecting adoption.

The adoption of the e-business application in the SME collapsed in the **infusion stage** because the venture was only able to sell a limited number of products to its customers. This eventual infusion of the e-business system depended on adoption by their customers (buyers). However, the attempts to influence buyer adoption were unsuccessful.

6.2 Review of the Assistance

Although the process collapsed in the infusion stage, we need to tease out the various considerations of when and how the program did and could have influenced this outcome. Although it could be assumed that the venture failed despite good and targeted program interventions, the program intervention can be questioned from several points of view.

The partners did not accept most of the advice provided by the program. The advice of the delivery charges was not accepted and the advice of the presentation of the e-marketplace by shops was reversed after the MBA project. The advice that was accepted was for the look and feel of the web site. This could suggest that if the advice was accepted, or was rejected in the case of the look and feel, the venture would have succeeded. However, various case data suggests that the rejected advice was inappropriate, and the advice that was accepted was advice that could have been generated by the venture itself. For the latter, the SME had expert web site design knowledge with their partners. For the former, the negative opinion of the managing directors suggests that both the intervention methodology and the knowledge and experience of the consultant were poor.

Assuming that the advice was valid and was implemented by the partners, it is possible it was incomplete, taking into account other reasons for closing down the venture, such as sector knowledge. Finally, the assistance was given by a program that was created for another type of service. Program A was created to provide coaching and mentoring based on e-learning techniques as well as to complement it with face-to-face teaching methods, and not for traditional consultancy services.

6.3   Recommendations for the Intervention

In addition to the irrelevant advice that was already available to the SME, or the poor advice that was rejected, there were other gaps in the SME knowledge that needed filling if the venture was to succeed. This suggests various possibilities for a more actively engaged public program participant. The program personnel could have not **selected** SME A because of the insufficiency of the advice, or in **designing** the assistance, program workers could have taken into account the other barriers that were affecting the adoption process of the SME. To address these knowledge gaps, program personnel could have **connected** SME A with other programs or contracted third-party service providers to overcome the barriers of sector know-how and business knowledge for the web presence. Program workers could then have focused their intervention on those barriers for which they could have **delivered** acceptable and practical advice. As a final step, an assessment of the entire adoption process could have been done through an independent **follow-up** of the final outcomes of the adoption process.

However, the program personnel did not address these other knowledge needs, and so the funds were, to a large extent, blindly applied without full consideration of SME needs. Certainly, the **evaluation** form did not reflect either the final result of the adoption process or the impact of the assistance on it. We recommend modification of the measurement instruments, and rethinking the methodology of getting this information. Appropriate and complete evaluation mechanisms represent systemic issues that deserve to be studied and implemented.

6.4   Context Around Program Personnel

Beyond the specific recommendations above, we can examine the context around the program personnel to understand what factors influence their actions and decision. The program targets and measures provided little to explain the quality of the assistance. In addition, the quantitative information was **difficult to measure**. For example, an increase in sales of £67,000 could have been caused by the venture's growth and increasingly favorable market conditions, unrelated to public assistance. However, we also suggest that clients can **manipulate** the evaluation data because they feel they may need the assistance of the agency in the future. This client behavior could be a manifestation of a relatively **powerful position** of the public workers over the clients (Lipsky 1980).

Both the lack of proper performance measures and the relatively powerful position of public workers left program personnel free to choose the level and quality of the program intervention. At this point, there is a **conflict** between **client-centered goals** and **program-centered goals**. On the one hand, program personnel could have met completely the requirements of the clients in a proper way. On the other hand, public workers could have decided to produce a minimal service because the performance measurements did not effectively capture more important outcomes for the client.

There are three factors that could have played in favor of program-centered goals. The first is the **alienation** of the consultant from clients. This problem could result from the fact that the program capabilities were only a **part** of the total needs of the client. This limitation of the program personnel to consider all elements of the SME's needs may have contributed to this outcome. For example, program personnel did not take into account the **circumstances** of SME A in proposing the delivery charges. According to the managing director, the advice was impractical because it did not match with the e-business model of the company. Additionally, program workers were **disconnected** from the next stages of the adoption process by SME A. This was evident when the program consultant was unsure about which recommendations were implemented by the client. What is more, the consultant did not realize there were other barriers to SME A's business plans and e-business strategies, and was therefore unable to connect the client with other programs to address these needs.

A second reason for program-centered goals may be the **inadequacy of resources**. We believe the one week of time provided by one consultant was not enough **time** to deliver a proper program outcome. The managing director of SME B questioned the lack of data to justify the advice. In this case, the seriousness of the advice should have been justified by primary data (e.g., surveys or focus groups), as was done in the MBA project. In addition, the consultant was very young at the time of the service, and appears to have only had basic **knowledge** of web design and marketing. Finally, any limitations on time or expertise could be overcome by contracting third-party service providers. However, we need to gather additional data to determine if there was a **budget** for this activity.

The last reason to focus on program-centered goals is the **demand**. The demand for program A was extremely low. Public workers may have felt the pressure to meet the targets of the entire program. This was evident when the consultant delivered a service that was not in the purview or expertise of the program consultants. So, the inadequacy of resources and the low demand caused a goal displacement when client needs were subordinated to the needs of the program.

7   CONCLUSIONS

The research agenda on e-business innovation and SMEs is traditionally represented by the DOI. The SIA concepts of activities, organizations, institutions, and linkages depict the real-life complexities of innovation. In general, they broaden the research agenda for the adoption of complex innovations to a systemic examination of the contexts and innovations around focal innovations. Accordingly, our study of public program intervention showed additional systemic issues that need to be researched, for example, the dependency of multiple adoption processes, consultancy training, power relationships between public workers and clients, cross-program collaboration, program targets definition and measurement methods, and program demand generation. Program interventions and the focal innovations they target depend on these systemic issues.

The study of the implementation of public programs demonstrated that the research of systemic issues has to rely on theoretical models that go further than the DOI. We used concepts from the study of bureaucracies to explain the reciprocal relationship between public programs and adoption. These concepts were developed in the political science field. In fact, program intervention is explained by concepts such as the lack of program delivery knowledge, limited time for the interventions, low demand of public services, conflict between client and program-centered goals, incorrect program targets and evaluation mechanisms, powerful position of program personnel over clients, and alienation of the personnel from clients. Nevertheless, the adoption process is also necessary to explain the evolution of the different stages of the program process. Concepts from bureaucracies and the DOI are general frameworks which can be used to explain program intervention for the adoption of other complex innovations and types of organization. This consideration enhances the usability of the theoretical model.

To conclude, the practical implications of the research stem from both theoretical and empirical contributions. For instance, the research will help program managers to select SMEs with greater chances of finishing the adoption processes, to help assistance brokers identify programs that can address specific SME issues, to help program officers think about the resources and needs of SMEs to shape effective interventions, to allow SME decision-takers to understand the complexities of the adoption processes, and to identify and employ information technology suppliers to work effectively with public programs.

References

Argyris, C. *Integrating the Individual and the Organization*, New York: John Wiley, 1964.

Attewell, P. "Technology Diffusion and Organizational Learning: The Case of Business Computing," *Organization Science* (3:1), 1992, pp. 1-19.

CEPAL. "Information Society Programme," Division of Production, Productivity and Management, Economic Commission for Latin America and the Caribbean, Santiago, Chile, 2006 (available online at http://www.eclac.cl/socinfo/default.asp?idioma=IN).

Cooper, R., and Zmud, R. "Information Technology Implementation Research: A Technological Diffusion Approach," *Management Science* (36:2), 1990, pp. 83-102.

Dierckx, M., and Stroeken, J. "Information Technology and Innovation in Small and Medium-Sized Enterprises," *Technological Forecasting and Social Change* (60), 1999, pp. 149-166.

Edquist, C. "The Systems of Innovation Approach and Innovation Policy: An Account of the State of the Art," Lead Paper presented at the Danish Research Unit for Industrial Dynamics (DRUID) Conference, Aalborg, Denmark, June 12-15, 2001 (available online at http://www.druid.dk/conferences/nw/paper1/edquist.pdf).

Edquist, C. "Systems of Innovation: Perspectives and Challenges," in J. Fagerberg, D. Mowery, and R. Nelson (eds.), *The Oxford Handbook of Innovation*, Oxford, England: Oxford University Press, 2005, pp 181-208.

European Union. "Helping SMEs to 'Go Digital,'" Enterprise and Industry DG–Technology for Innovation, ICT Industries and E-Business Unit, Brussels, Belgium, 2001 (available online: http://europa.eu/eur-lex/lex/LexUriServ/LexuriServ.do?uri=COM:2001:0136:FIN:EN:PDF).

Eveland, J., and Tornatzky, L. "The Deployment of Technology," in L. Tornatzky and M. Fleischer (eds.), *The Processes of Technological Innovation*, Lexington, MA: Lexington Books, 1990, pp. 117-148.

Gengatharen, D., Craig, S., and Burn, J. "Government-Supported Community Portal, Regional E-Marketplaces for SMEs: Evidence to Support a Staged Approach," *Electronic Markets* (15:4), 2005, pp. 405-417.

Grandon, E., and Pearson, M. "Electronic Commerce Adoption: An Empirical Study of Small and Medium US Businesses," *Information & Management* (42), 2004, pp. 197-216.

Hira, N. *Electronic Commerce and Manufacturing Supply Chain Integration and Management: Approach to Improve Government Policies*, unpublished Ph.D. dissertation, George Mason University, Fairfax, VA, 2002.

Jansen, A. "Technology Diffusion and Adoption in Small, Rural Firms," in T. J. Larsen and and E. McGuire (eds.), *Information Systems Innovation and Diffusion: Issues and Directions*, Hershey, PA: Idea Group Publishing, 1998, pp. 345-372.

Juma, C., and Clark, N. "Policy Research in Sub-Saharan Africa: An Exploration," *Public Administration and Development* (15), 1995, pp. 121-137.

King, J., Gurbaxani, V., Kraemer, K., McFarlan, F., Raman, K., and Yap, C. "Institutional Factors in Information Technology Innovation," *Information Systems Research* (5:2), 1994, pp. 139-170.

Lipsky, M. *Street-Level Bureaucracy: Dilemmas of the Individual in Public Services*, New York: Russell Sage Foundation, 1980.

Long, N. "The Multiple Optic of Interface Analysis. Background Paper on Interface Analysis," Working Paper, UNESCO. Wageningen University, The Netherlands, 1999 (available online: http://www.utexas.edu/cola/insts/llilas/content/claspo/PDF/workingpapers/multipleoptic.pdf).

Lundvall, B.,and Borras, S. "Science, Technology and Innovation Policy," in J. Fagerberg, D. Mowery, and R. Nelson (eds.), *The Oxford Handbook of Innovation*, Oxford, England: Oxford University Press, 2005, pp. 599-631.

McGowan, M., and Madey, G. "Adoption and Implementation of Electronic Data Interchange," in T. J. Larsen and E. McGuire (eds.), *Information Systems Innovation and Diffusion: Issues and Directions*, Hershey, PA: Idea Group Publishing, 1998, pp. 116-140.

Mohr, L. *Explaining Organizational Behavior: The Limits and Possibilities of Theory and Research*, San Francisco: Jossey-Bass, 1982.

Morgan, A., Colebourne, D., and Thomas, B. "The Development of ICT Advisers for SME Businesses: An Innovative Approach," *Technovation* (26:8), 2006, pp. 980-987.

Nyholm, J., Normann, L., Frelle-Petersen, C., Riis, M., and Torstensen, P. "Innovation Policy in the Knowledge-Based Economy: Can Theory Guide Policy-Making?," in D. Archibugi and B. Lundvall (eds.), *The Globalizing Learning Economy*, Oxford, England: Oxford University Press, 2002, pp. 253-272.

OECD. "ICT, E-Business and SMEs," Organisation for Economic Co-Operation and Development, Directorate for Science, Technology and Industry and Center for Entrepreneurship, SMEs and Local Development, Istanbul, Turkey, 2004 (available online: http://www.oecd.org/dataoecd/32/28/34228733.pdf).

Rogers, E. M. *Diffusion of Innovations* (5th ed.), New York: The Free Press, 2003.

Thong, J. "An Integrated Model of Information Systems Adoption in Small Businesses," *Journal of Management Information Systems* (15:4), 1999, pp. 187-214.

Yap, C., and Thong, J. "Program Evaluation of a Government Information Technology Program for Small Business," *Journal of Information Technology* (12), 1997, pp. 107-120.

Yin, R. *Case Study Research: Design and Methods* (3rd ed.), London: Sage Publications, 2002.

About the Authors

Arturo Vega is a doctoral candidate at Lancaster University Management School where he received his MBA. He earned his B.Eng. from Ricardo Palma University in Peru. He has 10 years of international experience in multinationals. His research interest is a mix of information technology, business strategy, innovation, and public policy. He can be reached by e-mail at a.vega1@lancaster.ac.uk.

Mike Chiasson is a senior lecturer in the Department of Management Science at Lancaster University. Mike's research examines the relationships between institutional contexts and the development and implementation of information systems. His work includes action research, user involvement, IT diffusion, privacy, outsourcing, and social foundations of IS development and use. He can be reached by e-mail at m.chiasson@lancaster.ac.uk.

David Brown is a professor of Strategy and Information Systems at Lancaster University Management School. He is also director of the Lancaster Center for Management in China. His research interests include strategic management, strategy, and IT and management in transitional economies. He has published widely in these topics, including books. He can be reached by e-mail at d.brown@lancaster.ac.uk.

26 EXPLORING THE ROLE OF GOVERNMENT IN INFORMATION TECHNOLOGY DIFFUSION: An Empirical Study of IT Usage in Shanghai Firms

Cheng Zhang
Lili Cui
Lihua Huang
Chenghong Zhang
Fudan University
Shanghai, China

Abstract   *By analyzing survey data from 1,211 firms across 14 industries in Shanghai, this study examines factors that influence information technology usage in Chinese firms applying a technology–organization–environment framework and institutional theory. This study provides an in-depth examination of governmental impact on Chinese firms' IT adoption. Although government cannot directly influence firms' IT adoption, it does so indirectly by influencing firms' IT infrastructure construction and management. Firms' IT infrastructure development and IT management decisions act as a mediator between government policies and firms' IT adoption. Furthermore, firms adapt to governmental impact in distinct ways. The findings suggest that e-government approaches and government promotion policies have a significant impact on IT usage in manufacturing firms, in local firms, and in national-background firms.*

Keywords   IT adoption, TOE framework, institutional theory, government

Please use the following format when citing this chapter:

Zhang, C., Cui, L., Huang, L., and Zhang, C., 2007, in IFIP International Federation for Information Processing, Volume 235, Organizational Dynamics of Technology-Based Innovation: Diversifying the Research Agenda, eds. McMaster, T., Wastell, D., Ferneley, E., and DeGross, J. (Boston: Springer), pp. 393-408.

1   INTRODUCTION

With the development of information technology, more and more Chinese firms have investing heavily in IT in order to catch up with the "age of the information economy." A recent report puts China's total IT investment in 2004 at 286.5 billion RMB, 13.7 percent higher than in 2003 (CCW 2004b). The rate of increase reached 15.2 percent in 2005 and will be around 20 percent for 2006 (CCIDNet 2006). Shanghai, as one of the biggest and most modern cities in China, ranks at the top in IT adoption (ISIC 2004).

However, as a developing country, China is still in transition to a market economy and is in the initial phase of IT usage. Compared with firms in developed countries, information technology usage in Chinese firms is far from mature and is uneven across different types and scales of enterprises. A report from ChinaLabs (2004) shows that, out of 1,000 surveyed firms, only 3.7 percent achieved mature IT usage. A survey by the Chinese National Informatization Evaluation Center (NIEC 2004) also shows that the top 500 informatization[1] enterprises in China are mostly large manufacturing enterprises with revenue above 500 million RMB. Large SOEs (state-owned enterprises) tend to be leaders in the national informatization process (NIEC 2004), while only 5 percent of SMEs (small- and medium-sized enterprises) have IT application systems (CCW 2004a).

In the information systems field, factors that affect IT adoption, usage, and valuation have long constituted an active research area (Straub et al. 2002). Many researchers and practitioners have sought theoretical models and empirical evidence to explain these factors and to give suggestions regarding firms' IT decisions. Most of the research to date has focused on developed countries. However, since developing countries have different markets, legal systems, and cultural factors, models from developed countries may not be adaptable to developing countries' environments (Shenkar and Glinow 1994) and such factors may have different effects. It seems clear that government and culture factors have a greater impact on firms' IT usage in developing countries than they do in developed countries (Thatcher and Foster 2003). Research also points out that government regulation plays a more important role than culture in Chinese firms' decisions and IT usage (Xu et al. 2004).

To better understand factors that influence IT adoption in Chinese firms, we developed a research model based on the technology–organization–environment (TOE) framework (Tornatzky and Fleischer 1990) and focused more on government-related factors. With survey data from 1,211 firms across 14 industrial fields, the study provides insightful managerial implications for Chinese firms and valuable practical suggestions to the Chinese government. We explored the following research issues:

(1) The importance of technological, organizational, and environmental factors for firms deploying IT.
(2) The influence of different industry types, investment property types, and ownership types on IT adoption by firms in developed Chinese cities such as Shanghai.

---

[1]*Informatization* refers to IT usage and adoption in organizations and is a widely accepted concept in China.

Focusing on measuring Shanghai's government initiatives can largely reduce the potential interference of different influences on policy execution by various local governments and enhance our observation of the government's role. To make the results generalizable, firms with either headquarters or branches registered in Shanghai were included in the sample.

2 LITERATURE REVIEW

Many studies have explored the factors that drive the business value of IT. The research relevant to this study can be divided into two streams. One is the technology–organization–environment framework (Tornatzky and Fleischer 1990), which is used to identify technological, organizational, and environmental factors that affect IT diffusion in organizations. Here, we concentrate more on external institutional elements as a unique environmental factor. The second research stream is institutional theory perspective, which is used to explore the effects of path dependency, governmental intervention, and historical context on the evolution of organizational rules (Zucker 1987). These streams provide evidence of environment constructs, especially government related factors in the model.

2.1 The Technology–Organization–Environment Framework

The technology–organization–environment (TOE) framework(Tornatzky and Fleischer 1990) was developed to study the adoption of general technological innovations in organizations. The framework features three aspects that influence the process of technology diffusion in organizations: technological context, organizational context, and environmental context. Technological context refers to technologies that are relevant to firms. Organizational context generally refers to organizational characteristics, such as size, scope, and resources available within a firm. Environmental context involves the macro-circumstances in which a firm conducts its business. Environmental factors include industry, competitors, government relations, etc. The framework is suitable to identify factors shaping innovation adoption (Xu et al. 2004) and provides a reliable theoretical basis for this study.

The impact of technological factors on information system adoption and business values may be enhanced in the Chinese context. Because the overall IT usage in Chinese firms is immature (ChinaLabs 2004), better IT resources are comparatively rare and probably exert greater influence on firms' IT adoption. A report from National Informatization Evaluation Center (NIEC 2005) also showed that high IT adoption has successfully helped some large firms gain a competitive advantage and support their core value realization.

Organizational and management factors also play an important role in firms' IT usage. Research shows that SMEs are more likely to focus on the alignment between IT and business strategy (Levy and Powell 2003; Tsao et al. 2004), but tend to lack management support (such as technical consultation), IT management knowledge, and business transformation guidelines (Yeung et al. 2003). In China, those obstacles seem to be common. Suffering from an immature IT service market and poor IT management knowledge, most Chinese enterprises have low performance in IT usage and value creation (NIEC 2004). Therefore, effective IT management has become one of the most critical and urgent problems Chinese enterprises face.

External environmental factors, such as trading partners, competitors, government, and socio-political conditions, may play an important role in firms' IS/IT adoption and business value generation (Melville et al. 2004). Due to an immature market, different culture, and other reasons, China has environmental characteristics distinct from Western countries (Boisot and Child 1999). For example, studies find that culture and philosophy have impacts on firms' IT adoption (Davison 2002; Martinsons and Westwood 1997). Tan and Ouyang (2004) examined the diffusion of e-commerce in China and found that the current e-commerce barriers include legal, cultural, and governmental issues. Xu et al. (2004) further confirmed that government regulation plays a more important role in China than in the United States. As a new method of delivering public services, e-government initiatives and activities, differing from traditional incentive policies such as legislation and promotion, became a new way through which government could potentially participate in e-business affairs and affect IT diffusion. Government influence can be particularly significant in a government-directed economy or where the private sector is not yet fully developed (Blakeley and Matsuura 2004).

Overall, the TOE framework provides a theoretical basis for understanding factors that affect firms' IS/IT adoption. In this study, IT infrastructure, IT management, and government factors are all investigated.

2.2 Institutional Theory Perspective

From an institutional perspective, organizations can be influenced by varied pressures arising from either external environment or internal organizational factors. Firms become more similar due to isomorphic pressures and pressures for legitimacy by three important legitimization processes: coercive, imitative, and normative (DiMaggio and Powell 1983).

The institutional factors provide a useful research view on an IT adoption study. The institutional environment in which the organization is embedded exerts an influence on the adoption process exhibited by individual organizations. In IT diffusion, firms tend to be induced to adopt and use certain information systems by external isomorphic pressures form competitors, trading partners, customers, and government. Recent studies have taken an institutional approach to e-commerce diffusion (Gibbs and Kraemer 2004; Teo et al. 2003), which reveals the importance of external pressures, government promotion, and legislation in e-commerce adoption and use. Regulatory agencies, such as the government or industrial consortiums, may create incentives or barriers to adoption and use. On the other hand, firms tend to learn and copy successful IT practices from industry leaders and accept a normalized best practice on IT adoption in a fast-changing environment.

From an institutional view, firms with strong ties to the public sector are likely to adopt innovations required or supported by government policy (Hinings and Greenwood 1987; Zucker 1987). In China, the government has determined informatization-driven industrialization as part of its national policy. The Ministry of Information Industry (MII) of China indicates that, in the future, China will persist in promoting a national plan of enterprise informatization, led by large-scale backbone enterprises. Given different investment property and ownership, firms' IT adoption may be influenced differently by government policies and actions. Studies also found that firms' ownership strongly influences their IT implementation (see Reimers 2002), and government regulation plays a more important role in Chinese firms' IT decisions and usage than in the United States (Xu et al. 2004). These environmental factors may play a crucial role in firms' IT adoption in China.

3 RESEARCH MODEL AND HYPOTHESES

With theoretical support by the TOE and institutional theory, we developed the research model shown in Figure 1. Our framework is inspired by the TOE, while environmental factors here are examined by institutional factors of government: e-government, promotion, and regulation. Three major factors—IT infrastructure, IT management, and government factors (Melville et al. 2004; Tan and Ouyang 2004; Wade and Hulland 2004; Xu et al. 2004)—are proposed in the model to analyze their impact on IT usage. We also consider the possible relationships between different government factors, firms' IT factors, and organizational factors and explore how different government policies may influence firms' IT infrastructure and management decisions, respectively. Furthermore, we sought to determine whether government impacts are diverse across multiple industries, investment properties, and ownerships.

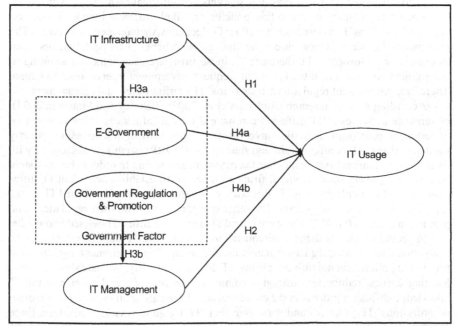

Figure 1. **The Research Model**

IT infrastructure is a collection of physical technology resources, including shared technology and technology services across the organization (Melville et al. 2004), which facilitate firms' connectivity and operations. Depending on its use, IT infrastructure can be an important source to influence firms' business value (Kumar 2004). Firms can develop unique capabilities and business value by using their IT infrastructure (Zhu 2004). Research shows that IT factors, including infrastructure and expertise, play a significant role in IT usage (Zhu et al. 2002). Therefore, we propose

H1: The more developed a firm's IT infrastructure, the greater the firm's IT usage.

Another type of factor is IT management capability (ITMC) in organizations, which denotes firms' technical and managerial knowledge (Byrd and Turner 2000; Melville et al. 2004) of IT. Compared with physical IT infrastructure, IT management is a set of soft abilities that help firms to deploy IT in an effective manner (Lee et al. 1995; Swanson 1994). In order to utilize IT physical assets economically, firms need to pursue a good fit between IT functionalities and business strategies (Grabowski and Lee 1993; McLaren et al. 2004) and manage IT infrastructures to improve organization performance (Markus and Soh 1993). Therefore, we propose

H2: The greater a firm's IT management capability, the greater the firm's IT usage.

Considering the relatively immature markets and information asymmetry in China, government regulations or promotion policies are likely to have broader impact on Chinese local firms' behavior, including their IT decisions, management, and usage. The government influence is more direct and visible than other environmental factors, such as culture or philosophy. Furthermore, Chinese firms are accustomed to adapting to government policies, given the history of frequent government interventions in China. Therefore, government regulation affects firms' IT configuration and management.

According to prior research (Anderson et al. 2003; Blakeley and Matsuura 2004), governance activities in IT diffusion can have different influences. One category of government promotion activities involves the e-government initiatives to directly influence firms' IT configurations and thus usage (GDRP), such as transactions with firms in e-government systems, online tax payment, and so on. In order to be consistent with these e-government activities, firms are coerced to establish accordant IT infrastructure and IT configuration. In this way, e-government will affect firms' IT plans, especially their IT infrastructure. The other category deals with their regulations and promotion policies (GIRP). These are intended to improve firms' IT-related knowledge and to provide a standardized environment by establishing IT application standards, evaluation frameworks, regulation standards, and so on. The government regulations or promotion policies cannot influence firms' IT decisions directly, but may shorten firms' learning curves, reduce information asymmetry, and improve and accelerate the IT knowledge-diffusion process in the entire market. Firms are motivated to imitate other organizations' IT practices and normalize their IT usage behavior. Therefore, these regulations or policies can affect firms' IT knowledge and, consequently, their IT management quality. Accordingly, we propose

H3: Government IT promotion policies have positive impact on firms' IT infrastructure and IT management.

    H3a: E-government initiatives positively affect firms' IT infrastructure construction.

    H3b: Government regulation and IT promotion policies help firms improve their IT management.

Prior research shows that nontechnical environmental factors affect innovation adoption (Kraemer et al. 2002; Tornatzky and Fleischer 1990). While firms in e-commerce surveys frequently cite environment issues like security, credibility of the system, and legal matters as their major concerns, they also point out that incentives provided by the government are key drivers for their new IT and e-commerce usage (Tan and Ouyang 2004; Xu et al. 2004). The results denote that government regulation (GRDP) and IT-related promotion policies can affect firms' IT configuration and improve their IT usage. Thus, we propose

H4: Government IT-related policies positively affect firms' IT usage.

    H4a: E-government initiatives help firms improve their IT usage.

    H4b: Government regulation and IT promotion policies help firms improve their IT usage.

Firms with strong ties to the public sector are likely to adopt IT innovations supported by government policy (Hinings and Greenwood 1987; Zucker 1987) and to follow up government IT-usage actions. The extent of environmental effect can be defined by firms' ownership, investment property, and industry type. Firms with a national background are more easily influenced by government actions and regulations. Government may influence firms' IT adoption in diverse ways. With e-government implementation, firms are coerced to adopt their technology infrastructure to align with the government's system. With government promotion and regulation of IT standards and practices, firms can imitate other organizations' IT practices and normalize their IT usage behavior. In order to examine whether government effects are the same across different firm types, we will divide the full sample into subsample sets according to firm type and run *post hoc* analysis to further explore government's role in firms' IT adoption.

4 METHODOLOGY

4.1 Data and Method

A questionnaire survey method was adopted for the study. The sample frame includes enterprises in Shanghai from 14 industries: machinery manufacturing; transportation services; retail business/wholesale trade; food, beverage, and tourism services; food processing; textile; oil and coking processing; pharmaceutical manufacturing; chemical fiber/rubber/plastic products; metal smelt and mangle processing; transport manufacturing; electronic and telecommunication equipment manufacturing; sporting, cultural, and educational goods manufacturing; and real estate. Overall, 1,912 random firms received questionnaires, resulting in 1,211 valid returned questionnaires. We used the partial least squares (PLS) approach, a structural equation modeling (SEM) technique, to examine the model and hypotheses. The software used to apply PLS to the model is PLS-Graph (Chin 2001).

4.2 Measures and Validity

Three items (i.e., firms' IT hardware, software, and network status) were used to measure IT infrastructure; these items were also used in prior work (Byrd and Turner 2000; Duncan 1995). To measure the IT management factor, we studied the practice of IT-related planning, evaluation, and management activities in firms (Byrd and Turner 2000). To measure the regulatory environment, questions about how government actions, including online procurement requirement, incentives, laws, and legal protection, would affect firms' IT adoption were adapted from prior research (Tan and Ouyang 2004, Xu et al. 2004). Other new items, including funding, e-government service, establishing application standards, and establishing evaluation framework were added after careful discussion among professionals and were validated in the pretest. Among these, adopting web-based online e-government services is categorized as e-government, and others are attributed to government regulations and promotion policies. Finally, IT usage included measures on firms' computer usage and application usage.[2]

To validate the instruments, we examined internal consistency, convergent validity, and discriminant validity. The result shows that the composite reliability values for the constructs in the model were all above the suggested threshold of 0.7 (Chin 1998; Straub 1989). All items had a loading above 0.55 as suggested by Falk and Miller (1992) while average variance extracted (AVEs) of the construct were above the limit of 0.50 advised by Fornell and Larcker (1981). The squared root of average variance extracted for each construct was higher than the correlation coefficient between two constructs.

5 DATA ANALYSIS

5.1 Full Sample Analysis

All hypothesized paths, except the link between government factors and IT usage, are found to be significant ($p < 0.01$). The path coefficient from infrastructure to usage is 0.453, and from IT management to usage is 0.147, which suggests significant impacts of IT infrastructure and management issues on appropriate IT usage in firms. Furthermore, the paths from e-government to the infrastructure and from government regulation and promotion to IT management are also significant. The path coefficients are 0.189 and 0.246, respectively. The results suggest a clear influence of government on firms' IT configuration and management. However, the impact of government factors on firms' IT usage is not significant. This result suggests that government affects firms' IT usage in an indirect manner. The mediating factors are firms' IT infrastructure and IT manage-

---

[2]Details of the questionnaire are available upon request from the second author (cuilili@ fudan.edu.cn).

ment. The important dependent construct (i.e., IT usage) has R^2 of 0.331, suggesting a reasonable explanation of data variation in the TOE framework. In summary, H1, H2, H3a, and H3b are supported, while H4a and H4b are not supported.

To verify the mediating effect of IT management and IT infrastructure on government factors and IT usage, we removed the paths between government factors and IT infrastructure and IT management and the model was rerun. Result shows that the paths from government factors to IT usage are not significant, while other paths are still significant. The test demonstrates that government factors affect firms' IT usage indirectly, with IT infrastructure and IT management as mediators.

5.2 Subsample Analysis

5.2.1 Industry Difference Analysis

To test for industry differences in the model, we split the full sample set into two sub-samples, one including 988 survey responses from the manufacturing industry (MI) and the other 223 responses from the service industry (SI). According to China's national standard of statistics, the service industry includes retail business/wholesale trade, as well as food, beverage, and tourism services and real estate. The remaining industries belong to the manufacturing category. After examining the internal consistency, convergent validity, and discriminant validity of the model with each subsample set, we ran a PLS analysis.

The path coefficient from infrastructure to usage and from management to usage, respectively, is of the same significance as those in the full-data mode. The result suggests that the model applies across industries. However, the effect of government on firms' IT infrastructure and IT management is only significant in manufacturing, suggesting a distinct government impact on firms' IT decision from different industries. Therefore, the process of IT adoption proves to be similar across industries, while government actions and policies influence only the manufacturing industry significantly.

5.2.2 Investment Property and Ownership Difference Analysis

To further explore whether different types of firms have different IT adoption behavior, we divided firms into several groups according to their investment property and ownership types. With respect to investment property, firms were divided into three groups: local invested, joint invested, and foreign invested. In terms of ownership, firms were divided into three groups: state owned, private owned, and semi-national (private) owned.

The impacts of technological and organizational factors on firms' IT adoption are significant across firms investment property. However, the government influence on firms' IT infrastructure and IT management is only significant in local firms, suggesting a distinct government impact on firms' IT decision from different investment property. Furthermore, IT management plays a more important role in foreign-invested firms than in local- and joint-invested firms, which may suggest a different focus on IT strategy among local, joint, and foreign firms. Therefore, government's actions and policies influence local firms' IT adoption only.

The impacts of technological and organizational factors on firms' IT adoption are significant across firms' ownership. However, government influence on firms' IT infrastructure and IT management is not significant in private firms. The result suggests a distinct government impact on firms of different ownership. Government's actions and policies influence national-background firms significantly.

6   DISCUSSION AND CONCLUSIONS

To study IT adoption in the context of China's governmental regulation, we developed a research model and examined the model with empirical data from 14 selected vertical industries in Shanghai. The empirical analysis provides several major findings.

Finding 1: Government actions affect firms' IT adoption via different paths. Firms' IT infrastructure development and IT management decisions act as mediators between government actions and firms' IT adoption

China, with its booming economy and large population, has been gaining increasing interest from both the business world and the academy. Considering the relatively immature markets, information asymmetry, and relatively strong cultural tradition of subservience to government authority in China, government regulation may have broad impacts on local firms. Although prior research often concluded that government regulation, as an important environmental factor, would significantly influence firms' operation and decisions, exactly how government factors work is not as clear. Few studies have empirically examined the role of government in driving IT adoption in Chinese firms.

In this study, government actions are initially classified into two categories: e-government approach and regulation approach. The data suggests that different government actions affect firms' IT adoption in different ways. Although the government cannot directly influence firms' IT adoption, it does so by influencing firms' IT infrastructure construction and management. Further examination of mediating effects proves that IT infrastructure and management are mediators between government factors and IT usage. In other words, firms' IT infrastructure development and IT management decisions act as mediators between different government actions and firms' IT adoption.

By exploring the government's intervention power over firms' IT infrastructure construction and IT application usage, we find that e-government can affect firms' IT adoption by affecting their IT infrastructure construction. The finding seems reasonable. For example, when adopting online tax-payment systems, firms have to configure proper hardware, network connections, and software to pay the taxes online. Similarly, if firms want to evolve into government e-procedure, they have to be accordant with the e-government systems. Since government regulation and promotion policies can improve firms' IT-related knowledge, the promotion policies interactively act on firms' IT management.

The results also suggest that government regulation and promotion policies affect firms' IT adoption by influencing their IT management decisions. The finding seems reasonable and practical. Because IT adoption is emergent as a technological innovation for most Chinese firms in recent years, firms lack knowledge and experience on how to adopt IT to support their management and business practices. Without theoretical advancement or empirical examination in the context of China, firms cannot receive useful suggestions from the academy, either. Given these reasons, government actions (such as establishing case studies and an IT adoption evaluation framework, promoting IT learning and firms' IT practice, and adopting web-based tax reporting, inspection, and government e-procurement transaction) give firms a greater opportunity to learn and act. For example, case studies and IT research can help firms know more about IT, providing an IT adoption evaluation framework that can help firms clarify their direction of IT adoption, while promoting IT practices and e-government systems can directly motivate firms to initialize their IT adoption process.

However, since China is gradually transforming to a market economy, the government's impact on firms is decreasing. Although the government's promotion gives firms useful information to configure IT infrastructure and set up management rules, firms are likely to determine their own usage of IT according to their specific conditions and purposes, rather than following exactly what the government has provided. Also, because IT usage is a complex process of fitting IT assets with business operations and strategies, government promotion policies cannot influence manufacturing firms' IT usage directly, but do so indirectly by affecting firms' IT infrastructure and management. This observation will help the government assess its IT policies. For example, when considering new regulations, the government may find it more effective to help firms improve their IT management knowledge, rather than to intervene on their IT usage or direct investment.

Finding 2: Firms adapt to governmental impact in distinct ways. Government impacts on firms' IT adoption are most obvious in the manufacturing industry and are different among firms of different investment property and ownership types

The manufacturing industry is one of the most vital industries in China. With fast globalization and industrialization, China is playing an important role in the global production network (Ernst 2003), and facing more pressure from global competition. Since China has determined informatization-driven industrialization to be its national development strategy, the government has directed more attention to manufacturing firms' IT usage than usage by service firms. Comparing the manufacturing industry with the service industry provides clear evidence of how local government can influence firms' IT usage.

Firms' investment property types and ownership types indicate different degrees of control by government and probably different IT usage and management style in firms. From the empirical data, it seems clear that government policies show differing impacts on local-, joint-, and foreign-invested firms. It is clear that both e-government approaches and promotion policies play a significant role on local firms' IT adoption. In other words, local firms' IT usage is more influenced by government than in the case of firms with foreign investment. Compared to firms with foreign investment, local firms usually have less experience with how Western firms operate and less mature ways of using IT. As a result, local firms are willing to receive support from government when making IT-related decisions. Besides, government influence on local firms is historically strong in a government-directed economy. As market economics in China matures, government influence is weakening, but the empirical data in the study still suggest a stronger influence on local firms, compared with foreign-invested firms. The result also suggests that government policies and actions in China are critically important factors influencing firms' IT usage.

Government policies show distinct impacts on national, semi-national, and private firms. It is clear that firms with a national background are more significantly influenced by government policies. The reason is straightforward: national firms are more used to following government policies than other ownership type firms. On the other hand, national firms constitute the major focus of government regulation in China. Government usually targets national firms when making decisions and policies. Therefore, it is not surprising to see a more significant role of government in such firms' operation and management activities in China.

Overall, e-government approaches and government promotion policies have shown a significant impact on manufacturing firms, on local firms, and on national-background firms. The results suggest that environmental factors, such as government policies, may have varying impacts on different types of firms. Future studies should pay more attention to industry type, investment property type, and ownership type in examining firms' IT adoption, particularly in developing countries like China.

Acknowledgments

This research has been financially supported by Fudan Research Award for Young Scholars (Grant No. CHH1019035), National Science Fund of China (Grant No. 70571016), and National Philosophy and Social Science Foundation (No. 06BZZ020). The authors would like to thank the anonymous reviewers, Dr. Ken Kraemer, and Dr. Kevin Zhu for their valuable comments on the manuscript.

References

Anderson, K. V., Bjørn-Andersen, N., and Dedrick, J. "Governance Initiative Creating a Demand-Driven E-Commerce Approach: The Case of Denmark," *The Information Society* (19), 2003, pp. 95-105.

Blakeley, C. J., and Matsuura, J. H. "The Use of E-Government to Encourage E-Commerce Development," in *Proceedings of the International Conference on Information and Communication Technologies: From Theory to Applications*, April 19-23, 2004, pp. 15-16.

Boisot, M., and Child, J. "Organizations as Adaptive Systems in Complex Environments: The Case of China," *Organization Science* (10), 1999, pp. 237-252.

Byrd, T. A., and Turner, D. E. "Measuring the Flexibility of Information Technology Infrastructure: Exploratory Analysis of a Construct," *Journal of Management Information Systems* (17), 2000, pp. 167-208.

CCIDNET. "Increase Rate at Industrial Informatization Investment Will Reach 20% in 2006," China Market Information Center, 2006 (available online through http://industry.ccidnet.com/art/7/20060217/431185_1.html).

CCW. "China (Both Government and Enterprises) Informatization Situation and Demand Survey Report," China Computer World, 2004a (available online at http://219.141.209.201/article/zhengfuzhuanlan/bulingdao/wangxudong/y2004/2006-11-20/20061120163553.html; in Chinese).

CCW. "High-Speed Development of China it Market from 2005 to 2009," China Computer World, 2004b (available online at http://www.ccw.com.cn/htm/center/ccw/ccwresearch1.asp; in Chinese).

Chin, W. W. "Issues and Opinion on Structure Equation Modeling," *MIS Quarterly* (22:1), 1998, pp. vii-xvi.

Chin, W. W. *PLS-Graph User's Guide*, Soft Modeling Inc., 2001 (available online at http://www.cis.gsu.edu/~ghubona/info790/PLSGRAPH3.0Manual.pdf).

ChinaLabs. "China Informatization Report (2004 Q2, Chinese)," ChinaLabs, 2004 (available online through http://www.chinalabs.com/cache/doc/04/06/29/2790.shtml; in Chinese).

Davison, R. "Cultural Complications of ERP," *Communications of the ACM* (45:7), July 2002, pp. 109-111.

DiMaggio, P. J., and Powell, W. W. "The Iron Cage Revisited: Institutional Isomorphism and Collective Rationality in Organizational Fields," *American Sociological Review* (48), 1983, pp. 147-160.

Duncan, N. B. "Capturing Flexibility of Information Technology Infrastructure: A Study of Resource Characteristics and Their Measure," *Journal of Management Information Systems* (12), 1995, pp. 37-57.

Ernst, D. "The New Mobility of Knowledge: Digital Information Systems and Global Flagship Networks," Economics Series No. 56, East-West Center Working Papers, Honolulu, HI, June 2003 (available online at http://www.eastwestcenter.org/stored/pdfs/ECONwp056.pdf).

Falk, R. F., and Miller, N. B. *A Primer for Soft Modeling*, Akron, OH: University of Akron Press, 1992.

Fornell, C., and Larcker, D. F. "Evaluating Structural Models with Unobserved Variables and Measurement Errors," *Journal of Marketing Research* (18), 1981, pp. 39-50.

Gibbs, J. L., and Kraemer, K. L. "A Cross-Country Investigation of the Determinants of Scope of E-Commerce Use: An Institutional Approach," *Electronic Markets* (14), 2004, pp. 124-137.

Grabowski, M., and Lee, S. "Linking Information Systems Application Portfolios and Organizational Strategy," in R. D. Banker, R. J. Kauffman, and M. A. Mahmood (eds.), *Strategic Information Technology Management: Perspectives on Organizational Growth and Competitive Advantage,* Harrisburg, PA: Idea Group Publishing, 1993, pp. 33-54.

Hinings, C. R., and Greenwood, R. *The Normative Prescription of Organizations,* Cambridge, MA: Ballinger Press, 1987.

ISIC. "The Measuring and Comparative Research of Regional Imformatization Level from 1999 to 2001 of China," *Statistical Research* (3), 2004, pp. 3-11.

Kraemer, K., Gibbs, J., and Dedrick, J. "Environment and Policy Facilitators Shaping E-Commerce Diffusion: A Cross-Country Comparison," in L. Applegate, R. Galliers, and J. I. DeGross (eds.), *Proceedings of the 23rd International Conference on Information System,* Barcelona, Spain, 2002, pp. 325-335.

Kumar, R. L. "A Framework for Assessing the Business Value of Information Technology Infrastructures," *Journal of Management Information Systems* (21), 2004, pp. 11-32.

Lee, D. M. S., Trauth, E., and Farwell, D. "Critical Skills and Knowledge Requirements of IS Professionals: A Joint Academic/Industry Investigation," *MIS Quarterly* (19:3), September 1995, pp. 313-340.

Levy, M., and Powell, P. "Exploring SME Internet Adoption: Towards a Contingent Model," *Electronic Markets* (13), 2003, pp. 173-181.

Markus, M. L., and Soh, C. "Banking on Information Technology: Converting IT Spending into Firm Performance," in R. D. Banker, R. J. Kauffman, and M. A. Mahmood (eds.), *Strategic Information Technology Management: Perspectives on Organizational Growth and Competitive Advantage,* Harrisburg, PA: Idea Group Publishing, 1993, pp. 364-392.

Martinsons, M. G., and Westwood, R. I. "Management Information Systems in the Chinese Business Culture: An Explanatory Theory," *Information and Management* (32), 1997, pp. 215-228.

McLaren, T., Head, M. M., and Yuan, Y. "Strategic Fit of Supply Chain Management Information Systems: A Measurement Model," in R. Agarwal, L. Kirsch, and J. I. DeGross (eds.), *Proceedings of the 25th International Conference on Information Systems*, Washington, DC, 2004, pp. 597-606.

Melville, N., Kraemer, K., and Gurbaxani, V. "*Review*: Information Technology and Organizational Performance: An Integrative Model of it Business Value," *MIS Quarterly* (28:2), June 2004, pp. 283-322.

NIEC. "Survey Report of Top 500 China Informatization Enterprises," National Informatization Evaluation Center, 2004 (available online at http://www.ipower500.com/2004/report.htm; in Chinese).

NIEC. "Top 500 of Chinese Enterprise Informatization," National Informatization Evaluation Center, 2005.

Reimers, K. "Implementing ERP Systems in China," in *Proceedings of the 35ᵗʰ Hawaii International Conference on System Sciences*, Los Alamitos, CA: IEEE Computer Society Press, 2002.

Shenkar, O., and Glinow, M. A. V. "Paradoxes of Organizational Theory and Research: Using the Case of China to Illustrate National Contingency," *Management Science* (40), 1994, pp. 56-71.

Straub, D. "Validating Instruments in MIS Research," *MIS Quarterly* (13:2), June 1989, pp. 147-169.

Straub, D., Hoffman, D., Weber, B., and Steinfield., C. "Toward New Metrics for Net-Enhanced Organizations," *Information Systems Research* (13), 2002, pp. 227-238.

Swanson, E. B. "Information Systems Innovation among Organizations," *Management Science* (40), 1994, pp. 1069-1092.

Tan, Z., and Ouyang, W. "Diffusion and Impacts of the Internet and E-Commerce in China," *Electronic Markets* (14), 2004, pp. 25-35.

Teo, H. H., Wei, K. K., and Benbasat, I. "Predicting Intention to Adopt Interorganizational Linkages: An Institutional Perspective," *MIS Quarterly* (27:1), March 2003, pp. 19-49.

Thatcher, S. M. B., and Foster, W. "B2B E-Commerce Adoption Decisions in Taiwan: The Interaction of Organizational, Industrial, Governmental and Cultural Factors," in *Proceedings of the 36ᵗʰ Annual Hawaii International Conference on System Science*, Los Alamitos, CA: IEEE Computer Society Press, 2003.

Tornatzky, L. G., and Fleischer, M. *The Processes of Technological Innovation*, Lexington, MA: Lexington Books, 1990.

Tsao, H. Y., Lin, K. H. C., and Lin, C. "An Investigation of Critical Success Factors in the Adoption of B2BEC by Taiwanese Companies," *Journal of American Academy of Business, Cambridge* (5:1-2), September 2004.

Wade, M., and Hulland, J. "*Review*: The Resource-Based View and Information Systems Research: Review, Extension, and Suggestions for Future Research," *MIS Quarterly* (28:1), March 2004, pp. 107-142.

Xu, S., Zhu, K., and Gibbs, J. "Global Technology, Local Adoption: A Cross-Country Investigation of Internet Adoption by Companies in the United States and China," *Electronic Markets* (14), 2004, pp. 13-24.

Yeung, J. H. Y., Shim, J. P., and Lai, A. Y. K. "Current Progress of E-Commerce Adoption: Small and Medium Enterprises in Hong Kong," *Communications of the ACM* (46:9), September 2003, pp. 226-232.

Zhu, K. "The Complementarity of Information Technology Infrastructure and E-Commerce Capability: A Resource-Based Assessment of Their Business Value," *Journal of Management Information Systems* (21), 2004, pp. 167-202.

Zhu, K., Kraemer, K. L., and Xu, S. "A Cross-Country Study of Electronic Business Adoption Using the Technology–Organization–Environment Framework," in L. Applegate, R. Galliers, and J. I. DeGross (eds.), *Proceedings of the 23ʳᵈ International Conference on Information Systems*, Barcelona, Spain, 2002, pp. 337-348.

Zucker, L. G. "Institutional Theories of Organization," *Annual Review of Sociology* (13), 1987, pp. 443-464.

About the Authors

Cheng Zhang is a lecturer in the MIS Department, at Fudan University. His research interests include IT diffusion and e-business. His work has appeared in including *Omega, Electronic Markets,* and *Simulation Modeling Practice and Theory,* and in conference proceedings including Decision Sciences Institute and the Americas Conference on Information Systems.

Lili Cui is a Ph.D.candidate in the MIS Department at Fudan University and a senior analyst of SIECC. Her research focuses on IS diffusion. She has published in *Electronic Markets* and various conference proceedings. Lili can be reached by e-mail at cuilili@fudan.edu.cn.

Lihua Huang is a professor in the MIS Department at Fudan University. Her research interests include e-commerce and information system implementation. Her research work has been published in *Information and Management, Electronic Markets,* and various conference proceedings

Chenghong Zhang is an associate professor in the MIS Department at Fudan University. His research interests include e-commerce, information system planning, and knowledge management.

27 SME ADOPTION OF ENTERPRISE SYSTEMS IN THE NORTHWEST OF ENGLAND: An Environmental, Technological, and Organizational Perspective

Boumediene Ramdani
Peter Kawalek
Manchester Business School
University of Manchester
Manchester, United Kingdom

Abstract   *The attention of software vendors has moved recently to SMEs (small- to medium-sized enterprises), offering them a vast range of enterprise systems (ES), which were formerly adopted by large firms only. From reviewing information technology innovation adoption literature, it can be argued that IT innovations are highly differentiated technologies for which there is not necessarily a single adoption model. Additionally, the question of why one SME adopts an ES while another does not is still understudied. This study intends to fill this gap by investigating the factors impacting SME adoption of ES. A qualitative approach was adopted in this study involving key decision makers in nine SMEs in the Northwest of England. The contribution of this study is twofold: it provides a framework that can be used as a theoretical basis for studying SME adoption of ES, and it empirically examines the impact of the factors within this framework on SME adoption of ES. The findings of this study confirm that factors impacting the adoption of ES are different from factors impacting SME adoption of other previously studied IT innovations. Contrary to large companies that are mainly affected by organizational factors, this study shows that SMEs are not only affected by environmental factors as previously established, but also affected by technological and organizational factors.*

Keywords   SMEs, adoption, ICT, enterprise system

Please use the following format when citing this chapter:

Ramdani, B., and Kawalek, P., 2007, in IFIP International Federation for Information Processing, Volume 235, Organizational Dynamics of Technology-Based Innovation: Diversifying the Research Agenda, eds. McMaster, T., Wastell, D., Ferneley, E., and DeGross, J. (Boston: Springer), pp. 409-430.

1   INTRODUCTION

New information and communication technologies (ICT) such as enterprise systems (ES) provide small- to medium-sized enterprises (SMEs) with opportunities that are largely unexploited. Most small firms still underutilize the potential value of ICT by restricting it to administrative tasks (Brock 2000). The UK Department of Trade and Industry (DTI) literature claims that ICT adoption and implementation is crucial to the survival and growth of the economy in general, and the small-business sector in particular (Martin and Matlay 2001). Although SMEs form a substantial constituent of the global economy and ICT adoption is nowadays economically and strategically feasible for the smallest organizations (Raymond 1989; Thong et al. 1994), limited research has addressed the specifics of new ICT adoption, implementation and use in the context of small firms (Brock 2000; Shiels et al. 2003).

The SMB global model study predicts spending worldwide by SMEs on information technology and telecommunications will exceed U.S.\$1.1 trillion during 2008 (AMI-Partners 2004). Furthermore, predictions are that the global level of spending by SMEs on CRM software packages alone will double, reaching U.S.\$2 billion by 2008 (Datamonitor 2004). As a result, the attention of software vendors has moved to SMEs, offering them a vast range of ES. The question of why one SME adopts an ES while another does not is still understudied. This study intends to fill this gap by answering the following research questions:

- What framework can be used as a theoretical basis for studying SME adoption of ES?
- What is the impact of the identified factors within this theoretical framework on SME adoption of ES?

Before reviewing IT innovation adoption research, the following section gives an overview of SMEs and their ICT adoption.

2   SME ADOPTION OF ICT

SMEs are considered to be major economic players and a potent source of national, regional, and local economic growth (Taylor and Murphy 2004). Without a better understanding of the complex processes and the differentiating factors that affect the ICT adoption level, the drive of ICT adoption and development will not successfully contribute to SMEs' competitiveness (Martin and Matlay 2001). There were 4.3 million small business enterprises in the United Kingdom at the start of 2005 representing 99 percent of all business and accounting for more than half of the employment (58.7 percent) and turnover (51.1 percent) in the UK (SBS 2006).

The European Commission defines small businesses based on the number of employees, annual turnover, annual balance sheet total, and level of autonomy (European Commission 2003). Most definitions of SMEs emanate from the 1971 Bolton Committee Report, which defines a small firm as independent, owner-managed, and with small market share (Simpson and Docherty 2004). The DTI categorizes SMEs into micro firms with fewer than 10 employees; small firms with 10 to 49 employees; and medium sized firms with 50 to 249 employees. Story (1994) argues that the number of employees is considered to be an appropriate measure of SMEs because of the differences in organizational structures that occur with size. Using number of employees as a measure, the European Commission and DTI definitions are compatible and therefore will be used in this study.

New ICT provides SMEs with opportunities that are largely unexploited (Brock 2000; Corso et al. 2001). It is hard nowadays to imagine SMEs operating without some use of ICT. However, SMEs differ in the level of ICT usage (Blackburn and McClure 1998). Southern and Tilley (2000) identify three categories of small firms with different attitudes to ICT.

- *SMEs with low-end ICT use,* where there is not a good fit between ICT and the owner-manager's concept of the business
- *Medium-level ICT users,* with more expertise, separate IT and communications systems, open access to company data (network and files servers), IT in production, e-mail, and a plan for and delegation of the management and routine upgrading of IT
- *High-end ICT users,* leading-edge and innovative IT use, ICT integrated in the business process, a full digital information and communication system, ICT as a formal responsibility with a dedicated manager

ICT is a broad term used to refer to any technology from the simple acquisition of hardware to the full implementation of an enterprise resource planning (ERP) system. This study focuses on enterprise systems (ES), which are defined as "commercial software packages that enable the integration of transaction-oriented data and business processes throughout an organization (and perhaps eventually throughout the entire interorganizational supply chain)" (Markus and Tanis 2000, p. 176). These application software packages started as the support for a variety of transaction-based back-office functions at which time they were called ERP systems (Volkoff et al. 2005). Since then, they have evolved to include support for front-office and interorganizational activities including supply chain management (SCM) and customer relationship management (CRM) (Davenport 2000; Markus and Tanis 2000; Volkoff et al. 2005).

In our definition, ES include ERP, CRM, SCM, and eProcurement software (Shang and Seddon 2002). Markus and Tanis (2000) claim that small firms can benefit technically and strategically from their investment in ES. Business and technical reasons for adopting ES in small firms are highlighted in Table 1.

SMEs differ from large companies in important ways affecting their information-seeking practices (Buonanno et al. 2005; Lang and Calantone 1997). These differences include

- Lack of (or substantially less sophisticated) information system management (Kagan et al. 1990)
- Frequent concentration of information-gathering responsibilities into one or two individuals, rather than the specialization of scanning activities among top executives (Hambrick 1981)
- Lower levels of resource available for information-gathering
- Quantity and quality of available environmental information (Pearce et al. 1982)

Table 1. **Reasons behind SME Adoption and Enterprise Systems (based on Markus and Tannis 2000)**

Business Reasons	Technical Reasons
• Accommodate business growth • Acquire multilanguage and multicurrency IT support • Improve informal and/or inefficient business processes • Reduce business operating and administrative expenses • Reduce inventory carrying cost and stockouts • Eliminate delays and errors in filling customers' orders for merged businesses	• Solve Y2K and similar problem • Integrate application cross-functionally • Replace hard-to-maintain interfaces • Reduce software maintenance burden through outsourcing • Eliminate redundant data entry and concomitant errors and difficulty analyzing data • Improve IT architecture • Ease technology capacity constraints • Decrease computer operating costs

A recent study by Buonanno et al. (2005) found that SMEs disregard financial constraints as the main cause for not adopting an ERP system, suggesting structural and organizational reasons as major ones. This pattern is partially different from what was observed in large companies where the first reason of ERP system non-adoption is organizational. Moreover, the decision process regarding the adoption of ERP systems within SMEs is still more affected by exogenous reasons than business-related factors, contrary to large companies that are more interested in managing process integration and data redundancy/inconsistency through ERP implementation. Before investigating the factors affecting SME adoption of ES, the IT innovation adoption literature will be reviewed.

3   IT INNOVATION ADOPTION RESEARCH

IT innovation adoption research has become increasingly popular as IT continues its relentless march into almost every aspect of organizational life (Fichman 2004), and as innovation becomes an important driver of organizational competitiveness (Hamel 1998). A recent review of the predictors, linkages, and biases in IT innovation adoption research by Jeyaraj et al. (2006) highlights that a rich but diverse body of *theoretical* and *empirical* work has accumulated on the adoption and diffusion of IT-based innovations. A large number of theories have been tested, including the theory of reasoned action (Fishbein and Ajzen 1975), the innovation diffusion theory (Rogers 1983), the social cognitive theory (Bandura 1986), the diffusion/implementation model (Kwon and Zmud 1987), the technology acceptance model (TAM) (Davis 1989), the theory of planned behavior (Ajzen 1991), perceived characteristics of innovating (Moore and Benbasat 1991), the tri-core model of IS innovations (Swanson 1994), the innovation diffusion theory for organizations (Rogers 1995), TAM2 (Venkatesh and Davis 2000), and the unified theory of acceptance and use of technology (Venkatesh et al. 2003). Empirically, qualitative (Agarwal and Prasad 1997), quantitative (Igbaria and Tan 1997), and a combination of

Table 2. **Theoretical Models Used to Examine SME Adoption of IT Innovations**

Theory	Sources
Technology Acceptance Model (TAM)	Grandon and Pearson (2004) Igbaria et al. (1997)
Theory of Planned Behavior (TPB)	Harrison et al. (1997)
Combined TAM and TPB	Riemenschneider et al. (2003)
TAM2	Venkatesh and Davis (2000)
Innovation Diffusion Theory (IDT)	Cragg and King (1993) Iacovou et al. (1995) Mehrtens et al. (2001) Scupola (2003) Thong et al. (1994)
Resource-Based Theory	Braun (2002) Caldeira and Ward (2003) Chau (2001) Feeny and Willcocks (1998) Grewal (2001) Iacovou et al. (1995) Mata et al. (1995) Mehrtens et al. (2001) Scupola (2003) Thong (2001)
Stage Theory	Daniel et al. (2002) DTI (2001) Levy et al. (2002) Poon and Swatman (1997) Prananto et al. (2003) Rao et al. (2003)
Unified Theory of Acceptance and Use of Technology (UTAUT)	Anderson and Schwager (2003)

both methods (Thong and Yap 1995) have been used. Theories used to examine IT innovation adoption research in a small business context are highlighted in Table 2.

According to Fichman (2004), a dominant research paradigm for IT innovation has emerged. He argues that this dominant paradigm assumes that organizations with a greater quantity of the "right stuff" will exhibit a greater quantity of IT innovation. Although IT innovation adoption research tends to address the same research question— *What factors facilitate or hinder the adoption and diffusion of IT-based innovations within a population of potential adopters?* (Jeyaraj et al. 2006)—it is essential to understand different factors impacting the adoption of new IT innovations. Jeyaraj et al. (2006) argue that different theories have been used to examine the organizational adoption of IT innovations. Table 2 highlights the main theories used to examine SME adoption of IT innovations. In order to state the factors impacting the adoption of different IT innovations, the technology–organization–environment frameworks will be reviewed.

4   THE TECHNOLOGY–ORGANIZATION–ENVIRONMENT (TOE) FRAMEWORK

Tornatzky and Fleischer (1990) developed the technology–organization–environment (TOE) framework to study adoption of IT innovations. This framework included three aspects of a firm's context that influence the process by which it adopts and implements IT innovations: technological, organizational, and environmental. The TOE framework can be used to study organizational adoption of IT innovations. These innovations are classified into three types: Type I innovations are confined to the technical tasks; Type II innovations support business administration; and Type III innovations are embedded in the core of the business (Swanson 1994). Taking this typology into consideration, ES can be categorized as Type III innovations because they are embedded in a firm's core business processes. Shang and Seddon claim "ES...can be used by firms as their primary engine for integrating data, processes and information technology, in real time, across internal and external value chain" (2002, p. 272).

The TOE framework has been examined by a number of empirical studies on various IT innovations (as illustrated in Table 3). From reviewing these empirical studies, it is not clear which factors to include in the TOE framework to study SME adoption of ES. Within the three contexts, it seems that different factors impact the adoption and imple-

Table 3.   TOE Frameworks of SME Adoption of IT Innovations (Only factors that are shown to be significant are listed in this table)

Authors	ICTs Innovation	Technological Context	Organizational Context	Environmental Context
Lertwongsatien and Wongpinunwatana 2003	Electronic commerce	Technology factors (perceived benefits, perceived compatibility)	Organizational factors (size, top management support for e-commerce, existence of it department)	Organizational environment (competitiveness)
Scupola 2003	Electronic commerce	Electronic commerce barriers, electronic commerce benefits, related technologies	Employees' is knowledge	Pressure from competitors, buyers, and suppliers; role of government; technology support infrastructure
Kuan and Chau 2001	EDI (electronic data interchange)	Perceived direct benefits	Perceived financial cost, perceived technical competence	Perceived industry pressure, perceived government pressure
Thong 1999	IS (information systems)	IS characteristics (relative advantage/compatibility, complexity)	Organizational characteristics (business size, employee's is knowledge)	Environmental characteristics (competition)
Fink 1998	IT (information technology)	IT benefits	Organizational culture, in-house IT expertise and resources, IT implementation and selection	External environment, outside support, external resources
Iacovou et al. 1995	EDI	Perceived benefits	Organizational readiness	External pressure

mentation of different IT innovations. In addition, different factors impact the same studied IT innovation (e.g., e-commerce). Thus, extending the TOE framework to study other IT innovations has been suggested (Chau and Tam 1997). As a result, this study investigates the TOE factors that impact SME adoption of ES.

5 THEORETICAL FRAMEWORK

From reviewing the IT innovation adoption literature, it can be argued that IT innovations are highly differentiated technologies for which there is not necessarily a single adoption model. Based on the TOE framework discussed earlier, Figure 1 presents a conceptual model of SME adoption of ES.

5.1 Technological Context

Premkumar (2003) argues that there are very few studies that have examined the impact of technological characteristics. Rogers' innovation diffusion theory for organizations will be used as a theoretical basis for studying the impact of technological factors. Earlier

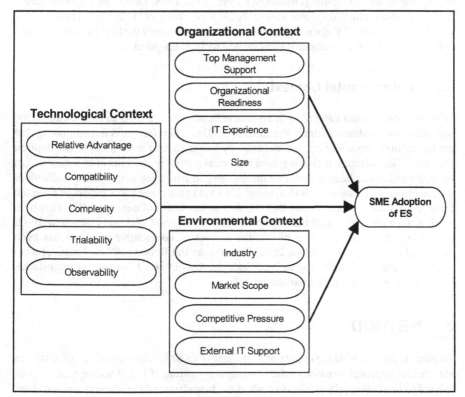

Figure 1. **TOE Framework of SME Adoption of Enterprise Systems**

studies, such as Igbaria et al. (1997), used TAM to examine the impact of *relative advantage* and *complexity* on IT adoption and usage. Grandon and Pearson (2004) examined the impact of *perceived usefulness* (*relative advantage*) and *perceived ease-of-use* (*complexity*) and included *compatibility* as a significant factor. *Relative advantage*, *compatibility*, and *complexity* have been examined in previous studies, and have been shown to be significant. As an extension, this study intends to examine all five technological characteristics.

5.2 Organizational Context

The characteristics in the organizational context seem to be the primary focus of many SME studies (Premkumar 2003). *Top management support* has been found to be one of the best predictors of IT adoption by organizations (Jeyaraj et al. 2006). This factor has also been studied in the small business context (Guinea et al. 2005; Premkumar 2003). Furthermore, *organizational readiness* has been shown to be a significant organizational factor that impacts the adoption of IT innovations (Iacovou et al. 1995; Mehrtens et al. 2001). Relevant *IT experience* variables have been examined in many studies (Lee 2004; Lertwongsatien and Wongpinunwatana 2003). Finally, empirical evidence on the impact of *size* shows mixed results (Damanpour 1996; Fink 1998; Goode and Stevens 2000; Lertwongsatien and Wongpinunwatana 2003; Levenburg et al. 2006). The study by Goode and Stevens (2000) shows that business size, previously the best indicator of technology adoption, was not significantly related to Web adoption.

5.3 Environmental Context

IT innovations do not cater for just an internal audience, but also to firm's customers, suppliers, and business partner (Premkumar 2003). Therefore, it is not surprising that environmental characteristics are increasingly being studied in IT innovation adoption research. The literature includes mixed empirical results on the impact of *industry*. On the one hand, it has been argued that the industry in which the firm operates influences the adoption of IT innovations (Raymond 2001). On the other hand, evidence from the Levy et al. (2001) study shows that the sector has little influence on ICT adoption. Studies have also examined the impact of *market scope* (Daniel and Grimshaw 2002; Levenburg et al. 2006). In addition, the impact of *competitive pressure* has been examined (Daniel and Grimshaw 2002; Premkumar and Roberts 1999). Finally, recent studies (Guinea et al. 2005; Thong 2001) indicate that *external IT support* is a significant factor in the adoption of IT innovations.

6   METHOD

To empirically examine the impact of TOE factors on SME adoption of ES, case studies are a useful approach because of the contemporary nature of ES. This approach is considered to be particularly appropriate when the boundaries of the research are not clear, there is a need to investigate the issue within a real-life context, or the views from a number of sources need to be examined (Yin 1994). Additionally, case study research provides a means to review theory and practice iteratively (Levy and Powell 2003).

The case studies employed here all examine SMEs located in the Northwest of England. The chosen firms satisfy both of DTI and European Commission definitions of an SME. This a convenient rather than a random sample of SMEs that were selected from manufacturing, retail/wholesale, and services industry sectors because they have greater dependence on IT innovations (Goode and Stevens 2000). The major method of data collection was through face-to-face semi-structured interviews, lasting between one to two hours, with personnel who had been key decision makers regarding IT innovation adoption in the firm (managing director or IT manager). At least two interviews were conducted for each SME. Key personnel were contacted by phone to arrange for an interview. Most interviews were conducted at the firm's site. The interview questions were formulated to gather information on the factors that impact the adoption of ES within the three contexts of Tornatzky and Fleischer's model. The questions covered the firm's background, the level of ICT sophistication and use in the firm, and the impact of TOE factors on ES adoption. Interview were transcribed and reports were sent to the interviewees subsequently for validation and refinement. Moreover, information was gathered from secondary sources such as internal company documentation and firm websites.

To overcome the pro-adoption bias (Rogers 2003), this study focuses on both adopters and non-adopters of ES. Using Rogers' (2003) adopter categorization on the basis of innovativeness, nine cases have been categorized into three main groups based on the extent to which an SME is relatively earlier to adopt an ES than others (Table 4). First, *early adopters* are firms that have already adopted and implemented ES. Second, *prospectors* are firms that have not adopted ES yet, but intend to adopt at least one of these systems in the next 3 years. Finally, *laggards* are firms that have not adopted ES and do not intend to adopt them in the future. Table 4 briefly describes the investigated SMEs.

Table 4. Description of SMEs Investigated

Classification	Firms	Industry	Type of Business	Market Scope	Number of Employees
Early Adopters (Already adopted ES)	F1	Manufacturing	Manufacturer of feeders and controls	International	42
	F2	Manufacturing	Manufacturer and supplier of air filters	National	40
	F3	Retail/Wholesale	Retailer of domestic appliances	Local	15
Prospectors (Intend to adopt ES in next 3 years)	F4	Service	IT and management services consultancy	International	200
	F5	Manufacturing	Food manufacturing	Local	12
	F6	Retail/Wholesale	Retailer of PCs and components	Regional	124
Laggards (Do not intend to adopt ES)	F7	Manufacturing	Manufacturer of paints and powder coatings	International	160
	F8	Service	Change management consultancy	International	5

7   EMPIRICAL FINDINGS

An iterative, cyclical model of data analysis was adopted consisting of three components: data reduction, data display (within-case analysis; cross-case analysis), and conclusion drawing/verification (Miles and Huberman 1994). To ensure the robustness of the analysis, data reduction was performed by both authors independently inspecting the interview notes and transcripts. The analysis of the empirical findings is structured around the three contexts outlined in the TOE framework of SME adoption of ES. Relative advantage, compatibility, complexity, trialability, observability, top management support, organizational readiness, IT experience, size, industry, market scope, competitive pressure, and external IT support are factors that impact SME adoption of ES.

7.1   Technological Context

This study found that not only relative advantage, compatibility, and complexity, but also trialability and observability are factors impacting SME adoption of ES.

7.1.1 Relative Advantage

On the one hand, findings indicate that laggards seem to be unaware of the benefits of adopting ES. On the other hand, both firms F1 and F2 were aware of the benefits before adopting an ES. F3 claims that benefits that were the initial motive to the adoption of an ES were very limiting, because other benefits, such as quick customer response rate, were not initially stated. Prospectors expressed their concerns with regard to which of the available ES could deliver their business needs.

7.1.2 Compatibility

Firms intending to adopt ES seem to have compatible working styles to those firms who have already adopted ES, whereas firms that do not intend to adopt ES appear to be comfortable with traditional IT systems in place. F7 designed a system internally to take care of the bill-of-materials. F8 expressed its comfort with producing the quotes manually, because of its limited customer base.

7.1.3 Complexity

It has been found that prospectors emphasize the need for systems that are easy-to-use by employees. F5 expressed that systems are too advanced for employees to use. F7 and F9 seem to be deterred from adopting these technologies because ES are perceived to be complex systems for complex organizations. Early adopters of ES have expressed that they are comfortable with the complexity level of the adopted systems.

7.1.4 Trailability

Although this factor has not yet been examined in the small business context, this study has found that the relationship between trialability and the adoption of ES is strong. Both

F1 and F2 had the opportunity to try the system before fully implementing it. Both expressed that having the system on a trial basis contributed to their final decision of adopting ES. The availability of ES on a trial basis would show its performance and would resolve any problems before committing to a full implementation (F2). F5 seem to be willing to try an ES as long as it did not disrupt its daily productivity. All of the firms intending to adopt an ES perceive trialability as a crucial phase before full implementation.

7.1.5 Observability

It has been found that early adopters agree that ES are adopted by many firms in the industry in which they operate. However, laggards are unaware of any firms that adopted such systems. Prospectors seem to have mixed views of the visibility of ES in their industries. On the one hand, F4 seems to be willing to adopt an ERP system even though firms in the same industry have not yet adopted such systems. On the other hand, F5 and F6 have observed other firms implementing ES and have been advised to adopt similar ES.

7.2 Organizational Context

In addition to the technological characteristics mentioned earlier, this study found that top management support, organizational readiness, IT experience, and size are also factors impacting SME adoption of ES.

7.2.1 Top Management Support

It has been found that early adopters have a strong managerial commitment to adopting new technologies. This commitment has been characterized by inviting software companies on-site to demonstrate how the technology can help them manage their operations. However, it was found that laggards and prospectors have less enthusiastic top management compared to early adopters.

7.2.2 Organizational Readiness

This study found that the overall organizational readiness of SMEs is not high enough for the adoption ES. Investing major organizational resources seems to have a strong influence on the adoption of ES (F5 and F6). Companies with very limited resources (F8 and F9) are not intending to adopt ES. F4 has the resources to adopt an ES, but the main reason of not adopting it yet is not being aware of its potential. All three adopting firms appeared to be technologically and financially ready to adopt ES.

7.2.3 IT Experience

According to the classification scheme developed by Southern and Tilley (2000), early adopters can be categorized as high-end ICT users. These firms have integrated ICT in their business process. However, laggards seem to be on the low end of ICT use. F7 has been operating in the industry for 76 years with a minimal use of ICT and has been doing well without the need for adopting an ES. Prospectors can be categorized as medium-level ICT users. These firms had implemented at least one software application (i.e., accounts). Either they have not found an ES that has all the functions they need (F4 and F6) or they could not commit to any vendor (F5).

7.2.4 Size

On the one hand, only larger firms were able to adopt ES, as they are more likely to have the necessary resources, skills, knowledge, and experience (Damanpour 1996; Montazemi 1988). Many new technologies are less expensive, require less support infra-structure, and offer firms a way to compete with larger firms (Goode and Stevens 2000). Although the adoption of ES does not strongly depend on company size (F7 is a large non-adopting firm), it has been found that micro-firms are unlikely to adopt ES (F8 and F9). Both F8 and F9 expressed that the need to adopt these systems was not apparent to them since the workload is manageable with the existing systems. Furthermore, F9 expressed that ES are not needed at this stage because it only deals with 10 invoices a week and one or two purchase orders a day.

7.3   Environmental Context

In addition to technological characteristics and organizational characteristics, this study found that industry, market scope, competitive pressure, and external IT support are factors impacting SME adoption of ES.

7.3.1 Industry

Although Levy et al. (2001) claim that the evidence shows that the sector has a little influence on ICT adoption, the industry of which the SME is a member has been found to be a factor impacting the adoption of IT innovations (Levenburg et al. 2006; Raymond 2001; Yap 1990). Because it has been shown that the industry is a significant factor in the adoption of new IT innovations (Goode and Stevens 2000), this study concentrated on the three industries that make more use of ICT. It has been found that manufacturing and retail/wholesale firms are more likely to adopt ES than firms in the service sector. It has been noted that service industry make use of different systems than manufacturing and retail industries (Premkumar and King 1994; Reich and Benbasat 1990). Although service industries are reliant on information and can be more prolific in the adoption of information systems (Goode and Stevens 2000), this has not been the case in adopting ES.

7.3.2 Market Scope

With the availability of ICT, smaller firms are able to reach broader markets. It was harder for SMEs to reach broader markets with their limited resources (Levenburg and Klein 2006). Because SMEs are now operating internationally, there is a clear need for SMEs to adopt ES in order to reduce costs and accommodate their business growth.

Even though laggards are operating internationally, they still have no plans to adopt ES. All of the firms intending to adopt ES have expressed their intentions for market expansion.

7.3.3 Competitive Pressure

The use of IT innovations to respond to competitors, provide enhanced customer service, and improve relationship with suppliers were driving the uptake by smaller businesses compared to their larger counterparts (Daniel and Grimshaw 2002). Early adopters expressed that one of the main reasons for adopting ES is competitive pressure. F3 argues that if an SME is willing to continue operating, it has to be up-to-date with IT market offerings. Also, F1 stressed that if direct competitors are faster in adopting ES, they have a better chance to increase their market share. Firms not intending to adopt ES seem to have less pressure although operating internationally. One reason for this could be the business niche that these SMEs serve.

7.3.4 External IT Support

Driven by the need for lower costs, faster implementation, easier-to-use applications and effective use of scarce resources, internal information system development is increasingly moving to an external development and provision model: outsourcing (Ward and Peppard 2002). Lockett et al. (2006) emphasize that the provision of hosted applications by ASPs (application service providers), on a rented basis is viewed as being of particular relevance to SMEs. None of the early adopters has a hosted ES, but they still seek IT support from the leasing vendors. F4 is considering adopting a hosted ES. However, F5 expressed their concern with hosted ES and stated that it would only invest in client/ server in-house ES.

8 DISCUSSION OF FINDINGS

This study has shown that the TOE framework can be used as a theoretical basis for understanding the factors impacting SME adoption of new IT innovations. The application of this framework has contributed to the discussion of the impact of technological, organizational and environmental factors on SME adoption of ES. Previous studies have focused on factors affecting other IT innovations (see Table 5). This study has shown that factors impacting the adoption of ES are different from factors impacting SME adoption of other, previously studied IT innovations such as e-commerce and EDI. Relative advantage, compatibility, complexity, trialability, observability, top management support, organizational readiness, IT experience, size, industry, market scope, competitive pressure, and external IT support are found to be factors impacting SME adoption of ES.

   With regard to the technological context, this study has found that relative advantage, compatibility complexity, trialability, and observability impact SME adoption of ES. Relative advantage and compatibility have been shown to impact previously studied IT innovations (Table 5). This study has highlighted the need for SMEs to be aware of the relative advantage of ES, and the need for these systems to be compatible

Table 5. Different Factors Impacting the Adoption of
Different IT Innovations

| Factors | Studies of the Factors Impacting Different IT Innovations | | | | |
	IT	IS	EDI	E-Commerce	ES
Relative Advantage	Fink 1998	Thong 1999	Iacovou et al. 1995; Kuan and Chau 2001	Lertwongsatien & Wongpinunqatana 2003; Scupola 2003	*Current study*
Compatibility		Thong 1999		Lertwongsatien & Wongpinunqatana 2003	*Current study*
Complexity		Thong 1999			*Current study*
Trailability					*Current study*
Observability					*Current study*
Top Management Support				Lertwongsatien & Wongpinunqatana 2003	*Current study*
Organizational Readiness	Fink 1998		Iacovou et al. 1995; Kuan and Chau 2001		*Current study*
IT Experience		Thong 1999		Lertwongsatien & Wongpinunqatana 2003; Scupola 2003	*Current study*
Size		Thong 1999		Lertwongsatien & Wongpinunqatana 2003	*Current study*
Organizational Culture	Fink 1998				
IT Implem. and Selection	Fink 1998				
Location				Scupola 2003	
Industry					*Current study*
Market Scope					*Current study*
Competitive Pressure		Thong 1999	Kuan and Chau 2001	Lertwongsatien & Wongpinunqatana 2003; Scupola 2003	*Current study*
External IT Support	Fink 1998				*Current study*
Government Pressure			Kuan and Chau 2001	Scupola 2003	
External Environment	Fink 1998		Iacovou et al. 1995		
External Resources	Fink 1998				

with their existing IT systems. Although complexity does not seem to matter in studying information technology, EDI, and e-commerce, this study emphasizes the need for these new technologies to be easy-to-use. One misconception SMEs have about ES is that these technologies are created for complex organizations. It seems that SMEs are not only unaware of the relative advantage of these technologies, but they seem to be unaware of the complexity level of these systems. Unlike previously studied IT innovations, it has been found that SME adoption of ES is highly dependent on whether it is possible for an SME to adopt an ES on a trial basis and observe its adoption by other firms in the same industry. This might due to the high risk involved in implementing such technologies. Adopting an ES might affect not only the day to day operations of a small business, it may cause a total breakdown that an SME cannot afford. Most of the non-adopting SMEs are comfortable with their existing IT systems. Prospectors appear to be willing to adopt ES as long as they have the opportunity to try these systems out before committing to fully implementing them.

With regard to the organizational context, this study found that top management support, IT experience, organizational readiness and size impact SME adoption of ES. Non of the previously studied IT innovations has emphasized the importance of top management support apart from the e-commerce study (Lertwongsatien and Wongpinunwatana 2003). Without top management commitment and support, SMEs will not adopt ES. Academic and industry literature cannot overemphasize the importance of adopting ES. However, it is not possible for top management of an SME to support the adoption of ES unless they observe the relative advantage of adopting such technologies, which can be achieved by allowing SMEs to test these systems. Investing organizational resources to adopt ES might be one of the difficult decisions taken by top management of an SME. It has been shown that IT and EDI were technologies that needed organizations to be ready technologically and financially before adopting them. In the case of ES adoption, SMEs still consider their organizational readiness as an important factor in deciding whether to adopt ES. Having relevant IT experience is perceived by SMEs to be an important factor in helping them decide which system to adopt from the wide range of available ES. Size has been shown to be a significant factor in adopting IS and e-commerce. In the case of ES adoption, micro-firms were found to be unwilling to adopt ES. This might be because they are not technologically and financially ready to adopt such systems. Also, it might be because they do not need these systems at this early stage of their business growth.

With regard to the environmental context, this study found that industry, market scope, competitive pressure, and external IT support impact SME adoption of ES. Unlike previously studied IT innovations, this study has shown the importance of industry and market scope in SME adoption of ES. It has been found that the manufacturing and retail/wholesale industries are more likely to adopt ES than firms in the service sector. This might be because ES are more relevant to the manufacturing and retail/wholesale industries. Firms in the service sector do not seem to need such systems because of the nature of their business operations. Also, it has been found that the wider the market area in which an SME operates, the more likely it is to adopt an ES to support its business operations. Like other previously studied IT innovations, competitive pressure is shown to be an important factor. Finally, external IT support can prove to be the most challenging factor for vendors, since SMEs intending to adopt ES are willing to adopt hosted ES.

9 CONCLUSIONS AND LIMITATIONS

IT innovations are highly differentiated technologies for which there is not a single adoption model. Contrary to large companies that are mainly affected by organizational factors, this study shows that SMEs are not only affected by environmental factors as previously established, but also affected by technological and organizational factors. This study also confirms that factors impacting the adoption of ES are different from factors impacting SME adoption of other previously studied IT innovations. Using the TOE framework as a theoretical basis, the major contribution of this study is highlighting these factors, which are relative advantage, compatibility, complexity, trialability, observability, top management support, organizational readiness, IT experience, size, industry, market scope, competitive pressure, and external IT support.

The main implications for this study are twofold.

* Software vendors can increase ES rate of adoption among SMEs by offering trial periods before full implementation of ES. This would create awareness and demonstrate what an ES can do for an SME. Also, an SME will be able to assess an ES compatibility with its existing systems and examine the ES complexity level. Once these systems are adopted, their visibility in different sectors will increase.
* Because of the heterogeneity of SMEs, software vendors should not only consider segmenting SME market according to size, but also consider the industry sector. Targeting specific industries will help ES vendors understand further what SMEs need and increase the take-up of industry-specific ES.

The key limitations of this study are as follows. First, the study focused on a limited geographical area, which makes it difficult to generalize the results to other UK regions. Second, although the small number of the investigated cases has drawn a good picture of the factors impacting SME adoption of ES, a survey with a large sample would help generalize the results in the region. Third, this study focused only on adoption. To gain a holistic understanding of ES, the implementation process and the impact of ES adoption on firm performance should also be examined. With the recent popularity of hosted software applications (Lockett et al. 2006), future studies could empirically examine further the factors impacting the adoption of these technologies and how they differ from the findings presented in this study. Finally, because factors impacting adoption of ES are different from factors impacting SME adoption of previously studied IT innovations, future research could examine factors impacting the adoption of new IT innovations.

References

Agarwal, R., and Prasad, J. "The Role of Innovation Characteristics and Perceived Voluntariness in the Acceptance of Information Technologies," *Decision Sciences* (28:3), 1997, pp. 557-582.

Ajzen, I. "The Theory of Planned Behavior," *Organizational Behavior and Human Decision Processes* (50:2), 1991, pp. 179-211.

AMI-Partners. "The SMB Global Model," Access Markets International Partners, Inc., New York, 2004 (http://www.ami-partners.com).

Anderson, J. E., and Schwager, P. H. "SME adoption of Wireless LAN Technology: Applying UTAUT Model," in *Proceedings of the 7th Annual Conference of the Southern Association for Information Systems*, 2003, pp. 39-43 (available online at http://sais.aisnet.org/sais2004/Anderson%20&%20Schwager.pdf).

Bandura, A. *Social Foundations of Thought and Action: A Social Cognitive Theory*, Englewood Cliffs, NJ: Prentice Hall, 1986.

Blackburn, R., and McClure, R. *The Use of Information and Communication Technologies (ICTs) in Small Business Service Firms*, Report to Midland Bank, Small Business Research Centre, Kingston Business School, London, UK, 1998.

Braun, P. "Digital Knowledge Networks: Linking Communities of Practice with Innovation," *Journal of Business Strategies* (19:1), 2002, pp. 43-54.

Brock, J. K. "Information and Communication Technology in the Small Firm," in D. Jones-Evans and S. Carter (eds.), *Enterprise and Small Business: Principles, Practice and Policy*, Harlow, UK: FT-Prentice Hall, 2000, pp. 384-408.

Buonanno, G., Faverio, P., Pigni, F., Ravarini, A., Sciuto, D., and Tagliavini, M. "Factors Affecting ERP System Adoption: A Comparative Analysis Between SMEs and Large Companies," *Journal of Enterprise Information Management* (18:4), 2005, pp. 384-426.

Caldeira, M. M., and Ward, J. M. "Using Resource-Based Theory to Interpret the Successful Adoption and Use of Information Systems and Technology in Manufacturing Small and Medium-Sized Enterprises," *European Journal of Information Systems* (12:2), 2003, pp. 127-141.

Chau, P. Y. K. "Inhibitors to EDI Adoption in Small Businesses: An Empirical Investigation," *Journal of Electronic Commerce Research* (2:2), 2001, pp. 78-88.

Chau, P. Y. K., and Tam, K. Y. "Factors Affecting the Adoption of Open Systems: An Exploratory Study," *MIS Quarterly* (21:1), 1997, pp. 1-24.

Corso, M., Martini, A., Paolucci, E., and Pellegrini, L. "Information and Communication Technologies in Product Innovation Within SMEs: The Role of Product Complexity," *Enterprise and Innovation Management Studies* (2:1), 2001, pp. 35-48.

Cragg, P. B., and King, M. "Small-Firm Computing: Motivators and Inhibitors," *MIS Quarterly* (17:1), 1993, pp. 47-60.

Damanpour, F. "Organizational Complexity and Innovation: Developing and Testing Multiple Contingency Models," *Management Science* (42:5), 1996, pp. 693.

Daniel, E. M., and Grimshaw, D. J. "An Exploratory Comparison of Electronic Commerce Adoption in Large and Small Enterprises," *Journal of Information Technology* (17:3), 2002, pp. 133-147.

Daniel, E. M., Wilson, H., and Myers, A. "Adoption of E-Commerce by SMEs in the UK: Towards a Stage Model," *International Small Business Journal* (20:3), 2002, pp. 253-268.

Datamonitor. "CRM For Small to Medium Business," 2004 (http://www.datamonitor.com).

Davenport, T. H. *Mission Critical: Realizing the Promise of Enterprise Systems*, Boston, MA: Harvard Business School Press, 2000.

Davis, F. D. "Perceived Usefulness, Perceived Ease of Use, and User Acceptance of Information Technology," *MIS Quarterly* (13:3), 1989, pp. 319-340.

DTI. "Business in the Information Age: International Benchmarking Report," Department of Trade and Industry, London, 2001.

DTI. "Business in the Information Age: International Benchmarking Study 2004, Department of Trade and Industry, London, 2004.

European Commission. "SME User Guide Explaining the New SME Definition," Enterprise and Industry Directorate, Brussels, 2003 (available online at http://ec.europa.eu/enterprise/enterprise_policy/sme_definition/index_en.htm)

Feeny, D. F., and Willcocks, L. P. "Re-Designing the IS Function Around Core Capabilities," *Long Range Planning* (31:3), 1998, pp. 354-367.

Fichman, R. G. "Going Beyond the Dominant Paradigm for Information Technology Innovation Research: Emerging Concepts and Methods," *Journal of the Association for Information Systems* (5:8), 2004, pp. 314-355.

Fink, D. "Guidelines for the Successful Adoption of Information Technology in Small and Medium Enterprises," *International Journal of Information Management* (18:4), 1998, pp. 243-253.

Fishbein, M., and Ajzen, I.   *Belief, Attitude, and Behavior: An Introduction to Theory and Research*, Reading, MA: Addison-Wesley, 1975

Goode, S., and Stevens, K.   "An Analysis of the Business Characteristics of Adopters and Non-Adopters of World Wide Web Technology," *Information Technology and Management* (1:1-2), 2000, pp. 129-154.

Grandon, E. E., and Pearson, J. M.   "Electronic Commerce Adoption: An Empirical Study of Small and Medium US Businesses," *Information and Management* (42:1), 2004, pp. 197-216.

Grewal, R.   "An Investigation into the Antecedents of Organizational Participation in Business-to-Business Electronic Markets," *Journal of Marketing* (65:3), 2001, pp. 17-33.

Guinea, A. O., Kelley, H., and Hunter, M. G.   "Information Systems Effectiveness in Small Businesses: Extending a Singaporean Model in Canada," *Journal of Global Information Management* (13:3), 2005, pp. 55-79.

Hambrick, D. C.   "Specialization of Environmental Scanning Activities among Upper Level Executives," *Journal of Management Studies* (18:3), 1981, pp. 299-320.

Hamel, G.   "The Challenge Today: Changing the Roles of the Game," *Business Strategy Review* (9:2), 1998, pp. 19-26.

Harrison, A. D., Mykytyn Jr., P. P., and Riemenschneider, K. C.   "Executive Decision About Adoption of Information Technology in Small Business: Theory and Empirical Tests," *Information Systems Research* (8:2), 1997, pp. 171-195.

Iacovou, C. L., Benbasat, I., and Dexter, A. S.   "Electronic Data Interchange and Small Organizations: Adoption and Impact of Technology," *MIS Quarterly* (19:4), 1995, pp. 465-485.

Igbaria, M., and Tan, M.   "The Consequences of Information Technology Acceptance on Subsequent Individual Performance," *Information and Management* (32:3), 1997, pp. 113-121.

Igbaria, M., Zinatelli, N., Cragg, P., and Cavaye, A. L. M.   "Personal Computing Acceptance Factors in Small Firms: A Structural Equation Model," *MIS Quarterly* (21:3), 1997, pp. 279-302.

Jeyaraj, A., Rottman, J. W., and Lacity, M. C.   "A Review of the Predictors, Linkages, and Biases in IT Innovation Adoption Research," *Journal of Information Technology* (21:1), 2006, pp. 1-23.

Kagan, A., Lau, K., and Nusgart, K. R.   "Information System Usage Within Small Business Firms," *Entrepreneurship: Theory and Practice* (14:3), 1990, pp. 25-37.

Kuan, K. K. Y., and Chau, P. Y. K.   "A Perception-Based Model for EDI Adoption in Small Businesses Using a Technology-Organization-Environment Framework," *Information and Management* (38:8), 2001, pp. 507-521.

Kwon, T. H., and Zmud, R. W.   "Unifying the Fragmented Models of Information Systems Implementation," in R. J. Boland and R. A. Hirschheim (eds.), *Critical Issues in Information Systems Research*, New York: John Wiley and Sons, 1987, 227-251.

Lang, J. R., and Calantone, R. J.   "Small Firm Information Seeking as a Response to Environmental Threats and Opportunities," *Journal of Small Business Management* (35:1), 1997, pp. 11-23.

Lee, J.   "Discriminant Analysis of Technology Adoption Behavior: A Case of Internet Technologies in Small Businesses," *Journal of Computer Information Systems* (44:4), 2004, pp. 57-66.

Lertwongsatien, C., and Wongpinunwatana, N.   "E-Commerce Adoption in Thailand: An Empirical Study of Small and Medium Enterprises (SMEs)," *Journal of Global Information Technology Management* (6:3), 2003, pp. 67-83.

Levenburg, N., Magal, S. R., and Kosalge, P.   "An Exploratory Investigation of Organizational Factors and E-Business Motivations Among SMFOEs in the US," *Electronic Markets* (16:1), 2006, pp. 70-84.

Levenburg, N. M., and Klein, H. A.   "Delivering Customer Services Online: Identifying Best Practices of Medium-Sized Enterprises," *Information Systems Journal* (16:2), 2006, pp. 135-155.

Levy, M., and Powell, P. "Exploring SME Internet Adoption: Towards a Contingent Model," *Electronic Markets* (13:2), 2003, pp. 173-181.

Levy, M., Powell, P., and Yetton, P. "The Dynamics of SME Information Systems," *Small Business Economics* (19:4), 2001, pp. 341-354.

Levy, M., Powell, P., and Yetton, P. "SMEs: Aligning IS and the Strategic Context," *Journal of Information Technology* (16:3), 2001, pp. 133-144.

Lockett, N., Brown, D. H., and Kaewkitipong, L. "The Use of Hosted Enterprise Applications by SMEs: A Dual Market and User Perspective," *Electronic Markets* (16:1), 2006, pp. 85-96.

Markus, M. L., and Tanis, C. "The Enterprise System Experience—From Adoption to Success," in R. W. Zmud (ed.), *Framing the Domain of IT Management: Projecting the Future... Through the Past*, Cincinnati, OH: Pinnaflex Educational Resources, Inc., 2000, pp. 173-207.

Martin, L. M., and Matlay, H. "'Blanket' Approaches to Promoting ICT in Small Firms: Some Lessons from the DTI Ladder Adoption Model in the UK," *Internet Research: Electronic Networking Applications and Policy* (11:1), 2001, pp. 399-410.

Mata, F. J., Fuerst, W. L., and Barney, J. B. "Information Technology and Sustained Competitive Advantage: A Resource-Based Analysis," *MIS Quarterly* (19:4), 1995, pp. 487-505.

Mehrtens, J., Cragg, P. B., and Mills, A. M. "A Model of Internet Adoption by SMEs," *Information and Management* (39:3), 2001, pp. 165-176.

Miles, M. B., and Huberman, M. A. *Qualitative Data Analysis: An Expanded Sourcebook* (2nd ed.), London: Sage Publications, 1994.

Montazemi, A. R. "Factors Affecting Information Satisfaction in the Context of the Small Business Environment," *MIS Quarterly* (12:2), 1988, pp. 238-256.

Moore, G. C., and Benbasat, I. "Development of an Instrument to Measure the Perceptions of Adopting an Information Technology Innovation," *Information Systems Research* (2:3), 1991, pp. 192-222.

Pearce, I. J. A., Chapman, B. L., and David, F. R. "Environmental Scanning for Small and Growing Firms," *Journal of Small Business Management* (20:3), 1982, pp. 27-34.

Poon, S., and Swatman, P. M. C. "Small Business Use of the Internet: Findings From Australian Case Studies," *International Marketing Review* (14:5), 1997, pp. 385-402.

Prananto, A., Marshall, P., and McKay, J. "A Study of the Progression of E-Business Maturity in Australian SMEs: Some Evidence of the Applicability of the Stages of Growth for E-Business Model," in M. Hiller, D. Falconer, J. Hanish, and S. Horrocks (eds.), *Proceedings of the 7th Pacific Asia Conference on Information Systems (PACIS)*, Adelaide, South Australia, 2003.

Premkumar, G. "A Meta-Analysis of Research on Information Technology Implementation in Small Business," *Journal of Organizational Computing and Electronic Commerce* (13:2), 2003, pp. 91-121.

Premkumar, G., and King, W. R. "Organizational Characteristics and Information Systems Planning: An Empirical Study," *Information Systems Research* (5:2), 1994, pp. 75-109.

Premkumar, G., and Roberts, M. "Adoption of New Information Technologies in Rural Small Businesses," *Omega* (27:4), 1999, pp. 467-484.

Rao, S. S., Metts, G., and Mora, M. C. A. "Electronic Commerce Development in Small and Medium Sized Enterprises: A Stage Model and its Implications," *Business Process Management* (9:1), 2003, pp. 11-32.

Raymond, L. "Determinants of Website Implementation in Small Businesses," *Internet Research* (11:5), 2001, pp. 411-422.

Raymond, L. "Management Information Systems: Problems and Opportunities," *International Small Business Journal* (7:4), 1989, pp. 44-53.

Reich, B. H., and Benbasat, I. "An Empirical Investigation of Factors Influencing the Success of Customer Oriented Strategic Systems," *Information Systems Research* (1:3), 1990, pp. 325-347.

Riemenschneider, K. C., Harrison, A. D., and Mykytyn Jr., P. P. "Understanding IT Adoption Decisions in Small Business: Integrating Current Theories," *Information and Management* (40:4), 2003, pp. 269-285.

Rogers, E. M. *Diffusion of Innovations* (3rd ed.), New York: Free Press, 1983.

Rogers, E. M. *Diffusion of Innovations* (4th ed.), New York: Free Press, 1995.

Rogers, E. M. *Diffusion of Innovations* (5th ed.), New York: Free Press, 2003.

SBS. "Statistical Press Release," DTI News Release, August 31, 2006 (http://www.sbs.gov.uk/SBS_Gov_files/researchandstats/SMEstats2005pr.pdf).

Scupola, A. "The Adoption of Internet Commerce by SMEs in the South of Italy: An Environmental, Technological and Organizational Perspective," *Journal of Global Information Technology Management* (6:1), 2003, pp. 52-71.

Shang, S., and Seddon, P. B. "Assessing and Managing the Benefits of Enterprise Systems: The Business Manager's Perspective," *Information Systems Journal* (12:4), 2002, pp. 271-299.

Shiels, H., McIvor, R., and O'Reilly, D. "Understanding the Implications of ICT Adoption: Insights from SMEs," *Logistics Information Management* (16:5), 2003, pp. 312-326.

Simpson, M., and Docherty, A. J. "E-Commerce Adoption Support and Advice for UK SMEs," *Journal of Small Business and Enterprise Development* (11:3), 2004, pp. 315-328.

Southern, A., and Tilley, F. "Small Firms and Information and Communication Technologies (ICTs): Toward a Typology of ICTs Usage," *New Technology, Work and Employment* (15:2), 2000, pp. 138-154.

Story, D. *Understanding the Small Business Sector*, London, UK: Routledge, 1994.

Swanson, E. B. "Information Systems Innovation Among Organizations," *Management Science* (40:9), 1994, pp. 1069-1092.

Taylor, M., and Murphy, A. "SMEs and E-Business," *Journal of Small Business and Enterprise Development* (11:3), 2004, pp. 280-289.

Thong, J. Y. L. "An Integrated Model of Information Systems Adoption in Small Businesses," *Journal of Management Information Systems* (15:4), 1999, pp. 187-214.

Thong, J. Y. L. "Resource Constraints and Information Systems Implementation in Singaporean Small Businesses," *Omega* (29:2), 2001, pp. 143-156.

Thong, J. Y. L., and Yap, C. S. "CEO Characteristics, Organizational Characteristics and Information Technology Adoption in Small Businesses," *Omega* (23:4), 1995, pp. 429-442.

Thong, J. Y. L., Yap, C. S., and Raman, K. S. "Engagement of External Expertise in Information Systems Implementation," *Journal of Management Information Systems* (11:2), 1994, pp. 209-231.

Tornatzky, L. G., and Fleischer, M. *The Process of Technological Innovation*, Lexington, MA: Lexington Books, 1990.

Venkatesh, V., and Davis, F. D. "A Theoretical Extension of the Technology Acceptance Model: Four Longitudinal Field Studies," *Management Science* (46:2), 2000, pp. 186-204.

Venkatesh, V., Morris, M. G., Davis, G. B., and Davis, F. D. "User Acceptance of Information Technology: Toward a Unified View," *MIS Quarterly* (27:3), 2003, pp. 425-478.

Volkoff, O., Strong, D. M., and Elmes, M. B. "Understanding Enterprise Systems-Enabled Integration," *European Journal of Information Systems* (14:2), 2005, pp. 110-120.

Ward, J., and Peppard, J. *Strategic Planning for Information Systems*, Chichester, UK: John Wiley and Sons, 2002.

Yap, C. S. "Distinguishing Characteristics of Organizations Using Computers," *Information and Management* (18:2), 1990, pp. 97-107.

Yin, R. *Case Study Research: Design and Methods*, Newbury Park, CA: Sage Publications, 1994.

About the Authors

Boumediene Ramdani is a doctoral student at Manchester Business School. He is currently researching SME adoption of ES. He has been involved in projects that look at diffusion of IT innovations in the public sector. His research interests include diffusion of IT innovations, SMEs, and e-government. Boumediene can be reached by e-mail at b.ramdani@gmail.com.

Peter Kawalek is a professor of information systems at Manchester Business School. He is currently involved in research projects that look at the diffusion of IT innovations in the public sector. His research interests include diffusion of IT innovations, process modeling, business process development, e-government; and IT strategy. Peter can be reached by e-mail at peter.kawalek@dom01.mbs.ac.uk.

28 INFORMATION TECHNOLOGY DIFFUSION IN THE JORDANIAN TELECOM INDUSTRY

Ala M. Abu-Samaha
Amman University
Amman, Jordan

Ibrahim Mansi
The Arab Academy for Banking
and Financial Sciences
Amman, Jordan

Abstract   *The aim of this paper is to analyze the diffusion of information technologies, applications, and systems in the Jordanian telecommunication industry. The paper introduces changes and challenges facing the public switched telephony network (PSTN) providers in Jordan and a number of strategies to face or even to exploit such changes and challenges to PSTN providers' advantage.*

Keywords   Information technology diffusion, public switched telephony network provider, mobile telephony provider, challenges

1   INTRODUCTION

A key driver of unrelenting change in organizations is the ever-increasing rate of information technologies and systems implementation and replacement. The introduction of new information technology applications is often associated with changes to organizational structure, the distribution of power, and user working practices/styles (Clegg et al. 1996; Clegg et al. 1997; Doherty and Perry 2001; Poulymenakou and Holmes 1996; Raymond et al. 1995). IT development and utilization provide insights into the nature

Please use the following format when citing this chapter:

Abu-Samaha, A. M., and Mansi, I., 2007, in IFIP International Federation for Information Processing, Volume 235, Organizational Dynamics of Technology-Based Innovation: Diversifying the Research Agenda, eds. McMaster, T., Wastell, D., Ferneley, E., and DeGross, J. (Boston: Springer), pp. 431-442.

of the complex relationship between the technology and the organization (Bloomfield and McLean 1996; Zuboff 1988). In its broadest sense, implementation refers to all organizational activities involved in the adoption, management and utilization of an innovation. Specifically, in the realm of information systems, adoption is the process of introducing, developing, and deploying/installing a system within an organizational setting whether intra- or interorganizational (i.e., internal to the organization or across a supply chain). Such a process can be considered as a complex process of deliberate organizational change(s) as many organizations seize the chance to introduce deliberate and reactive changes to the organizational setting entailing structure, processes, tasks, roles, job descriptions, relationships to others, and power structure (Orlikowski and Hofman 1997).

This paper introduces an analysis of future IT diffusion in the Jordanian tele-communication industry. The paper starts with the history of telecommunications in Jordan. The third section introduces Jordan Telecom Group (JTG) as a counter to the environmental changes and challenges facing the public switched telephony network (PSTN) providers in Jordan. The fourth section introduces statistical data to show the size and effect of environmental changes and challenges to PSTN services provision. The fifth section introduces a number of strategies adopted by JTG to face or even to exploit the environmental changes and challenges to PSTN providers' advantage. The paper ends with a number of lessons learned and conclusions.

2   HISTORY OF TELECOMMUNICATIONS IN JORDAN

Jordan Telecom (JT) is a PSTN provider operating and managing a fixed public telecom-munication network that provides local, national, and international fixed telephony services and leased lines. In addition to JT, the Jordanian Telecommunications Regula-tory Commission granted a class license in May 2005 to BATELCO Jordan to provide PSTN services in the near future.[1] JT was the exclusive provider of these services until the end of 2004. In addition to PSTN, JT was granted a license for providing GSM900 public mobile telephony on September 15, 2000, through an affiliate (MobileCom). JT enjoyed dual exclusivity (duopoly) for providing GSM900 public mobile telephony service until the end of 2003 when a third player was granted a third license.[2]

In terms of history, Britain's Cable and Wireless Company assisted the Jordanian Department of Post and Telegraph in developing telecommunication services and international links in 1930. The Telecommunications Corporation (TCC) was established as a government controlled entity responsible for various telecom services, including telephone, telegraph, and telex in 1971. In 1997, TCC was transformed into a govern-ment-owned company operating on a commercial basis, as a first step toward privatiza-tion, and was then renamed Jordan Telecommunications Company (JTC). A consortium

---

[1]From the Telecommunications Regulatory Commission website (http://www.trc.gov.jo/ Static_English/market.shtm; accessed on November 12, 2005).

[2]From the Telecommunications Regulatory Commission website (http://www.trc.gov.jo/ Static_English/telecomss.shtm; accessed on November 12, 2005).

led by France Telecom and the Arab Bank, the largest independent bank in Jordan, purchased 40 percent of JTC in 2000.[3]

3 JORDAN TELECOM GROUP

Jordan Telecom Group (JTG) represents the integrated operations, infrastructure and management of Jordan Telecom (the telephony provider), MobileCom (the mobile telephony provider), Wanadoo (the Internet service provider), and e-Dimension (an electronic content and service provider). Jordan Telecom Group aims to provide a higher quality service and a better added value to customers by combining four operating companies into a single one-stop-shop operator.

3.1 Jordan Telecom (JT Fixed Retail Business Unit)

Jordan Telecom, initially established by the government of Jordan, is currently considered as a privately owned public company dominated by France Telecom, the largest shareholder in the company. With more than 600,000 customers, Jordan Telecom's priorities include (1) developing and improving the fixed line telephone network, (2) extending the reach of the national data transmission network to ensure that every citizen/customer has the opportunity of being globally connected, and (3) lowering telephony tariffs.

3.2 MobileCom (JT Mobile Business Unit)

MobileCom, a subsidiary of Jordan Telecom, is one of four mobile telephone service providers in Jordan. The company was established in September 1999 with the aim of building a new, highly advanced mobile communications network. MobileCom is committed to continually introducing new levels of customer service, satisfaction, and quality, enabling Jordanians to benefit from the advantages of mobile communication. By coupling advanced technology and quality with value for money services, today MobileCom has more than 1,000,000 customers and a GSM network coverage reaching over 99 percent of the Jordanian population.

3.3 Wanadoo (JT Internet and Data Business Unit)

Previously known as Global One and Equant, Wanadoo emerged on the Jordanian market in 2001 following a strategic partnership with France Telecom. Wanadoo, Europe's largest Internet service provider, is leading the Internet service provision (ISP) market in Jordan with more than 50 percent of market share. Wanadoo continues to lead the Jordanian ISP market through introducing first-to-market services such as ADSL (asymmetric digital subscriber line), Cool Net Pre-Paid Internet Cards, Internet accessibility via 0900 service, full-fledged data communication and Internet roaming, to name just a few.

---

[3]Ibid.

3.4   e-Dimension (JT Content Business Unit)

Inaugurated in 2002 to address the needs of JT Group and the local/regional markets, e-Dimension, a *de facto* industry standard, is a leader in the IT solutions and content provision markets with an array of products including web software solutions development, ASP (application service provider), ICDN (Internet content delivery network) technologies, integration, specialized high-end PSP (payment service provider), and IPTV and triple play content provision. Exploiting the expertise of its highly experienced and internationally recognized team, e-Dimension successfully launched Jordan's first and only e-Payment gateway in 2003. e-Dimension was the first to develop and integrate an online real-time rating and billing engine for JT Double Play. e-Dimension integrated and provisioned the SVI/IVR and Saga800 virtual call centers for JT, which enables operator-class deployment of any combination of human resources at any location for customer interaction. e-Dimension has recently partnered with local, regional and international content providers to pave the way for developing the infrastructure for triple play and IPTV services, which offers a combination of voice, data, and video to be launched soon.

3.5   The Wholesale Business Unit

The wholesale business unit was created to address the business requirements of the existing and newly licensed service providers in a consistent, regulatory compliant, and time effective manner. The significant strategic partnership with France Telecom has enabled the Group to open up wider perspectives with new wholesale services, new technologies, and a worldwide presence.

4   CHALLENGES TO FIXED LINE PENETRATION

Public switched telephony network providers face serious challenges from the mobile and Internet service providers, mainly the high penetration rate of mobile devices compared to the decreasing penetration rate of fixed lines and the accelerated move to voice over IP services.

In terms of national infrastructure, Jordan has one telecommunication company (JT), four mobile network operators mostly owned by the private sector, and an extended number of ISPs, all of which are owned and operated by the private sector. In order to meet the increasing demand for high quality, high bandwidth Internet connectivity, the government of Jordan has issued 21 additional ISP licenses.[4] In addition, the Telecommunications Regulatory Commission also granted a class license to BATELCO Jordan May 2005 to provide PSTN services in the near future to the Jordanian market and a class license to Thuraya Satellite Telecommunications Company to provide global mobile personal communications by satellite (GMPCS).[5]

---

[4]For information on ISP licenses in Jordan, see the Telecommunications Regulatory Commission's website (specifically, http://www.trc.gov.jo/Static_English/market.shtm) and Arab Advisors Press Room (http://www.arabadvisors.com/Pressers/presser-181005.htm).

[5]From the Telecommunications Regulatory Commission's website (specifically, http://www.trc.gov.jo/Static_English/telecomss.shtm).

Jordan's cellular subscribers grew at a rate of 46.8 percent between 2000 and 2004. Reduced rates, per second billing, extended validities and special offers, were expected to cause the market to grow at a rate of 46 percent in 2005. Between 2006 and 2009, the Arab Advisors Group expects the Jordanian cellular market to grow at a rate of 10 percent, to exceed 3.43 million subscribers by 2009; with a penetration rate of more than 57 percent.[6] The number of fixed line/PSTN subscribers decreased from 629,000 in 2002 to 623,000 in 2004 and currently is estimated at 600,000. In the same period of time, the number of mobile subscribers rose to 1,624,000 in 2004 from 1,219,000 in 2002.[7] Abu-Ghazaleh & Co. Consulting (2005) estimated the penetration rate of cellular/mobile phone at 30.9 percent in 2004, with a total number of mobile owner population of 1,801,100. Regarding Internet accessibility, on the other hand, Abu-Ghazaleh and Co. estimated the number of Internet users in Jordan at 111,054 in 2004, up from 62,242 in 2002.

5 INFORMATION TECHNOLOGY DIFFUSION IN JORDAN TELECOM

Basically, telecommunication technologies were developed to transfer voice. Initially such transmission was achieved through analog systems based on microwave technology, which were limited in capacity. The disadvantages of the analog transmission and switching system pushed developers and technology manufacturers to look for more enhanced and effective telecommunication systems based on PCM (pulse code modulation). PCM is a digital signal of 2048Kb/s speed that can transfer up to 30 voice channels. The need for enhanced channel capacity for data and voice transmission during the late 1980s resulted in PDH (plesynchronous digital hierarchy) followed with SDH (synchronous digital hierarchy). This higher technology capacity matches the needs for data transmission caused by increased Internet traffic. Initially, Internet connectivity was available via dial up connections to pass through digital circuit switches which provide limited bandwidth, continuous billing during connectivity, and a busy analog telephone set. In order to meet the even higher needs for Internet connectivity, ADSL (asymmetrical digital subscriber line) over soft switch was introduced to provide wireless connectivity. By the year 2012, all telecommunication media (voice, data, and video) will be integrated through soft switch by using complete packet switching technology. By doing so, JTG as a telecommunication operator will provide its customers all the services needed through one platform, which will lead to reduced service cost, the possibility of increasing the bandwidth needed by customers, and interconnection with international operators to enhance services provision globally via satellite between JTG and France Telecom.

In order to absorb the accelerating move to IP-based services and the ever-increasing challenge from mobile telephony, the industry's network management paradigm is rapidly shifting from traditional infrastructure management to the management of next-

---

[6]See Arab Advisors Press Room, http://www.arabadvisors.com/Pressers/presser-181005.htm.

[7]Information taken from Department of Statistics website (www.dos.gov/jo; accessed November 12, 2005).

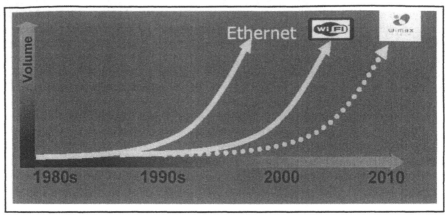

Figure 1. Jordan Telecom Technology Changes

generation, converged infrastructure (bearing both traditional and packet traffic) and the revenue-generating component of network services. While network element and domain monitoring remain critically important, today's quality of service commitments require a clear, real-time view of traffic and performance to ensure services are delivered end-to-end to the customer. Figure 1 depicts the JT technology changes reaching the vision of 2010.

Currently, JT is considering three major emerging technologies to be included within its current suit of services and products; these are voice over IP (VoIP), WiFi and WiMax. The costs of ownership and life cycle are posing important embodiments for implementing these technologies. The following sections provide a brief overview of these technologies and their JT Group implementation.

5.1 Voice Over IP

Protocols which are used to carry voice signals over the IP network are commonly referred to as **voice over IP** or **VoIP** protocols. Some cost savings are due to utilizing a single network to carry voice and data, especially where users have existing, under-utilized network capacity. VoIP to VoIP phone calls are typically free, while VoIP to PSTN calls generally require an added cost to the VoIP user. VoIP is gaining an advantage over PSTN, replacing the regular switching with new soft IP-based switches and it is generally under-implemented in JT Group. VoIP offers features and services that are not available via traditional phones. Where there is a broadband Internet connection, there is no need to maintain and pay the additional cost for a line just to make telephone calls. Figure 2 provides a diagrammatic representation of the VoIP environment.

5.2 WiFi Network Technology in JT Group

WiFi (wireless fidelity) is a data transmission system designed to provide location independent network access between computing devices by using radio waves rather than a

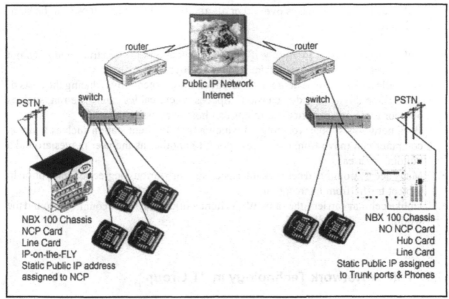

Figure 2. **Voice over IP in Jordon Telecom Group**

cable infrastructure. In the corporate enterprise, wireless LANs are usually implemented as the final link between the existing wired network and a group of client's computers, giving these users wireless access to the full resources and services of the corporate network across a building or campus setting.[8] Figure 3 provides a diagrammatic representation of a WiFi environment.

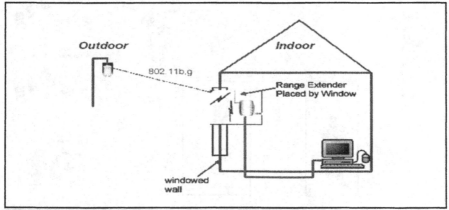

Figure 3. **WiFi Network**

---

[8]From the TelecomSpace web site, http://www.telecomspace.com/wirelessnw-wifi.html, accessed on January 10, 2006.

WiFi has many advantages over other alternative technologies; these can be summarized as follows:

- Unlike packet radio systems, WiFi uses unlicenced radio spectrum and does not require regulatory approval for individual deployments.
- WiFi allows LANs to be deployed without cabling, potentially reducing the costs of network deployment and expansion. Spaces where cables cannot be run, such as outdoor areas and historical buildings can host wireless LANs.
- WiFi networks support roaming, in which a mobile client station such as a laptop computer can move from one access point to another as the user moves around a building or area.
- Many access points and network interfaces support various degrees of encryption to protect traffic from interception.
- Unlike cellular carriers, the same WiFi client works in different countries around the world.[9]

5.3 WiMax Network Technology in JT Group

WiMax is a worldwide interoperability for microwave access allowing broadband wireless access of information in the form of data packet. Figure 4 describes the JT Group WiMax trial.

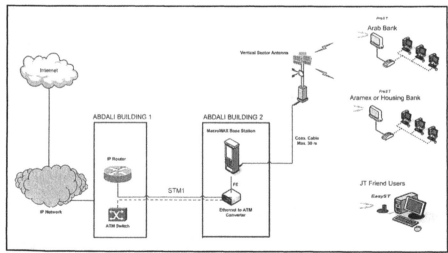

Figure 4. JT Group WiMax Trial

---

[9]Ibid.

WiMax is a technology that delivers last mile broadband connectivity in a larger geographic area than WiFi, enabling service to business customers and cable DSL-equivalent access to residential users providing coverage anywhere from 1 to 10 km. WiMax will enable greater mobility, range, and throughput for high speed data applications. The motivators for WiMax are

- low-cost high-performance solution to deliver broadband wireless data
- new business opportunities for broadband services reaching developed, emerging, and rural markets
- designed to operate as a complementary network to the third generation technologies

5.4 The NMC Project

In addition to the technologies mentioned, JTG launched the Jordan Telecom Group Network Centre (NMC) to revolutoinize the way the company manages its infrastructure. The Jordon Telecom Group NMC project came to meet many objectives, which motivated the movement tothe next generation of network management. These are

- increasing revenue through increasing the call completion rate
- reducing operating cost through improved operations and maintenance of the network
- making better use of people *(rightsizing not downsizing, too high staff/line ratio)*
- meeting regulatory standards
- minimizing service restoration time
- improving quality of the network and services
- managing the resources and reducing duplication of resources
- better informing the customers
- centralizing the work in one location
- managing and coordinating fieldwork through resources management and good field team piloting and handling of faults
- identifying cause, effect and status of system failures
- preparing for deregulation

In order to realize the objectives of the NMC project, NetBoss was selected by JTC to deliver reliable, flexible network management systems to commercial, government, and utility communications providers globally for the next a decade. NetBoss Network Management focuses on the service assurance and service fulfilment needs of complex, multi-vendor, multi-protocol network operators. A full-featured suite of applications covering real-time fault management, performance management, service activation, billing mediation, e-bonding, and enterprise application integration is available for a broad range of network operators—from telecommunications service providers to large private networks. NetBoss manages everything from legacy to next-generation, IP-based network infrastructure and services, offering a scalable, future-proof solution for convergent service providers. This movement and convergence of fault and performance management enables the operators to truly plan and manage service quality and proactively correct problems before they significantly impact the customers, which will increase the company performance and reliability.[10] NetBoss supported the major goals of the JTG-NMC project and is one of the best solutions for network management. NetBoss is an integrated communications management platform that supports wireless, wire line, and Internet services.

The strategic benefits of NetBoss include lower life cycle costs, maximization of the existing investment; reduced IT and administration costs; bundled solution pricing; and faster delivery of new services. Operational operational benefits include rapid deployment; improved network and service reliability; redundant and scalable solution; multi-vendor, multi-service, multi-protocol solutions; an open architecture; and single vendor for faster response. The added values for this movement include

- Flexible, scalable, proven solution: Regardless of the equipment and service mix in the network, NetBoss offers powerful element, shelf, rack, segment, and full network views, as well as fault management, proactive network control, database and application monitoring and automated processes.
- Trouble ticketing: NetBoss is already integrated with a powerful alarm reporting system, which is a dynamic tool to automatically assign a given alarm at the NetBoss fault management system screen to the related team.
- Service management quality and service level management: As the new economic models have evaporated and management attention has returned to fundamentals, there has been a corresponding increase in the level of discussion surrounding the concept of service level management. While there is much discussion about the need to invest significant resources in new and sophisticated applications, service providers can leverage existing resources significantly by building relatively simple, integrated service-level views of their networks. These views provide network managers and customer account managers with the information they need to proactively work with key clients while addressing network infrastructure issues on a priority basis.[11]

Figure 5 shows the NMC work flowchart.

6   CONCLUSIONS

This paper has produced an analysis of the major challenges that face the Jordanian PSTN market and few of the strategies undertaken by the sole PSTN provider to counter these challenges. The paper has provided a number of statistics to show the severe migration from traditional fixed accessibility to mobile and Internet accessibility. The paper presented three communication technologies—voice over IP, WiFi, and WiMax—to be included within the current suit of services and products offered by PSTN providers. This new mix of products is expected to recapture the telecommunication market by Jordan Telecom Group that was lost over the past few years to mobile telephony operators and ISPs.

---

[10]From the NetBoss Manual (http://www.networksupport.harris.com/support/documents/1000.pdf; accessed January 10, 2006).
    [11]Ibid.

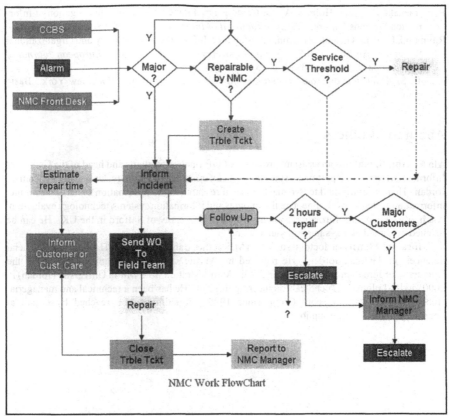

NMC Work FlowChart

Figure 5. **The NMC Work Flowchart**

References

Abu-Ghazaleh and Co. Consulting. "Market Brief on Telecommunications Sector in Jordan," 2005.

Bloomfield, B. P., and McLean, C. "Madness and Organization: Informed Management and Empowerment," in W. J. Orlikowski, G. Walsham, M. R. Jones, and J. I. DeGross (eds.), *Information Technology and Changes in Organizational Work*, London: Chapman & Hall, 1996, pp. 371-393.

Clegg, C., Axtell, C., Damadoran, L., Farbey, B., Hull, R., Lloyd-Jones, R., Nicholls, J. Sell, R., and Tomlinson, C. "Information Technology: A Study of Performance and the Role of Human and Organizational Factors," *Ergonomics* (40:9), 1997, pp. 851-871.

Clegg, C., Coleman, P., Hornby, P., McClaren, R., Robson, J., Carey, N., and Symon, G. "Tools to Incorporate Some Psychological and Organizational Issues During the Development of Computer-Based Systems," *Ergonomics* (39:3), 1996, pp. 482-511.

Doherty, N. F., and Perry, I. "The Cultural Impact of Workflow Management Systems in the Financial Services Sector," *Service Industries Journal* (21:4), 2001, pp. 147-166.

Orlikowski, W. J., and Hofman, D. "An Improvisational Model of Change Management: The Case of Groupware Technologies," *Sloan Management Review* (38:2), 1997, pp. 11-21.

Poulymenakou, A., and Holmes, A. "A Contingency Framework for the Investigation of Information Systems Failure," *European Journal of Information Systems* (5), 1996, pp. 34-46.

Raymond, L., Pare, G., and Bergeron, F. "Matching Information Technology and Organizational Structure: An Empirical Study with Implications for Performance," *European Journal of Information Systems* (4), 1995, pp. 3-16.

Zuboff, S. *Dilemmas of Transformation in the Age of the Smart Machine*, New York: Basic Books, 1988.

About the Authors

Ala M. Abu-Samaha is an assistant professor of Information Systems and head of the Computer Information Systems Department at the Faculty of Information Technology, University of Amman, Jordan. He has contributed to two major areas of research in the information systems discipline: information systems development methodologies and information systems/technology evaluation. Ala holds a Ph.D. in Information Systems from the University of Salford in the UK. He can be reached by e-mail at ala_samaha@yanoo.com.

Ibrahim Mansi is a doctoral student in MIS at the Arab Academy for Banking and Financial Sciences, in Amman, Jordan. He received his Master's in Public Administration from the University of Jordan in 2003, a B.Sc. in Public Administration from Mu'ta University (Jordan) in 2000, and a diploma in Technical Engineering in 1994. He has been a technical and managerial employee in Jordan Telecom Group since 1995. Ibrahim can be reached by e-mail at imansi@jordantelecomgroup.jo.

Part 7:

Position Papers

29 CHALLENGES FOR CREATIVITY AND INNOVATION IN MOBILE AND TRANSIENT VIRTUAL ENVIRONMENTS

Carl Adams
University of Portsmouth
Portsmouth, UK

Abstract   *This position paper examines the processes of creativity and innovation within the current context of virtual working. There is a discrepancy between innovation practice and support techniques: techniques are dominated by group activity, yet much of the work on instances of creativity indicate individual activity. There are considerable challenges in supporting creativity and innovation in virtual groups, however it is an area calling for innovation and the paper proposes where this innovation may take place.*

Keywords   Creativity and innovation, mobile and transient e-collaboration, diffusion of innovation

1   INNOVATION AND TECHNOLOGICAL PROGRESS

Innovation has fueled the development and progress in technology, business, and social activity and played an important role throughout the development of mankind (Gabor 1970). One current set of innovations has resulted in the virtual world, which is redefining business and working practices, organizations, markets, trade, and social interaction (Gibson 2003). The virtual organization is typically dynamic and flexible involving transient groups of people coming together for specific tasks (Cascio 1999, p. 7). Information systems development and support are sectors actively engaged in virtual working: Teams often consist of international group members, consisting of a mix of

Please use the following format when citing this chapter:

Adams, C., 2007, in IFIP International Federation for Information Processing, Volume 235, Organizational Dynamics of Technology-Based Innovation: Diversifying the Research Agenda, eds. McMaster, T., Wastell, D., Ferneley, E., and DeGross, J. (Boston: Springer), pp. 445-451.

outsourced and offshored elements and transient work workforces (Aalder 2001). However, the virtual organization, like any other, is based on collaboration and it is within this virtual environment that creativity and innovation will have to develop. Achieving creativity and innovation within virtual environments will face extra challenges in fostering and maintaining collaboration among dispersed and transient groups of people, often with their own goals and objectives.

2   INNOVATION AND CREATIVITY

Innovations are not just *technology*. For instance, Gabor (1970) includes 137 inventions and innovations in his book, 73 of them classed as hardware, 27 as biological, and 37 as social. A good example of social innovations is the development of the PERT planning system that evolved when developing the Polaris submarine and so enabled coordination on large-scale projects. Gibson (2003) gives further examples. Innovations and inventions take place when someone identifies a set of problems that need addressing or notices a potential opportunity to do something different. Roberts (1989) describes 36 fairly major discoveries that had considerable pseudo-serendipity in the discovery process, the accidental discovery activity when the inventor is looking for something, though possibly not the thing they eventually found. This concept has similarities with Pasteur's "prepared mind." Roberts' examples are predominantly of individual innovative and creative activity. Many of the examples given rely on an environment enabling a free flow of ideas to develop and so enabling insight. This free flow of ideas supports work by de Bono (1969, 1977).

There seem to be distinct elements in the creative problem solving process. First the identification of the need or problem to be addressed, which itself may involve, even require, some creativity. The mind has to be well prepared with sufficient knowledge of the problem domain. The next stage seems to involve a free flow of ideas where different alternatives are considered. The examples found in the literature indicate that these moments of innovation are predominantly individual activities. This is supported by the high proportion of individual patents filed (Huebner 2005). Harrison's (2006) *Book of Inventions,* also provides insightful snapshots of the activity behind many inventions and their inventors: inventions usually have single inventors, although several inventors often examine the same problem, creating competitive forces to driving innovation. The group activity in the main seems to involve the later stages, that of comparing alternatives and choosing. Of course, there will be examples where moments of innovations and creativity arise out of group activity, but the majority of the examples recalling such moments are individual events.

3   LITERATURE ON INNOVATION
AND CREATIVE SUPPORT

The literature on support for innovation and creativity covers a range of different techniques. Jantsch (1967) examined over 100 techniques for general business and technological forecasting; the Royal Society's work on *risk assessment* (Royal Society 1992) provided numerous techniques from several business areas; Bicheno's (1994) descriptions of 50 techniques and business tools; Obolensky's (1994) studies of a range of business reengineering techniques; and nearly 100 further techniques from de Bono (1969, 1977), Adams (1987), Couger (1995), and Adams and Avison (2003) to improve creativity, innovation, and general problem solving in a variety of domains from general business to information systems development. There are, of course, similarities between many of these techniques, and many are effectively a re-badging of earlier techniques. However, the majority of these are based around group activity involving collaboration between team members. There seems to be a tension here between the practice, involving *individual* creative moments, and the group interaction norms suggested in the techniques. To understand these tensions, we will have to examine what the innovation and creativity support techniques do. Adams and Avison, while examining a range of techniques used in information system development, identify some of the attributes and advantages that techniques bring:

The use of a technique may offer one or more of the following advantages:
- Reduces the solution of a problem to a manageable set of tasks.
- Provides guidance on addressing the problem situation.
- Adds structure and order to tasks.
- Provides focus and direction to tasks.
- Provides cognitive tools to address, describe and represent the problem situation.
- Provides the basis for further analysis or work.
- Provides a communication medium between interested parties.
- Provides an output of the problem solving activity
- Provides support to the practitioner (Adams and Avison 2003, p. 205).

Techniques support goes beyond the creativity and innovation activity and includes providing support for people to work together and developing common problem definitions and acceptance, or buy-in, of the problems and any solutions. This is very similar to the concept of the *collective mind* and mindful interaction that Weick and Roberts (1993) identify as essential for efficient and reliant teams.

However, there seems to be a tension between individual and group creativity, especially with the personal creativity tasks (Gladstein 1984). Bharadwaj and Menon (2000, p. 424) examine individual and organizational creativity mechanisms and identify a range of tensions. Clearly the tensions between individual and groups creativity are complex and involved. These tensions are resolved in some part by the designed tasks within the support techniques, and also through the embedded structures within the organization. In the pre-virtual world, this mostly meant face-to-face interaction within organizations where clear official structures and business protocols evolved to support business activity. At the same time, corresponding informal structures and protocols also evolved alongside the formal (Hutchison and Rosenberg 1994, p. 7; Adams 2005). This is a theme taken up by Bloomfield (1992), who argues for a "socially adequate view of organizations" (p. 204).

The informal and formal aspects are both important for effective collaboration (Adams 2005). However, fully functional teams take time to develop and work out responsibilities and protocols (Stewart 1991). It seems clear that the more transient teams are, then the bigger challenges they will have in achieving cohesion, shared goals, and a collective mind set. Weick and Roberts identify the need for rich communication structures between individuals within working groups. In addition, the type of interaction with newcomers into the group is also an indicator of the level of collective mind: "The quality of collective mind is heavily dependent on the way insiders interact with newcomers" (Weick and Roberts 1993, p. 368). A developed collective mind provides key elements of common problem framing and integrating new members into the common mind set.

Many authors on using creativity/innovation techniques recommend some consideration of the make-up of different groups (e.g., Bicheno 1994; Couger et al. 1993), although they give limited practical guidance on doing so. It seems that support techniques are performing a complex set of roles, not least getting common mind sets, mindful interaction, and buy-in of problems and solutions. Addressing the limitations of the virtual environment in achieving group cohesion as well as utilizing the capabilities of the environment to foster creativity and innovation is an area calling for innovation.

4   CONCLUSION AND WAY FORWARD

This paper has explored the processes of creativity and innovation within the current context of virtual working. The paper identified a discrepancy between works on innovation practice and the works covering support for innovation: Work on innovation and creative problem solving techniques is dominated by group activity, yet many actual instances of innovation and creativity indicate a predominance of individual activity. This tension between *individual* practice and *group* support is typically resolved in traditional face-to-face environments by the embedded social and formal structures. However, more challenges occur within the current climate of virtual working environments where social and formal structures are less strong. The virtual context also involves more transience and mobility of group members. Achieving buy-in for common problems, and any creative innovations to address those, are more difficult.

There seems to be an opportunity for creative and innovative solutions to emerge which address limitations of the virtual environment in achieving group cohesion. The traditional creativity and innovation support techniques need to be adapted to foster virtual interaction, and collaboration. Use of rich media, frequent interaction and informal interaction are areas that clearly offer potential for developing and supporting trust within development groups and achieving common mind sets, mindful interaction, and buy-in of problems and solution. Possibly the biggest impact will be by social innovations, developing new interaction activity and norms for virtual and reliant groups. There also seems to be an opportunity for utilizing the capabilities of the virtual environment to foster creativity and innovation at the individual level. After all, that is where omst creative moments take place. There is clearly a need for more research into the complex creative problem-solving activity with the trend toward virtual working and involving dispersed and often mobile transient groups.

References

Aalder, R. *The Outsourcing Guide*, New York: Wiley, NY, 2001.

Adams, C. "Supporting Structures for Evolving Systems Development," *International Journal of Information Technology and Management* (4:4), 2005, pp. 423-442.

Adams, C., and Avison D. E. "Dangers Inherent in the Use of Techniques: Identifying Framing Influences," *Information Technology & People* (16:2), 2003,pp. 203-234.

Adams, J. *Conceptual Blockbusting: A Guide to Better Ideas*, Harmondsworth, UK: Penguin, 1987.

Bharadwaj, S., and Menon, A "Making Innovation Happen in Organizations: Individual Creativity Mechanisms, Organizational Creativity Mechanisms or Both?," *Journal of Product Innovation Management* (17:6), 2000, pp. 424-434.

Bicheno, J. *The Quality 50: A Guide to Gurus, Tools, Wastes, Techniques and Systems*, Buckingham, UK: PICSIE Books, 1994.

Bloomfield, B. P. "Understanding the Social Practice of Systems Developers," *Journal of Information Systems* (2), 1992, pp. 189-206.

Cascio, W. F. "Virtual Workplaces: Implications for Organizational Behavior," in C. L. Cooper and D. M. Rosseau (eds.), *The Virtual Organization*, Chichester, UK: Wiley, 1999, pp. 1-14.

Couger, J. D. *Creative Problem Solving and Opportunity Finding*, Boston: Boyd and Fraser, 1995.

Couger, J. D., Higgins, L., and McLntyre, S. "(Un)Structured Creativity in Information Systems Organizations," *MIS Quarterly* (17:4), 1993, pp. 375-397.

de Bono, E. *Lateral Thinking: A Textbook of Creativity*, Harmondsworth, UK: Penguin, 1977.

de Bono, E. *The Mechanism of Mind*, Harmondsworth, UK: Penguin, 1969.

Gabor, D. *Innovations: Scientific, Technological and Social*, New York: Oxford University Press, 1970.

Gibson, R. *Rethinking the Future*, London: Nicholas Brealey Publishing, 2003.

Gladstein, D. L. "Groups in Context: A Model of Task Group Effectiveness," *Administrative Science Quarterly* (29), 1984, pp. 499-517.

Harrison, I. *The Book of Inventions: The Stories Behind the Inventors of the Modern World*, London: Casselli Illustrated/Octopus Publishing, 2006.

Huchinsonm C., and Rosenberg, D. "The Organization of Organizations: Issues for Next-Generation Office IT," *Journal of Information Technology* (9:2), 1994, pp. 99-117.

Huebner, J. "The Decline of Innovation," *Technological Forecasting and Social Change* (72:8), 2005, pp. 980-986.

Jantsch, E. "Technological Forecasting in Perspective," report for the Organization for Economic Co-operation and Development (OECD), Paris, 1967.

Obolensky, N. *Practical Business Re-engineering: Tools and Techniques for Achieving Effective Change*, London: Kogan Page, 1994.

Roberts, R. M. *Serendipity*, New York: John Wiley, 1989.

Royal Society. *Risk Analysis Perception and Management*, London: The Royal Society, 1992.

Stewart, R. "The Use of Social Paradigms in the Analysis of Team Behaviour During Organisational Change," in *Proceedings of the United Kingdom Systems Society Conference*, New York: Plenum, 1991, pp. 377-382.

Weick, K., and Roberts, K. "Collective Mind in Organizations: Heedful Interrelating on Flight Decks," *Administrative Science Quarterly* (38), 1993, pp. 357-381.

About the Author

Carl Adams had over a decade of professional experience in software development before entering academia. His research interests include information systems development (particularly creativity/problem solving activities), current technologies (e/m-commerce), and their impact on people and organizations. His Ph.D. (Southampton University) was in dealing with uncertainty within ISD. Carl can be reached by e-mail at carl.adams@port.ac.uk.

30 ATTAINING ORGANIZATIONAL INNOVATIONS: Better Smart than Fast

Peter Baloh
University of Ljubljana
Ljubljana, Slovenia

Maria E. Burke
University of Salford
Salford, UK

1 INTRODUCTION

Is never-ending innovation really the key to the ultimate success? Reading marketing and technological innovation literature, it is easy to get the impression that businesses today cannot survive without the continuously innovating processes and technology that new products are based upon. Yet, it seems that truly successful businesses know better. Asked about the rate of innovation and measuring innovation process success, the executive director of development in a successful manufacturing company responded:

> *Sure, we do set goals, we do measure, and we do assess the rate of innovation. But this is only for incremental innovation, small ideas that improve daily working practices and result in minor product changes. We are situated in a mature industry with narrow profit margins and products with approximately 5 to 7 years of shelf-life....So our development goals are not oriented toward rapid renewal of product lines and our activities are not labeled with aching urge to replace existing products. Rather, we are harvesting our crops from well-designed products throughout the life-cycle and definitely don't cut the mature stage too early as it is the most profitable stage. Also we don't cut the development cycles as the teething troubles do more harm than good to our image. We are even so working hard on figuring out the future trends and*

Please use the following format when citing this chapter:

Baloh, P., and Burke, M. E., 2007, in IFIP International Federation for Information Processing, Volume 235, Organizational Dynamics of Technology-Based Innovation: Diversifying the Research Agenda, eds. McMaster, T., Wastell, D., Ferneley, E., and DeGross, J. (Boston: Springer), pp. 451-456.

steadily and prudently updating our product portfolio—when the time is right
and with the features and products that are aligned with customers' needs and
which promise the best margins.

This echoes Gottfredson and Aspinall (2005) on the topic of innovation versus complexity. They suggest that firms can identify the point at which innovation maximizes
profits and revenues and argue that, for most firms, the number of product and service
offerings that would optimize profits and revenues is considerably lower than the number
they offer today. Continual launches of line extensions add complexity throughout
operations, and as the costs of managing that complexity multiply, margins shrink. Firms
that fail to check proliferating and overly customized products lose efficiency and
confuse their customers.

After thinking about this, "24/7 innovation" seems like hype. It appears that the best
way to success is to make competition irrelevant by redesigning buyer value to expand
existing markets and create entirely new ones (Kim and Mauborgne 1997), while
simultaneously keeping in mind the product portfolio and tracking how new products
grow in complexity from the consumer, operational, supply chain, and financial criteria.
Looking at the *inside* face of the innovation, we can see the same issue with regard to
processes and operations. Continuous organizational, business process, and IT innovations: yes, but only to the point where it doesn't start to burden the organization's ability
to sense and respond to challenges that will truly add value.

The natural question is, how do we get to the point of being a smart innovator? The
existing literature argues that this is the case of knowledge management (KM), which as
a field is concerned with how to create, mobilize, store, retrieve, and apply organizational
know-how with the goal of attaining business objectives (Desouza and Awazu 2005).
The results of good KM practices are tempting: improved decision making, accelerated
learning, improved innovation assimilation, increased productivity, and minimized reinvention and duplication are just a few of the commonly cited benefits (see Wing and
Chua 2005).

These factors are associated with the organization's capacity to absorb innovation
as it moves through assimilation stages of initiation, adoption, adaptation, acceptance,
routinization, and infusion (Cooper and Zmud 1990). In the initiation and adoption
phases, acquisition of facts and learning skills are especially relevant. In the adoption
and adaptation phases, imbibing knowledge and skill of understanding is important.
Using knowledge is crucial in the adaptation, acceptance, and routinization phases.
Finally, exploitation of knowledge and new knowledge creation relate to the routinization
and infusion phases of innovation assimilation (Sherif and Menon 2004; Zahra and
George 2002).

KM practices can thus lead to wisdom and result in more successful innovation. For
smarter innovation, organizations should be constantly and consciously paying attention
and introducing such management interventions that lead to creation of new, and
utilization of existing, knowledge. The aim of this paper is to consider the organizational
interventions that can be deployed in order to innovate smartly. In order to encourage
development of the field, another aim is to ask some of the questions that the research has
yet to answer.

The findings presented are based on extant literature and are enriched with our
experience from several research and consulting projects.

2   IMPLEMENTING KNOWLEDGE MANAGEMENT FOR SMARTER INNOVATION

As actual implementation of knowledge management can be seen as diffusion and implementation of innovation, we can refer to rich body of knowledge in the field of adoption of technological innovations. Innovating in firms is accompanied by a need to change. In order to adopt a new process, the firm must successfully utilize technological and process capabilities. This assimilation of innovation (Armstrong and Sambamurthy 1999) presents an organizational change and is thus naturally subject to inertia. Comprehensive advice has been given by Sherif and Menon (2004), who argue that actors at different organizational levels need to implement strategy, process, and culture changes. These are now considered in more detail, and critical success factors are highlighted.

2.1   Strategic Changes

Senior managers need to provide the strategy change. They need to develop administrative guidelines and new corporate strategy (i.e., set appropriate mission and vision statements). Furthermore, top management needs to allocate appropriate resources (Kwon and Zmud 1987).

Sometimes organizational change is evolutionary, and at other times it is radical. Senior management determines the scope of change, and delimits the processes and individuals affected by the change. In the view of KM, the change is complex and the results difficult to predict, so some authors (e.g., Sherif and Menon 2004) advise a step-by-step approach to changes (i.e., process-by-process).

In addition, senior management needs to develop educational and training programs to lower the knowledge barrier and, very importantly, appoint the change agent who fosters the adoption of the KM program throughout the organization (Sherif and Menon 2004).

From the aspect of smart innovators, research is needed to investigate the differences between successful innovators and other organizations with regard to top management support.

2.2   Process Changes

Middle and project managers are the ones that need to enact in the process change. They are the ones that understand, convert, and internalize visionary ideas of top management into down to earth, operationalizable organizational design. They do that by developing the methods for implementing new processes (e.g., business processes injected with KM practices), implementing the tools to support those processes, creating scales for progress measurement, and crafting financial and nonfinancial reward systems.

Middle and project managers are thus very important players in KM implementation. We would agree that senior management needs to act as sponsors and vision-providers, and without actual performers (employees) knowledge could not be created and utilized. However, middle and project managers need to move the vision of senior managers into everyday reality by transferring high-flying ideas and often metaphorical visions into new processes and adapt them to particular business context (Nonaka and Takeuchi 1995; Sherif and Menon 2004).

Reflecting the smart innovation orientation, middle and upper management have a crucial role in devising the performance measures that will be aligned with and will help attain top management's strategies and visions.

One area of further research should investigate nonquantitative measures of innovation, as the speed and number of innovations might not be the most suitable measures. Examples include quality of innovation or alignment of innovation programs with specifics of the company. For example, deviance from *innovation fulcrum* (optimal product and service structure, see Gottfredson and Aspinall 2005) is one possible measure.

2.3 Culture Changes

Operational staff needs to be able to exploit existing knowledge and create new knowledge. For KM practices to become accepted, routinized, and infused in everyday work practices, a culture change must occur (Sherif and Menon 2004). This is due to the all-pervading impact of culture on the organization, for example, culture impacts on both the formation and implementation of strategy and on the processes that take place within the organization.

Studies regarding systems theory included aspects such as culture, politics, and human emotions. These studies recognized the importance of organizational culture as an attribute in managing organizations (Bertalanffy 1968; Checkland 1981). Scott and Gable (1997) highlight how culture is about the way organizations do things, and is associated with an organization's underlying assumptions, characteristics, objectives, beliefs, and values. Presthus (1958), a political scientist, highlights the fact that we live in an organizational society, where employees build their life around organizations. To an outsider, life in organizations would be "full of peculiar beliefs, routines, and rituals that identity is as a distinctive cultural life when compared with that in more traditional societies" (Morgan 1997, p. 121). Although culture exists within all organizations, a strong culture is associated with how things happen (or don't) within the organization (Lee and Yu 2004; Robbins 2001).

As strong culture creates resistance to change, organizations must find ways of dealing with this in order to determine the success of new strategies and processes. Innovation, at the end of the day, "can be accomplished only by large numbers of individuals trying things they have not tried before" (Slevin 1971, p. 515).

Again, cultural characteristics of smart innovators as opposed to others should be investigated. What are the characteristics that the first have and the latter don't? Gaining an understanding of the type of culture that exists within an organization is important and useful as changing an organization's culture is particularly demanding.

3 CONCLUSION

The literature and our experience shows that any organizational intervention needs to be studied on strategic, process, and cultural levels. When pursuing innovation, managers need to be particularly focused on setting up an environment (organizational design, human and financial resources, etc.) that will enable new knowledge creation, its diffusion, and appropriate application. This will assist management in changing the organization's culture to one that nurtures knowledge sharing and open communication, resulting in new knowledge creation and an ability to compete in an ever-changing environment.

Organizational culture appears to be the prime antecedent to successful interventions, as it is about the core values and beliefs inherent in the fabric of the organization, including traditions, underlying assumptions, and the way employees communicate throughout the firm. Yet the culture can only be nurtured when top management envisions it as a desirable future and when middle management can operationalize it in appropriate goals.

We have listed some of the issues that will need to be answered in order for companies to innovate smarter and not to over-innovate nor lag behind the best. We can see comparative longitudinal studies as an especially useful and fruitful approach to the phenomena.

References

Armstrong, C. P., and Sambamurthy, V. "Information Technology Assimilation in Firms: The Influence of Senior Leadership and IT Infrastructures," *Information Systems Research* (10:4), 1999, pp. 304-327.

Bertalanffy, L. v. *General System Theory: Foundations, Development, Applications*, New York: G. Braziller, 1968.

Checkland, P. *Systems Thinking, Systems Practice*, Chichester, UK: Wiley, 1981.

Cooper, R. B., and Zmud, R. W. "Information Technology Implementation Research: A Technological Diffusion Approach," *Management Science* (36:2), 1990, pp. 123-140.

Desouza, K. C., and Awazu, Y. *Engaged Knowledge Management: Engagement with New Realities*, Basingstoke, UK: Palgrave Macmillan, 2005.

Gottfredson, M., and Aspinall, K. "Innovation Versus Complexity: What Is Too Much of a Good Thing?," *Harvard Business Review* (83:11), 2005, pp. 62-71.

Kim, W. C., and Mauborgne, R. "Value Innovation: The Strategic Logic of High Growth," *Harvard Business Review* (75:1), 1997, pp. 103-112.

Kwon, T. H., and Zmud, R. W. "Unifying the Fragmented Models of Information Systems Implementation," in R. J. Boland and R. A. Hirschheim (eds.), *Critical Issues in Information Systems Research*, New York: John Wiley, 1987, pp. 227-251.

Lee, S. K. J., and Yu, K. "Corporate Culture and Organizational Performance," *Journal of Managerial Psychology* (19:4), 2004, pp. 340-359.

Morgan, G. *Images of Organization*, Thousand Oaks, CA: Sage Publications, 1997.

Nonaka, I., and Takeuchi, H. *The Knowledge-Creating Company: How Japanese Companies Create the Dynamics of Innovation*, New York: Oxford University Press, 2001.

Presthus, R. "Toward a Theory of Organizational Behavior," *Administrative Science Quarterly* (3:1), 1958, pp. 48-72.

Robbins, S. P. *Organizational Behavior*, Englewood Cliffs, NJ: Prentice Hall, 2001.

Scott, J. E., and Gable, G. "Goal Congruence, Trust, and Organizational Culture: Strengthening Knowledge Links," in K. Kumar and J. I. DeGross (eds.), *Proceedings of the 18th International Conference on Information Systems*, 1997, pp. 107-120.

Sherif, K., and Menon, N. M. "Managing Technology and Administration Innovations: Four Case Studies on Software Reuse," *Journal of the Association for Information Systems* (5:7), 2004, pp. 247-281.

Slevin, D.   "The Innovation Boundary: A Specific Model and Some Empirical Results,"
    Administrative Science Quarterly (16), 1971, pp. 515-531.
Wing, L., and Chua, A.   "Knowledge Management Project Abandonment: An Exploratory
    Examination of Root Causes," *Communications of AIS* (16), 2005, pp. 723-743.
Zahra, S. A., and George, G.   "Absorptive Capacity: A Review, Reconceptualization, and
    Extension," *Academy of Management Review* (27:2), 2002, pp. 185-203.

About the Authors

Peter Baloh is an assistant lecturer at the Faculty of Economics, Ljubljana University. His main research interest is concentrated in the areas of knowledge management and technological innovation, which are considered through the lens of successful implementations. He is on the editorial review board of *International Journal of Knowledge Management*, and has authored articles for *IEEE Software, Research-Technology Management, Knowledge and Process Management Journal*, and *Manager*, among others.   Peter can be reached by e-mail at peter@baloh.net.

Maria E. Burke currently holds a position at the University of Salford's Information Systems Institute.   Her research is based in the area of information management.   She is a member of the editorial boards for the journals *Management Decision, Journal of Documentation, New Library Review*, and *International Journal of Electronic Marketing and Retailing*.   Her interests are in information fulfilment, business intelligence, KM, and the way in which organization structures and strategies are developing within economies of Central and Eastern Europe.   Maria can be reached by e-mail at m.e.burke@salford.ac.uk.

31 KNOWLEDGE ECOSYSTEMS: A Theoretical Lens for Organizations Confronting Hyperturbulent Environments

David Bray
Emory University
Atlanta, GA, U.S.A.

1 CONJECTURE

Adopt the viewpoint of a U.S. citizen and recall the contribution of knowledge exchanges (or lack thereof) to the major events of the last 6 years: incorrect estimates of the Al-Qaeda threat prior to the 9/11 attacks, failing to apprehend the culprit behind the anthrax events of 2001, inadequate response to Hurricane Katrina in 2005. Repeat investigations and comprehensive certifications by the U.S. General Accounting Office all report the same theme: more than sufficient knowledge existed to mitigate these events, but the knowledge was in a highly distributed and fragmented form across multiple departments, agencies, and the White House (Kean and Hamilton 2004; U.S. GAO 2003, 2004a, 2004b, 2006a, 2006b).

According to the **knowledge-based theory of the firm**, knowledge is the most strategically significant resource of an organization (Alavi and Leidner 2001; Argote and Ingram 2000). Capturing and sharing knowledge of expert and innovative employees provides a strategic advantage influencing performance outcomes (Nonaka 1994; Singh 2005). However, in order for distributed, heterogeneous knowledge bases to be intentionally leveraged as a strategic asset, an organization not only needs to identify what its employees know (and do not know) so it can appropriately target the transfer of knowledge, but also needs to discern when such knowledge will be valuable both now and in the future. To perform these feats with any certainty, an organization has to predict future events and knowledge needs.

Please use the following format when citing this chapter:

Bray, D., 2007, in IFIP International Federation for Information Processing, Volume 235, Organizational Dynamics of Technology-Based Innovation: Diversifying the Research Agenda, eds. McMaster, T., Wastell, D., Ferneley, E., and DeGross, J. (Boston: Springer), pp. 457-462.

Thus, there is a temporal dimension to knowledge. Knowledge can be time sensitive, potentially losing its relevance as environments change. Relaying information facilitates the exchange of tacitly stored knowledge (Galbraith 1982). Such exchanges allow humans to relay thoughts, to relay perceptions of the environment, and to adapt. Knowledge exchanges allow interindividual awareness of reality, opportunities, environmental changes, and trends. Ultimately, knowledge exchanges allow humans to become more "fit" to their environment (Clippinger 1999; Cummings 2004).

Knowledge itself may rapidly **lose its relevance due to hyperturbulent environments** involving rapid changes in human systems. Compared to "ordinary" turbulent environments, hyperturbulent environments require greater interindividual knowledge exchanges to adapt. Examples of such environments include 9/11, the anthrax events of 2001, and Hurricane Katrina in 2005. As confirmed by documented investigations, these historical events are examples where sufficient knowledge existed (and insufficient exchanges occurred) to mitigate negative outcomes. Organizations that must confront such seemingly chaotic environments include those involved with intelligence gathering and public health emergency response, to include the U.S. Central Intelligence Agency, U.S. Centers for Disease Control and Prevention, and the Federal Emergency Management Agency.

I contend that **organizations like the CIA and CDC represent the future of business**. Both organizations comprise globally distributed individuals, who must exchange time-sensitive knowledge to deal with hyperturbulent environments, increase organizational adaptedness, and increase organizational survivability (Clippinger 1999; U.S. NIC 2000, 2003).

Both the CIA and CDC must confront hyperturbulent environments in which organic, information-intensive changes occur rapidly with little warning. Moreover, no one individual harbors sufficient knowledge to either mitigate negative outcomes or capitalize on positive opportunities. Within these organizations, interindividual exchanges must transcend physical group proximity, social networks, and the institutions themselves (Daft and Weick 1984; U.S. GAO 2003; Kerr et al. 2005, 2006).

For these organizations, it may be **nearly impossible** (unless organizations assume omniscience) to discern in advance not only what knowledge is known and not known by their employees, but what knowledge is worth capturing for both present and future reuse, when such reuse will be appropriate, and when creating entirely new knowledge will be required. Under such circumstances, attempts at top-down management of knowledge are infeasible, since hyperturbulent events confronting an organization are too dynamic and organic. An organization cannot discern deterministically what knowledge is valuable in its employees rapidly enough to keep pace with environmental changes (Bray 2006; Carley and Lin 1997).

Instead, my contention here is that such organizations can **cultivate indirectly a knowledge ecosystem** that both fosters knowledge exchange opportunities among employees and allows dynamic (versus statically defined) knowledge exchange activities to occur and evolve as environmental circumstances require (Heckscher and Donnellson 1994). Such an approach frees an organization from the nearly impossible task of identifying what knowledge its employees have, need now, and will later find valuable. Rather, ecosystem-framed solutions require pragmatic approaches to maximize interindividual knowledge exchange opportunities and "seed" positive behavioral antecedents.

2   IMPLICATIONS

For academic theory, knowledge ecosystems bridge ongoing research regarding complex adaptive systems with theories of organizational learning. Complex adaptive systems literature supports the premise that bottom-up (i.e., grassroots) approaches are more resilient to volatility (Anderson 1999; Clippinger 1999). This literature also suggests that bottom-up approaches will cultivate emergent knowledge exchanges that **should prove more optimal than directed, top-down alternatives** (Heckscher and Donnellson 1994). As researchers, we should seek to test these theories.

The lens offered by knowledge ecosystems also links findings from social dilemmas research (Dawes et al. 1986; Frey and Iris 1996). Social dilemmas involve situations where individuals confront a shared situation in which each receives a higher personal payoff for defecting rather than cooperating as a group, but cumulatively all individuals would be better off if they cooperated rather than defected. **Deciding whether to exchange knowledge is akin to social dilemmas**: (1) should an individual contribute knowledge to the group, with a future possible return, or (2) should an individual opt not to contribute and free ride?

When it comes to exchanging knowledge, each individual may potentially receive a higher personal payoff for defecting rather than cooperating and exchanging knowledge, but cumulatively all group members would be better off if they cooperated. Most government managers run the risk of having parts of their divisions subsumed by other divisions if they choose to be transparent as to their budget and projects, and openly share knowledge with other organizations. **The current benefits of defecting outweigh the benefits of collaborating**. Other government divisions may claim these projects fall into their sphere of influence or represent work that they are already doing (Kerr et al. 2005, 2006).

If, however, a sufficient number of government divisions equally make the same decision to openly share knowledge and collaborate, all individuals in the organization will ultimately benefit (Kling 1991; Wade-Benzoni et al. 1996). Organizations need to find ways to encourage fewer individuals to defect from exchanging knowledge, and instead opt to collaborate; ergo, researchers need to discover methods of cultivating vibrant knowledge ecosystems.

Past research into social dilemmas supports the premise that technology not only enables individuals to exchange knowledge, but also mediates human perceptions with regard to the opportunities and motivations surrounding the exchange of knowledge. Experiments show that allowing electronic communication among individuals improves the rate of contributions in a social dilemma scenario (Dawes et al. 1986; Orbell and Dawes 1991). Intriguingly, the treatment of costly communication, where individuals must pay to communicate with each other, is itself sufficient to encourage individuals to contribute more to the public good of the group than defect (Ostrom et al. 2002).

Technology both facilitates knowledge exchanges and provides opportunities not afforded by physical proximity to collaborate. Extrapolating from social dilemmas research, I posit that the mere existence of these opportunities to exchange knowledge or ideas can reshape whether or not human individuals actually **deem such exchanges worthwhile**. Knowledge exchange opportunities influence human motivations, which in turn influence knowledge exchange behaviors and processes, which ultimately shape outcomes, including organizational performance.

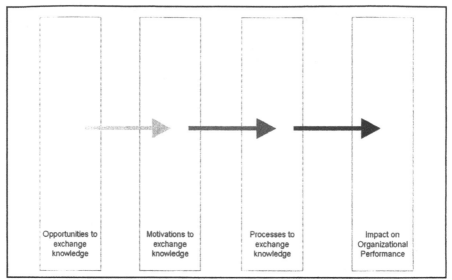

Opportunities to exchange knowledge → **Motivations to exchange knowledge** → **Processes to exchange knowledge** → **Impact on Organizational Performance**

Figure 1. The Key Steps to Designing a Knowledge Ecosystem

   Cumulatively, if top-down knowledge management is indeterminate and not possible for hyperturbulent environments, perhaps instead researchers should piece together a puzzle by uncovering (1) who had opportunity, (2) who had motive, and (3) how was it done regarding method? These three questions establish knowledge exchange opportunities, behavioral antecedents, and knowledge exchange activities for individuals comprising an organization (Daft and Weick 1984). These three factors form the pieces of the puzzle that promote cultivation of a knowledge ecosystem. For governments and business alike, the vibrancy of their knowledge ecosystem determines the veracity and relevance of organizational knowledge. The challenge for us, as researchers, will be to clarify how best to design such ecosystems, further discern the role of technology as an intervention, and to determine what influential variables determine positive or negative performance outcomes.

References

Alavi, M., and Leidner, D. *"Review:* Knowledge Management and Knowledge Management Systems: Conceptual Foundations and Research Issues," *MIS Quarterly* (25:1), 2001, pp. 107-136.

Anderson, P. "Complexity Theory and Organization Science," *Organization Science* (10:3), 1999, pp. 216-232.

Argote, L., and Ingram, P. "Knowledge Transfer: A Basis for Competitive Advantage in Firms," *Organizational Behavior and Human Decision Processes* (82:1), 2000, pp. 150-169.

Bray, D. "Exploration, Exploitation, and Knowledge Management Strategies in Multi-Tier Hierarchical Organizations Experiencing Environmental Turbulence," in D. Sallach and M. Prietula (eds.), *North American Association for Computational Social and Organizational Sciences*, Notre Dame, IN, June 22-23, 2006.

Carley, K., and Lin, Z. "A Theoretical Study of Organizational Performance Under Information Distortion," *Management Science* (43:7), 1997, pp. 976-997.

Clippinger, J. (ed.). *The Biology of Business: Decoding the Natural Laws of Enterprise*, San Francisco: Jossey-Bass, 2004.

Cummings, J. "Work Groups, Structural Diversity, and Knowledge Sharing in a Global Organization," *Management Science* (50:3), 2004, pp. 352-364.

Daft, R., and Weick, K. "Toward a Model of Organizations as Interpretation Systems," *Academy of Management Review* (9:2), 1984, pp. 284-295.

Dawes, R., Orbell, J., Simmons, R., and Van De Kragt, A. "Organizing Groups for Collective Action," *American Political Science* Review (80:4), 1986, pp. 1171-1185.

Frey, S., and Iris, B. "Cooperation, Communication and Communitarianism: An Experimental Approach," *Journal of Political Philosophy* (4:4), 1996, pp. 322-336.

Galbraith, J. "Designing the Innovating Organization," *Organizational Dynamics* (10:3), 1982, pp. 4-25.

Heckscher, C., and Donnellson, A. (eds). *The Post-Bureaucratic Organization: New Perspectives on Organizational Change*, Thousand Oaks, CA: SAGE Publications, 1994.

Kling, R. "Cooperation, Coordination and Control in Computer-Supported Work," *Communications of the ACM* (34:12), 1991, pp. 83-88.

Kean, T., and Hamilton, L. *The 9/11 Commission Report: Final Report of the National Commission on Terrorist Attacks upon the United States*, Washington, DC: U.S. General Printing Office, 2004.

Kerr, R., Wolfe, T., Donegan, R., and Pappas, A. "A Holistic Vision for the Analytic Unit," *Studies in Intelligence* (50:2), 2006, pp. 47-55.

Kerr, R., Wolfe, T., Donegan, R., and Pappas, A. "Issues for the US Intelligence Community," *Studies in Intelligence* (49:3), 2005, pp. 47-54.

Nonaka, I. "A Dynamic Theory of Organizational Knowledge Creation," *Organizational Science* (5:1), 1994, pp. 14-37.

Orbell, J., and Dawes, R. "A 'Cognitive Miser' Theory of Cooperators' Advantage," *American Political Science Review* (85:2), 1991, pp. 515-528.

Ostrom, E., Dietz, T., Dolsak, N., Stern P., Stonich, S., and Weber, E. (eds.). *The Drama of the Commons*, Washington, DC: National Academy Press, 2002.

Singh, J. "Collaborative Networks as Determinants of Knowledge Diffusion Patterns," *Management Science* (51:5), 2005, pp. 756-770.

U.S. General Accounting Office. *Department of Homeland Security: Formidable Information and Technology Management Challenge Requires Institutional Approach*, GAO-04-702, 2004a.

U.S. General Accounting Office. *Katrina: GAO's Preliminary Observations Regarding Preparedness, Response, and Recovery*, GAO-06-442T, 2006a.

U.S. General Accounting Office. *More Comprehensive National Strategy Needed to Help Achieve U.S. Goals and Overcome Challenges*, GAO-06-953T, 2006b.

U.S. General Accounting Office. *Public Health Response to Anthrax Incidents of 2001*, GAO-04-152, 2003.

U.S. General Accounting Office. *9/11 Commission Report: Reorganization, Transformation, and Information Sharing*, GAO-04-1033T, 2004b.

U.S. National Intelligence Council. *Global Trends 2015: A Dialogue About the Future with Nongovernment Experts*, NIC 2000-02, 2000.

U.S. National Intelligence Council. *SARS: Down But Still a Threat*, NIC ICA 2003-09, 2003.

Wade-Benzoni, K., Tenbrunsel, A., and Mazerman, M. "Egocentric Interpretations of Fairness in Asymmetric, Environmental Social Dilemmas: Explaining Harvesting Behavior and the Role of Communication," *Organizational Behavior and Human Decision Processes* (67:2), 1996, pp. 111-126.

About the Author

David A. Bray is currently a Ph.D. candidate at the Goizueta Business School, Emory University. His research focuses on bottom-up (i.e., grassroots) socio-technological approaches for fostering interindividual knowledge exchanges. Before academia, he served as the IT chief for the Bioterrorism Preparedness and Response Program at the Centers for Disease Control, where he led the technology response to 9/11, anthrax, WNV, SARS, and other major outbreaks. David can be reached by e-mail at dbray@bus.emory.edu.

32 THE TRIPLE HELIX, OPEN INNOVATION, AND THE DOI RESEARCH AGENDA

Gabriel J. Costello
Galway-Mayo Institute of Technology and
National University of Ireland
Galway, Ireland

Brian Donnellan
National University of Ireland
Galway, Ireland

Ivor Gleeson
Central Applications Office
Ireland

Colm Rochford
American Power Conversion
Castlebar, Ireland

Abstract   *This paper examines the implications for research on the diffusion of innovations (DOI) arising from a growing body of literature in two related fields. The first area concerns the debate on the role of regional and national systems of innovation in the innovation process. The second area deals with the argument that enterprises must move from a "closed innovation" to an "open innovation" paradigm. The review is presented in the context of a case study being undertaken in a subsidiary of American Power Conversion (APC) located in the West of Ireland. Based on the preliminary stages of our work, we present a conceptual 3-D model of Rogers' innovation-decision process and suggest a series of propositions to stimulate future research efforts.*

Please use the following format when citing this chapter:

Costello, G. J., Donnellan, B., Gleeson, I., and Rochford, C., 2007, in IFIP International Federation for Information Processing, Volume 235, Organizational Dynamics of Technology-Based Innovation: Diversifying the Research Agenda, eds. McMaster, T., Wastell, D., Ferneley, E., and DeGross, J. (Boston: Springer), pp. 463-468.

1   INTRODUCTION

Over the last decade, significant literature has emerged in two areas related to innovation, first with the debate on the role and composition of national systems of innovation and second with the argument that enterprises must move from a *closed innovation* to an *open innovation* paradigm.   The aim of this paper is to examine the consequences of this literature for research on the diffusion of innovations (DOI) and in particular on Rogers' (2003) work on the innovation-development process.   The paper is presented in the context of a case study in a subsidiary of American Power Conversion (APC) located in Ireland's Border, Midland, and Western (BMW) region.   The paper proceeds as follows. First, the research context is outlined in terms of the evolving Irish economy and the regional situation.   A brief literature review is then presented of enterprise innovation models and of national systems of innovation.   The next section provides an overview of an ongoing longitudinal case study on innovation being carried out in APC.   Following this, a perspective is presented that realigns Rogers' two-dimensional innovation process to a more externally focused three-dimensional model.   Finally, based on the context and literature, we propose a revised DOI research agenda together with suggestions for future work.

2   BACKGROUND

Over the last 40 years, Ireland has leapfrogged from a traditional agrarian economy to a deliberately created information economy (Trauth 2000).   The initial impetus was fueled by foreign direct investment from North American multinational corporations setting up offshore manufacturing facilities to avail of tax incentives; a young, educated workforce; and proximity to their growing number of European customers.   However, this initially successful model is increasingly being threatened by the low cost economies of Eastern Europe, India, and China.   Irish enterprises rapidly need to build new sources of competitive advantage to sustain employment and standards of living.   The Border, Midland, and Western (BMW) region of Ireland is designated by the European Union as "Objective 1": a less well developed area that qualifies for additional structural funds under the European Union state aid scheme.   It is also one of the fastest growing regions of Europe but needs to increase absorptive capacity.   Ireland is now entering a new era which, according to Porter (2003), requires a transition to an innovation economy

3   CHANGING INNOVATION PARADIGMS

The innovation-development process as defined by Rogers (2003, p. 138) consists of the six steps shown in Figure 1.   The methodology includes all the decisions, activities, and their impact from the initial recognition of a need, followed by research, development, and commercialization through to diffusion and evaluation of the consequences.

Chesbrough (2003) argues that, in many industries, the centralized approach to R&D described above, which he terms *closed innovation* has become obsolete.   This paradigm, he contents, must be replaced by *open innovation*, which adopts external ideas and knowl-

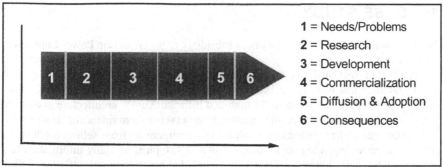

Figure 1. The Innovation-Decision Process (adapted from Rogers 2003, p. 138)

edge in conjunction with the internal process. A number of factors are influencing this change such as the mobility of skilled people, the increasing presence of venture capital, emergent high-tech start-ups, and the significant role of university research. The increasingly important role of academia in supporting innovation in knowledge-based societies has led to the development of a number of models from national systems of innovation (Lundvall 1995) to the more recent triple helix model of university–industry–government relations (Etzkowitz and Leydesdorf 2000). The latter is illustrated in Figure 2, which has been adapted to emphasize the focal area of interaction, highlighted in the Venn diagram.

However, while the reality of the growing association between academia and enterprises is widely accepted, the nature of the involvement is still a matter of lively debate (Manimala 1997, p. 111).

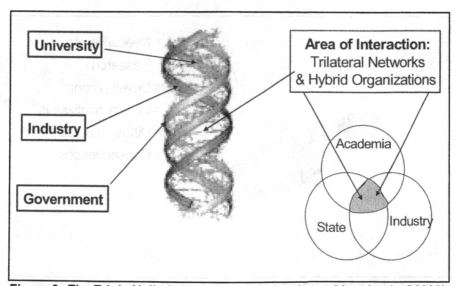

Figure 2. The Triple Helix (adapted from Etzkowitz and Leydesdorf 2000)

4   CASE STUDY

The case study is based in APC Ireland, a subsidiary of the American Power Conversion (APC) Corporation. APC designs, manufactures, and markets back-up products and services that protect hardware and data from power disturbances. The explosive growth of the Internet has resulted in the company broadening its product offerings from uninterruptible power supplies to the high-end InfraStruXure™ architecture in order to meet the critical availability requirements of Internet service providers and data centers. This phenomenon has resulted in a value chain realignment from selling products or services to providing integrated customer solutions, typical of many information and communication technology corporations in knowledge-based economies (Grimes 2003). APC entered a major period of transition in the second-half of 2006 with the announcement of its merger with Schneider Electric.

5   IMPLICATIONS FOR THE DOI RESEARCH AGENDA

Figure 3 illustrates the conceptual model of a 3-D innovation process that realigns the 2-D model of Figure 1 to include the dynamics of the triple helix. Using this perspective, we contend that organizations with closed innovation processes need to accommodate the dimensions of open innovation and engage with other significant regional actors.

Having illustrated our argument that Rogers diffusion theory needs to be updated based on the current debates on the concepts and structures of national systems of innovation and open innovation models, we will now discuss the implications for research.

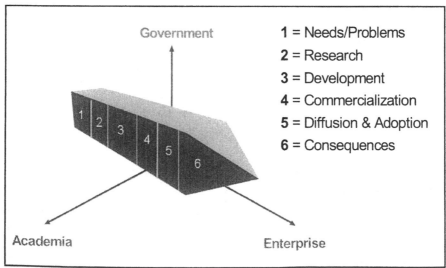

Figure 3. **3-D Representation of Rogers' Innovation-Decision Process**

5.1 Issues for the Research Agenda

A research agenda provides the impetus for planning and developing more detailed studies of a particular area. Arising from our previous discussion, we now propose the examination of the following issues that could contribute to refreshing the DOI research agenda:

1. Issues associated with regional innovation.
2. Issues associated with the innovation process within open organizations.
3. Issues associated with developing more integrated and interactive collaboration between a region and its organizations.
4. Issues associated with management of the innovation process in a 3-D reference frame.

5.2 Suggestions for Future Work

Arising from the issues presented above, we suggest a number of topics to stimulate future work.

1. Developing a triple helix model of, for example, the BMW region, showing the main actors, roles, and areas of interaction.
2. Examining the phases and deliverables of current closed innovation methodologies in the light of the open innovation paradigm.
3. Identifying the main areas of interaction between the regional model and the organizational innovation process with a view to more productive collaboration. We also raise the question whether each of Rogers' six steps needs its own triple helix.
4. Exploring the implications for innovation project and portfolio management arising from the 3-D perspective. Associated with this, we suggest investigating the consequences of moving from product and service innovation to "solutions" innovation.

6 CONCLUSIONS

This paper has provided a review of Rogers' innovation-development process in the light of a movement to open innovation within the triple helix of academia–enterprise–government. Following a review of the literature and the regional context, a conceptual model of a 3-D innovation process that realigns the current 2-D model to include the dynamics of the triple helix was illustrated. The paper argued that Rogers' innovation process needs to be updated to take into account these paradigms. Future work was suggested for a more detailed investigation of the implications of this perspective on the integration of regional and organizational innovation structures and methodologies.

References

Chesbrough, H. W. *Open Innovation: The New Imperative for Creating and Profiting from Technology*, Boston: Harvard Business School, 2003.

Etzkowitz, H., and Leydesdorf, L. "The Dynamics of Innovation: From National Systems and 'Mode 2' to a Triple Helix of University–Industry–Government Relations," *Research Policy* (29), 2000, pp. 109-123.

Grimes, S. "Ireland's Emerging Information Economy: Recent Trends and Future Prospects," *Regional Studies* (37:1), 2003,pp. 3-14.

Lundvall, B.-A. *National Systems of Innovation: Towards a Theory of Innovation and Interactive Learning*, London: Pinter, 1995.

Manimala, M. J. "Higher-Education-Enterprise Co-operation and the Entrepreneurial Graduate: The Need for a New Paradigm," in J. Mitra and P. Formica (eds.), *Innovation and Economic Development: University–Enterprise Partnerships in Action*, Dublin: Oak Tree, 1997.

Porter, M. "Irish Competitiveness: Entering a New Economic Era," IMI Top Management Briefing, Dublin, Ireland, October 9, 2003 (available online at http://www.isc.hbs.edu/pdf/CAON_Ireland_2003.10.09_CK.pdf).

Rogers, E. M. *Diffusion of Innovations* (5th ed.), New York: Free Press, 2003.

Trauth, E. M. *The Culture of an Information Economy: Influences and Impacts in the Republic of Ireland*, Boston: Kluwer Academic Publishers, 2000.

About the Authors

Gabriel J. Costello is a lecturer at the Galway-Mayo Institute of Technology. Presently, he is also a researcher at the Centre for Innovation and Structural Change (CISC), National University of Ireland, Galway, and is undertaking a Ph.D. in MIS. Prior to this he worked for 20 years in the telecommunications industry. He can be reached by e-mail at gabrielj.costello@gmit.ie.

Brian Donnellan is a lecturer in Information Systems at NUI Galway. His research interests lie primarily in the area of knowledge management systems, which encompasses the use of information systems to support knowledge management, innovation, new product development, and technology management. Prior to this he worked for 20 years in the electronics industry. He can be reached by e-mail at brian.donnellan@nuigalway.ie.

Ivor Gleeson is the general manager and chief executive officer of Ireland's higher education Central Applications Office (CAO). Presently, he is undertaking a Ph.D. in Economic and Strategic Management Considerations in the Provision of Computer Software at the National University of Ireland, Galway. He has over 30 years experience in computer programming analysis and design. He can be reached by e-mail at ivor@cao.ie.

Colm Rochford is the plant manager for APC Castlebar. His areas of interest include developing cultures that promote innovative thinking and lean transformation. Prior to this, he held lean transformation and product support roles in APC. He previously worked as a design engineer in the power electronics industry. He can be reached by e-mail at colm.rochford@apcc.com.

33 BRINGING AN INTEGRAL APPROACH TO THE FIELD OF TECHNOLOGY DIFFUSION RESEARCH

Michael L. Ginn
Fielding Graduate University
Santa Barbara, CA, U.S.A.

Abstract   *The intention in this position paper is to propose a possible new future for the technology diffusion research community, based on the integral approach of American philosopher Ken Wilber. The trends and current state of technology diffusion research are reviewed, and relevant aspects of Wilber's integral approach and its possible contributions are described. These aspects include Wilber's basic quadrants model and integral methodological pluralism, as well as the metapractices from which they arise.*

Keywords   Diffusion, integral, quadrants, Wilber

1   A BRIEF HISTORY OF TECHNOLOGY DIFFUSION RESEARCH

For much of the past 50 years, the field of technology diffusion has been dominated by a single theoretical leader: Everett Rogers. His 1962 classic, *Diffusion of Innovations*, is now in its fifth printing, and joins his 30 other books and some 500 articles. Useful models introduced by Rogers include the adopter curve, a five-stage process model of diffusion, elements of diffusion, the history of diffusion research, innovation roles, change agent characteristics, and the consequences of innovations. I have been greatly influenced by Rogers' models, extending his conception of innovator roles and their distinct concerns (Ginn 1994). Rogers' adopter curve, as adapted by Geoffrey Moore (2002), has introduced a generation of high-tech and marketing professionals to basic technology diffusion principles. Rogers has extended his diffusion principles to social issues such as family planning, drunk driving, and cancer prevention.

Please use the following format when citing this chapter:

Ginn, M. L., 2007, in IFIP International Federation for Information Processing, Volume 235, Organizational Dynamics of Technology-Based Innovation: Diversifying the Research Agenda, eds. McMaster, T., Wastell, D., Ferneley, E., and DeGross, J. (Boston: Springer), pp. 469-474.

Over the past decade, however, diffusion research has diverged from this common ground. For instance, nearly half of the papers in the 1994 IFIP 8.6 proceedings cited Rogers, while only 4 out of 19 papers did so in 2006. Similar developments in other research communities suggest that our field's decamping is a result of a broad historical movement rather than defects with or resolution of Rogers' theories. For example, the broader field of organizational science recently examined a similar theoretical divergence (Schoonhoven et al. 2005a, 2005b), and noted a mix of likely causes: a growing number of researchers, institutions, and consumers engaged in research; a growth in the number of acceptable epistemological stances and research methodologies; and an explosion of journals with varied viewpoints and requirements. Some suggested that this divergence could be best understood using a theory of paradigmatic change as introduced by Kuhn (1996) which explores an essential tension between tradition and novelty. However, I believe a more productive approach is a lens proposed by Tsoukas and Knudsen (2003). They reviewed how major historical movements in epistemology have impacted organizational theorists and their methodologies, building toward a framework which includes and relates research done from fundamentally different perspectives.

I propose that we adopt a similar, but a richer and more general approach to our research divergence: the integral theory of American philosopher Ken Wilber. This would not replace Rogers' seminal work, but rather include the important but partial truths of it and the divergences that have and will continue to take place.

2   HOW AN INTEGRAL APPROACH COULD BE USEFUL TO TECHNOLOGY DIFFUSION RESEARCH

What might Wilber's integral approach offer to our technology diffusion research community?

First, it may address the divergence of our research more powerfully that can cross-disciplinary, multiple methods, and other approaches we currently use. It might provide a more satisfactory theoretical framework from which to describe and work with the state of and trends of our technology diffusion research. It could also offer our research community a core set of social practices and methodologies that would powerfully relate our diverse elements and at the same time validate each of the methodologies currently in use. Finally, this integral approach offers the possibility of more powerful research with broader impact.

3   QUADRANTS: A BASIC INTEGRAL MODEL

Integral can be defined as comprehensive, balanced, inclusive, and essential for completeness. Wilber has refined this basic idea over the past several decades in some 30 books, including *Sex, Ecology, and Spirituality* (2001). A key model in his integral approach is the quadrants, as shown in Figure 1. It is a simple 2 × 2 matrix of singular/ plural and interior/exterior pairs.

The resulting intentional, behavioral, cultural, and social perspectives are not new inventions, but rather fundamental aspects of human experience. For example, most

	Interior	Exterior
Singular	"I" Intentional The Beautiful Art	"It" Behavioral The True Science
Plural	"We" Cultural The Good Morals	"Its" Social The True Science

Figure 1. **Wilber's Basic Quadrants**

human languages have first-, second-, and third-person pronouns such as I, you/we, and it. Socrates recognized these three dimensions of our language-given reality as the Beautiful, the Good, and the True. Later, Max Weber and others would distinguish the cultural value spheres of **art** or the aesthetic expression of "I," the **morals** of "we," and the objective "its" of **science**. Habermas has in a similar way pointed to subjective, intersubjective, and objective domains.

It is useful to think of the quadrants as aspects of ourselves or perspectives though which we see the world, rather than as containers in which to put things.

4   INTEGRAL METHODOLOGICAL PLURALISM

Adding a bit of complexity to this basic idea of four quadrants is the idea that a perspective given by each quadrant can be further distinguished by objective or subjective approaches. For example, a subjective approach to interior, singular phenomena results in epistemologies and research practices like phenomenology, whereas an objective approach would result in structuralist approaches such as developmental psychology.

The primary defining characteristic of integral methodological pluralism (IMP) is acknowledging the importance and validity of each set of practices and methodologies that are in use: each has some important if partial truth. IMP can be seen as what will help establish a multipurpose toolkit that will enhance a tradition's chances of making a striking contribution to knowledge or to the conduct of industry or government. Alternatively, IMP can be seen as contributing to a mutual regard in which a richer diversity of interpretations can be held as a whole. IMP can also be seen as a framework that will embrace these enduring practices and methodologies yet transcend their partialisms, absolutisms, and exclusionary practices.

5   IMPLICATIONS FOR PRACTICE

Wilber, in his Excerpt B, describes how an integral methodological pluralism has two main parts. There is a paradigmatic aspect that is the result of a careful compilation of

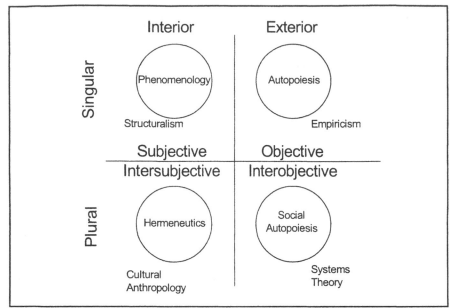

Figure 2. Eight Major Paradigms or Methodologies (Wilber, Excerpt D)

the accepted methods of a research community. These could be mapped using the IMP extension of the basic quadrants model as shown in Figure 2. This compilation would show major methodologies which currently enact, illume, bring forth the various world spaces and ways of being.

The second main part is a meta-paradigmatic set of practices that relate the various paradigmatic strands to each other. A new set of practices and methodologies weave these strands into "radically nonexclusionary ways of being-in-the-world." This follows from one of the basic heuristics of Wilber's integral approach, that "everyone is right" or holds an important if partial truth.

What practices can build bridges between other practices? While many will be uniquely developed by researchers in their various traditions, Wilber (Excerpt B) offers simultracking as one example. Phenomena of various domains are simultaneously tracked according to the accepted methodologies of those domains. The second main part of IMP, the meta-paradigmatic aspect, requires that the different methodologies address the same phenomena in such a way that correlations can be noted and also so that practices can be engaged to bring forth previously unrealized interrelationships between the world views enacted by their respective methodologies.

In addition to these social practices and methodologies, individual practices are critical to developing the capacity to be integrally informed. For example, an integrally informed researcher will be able to distinguish transdisciplinary studies, which "enact a new territory of integral displays between old rivals" (Wilber, Excerpt B), from cross-disciplinary ones, which simply confirm each other's prejudices. Another capacity would be to bring forth a radically nonexclusionary way of being-in-the-world. This involves more than accomplishing an intellectual understanding, adopting a belief, or taking a certain position such as pluralism for its own sake.

Integral methodological pluralism ultimately makes central the development of the researcher. This development is broad based, involving not just cognitive development, but also emotional, social, somatic, spiritual, and integrative development as well. It holds the intention and promise of higher development as suggested by, for example, Kegan (1986). It suggests a facility with human types such as gender differences and the Enneagram typology. It is grounded in a personal experience of various states of experience or consciousness and an adequate conception of how these are related to more general development.

One generic example of such a development approach is Wilber's (2006) integral life practice, which simultaneously engages and exercises a full range of human potentials and perspectives such as those suggested by his quadrants model. Another way to explain the scope of an integral life practice is to say that it both addresses the short-comings and celebrates the advances of the modern world that most of us grew up in and still inhabit. It will work on resolving how, in us, arts and morals have been colonized by science. It will work on the disassociation of feeling from reason. It will celebrate and further develop empirical science's challenges to premodern myths.

6   SUMMARY

Wilber's integral approach and IMP present us with an opportunity to observe ourselves as a research community in a process of adoption, and then, as we master it, in a process of diffusion to other research communities. Ultimately these complex streams of discourse, centered on methodology, will become generalized and streamlined and enter the culture at large. This is an opportunity for us to be engaged in a historic forming of a broad societal shift in consciousness.

References

Ginn, M. L. "The Transitionist as Expert Consultant: A Case Study of the Installation of a Real-Time Scheduling System in an Aerospace Factory," in L. Levine (ed.), *Diffusion, Transfer and Implementation of Information Technology*, Amsterdam: North Holland, 1994, pp. 179-198.

Kegan, R. *The Evolving Self: Problem and Process in Human Development*, Boston: Harvard University Press, 1986.

Kuhn, T. *The Structure of Scientific Revolutions* (3rd ed.), Chicago: University of Chicago Press:, 1996.

Moore, G. *Crossing the Chasm* (Revised ed.), New York: HarperCollins, 2002.

Rogers, E. *Diffusion of Innovations* (5th ed.), New York: Free Press, 2003.

Schoonhoven, C. B., Meyer, A. D., and Walsh, J. P. "Moving Beyond the Frontiers of Organization Science," *Organization Science* (16:5), 2005a, pp. 453-455.

Schoonhoven, C. B., Meyer, A. D., and Walsh, J. P. "Pushing Back the Frontiers of Organization Science," *Organization Science* (16:4), 2005b, pp. 327-331.

Tsoukas, H., and Knudsen, C. (eds.). *The Oxford Handbook of Organization Theory: Meta-Theoretical Perspectives*, New York: Oxford University Press, 2003.

Wilber, K. "Excerpt B: The Many Ways We Touch: Three Principles Helpful for Any Integral
    Approach," (available online at http://wilber.shambhala.com/html/books/kosmos/excerptB/
    part1.cfm).
Wilber, K. "Excerpt D: The Look of a Feeling: The Importance of Post/Structuralism,"
    (available online at http://wilber.shambhala.com/html/books/kosmos/excerptD/part1.cfm).
Wilber, K. *Sex, Ecology, and Spirituality: The Spirit of Evolution* (2nd ed.), Boston: Shambhala
    Publications, 2001.
Wilber, K. *Integral Life Practice Kit Starter Kit: The Simplest Practice You Can Do To Wake Up*,
    Boston: Shambhala Publications, 2006.

About the Author

Mike Ginn lives in Carmel, California, with his wife Carol. He has worked at the Software
Engineering Institute and Sun Microsystems. He is currently a doctoral student in Human and
Organizational Systems at Fielding Graduate University where his research interests are driven by
the integral approach of Ken Wilber. Mike can be reached by e-mail at mikeginn@
bethechange.com.

34   SOFTWARE INNOVATION AS MAINTENANCE: Theorizing the Social in Software Maintenance

Allen Higgins
University College Dublin
Dublin, Ireland

Abstract   *This paper entertains the notion that software maintenance and innovation are more closely related than is commonly accepted. We consider perspectives where innovation projects are understood as attempts to engineer both the social and the technological, where processes of innovation imply the configuring of users, communities, and artifacts through the work of maintenance, manifest perhaps as bricolage or drift. If this alternate interpretation of innovation is accepted, it implies a renewed sensitivity to research and method aligned to innovation settings, emphasizing subjects' interpretations, language, perceptions, behavior and even culture. This has implications for developing a deeper and more intimate understanding of processes surrounding software development.*

Keywords   Software development, maintenance, programming, information systems development, diffusion of innovation

1   INTRODUCTION

Software undergoing maintenance is often regarded as a "mutable immutable," where the idiom of maintenance is employed even though software does not wear out or degrade (Swanson 1976). Maintenance work is difficult and messy; patches must satisfy new demands without breaking existing installations and work as before (only better). It is better for your career to work on next generation technology, rather than being stuck on bug fixing or maintaining old versions within the straight jacket constraints of compatibility and legacy codebases (Riain 2000). Maintenance jobs are outsourced to low

Please use the following format when citing this chapter:

Higgins, A., 2007, in IFIP International Federation for Information Processing, Volume 235, Organizational Dynamics of Technology-Based Innovation: Diversifying the Research Agenda, eds. McMaster, T., Wastell, D., Ferneley, E., and DeGross, J. (Boston: Springer), pp. 475-479.

cost locations or shunted into the background noise of the workplace, and so the work of maintaining a venerable old version is often shunned by developers as they jockey for assignment to new product projects.

An alternate perspective, however, revalues the commonplace observation that software maintenance activities comprise merely the thick dynamic between customers and developers. E-mail and bug reports negotiate complaints, desires, trade-offs, insights, and solutions. These aspects of maintenance work, performed day-to-day on software still in development, suggest that the *idiom* of maintenance (connoting breakage, wear, and degradation over time) is not commensurate with the *activity* of maintenance (the co-production and mutual configuration of both users and objects).[1] What then if we adopt this alternate stance, that the work of software maintenance is instead a rich and messy process of innovation? This paper briefly explores the implications of conflating maintenance with innovation (suitably defined), and sketches a need for research attending to the situation and performance of maintenance work, to programming and configuring software as collective and multi-sited activities.

2   INNOVATION

Innovation is defined as the *bringing in* or *introduction of change* but the burgeoning innovation literature is largely concerned with the strategic production of novelty, usually conceived as new technology under the constraints of structural or individualist factors (Amabile et al. 1996; Christensen 1997; Schilling 2005; Trott 2005). Formal accounts of the organized production of software under the banner of innovation are likewise presented as processes of planned, purposeful engineering of novel products (Schilling 2005; Trott 2005). Software development is conceived as new product development (NPD), and the subsequent success (or otherwise) of technological innovation is considered to be path dependent; determined by factors like timing, market preparedness, technological superiority, or organization strategy. Key figures such as the engineer or architect, although central to these conceptions of invention and production, are rarely seen to be actively engaged with distant others in constructing the social contexts for their technological innovations. However, an alternate literature bedded in sociology presents another view, where so called engineer-sociologists are themselves engaged in building both the technologies and the social networks intended to take up an innovation (Callon 1987). This hints at another interpretation of innovation, revaluing the notion of *introduction* or *bringing in*, and shifting us toward a deeper concern with the use, appropriation, and adoption of changed technology by users or consumers. From this perspective we anticipate that innovation narrowly conceived under the rubric of NPD will lead to partial accounts, ignoring or dealing superficially with concepts of social power, interests, and action implicit in the sociality of *introduction*.

---

[1]This position is informed by the author's on-going study in a software development company. Although new product development (NPD) is the high profile, strategic activity in the company, the metaphor of maintenance is found to be a dominant idiom within the workplace. The maintenance idiom is shared and employed by developers, testers, users, and others to describe, interpret, and explain much of their daily work.

Let us entertain this alternate paradigm, of software innovation as maintenance, where the idea of *maintenance* carries a stronger sense of *bringing in* or *introduction*. In this case introduction patterned on the notion of *xenia* (the Greek concept of hospitality or host-guest relations employed by Ciborra (2002)), transforms the ideation of innovation into a process of *hosting* technology within the social. Bringing in an innovation lets us blur the boundary between the host and the stranger (technology cast as the guest), as each accommodates the other if the materiality of software remains open-ended. What are the implications if maintenance work surrounding software is revealed as a valid location for processes and activities constituting innovation, and where might this understanding be positioned within the information systems literature?

3   PROCESSUAL INNOVATION

The concept of *processual* innovation (Brown and Eisenhardt 1995; Slappendel 1996; Von Hippel 2005) enriches an understanding of this setting, accounting for the generation of meaning by actors both using and developing software, through its maintenance and production. Slappendel (1996) reviewed the innovation literature and its underlying theoretical perspectives. Earlier studies implied two main levels of analysis (individualist and structuralist), but she also noted the growing acceptance of a third approach she termed the *interactive process* perspective. An integrative process view of innovation is an attempt to overcome the dialectic between individualist and structural perspectives, resolving the tension of their commensurability through an interactive dynamic. Von Hippel (2005), tracing the history of selected technology innovations, arrived at the pragmatic realization that products continue to be developed even when they leave the confines of a laboratory or engineering shop. He develops the concepts of *lead user* and *innovation communities* and concludes that innovation is a process of coproduction shared between the producer and the consumer of a new product. In a similar vein Ciborra (2002) discredits the appeal of new product development as the source of innovation, proposing instead to celebrate the situated activity of tinkering (or bricolage) as an incremental route to producing the technologies with which we work. Processes like *dérive* or technology *drift* present a "phenomenological middle ground, where the intentions of humans and non-humans mingle and blur; where learning and recalcitrance, hacking and inertia show up simultaneously" (Ciborra 2002, p. 84). Drift is a process of development and maintenance, a concept that links technology developed in the laboratory and the technology installed in the users' environments and those in between: customers, support engineers, and programmers writing code. "[D]rifting is about situated technology....It is about technology in use, as experienced and seen from the swamp of contingent situations and practices, and not from the crisp, crystal-clear high ground of method" (Ciborra 2002, p. 90).

Processual perspectives on innovation, therefore, attend naturally to the diversity of actors interacting to stabilize their objectives through dynamics of crises, negotiation, and agreement. These strands of the IS literature claim that innovations are never fully designed top-down nor introduced in one shot, instead they are tried out through prototyping and tinkering. Innovation as *maintenance* would then be a collective and intrinsically social phenomenon resulting from the fluidity of software undergoing cycles of packing and unpacking (construction, deconstruction, and reconstruction). Maintenance as bricolage, drift, and xenia offers a language for the production of innovation as *coproduction* (Grint and Woolgar 1997) involving the many actors participating in slow processes of transformation. We might think of ourselves then as hosts to the "gift" of software as it enters into the workplace, where it is shaped by, and in turn shapes, the lived phenomena of our work.

4   IMPLICATIONS FOR STUDIES OF SOFTWARE DEVELOPMENT WORK

A sketch of future research attending to the practices of maintaining software (software still in development) implies the necessity of observing those involved, as they interact, while maintaining and recreating software in use. It entails recording, tracing, and interpreting episodes of communication, dialectical conflict, and control (overt or pervasive), giving rise to adapted objects and conceptions of usage in maintenance settings. Field work patterned on ethnographic methods (Garfinkel 1967; Geertz 1973; Marcus 1998) provides a methodological approach to studying the domain through multi-sited ethnography (Marcus 1995) encompassing involved, detailed, longitudinal studies which privilege intersubjectivity generated in the contested environment of software maintenance.

References

Amabile, T. M., Conti, R., Coon, H., Lazenby, J., and Herron, M.   "Assessing the Work Environment for Creativity," *Academy of Management Journal* (39:5), 1996, pp. 1154-1184.

Brown, S. L., and Eisenhardt, K. M.   "Product Development: Past Research, Present Findings, and Future Directions," *Academy of Management. The Academy of Management Review* (20:2), 1995, pp. 343-378.

Callon, M.   "Society in the Making: The Study of Technology as a Tool for Sociological Analysis," in W. E. Bijker, T. P. Hughes, and T. Pinch (eds.), *The Social Construction of Technological Systems*, Cambridge, MA: MIT Press, 1987, pp 83-103.

Christensen, C. M.   *The Innovator's Dilemma: When New Technologies Cause Great Firms to Fail*, Boston: Harvard Business School Press, 1997.

Ciborra, C.   *The Labyrinths of Information: Challenging the Wisdom of Systems*, Oxford, UK: Oxford University Press, 2002.

Garfinkel, H.   *Studies in Ethnomethodology*, Englewood Cliffs, NJ: Prentice-Hall, 1967.

Geertz, C.   *The Interpretation of Cultures*, London: Fontana, 1973.

Grint, K., and Woolgar, S.   *The Machine at Work: Technology, Work and Organization*, Cambridge, UK: Polity Press, 1997.

Marcus, G. E.   "Ethnography in/of the World System: The Emergence of Multi-sited Ethnography," *Annual Review of Anthropology* (24), 1998, pp. 95-117.

Marcus, G. E.   *Ethnography Through Thick and Thin*, Princeton, NJ: Princeton University Press, 1995.

Riain, S. Ó.   "Working for a Living: Irish Software Developers in the Global Workplace," in M. Burawoy (ed.), *Global Ethnography: Forces, Connections, and Imaginations in a Postmodern World*, Berkeley, CA: University of California Press, 2000.

Schilling, M. A. *Strategic Management of Technological Innovation*, New York: McGraw-Hill Irwin, 2005.

Slappendel, C. "Perspectives on Innovation in Organizations," *Organization Studies* (17:1), 1996, pp. 107-129.

Swanson, E. B. "The Dimensions of Maintenance," in *Proceedings of the Second international Conference on Software Sngineering*, Los Alamitos, CA: IEEE Computer Society Press, 1976, pp. 492-497.

Trott, P. *Innovation Management and New Product Development*, Upper Saddle River, NJ: Financial Times Prentice Hall, 2005.

Von Hippel, E. *Democratizing Innovation*, Cambridge, MA: MIT Press, 2005.

About the Author

Allen Higgins is a researcher at University College Dublin and doctoral student at the University of Warwick under the supervision of Joe Nandhakumar. His studies are focused on the intersubjectivity of software development work, accessed ethnographically; seeking to describe aspects related to how programmers and users understand and access the objects they create; and processes of creating and maintaining the ensembles of actors composing processes of innovation. He can be reached by e-mail at allen.higgins@ucd.ie.

35 EXPLORING STRUCTURAL CHANGES OF THE COMMUNICATIONS NETWORK DURING ORGANIZATIONAL CRISIS

Liaquat Hossain
Zhao Shenshen
Shahriar Hasan Murshed
University of Sydney
Sydney, Australia

Abstract   *In this study, we explore patterns of organizational communication during normal state and crisis state using e-mail communications data. We apply social networks analysis (SNA) to understand the communication behavior and its structural changes during crisis from a real-world organization's communication data. By applying SNA, we first analyze the changes of social network structures from normal organizational state to crisis state. Second, we explore the changes of different positions or roles of the organizational communication networks during the crisis. Third, we apply measures of centrality (i.e., degree, betweenness, and closeness) for studying how different structural changes in social networks correlate to organizational hierarchy during normal and crisis state.*

Keywords   Organizational crisis, centrality measures, e-mail communications, SNA

1   INTRODUCTION AND BACKGROUND

E-mail communication is becoming an integral component of organizational communication networks. E-mail has also become one of the most popular methods of communication adopted by organizations today. Therefore, e-mail logs can serve as a useful resource for research in fields such as link analysis, social network analysis, and textual

Please use the following format when citing this chapter:

Hossain, L., Shenshen, Z., and Murshed, S. H., 2007, in IFIP International Federation for Information Processing, Volume 235, Organizational Dynamics of Technology-Based Innovation: Diversifying the Research Agenda, eds. McMaster, T., Wastell, D., Ferneley, E., and DeGross, J. (Boston: Springer), pp. 481-486.

analysis. In May 2002, the U.S. Federal Energy Regulatory Commission publicly released a large set of e-mail, the Enron corpus, which contains 619,446 e-mails belonging to 158 users over a period of 3.5 years. Shetty and Adibi (2004) created a MySQL database of this corpus. They also cleaned the database by removing a large number of duplicate e-mails, computer generated folders, junk data, invalid e-mail addresses, blank messages etc. The resulting dataset contains 252,759 messages from 151 employees distributed in about 3,000 user-defined folders. We have used this database to perform our study. We explore if the organizational crisis state reflects a different social network structure than the normal state of an organization. We argue that this type of dataset, representing actual communications behavior, is best suited to study the relationships between structural changes of communication networks and organizational crisis.

2   EXPLORING STRUCTURAL CHANGES OF COMMUNICATIONS NETWORK

Diesner at el. (2005) argue that when an organization encounters crisis, the social network analysis (SNA) measures will change accordingly. Those changes, they contend, reflect the organizational structural changes. The exploration of those SNA measures corresponding to the crisis stage might support decision making on the prediction of any future crisis.

Centrality is the state or quality of being central in a network structure (Faust 1997). It is considered to be the structural attribute of nodes in a network, not an attribute of actors themselves, but of their structural position in the network. Centrality has been defined as a measure of the potential importance, influence, and prominence of an actor in a network (Borgatti et al. 2002; Freeman 1979). Freeman (1979) defined three measures of centrality and explained their structural implications: degree, betweenness, and closeness. Freeman stated that the degree of a point seemed to be an index of that position's potential for activity in the network. Betweenness is the extent to which a point falls between others on the shortest paths connecting them. It was taken to be an index of potential for control of communication. Closeness measures the distance of a point to all others. This was viewed as a measure of independence from control.

3   METHODS

We extracted data from the MySQL database by using PHP (hypertext preprocessor). The result contained the e-mail addresses suggesting who send e-mail to whom for every month. We converted our files to text files and then converted them into VNA format, supported by UCINET software (Borgatti et al. 2006). Using NETDRAW, we then drew the network diagram and calculated the centrality measures in terms of degree, betweenness, and closeness. We transferred the data in to MS Excel and plotted them as a chart, showing how every centrality measure goes from the normal organizational state to the organizational crisis state. We repeated the procedure in order to collect the data for every month. We tried to understand why the SNA measure changes followed that trend by reviewing the corresponding organizational context, and tried to give possible and reasonable explanation.

4   RESULTS AND ANALYSIS

This section displays the results containing the undirected centrality measures based on
the organizational hierarchy and the overall view of the entire organization over time.
Figure 1 contains the degrees based on the various organizational roles. The simple
count of the degree measures for every organizational role indicates that every role in
Enron was having more e-mail connections with others during the crisis period (2000 –
2001) than during the noncrisis period (pre-2000). We further observed the difference
of degree measures' changes between the lower level positions and the higher level
positions during crisis state. The increment of the degree measure of higher lever
employees is found to be much more rapid than that of lower level employees as the
organizational crisis intensifies. We also discovered that higher level employees had
more absolute degrees than the lower ones during the organizational crisis. However, the
lower level employees (e.g., employees and traders) had even more absolute connections
than those of middle level employees (e.g., directors and managers). We argue that the
middle level employees had less importance during the crisis time. We also found that
the degree of lawyers was quite high, implying that the organization was facing many
legal problems during the crisis state. Freeman (1979) suggested that the degree is a kind
of index of communication activities. We can also conclude that during the crisis, both
senior management and executive employees were having more communication activities
than was middle management; while there is not much difference in the degree measure
of all positions during the normal noncrisis state.

    Figure 2 shows the betweenness measure based on the organizational hierarchy.
Like the trend of the degree, the betweenness of almost all positions in the crisis period
is far more than that of every position during the noncrisis period. During the crisis, we
found that senior management had a high value of betweenness. Lower level employees
had relatively higher betweenness value than middle management. The lawyers also had
high betweenness values during the crisis period. Based on Freeman's explanation of

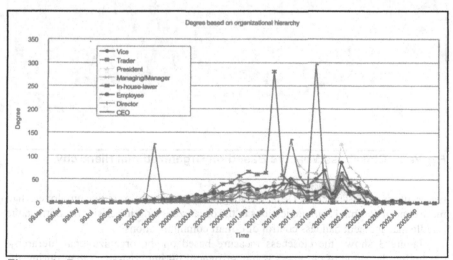

Figure 1. **Degree Measure Based on Organizational Hierarchy**

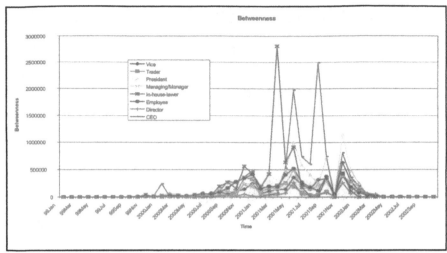

Figure 2. Betweenness Measure Based on Organizational Hierarchy

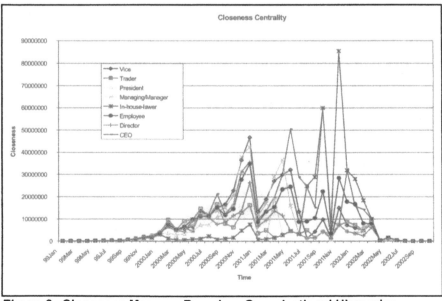

Figure 3. Closeness Measure Based on Organizational Hierarchy

betweenness, we assumed that senior management and lower executive employees had more control of e-mail communications in the organization during crisis. In contrast, the middle management had less control of e-mail communications.

Figure 3 shows the closeness measure based on the organizational hierarchy. Generally, the value of closeness is higher overall during crisis state than during the normal state. One of the interesting points is that middle management had higher closeness value during most of the crisis period, whereas the lawyers had very low closeness value. This indicates that the lawyers did not have a very important role, which was close to many other employees. This lower closeness value is also observed with traders and even the president. Unlike lower degrees and the betweenness values, middle management had relatively higher closeness value during most of the crisis period. Overall, we conclude that the actors or groups (such as middle management) with fewer connections to others could be globally close to many others in the networks, a claim supported by Scott (2000). Although middle management have fewer communication activities, they are still in a position which is close to both senior management and lower level employees. The CEO and the vice president were still having very high closeness value, which is quite understandable in the sense that the CEO and vice president had high independency and efficiency, as Freeman pointed out in his literature review on centrality measures.

5 CONCLUSIONS

This study suggests that there are some relations between structural changes of the communications network and organizational crisis. We applied measures of network *centrality* to study the changes of communications network structure in both the normal state and the crisis state. Based on the assumptions of centrality measures, we compare the centrality measures in different organizational states so that we can discover and analyze the centralization and decentralization of organizational communication networks in both the normal organizational state and the crisis state. By exploring the Enron e-mail corpus dataset, we found that different organizational positions have different social network attributes during crisis. By exploring different centrality measures such as group degree, betweenness, and closeness, we discovered that the organizational communication network becomes more decentralized during crisis. We further explored the relationship between formal organizational hierarchy and the changes in measures of centrality during crisis.

References

Borgatti, S. P., Everett, M. G., and Freeman, L. C. *UCINET6 for Windows Software for Social Network Analysis*, Harvard, MA: Analytic Technologies, 2002.

Diesner, J., Franz, T. L., and Carley, K. M. "Communication Networks from Enron Email Corpus: 'It's Always About the People. Enron is no Different,'" *Computational & Mathematical Organization Theory* (11), 2005, pp. 201-228

Faust, K. "Centrality in Affiliation Networks," *Social Networks* (19:2), 1997, pp. 157-191.

Freeman, L. C. "Centrality in Social Networks Conceptual Clarification," *Social Networks* (1), 1978/1979, pp. 215-239.

Scott, J. *Social Network Analysis: A Handbook*, London: SAGE Publications, 2000.

Shetty, J., and Adibi, J. "The Enron Dataset Database Schema and Brief Statistical Report," unpublished paper, 2004 (available online at http://www.isi.edu/~adibi/Enron/Enron_Dataset_Report.pdf).

About the Authors

Liaquat Hossain is a senior lecturer and director of the postgraduate program at the School of Information Technologies at the University of Sydney, Australia. His research interests are primarily in the area of CSCW, computer mediated communication, human–computer interaction, structural properties of group work and their behavior, distributed coordination, and social networks. Liaquat can be reached by e-mail at lhossain@it.usyd.edu.au.

Zhao Shenshen is a postgraduate student in Information Technologies at the University of Sydney, Australia.

Shahriar Hasan Murshed is an M.Sc. research student in Information Technologies at the University of Sydney, Australia. His current research is in the area of communication networks and organizational disintegration. He can be reached by e-mail at tanvir@it.usyd.edu.au.

36 RESEARCH AND INFORMATION SYSTEMS: How Information Systems Are Transforming the Nature of Science (And What Does This Mean for IS Researchers)

Laurie J. Kirsch
University of Pittsburgh
Pittsburgh, PA, U.S.A.

Sandra A. Slaughter
Carnegie Mellon University
Pittsburgh, PA, U.S.A.

Mark H. Haney
University of Pittsburgh
Pittsburgh, PA, U.S.A.

It is well known that information systems and technology can facilitate innovation in organizations. For example, companies in the automotive industry are leveraging product lifecycle management systems and advanced information technologies such as automated product design and testing tools, digital simulation and visualization, knowledge repositories of best practices, and collaboration tools linking globally distributed design teams. These technologies are revolutionizing the automotive product development process, facilitating the development of novel products, significantly reducing product development time and eliminating inconsistencies in product design, creation, and production (Rosencrance 2002).

What is perhaps less well recognized is the impact that IT is having on the very nature of science. In fields as diverse as particle physics, education, oceanography, and engineering, information systems and technology are having a profound effect on how researchers and scientists go about their work. Moreover, many government agencies are

Please use the following format when citing this chapter:

Kirsch, L. J., Slaughter, S. A., and Haney, M. H., 2007, in IFIP International Federation for Information Processing, Volume 235, Organizational Dynamics of Technology-Based Innovation: Diversifying the Research Agenda, eds. McMaster, T., Wastell, D., Ferneley, E., and DeGross, J. (Boston: Springer), pp. 487-490.

encouraging this transformation by funding the development and diffusion of innovative information and computing technologies. In the UK, for example, an "e-Science" initiative was launched in 2001 to nurture the development of grid and other high-performance computing, and to foster and encourage research activities that utilize such technologies in a wide range of disciplines including astronomy, particle physics, environmental science, and biology.[1] Similar initiatives can be found in the US as well as other regions of the world.

In this position paper, we first briefly examine how the diffusion of innovative technologies is transforming the way in which science is conducted. We then explore the implications of these changes for the Information Systems community. We suggest there are many avenues for IS researchers to pursue. Further, we propose that IS researchers are missing an enormous opportunity to play a significant role in the larger scientific community, as many in this community are struggling, sometimes successfully but other times not as successfully, in diffusing information systems and technologies into their research practices. We also suggest that IS researchers should envision how information systems and technologies can be leveraged to transform how IS research itself is conducted.

Although scientists espouse different epistemologies, there is a large degree of consensus across scientific communities about the purpose of science and the nature of the scientific process. Broadly speaking, the purpose of science is to understand, describe, and explain some aspect of the world; the goal is to produce knowledge. The scientific process is a cycle involving theories, predictions, observations, and generalizations (Creswell 2003; Singleton et al. 1988). Thus, scientists in many fields develop hypotheses from a theory, collect data to test the hypotheses, and draw conclusions based on the hypothesis testing. The role of data in this process is critical as science is based on empiricism (Singleton et al. 1998). Although the role of data in research hasn't changed, information technology has changed the way in which data are often collected. With information technology, researchers can now collect and store vast amounts of data. Moreover, IT allows researchers to collect data remotely. For example, oceanographers and environmental researchers can now place sensors and monitors in the field and, instead of traveling to field sites, they can access data that is streamed directly from the sensors and monitors. In addition, scientists can leverage data mining and simulation technologies to conduct "virtual" experiments and to explore conditions that would be difficult, if not impossible, to replicate or control in the field.

Besides impacting the way data are collected and analyzed, IT has had another radical change on the nature of science for many communities: it has enabled the growth of extremely large, complex, distributed projects that are undertaken by a large community of geographically dispersed scientists and technicians. GENI (Global Environment for Network Innovations) is an example of such a project.[2] GENI is an ambitious, ground-breaking initiative of the National Science Foundation (NSF) in the United States. The goal of GENI is to enable the computer science and engineering research communities to invent and build novel and revolutionary networks and architectures of the future. A critical component of GENI is the development of a large-

---

[1] See the website http://www.rcuk.ac.uk/escience/default.htm for more information.
[2] For additional information on GENI, see http://www.geni.net.

scale "cyber" network that connects researchers and experimental apparatus around the world. The project to create this network requires the development of a significant and large software system, which contributes enormously to its risk and complexity as software projects are often prone to mismanagement and failure.

Projects such as GENI are huge, spanning years, even decades, and costing millions of dollars. But these projects can also have significant impacts on a variety of stakeholders. GENI, for example, will ultimately affect many areas of computer science and engineering research, in addition to networking and distributed systems. Projects such as GENI are intended to promote innovation because they connect individuals and equipment. However, the deployment of the technologies created in the GENI project have the potential to fundamentally alter the nature of scientific research from small research projects conducted by individual computer scientists to large, collaborative research efforts performed by a distributed community of scientists. With the help of IT, these projects help to break barriers by cutting across geographic and disciplinary boundaries.

The transformational effect of IT on scientific communities is not limited to the hard sciences or to huge projects such as GENI. Information technology is also changing the way educational research is conducted. For example, the Pittsburgh Science of Learning Center (PSLC), funded by the NSF, is creating an international resource for the study of robust learning by developing IT tools that enable educational research combining the rigor of experimental research with the realism of a classroom setting, deploying these tools in highly instrumented LearnLab courses, and storing structured longitudinal data on student learning interactions.[3]

PSLC authoring tools facilitate the creation of interactive computer-based tutors that enable the administration of systematic educational treatments and logging of fine-grained data on student interactions with the tutors, categorized by a hierarchical structure of knowledge components, to a central data repository (Data Shop). The PSLC is using these technologies to establish LearnLab courses, which are real courses for which a large percentage of student learning interactions is logged to the Data Shop. The Data Shop is enhanced with a selection of data analysis and reporting tools, all of which are accessible to instructors and researchers via the web. The analysis and reporting tools enable researchers to quickly view data on student interactions with the learning tools, such as error rates and learning curves at the individual exercise level or at the level of knowledge components. Researchers around the world are invited to use the authoring tools, to submit projects for conducting learning experiments in the PSLC LearnLab courses, or to analyze data on student interactions that is stored in the Data Shop.

Clearly, information technology and systems are impacting how many scientists approach and conduct their research. What are the implications of these changes for the IS research community? We see at least three areas of implication. **First**, because more large projects like GENI are being proposed, there is a need for research that investigates project management in this context. Understanding how to manage information technology projects that are large, complex, dynamic, and distributed is crucial to the success of these efforts. **Second**, while many scientific fields are experimenting with information systems and technologies to facilitate data collection and analysis and new

---

[3]See http://www.learnlab.org for more information on the PSLC.

ways of conducting research, few IS researchers seem to be engaged with these efforts. The IS community has examined innovation and diffusion, implementation, and technology-enabled change for years, yet little of this research has made its way to physicists, educators, engineers, and other scientific communities. Thus, IS researchers need to find a way to participate in cross-disciplinary work and bring our expertise to researchers in other fields. These efforts would potentially enhance our reputation, facilitate the use and deployment of technology in these communities, and enable the innovations promised by technology usage. **Third**, it is interesting to consider the question of whether and how information technology might transform the nature of IS research itself. Will we see large, complex, distributed research projects being undertaken by the IS community, as the computer science community is undertaking with GENI? Will IS scholars learn how to work as a united community in order to secure large-scale funding and projects from government agencies to build the technological infrastructure needed to support such research, in the way that the particle physics community has? In short, how will IS research and the IS research community evolve as information technology and systems become increasingly sophisticated and widespread in science?

In this paper, we have argued that information systems and technologies have already begun to transform how science is being conducted in a range of communities. We have speculated on the implications of those changes for the IS research community, and have proposed that IS researchers become more engaged in the efforts to diffuse information technology and systems into scientific research.

References

Creswell, J. W. *Research Design: Qualitative, Quantitative, and Mixed Methods Approaches* (2nd ed.), Thousand Oaks, CA: Sage Publications, CA, 2003.
Rosencrance, L. "Speed: Automakers Rely on IT to Build Cars Faster (and Cheaper)," *Computerworld*, August 12, 2002 (available online at http://www.computerworld.com/industrytopics/automotive/story/0,10801,73334,00.html).
Singleton, Jr., R., Straights, B. C., Straits, M. M., and McAllister, R. J. *Approaches to Social Research*, New York: Oxford University Press, 1988.

About the Authors

Laurie J. Kirsch (Ph.D., University of Minnesota), is a professor of Business Administration at the University of Pittsburgh. Her research explores how to better manage IS projects and initiatives. She has published her work in leading scholarly journals, serves on several editorial boards, and is active in various conferences. Laurie can be reached by e-mail at lkirsch@katz.pitt.edu.

Sandra A. Slaughter (Ph.D., University of Minnesota), is an associate professor in the Tepper School of Business at Carnegie Mellon University. Her research examines performance in software development projects and has been published in leading research journals, conference proceedings, and edited books. She also serves on several editorial boards. Sandra can be reached by e-mail at sandras@andrew.cmu.edu.

Mark H. Haney is a Ph.D. candidate in Management Information Systems at the Katz Graduate School of Business at the University of Pittsburgh. His research explores the management of the information systems development process, global information systems, and knowledge management. Mark can be reached by e-mail at mhaney@katz.pitt.edu.

37 PSYCHOLOGICAL REACTANCE AND INFORMATION SYSTEMS ADOPTION

Thomas Matthias
Leonie Miller
Peter Caputi
Rohan Jayasuriya
University of Wollongong
North Wollongong, NSW, Australia

David Willis
BlueScope Steel Limited
Port Kembla, NSW, Australia

Abstract *According to Brehm (1966), if a person's freedom to behave as they choose is threatened in some way, then they will become motivationally aroused to either reestablish the lost freedom, or to ensure that there is no further loss. This hypothetical motivational state is referred to as psychological reactance. While resistance is defined as behavior against compliance, psychological reactance is a motive to behave to recover a lost freedom, and may result in behavior against compliance. It is argued that negative behaviors, which contribute to the poor record of information system implementation, likely contain some element of psychological reactance and that the latter may be brought about by threats directly or indirectly related to the implementation at hand. Therefore, an understanding of the interactions between system implementation, broader contextual influences, such as organizational climate and the formation of reactance, offer an opportunity to base interventions in strategies that avoid or minimize the motive to adopt negative behaviors, and therefore enhance the implementation of information systems in organizational settings.*

Keywords Psychological reactance, resistance, motivation, IS adoption

Please use the following format when citing this chapter:

Matthias, T., Miller, L., Caputi, P., Jayasuriya, R., and Willis, D., 2007, in IFIP International Federation for Information Processing, Volume 235, Organizational Dynamics of Technology-Based Innovation: Diversifying the Research Agenda, eds.McMaster, T., Wastell, D., Ferneley, E., and DeGross, J. (Boston: Springer), pp. 491-495.

1   INTRODUCTION

Resistant behavior associated with the implementation of information systems has been described by a number of authors. Ang and Pavri (1994) considered *resistance to change* as an end user attitude operating at an individual level within an organization. Lapointe and Rivard (2005) suggest that resistant behaviors occur as a result of perceived threats that arise from the interaction between initial conditions and a given phenomenon, in this case the implementation of an information system. Examples of resistant behaviors included passive resistance, sabotage, not using the system, and oral defamations. Hartwick and Barki (1994) also observed that some users begrudgingly accepted that they would have to use a mandated information system, behavior that they termed *unwilling compliance*.

It is suggested that, in an organizational setting, "negative" behavior directed at an information system may be situationally generated, perhaps as a reaction to an act of mandate, rather than as a result of aspects of the system in question. Brehm's (1966) theory of psychological reactance is proposed as an explanation for such negative behavior (i.e., when a specific freedom is eliminated, or threatened with elimination, an individual may be motivationally aroused to recover the freedom). The freedom threatened in the case of mandated information system usage could be a loss of job control, or perhaps the replacement of an existing system to which a user has some level of investment or allegiance. Reactance could be expressed in negative behaviors such as incorrectly or inefficiently using the new system so as to preserve the sense of control. Psychological reactance is seen as a motive to behave negatively toward something upon which individual focuses upon (i.e., the object is not necessarily part of the causal mechanism). This is different to the concept of resistance, which describes negative behavior toward a phenomenon such as an information system implementation (Marakas and Hornich 1996). Recognizing psychological reactance in an organizational setting should enable us to formulate strategies to minimize or negate its motivational impact, and thereby improve the success rate of systems implementation.

2   PSYCHOLOGICAL REACTANCE

According to Brehm (1966), most of the time people hold a belief that they are relatively free to behave in the ways that they choose. It can be argued that given some level of knowledge about oneself and the environment, freedom to choose is potentially beneficial in terms of survival. It follows, then, that if a person's freedom to behave as they choose is threatened in some way, they will become motivationally aroused to either reestablish the lost freedom, or to ensure that there is no further loss. This hypothetical motivational state is referred to as *psychological reactance*. Brehm further argues that the size of the psychological reactance is a direct function of (1) the salience or importance of the threatened freedoms, (2) relative proportion of free behaviors that are threatened or eliminated, and (3) where there is perceived threat only, the size of the threat.

In any social situation, there will always be a number of competing pressures influencing the way that people choose to behave. If, for example, the magnitude of reactance is less than the social pressure to comply, then the person will do what is suggested, albeit in a less enthusiastic way than if there was no reactance component. *Psychological reactance* is a *motive*, which *may* result in observable negative behavior. It is proposed that reactance is a likely underlying motivational state to a number of noncompliant activities in which potential information system users engage, and perhaps the source of dissatisfaction experienced by users when they are seen to comply with usage at a minimum level.

While Brehm's theory does not emphasize individual differences (Brehm and Brehm 1981, pp.213-228), it can be accepted that different life experiences would generally shape an individual's perception of what freedoms they have and value as being important. This perception would have direct influence over the amount of reactance aroused in a given situation. Therefore, it is reasonable to assume in a given context, such as an organizational setting into which an information system is introduced, that there would be individual differences in the amount of any psychological reactance generated.

3 REACTANCE IN AN ORGANIZATIONAL SETTING

People in an organizational setting are exposed to many influences. For the majority of workers, their "psychological workplace" (Statt, 1994, p. 25) is an organization of some type, and organizations are characterized by three common attributes. People within organizations share a *social identity* or sense of belonging in some way. The activities of the people in an organization are *coordinated* so that they interact with each other in what is supposed to be a supportive and complementary manner. The reason for the coordinated interaction is to *accomplish the stated goals* of the organization. However, organizations are not just about what people collectively do, but inherently involve who the individuals are, what they want, and how they feel about things. The freedom to choose what to do and how to do it is likely to be one important aspect of work in organizations.

Given these organizational influences, looking at information systems from an organizational perspective thus brings into focus social factors, as well as business and technology factors, organizational behavior, and organizational culture and climate. Past research has identified a number of aspects of organizations that contribute to the success of information system implementation. For example, Rivard et al. (2004) discuss system adoption in terms of organizational transformation and identify four pieces of the trans-formational "puzzle," namely, strategy in terms of positioning, capability, and govern-ance; structure in terms of boundaries and success factors; the information system itself in terms of its place in the organization; and aspects of leadership. Within the framework defined by these factors, however, lie the perceived freedoms of individual users that may or may not be disrupted by any implementation activities. Any perceived loss of free-dom, whether it arises from the nature of the information system, the implementation, or from existing social factors, can result in negative behaviors toward the implementation.

If we look at this organizational landscape through the lens of reactance, we can see that there are many situations where individuals can experience actual or threatened loss of freedom when new systems are introduced into a work environment. Broeng (2006), for example, suggests that the task of ERP implementation is typically bigger than initially estimated, and one of the major issues is that of *ownership*. The new system will likely need to be resold internally as often the nature of jobs can be changed, and "uncommitted people can derail the process very quickly" (p. 35). Lack of ownership of a mandated system (e.g., where the user cannot foresee that they can comfortably integrate the system within their work practices) is likely to be perceived as a threatened loss of freedom and hence will trigger reactance.

In terms of systems research, it is likely that researchers have noted reactance-driven behavior, but not recognized it as such. In a study of safety culture attitudes in a highly regulated environment (Harvey et al. 2002), the authors describe hierarchical situations whereby management expect "compliance with regulations" and utilize downward instruction, whereas shop floor workers are characterized as "being resigned to high levels of prescription" with a minimum of participation in the workplace (Dake 1992, cited in Harvey et al. 2002, p. 21). The workers are described as being "fatalist" (Dear 1995, cited in Harvey et al. 2002, p. 21) and their varied adherence to safety system requirements is attributed to this mind set. Such an organizational setting would likely generate differing levels of reactant motivation, and varied levels of adherence to safety systems by the workers might be better understood through this lens, an apparent loss of freedoms brought about by adherence to the new safety system expectations.

4   IMPLICATIONS FOR FURTHER RESEARCH

Psychological reactance is likely to be an important motivator of behavior in organizational settings. It may be that the perceived or actual loss of freedom, which triggers the reactance, is associated directly with implementation of an information system, but in the implementation context it is also possible that there are other organizational factors responsible. This perspective represents an opportunity for interventions in the pre-implementation phase of information system projects to reduce or eliminate the psychological reactance, and in doing so increase the likelihood of implementation success. Core to this approach is the need to understand such factors as the climate prevailing within an organization within which reactance can be generated. According to Bock et al. (2005) "climate" can be thought of as a contextual situation that occurs at some definable point in time, and this contextual situation frames the behaviors of organizational members. It would follow, then, that an assessment of an information system implementation within the context of an organization's climate, with particular emphasis on reactance, could provide cues to the development of an appropriate strategy to minimize both psychological reactance and its effects.

References

Ang, J., and Pavri, F. "A Survey and Critique of the Impacts of Information Technology," *Journal of Information Management* (14:2), 1994, pp. 122-133.

Bock, G.-W., Zmud, R.W., Kim, Y-G, and Lee, J-N. "Behavioral Intention Forming in Knowledge Sharing: Examining the Roles of Extrinsic Motivators, Social-Psychological Forces, and Organizational Climate," *MIS Quarterly* (29:1), 2005, pp. 87-112.

Brehm, J. W. *A Theory of Psychological Reactance*, New York: Academic Press, 1966.

Brehm, S. S., and Brehm, J. W. *Psychological Reactance: A Theory of Freedom and Control*, New York: Academic Press, 1981.

Broeng, M. "Outside the Comfort Zone," *Logistics* (13), 2006, pp. 34-35.

Dake, K. "Myths of Nature: Culture and the Social Construction of Risk," *Journal of Social Issues* (48:4), 1992, pp. 21-37.

Dear, L. "Negotiated Safety, What You Don't Know Won't Hurt You, or Will It?," *Drug and Alcohol Review* (14), 1995, pp. 323-329.

Hartwick, J., and Barki, H. "Explaining the Role of User Participation in Information System Use," *Management Science* (40:4), 1994, pp. 440-465.

Harvey, J., Erdos, G., Bolam, H., Cox, M. A. A., Kennedy, J. N. P., and Gregory, D. T. "An Analysis of Safety Culture Attitudes in a Highly Regulated Environment," *Work & Stress* (16:1), 2002, pp. 18-36.

Lapointe, L., and Rivard, S. "A Multilevel Model of Resistance to Information Technology Implementation," *MIS Quarterly* (29:3), 2005, pp. 461-492.

Marakas, G. M., and Hornick, S. "Passive Resistance Misuse: Overt Support and Covert Recalcitrance in IS Implementation," *European Journal of Information Systems* (5), 1996, pp. 2-8-219.

Rivard, S., Aubert, B. A., Patry, M., Pare, G., and Smith, H. A. *Information Technology and Organizational Transformation: Solving the Management Puzzle*, Oxford, UK: Elsevier Butterworth-Heinemann, 2004.

Statt, D. A. *Psychology and the World of Work*, Basingstoke, UK: Palgrave, 1994.

About the Authors

Thomas Matthias is a Ph.D. candidate in the School of Psychology at the University of Wollongong and works for BlueScope Steel. Currently he is working on the implementation of an enterprise-wide SAP system in the role of a change agent. Thomas can be reached by e-mail at tmm03@uow.edu.au.

Leonie Miller is a Ph.D. candidate in the School of Psychology at Wollongong University with 13 years experience in the manufacturing industry. She can be reached by e-mail at lmm17@uow.edu.au.

Peter Caputi is a senior lecturer in the School of Psychology at the University of Wollongong. His research in information systems has focused primarily on the behavioral determinants of IS adoption. He has published in the area of computer anxiety and subject computer experience. Dr. Caputi can be reached by e-mail at pcaputi@uow.edu.au.

Rohan Jayasuriya is an associate professor in the School of Health Science at Wollongong University. His research interests are in the are in the adoption and diffusion of technology, IT evaluation, health informatics, and post-adoption behavior. He has previously presented research at the International Conference on Information Systems as well as IFIP conferences. Dr. Jayasuriya can be reached by e-mail at ajayasur@uow.edu.au.

David J. Willis is Manager of Research Services at BlueScope Steel Research in Port Kembla, Australia. He received his Ph.D. in Physical Metallurgy from the University of New South Wales. His research has focused on metallic coatings with a particular interest in the properties and processing of 55 percent Al-Zn coated steel. More recently, he also has a responsibility for knowledge management and, as a result, is involved with introducing new technology (e.g., a wiki) and implementing changes to work practices in order to improve knowledge sharing and information capture. Dr. Willis can be reached by e-mail at david.willis@bluescopesteel.com

38 THE NEW CHALLENGE OF BUSINESS VALUE: Time to Link Project Management Performance with Adoption Research?

Chris Sauer
Saïd Business School, Oxford University
Oxford, United Kingdom

Blaize Horner Reich
Andrew Gemino
Simon Fraser University
Burnaby, Canada

1   INTRODUCTION

When Working Group 8.6 was formed, there was only partial recognition among academics and practitioners that implementation of information technology did not automatically translate into adoption and diffusion. Rigorous study of these issues was thus well-motivated. In the last decade, focus on adoption has become mainstream for practice. For example, the UK's National Health Service *Connecting for Health* program has contractually required its suppliers not only to implement new medical record and booking systems, but also to secure their adoption.

Today, organizations increasingly recognize the need to manage IT project investments to achieve business value. Project managers are tasked with more than just delivering an implemented or adopted IT system. According to our informants, delivery requires process change, organizational redesign, and benefits capture. Thus, in the National Health Service example, value will only be achieved when hospitals and primary care trusts deliver better health and service outcomes because they have restructured, adopted new processes, and managed for the value outcomes that the tech-

Please use the following format when citing this chapter:

Sauer, C., Reich, B. H., and Gemino, A., 2007, in IFIP International Federation for Information Processing, Volume 235, Organizational Dynamics of Technology-Based Innovation: Diversifying the Research Agenda, eds. McMaster, T., Wastell, D., Ferneley, E., and DeGross, J. (Boston: Springer), pp. 497-502.

nology makes possible. Put crudely, if the objective is to save costs by reducing head-count in a business unit, the value is only achieved when the relevant number of employees has left the building.

One consequence of these changes is that the study of adoption and diffusion of information technology remains useful because they are a necessary prerequisite to securing value. However, they are no longer sufficient. We should be trying also to understand the point where the real interest lies, vis. value delivery and its antecedents.

Our reason for making this observation is that we believe there would be mutual benefit from connecting the WG 8.6 agenda with our own area of research—project management performance—against which similar criticisms can be leveled. In this area, research has focused principally on understanding performance as a function of risk and project management practice (Figure 1). Performance has been most commonly construed as process performance (i.e., delivery against budget and schedule). Less commonly it has been construed as the extent to which the product delivered was of the scope and quality required. Only occasionally have researchers collected data about benefit achievement by the business. (And, curiously, almost never is adoption considered as a relevant dependent variable!)

Our own research has sought to improve the accuracy and explanatory power of this kind of model by developing it into the interactive model shown in Figure 2. Changes we have made include

- Separating risks according to the time they occur in a project. *A priori* risks are known at project kickoff time and emergent risks occur during the life of the project.
- Employing more sophisticated data collection and data analysis techniques to explore the full range of performance and to investigate the interaction between the antecedents of project performance.
- Categorizing risks into risks and resources. We hypothesized that risks (i.e., size/complexity and project volatility) and resources (i.e., knowledge resources and organizational support) would differentially interact with project management practices.

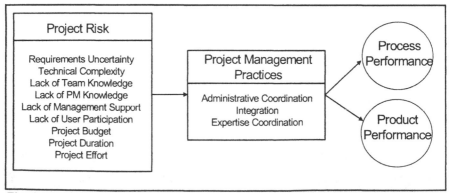

Figure 1. **Project Risk Mediated by Project Management Practices**

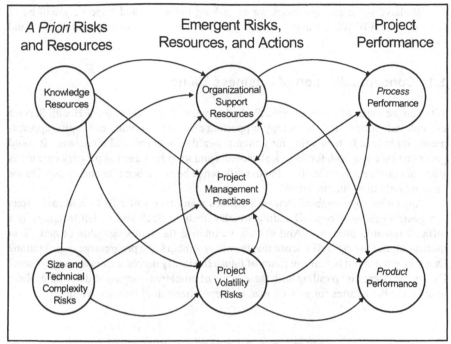

Figure 2. An Interactive Model of IT Project Performance

- Adding a knowledge resources construct. This was suggested by our knowledge management research (Reich 2007; Reich and Wee 2006). It represents the knowledge and experience (or lack thereof) of the sponsor, client manager, project manager, and project team.
- Adding a project volatility risk construct. This construct, developed from a prior analysis (Sauer et al. 2007) includes changes in project personnel, project targets, and unexpected exogenous changes. Project volatility risk is an emergent risk.

Testing this model using data from 194 IT projects, we found it was able to explain 39 percent of the variance in process performance, whereas the traditional model depicted in Figure 1, using the same data, could only explain 16 percent of variance (Gemino et al. 2006a, 2006b).

The good news here is that the form of interactive modeling we have pioneered appears to generate strong explanatory power for process performance. The bad news is that it is the wrong dependent variable. As we argued earlier, what counts today is value achievement. To the extent that we have been able to model value achievement (i.e., product performance), we are only able to explain 20 percent of the variance. This has caused us to reflect on our approach to this research. And, to the extent that IFIP WG 8.6 should be likewise concerned with understanding project value, the questions and issues we have raised should be of interest.

We have some key questions we are asking ourselves and hope they will be of interest to the IFIP WG 8.6 audience. They deal with the issues of conceptualization and measurement.

1.1   Conceptualization of Business Value

What do we mean by business value? And to whom? In the National Health Service example, adoption of the technology supporting electronic booking of hospital appointments might lead to new value for patients, health managers, and clinicians. It could generate new costs both for these stakeholders and for others such as primary care trusts who gain no direct benefit. Is value the difference between benefits and costs? Do we measure only in economic terms?

Any technology-enabled change generates many layers of effect—and each effect can generate more effects. Deciding which effects to track and which to ignore is a difficult research problem. And should we include the symbolic value of new IT in motivating and giving staff a sense that they are members of a progressive organization? Or again, what about benefits in terms of future flexibility deriving from a new platform? Our research team is wrestling with these kinds of problems in trying to determine where to draw the boundaries for a theoretical conceptualization of business value.

1.2   Measurement of Business Value

Assuming we could agree on a definition of business value and, therefore, where we might start to measure it, there are significant issues still to face.

One approach to measurement of benefits is to make comparisons between expectations and actual achievement. That way we could say that 108 percent of the expected economic benefits and 23 percent of the expected health benefits were achieved. That approach leaves us with the problem of whether different outcomes should be equally or differentially weighted. It also leaves a question about the baseline expectations. Is it original expectations that matter or subsequent modifications? Our research (Gemino et al. 2006b) has found that targets (i.e., scope, time, budget) change on average eight times in an IT project, so determining a baseline for measurement is problematic. If the business conditions change, modified targets may be justified as a new baseline. If the project underperforms and targets are adjusted downward to reflect this situation, it is less obviously appropriate to use the modified targets.

There is also the question of who is authoritative as a provider of information about value and at what stage to collect it. So, can a project manager provide us with reliable data about benefits or must we ask the stakeholders? Which stakeholders? When do we ask? A month after implementation, a year after, or longer? As the period lengthens, more extraneous factors affect the value experienced and stakeholders' perceptions. It is clear then that there are some serious questions to be answered if researchers are to model and measure the antecedents of business value.

One possible reason why we have thus far been unable to explain much variance on value-related project outcomes is that traditional research on the antecedents of performance have concentrated on risks and project management practices more relevant to budget and schedule targets. Traditional thinking on project management practice has focused on a restricted set of behaviors relating to control and coordination such as administrative control, team-building, and knowledge management (*pace* the value management literature in engineering management).

We need a more fundamental reexamination of project performance and management practice. We must ask project managers what they do differently to achieve outcomes beyond the traditional targets. We may have to frame elements of project management in entirely new ways. For example, it has been commonplace that time, cost, and quality are often traded off against each other. In the future, it may prove preferable to think of them not as targets but, say, as repositories of slack resources that can be accessed to help manage changing requirements. Or, it may be that project managers who secure value are obliged to embrace changing requirements rather than resist them. The whole emphasis on process control may need to be re-thought.

2 SUMMARY

Our argument is that research into project performance and adoption and diffusion face a shared problem. Both fields may need to move away from reliance on intermediate measures and toward researching delivery of business value and its antecedents. We have tried to show that there are some substantial issues that will require serious research effort to resolve.

We want to push the argument further by suggesting that the project manager has not figured as a major unit of analysis in adoption and diffusion studies, but that given the increased requirement for project managers to deliver targets that go beyond implementation, it would be appropriate to rectify this. Equally important is the absence of the adoption construct in project performance literature. There may be an important opportunity for project management research to incorporate the findings relating to adoption and diffusion into our models.

Our proposal is that investigators of both IT project performance and adoption and diffusion could usefully combine forces to develop more comprehensive models that are methodologically rigorous and more directly useful to practitioners.

References

Gemino, A., Reich, B. H., and Sauer, C. "Factors Influencing IT Project Performance," in *Proceedings of the 12th Americas Conference on Information Systems*, Acapulco, Mexico, August 4-6, 2006a, pp. 3733-3740.

Gemino, A., Reich, B. H., and Sauer, C. "Inside the Black Box: Developing a Model for IT Project Performance," unpublished working paper, Simon Fraser University, 2006b.

Reich, B. H. "Managing Knowledge and Learning in IT Projects: A Conceptual Framework and Guidelines for Practice," *Project Management Journal*, 2007 (forthcoming).

Reich, B. H., and Wei, S. Y. "Searching for Knowledge in the PMBOK Guide," *Project Management Journal* (37:2), June 2006, pp. 11-27.

Sauer, C., Gemino, A., and Reich, B. H. "Managing Projects for Success: The Impact of Size and Volatility on IT Project Performance," *Communications of the ACM*, 2007 (forthcoming).

About the Authors

Chris Sauer is a fellow in Information Management at Oxford University's Saïd Business School, University of Oxford, Egrove Park, United Kingdom. He was Secretary and then Deputy-Chair of WG8.6 from 1994 through 2001. Chris can be reached by e-mail at Chris.Sauer@sbs.ox.ac.uk.

    Blaize Horner Reich is professor in management information systems of the Faculty of Business Administration at Simon Fraser University, Vancouver, Canada. Blaize can be reached by e-mail at breich@sfu.ca.

    Andrew Gemino is an associate professor in management information systems of the Faculty of Business Administration at Simon Fraser University, Vancouver, Canada. Andrew can be reached by e-mail at gemino@sfu.ca.

39 SOCIO-TECHNICAL DESIGN OF THE 21ST CENTURY: A Vision

Ramanjit Singh
Bob Wood
Trevor Wood-Harper
University of Manchester
Manchester, United Kingdom

Abstract   *The norm of the 21st century has been decentralization as competition in the marketplace has increased significantly. Organizations commonly freelance or outsource work to other professionals or manufacturers where it can be performed at lower cost. Thus, due to the changing nature of work, there is a need to reconsider the ETHICS of the past. Based upon the new work order, changes in ETHICS are proposed and will be discussed in this paper.*

Keywords   Decentralized work, freelancing, outsourcing, socio-technical theory, SSM, ETHICS, balanced scorecard

1   INTRODUCTION

The norm of the 21st century has been decentralization as competitive pressures in the market have increased considerably. Firms commonly freelance or outsource work to other professionals or manufacturers to cut operating costs. Instead of hiring people to conduct work on a permanent basis, temporary workers are employed. In the case of manufacturing organizations, one or more production functions are outsourced to other firms. Although the global outsourcing of manufactured goods has been practiced for many years, the outsourcing of software development is still a relatively new phenomenon. In 2001, major software users in the United States such as Cisco, IBM, GE, and Ford made significant investments in joint development programs with Indian firms (Ramamoorthy 2001; Sahay et al. 2003). Historically, the socio-technical prin-

Please use the following format when citing this chapter:

Singh, R., Wood, B., and Wood-Harper, T., 2007, in IFIP International Federation for Information Processing, Volume 235, Organizational Dynamics of Technology-Based Innovation: Diversifying the Research Agenda, eds. McMaster, T., Wastell, D., Ferneley, E., and DeGross, J. (Boston: Springer), pp. 503-506.

ciples of ETHICS (Mumford 1993) have proved fruitful in the design of information systems in the workplace. However, given the changing nature of work and a dramatic increase in abnormal crises, ETHICS may need a modification to better meet the demands of future system development projects. In line with this thinking, a number of shortcomings in the ETHICS methodology will be identified and various improvements put forward.

2   THE ESSENCE OF ETHICS

Mumford's ETHICS methodology for system design is essentially systems development by democracy. Just like Florence Nightingale, Enid Mumford had a passion for human beings, and worked extremely hard to improve the human work space. Mumford developed ETHICS to effectively design and develop information systems that cater for both the social and technical concerns of users. The ETHICS methodology was used in many industrial projects with fruitful results in the 1970s and 1980s. Today, ETHICS is still used in industrial projects and is also taught at universities around the world. The ETHICS method has three principle objectives. First, to enable future users to play a major role in system design (this involves a learning process and a set of simple diagnostic and socio-technical design tools). Second, to ensure that new systems are acceptable to users. Third, to assist users in developing skills for managing organizational change (Avison et al. 2006; Mumford 1993, 2003, 2006).

3   THE SHORTCOMINGS OF ETHICS

As the nature of work is clearly changing so the socio-technical design principles of ETHICS need to be reconsidered. Several academics are calling for a reconsideration of the socio-technical view. According to Wood-Harper and Wood, for example, although the benefits of ETHICS have been substantial in the past, ETHICS may need rethinking in order to tackle the future requirements of work (e.g., mobile work and the design of wireless technologies to accommodate work and social needs). According to Bend Carsten, there are some practical contradictions in Mumford's ETHICS. If worker "needs" were truly management requirements, then participative methods would have been accepted more widely. Thus, some of Mumford's basic assumptions with respect to participative work may be false. Insufficient analysis of the capitalistic systems in which information systems are designed and situated is another shortcoming. For instance, the conflicting interests of stakeholders and the political interplay may clash with the belief that management is there to serve the best interest of employees. Mumford also accepted technology as is and never went on to criticize or conceptualize it differently. Therefore, some notions of ETHICS may be relatively superficial and require further development. Mumford applied concepts of relativism, contractualism, natural rights, and consequentialism without defining her own position clearly. According to Carsten Sorensen, decentralization is the norm of the 21st century, as work is commonly performed outside the office. Nevertheless, this certainly does not mean that Mumford's ETHICS is now obsolete. On the contrary, it is important that the IS community reassess Mumford's relational concepts to meet the social challenges of the 21ˢᵗ century (Avison et al. 2006).

To respond the arguments above, a set of changes in ETHICS are proposed and will be discussed in more detail.

4   SOCIO-TECHNICAL DESIGN OF 21ˢᵗ CENTURY

The traditional goals of socio-technical design have been twofold: the humanization of work through better job design and increased democracy in both workplace and society as a whole. However, as the social, political, economic, and technological environments change, it is important that the consequences of such changes are incorporated in the socio-technical methodologies of the past. According to Avison (as cited by Wood-Harper and Wood 2006), in order to realize the true benefits of the above-mentioned socio-technical design principles, changes in the roles of actors are essential in the system design process. First, he suggests the designer be a facilitator and not an expert since this would ensure that a new solution is based on the social requirements of work and not merely technical requirements. Second, he recommends that the worker be a designer of the system since this would ensure that the new system fits workers' daily routines and not vice versa. Third, he proposes that the manager be a boundary manager and not a supervisor of employees since this would provide freedom and discretion in carrying out work (Sahay et al. 2003; Wood-Harper and Wood 2006). According to Mumford, *participation* has a different meaning for different people. For her, a facilitator is required in the team and the role of the facilitator is to help the design group select and implement an appropriate problem solving methodology and to keep members motivated and interested in the design task. Although Mumford's work highlights the need for participative design and democracy in work the place, it does not result in individuals being empowered to own and control their own design processes. Due to the decentralized nature of work, a facilitator may not be available during project meetings. Thus, it is important to devise vehicles to improve two-way communication between group members. One solution is to provide the design group with video conferencing capabilities to lessen space and time constraints. Soft systems methodology (SSM) (Checkland 1999) has been a choice for system inquiry in the problem area in the past; however, it does not provide any clear guidelines for furthering a project. Researchers recommend that the principles of SSM be incorporated into steps 1 through 3 of ETHICS. This would modify ETHICS to include a more explicit questioning, and to critically review the problem area and the greater system boundaries. Although ETHICS have been used widely in academia, the principles of socio-technical theory have not been very successful in the commercial sector and numerous socio-technical failures were noted the 1980s and 1990s (Mumford, 2006). In management schools, socio-technical approaches are introduced in the classroom but they tend to be used more or less as buzz words. Hence, in order to reduce the likelihood of socio-technical failures in the commercial world of the future, it is suggested that elements of the balanced scorecard be incor-porated to assess the economic, political, and, most importantly, the social climate of an organization (Land 2000).

5   CONCLUSION

Although Mumford strove to improve people's work and lives through ETHICS, there are still a number of shortcomings that need attention. Specifically, steps 1 through 3 of ETHICS need revision. Suggestions include incorporating ETHICS with SSM so that more accurate requirements can be obtained. This, however, is only possible if the *user* is perceived as an *actor* and involved more actively in the system analysis phase. It is also suggested that the balanced scorecard be used in steps 1 through 3 of ETHICS for a structured assessment of the social climate of an organization.

References

Avison, D., Bjørn-Andersen, N., Coakes, E., Davis, G. B., Earl, M. J., Elbanna, A., Fitzgeral,dG., Galliers, R. D., Hirschheim, R., Iivari, J., Klein, H. K., Land, F., de Marco, M. Pettigrew, A. M., Porra J., Carsten Stahl, B., Sørensen, C., Wood, B., and Wood-Harper, T. "Enid Mumford: A Tribute," *Information Systems Journal* (16), 2006, pp. 343-382.

Land, F. F. "Evaluation in a Socio-Technical Context," paper presented at Organizational and Social Perspectives on IT, Aalborg, Denmark, 2000.

Mumford, E. "The ETHICS Approach," *Communications of the ACM* (36:6), 1993, p. 82-83.

Mumford, E. *Redesigning Human Systems*, Hershey, PA: Idea Group Publishing, 2003.

Mumford, E. "The Story of Socio-Technical Design: Reflections on its Successes, Failures and Potential," *Information Systems Journal* (16), 2006, pp. 317-342.

Ramamoorthy, G. "U.S. Firms Bullish on India Development Centers," *Netscribes*, Retrieved October, 2006 (http://www.rediff.com/money/2001/mar/20spec.htm).

Sahay, S., Nicholson, B., and Krishna, S. *Global IT Outsourcing: Software Development Across Borders,* Cambridge, UK: Cambridge University Press, 2003.

Wood-Harper, T., and Wood, B. *Enid Mumford: Your Way and Our Way for the Future,* Manchester, UK: University of Manchester, 2006.

About the Authors

Ramanjit Singh is a second year Ph.D. student at the University of Manchester. His research interests include the use of wireless technology in developing countries. In addition to his Ph.D. research, he has published a report at the University of Trento, Italy. He can be reached by e-mail at ramanjit.singh@postgrad.manchester.ac.uk.

Bob Wood has been a professor of Information Systems and head of the School of Informatics at the University of Manchester since 2003. Before that, he spent 10 years at the University of Salford as a professor and associate dean for research within the Faculty of Business and Informatics. He can be reached by e-mail at bob.wood@manchester.ac.uk.

Trevor Wood-Harper is a professor of Information Systems and director of graduate research at the School of Informatics, University of Manchester. He has authored, coauthored, or coedited 20 books and proceedings, and has published over 200 research articles. He has supervised or co-supervised more than 30 Ph.D. students. He can be reached by e-mail at t.wood-harper@manchester.ac.uk.

40 WHEN COUNTERFACTUAL THINKING MEETS THE TECHNOLOGY ACCEPTANCE MODEL: An Investigation

Chuan-Hoo Tan
Xue Yang
Hock-Hai Teo
National University of Singapore
Singapore

Abstract   *Technology offers great benefits to employees. This study draws from the theory of the technology acceptance model (TAM) and counterfactual thinking theory and posits anticipated emotion to be an important intermediate variable between adoption intention and exogenous factors (i.e., perceived usefulness and perceived ease of use). The proposed model lays the foundation for a richer understanding of employee's adoption of technology.*

Keywords   Technology acceptance model, counterfactual thinking

1   INTRODUCTION

A fundamental understanding of factors affecting user adoption of information technology related business applications is of great importance to Information Systems researchers and practitioners. While much extant research focuses on identifying factors leading to higher propensity for technology adoption, we posit that identifying the determinants requires a model that takes into account the judgments associated with the technological evaluation. Toward this goal, we seek to synergize extant studies in technology adoption and counterfactual thinking to propose an alternative examination of the technology adoption model.

Please use the following format when citing this chapter:

Tan, C.-H., Yang, X., and Teo, H-H., 2007, in IFIP International Federation for Information Processing, Volume 235, Organizational Dynamics of Technology-Based Innovation: Diversifying the Research Agenda, eds. McMaster, T., Wastell, D., Ferneley, E., and DeGross, J. (Boston: Springer), pp. 507-511.

2   TECHNOLOGY ACCEPTANCE MODEL

The technology acceptance model (TAM), the most commonly referenced model, posits that perceived usefulness and perceived ease of use together determine an individual's attitude toward adopting and using a certain technology (Davis 1989). According to TAM, attitude drives usage intentions, and such intentions, in turn, drive realized adoption and usage behavior. TAM also posits a direct link from perceived usefulness as reflection of perceived task performance consequences of using (or not using) the system to intention and behavior, bypassing attitude. Subsequent research has expanded TAM in multiple directions. In general, the model has been shown to have good predictive validity for the use of several information technologies (Adams et al. 1992).

3   COUNTERFACTUAL THINKING

The counterfactual thinking principle posits that when a user makes a decision, he will mentally simulate what would happen if choosing one option and compare it to what otherwise might have happened if choosing the foregone option (Kahneman and Tversky 1982). Based on these simulations, one can decide whether the outcomes of different choices would be able to prevent something from happening (e.g., negative emotions), or to prompt the occurrence of other things (e.g., positive emotions). From this perspective, a basic understanding can be derived: users would attempt to reduce anticipated negative emotions (e.g., regret) and increase anticipated positive emotions (e.g., satisfaction) (Medvec et al. 1995).

4   PROPOSED RESEARCH MODEL

This study proposes that an individual's propensity to adopt a technology can be affected by perceived usefulness, perceived ease of use, and anticipated emotions (Figure 1).

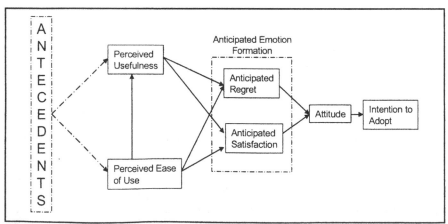

Figure 1. **Research Model**

Anticipated Regret: Regret is "a negative, cognitively based emotion that we experience when realizing or imagining that our present situation would have been better had we acted differently" (Zeelenberg 1999, p. 94). Regret theory conceives that a decision maker is aware that he will feel regretful if he makes a wrong choice (Bell 1982) and, hence, he will take into account this anticipated regret when deciding. When individuals evaluate outcomes, they compare what they have received with what they would have received had they made a different choice. If a different choice would have led to a better outcome, then the person will feel regret about the decisions. Conversely, if a different choice would have led to a worse outcome, then less regret results. Regret aroused through decisional choice should motivate a user to engage in a regret-minimizing coping strategy to reduce the possibility in forgoing an optimum choice. With this in mind, one is likely to evaluate the magnitude of anticipated regrets resulting from different choices prior to drawing a conclusion. Applying this to our research context, it is postulated that the higher the anticipated regret of using a technology, the lower the attitude toward adoption and, hence, the lower the intention to adopt.

Anticipated Satisfaction: Compared to regret, satisfaction focuses on the comparison between expected and actual performance (Tsiros and Mittal 2000). Satisfaction is not the opposite emotion of regret. For instance, it is observed that while a runner-up in a competition is satisfied with the fact that he won a metal, he would also report regret for not being first (Tsiros and Mittal 2000).

Satisfaction is not merely an emotion itself, but also is formed from the evaluation of certain experience. The expectation-disconfirmation paradigm suggests that satisfaction perception is processed through predefined steps during which users form expectations toward the outcomes, evaluate the actual performance and compare performance, with the expectations, resulting in either positive or negative disconfirmations (McKinney et al 2002). Thus, satisfaction is more of a hybrid of cognition-emotion (Oliver 1997), that is, neither the cognitive processing nor the emotional perception resulting from previous experience or expectation and current conditions should be neglected during the satisfaction formation process. Applying this to our research context in which anticipated satisfaction is conjectured by comparing current expectation with possible future outcomes of adopting a technology, it is hypothesized that the higher the anticipated satisfaction, the higher the attitude toward adoption and, hence, the higher the intention to adopt.

Perceived Usefulness: "Usefulness" refers to the individual's perception that using the technology will enhance or improve his/her performance (Davis 1989). Applying this definition to this study, usefulness reflects a user's perceptions that technology enhances the outcome of his/her experience. These perceptions should positively influence anticipated satisfaction and negatively influence anticipated regret. Should using a technology meet the expectation with which judgments are formed prior to adoption decision, a user will judge that technology positively. In other words, if the initial judgment of technology is positive (i.e., useful), then one would anticipate higher satisfaction and lower regret from using it.

Perceived Ease of Use: "Ease of use" refers to the individual's perception that using the technology will be free of effort (Davis 1989). Whereas usefulness refers to a user's perceptions regarding the outcome of a technology usage experience, ease of use refers to the perceptions regarding the process leading to the final usage outcome.

According to TAM, ease of use has a dual effect, direct as well as indirect through usefulness, on a user's intention to adopt. The direct effect is explained by the fact that the user attempts to minimize effort in his/her behaviors when making a decision. Applying this to our research context, we postulate that the easier and more effortless it is to engage in a task (i.e., higher perceived ease of use), the less likely one would be to anticipate regret. By investing less effort in learning to use a technology effectively, the user would not experience greater disappointment, which can trigger regret feelings when the outcome does not turn out as expected, but greater satisfaction when superior outcomes are yielded.

5   DISCUSSION

To develop an in-depth understanding of employees' intention to adopt a technology, this research takes a specific perspective by arguing that between intentions to adopt and constructs of perceived usefulness and perceived ease of use in the TAM model, there is anticipated emotion. The posited model, by incorporating anticipated emotion formation prior to making an adoption decision, may be able to better reflect the mental evaluation and assessment of the technology available. The research model proposed is of great importance because it helps organizations to make adequate strategic, technological, and marketing decisions to increase a user's propensity to adopt. Although we based our model on a combination of prior psychological studies in identifying anticipated satisfaction and anticipated regret, there can always be other emotional factors influencing a user's intention to adopt. However, we are confident that two pertinent emotional factors are discussed.

References

Adams, D., Nelson R. R., and Todd, P. "Perceived Usefulness, Ease of Use, and Usage of Information Technology: A Replication," *MIS Quarterly* (16:2), 1992, pp. 227-248.
Bell, D. E. "Regret in Decision Making Under Uncertainty," *Operations Research* (30), 1982, pp. 961-981.
Davis, F. D. "Perceived Usefulness, Perceived Ease of Use and User Acceptance of Information Technology," *MIS Quarterly* (13:3), 1989, pp. 319-340.
Kahneman, D., and Tversky, A. "The Psychology of Preferences," *Scientific American* (246), 1982, pp. 160-173.
McKinney, V., Yoon, K., and Zahedi, F. M. "The Measurement of Web-Customer Satisfaction: An Expectation and Discontinuation Approach," *Information Systems Research* (13:3), 2002, pp. 296-315.
Medvec, V. H., Madey, S. F., and Gilovich, T. "When less Is More: Counterfactual Thinking and Satisfaction among Olympic Athletes," *Journal of Personality and Social Psychology* (69), 1995, pp. 603-610.
Oliver, R. L. *Satisfaction: A Behavioral Perspective on the Consumer,* New York: McGraw-Hill, 1997.
Tsiros, M., and Mittal, V. "Regret: A Model of its Antecedents and Consequences in Consumer Decision Making," *Journal of Consumer Research* (26:4), 2000, pp. pp. 401-417.
Zeelenberg, M. "Anticipated Regret, Expected Feedback and Behavioral Decision Making," *Journal of Behavioral Decision Making* (12), 1999, pp. 93-106.

About the Authors

Chuan-Hoo Tan is an instructor at the National University of Singapore, where he is pursuing his doctoral degree. His research interests include agent design, online market institutions, and IT innovation adoption. He has published in journals such as *IEEE Transactions of Engineering Management* and *Communications of the ACM*, and conferences, such as ICIS. He can be reached by e-mail at tanch@comp.nus.edu.sg.

Xue Yang is a doctoral student at the National University of Singapore. Her research interests include electronic commerce, consumer behavior and consumer psychology. She has published in conferences including ICIS, AMCIS, and PACIS. She can be reached by e-mail at yangxue@comp.nus.edu.sg.

Hock-Hai Teo is an associate professor of Information Systems at the National University of Singapore. His research interests include IT innovation adoption, assimilation and impacts, information privacy, and electronic market institutions. Dr. Teo has published in many journals including *MIS Quarterly*, *Journal of MIS*, and *IEEE Transactions on Engineering Management*. He can be reached by e-mail at teohh@comp.nus.edu.sg.

41 THE MYTH OF ALIGNMENT

David Wastell
Nottingham University Business School
Nottingham, UK

> The greatest gap between the practices of Hall of Fame organizations occurs for organization alignment...and this indicates that alignment, much like the synchronism achieved by a high-performance rowing crew, produces dramatic benefits. Understanding how to create alignment in organizations is a big deal, one capable of significant payoffs for all types of enterprises (Kaplan and Norton 2006).

Colloquially, myth denotes a widely held belief that is fictional or erroneous. Its anthropological usage, however, does not carry the same pejorative charge: myths are simply conceptual schemata, embodying core metaphysical concepts and moral wisdom. It is in this latter sense that I dub alignment as a myth; not to question its factuality (a nonsensical property in the case of a belief) but to highlight and interrogate the cultural work that it does (Stillman, 1985). Barthes (1973) defines myth as a type of speech, a "second order semiological system" of signs drawn from the medium of language in which their original meanings are modified to suit the myth-building role. Any elementary *linguistic object* (the definition is broad, encompassing visual imagery as well as language) can be symbolically coopted as raw material by the mythical system. Barthes uses a cover page of *Paris Match* depicting a French negro soldier saluting the tricolour as an exemplar. Beyond the naive meaning, the second-order mythical signification is easily read: "France is a great Empire, that all her sons, without colour discrimination, faithfully serve under her flag..." (Barthes 1973, p. 116). Other symbols conveying the same underlying idea may readily be imagined. Through a matrix of such varied *forms*, the myth of French colonialism as a beneficent force is constituted.

By appropriating signs, promiscuously and parasitically, mythical speech thus builds chains of signifiers mediating abstract, metaphysical concepts, often complex and protean, and with strong moral content. An illustrative case study from Kaplan and Norton featuring the strategic alignment of IS/IT provides a relevant example. Strategic align-

Please use the following format when citing this chapter:

Wastell, D., 2007, in IFIP International Federation for Information Processing, Volume 235, Organizational Dynamics of Technology-Based Innovation: Diversifying the Research Agenda, eds. McMaster, T., Wastell, D., Ferneley, E., and DeGross, J. (Boston: Springer), pp. 513-518.

ment has been a hot topic in the information systems field for many years (Luftman 2004), although with a handful of distinguished exceptions (Ciborra 2004), much of this discourse lacks a critical edge. In Kaplan and Norton's own words, here is an elliptical rendering of their tale, abridged from the full account (on pages 149-162).

> Lockheed Martin's EIS [enterprise information system] organization has more than 4000 employees working in its Orlando HQ and decentralized units around the US. Business leaders, especially since the 1995 merger, were concerned because the IT units operated in stovepipes and silos. To meet its new challenges as a value-added IT provider, EIS launched a balanced scorecard program to align its various departments with the overall EIS strategy and the strategies of the corporation. The BSC would help EIS become the credible innovator and supplier of cutting-edge, net-centric capabilities. Figure 5.12 [see Figure 1] shows the EIS strategy map....By mid-2005, EIS had cascaded this Strategy Map into its ten functional areas and was already seeing heightened awareness and engagement with the strategy among its workforce.

The linguistic and mythical levels in the narrative are easily differentiated. At the elementary level, we have an apparently straightforward piece of factual reporting: a short historical account of a turnaround in Lockheed-Martin due to the intercession of the balanced scorecard (BSC). The meanings are all perfectly clear and unambiguous. But the account can also be read mythically, as a single compound signifier, a kind of moral parable, exemplifying the virtues of alignment and implicitly warning of the dangers of transgression. Its mythical function is an ideological one, and at this level its truth is simply not relevant: the factual detail is pure ornamentation to lend rhetorical force through verisimilitude. The rest of the book is replete with fables of a similar genre, as well as simplistic formulae for achieving alignment, often conveyed diagrammatically. The business organization is consistently depicted as an orderly commonwealth, where managerial agency is sovereign with all working harmoniously for the public good.[1]

> Each individual in the organization develops a personal scorecard. The objectives and targets on those scorecards for the following year are agreed in December. These scorecards are linked to the business or service unit scorecard to which the person belongs, thus ensuring complete top to bottom alignment (Kaplan and Norton 2006, p. 24).

---

[1]There is, of course, something of a much older myth at work here, the myth of an idealized realm where all live in peace and prosperity in a community governed by a wise and benign authority. Plato's Republic, Hobbes' Leviathan, More's Utopia provide relevant examples from political philosophy, whilst literature invokes the motif allegorically through the pastoral idiom with its Arcadian depiction of idyllic rural life. The figure of the shepherd provides an ingenious double emblem of the natural pastoral order, both as model subject (of the polity) and model ruler (of his sheep). Stillman (1985) offers an exegesis of Sydney's "Old Arcadia" based on Barthes, emphasizing the role of myth in the naturalization of aristocratic power. The relationship between pastoral power (in its Christian embodiment) and Foucault's concept of governmentality is discussed by Blake (1999).

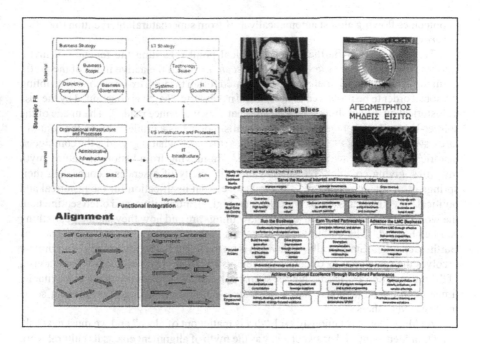

***Figure 1.* Collage**
Clockwise from bottom left: a random image of alignment found on the Internet; Henderson and Venkatraman's (1993) seminal model of strategic alignment (SAM); Marshall McLuhan; a pastry cutter; motto from the entrance to Plato's Academy; two lemmings; Oxford vs. Cambridge boat race (1951), and Figure 5.12 from Kaplan and Norton (the illegibility of the latter is deliberate, partly for copyright purposes, partly to emphasize the form of the diagram over its content). The relevance of some of the images to the text is direct; the symbolism of others is encoded in heuristic juxtapositions and left to speak for itself!

Like so many business case studies, these "parables of alignment" share a simple canonical structure, lacking even the limited sophistication of fairy tales where villains and evil forces figure to provide moral depth and complexity (Monin and Monin 2005). The formula usually goes as follows: a looming crisis, the arrival of a savior, choice between redemption or calamity, a happy ending when the prescriptions are followed, apocalypse otherwise. The pervasive use of diagrams throughout the alignment literature (Figure 1) is an interesting semiotic device is its own right. As McLuhan gnomically observed, the medium is the message, and potent metaphysical messages are subliminally conveyed through such imagery: that the organisational world is an orderly domain, inhabited by well-defined concepts, entities, and processes, governed by simple laws of causality and managerial agency. The geometric regularities are themselves aesthetically enchanting, powerfully reinforcing the sense of natural order. This is a mythical world of magical thinking, of reified concepts standing in fixed determinate configurations, and of outcomes flowing almost automatically as if from supernatural intervention (the BSC *ensures*, etc.).

This brings us to Barthes' second critical point regarding the function of myth. Barthes describes myth as *de-politicized speech*, in which the active mode of the prefix is emphasized. Political interests are obfuscated (often through *ex-nomination*) enabling the social order to be portrayed as natural and necessary: "Myth is constituted by the loss of historical quality of things...the quality that they were once made." The image of the soldier-Negro does not deny French imperialism or act as a crude alibi; on the contrary its existence as a benign force is intentionally affirmed: "what is got rid is the contingent, historical, *fabricated* quality of colonialism." In moving from history to nature, myth mystifies, giving complex, human acts the "simplicity of essences," concealing their springs-of-action and endowing a natural and eternal justification for the historical and political. Mythical language is typically tautological, intransitive, and often sentimental: the world is the way it is because that's how things are and how they should be; nothing can be changed. The cultural work of myths is thus to naturalize the *status quo*: as Barthes remarks, "Statistically, most myth is on the Right." The mythology of alignment involves the same process of conservative mystification. Not only does it paint a vista of the organization as a harmonious system, but this depiction is normalized as inevitable, timeless and natural rather than a fabricated, cultural arrangement privileging some interests over others.

As Mary Douglas famously said, "dirt is matter out of place" and we must next ask, what is hidden, banished or swept away as the myth of alignment enacts its cultural work of ordering the world. The answer should by now be clear, but to assist in this demystification, I will detour with a vignette of my own. Wastell et al. (2007) report a short ethnography of how alignment was accomplished in one organization, a UK local authority. Today, the IS function considers itself well-aligned, having gained a "seat of at the top table," and the organization as a whole has achieved fame and distinction for its e-Government achievements, winning a range of prestigious national awards. This prowess contrasts starkly with the beleaguered, hopelessly misaligned position of the IS function toward the end of the 1990s. Then they were demeaned as "the people who put PCs on desks" with the Damoclean sword of "out-sourcing" poised to strike. How has this transformation come about? There was no top-level imperative to align, no messianic saviour, no methodological bromide. Instead, a human story is told, of front line improvisation and renegade action.[2] The story speaks romantically of a group of senior professionals taking fate into their own hands and through a determined and resourceful campaign of opportunism and political manipulation eventually gaining the influence and status which they coveted. The historical reality inverts the alignment myth: misalignment becomes a force for good not ill, a stimulus for innovation without which the glittering prizes would never have been won. The demystification creates the potential for new mythical readings, of David-versus-Goliath, the heroic few winning out against the many (Gertz, 1986). More seditiously, by romanticizing misbehavior (Trickster as victorious folk-hero) core elements of alignment mythology are destabilized, particularly the idea of power as the concentrated monopoly of a senior, managerial elite.

---

[2] A less starry eyed version may be found in McMaster and Wastell (2005)!

Alignment provides a totalizing myth of the organization as a happy family, a perfect society in which the manager/worker divide has been forever sutured and all work for the common good. It undergirds a range of management fads such as BPR and TQM, and is the *sine qua non* of the systems paradigm (entirely predicated on the notion of functional unity) which has so dominated orthodox organizational theory (Parsons, 1956). But by naturalizing the world, myths inevitably pathologize. There is no place for resistance or subversion in this mythical world of "designer employees" (Ackroyd and Fleming, 2003): all act as "docile bodies," rationally and obediently serving the "primary goal" vouchsafed by the organization's priesthood. Dissent is automatically cast as deviant and irrational, as a dangerous pollution (dirt). Describing alignment as a right-wing myth is not to judge it good or bad, true or counterfactual. This essay is no anti-bourgeois crusade (and satirical temptations are also tightly reined): such polemical demystifications so often turn into remystifications, with authors infiltrating their pet social theories in tendentious re-readings. Rather, it is an invitation to interrogate writing and scholarship in this area more critically and ironically. As an exercise in de-politicized speech, Kaplan and Norton is a *tour de force*: organizational politics are utterly elided; the only agency in town is the hybrid agency of senior managers hand-in-glove with the technology of the balanced scorecard; there is no allusion anywhere to dissent, critique, or alternative views. Dubbing alignment as a myth is not to denigrate it, but merely to bring out its latent ideological content, to analyze its semiotics and the cultural work it does in converting history into nature.

References

Ackroyd, S., and Thompson, P. *Organizational Misbehaviour,* London: SAGE Publicatoins, 2003.

Barthes, R. *Mythologies*, St. Albans, UK: Paladin, 1973.

Blake, L. A. "Pastoral Power, Governmentality and Cultures of Order in Nineteenth Century British Columbia," *Transactions of the Institute of British Geographers* (24), 1999, pp. 79-93.

Ciborra, C. *The Labyrinths of Information: Challenging the Wisdom of Systems,* Oxford, UK: Oxford University Press, 2003.

Gertz, N. "Social Myths in Literary and Political Texts," *Poetics Today* (7:4), 1986, pp. 621-639.

Henderson, J. C., and Venkatraman, N. "Strategic Alignment: Leveraging Information Technology for Transforming Organizations," *IBM Systems Journal* (32:1), 1993, pp. 4-16.

Kaplan, R. S., and Norton, D. P. *Alignment: Using the Balanced Scorecard to Create Corporate Synergies*, Cambridge, MA: Harvard Business School Press, 2006.

Luftman, J. "Key Issues for IT Executives 2004," *MISQ Executive* (4:2), 2004, pp. 269-285.

McMaster, T., and Wastell, D. "Diffusion or Delusion? Challenging an IS Research Tradition," *Information Technology and People* (18), 2005, pp. 383-404.

Monin, N., and Monin, J. "Hi-Jacking the Fairy Tale: Genre Blurring and Allegorical Breaching in Management Literature," *Organization* (12:4), 2005, pp. 511-528.

Parsons, T. "Suggestions for a Sociological Approach to the Theory of Organizations," *Administrative Science Quarterly* (1), 1956, pp. 63-85.

Stillman, R. "The Politics of Sidney's Pastoral: Mystification and Mythology in the Old Arcadia," *English Literary History* (52:4), 1985, pp. 795-814.

Wastell, D. G., McMaster, T., and Kawalek, P. "The Rise of the Phoenix: Methodological Innovation as a Discourse of Renewal," *Journal of Information Technology* (22:1), 2007, pp. 59-68.

About the Author

David Wastell is a professor of Information Systems at Nottingham University Business School. He began his research career as a psycho-physiologist before moving into information systems. His research interests are in public sector reform, innovation and design, management epistemology, and cognitive ergonomics. He has co-organized two previous IFIP conferences as well as the present meeting, and has extensive consultancy experience, especially in the public sector. David may be contacted at dave_wastell@hotmail.com.

42   COACHING THE APPLICATION OF AGILE SOFTWARE DEVELOPMENT

Peter Wendorff
ASSET GmbH
Oberhausen, Germany

Abstract   *The success of agile software development has drawn attention to coaching as an alternative management style. In this paper, we argue that coaching, with its focus on trustful relationships, empathetic communication, mental models, and experiential learning, is suitable to facilitate the sustainable application of agile software development.*

Keywords   Agile, management, leadership, coaching

1   INTRODUCTION

A central element of the people-centric project management strategy practiced in agile software development (ASD) is coaching. Highsmith (2004, p. 182) characterizes it in the following way: "The objective of coaching and team development is to unleash the capability of the team by helping team members continuously improve their domain knowledge (technical, business), self-discipline, and 'teaming' skills."

The application of eXtreme Programming, currently the most popular agile method, is typically facilitated by a coach. As Beck (2005, pp. 143-144) notes, "A coach is responsible for the process as a whole, keeping the team working at a sustainable pace and continuing to improve. A coach communicates what he sees in such a way that the team can address problems."

This statement highlights a fundamental principle of coaching in ASD: A coach typically identifies issues that might need attention and communicates his perspective to the team, but leaves the responsibility for decisions and their implementation to the team. A coach facilitates, but he does not direct.

Please use the following format when citing this chapter:

Wendorff, P., 2007, in IFIP International Federation for Information Processing, Volume 235, Organizational Dynamics of Technology-Based Innovation: Diversifying the Research Agenda, eds. McMaster, T., Wastell, D., Ferneley, E., and DeGross, J. (Boston: Springer), pp. 519-523.

Successful coaching results in human growth and encourages independence from the coach. This position is firmly expressed by Beck (p. 144): "Finally, and most importantly, a coach should encourage independence, not dependence. A good coach moves on a little before you think you're ready and leaves behind a team that finds itself firmly on a path to sustainable, profitable, stable, fast, fun software development."

This statement suggests that coaching enables the sustainable application of agile practices.

2   MANAGEMENT, LEADERSHIP, AND COACHING

The classical management theorists—Taylor, Fayol, and Weber—viewed managers as commanding and controlling executioners of authority, who use rewards and punishments to direct the behavior of staff. This command-and-control style of management can be very effective in the short run, because it addresses the behavioral level directly, but it often fails to create lasting motivation (Robbins and Coulter 1999).

The famous Hawthorne studies gave rise to the organizational behavior school of thought, which claims that human behavior, driven by emotional and rational factors, is key to understanding organizational phenomena. This school focused much attention on leadership in organizations.

Leaders create an emotionally satisfying social bond with their followers. They use the emotional needs of other people effectively to influence their behavior and inspire followership. Leaders can achieve a high degree of commitment and loyalty among their followers (Bennis 1989). However, strong leadership often results in dependence of followers on their leaders, making organizational performance dependent on a few key leaders (Robbins and Coulter 1999).

In the late 1980s, there was a growing realization that traditional management and leadership had one common flaw: Frequently, their effects were not lasting, because they mainly focus on direct behavior control rather than change of the underlying mental models (Hudson 1999).

As a reaction to that, coaching became popular as a management style. The key idea was for coaches to work with individuals in order to promote lasting human growth and organizational change by facilitating natural processes of human development in the context of the workplace. In that role a coach acts as a catalyst, or as Hudson (1999, p. 4) writes, "leaven in bread."

Hudson (p. 6) characterizes a coach as

> a person who facilitates experiential learning that results in future-oriented abilities....A coach is someone trained and devoted to guiding others into increased competence, commitment, and confidence. The most profound way to learn skills, culture, and values is directly from other human beings who already possess those qualities and who are available to offer guidance and counsel.

Cunningham, Dawes, and Bennett (2001, p. 13) point out that coaching leads to self-motivation because it focuses on skills of immediate relevance resulting in "the motivation to learn them, the desire to integrate them, and the will to express them in action."

Coaching achieves lasting results by addressing the level of mental models as drivers of human behavior. Based on a trustful, collaborative working relationship with a coach, mental models are explored, and change is firmly based on increased understanding of perceptions, experiences, and interpretations, resulting in self-motivated learning (Whitmore 2004).

3 INDIVIDUAL COMPETENCES

Coaching is a young discipline with a diverse theoretical base (Hudson 1999). Nevertheless, there are some individual competences that are developed in practically every approach to coaching. These competences are shown in Figure 1 as a ramp. The ramp symbolizes how the competences help a person or team to ascend from a given state to a desired state. During that ascent the lower competences support the development of the higher competences. For example, the ability to trust another person is needed before two persons can effectively explore a given situation together. The individual competences are

- Trusting: The ability to establish a collaborative, supportive working relationship, in which sympathy, respect, and care lead to a climate of comfort and safety.
- Exploring: The ability to understand a given problem situation through empathic communication based on dialogue with another person, using structuring techniques like active listening, questioning, and feedback.
- Changing: The ability to identify goals, to develop options for their attainment based on appropriate mental models of reality, and to implement targeted action plans.
- Learning: The ability to adapt own behavior based on a process of emotional and intellectual reflection, insight, and integration.

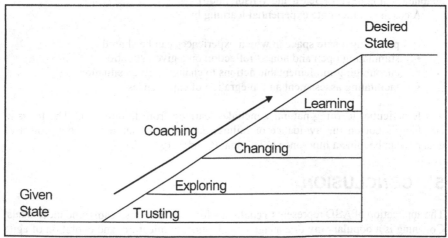

Figure 1. Development of Individual Competences Through Coaching

4   RATIONALE BEHIND COACHING

Coaching is built on two theories: humanistic psychology and experiential learning.

4.1 Humanistic Psychology

Humanistic psychology focuses on the mental capacities that enable humans to grow and fulfil their unique potential for responsibility, creativity, and self-determination. It is a value orientation that emphasizes the development of personal competence in the context of social networks.

This approach views the unique mental models held by humans as main drivers of their behavior (Bernstein et al. 2003).

Typical humanistic positions adopted in coaching assume that humans

- can accept responsibility for their lives
- have the inherent capacity to solve problems
- show motivation to engage in satisfying occupations
- want to form mutually satisfying and supporting relationships
- have a lifelong drive to develop in their search for self-actualization

Coaching is critically dependent on social relationships. From the perspective of the humanistic framework it can be described as the relationship-centric use of communication aiming for the facilitation of human growth.

4.2 Experiential Learning

A fundamental principle of coaching is learning through own experience (Zeus and Skiffington 2000). The careful observation of own behavior and the conscious experience of its results are an important condition for learning that enables future-orientated adaptation of behavior (Beard and Wilson 2006).

A coach can facilitate experiential learning by

- providing a safe space in which experiences can be shared
- stimulating open and honest reflection on a given situation
- encouraging implementable actions to change a given situation
- facilitating assessment and integration of experiences

Experiential learning naturally includes learning from failure, too. The focus in coaching is not on the avoidance of failure, but rather on learning. Overprotective coaches can become a hindrance to learning (Landsberg 2002).

5   CONCLUSION

The application of ASD represents a challenge for organizations, teams, and individuals. Coaching is a popular way to manage the adoption, application, and evolution of agile processes.

Coaching differs from more traditional management and leadership significantly in a number of ways. The success of coaching is critically dependent on

- a mutually trustful work relationship
- empathic, structured communication
- change based on realistic mental models
- emotional and intellectual experiential learning

Coaching is firmly based on the values of humanistic psychology and the principles of experiential learning. It shares this theoretical base with ASD and is a bottom-up approach to the application of agile methods, built on democratic involvement and consultation.

A coach only facilitates the application of an agile process and does not make decisions on behalf of others. This encourages motivation, commitment, and a sense of responsibility, that reduces the need for external control by managers or leaders.

Successful coaching encourages self-regulating maintenance processes and increasing independence from the coach over time. This makes it particularly suitable to ensure the sustainable application of ASD.

References

Beard, C., and Wilson, J. P. *Experiential Learning: A Best Practice Handbook for Educators and Trainers* (2nd ed.), London: Kogan Page, 2006.

Beck, K. *Extreme Programming Explained: Embrace Change* (2nd ed.), Boston: Addison-Wesley, 2005.

Bennis, W. *On Becoming a Leader*, London: Random House, 1989.

Bernstein, D. A., Penner, L. A., Clarke-Stewart, A., and Roy, E. J. *Psychology* (6th ed.), Boston: Houghton Mifflin, 2003.

Cunningham, I., Dawes, G., and Bennett, B. *The Coaching Skill-Builder Activity Pack*, New York: AMACOM Books, 2001.

Highsmith, J. A. *Agile Project Management*, Boston: Addison-Wesley, 2004.

Hudson, F. M. *The Handbook of Coaching*, San Francisco: Jossey-Bass, 1999.

Landsberg, M. *The Tao of Coaching*, London: Profile Books, 2002.

Robbins, S. P., and Coulter, M. *Management* (6th ed.), Upper Saddle River, NJ: Prentice-Hall, 1999.

Whitmore, J. *Coaching for Performance: GROWing People, Performance and Purpose* (3rd ed.), London: Nicholas Brealey Publishing, 2004.

Zeus, P., and Skiffington, S. *The Complete Guide to Coaching at Work*, Sydney: McGraw-Hill, 2000.

About the Author

Peter Wendorff holds university degrees in business and engineering. Since 1993, he has been working as an IT consultant in a variety of technical and managerial roles. His professional and academic interests include software engineering, corporate management, organizational theory, humanistic psychology, research methods, and the philosophy of science. Peter can be reached by e-mail at peter.wendorff@integrative-paradigm.com.

Part 8:

Panels

43 COMPLEXITY THEORY AND THE DIFFUSION OF INNOVATIONS

Frank Land
Emeritus Professor,
London School of Economics

Antony Bryant
Leeds Metropolitan University

Ken Eason
Emeritus Professor,
Loughborough University, and
Director, Bayswater Institute

Eve Mitleton-Kelly
Director, Complexity Research Programme
London School of Economics

David Wastell
Nottingham University Business School

In recent years, complexity theory has been shown to throw light on a number of issues related to the management of organizations. Examples include the use of complexity notions to help understand situations such as mergers and acquisitions and assist in the successful facilitation of these events by suggesting appropriate enabling infrastructures (Mitleton-Kelly 2004). Complexity theory has similarly helped in an understanding of information systems failures and perhaps goes some way to explaining perennial problems such as the alignment problem: a problem near the top of serious issues reported by researchers into concerns expressed by CIOs and business managers.

Complexity theory may also be useful in providing a framework for helping to understand the diffusion of innovations. An innovation can be regarded as a disturbance

Please use the following format when citing this chapter:

Land, F., Bryant, A., Eason, K., Mitleton-Kelly, E., and Wastell, D., 2007, in IFIP International Federation for Information Processing, Volume 235, Organizational Dynamics of Technology-Based Innovation: Diversifying the Research Agenda, eds. McMaster, T., Wastell, D., Ferneley, E., and DeGross, J. (Boston: Springer), pp. 527-528.

of a system in some kind of equilibrium. Complexity theory shows how systems respond to such disturbances.

Frank Land will introduce and chair the panel. He was a research associate of the ESRC-funded ICOSS project at the London School of Economics, which explored complexity in the context of major initiatives such as mergers and acquisitions, so-called incubator projects, and new business directions by its research partners.

Tony Bryant will discuss the ways in which the concepts of complexity and chaos can be seen against a background of constant demands for innovation, novelty, and invention with specific reference to liquid modernity, auto-destructive art, and turbulence (Bryant 2007). These concepts have an impact on the ways in which technological development and innovation are understood, since innovation becomes seen as an end in itself, one that can never actually be fully realized.

Ken Eason will draw on his extensive research on the socio-technical issues of implementing information systems and his action research projects on change programs in order offer some insights into the value of complexity science principles in understanding the responses of NHS Trusts to the National IT Programme that is now being rolled out.

Eve Mitleton-Kelly will highlight some of the relevant principles of complexity theory as applied to socio-technical systems.

Dave Wastell will address the dynamic interplay of human agency and social structure in organisational change, combining ideas from evolutionary theory (e.g., colonial systems) and complexity science (e.g. dissipative structures). He will apply these ideas in a case study of strategic alignment and business process reengineering in a local authority.

References

Bryant, A. "Liquid Modernity, Complexity and Turbulence," *Theory, Culture and Society* (24:1), 2007, pp. 127-135.
Mitleton-Kelly, E. "An Integrated Methodology to Facilitate the Emergence of New Ways of Organising," in A. Minai and Y. Bar-Yam (eds.), *Proceedings of the Fifth International Conference on Complex Systems*, Boston, May 16-21, 2004 (available online at http://necsi.org/events/iccs/openconf/author/papers/f659.doc).

44 GLOBAL DIFFUSION OF BROADBAND: Current State and Future Directions for Investigation

Michael D. Williams
Yogesh Kumar Dwivedi
Swansea University, UK

Catherine Middleton
Ryerson University, Canada

Diana Wilson
Trinity College, Dublin, Ireland

Morton Falch
Technical University of Denmark

Alex Schulz
De Montford University, UK

Vishanth Weerakkody
Anastasia Papazafeiropoulou
Brunel University, UK

Ben Ramdani
University of Manchester, UK

Roya Gholami
Aston University, UK

Please use the following format when citing this chapter:

Williams, M. D., Dwivedi, Y, K., Middleton, C., Wilson, D., Falch, M., Schultz, A., Weerakkody, V., Papaza-feiropoulou, A., Ramdani, B., and Gholami, R., 2007, in IFIP International Federation for Information Processing, Volume 235, Organizational Dynamics of Technology-Based Innovation: Diversifying the Research Agenda, eds. McMaster, T., Wastell, D., Ferneley, E., and DeGross, J. (Boston: Springer), pp. 529-532.

1   INTRODUCTION

Governments all over the world are encouraging broadband Internet connectivity to both residential and small business consumers. Despite large investments for developing the enabling infrastructure and the provision of access at affordable prices, however, demand for broadband has not increased the expected rate in many countries. The slow rate of broadband adoption can be viewed as being "supply constrained" in the developing world where countries are lagging behind in infrastructure development, but "demand constrained" in countries where high-speed access is already available to the majority of the population. In order to achieve greater uniformity in rates of adoption and use of broadband in both residential and small business contexts, and to reduce the digital divide, it is essential to focus upon understanding both macro- and micro-level factors influencing adoption and consequent use of broadband. The overall aim of this panel is to stimulate discussion and contribute to an understanding of the diffusion of broadband from a global perspective. In order to realise the overall aim, a number of studies from a range of different countries (including Australia, Canada, Denmark, Germany, Ireland, Kingdom of Saudi Arabia, Singapore, and United Kingdom) are integrated within the panel discussion.

2   PANEL STRUCTURE AND CONTENT

Williams and Dwivedi will introduce and chair the panel. Both chairs have been involved in a number of projects on broadband adoption and the information society.

   Middleton will identify areas that have been holding up broadband development in Australia. In examining multiple areas for attention (competition, user characteristics and behaviors, applications, network characteristics, and pricing), the experience of Canada, a leader in broadband deployment, is used to show the differences in each area. This part of the panel outlines objectives for the development of a more user-friendly broadband environment in Australia, which would encourage broadband adoption. Although both countries discussed here have their own policy agendas and some unique circumstances related to broadband deployment, Middleton will provide valuable insights for policy makers and industry leaders in Australia, and in other countries struggling to develop widespread broadband deployment.

   Wilson will consider from a marketing perspective the political, cultural/social, and economic factors, both micro and macro, affecting the supply/demand nexus of broadband services for the Irish consumer. She will highlight the development of broadband, its current situation of roll-out and uptake, and examine the reasons for its continuing poor performance and offer recommendations on how Ireland may close the gap and perhaps even move ahead.

   Falch will provide a comparison of broadband development in the OECD countries, which reveals that national policies are important for the penetration of broadband. Successful policies include direct intervention in the form of financial support to infrastructure development in disadvantaged areas, regulation ensuring facility based competition, and facility measures such demand stimulation and providing common visions for the information society.

Schulz will present a case study from East Germany where local politicians failed to take the demand for broadband seriously. Using the theoretical lens of responsibility, this section will also present an explanation of why the demand/supply model fails when free markets do not emerge or exist.

Weerakkody will present findings from a survey that explores the reasons for the slow progress of broadband adoption in the Kingdom of Saudi Arabia. Particular emphasis was placed on individual level factors such as social and cultural influences. The key findings were that the factors with the main influence on attitude toward adoption of broadband were (1) usefulness, (2) service quality, (3) age, (4) usage, (5) type of connection, and (6) type of accommodation. Contrary to prediction, although socio-cultural factors such as regulation through filtration of broadband were found to have no significant influence on the adoption of broadband, consumers were aware and largely did not like the regulation.

Papazafeiropoulou will argue that the existing diffusion of innovations theories are inadequate for the study of broadband diffusion and a more socio-technical approach is required for this purpose. Such an approach would be useful for SMEs considering the adoption of new technologies such as broadband, and for policy makers seeking to apply effective technological adoption policies.

Ramdani will argue that while most large European companies are connected to broadband, SME (small- to medium-sized enterprises) connectivity is lagging behind. The question of why one SME adopts broadband while another does not is still understudied. The purpose of this part of the panel is to fill this gap by investigating the environmental, organizational, and technological factors impacting broadband adoption in the small business context. Based on the ICTs innovation adoption literature, a framework of SME broadband adoption has been developed and empirically validated using key decision makers in nine SMEs in the Northwest of England.

Gholami will argue that in spite of the increasing significance of broadband Internet, there are not many research papers explicitly addressing issues pertaining to its adoption and post-adoption. Previous research on broadband has mainly focused on the supply side aspect at the national level, ignoring the importance of the demand side, which may involve looking more deeply into the use, as well as factors impacting organizational and individual uptake. This part of the panel empirically verifies an integrated theoretical model, comprising the theory of planned behavior and the information systems continuance model to examine factors influencing broadband Internet adoption and post-adoption behavior of some 1,500 organizations in Singapore. Overall, strong support for the integrated model has been manifested the results, providing insight into influential factors. At the adoption stage, perceived behavioural control has the greatest impact on behavioural intention. The findings also suggest that, as compared to attitude, subjective norms and perceived behavioural control more significantly affect the broadband Internet adoption decision. At the post-adoption stage, intention is no longer the only determinant of broadband Internet continuance; rather, initial usage was found to significantly affect broadband Internet continuance.

3   CONCLUSIONS

The panel participants will contribute to the existing body of broadband adoption research in two main areas: panelists Middleton, Wilson, Morten, Schulz,and Weerakkody will address issues related to national policies and individual/consumer level adoption, while Papazafeiropoulou, Ramdani, and Gholami will focus their discussions upon the issue of broadband adoption in the SME context. Needless to say, findings presented by all panelists will also be of interest to supply-side stakeholders including ISPs and governments. Finally, panelists will also formulate research issues requiring further investigation.

Index of Contributors